A History of Blacks in Kentucky
# From Slavery to Segregation, 1760–1891

By
Marion B. Lucas

The Kentucky Historical Society

*To Henry E. Cheaney*
—Marion B. Lucas

© 1992, 2003 by the Kentucky Historical Society. All rights reserved
First edition published 1992. Second edition 2003
Printed in the United States of America

Library of Congress Cataloging-in-Publication Data

Lucas, Marion Brunson, 1935-
   A history of Blacks in Kentucky.
   p. cm.
   Includes bibliographical references and index.
   1. African Americans—Kentucky—History.  2. Kentucky History.
3. Kentucky—Race relations.

ISBN 0-916968-32-4

## Contents

Introduction ............................................................. iv

Preface .................................................................. vii

Ackowledgments ................................................... viii

Prologue ................................................................. xi

Chapter 1. Labor, Living Conditions, and the Family ..... 1

Chapter 2. Slave Mobility, Recreation, Health, and Treatment ......................................................... 29

Chapter 3. Resistance to Slavery ........................................ 51

Chapter 4. The Slave Trade ................................................ 84

Chapter 5. Slave Hiring and Free Blacks ...................... 101

Chapter 6. Religion and Education before 1865 ........... 118

Chapter 7. Kentucky Blacks in the Civil War .................146

Chapter 8. Freedom's Pains: Life in the Immediate Postwar Period, 1865-1870 ........................... 178

Chapter 9. Post-Civil War Religion, 1865-1891 ............. 210

Chapter 10. Post-Civil War Education, 1865-1891 ..........229

Chapter 11. Labor, Living Conditions, and Recreation, 1865-1891 ......................................................... 268

Chapter 12. Civil Rights, Politics, and Society, 1865-1891 ......................................................... 292

Epilogue .................................................................. 326

Notes ....................................................................... 328

Bibliography .......................................................... 389

Index ....................................................................... 412

# Introduction

WHEN I began research on *A History of Blacks in Kentucky: From Slavery to Segregation, 1760-1891*, I appreciated the need to reconceptionalize and rewrite entirely the role of African Americans in Kentucky and in United States history. With the exception of herculean efforts by African American scholars, little had been done prior to the 1950s to research the records of African Americans and integrate their testimony into our nation's history. Consequently, African Americans, whether slave or free, were at best allowed a peripheral place in the history of our commonwealth and the nation.

Two seminal studies of slavery published in the 1950s changed the way both historians and the public viewed African Americans. Kenneth P. Stampp's *The Peculiar Institution: Slavery in the Ante-Bellum South* (New York, 1956) vigorously challenged older, racist interpretations. Stampp's argument that African Americans were fellow human beings who possessed the same hopes and desires as white Americans, and who were determined to end their enslavement, turned the historical profession on end. The uproar over Stampp's book still raged when Stanley Elkins's provocative book, *Slavery: A Problem in American Institutional and Intellectual Life* (Chicago, 1959), raised the significant question: What was the essential nature of black life, society, and culture during slavery? The genius of Elkins's scholarship was to move African American life and culture to center stage and, in the process, point historians in a new direction.

Following the lead of Stampp and Elkins, young historians began investigating every aspect of antebellum slavery, for the first time poring over sources that African American historians had thanklessly promoted for years. Thus, one hundred years after the Civil War, black testimony suddenly achieved the status of credible historical evidence. In addition to the slave narratives and postbellum autobiographies, historians began mining the Depression-era Works Progress Administration interviews with former slaves, most of whom were in their eighties and nineties when they were interviewed. Slave songs and spirituals also underwent scrutiny for insights into the African American psyche, and folk tales took on new meanings for interpreting day-to-day life. From these studies, a completely new picture of slave life, society, and culture materialized.

My 1992 book on black Kentuckians was part of this renaissance in the study of African American history, though when I began my research, I was unaware that a revolution in the study of black history was in progress. Utilizing previously disdained sources, I described in detail Kentucky's slave society and culture, the black family, and the institution most responsible for viable family relations, the black church. The result was a new and very different picture of the lives of black Kentuckians before 1891.

I had also hoped when researching and writing *A History of Blacks in Kentucky* that the book would stimulate additional research about Kentucky's African Americans. I am pleased to say that I believe that has happened. During the past decade, a number of seminal articles and books have reached fruition as historians worked to incorporate new evidence describing the place of African Americans in Kentucky society. I am convinced this only the beginning.

Marion B. Lucas<br>
January 2003

# *Preface*

IN histories of large groups of people, historians constantly struggle against the charge that they in fact wrote accounts of the middle classes, the successful, and the wealthy. That criticism, I hope readers will conclude, is not applicable to this book. As with other races, blacks who left extensive records of their people were, in most instances, those who had achieved success in one form or another. But because of race prejudice, Kentucky's small but energetic middle class continued to be the object of discrimination because of skin color as much as the poorer classes and thus remained an integral part of "the people." The accounts they left tell more than their own story and are representative of the lives of black Kentuckians at all levels of society.

A second problem historians of American blacks encounter is that they must write about a people who reside in a society dominated by whites, sometimes resulting in the criticism that their histories tell readers more about whites than blacks. I have attempted to solve this problem by not writing a history of Kentucky which included black, but by writing a history of black who lived in Kentucky. Since we know fairly well the views of Kentucky whites before 1891 regarding blacks and since space prevents retelling the story of white Kentuckians, i have mentioned whites only as they reflect upon the story of blacks. In this book, Kentucky's blacks—slaves, freemen, and freedmen, male and female—are at the center of the story.

Finally, where no race is given and the context does not indicate that a person is white, the reader may assume that the individual identified is black. Where comments of analyses of the actions of blacks are quoted, one may assume that they are from blacks unless other indicated. Comments by whites will be identified as "white" unless race is clear from the text.

# Acknowledgments

HISTORIANS are solitary people who somehow make lots of helpful friends. Without their support, few historians would see the product of their research in print. The assistance of library and archival professionals at Western Kentucky University and throughout the nation was absolutely essential for completion of this project. No amount of praise is sufficient to thank those who helped me complete this work.

At Western Kentucky University's Helm-Cravens Library, I am especially thankful for the assistance of Susan Knight Gore and her staff in Interlibrary Loan. Ever helpful, Susan went out of her way to assist me in finding documents, books, and newspapers which were necessary for my study. Government documents librarians Sara Gleaves and Gene Whicker also gave expert assistance, working tirelessly to fill my many requests. Riley Handy and the faculty and staff at Western Kentucky University's Kentucky Library were equally helpful. Elaine Harrison, Patricia M. Hodges, and Sue Lynn McGuire guided me to manuscript collections that I might otherwise have missed, while Constance Ann Mills, Nancy Disher Baird, and Jonathan D. Jeffrey fulfilled hundreds of requests for assistance. Nancy also read and criticized those portions of my manuscript dealing with health care, saving me from several errors.

I owe a special debt of appreciation to Gerald Roberts, director of the Berea College Archives, and to his associate, Sidney Farr. Gerald and Sidney assisted me in every possible way in researching Berea's excellent collection on black history, making my time there most memorable. Dwayne Cox, while on the staff at the University of Louisville Archives, pointed out numerous collections filled with important sources, as did Deborah Skaggs and Sherrill Redmon.

Several other Kentucky collections possessed source materials essential for this study. At the Kentucky Historical Society in Frankfort, James C. Klotter, Thomas H. Appleton, Jr., and the staff led me to numerous manuscripts and records that proved to be helpful. I am also indebted to Jennie M. Nelson, Virginia Keene, and former Military Records Supervisor Forest E. Dudley at the Military Records and Research Library in Frankfort and to Edna Milliken at the Kentucky Department for Libraries and Archives for invaluable assistance. At the Filson Club in Louisville, Nelson Dawson guided me through that fine manuscript collection, and Nettie Watson Oliver assisted in locating secondary sources. Sister Agnes Geraldine McGann at Nazareth Archival Center in Nazareth, Kentucky, and Sister Florence Wolfe of the Loretto Archives in Nerinx, Kentucky, facilitated research in those important collections. The Special Collections staff at Margaret I. King Library at the University of Kentucky, especially Terry Warth, Claire McCann, and Betty Matulionis, were indefatigable in locating manuscripts for me.

A number of black history archives housed sources valuable for this study. Florence E. Borders of the Amistad Research Center at Dillard University in New Orleans, Louisiana, was especially helpful, as were Betty Gubert and the staff at the Schomburg Center for Research in Black Culture of the New York Public Library, Janet L. Sims-Wood at the Moorland-Spingarn Research Center at Howard University, Washington, D.C., Mary Jo Pugh at the Bentley Historical Library at the University of Michigan, Michael P. Musick of the Military Reference Branch of the National Archives, Washington, D.C., and Paul T. Heffron at the Library of Congress, Washington, D.C.

No author could ask for more support than that given to me by members of the history department at Western Kentucky University. Lowell H. Harrison not only suggested the topic, but also critiqued each chapter, always making seminal suggestions. J. Drew Harrington, David D. Lee, Francis H. Thompson, Richard L. Troutman, and Richard D. Weigel read each chapter. Their suggestions significantly improved this work. Robert V. Haynes offered suggestions for each chapter on style and content. My old friend, Jack W. Thacker, gave me encouragement, and my close buddy and leader of the "Friday afternoon gang," Carlton L. Jackson, never ceased to demonstrate his support. And finally, thanks to Elizabeth A. Jensen, history department secretary, for her assistance.

I owe a special debt of appreciation to Frank D. Conley of Western Kentucky University's Industrial and Engineering Technology Department for his careful reading of each chapter, thereby saving me from more than one faux pas, to Shirley O. Gibbs of Western's Department of Home Economics and Family Living who generously evaluated the section on slave diet, and to John David Smith of North Carolina State University who offered valuable advice on every chapter of the manuscript.

Other friends and historians, at Western and universities across America, who contributed to the completion of this book include Linda Morrissett, Sallye R. Clark, Stanley S. Cooke, Alan B. Anderson, John Long, Howard Bailey, Lee Dew, Leslie Rowland, Juliet E.K. Walker, Roberta Hall Slade, Todd L. Savitt, Jacqueline G. Burnside, Paul M. Debusman, John M. Houchens, Kathleen C. Bryson, and George C. Wright.

Several Western students assisted with this project. While an undergraduate, my daughter, Amy A. Lucas, helped in the research, tracing references to secondary books and newspaper articles. Upon completion of the manuscript, my son, Scott J. Lucas, along with Sarah Goodfellow, received their introduction to one of the unpleasant chores of historical research when they spent several weeks checking footnotes. The gifted Thompson girls, Jo and future historian Delia, typed many hundreds of pages of note cards while working as student assistants in the History Department. Five history graduate students—Randy Bowling, Cheryl Ann Paterson Edelen, Julie Applegate, C. David Dalton, and Scott Sallee—also helped on this project.

Several ministers with special knowledge of black church history in Kentucky made a contribution to this work. They include J.H. Taylor, William J. Hodge, William H. Rogers, and Lincoln N. Bingham.

Finally, I want to express my appreciation to James C. Klotter, director of the Kentucky Historical Society, and his staff. This book and its companion volume by George C. Wright are the culmination of the "Black History Project" funded by a state appropriation in 1978. Over the years, Klotter and his associate, Thomas H. Appleton, Jr., and more recently Melba Porter Hay, in addition to offering their expert advice, have provided every possible assistance. I am also appreciative of the assistance of two other staff members at the Historical Society, Jean Criswell and James Russell Harris.

Marion B. Lucas<br>
January 1992

# *Prologue*

BLACKS and whites entered Kentucky together. As early as 1751 a black "servant" accompanied Christopher Gist as he explored territory bordering the Ohio River. Gist and his servant found another black man, a slave already at an Indian town on the Scioto River, then descended to within fifteen miles of the Falls of the Ohio before returning east.[1]

During one of Daniel Boone's early trips westward in 1760, a slave "guided" the young explorer across the Blue Ridge Mountains. Later, in 1773, Daniel and his brother Squire and their families, assisted by an unknown number of blacks, sought to settle Kentucky. En route, Boone sent his son, James, several whites, and slaves Charles and Adam back to a nearby settlement for provisions. During the return trip, Indians surprised the group. James and a lad were severely wounded. Charles and several whites were killed. Adam hid among river bank driftwood and watched in horror as Indians tortured and killed the wounded whites—including Boone's son. Adam returned to tell Boone the sad news.[2]

In 1775 Daniel Boone led another group of settlers, including a number of black laborers, into Kentucky. On March 25 Indians attacked just before dawn as Boone's party camped near the present site of Richmond. The first volley killed Sam, a black "body servant"; his owner, shot through the knees, also died. After driving off the Indians, the frontiersmen buried the two men side by side.[3]

In early 1778 blacks played an important part in both the attack on and defense of Boonesborough. While away from the fort making salt with a small party of men, Boone fell into the hands of four Shawnee scouts. Upon arriving at their camp, Boone met "Pompey," a huge black slave who served as the interpreter for Blackfish, the Shawnee chief. Pompey announced that Blackfish intended to kill Boone's men at the salt lick before destroying Boonesborough. Boone faced a painful dilemma. Only a few men remained in Boonesborough, the fort's defenses were in poor condition, and the men at the salt works were vulnerable. Boone agreed to secure the surrender of the men at the lick in return for a guarantee of their safety. Upon surrendering, Boone and the salt workers were taken to the Shawnee camp.

Pompey became the central character in the events which followed. Indians and Boone debated the fate of the pioneers. Pompey, who sat beside Boone during the ordeal, translated in hushed tones. The frontiersmen had no idea of what was transpiring until Boone made an audible peroration pleading for their lives, ultimately resulting in a Shawnee vote to spare their captives. Boone next persuaded Blackfish to delay the attack on Boonesborough, arguing through Pompey that the fort was strongly defended and that the chief should return in the spring with a larger force. Persuaded, the Indians marched off northward with their prisoners.

In spring 1778, before the Indians completed their plans to attack Boonesborough, Boone slipped away from an Indian hunting party. In four days he traveled 160 miles to Boonesborough, only to find the fort still in bad condition and defended by a handful of men. The settlers prepared as best they could before a force of about 450 warriors arrived in early September.

Pompey advanced ahead of the Indians and waved a white flag. The black interpreter invited Boone to come out and parley, promising no harm. After some delay, Boone met with Pompey and the Indian chief. Blackfish wanted Boone to surrender the fort, but Boone stalled for time. On the third day of discussions, the Indians attempted to subdue the pioneer negotiators. Two men were shot as the settlers ran to the fort.

Once the siege of Boonesborough began, armed slaves took their turn at the beleaguered fort's walls, and one slave, London, died when he bravely went beyond the walls to battle an Indian. When the Indians withdrew, the pioneers opened the fort's gates as a show of strength. On several occasions, Pompey attempted to creep close enough to ascertain the true strength of the garrison, only to be driven back by sharpshooters. Periodically during the siege, Pompey yelled demands for the garrison's surrender, usually followed by an exchange of profanity. Near the siege's end, as Pompey shot at settlers from a tree, several pioneers fired at Pompey, but Daniel Boone was credited with the shot that killed the black interpreter. When the Indians abandoned the siege, they left only Pompey's body.[4]

The events surrounding the attack on Boonesborough illustrate several points. First of all, a few blacks had fled white society and lived among the Indians. But they were exceptions. Overall, there existed a strong interdependence among blacks and whites on the Kentucky frontier. The primitive living conditions in the forest and the ever-present Indian threat forced them to depend upon each other for protection, though the white man was free and the black man usually a slave. Facing the hostile environment of wilderness and Indians, slaves knew that to run off into the forest might mean death from starvation, wild animals, Indians, or reenslavement by the aborigines, whose customs and manners they often did not understand. A safer, more secure life—but one also of unrelieved labor—awaited them in the forts. Thus the frontier years were probably the closest association blacks and whites experienced during slavery.

When Indians assailed homesteads in the Kentucky wilderness, they attacked the homes of blacks as well as whites, and slaves were as much a part of the system of defense as were their masters. Though Indians may have demonstrated less hostility toward blacks than whites, no accounts exist of slaves rising up to join an Indian assault against their masters. Indeed, loyal slaves or servants sometimes discovered the attackers and then joined with the whites to fight off the common enemy. In 1780 when Indians attacked a crew of workers building a ferryboat on the Kentucky River about a mile north of Boonesborough, a black laborer ran to the fort to warn the settlers. The Indians killed two whites and abducted two blacks, but the alerted fort remained secure.[5]

On another occasion, in 1782 near Crab Orchard, Indians attacked the cabin of a white woman and her daughter, defended only by an aged, lame slave. The black man struggled with an Indian who had entered the house before the woman bolted the door. While the servant held the Indian, the young girl, at the slave's urging, killed the invader with an ax.[6]

Another slave, "Black Sam," displayed equal bravery when Indians attacked his master's homestead. Sam awakened one evening to the screams of his owner's family. Looking toward their cabin, he saw an Indian run out with a small child, lay her down, and return for more spoils. Sam, unarmed, slipped through the weeds, picked up the child, and ran into the woods. He groped through the forest for four days before stumbling upon a settler's station. Leaving the baby at the fort, Sam returned to the burned-out cabin, where he found his despondent master, Edmund Cabell. Sam happily informed Cabell that his daughter had survived the ordeal.[7]

In March 1782 a slave also played a major role in preventing the destruction of Estill's Station, located about fifteen miles from Boonesborough. At a time when most men were away, a band of Wyandots surrounded the fort. During the siege the Indians murdered a white child caught outside the compound and took prisoner a "powerfully built" slave called Monk. Monk convinced the Indians that the fort was too strongly defended to be taken, though it actually contained mostly women and children. The Indians fled, taking their black prisoner.

When the pioneers returned to the station, they pursued the raiders, overtaking them near the present town of Mt. Sterling. During the battle, the clever Monk shouted to his owner across the lines, giving the strength of the Indians and urging the frontiersmen on. Though the settlers suffered heavy casualties, they rescued Monk, who helped carry wounded frontiersmen to the safety of Estill's Station, twenty-five miles away.

Monk's bravery during the Indian hostilities resulted in his emancipation. As a freeman he began manufacturing gunpowder from saltpeter he had discovered in a nearby Madison County cave and soon became the supplier for Boonesborough and Estill's Station. Monk is said to have been the father of the first black child born at Boonesborough. Another Boonesborough freeman, Richard Hind, a man with remarkable ingenuity, also contributed economically to the frontier community by developing new farm crops.[8]

Regardless of the frontier contributions and achievements of blacks, the institution of slavery that had developed in coastal areas routinely passed to the Kentucky wilderness. The freedoms of the frontier did not evolve to black slaves. From the earliest explorations, only a few white settlers viewed blacks as anything but slaves. When white Kentuckians drew up their first constitution in 1792, they incorporated their racial prejudices into the document, stating that all laws of Virginia regarding slavery were in force in Kentucky. This meant that those defined as slaves in Virginia, and all descendants of female bondswomen, were slaves in Kentucky. A small but vocal group of religious leaders failed in their attempt to prevent the continuation of slavery in the Commonwealth. In 1798 the Kentucky legislature adopted an elaborate slave code which relegated blacks, both freemen and slaves, to an inferior position in every aspect of life. Thus, black Kentuckians, from the very beginning, had to struggle against a view held by whites since the sixteenth century that blackness, in and of itself, meant permanent bond slavery.[9]

Farmers from Virginia, the Carolinas, Maryland, Pennsylvania, and elsewhere migrated by the thousands to the Kentucky frontier. Freemen and slaves worked with these white pioneers clearing paths through the wilderness, over mountain passes, and constructing rafts to ford streams. Blacks also built and loaded flatboats that deposited thousands of settlers on the southern bank of the Ohio River.

Prologue / xv

Upon reaching Kentucky, slave labor began the process of turning a wilderness into a civilized agricultural community. Blacks went to work clearing forests, erecting cabins, planting gardens, and building fences. When it came to hard labor, blacks had plenty of experience, and their general knowledge also proved beneficial to the communities that grew up around the early forts. One pioneer farmer boasted that Dick, his slave, instructed many of his neighbors in planting crops, felling trees, and building defenses against the Indians.[10]

The size of Kentucky's rapidly growing black population before 1790 is extremely difficult to estimate. The famous John Cowan census, the 1777 enumeration of the inhabitants at Harrod's Fort, listed twelve slaves over age ten and seven younger black children in a total population of 198, making blacks about 10 percent of the residents.[11] Blacks were probably never fewer than one in ten during the frontier period, and, based on John Filson's estimate of settlers, there were probably about 4,000 Kentucky blacks in 1784.[12] Settlers, with their slaves, took up land in Kentucky so rapidly in the 1780s that in a few places frontier conditions virtually ended by 1790.[13] The first Federal census, 1790, enumerated 11,830 slaves and 114 freemen on the Kentucky frontier, making blacks more than 16 percent of the population. Ten years later, blacks totaled 41,084, almost 19 percent of the inhabitants. Between 1790 and 1800 slaves lived in about one-fourth of the white households. During the same decade, freemen increased 550 percent, from 114 to 741, a growth rate almost three times that of the white population, and an indication that some freemen may have been settlers who migrated to frontier Kentucky as either free laborers or servants. In 1800 there was approximately one black person in every five inhabitants.[14]

Kentucky's black population experienced its greatest growth during the first forty years of statehood. In the period after 1790,[15] the black percentage of the total population increased about 2 percent each decade, reaching a peak at 24.7 percent in 1830. In each of these decades the growth rate of blacks was higher than that of whites. In 1830 Kentucky had 165,213 slaves and 4,917 freemen living among 517,787 whites, a ratio of one black for each three whites.[16] After 1830 the percentage of blacks among whites slowly declined, probably because of Kentucky's small-farm agriculture which did not require a large labor force, the 1833 law prohibiting the importation of slaves for resale, and the profitable southern slave trade.[17] Kentucky's 236,167 blacks made up only 20 percent of the population in 1860, or about one in every five inhabitants.[18]

Early in the migration to Kentucky, a pattern of settlement developed. Because of the absence of extensive tillable land, most farmers

Prologue Figure 1

## BLACKS IN KENTUCKY'S POPULATION 1790-1860

| | slaves | % of blacks | % of total pop. | total black pop. | % of blacks total pop. | whites | % of whites total pop. | total population |
|---|---|---|---|---|---|---|---|---|
| 1790 | 11,830 | 99.05 | 16.2 | 11,944 | 16.34 | 61,133 | 83.66 | 73,077 |
| 1800 | 40,343 | 98.2 | 18.26 | 41,084 | 18.59 | 179,871 | 81.41 | 220,955 |
| 1810 | 80,561 | 97.9 | 19.8 | 82,274 | 20.24 | 324,237 | 79.76 | 406,511 |
| 1820 | 126,732 | 97.9 | 22.46 | 129,491 | 22.95 | 434,644 | 77.05 | 564,135 |
| 1830 | 165,213 | 97.1 | 24.02 | 170,130 | 24.73 | 517,787 | 75.27 | 687,917 |
| 1840 | 182,258 | 96.14 | 23.37 | 189,575 | 24.31 | 590,253 | 75.69 | 779,828 |
| 1850 | 210,981 | 95.47 | 21.48 | 220,992 | 22.49 | 761,413 | 77.51 | 982,405 |
| 1860 | 225,483 | 95.48 | 19.5 | 236,167 | 20.44 | 919,517 | 79.56 | 1,155,684 |

moved beyond the eastern mountains and the adjacent narrow ridge of conical knobs, and settled with their slaves in the Bluegrass.[19] Thus, eastern Kentucky, about one-fourth of the state's land mass, from Lewis County on the Ohio River southwest to Clinton County on the Tennessee border, eastward to Virginia, had a small slave population.[20] During the existence of slavery, all eastern Kentucky counties except Bath had fewer than 10 percent black inhabitants. Bath County, with 2,641 blacks in 1860, contained about twice the black population of any other eastern Kentucky county. In contrast, Jackson County, with seven slaves and twenty-one freemen, had the fewest black residents. There was, however, one striking feature regarding slavery in eastern Kentucky. Blacks resided in towns in larger percentages than in the countryside, suggesting that most blacks in the mountain counties were either household servants or laborers.[21]

The Bluegrass area's eight thousand square miles in central Kentucky has an outer boundary that stretches from Mason County on the Ohio River southward to Garrard County, where it turns westward to Marion County before returning to the river at Louisville. From Jefferson County, the Bluegrass follows the river back to Mason County. The northernmost tier of counties, containing poor soil and hilly terrain, frequently interrupted by outcrops of shale which made the land less desirable agriculturally, proved unsuitable for slave labor.[22] The small black population in these counties increased from 7,920 in 1830 to only 9,982 in 1860, and declined in proportion to whites throughout the antebellum period. Like the mountainous East, the percentage of blacks residing in the towns was consistently higher than in the countryside. The remainder of the Bluegrass area consisted of level farm land and slightly rolling hills covered by deep, fertile soil with a high phosphorus content. Fayette, Woodford, and the tier of surrounding counties, the heart of the Bluegrass and perhaps the richest soil in Kentucky, became the hub of a large black population as early as 1790.[23]

The central Bluegrass counties experienced a remarkable growth in black population during the first half of the nineteenth century. Blacks made up more than 30 percent of Fayette, Woodford, Scott, Jessamine, and Jefferson counties by 1810, and they exceeded 20 percent in a majority of the remaining Bluegrass counties. In 1810 Lexington and Fayette County had 7,872 black residents while Jefferson, the second largest in terms of blacks, had 4,461. Ten years later blacks comprised over 40 percent of Fayette County, and surpassed 30 percent in ten others. In 1830 when the black portion of the population peaked, Fayette's blacks numbered 11,410, Jefferson's 7,264, Bourbon's 7,164, and Madison's 6,122. By 1840 Fayette and Woodford counties, with 11,309 and 5,924 blacks respectively, were more than one-half black, and Bourbon County almost matched that figure. A decade later all three counties were more than 50 percent black. In 1850 Louisville and Jefferson County, where the total black population had been second to Fayette County after 1820, emerged with the largest number at 12,548.

Among the Bluegrass counties in 1860, only Woodford County remained more than one-half black. The black population swelled to more than 40 percent in seven Bluegrass counties and 30 percent in eight others. Only Jefferson County, where blacks were one-third of the inhabitants in 1820, had a dramatic proportional decline in black residents. Though Jefferson County had 12,311 blacks in 1860, they accounted for only 13.8 percent of the population.

Though primarily rural, most counties in the Bluegrass had a population center where blacks were a sizeable portion of the community. Lexington, with 439 slaves, was one-quarter black in 1800, and never fell below 30 percent during the antebellum period. The town's black ratio reached its zenith in 1840 when it rose to 41 percent of the inhabitants. In 1860 Lexington contained 3,080 blacks among its 9,521 people. Louisville's population was quite small in 1810 when 495 blacks comprised about one-third of the town's residents. Though Louisville began growing rapidly shortly thereafter, the black ratio of the inhabitants steadily declined. In 1860 Louisville's 6,820 blacks, the largest urban concentration in the Commonwealth, comprised only 10 percent of the city's inhabitants. Frankfort began the century with only five freemen and 260 slaves, but they amounted to 42 percent of the town's population. During the 1820s and 1830s the capital was almost one-half black. Though Frankfort's black population grew to over 1,200 in the last two decades before the Civil War, blacks declined proportionally to slightly more than one-third of the inhabitants. The number of blacks was small in the other Bluegrass towns; however, they remained proportionally high in several. Blacks constituted almost 40 percent of the population of Harrodsburg and Danville after 1800, and Versailles was nearly one-half black after 1810. Versailles consistently had the highest percentage of black inhabitants for any Bluegrass town. Danville's black population increased fivefold between 1840 and 1860, reaching 2,076 in the latter year, to become the third-largest in the Bluegrass. Georgetown, with 912 slaves, was 63 percent black in 1840. Slavery, clearly, was more important to the economies of smaller Bluegrass towns than in the city of Lexington, and in Louisville bondsmanship was in a state of rapid decline.

Several large concentrations of blacks existed in western Kentucky, the region from the knobs that bordered the Bluegrass and the rolling, hilly, sometimes rugged landscape that touched the southeastern Kentucky mountains, westward to the Tennessee River. Their number grew with the increasing settlement of each decade. In the northern counties farmers settled on the gently rolling hills, divided by numerous streams that formed broad alluvial bottoms of fertile soils, and in the southern counties they flocked to the moderate-to-fair limestone soil which reminded settlers of the Bluegrass.[24]

The black population in the Ohio River counties in the west was consistently high, with Henderson County the largest center. Black residents never numbered below 30 percent of the county population after 1800, and totaled more than 40 percent in 1820 and in 1860. Henderson's blacks increased from 2,295 in 1820 to 5,844 in 1860. Union and Daviess counties, contiguous to Henderson County, contained the two other major concentrations of blacks along the river. Blacks comprised above 20 percent of the inhabitants of these counties after 1820, and each possessed more than 3,000 slaves in 1860. After 1830, however, all Ohio River counties except Henderson experienced a slight but steady decline proportional to their black populations. In 1860 only four counties in the northern half of western Kentucky—Meade, Daviess, Henderson, and Union, all bordering the Ohio River—were more than 20 percent black. Three northern counties had under 1,000 blacks in 1860. Grayson County's 354 blacks, the smallest number of any northern county, constituted only 5 percent of the population.

The growth of the black population in the southern counties in the western part of the state, especially along the Tennessee border, proved more dramatic. By 1810 blacks made up more than 10 percent of the inhabitants in every southern county, and in two, Logan and Green, accounted for more than one-fifth of the residents. From 1820 to 1840, blacks comprised over 20 percent of Green, Barren, and Warren, a tier of counties in southcentral Kentucky, and Trigg, a border county that touched the Tennessee River. In 1840 both Green and Barren counties contained about 4,000 black residents. Twenty years later, Trigg County, with 3,500 blacks, and Warren County, with 5,500, were 32 percent black. Blacks were also more than one-third of the population of Logan, Todd, and Christian counties, all bordering Tennessee, from 1820 to 1840. By 1860 Christian County's 10,008 blacks were 46 percent of the population, making it the third-largest county in black population in the Commonwealth. Logan's black population stood at 6,700 in 1860, the sixth largest concentration in Kentucky.

Henderson, Owensboro, Madisonville, and Hawesville were the

Figure 2

Counties and Regions of Kentucky in 1860

Percent Black in 1860

| Mountain | | Bluegrass | | Western | |
|---|---|---|---|---|---|
| Lewis | 3.0 | Mason | 22.8 | Lincoln | 33.7 |
| Greenup | 4.7 | Fleming | 17.1 | Casey | 11.1 |
| Carter | 4.1 | Bath | 21.8 | Adair | 17.4 |
| Boyd | 2.9 | Montgomery | 36.8 | Cumberland | 20.0 |
| Lawrence | 2.1 | Clark | 42.5 | Monroe | 11.0 |
| Morgan | 2.7 | Madison | 35.9 | Allen | 17.0 |
| Rowan | 6.2 | Garrard | 34.9 | Simpson | 29.5 |
| Powell | 6.6 | Boyle | 40.0 | Logan | 35.4 |
| Magoffin | 4.2 | Marion | 28.8 | Todd | 42.3 |
| Johnson | .9 | Nelson | 35.6 | Christian | 46.3 |
| Pike | 1.9 | Bullitt | 20.2 | Trigg | 31.6 |
| Floyd | 3.4 | Jefferson | 13.8 | Lyon | 21.5 |
| Breathitt | 4.3 | Oldham | 33.9 | Livingston | 17.4 |
| Owsley | 2.4 | Trimble | 14.2 | Crittenden | 10.9 |
| Estill | 7.6 | Carroll | 16.5 | Union | 24.4 |
| Jackson | 1.0 | Gallatin | 14.2 | Henderson | 40.9 |
| Rockcastle | 7.4 | Boone | 16.0 | Daviess | 23.1 |
| Laurel | 3.4 | Kenton | 2.6 | Hancock | 13.4 |
| Clay | 9.2 | Campbell | 1.0 | Breckinridge | 17.8 |
| Perry | 2.2 | Bracken | 7.6 | Meade | 22.0 |
| Letcher | 3.0 | Pendleton | 4.7 | Hardin | 16.9 |
| Harlan | 2.6 | Harrison | 24.9 | Larue | 13.1 |
| Knox | 8.7 | Nicholas | 16.0 | Taylor | 23.0 |
| Whitley | 2.9 | Bourbon | 47.6 | Green | 28.2 |
| Pulaski | 8.0 | Fayette | 47.3 | Metcalfe | 12.3 |
| Russell | 9.5 | Jessamine | 40.1 | Barren | 24.8 |
| Wayne | 9.9 | Woodford | 52.9 | Warren | 31.9 |
| Clinton | 4.8 | Anderson | 18.5 | Butler | 10.0 |
| | | Washington | 24.8 | Muhlenberg | 15.1 |
| Jackson Purchase | | Mercer | 25.9 | Hopkins | 17.2 |
| Marshall | 5.5 | Spencer | 38.5 | Caldwell | 26.2 |
| Calloway | 15.1 | Shelby | 41.3 | Webster | 14.8 |
| Graves | 17.5 | Henry | 28.0 | McLean | 14.9 |
| Fulton | 20.6 | Owen | 13.6 | Ohio | 10.8 |
| Hickman | 18.1 | Grant | 8.7 | Grayson | 4.4 |
| Ballard | 20.0 | Scott | 41.5 | Hart | 19.0 |
| McCracken | 17.4 | Franklin | 30.2 | Edmonson | 6.1 |

four largest towns in the northern counties of this section. Blacks were 25 percent of Henderson's population in 1800 and 37 percent in 1830. By 1850 almost half of the town's 1,775 residents were black. Owenboro's black population moved the opposite direction and dropped from 49 to 28 percent between 1830 and 1860. In the latter year there were 650 blacks among the town's 2,308 residents. Madisonville's population of 602 in 1860 included 165 black inhabitants. Blacks were 9 percent of Hawesville's 1,128 residents in 1860. In each of these towns, the percentage of black inhabitants was roughly proportional to the percentage of blacks in the county.

Hopkinsville was one of the largest towns in the southern counties of western Kentucky. Blacks comprised about 43 percent of the community in the early decades of the 1800s, and were more than one-half of the residents in 1860, when they totaled 1,268. From 1800 to 1850, about 40 percent of Russellville's residents were black, a figure slightly higher than the county's percentage of blacks, and in 1850 the town contained 560 blacks. Ten years later, in 1860, Russellville's blacks had declined to 280, still one-fourth of the residents. The 389 slaves in Cadiz in 1860 were 56 percent of that town's inhabitants, and in Bowling Green blacks increased from about one-third of the population during the first two decades of the nineteenth century to 40 percent in 1830, when 330 blacks lived among 491 whites. Franklin was one-third black in 1830 and 1860, but in real numbers jumped from 95 to 269. The black populations of southern Kentucky towns were consistently higher proportionally than in the rural areas during the antebellum period.

The Jackson Purchase, the area of Kentucky west of the Tennessee River, was not opened for settlement until bought from the Indians by the Federal government in 1818. The region, named in honor of one of the treaty negotiators, Andrew Jackson, is an undulating plain of fairly low elevation dissected by numerous streams and rivers, creating rich, alluvial bottom lands.[25] Settlers took their slaves into the Jackson Purchase, but in relatively small numbers. In 1830 there were only 1,737 blacks in the Purchase counties. Blacks were fewer than 20 percent of the population in three of the counties through 1840 and under 10 percent in the fourth. The black population grew to 4,000 in 1840 when there was a total of 31,000 settlers. During the next two decades the population grew rapidly, and the legislature carved three new counties out of the Purchase. In two of the new counties, Ballard and Fulton, blacks increased to 20 percent of the population by 1860, but in the third, Marshall, were only 6 percent of the inhabitants. The four other counties averaged about 16 percent black in 1860. Graves County possessed the largest number of blacks in 1860 at 2,847, and Marshall County, with 386, the fewest.

Few towns existed in the Jackson Purchase, and most of them experienced a decline in black residents, in proportion to whites, as 1860 approached. Black residents in Paducah, the largest town, decreased as a percentage of the population from 22 to 12 between 1830 and 1860, though the number of blacks had grown from 23 to 547. During those same years, the white population increased from 82 to 4,043. Columbus had 124 blacks in both 1830 and in 1860, but blacks dropped from 63 to 13 percent of the community. Only the hamlet of Clinton experienced a significant proportional growth in its black community, about 8 percent, between 1830 and 1860.

Blacks played an important role in the exploration and settlement of Kentucky, providing much of the labor. They worked closely with their masters or employers and during Indian hostilities demonstrated unyielding loyalty. While blacks were part of the history of every county, their contribution naturally proved greater in areas where their numbers were larger. Statistically, Fayette, Woodford, and the surrounding Bluegrass counties, along with their towns, possessed the largest concentration of blacks in the Commonwealth. Large pockets of blacks also lived in Ohio River cities and towns, especially west of Oldham County. Most of the Ohio River counties of western Kentucky contained high percentages of black residents, as did a tier of counties along the Tennessee border. Kentucky's smallest black populations lived in eastern Kentucky and the Jackson Purchase.

No matter where they lived, or in what numbers, black Kentuckians represented more than mere statistics. They were human beings who contributed mightily to the land their owners claimed and the prosperity whites monopolized; yet their rewards were few. But like other people around the world, they too hoped to improve their condition and to enjoy life as best they could, given their difficult circumstances under slavery. This book is an account of how blacks sought to share in the world they helped create and of their successes and failures. It is a story of struggle against overwhelming odds and of the human spirit.

*One*

# Labor, Living Conditions, and the Family

MIGRATION to Kentucky was a traumatic experience for many slaves. Francis Frederick, a twelve-year-old slave living in Fauquier County, Virginia, recalled learning in 1809 that his family would be moving with their master to frontier Kentucky. After thorough preparation, Frederick's family bid a tearful farewell to their friends, and several wagons loaded with "sobbing women" followed by "stony"-faced men began the journey through the forests with their owners. Living on meal cakes and salt herring, the "sorrowful cavalcade" crossed the Appalachian Mountains before turning northward toward Wheeling, Virginia, and the Ohio River. There they boarded a flatboat for Maysville, Kentucky, from where they trudged another twenty miles on foot to their new home in Mason County.[1]

For a few slaves the move to Kentucky proved beneficial. The son of William Webb's master married a Kentucky girl, and William moved northward by wagon with his youthful owner, away from the harsher conditions of Mississippi. After a hard journey of five weeks over poor roads, the migrants settled on a tobacco farm in Logan County.[2]

Josiah Henson left Maryland for Kentucky under unusual circumstances. On a cold February night in 1825, his financially troubled owner appeared unexpectedly in Henson's cabin and told him: "I want you to run away . . . to my brother Amos in Kentucky, and take all the servants with you." Josiah agreed to do as he was ordered. Leaving his home late one night with a pass for eighteen slaves and their families and carrying their supplies in a one-horse wagon, Henson shepherded his fellow slaves overland to Cumberland, Maryland. There they took the National Road to Wheeling, where Henson, following his master's orders, sold the wagon and purchased a flatboat. The slave band descended the Ohio River, stopping at Cincinnati where Henson learned they were on free soil. Local blacks could not understand why Henson and his fellow slaves did not grasp freedom while they had a chance, but Henson explained that he had given his word to deliver his charges to Kentucky. In April 1825 Henson arrived at the farm of his master's brother in Daviess County.[3]

Some slaves entered Kentucky under more unfortunate circumstances. Peter and Levin Still, free black children ages six and eight, were kidnapped when they wandered away from their home near Philadelphia, Pennsylvania. As darkness approached, "a tall dark man" riding by in a wagon offered to help them find their mother. Peter and Levin climbed into the wagon and began a journey into captivity. The two children lost track of time as they traveled first by wagon and then by boat until they reached Versailles, Kentucky. From there they were taken to Lexington and sold into slavery.[4]

Thousands more came to Kentucky in chains. Whether they tramped through Cumberland Gap along the Wilderness Trail before journeying northward to the heart of the Bluegrass or whether they floated down the Ohio River to counties in western Kentucky, they came in shackles. Handcuffed men chained together in long lines led women and children who plodded behind, followed by supply wagons and pack horses. Most came as slave laborers who undertook the drudgery of carving a farm from the Kentucky wilderness. In later years, when the demand for labor diminished in Kentucky, many of these slaves and their children eventually wound up in the Deep South.[5]

Most Kentucky bondsmen labored in a land of small, self-sufficient farms, a circumstance very different from the South as a whole where 25 percent lived on large plantations with at least fifty bondsmen. Geographic features and farmers' lack of capital meant that most whites never owned chattel labor, and as late as 1850 about one-fourth of the 38,385 masters possessed just one slave. Eighty-eight percent of Kentucky's slave owners had fewer than twenty bondsmen in 1850, about sixty slaveholders possessed as many as fifty, and only five masters owned more than one hundred. The average master had about five slaves. Still, only in Virginia and Georgia were slaves scattered among more owners. Missouri alone had a smaller slaveholding average than Kentucky. Nevertheless, black slavery became "ingrained and convenient" among small landholding white farmers, and with the passage of time and increased profits from farms where bondsmen worked the fields, the institution became almost sacred.[6]

Kentucky slaves usually labored side-by-side with their masters, working as farmers, handymen, cattlemen, and merchants. They performed jobs that were, for the most part, routine and could be learned easily and checked without difficulty. Bondsmen arose early and fed the horses, mules, and oxen. They tended the chickens and slopped the hogs. Slaves hauled salt blocks to the fields, counted the farm animals, and drove cattle and sheep from one pasture to another. Bondsmen plowed the fields and raised corn, sweet potatoes, and wheat for the farm, as well as the cash crops of tobacco, hemp, and flax. They weeded and harvested garden vegetables and trucked produce and staples to market. Bondsmen broke horses and mules, chopped out briar patches, cleared additional pasture or crop land, and shelled corn. Old or handicapped slaves, unable to work in the fields, sometimes carded wool, spun cotton or woolen thread, wove or dyed cloth, and tailored clothes. In short, they provided the labor that made Kentucky such a prosperous antebellum state.[7]

Those who toiled primarily as field hands were probably the most exploited slaves in Kentucky. Both blacks and whites judged the field hands' status and working conditions the lowest, with the fewest opportunities for improvement. Field hands performed the hardest, most monotonous jobs on the larger farms where the size of the work force tended to make relationships with owners less personal. The workday began at dawn for field hands and ended about dusk, with an hour or two of rest during the heat of the day. It was not unusual for females to work in the fields, especially during the pressure of harvest, an aspect of bondage many slave husbands found most disturbing. In the words of one former slave, the field hand, whether male or female, could look forward to little "but the setting of the sun." But as Steven A. Channing and Eugene D. Genovese point out, some slaves preferred working in the fields in spite of less favorable conditions, since it provided them with opportunities to express opinions to fellow bondsmen away from their masters' watchful eyes.[8]

The field hand's regimen varied from farm to farm, by the season and with each crop. A Madison County field hand, A.T. Jones, described being led to work on a typical day by his brother, a fellow slave who received orders from their owner and served as foreman for fifteen slaves. Once given assignments, the bondsmen acted as their "own managers," working in small groups in the fields, a system Jones believed less burdensome than others. Isaac Johnson's owner was a slave trader with a large farm on the Beech Fork River in Nelson County. The fifteen permanent slaves on that farm knew their jobs well, and after harvest in the fall they worked during the winter with little supervision shelling corn, making whiskey, and hauling grain to the mill.⁹

Bert Mayfield remembered from his youth the spring days on his farm when a horn blew at sun up and the slaves, both male and female, gathered their buckets and pots and walked to a nearby sugar maple grove. Mayfield watched the men tap the trees, insert the spikes, and begin collecting the sap in large troughs, while the women began preparations to boil the sap into sugar. "Sugar camp" represented one of the best times—among other, difficult ones—for Mayfield. Its sugar cakes for the children lessened the dread of the hard work and long hours involved in producing maple sugar.¹⁰

Working in hemp fields was the hardest, dirtiest, most laborious agricultural task performed by Kentucky field hands. Many antebellum Bluegrass farmers stated that the cultivation of hemp, a raw material used to make rope and a rough cloth, was the most profitable use of slave labor, and they often employed large groups of slaves under an overseer. The labor-intensive hemp crop began with hand-sown seeds in early spring and weeding during the summer. In August and September the slaves returned to the fields where they hand-cut and stacked the stalks in shocks. An adult slave was expected to cut a "land" and a half for a day's work, the equivalent of an eighteen-foot-wide swath across an eighty-acre field. After the winter rains began and the first frost appeared, the workers returned to the fields, this time to spread the dried stalks over the ground to allow dew, rain, and frost to soften them. Once ground rotting separated the desired fibers from the stalk, slaves returned to the field to re-shock the stalks and prepare for the "breaking" season, which had to be completed before spring plowing. Shortly after Christmas, the slaves marched through the shocks with their handmade wooden breaks and began the process that detached the desired fibers from the stalks. Slaves then tied the usable fibers together, discarding the "shives" to be burned.¹¹

Tobacco, which kept workers busy almost year-round, was another cash crop believed suited for chattel labor. After extensive preparation, slaves broadcast the tobacco seed into a seedbed in March or April and then covered it to prevent damage from frost. Weeks later they transplanted the seedlings by hand, with one worker punching holes in the soil with a stick and another placing the plant in the ground. During the spring and summer, slaves hoed weeds and picked worms off the crop. At midsummer they "topped" and "suckered" the plants. In August and September slaves cut the tobacco by hand, and after a period of wilting in the sun, hauled it to the barn for curing. In late fall, they stripped the leaves from the stalk and tied them into bundles. Bondsmen also frequently hauled the tobacco to market.

Early tobacco cultivation in the Bluegrass gave way to hemp, primarily because of price fluctuations and the difficulty of getting the leaf to market. Improvements in riverboat transportation shifted tobacco production, and with it large numbers of slaves, to the counties of western Kentucky. By the second quarter of the nineteenth century, Daviess, Christian, Todd, Henderson, and Barren counties, all with large slave populations, were the hub of tobacco culture.[12]

Many of Kentucky's slaves toiled not in the fields but in homes. Such service as personal or domestic bondsmen was apparently desired by all but a few. Some house slaves enjoyed an easier life, and their close relationship with their masters offered them perhaps their only opportunity for emancipation. But such proximity also made them always near, always subject to their owners' whims and wills. Still, there was strong competition for household positions, which sometimes produced class conflict within the slave community. Being chosen as a domestic servant occasionally resulted in hostility from those left behind in the fields, and bondsmen chosen for domestic service in the big house often developed a strong loyalty to their owner. Indeed, house servants had little option but to perform well and to display devotion for their owners, since failure to do so meant returning to the fields.

The most elite position among the house servants is represented in the career of Charles Dupuy, Henry Clay's favorite slave, the devoted major-domo at Ashland and valet to the senator when he traveled to Washington, D.C. Called a "perfect servant," the cultured Charles was a "kind of second master" at Ashland. He kept the keys to the wine cellar, and was appropriately "at the door, at the carriage, [or] at the gate." As a reward for his faithfulness, Clay emancipated Charles in 1844.[13]

Charles's duties at Ashland were similar to those of Alfred Robinson, the "house-man" at Greenbrier Plantation in Nelson County. As a young man, Alfred went through an "apprenticeship" during which his owner evaluated his performance. Eventually, Greenbrier's master chose Alfred as "valet," singling out the slave for "special" tasks around the house. Alfred's new responsibilities were largely managerial and ceremonial. He had to look nice, especially when his owner entertained, and to be at the beck and call of his master. Alfred met visitors at the door, bowed and scraped when they left, and coordinated the activities of "front-house" servants. When his master traveled, Alfred often accompanied him, and when Alfred traveled alone, he found that his position as valet made a pass unnecessary.[14]

In spite of the white stereotype of the well-treated, faithful bondsman, some slaves found no fulfillment in being personal servants. Thomas Hughes, the valet of a Louisville professional gambler, thought himself very fortunate when purchased by his owner from a Kentucky slave gang headed south. After three years of "miserable" service, Hughes again found himself on his way to Louisiana. Levi, another of Henry Clay's trusted personal servants, unlike Charles, temporarily chose running away over favored service with the senator. In 1849, while traveling with Clay in Newport, R.I., Levi fled to freedom, returned two days later, escaped again at Buffalo, N.Y., and finally turned himself in to a Clay relative in Louisville.[15]

While some wealthy farmers, lawyers, and businessmen in Kentucky had servants like Charles, Alfred, Thomas, and Levi, they were not typical household slaves. The most common domestic servants were, in fact, women, who lived in a world far less genteel and demonstrably less comfortable than Charles' male world. These female domestic workers performed the typical but tedious tasks required in every home. They served as cooks who rose early in the morning, built fires, milked cows, and prepared breakfast for the whites. They cleaned the farmhouse, washed clothes with lye soap in a pot of boiling water in the yard, and did the ironing while preparing the noon and evening meals. As time allowed, they made and mended clothes and when necessary tended the sick. Indeed, most of Kentucky's household servants, whether male or female, performed chores that took them outside the house, and they might be described more accurately, on the small slaveholding farms of the Commonwealth, as "primarily" indoor slaves.[16]

Caring for the master's children was a common task assigned house slaves. They more often than not slept in their owner's home so they could tend to the baby or nurse sick children during the night. Domestic slaves faced risks, even in the best of homes, when they assumed these tasks. A white Methodist minister whipped Mary because she "let" his daughter Helen fall against the stove, calling the servant's explanation a "falsehood." In Christian County a jury sent a slave girl to the gallows in 1812 when a child in her care died suddenly, though the community was quite "divided" on the question of responsibility. Those who called the verdict unjust believed the servant merely attempted to quieten a "fretful child" with laudanum, but others thought the slave deliberately administered an overdose.[17]

When the young son of the famous antislavery leader Cassius M. Clay suddenly became ill and, after three weeks of terrible suffering, died, Clay suspected the boy's nurse, Emily, of poisoning his child. Emily lived under the suspicion of murder for two years before being indicted. While she awaited trial, Clay, convinced of their complicity, sent her mother, brother, and sister to the New Orleans slave market. In spite of the malevolent atmosphere, a proslavery jury found Emily innocent, but Clay sold Emily south anyway.[18]

Having a mean-tempered mistress was another problem domestic servants faced. Henry Bibb, a household slave during his youth, called his mistress a "tyrant." Bibb built the fires in the kitchen and bedrooms, scrubbed the floors, washed clothes, and polished furniture, only to get frequent scoldings and his ears boxed. When napping in her rocking chair, Bibb's mistress required him to stand by to shoo flies that might interrupt her sleep, a task that convinced him that she was "too lazy to scratch her own head."[19]

Most male bondsmen were "primarily" outdoor slaves. Some were semiskilled or even skilled laborers whose training depended upon the number of slaves and the size and scope of their farm. While it is impossible to determine how many slaves fell into this category, it appears that farm owners and managers depended on slaves for much nonagricultural labor. George and Jim were skilled slave carpenters who lived on John Breckinridge's large Bluegrass farm in the early 1800s. Once Breckinridge gave them their instructions, they worked, for the most part, with little supervision, even going to the local merchant for plane irons, nails, and other supplies. The slave carpenters felled trees, prepared lumber, and built ox carts, stables, and outbuildings. In one of their larger projects, George and Jim weatherboarded the kitchen and began preparing planks, scantling, and shingles for an extensive expansion of Breckinridge's mansion. Breckinridge also had an "expert hostler," Johnny, who was in "charge" of training his horses.[20]

On farms all across Kentucky slaves were tanners, spinners, and weavers. George Conrad was a "stiller" on a Harrison County farm that produced a cash crop of three barrels of whiskey a day in the 1850s. Other slaves saved their owners money by learning the blacksmith trade, and wood-choppers kept the kitchen fires burning year-round and home fires blazing during winter on many Kentucky farms.[21]

Slaves with specific skills were a valuable asset, but because of their talents, many bondsmen were able to bargain for something they wanted. William Hayden, dissatisfied with his lot, began a work slow-down, forcing his owner to allow Hayden to hire his own time at ten dollars a month. Hayden worked in a rope factory and as a boot cleaner, ran errands, and played the tambourine at parties before taking up barbering. Eventually, his master built him a barbershop in Georgetown, greatly improving Hayden's lifestyle. Milton Clarke, the slave of a Presbyterian minister, was an accomplished musician who played bass drums and the bugle. Milton frequently entertained various white groups, and when he learned that his master was charging for these performances, the slave decided to force his owner to pay him a share. Milton sold his instruments, to his owner's dismay, saying he was "tired of playing." Eventually, using his talent as leverage, Milton and his master "compromised." Milton repurchased his instruments and agreed to play, but for half the profits. His manipulation of his master convinced Milton that, given the chance, he "could take care" of himself as a free person.[22]

Even before statehood, masters had utilized slave labor in manufacturing establishments and businesses. Such work increased thereafter. In 1807 bondsmen labored in the salt works of Mason County and later in the salt pits of Clay County. The Bourbon Iron Works Company used slave labor as early as 1791, and in 1810 an iron manufacturer located his mill in Louisville because of the abundance of cheap slave labor. In the 1850s slave gangs helped build the Louisville and Nashville Railroad, and during the Civil War slaves worked as iron moulders, wood choppers, charcoal makers, and teamsters at the iron furnaces of Mason, Fleming, Montgomery, Bath, and Clark counties. Bondsmen from southern Christian County toiled at the iron works just over the Tennessee line, and dominated the labor force in the iron and lead mines of Crittenden and Caldwell counties in the 1830s.[23]

While some cotton and woolen manufacturers used slave labor—a few plants employed as many as 150 workers—a greater number toiled in rope walks and hemp factories located in Fayette or surrounding counties. These factories, dating from before statehood, utilized locally produced hemp to manufacture twine, rope, bagging, and a cheap cloth. Those slaves working in the rope walks and bagging factories were not always, as some observers previously claimed, confined to the uncomplicated tasks. A visitor at a Lexington hemp factory in 1830 was surprised at the "skill" demonstrated by the sixty to one hundred "stout" and "healthy" bondsmen who performed the company's spinning and weaving. The constantly increasing utilization of slave labor in manufacturing left no doubt as to its growing profitability.[24]

Kentucky's rivers, connecting the Commonwealth with the free states and the Deep South, provided employment and travel opportunities for large numbers of bondsmen. While most slaves employed on the state's docks and rivers were hired out, others worked with or for their masters. Slaves moved the cargoes in Maysville, Covington, Frankfort, Bowling Green, Smithland, and Paducah, working on the docks and riverboats that plied the Ohio, Kentucky, Green, Cumberland, Barren, and Tennessee rivers. For five or six years Isaac Griffin of Trimble County worked on the Ohio and Mississippi, making numerous trips to the Lower South on flatboats. Griffin eventually saved enough of his extra earnings to buy freedom for himself, his wife, and one of his children. The situation of Aaron Siddles was similar. While being taken to the Lower South, Siddles persuaded Timothy Guard, a white man, to purchase him. Guard put Siddles to work as a steward on a steamboat where he improved his salary from thirty-five to a hundred dollars a month. Siddles saved enough money over the next seven years to purchase his freedom.[25]

Following rivers into the Deep South could be dangerous for slaves. In the early 1830s Josiah Henson and his master's son took a load of produce down the Mississippi. Henson suspected he might be sold in New Orleans, and upon reaching that city, his fears were confirmed. Before his sale, however, Henson's young master became gravely ill and begged the slave to help him return to Kentucky. Henson nursed his owner during the journey home, but his experience convinced him to run away at the first opportunity. Stephen Dickenson, Jr., was not so fortunate as Josiah Henson. Dickenson was a New York freeman stolen in 1837 off a ship docked in New Orleans and sold into slavery. A Kentuckian who had taken a load of horses south purchased Dickenson, eventually taking him to Hart County. Later, after contacting lawyers, Dickenson proved he was a freeman, but years passed before he secured his freedom.[26]

Kentucky slaves toiled at a host of different jobs, wherever labor was in demand. Slaves built roads, canals, and bridges, and tourists frequently commented on the number of bondsmen working in hotels and restaurants where they were waiters, maids, and cooks. A visitor to Lexington in 1807 reported that vegetables at the local market "were sold mostly by negro men and women" and that blacks were the most prominent "sellers and buyers." Peter Bruner wrote in his memoirs about a fellow bondsman, "Black John," who delivered his master's leather products to market in Winchester and Lexington. Slaves also worked as butchers, midwives, jockeys, groomsmen, and stablemen. A skilled furniture maker, Robert Boyd, is credited with inventing the "corded bed."[27]

Blacks also served as guides at two of Kentucky's famous tourist attractions. In Louisville, visitors from around the world listened to a slave guide who described at length an artesian well which brought water to the surface from over two thousand feet below. At Mammoth Cave, chattel labor helped map underground passages and guided tourists during much of the antebellum period.[28]

Carrying mail was another unlikely job occasionally performed by slaves. At least two carriers in one Kentucky county used blacks, probably their slaves, to assist them in delivering the mail in the early 1800s. In Louisville a slave apparently worked as a paralegal for his master. When he was put up for auction in 1849, his owner advertised him as a "good *rough lawyer*" who could "take depositions" and "make out legal writings." The slave possessed special expertise at "brow-beating witnesses and other tricks of the trade," the announcement claimed, and while not "fitted" to practice in the higher courts of the state, the bondsman was described as unbeatable in common-law cases or before county magistrates.[29]

In an era when child labor was generally accepted, slave children were particularly vulnerable and sometimes entered the world of work at a very early age. Smart Edward Walker remembered being given "little chores around the house" of his Kenton County owner when he was about four years old. By age ten, Walker was already in the corn field "with the grown-up slaves." At age six, Madison County slave Lewis George Clarke began training as a house boy. Clarke built fires early in the morning, rocked children to sleep at nap time, and made sure there was always plenty of water in the house. Before his sale at auction at age seventeen, Clarke acquired virtually all the skills needed to run a household, including spinning, weaving, and sewing.[30]

Children, like adults, generally preferred working inside their master's house. Francis Frederick was especially pleased, when at age twelve, he was promoted to "house" duties. Waiting tables and helping in the kitchen allowed him to eat as never before. Kitchen work also offered a hungry Robert Anderson the opportunity to "shake the biscuit plate" or trip slightly, allowing a small amount of food to fall to the floor, knowing he would "get it."[31]

Living close to the farm owner sometimes provided upward mobility, however slight. Shortly after he became a house servant, Francis Frederick's mistress began correcting words he mispronounced. Frederick did not believe that his ability to enunciate improved very much, and he never learned to read, but he was convinced that listening to kitchen and dinner-table conversation was beneficial in the long run, allowing him to learn things he could never have acquired in the field.[32]

For most children, however, the vast majority of their duties were outside the farmhouse and largely agriculture-related. Children often went into the garden to gather tomatoes or chop weeds. Robert Anderson remembered pulling weeds as a child, a job he considered "back breaking work for a little fellow." Other children planted and cultivated farm crops, laboring long hours in the fields. On a typical hot summer morning Madison Campbell, a lad of only ten, arose early and, with his father and three white youths, entered the corn field before sunrise. When the day was over, Campbell remembered, he was expected to have completed the work of a "full hand." Generally, children served as inexpensive but convenient laborers around the farmhouse.[33]

A number of tasks existed for children in tobacco and hemp. When he was only ten, Allen Allensworth's owners sent him from his family in Louisville to work on a tobacco farm in Henderson County. Lewis Clarke, who labored in a tobacco patch as a sixteen-year-old lad, described it years later as "work which draws most cruelly upon the back." Garrard County youth Bert Mayfield recalled getting lighter work in the hemp field before he was fifteen, but around age sixteen the work load increased to about two-thirds that of an adult male.[34]

Childhood ended early also for those children who performed very useful services for their owners in factories. As early as 1793, slave children of fourteen and fifteen provided the labor for a Lexington nail factory. Peter Bruner worked in a tannery at age ten doing what he believed to be "a man's work." Bruner hauled tanning bark in a wheelbarrow, cleaned out tanning vats, handled animal hides through most of the tanning process, and stacked the finished product. Several times a week he operated the engine that powered the mill.[35]

Slave children generally proved to be efficient workers in bagging factories and rope walks. In 1830 one factory in Lexington employed from eighteen to twenty boys between the ages of eight and fifteen to spin rope "filling." Each worker selected his raw material, or tow, and weighed it in front of an overseer, who recorded the amount the bondsman took. The child placed his tow beside his spinning wheel and went to work producing a rough hemp thread filler for ropes. He then wound the finished product on a reel which the overseer weighed. Factories of this type were common in the Bluegrass area.[36]

At age nine Peter Still worked as an *"off-bearer"* in his owner's brickyard, a business where slaves provided most of the labor. All workers, including the children, had a production quota, and two children were expected to unload three thousand bricks a day. When Peter and his co-worker fell behind, disrupting everyone's quota, the other slaves and their master became angry. Punishment consisted of standing in a wheelbarrow for a prolonged period.[37]

Apprenticing slave children was a convenient and inexpensive way for slaveholders to acquire skilled artisans for their farms. A farmer without a shoemaker, blacksmith, cabinetmaker, or "tobacconist" could apprentice a youthful slave, usually until age twenty-one, and thereby acquire a skilled servant. Being apprenticed might occasionally prove beneficial. In Nicholas County, William McClintock frequently placed his slaves in apprenticeships with the promise of emancipation once they learned a trade and could support themselves. As part of his benevolent program, he insisted that female slaves learn to read, weave, and sew before he emancipated them at age twenty-one. In another instance of apprenticeship, Henry Boyd learned cabinetmaking, acquired his freedom, and became a widely known, skilled craftsman after moving to Cincinnati.[38]

William Edward's story, however, was far less assuasive. Edward was born in Ohio and believed his mother was free, but a Kentuckian claimed her as a bondswoman. Edward and his mother passed through the hands of several slave owners before she was sold south. Edward "heard" that his mother had the option of taking him with her, but chose instead to leave him in Kentucky with the promise of eventual freedom. When Edward was thirteen, his "owner" apprenticed him to a "tobacconist" until age twenty-one. After his apprenticeship, Edward continued to work at the same job, afraid to broach the question of his freedom, but at age twenty-five Edward demanded his "freedom papers." When told that he must work two more years, Edward protested and won the right to hire his own time at twenty dollars a month. Each time Edward inquired about his freedom he was told he must "stay a while longer," and Edward began to believe, as slaves promised emancipation often concluded, that only death brought "freedom papers." Near his twenty-seventh birthday Edward acquired his "free papers" and promptly left for Ohio and then Canada.[39]

Bondage theoretically claimed all of a slave's working time. But what could be ironically called "free time" did exist, and bondsmen labored to improve their own living conditions after satisfying their masters. Whatever melioration slaves made in their lives and those of their families depended, in addition to what their owners allowed, upon their own initiative and their willingness to toil additional hours in a society where ten or twelve hours was a normal workday.

Housing, a major concern of slaves, usually reflected the prosperity of owners and their willingness to share with their bondsmen. Slaveholders knew that their bondsmen did not want to be "crowded together," and that healthful cabins should be built on dry ground, be well ventilated, and have a good fireplace. That some sufficiently prosperous and beneficent owners built slave quarters that met these standards can be seen in photographs of cabins which have survived into the twentieth century. Other slaves were not so fortunate.[40]

Most slave cabins were built of logs, were properly chinked, and had brick or stone fireplaces, though chimneys were sometimes constructed of sticks and clay. Wood slabs usually enclosed the gables. Slaveholders occasionally constructed brick cabins, but natural stone gathered from the countryside provided a more common building material. Roofs usually consisted of wooden shingles. Although the doors of slave quarters were low by current standards, once slaves entered the cabins, they found the height of the building sufficient. Not enough windows existed, even in the better-quality cabins, but usually there was at least one. Cabin floors were almost always dirt.[41]

The vast majority of bondsmen lived on farms with only one or two slave cabins, each with a single room totaling between one hundred and two hundred square feet. Most cabins had a loft, reached by a ladder, that almost doubled living space. Dan Bogie of Garrard County described his home, one room down and another in the loft, as a "one-room" cabin. Located about one hundred yards from his owner's residence, the cabin housed the farm's four slaves who tilled two hundred acres. Thomas Burton grew up in an identical cabin, but called it "two rooms." The loft, like the first floor, had a window, and there were front and back doors. Harry Smith spent part of his youth in slave quarters consisting of several cabins, about ten feet tall, all with clay floors, joined together by common walls. These cabins appear little different from those of many white families.[42]

Some bondsmen looked back on their days in slave cabins with bitter memories. Robert Anderson remembered "little one room log huts" where from one to three families occupied quarters unfit for pigs. Betty Guwn labeled the one-room cabin where she and her husband reared their fifteen children a "shack." The large cracks in the logs, she told an interviewer, allowed her husband to "shoot" barking dogs "without opening the door." George W. Buckner, a native Green County slave, described his childhood home as a crude log cabin with "holes" for windows. During the winter they covered the windows with "bark shutters" to prevent rain and snow from blowing in. *The Examiner*, a Louisville newspaper, estimated in 1849 that the cost of lodging an average "field hand" was five dollars per annum, one indication of the quality of slave housing.[43]

Not all slaves lived on farms. Thousands resided in villages, towns, and cities. In Lexington, many "live-in" bondsmen resided in their masters' homes in servants' quarters. Other urban slaves in Lexington lived behind their masters' houses in a shack or cabin. The more houses there were on a block, the greater the number of urban domestic slaves living nearby. Lexington alleys were lined with the "live-out" quarters of hundreds of slaves, creating patches of black neighborhoods throughout the city. Similar housing patterns existed in Louisville, where there were heavy concentrations of blacks in almost all wards. In the more expensive residential sections, homes with two, three, and even four servant rooms were common. Thousands of slaves lived in brick, stone, or wooden outbuildings in alleys behind the homes of their masters. Generally, slave housing was better in the nicer neighborhoods. Those slaves forced to seek their own lodging in the black community, however, were usually poorly housed.[44]

The quality of interior furnishings within slave cabins differed sharply. Most adults slept on a bedstead; their children slept on a trundle bed. Mattresses were usually straw ticks, and bed covers were often rough linsey quilts made from pieces of worn-out clothing. The trundle bed slid or rolled under the bedstead, allowing additional room in the cabin during the day. For many families, however, beds were little more than "a pile of straw or a shuck mattress." Some bondsmen possessed rude tables, chairs or stools, and even chests for storing clothes. But for most slaves, tables were "slabs" of lumber placed across wooden boxes, chairs were few or nonexistent, and storage might consist of nothing more than a peg on the wall. William Hayden's "wardrobe" closet was an "old flour barrel," and Robert Anderson described life in the cabin where he grew up as having "no luxuries, no conveniences, and no privacy." The large fireplace at one end of the cabin provided warmth in the winter and cooking facilities year-round. Most cabins apparently had enough cooking utensils for the occupants. Pots hung over the fire on racks or tripods. Heated rocks or a skillet placed on hot coals provided additional cooking space. Cabin fires occasionally robbed families in bondage of whatever "property" they owned.[45]

Most Kentucky slaves enjoyed an adequate, though sometimes repetitious, diet. Those who worked around the "big house" possessed a distinct advantage by obtaining a variety of food with little extra effort since leftovers often went to domestic workers, cooks, and their families. On some of the larger farms, where sizeable numbers of slaves toiled, owners, in a routine similar to that followed on the plantations of the Deep South, distributed staple food supplies to their bondsmen on a weekly basis. Slaves assembled at the smoke house each Sunday morning on one Bluegrass farm to receive their allotment. The overseer weighed each slave's weekly portion of meat, usually four pounds of pork, measured a peck of meal, and poured each person a half-gallon of molasses. Beans, potatoes, and other vegetables raised on the farm supplemented the slave family's diet. On special occasions, owners passed out wheat bread, coffee, sugar, and syrup as a bonus for their slaves. But slave diets were "nutritionally" adequate by nineteenth-century standards only. Application of a modern nutritional yardstick finds slave diets, because of the frequent dumping of vitamins B, C, and D in the processing and preparation of food, deficient in calories, nutrients, and vitamins and high in fat content.[46]

For the vast majority who lived on small farms, however, meals meant a female slave cooking for her family in a cabin fireplace or in the yard during the summer. The basic foods eaten in the slave cabin were often coarse and monotonous, to be sure, but food was reasonably plentiful in season during good crop years. Slaves regularly ate beans, potatoes, cabbage, blackeyed peas, greens, and a wide variety of other vegetables grown on the farm. Biscuits and wheat bread broke the monotony of cornbread. Pork was the usual meat, but slaves could often rely on a plentiful supply of dairy products. In most areas of Kentucky, slaves had access to apples, peaches, cherries, and other fruits which grew in abundance.[47]

Not all slaves ate as well. Some bondsmen complained of "mush and milk" diets, of being limited to two meals a day, of the "poorest kind" of "fat meat," and of "no vegetables." But it was usually difficult for slaveholders to deprive bondsmen of an adequate diet. Except in the most inhumane of circumstances, Kentucky slaves supplemented their food supply in a number of ways. Indeed, many owners encouraged, even expected, their bondsmen to provide a portion of their own food by growing a garden. Slaves usually raised whatever they desired, and most managed to grow "plenty of vegetables," frequently selling any surplus at local markets. Others raised chickens for meat and eggs, and some owned livestock.[48]

Slaves also supplemented their diet with wild game. Opossums, rabbits, squirrels, and birds were favorite foods shot or trapped in the woods, and the numerous streams and rivers were abundant with fish. Slaves used some of their spare time to pick wild berries. Those who did not get enough food at home sometimes ate at other farms. Mary Crane remembered "Doc," a bondsman from a nearby farm and frequent mealtime visitor to the farm where she was enslaved, being fed by her owner. "Give [Mr.] Heady's Doc something to eat," her owner told his cook, Christine, Mary's grandmother. "He looks hungry."[49]

Masters who did not allow slaves enough leisure time for gardening or hunting, or who willfully deprived them of an adequate diet, usually saw such treatment repaid, as some hungry slaves resorted to filching food. Some slaveholders took pilfering for granted. Indeed, Lewis Clarke, who grew up in Madison County in the 1820s and

1830s, reported that there was "a kind of first principle" in the moral code of many slaves that those who "*worked* had a right to eat." According to Clarke, pigs, hens, chickens, turkeys, geese, and eggs often "disappeared" without a trace as slaves sought a "greater variety" of food.[50]

Not all food was taken for consumption. Black John, a Clark County slave, sold stolen food to acquire money. Black John, a slave friend said, had an uncanny ability to clean out a "man's smoke house" without leaving a clue. Those who purchased his booty apparently asked no questions. Henry Bibb, accused by his owner after he ran away of stealing wheat and other farm "articles" and selling them to a neighbor, rejected the label of thief. Since he had helped produce his master's wealth, Bibb reasoned, taking "a little from the abundance" was not "stealing." "A slave has a moral right," Bibb argued, to partake of what was "within his reach." Being caught possessing unauthorized food, however, might mean severe punishment. Lewis Clarke reported that blacks were sometimes whipped "unmercifully" when found with a chicken or pig they did not own. Yet hunger could be a powerful motivation.[51]

Almost all slaves wore homespun clothes, often sewn from cloth woven on the farm and colored with dye extracted from sassafras bark or from wild berries. While blues and browns predominated, many slaves wore colored prints, plaids, and stripes. Linsey-woolsey, a coarse linen, and wool or cotton and wool cloth, was very common slave clothing, as were osnaburg, duffels, kerseys, bombazette, and cassimer. Cotton cloths included calico, Kentucky jeans, fustian, duck, and drilling. Tow linen, a coarse cloth make from poorer quality flax fibers, was the major linen material used for slave coats, trousers, pantaloons, jeans, shirts, and dresses. In winter most slaves had either wool or fur hats, socks, and russet brogans made from brownish, untanned leather.[52]

On many farms in Kentucky, slaveholders handed out clothes yearly. Bert Mayfield remembered from his childhood seeing slaves called together and "measured with a string" for clothes passed out at Christmas. The quality of the clothing worn by slaves varied among farms, but in general, slaves were clothed with inferior garments. Except where slaves worked in their owners' houses or on small farms where they received hand-me-downs, they did not wear the same apparel as whites.[53]

Harriet Mason, whose owner was a successful minister and physician, remembered being dressed well. She wore cotton and tow linen dresses in the summer, linsey-woolsey in the winter and her shoes were "good" quality. Lewis Clarke also was provided satisfactory clothing. For summer wear Clarke owned one pair of pants and two shirts, all made from tow linen. During winter he put on woolsey pants, a jacket, and brogans. Will Oats dressed in cotton shirts, heavy underwear, and rough shoes while growing up in Wayne County in the 1850s but recalled that if his shoes wore out before spring weather arrived, he had to wait until fall for another pair. Josiah Henson described slaves' clothes on the Daviess County farm where he lived in the late 1820s as adequate. The adult slaves wore mostly hard-time cotton clothes with little variation between winter and summer. The men donned trousers and shirts and the women cheap calico skirts and blouses. Winter clothing included a jacket or overcoat and a pair of brogans. Men received a wool hat every two or three years.[54]

Not all slaves believed, however, that their clothing was sufficient. John Eubanks complained that his garments were completely inadequate for Kentucky winters. Eubanks often went without shoes during the coldest days even though he worked outside much of the time. The skin on his feet became cracked and scabbed before winter yielded to barefoot weather. Robert Glenn recalled working shoeless on the farm where he was a slave, and Henry Bibb wrote of not wearing shoes through the end of November.[55]

Children's clothing was especially poor on many farms. Typically, smaller children ran around the farm with only a "tow-cloth" shirt covering them. Henry Bibb told of his embarrassment as a child when his owner barely furnished him enough clothes to conceal his "nakedness." When an interviewer asked a slave mother in 1863 about the apparel furnished her daughter, she displayed a dress that was virtually "rags."[56]

The slave family in Kentucky suffered from severe disabilities. Under both the Virginia and Kentucky constitutions, slaves were personal chattel, legally passed from one owner to another. Slave marriages were unrecognized by law. The children of a female slave were the property of her owner regardless of the status of their father. Parental relationships with children were almost wholly dependent upon the whims of owners. For slaves, "family" was what they made of the opportunities allowed by their owners. One foreign visitor to Kentucky in the 1820s captured the dilemma of the slave family when he commented that bondsmen were "reared with more or less tenderness, or sold to another," as the owner "thinks fit."[57]

Slaves on Kentucky farms, like white folk, fell in love and married, but the circumstances surrounding the process of love, courtship, and marriage differed drastically. Permission of their owners proved to be the critical consideration. If their owners consented, few impediments prevented an early marriage. The material prosperity of the slaves received, in most instances, slight consideration. The prosperity of the owner of one's betrothed was far more important in the eyes of many slaves, since marrying the slave of a wealthy owner potentially meant upward mobility.[58]

Slave marriages were easiest when both mates lived on the same farm. If their owner consented to the union, all was well. When slaves from separate farms desired to marry, the situation was more complicated. Often owners of the two slaves reached a settlement whereby one master became owner of both slaves. But sometimes slaves from different farms united in wedlock without a change in ownership. Depending upon distance, this usually meant visits by the husband one or two nights and weekends, but many slaves only enjoyed family life on Saturdays and Sundays.[59]

Henry Bibb's romance and marriage to Malinda illustrates the problems of separate owners. At age eighteen Bibb fell in love with Malinda, an Oldham County bondswoman who "moved in the highest circle of slaves, and free people of color." Mesmerized by her "smooth" skin, her "penetrating eyes," and her beautiful singing voice, Bibb temporarily postponed his goal of freedom to propose marriage. Malinda's mother, hoping her daughter might marry a slave owned by a more prosperous family, did not favor the union. Bibb's owner also opposed the match, but Malinda's master favored it. All parties agreed to wait one year as a test of devotion. A year later, during the 1837 Christmas holidays, the couple married.

Shortly after the marriage, Bibb's owner decided to move to Missouri. Apprehensive that his slave might run away to rejoin Malinda, Bibb's master sold him to a local farmer. During this early period of his marriage, Bibb only lived with his wife from the time he finished his chores on Saturday until sunrise on Monday. Difficulties arising from separate ownership eventually led Malinda's owner to purchase her husband, at least partially solving their problems. Bibb was fortunate since many slave marriages endured decades of problems arising from separate ownership.[60]

Some owners refused to allow their slaves to be married to someone living on another farm. When Green Campbell's owner died, he became the property of another Madison County slaveholder, William White. Though Samira, Campbell's wife of many years, lived on a nearby farm, his new owner demanded that the bondsman take a new wife on the White farm. The conflict that developed because of his separation from Samira eventually led to Campbell's sale south.[61]

Slave nuptials varied from receiving permission to marry and immediately cohabitating, to extensive, elaborate wedding celebrations.

The broom ritual was probably the best known marriage ceremony among slaves. Whether "married" by the slave owner who held an informal ceremony or by the local black preacher, "jumping over the broomstick" was often part of the observance. In this ancient practice, the couple became man and wife when they stepped over a new broom placed on the floor. Reflecting on the tenuousness of slave marriages, one of Kentucky's most famous black preachers, Rev. London Ferrill, often pronounced couples married until parted by "death or *distance.*" Slave marriage ceremonies in Kentucky, as John W. Blassingame's groundbreaking work on *The Slave Community* reveals, were remarkably similar to those performed in the Lower South.[62]

Slave weddings were usually a time of celebration. Madison Campbell recalled the story of his father's wedding which he often heard as a child. It was an "old fashioned" wedding, his father recounted with delight. A huge supper followed the ceremony and many area blacks participated. After the meal, the couple and their friends sang and danced away the night.[63]

Francis Frederick left a classic description of one of the more elaborate slave weddings. When Jerry decided he wanted to marry Fanny, a house slave on a nearby Mason County farm, he visited her mistress to ask permission. Convinced of Jerry's sincerity, Fanny's mistress told him to choose a black preacher to perform the ceremony. During the next two weeks, Fanny's owners planned the wedding. Invited guests included Jerry's owners, numerous white neighbors, and about one hundred friends of Fanny and Jerry. On the night of the wedding, January's Tom, the preacher, appeared in formal attire. Fanny wore white muslin, white shoes, and her head was "decked with white and red artificials." When time for the ceremony came, January's Tom recited the service from memory. Jerry kissed his bride and the entire entourage sat down to dinner. Jerry's toast was perceptive. He wished that Fanny's owners would remain prosperous and that he, his wife, and their children would never be separated. It was a time of laughter, merry-making, and joy for all.[64]

One of the most controversial questions regarding slave marriages is the charge that Kentucky masters required slave unions in order to "breed" slaves for the voracious southern market. In the 1850s Frederick Law Olmsted stated that Kentucky, like other border states, put as much effort into the "breeding and growth of negroes" as it did into producing "horses and mules." Extant evidence of slave breeding, however, is sparse. The slave narratives and autobiographies are essentially silent on this matter. Only Andrew Jackson, who grew up near Bowling Green, wrote that his master ordered him to "get married" and, as Jackson interpreted the command, "enrich his plantation by a family of young slaves." J. Winston Coleman wrote, without citing a source, of an "old colonel" who lived north of Louisville who was well-known for breeding slaves. The colonel, according to Coleman, selected "his healthiest and most vigorous young mulatto girls for breeding purposes" in his profitable enterprise. The lack of source material shrouds the whole question of slave breeding, but little doubt exists that Kentucky slaveholders, as Frederic Bancroft and Kenneth M. Stampp have suggested, sold southward the excess of the natural increase of their bondsmen.[65]

Though both a father and mother were not always present in every home, the Kentucky slave family was a viable institution. When speaking about their homes, bondsmen frequently described a family headed by a female. Will Oates grew up in a Wayne County cabin with his mother, brothers and sisters, and grandmother. William Edward remembered only his mother, and Peter Bruner described a fatherless home. Without a doubt, slavery disrupted numerous families, making many homes matriarchal, but Henry Bibb's claim that it was "almost impossible" for Kentucky slaves to trace their male ancestry was not true for many bondsmen.[66]

Many slaves knew both their parents well and remembered them fondly. Allen Allensworth was the son of Levi and Phyllis Allensworth, Louisville slaves. Allen attributed much of his success in life to an industrious father and a pious mother who took him to Sunday school. Separated from his parents at age ten, and later sold south, Allen returned to Louisville after the outbreak of the Civil War for reunion with his mother.[67]

Though Alexander Walters lived as a slave for only a short period, the strongest personalities in his life were his parents. His mother, Harriet, was a tall, powerful woman who weighed two hundred pounds. She worked hard, prayed loudly, and taught Alexander the meaning of justice, even in a system of slavery. His father, Henry Walters, provided Alexander with the example of a "hopeful spirit." Walters enjoyed a healthy family life. He had three brothers and sisters and relatives who lived close by. An uncle, Billy Hardin, whom Walters believed to be "the most intelligent man of color" in the Bardstown area, lived on a neighboring farm with his wife, Mahala. She was his favorite aunt, and Walters wrote, "the loveliest and best" person he knew. Old enough to be his grandmother, Mahala provided the Walters children with sympathetic understanding and encouragement during the uncertainty of childhood.[68]

Madison Campbell also lived in a close-knit family. His mother, Lucy, and his father, Jackson, grew up in Madison County. His maternal grandfather, Aaron, was a neighborhood slave until he purchased his freedom. Campbell had no memory of his maternal grandmother, a slave on a local farm until sold south. Campbell's maternal great-grandfather, Tobias, and his wife, Mato, had been slaves in the neighborhood until emancipated in their old age. Daniel and Lydia, Campbell's paternal grandparents, were also slaves, as were their parents.

Campbell's youth was a happy period of his life, but he believed himself more fortunate than most slaves. Though he saw little of the "barbarity" of slavery where he lived, he was not unfamiliar with the humiliation of bondsmanship nor unaware of its harshness on others. Born the same year as was his master's son, David Campbell, Madison and David played side-by-side for years. Then suddenly, David went to school and Madison to work. It came as a rude awakening for Madison, and for the first time he contemplated the meaning of being a slave.[69]

Physical punishments were not harsh on the farm where Campbell lived, and they did not shape his memory of slavery. For Campbell the most abhorrent aspect of slavery was its destruction of family life by selling men, women, and children separately to the Deep South. In his mind each individual sold south represented the mother, father, or relative of a fellow human being, a conviction that grew after he married and had his own family. Campbell's wife and their children lived on another farm, and he constantly feared for their future. Uncertainty about his family made Campbell wish he "had never been born a slave."

Campbell's worst fears became reality when his brother, who lived on an adjacent farm, was sold south. Shortly thereafter, Campbell's world crumbled when his owner died, and the slaves went on sale. Eventually, four of Campbell's brothers, his mother, a sister, and three nieces and nephews were sold. Campbell's "old mistress" retained him, his father, and one sister. Later, when hired out, Campbell persuaded his wife's owner to hire him, thus reuniting his family. A few years later Campbell's wife and three of his children were sold locally. Campbell managed to hold his family together by finding employment for himself and his wife. Finally, in October 1863, Campbell purchased his freedom, but the bondage of his wife and children did not end until after the Civil War.[70]

The ordeal of Rev. Elisha Green and his wife, Susan, further illustrates the strength and vitality of the slave family. Enslaved in northern Kentucky, they married in 1835, but three years later Elisha's owner moved from Mayslick to Maysville. Susan and the children were sold locally several times during the Greens' first twenty years of marriage, but their greatest family tragedy occurred with the sale of a son "down the river."

One December in the mid-1850s, while traveling to Paris by stage, Rev. Green and his wife unexpectedly came upon their son John at the Blue Lick Hills stop. Lightly clad and without a coat, his hands tied, John was being sold south by his owner. The journey to Paris began with John's riding outside the stage, but the driver relented after a few miles and allowed him to sit inside. At Paris the coachman placed John in jail, and Elisha Green began a frantic effort to delay his son's sale. Green even telegraphed the father of John's owner, pleading that he intercede with his son to delay the sale, to give the reverend time to find a local buyer. John's owner rejected all appeals and sold him to a trader. "The sight of this act I thought would break the heart of my wife," Green later recalled in his memoirs. Selling John was "wicked and mean," Green wrote, but the most degrading aspect was seeing his son bound, inexorably moving south, and "not having the power to assist him in the least."[71]

Family life was even more difficult for Lewis and Milton Clarke. When their "owner-grandfather" died, his estate was auctioned, splitting their family among relatives of their former owner. Lewis's father, mother, sister Delia, and brothers Cyrus and Milton moved to Lexington, the property of Judith and Joseph Logan. Lewis devolved to Betsy Banton, whom he served until about age twenty-one. Though forced to labor under difficult circumstances and constantly faced with harsh punishment, Lewis considered separation from his "mother, brothers and sisters" his most grievous experience in slavery. Over the next eleven years, Lewis visited his mother only three times, even though she lived only thirty miles away. During those years, Lewis later wrote, his thoughts were always of "mother and home." When his mother died in 1833, eighteen-year-old Lewis could not attend her funeral.

Eventually, Lewis, Milton, and Cyrus Clarke all acquired freedom by fleeing their native state. Shortly thereafter, Lewis described what happened to his family. Archy, their oldest brother, purchased his freedom with the assistance of Cassius Clay. Archy repaid Clay, but died before he could purchase his family, leaving his wife and several children in bondage. Brother Dennis, with the aid of two white friends, also gained his freedom, but remained in Kentucky where he had a "good business." Christiana, a sister, married a freeman, but her owner terminated the union, refusing to allow them to live together. Another brother, Alexander, suffered no serious hardships under slavery, and he had no great desire to change his status. His master, a benevolent physician, allowed Alexander to live "like a second-hand gentleman." Delia, an "uncommonly handsome" woman, experienced more ill-treatment in Kentucky than did any other member of the Clarke family. After Delia was sexually and physically abused by her owner, slave traders took her to New Orleans in chains. There Delia's fortune improved when she met and married a prosperous Frenchman. Lewis Clarke believed that his family's varied experiences were not unique.[72]

In addition to the traditional reasons why families ceased to live together, slave families faced "nontraditional" causes of family separation. Families in bondage occasionally broke up when their owners moved from one area to another. Though slaves sometimes viewed moving with one's owner or his relatives, leaving family behind, as a personal tragedy, there were at least two advantages for the bondsmen. It meant that they were not being sold, perhaps relieving anxiety regarding future treatment, and the possibility of continued contact with relatives and friends left behind remained.

Frank and his wife Peggy, slaves of Nathaniel Gist of Lexington, learned to their sadness in 1817 that they, though in their old age, were moving to Alabama with two of Gist's nephews. Though accompanied by their two sons, they believed it a mixed blessing, since they expected a harsher life for their children in the Deep South. Two youthful slaves, Levin Still and Alfred, were also chosen to go, each leaving a brother behind. Before the caravan left, the slaves stood around shaking hands, trying to be cheerful, but tears betrayed their feelings. For Levin and his brother, Peter, the separation proved especially bitter. This would be the first time they had to live apart since they had been kidnapped from their mother.

Occasionally, slaves threatened with transfer to another location prevented the move. When Nathaniel Gist died, nephew Levi returned to Lexington to collect more slaves. This time he announced his intention to take Mary, the long-time housekeeper, and her two sons to Alabama. Mary objected. Her husband Sam, in bondage on another farm, expected emancipation shortly. Mary threatened to "hang herself" rather than leave her husband and home. Levi alternately badgered and begged, but without success. When it finally became apparent that Mary would not go to Alabama, Levi sold the housekeeper and her two sons to his father, who lived in Lexington, enabling the faithful slave to live out her days in Kentucky.[73]

Hiring out slaves also disrupted family unity. Typically, hired slaves reared their children until they reached about age eleven, when, according to one mother's account, masters usually took them to do chores around their houses. When a surplus of chattel labor existed, masters frequently hired out the children. Henry Bibb reported being "taken away from my mother" and hired out as a lad for eight or ten years. While hired children could not appeal to their parents during abusive treatment, they often sought redress of grievances through their owners. When the tobacco factory owner who had hired Peter Still whipped him severely, Peter ran away to his master's home. Peter's owner gave the lad a week off to recover and refused to renew the contract when it expired.[74]

The sale of slaves was the most common method of destroying slave families. Though Kentucky newspapers, antislavery leaders, and even some slaveholders denounced the separation of families, the fact remained that Kentucky slaveholders often disrupted families by selling slaves in large numbers for profit or for relief from financial pressure.

Owners sometimes sold women, separating them from their husbands and children. The wife of Dick Coleman, a Lexington slave, was sold to New Orleans, and in 1846 an Owensboro slaveholder sold Mary Stowers and her small daughter, but retained her four-year-old son Willis. Robert Anderson's owner sold Anderson's mother to slave traders who took her to the Deep South. She left behind her husband, Bill, who lived on a nearby farm, two sons, Robert and William, and three daughters, Silva, Agga, and Emma. Silva, fourteen, became the surrogate mother for six-year-old Robert and three-year-old Emma. Robert's father later married a woman on another farm, and though the child saw his father frequently, it was not often enough to establish a satisfactory "father and son" relationship.[75]

Advertisements of women and children for sale were mute testimony of the dissolution of many slave families. Newspapers regularly advertised "likely" bondswomen and their "healthy" children. A Lexington master placed on the market a twenty-six-year-old mother and her sixteen-month-old child in 1834, and the Lexington *Intelligencer* listed a slave, trained in domestic work, and her three small children. An 1831 advertisement in the Paris *Western Citizen* offered for sale a twenty-four-year-old slave woman and her two male children, ages two-and-one-half and six months. One foreign visitor described an 1822 auction in Louisville of a pregnant slave and her two children. The mother stoically stood with her children as the auctioneer "indulged himself" with references to her "thriving condition."[76]

Occasionally, advertisements broached the question of splitting families, a possible indication that it posed no moral question for some slaveholders and newspaper owners. An 1809 Bardstown newspaper advertised a young slave couple and their two children who might be purchased together or separately. The Louisville *Weekly Journal* listed a slave woman, her husband, and their two children in 1845. Though ill-disposed to send them "down the river," their owner offered to sell the husband separately. An 1831 advertisement listed a six-year-old boy for sale, and that same year a Gallatin County master sold Squire, a six-year-old male slave, to a Nicholas County man. J.T. Underwood's 1849 Louisville newspaper advertisement left no doubt: "I wish to sell a negro woman and four children. The woman is 22 years old, of good character, a good cook and washer. The children are very likely, from 6 years down to 1 ½. I will sell them together or separately to suit purchaser."[77]

Isaac Johnson left a classic description of family destruction at an auction sale. At about age eleven, Isaac stood on an auction block. When the bidding ended, a man took Isaac's hand and said: "Come along with me, boy, you belong to me." Isaac asked to see his mother, but the man refused and "hitched" the lad to a "post." Isaac watched as Ambrose, his four-year-old brother went on the block next, followed by his mother, with her youngest son, Eddie, still in her arms. When the bidding lagged, Isaac heard someone shout: "Put them up separately." One buyer purchased his mother and another Eddie. "Thus," Isaac wrote in his memoirs, "in a very short time, our happy family was scattered, without even the privilege of saying 'Good by.'" Isaac never saw any member of his family again.[78]

Faced with the prospect of being sold, slaves sometimes, with the aid of friends, held their families together. Mary Crane grew up a slave in Larue County. Her father lived on a nearby farm, and her grandfather resided in the vicinity. When her father's owner fell into financial trouble, he put Mary's father up at auction. Mary's grandfather "begged" his owner, Bob Cowherd, to buy his son. Cowherd agreed to do so, but during the auction "Nigger-traders" raised the bid a few dollars higher than Cowherd believed to be a "fair price." To get Cowherd to bid higher, Mary's grandfather promised to contribute his life's savings, twenty-five dollars. Cowherd made the purchase, and Mary's family remained intact in the neighborhood.[79]

The members of the Pleasant Green Baptist Church, through an unusual set of circumstances, prevented their slave minister, George Dupee, from being sold south. After his owner died in 1847, Dupee remained part of the estate until his sale in 1856. Members of Dupee's congregation persuaded William Pratt, the white minister of the First Baptist Church, and his board of deacons to purchase George, promising to reimburse them. Pratt and his deacons agreed, provided the price did not exceed eight hundred dollars. The night before the sale, Pratt, in an unusual move, persuaded the auctioneer to agree to an eight-hundred-dollar price, but the next day a slave trader drove the bid up before Dupee was "struck off" to Pratt at $830. Dupee's grateful congregation repaid Pratt, sending installments, tied in a handkerchief, to his home each Monday morning. Sadly, no friend intervened in behalf of Dupee's two brothers, Henry and Logan, who were auctioned at the same sale.[80]

Other slaves facing auction were less fortunate, even when friends and relatives worked to prevent their sale south. Tony Lee, the father of two beautiful Lexington slave girls, purchased their freedom when they were quite young, but they apparently continued living on the farm of their former owner. After their father's death, slave traders obtained the girls' "freedom papers" from their unsuspecting mother. In 1860, when the girls were seventeen and nineteen, they went up for auction to pay their former owner's debts.

Before the auction, Letty, the older of the girls, tried to get Lexingtonians to pledge toward her purchase, but secured subscriptions totaling only two hundred dollars. Nancy Lee, their grandmother, worked through influential white friends to persuade potential buyers not to bid, with only partial success. By the day of the auction, when the futility of their efforts was apparent, Nancy Lee, in desperation, told her story to Rev. William Pratt. Pratt agreed to bid for the girls, though aware of the hopelessness of the situation. He began bidding at eight hundred dollars. At a thousand dollars Pratt stepped forward and explained the situation of Nancy Lee and her granddaughters to the crowd, but without effect. The bidding resumed briskly, and at fifteen hundred Pratt withdrew. A well-known Lexington slave trading firm bought Letty for $1,700. A Covington slave trader purchased her younger sister for $1,600. Pratt called down God's anathema upon slave traders in his diary, but his curse did not prevent similar scenes of family disruption from occurring.[81]

Slaveholders were not responsible for all family destruction among bondsmen. Some slaves simply refused to continue living as husband and wife, regardless of the consequences. If sold, they accepted their sale as the inevitable end of their marriage. A forty-five-year-old mother of six waiting to be sold in a Louisville slave dealer's jail told an interviewer that her children were distraught when sold away from their father, but the woman expressed little concern regarding her own future. Another slave couple, interviewed while confined with their children in a Lexington slave dealer's pen, exhibited apathy regarding their future as a family.[82]

Still, most slaves separated from their families and friends showed a more than casual interest in their relatives and loved ones left behind, another indication of the vitality of the slave family. Slaves who ran away, who moved to Liberia, Africa, after emancipation, or who were sold south, occasionally communicated with their Kentucky owners to ask about relatives. Gooley's family split when she and her husband were moved to South Carolina. Gooley wrote her former owner asking about the health of her children—especially her "little daughter Judith"—her sister Clary, and other friends. Her life, she wrote her former mistress, had become more complicated since arriving in South Carolina. After giving birth to a new baby boy, Gooley wrote, she faced the prospect of seeing her husband, Joshua, with whom she preferred to remain, sold. It's "very bad to part man & wife," Gooley commented to her former mistress.[83]

Some slaves visited relatives and friends after being separated. "Black Ann" of Logan County occasionally visited her mother in Clarksville, Tennessee, through the assistance of her owner. In 1830 Josiah Henson, while on a trip from Kentucky to New Orleans, visited several "old companions" sold from his farm to a plantation in Mississippi. Though overjoyed to see each other, Henson became despondent after their description of their daily lives and work routine. His sojourn with his friends, Henson later recounted, was one of the saddest days of his life. In 1839, several years after the sale of Lewis Clarke's sister Delia, she returned to Madison County to visit her family. Received with "politeness" by her former owner, Delia remained in Madison County for several months, while she made arrangements to purchase the freedom of two of her brothers. Unfortunately, her plans never materialized because of her untimely death after returning to New Orleans.[84]

Advertisements for fugitives reveal that one of the major motives for running away was to visit family members. Mary Elizabeth, about fourteen years old, escaped from her Lexington owner in the fall of 1838 "to see her mother at Maysville." When twenty-three-year-old Spencer disappeared, his Lexington owner surmised that his slave was on his way to Bowling Green, where he had recently been purchased, or to Louisville, where he had grown up. Cynthia ran away from her Lexington owner, taking her two-month-old daughter with her. Having recently purchased her in Grant County, Cynthia's owner assumed she was returning there to visit her "relations." When Betsy, age forty, ran away, her Lexington owner suspected that she was hiding near a farm on the Richmond Road where her husband lived, and the master of twenty-seven-year-old Anthony believed the fugitive would go to the Cincinnati area where his family resided.[85]

Though vastly more difficult, bondsmen sold south occasionally returned to see their Kentucky relatives. A Yazoo County, Mississippi, slave owner advertised in a Lexington paper for his runaway, Henry, a man between thirty-five and forty, who had been "much scarred with the whip." The owner believed Henry was on his way back to his former Lexington home. When forty-five-year-old Jess fled a Georgia farm, his master concluded Jess would "doubtless" go to Lexington where he was reared, and the owner of Jacob, a Lowndes County, Mississippi, fugitive, decided that the bondsman was on his way to Fayette County to see his friends and relatives. In at least one instance, a Kentucky fugitive followed a loved one sold to the Deep South.[86]

While most Kentucky bondsmen worked alongside their masters, toiling at a wide variety of tasks, perhaps lessening some of the harsher aspects inherent in the institution of slavery, the belief of most whites in the inferiority of blacks condemned slaves to a life of unrelieved labor and vastly inferior living conditions. Those who hoped to improve their situation could only look forward, if opportunity allowed, to still longer work days. Even worse, Kentucky law did not recognize slave marriages, making parental relationships difficult, and in many instances impossible, since family disruption or destruction through hiring out practices or the slave trade were constant fears for all. In spite of their situation, the slave family was probably the strongest institution among bondsmen, demonstrating a remarkable resilience throughout the antebellum period. Unable to redress grievances on terms of fairness and possessing few viable alternatives, Kentucky slaves seemingly had little to look forward to but the "setting of the sun." Nevertheless, bondsmen built a society among themselves where hope for a better day prevailed over abject despair.

*Two*

# Slave Mobility, Recreation, Health, and Treatment

KENTUCKY law strictly regulated the movement of slaves. The first slave code, adopted in 1798, required slaves who were away from their residences for longer than four hours to possess a pass. This confined bondsmen to a distance of eight to ten miles from their homes. Only members of the slave owner's family, employers, or overseers could issue passes, and regulations provided stiff penalties for offenders. State law fixed a slave's punishment for not having a pass at "ten lashes on his or her bare back." Bondsmen who contemplated clandestine "unlawful assemblies" faced arrest by any white citizen who discovered them and severe punishment from the state.[1]

Town ordinances, usually designed to meet specific problems, frequently supplemented state restrictions on slave mobility. In Bardstown any slave entering the county seat on Sunday without a pass ran the risk of receiving ten lashes. An early Louisville ordinance prohibited more than three blacks from assembling at the market or other public places, and slaves who disturbed the peace on Sunday got fifteen lashes. An 1853 Falls City ordinance which called for increased scrutiny of black church gatherings limited services to Sundays from sunrise to 10:00 P.M. and Wednesdays from sunset to 10:00 P.M. The 10:00 P.M. tolling of the Louisville watch bell warned slaves without a pass that they had thirty minutes to scurry home. Those apprehended without a "good excuse" faced harsh punishment.[2]

Henderson's officials authorized as many as twenty stripes for slaves found on the streets in violation of the 10:00 P.M. curfew, and Bowling Green's trustees, slightly more lenient, ordered watchmen to administer up to ten stripes to slaves found away from their homes after 10:00 P.M. without a "satisfactory excuse." The town of Paris forbade slaves from entering its corporate limits, day or night, without a pass. Even bondsmen sent to Paris on errands, or selling their master's produce at the market, had to possess papers describing their exact activities, and resident slaves had to be off the streets by 9:00 P.M.[3]

Lexington's efforts to regulate the movement of blacks began in 1796. By the early 1800s, the city prohibited large gatherings of blacks on Saturdays and Sundays, and night watchmen patrolled the streets from 10:00 P.M. to 6:00 A.M. during the week to arrest bondsmen violating the curfew. This policy continued with only slight variation for more than sixty years. Because of the tendency of many of the blacks working at the market to linger in the area after the watch bell, Lexington trustees decided in 1854 to require slaves employed there to have a pass with them at all times.[4]

Additional patrols operated in almost every Kentucky county. They looked for runaways, slaves away from their cabins without passes, and watched suspected gathering places. State law required special vigilance by citizens of counties bordering the Ohio River. They had to monitor water craft tied to the Kentucky shore and guard local crossings. Their patrols could arrest on sight any slave found "lurking about" the river.[5]

Common carriers also impeded the mobility of slaves. Ferrymen who took slaves without a pass across the Ohio River faced a two-hundred-dollar fine and forfeiture of a three-thousand-dollar bond. State law provided heavy fines for stage coach lines that did not enforce the pass system, and railroad companies frequently limited the access of slaves to their facilities. Officials of the Lexington and Frankfort Railroad Company, for instance, announced in 1853 that the mere possession of a ticket would not enable a black person to ride the train. Management required that a slave have a pass, in duplicate, and if personally unknown to the conductor and his owner's handwriting was not recognized by railroad officials, the bondsman must get "some respectable white known to the officers" to corroborate his identity.[6]

Masters, convinced that it was detrimental to the "peculiar institution" for slaves to leave their farms, made strong efforts to restrict slave mobility. To prevent unwarranted movement at night, owners visited slave quarters "at unseasonable Hours"; to restrict mobility at all times masters issued two kinds of passes. When most bondsmen left their farms, they possessed a pass to perform a specific act. It often described the slave, usually making some reference to an identifying trait or scar. The pass of Sam, a Boyle County slave, for instance, gave his age, build, the fact that he was in Danville on his owner's "business," and limited his absence to sundown. Some Bluegrass masters supplied identifying tags that allowed bondsmen to visit neighborhood black churches or adjacent farms.[7]

Many slaveholders gave their bondsmen general passes—some of which were open-ended—that allowed extensive travel both inside and outside the state. Tom, a slave preacher and loyal servant, received permission to travel to Louisville for several weeks before returning to his Lexington home. The pass to Willis Lago, allowing him to "go to any free state and there remain," essentially gave him freedom of movement. Milton Clarke, who worked on steamboats that stopped at Ohio River Valley cities, obtained a pass to visit his sister in New Orleans. From New Orleans Clarke journeyed to Galveston, Texas, before returning to Cincinnati. It was Clarke's pass which ultimately allowed him to flee to Canada. In 1828 Josiah Henson received a pass to return to Maryland. During the trip, Henson spent about three months in free states, where he made numerous friends among free blacks and accumulated about $275 preaching in black churches. Henson returned to Kentucky in March 1829, having been away for six months.[8]

An open-ended pass might solve some problems for bondsmen who traveled frequently, but it sometimes caused trouble for others. Allen, a Livingston County slave, had written permission to "pass and repass" from his home to Morgantown, Virginia. While traveling through Fayette County, however, Allen was apprehended as a runaway and spent several months in jail before his owner retrieved him. Rev. Elisha Green's general pass allowed him to preach throughout the Bluegrass and northern Kentucky. For years, as pastor of churches in Maysville and Paris, Green regularly traveled by train and stage between those towns and occasionally visited the Lexington and Louisville areas to fill pulpits, but not always without difficulty. After preaching for Rev. George Dupee in 1855, Green, a stranger to the Lexington ticket agent, could not obtain passage to Paris. Told that he must find someone to vouch for him, Green returned to the window with a well-known Maysville citizen, but the ticket agent again refused, stating that he did not know the man. Unable to purchase a ticket, Green resorted to a strategy suggested by Rev. Dupee, who advised him to stand on the platform near the train until it started moving and then to jump aboard. "You will get half way to Paris before the conductor gets to you," Dupee suggested to Green, "and should he put you off, you can walk the balance of the way." Sure enough, about halfway to Paris, the conductor reached Green and asked for his ticket. After Green explained why he did not have one, the conductor allowed him to continue to Paris.[9]

For whatever reason, small numbers of slaves, doubtless with passes in their pockets, constantly traveled along Kentucky's highways and railroads. London Ferrill, the famous Lexington minister, preached throughout the Bluegrass area before acquiring his freedom, and Rev. Henry H. Lytle on occasion walked from Lexington to Louisville to preach at gospel meetings. Nor was it unusual for pastors and deacons of Louisville congregations to participate in ordination services at regional churches, including some in New Albany, Indiana. A considerable amount of mobility existed among slave members of black churches, though it is impossible to ascertain whether they moved in conjunction with their owners. During the 1840s blacks, some of whom were bondsmen, left churches at Goose Creek, Bear Grass, Jefferson County, Bullitt County, Green County, Elizabethtown, Lexington, and even New Orleans to join Fifth Street Baptist Church in Louisville. Green Street Baptist Church, during those same years, received members from other Louisville churches, the Bear Grass Baptist Church, and from Shelbyville, Frankfort, and Nicholasville.[10]

Foreign travelers also mentioned seeing slaves on stage coaches and trains in Kentucky. James S. Buckingham met a bondswoman on a stage he rode from Maysville to Lexington in 1841. The quiet, well-dressed woman had remained behind the previous day because there was not enough room. Buckingham noted that no one thought it strange that she traveled alone. Isabella Trotter, while traveling with her husband from Louisville to Lexington by train in 1858, reported a large number of "merry" slaves in their car. The bondsmen conversed freely and frankly with the British visitors, some speaking of saving money to purchase their freedom, others of kind or dishonorable masters, and another of having no desire for freedom. The slaves intended to "pass their Sunday" visiting friends and relatives in Lexington.[11]

The effectiveness of the patrol in hampering the mobility of slaves remains a disputed matter. Some slaves maintained that they always carried a pass while traveling from home but never saw the patrol. Others reported that though the patrol posed a major problem, it was not difficult to slip away from home at night and return before morning without being detected. Those actually forced to deal with the patrol, however, described its activities as ranging from simple harassment to malicious abuse.[12]

Much of the difficulty slaves faced from the patrol stemmed from its composition. Methods for selecting patrol members were irregular, and unscrupulous whites often constituted the majority. Left to their own devices and discretion, patrols chosen to enforce the law sometimes turned to horseplay or even lawlessness. "Negro hunting,

Negro catching, Negro watching and Negro whipping," J. Winston Coleman concluded, occasionally "constituted the favorite sport of many youthful whites" who served on the patrols. Blacks suffered further from the fact that they provided a convenient scapegoat for whatever evils befell the white community. At times it proved useful to blame unexplained fires or unsolved murders on slaves seized away from their cabins at night.[13]

Blacks in general scoffed at the "iniquitous" patrols which they perceived as less a system of law and order and more an instrument of "horror." Patrols sometimes broke up Sabbath schools where slaves were learning to read or write, though such activities did not violate the law. At other times patrollers confiscated passes and then flogged bondsmen for being out "illegally," or wantonly shot into the crowd at an unauthorized slave "frolic" without regard to loss of life. The greatest abuses of the patrol system, however, occurred within slave cabins. On occasion patrollers rousted black families in the middle of the night, searched their homes on the pretense of looking for weapons or runaways, and abused members of the family, including women and children.[14]

In spite of the regulatory efforts, bondsmen in Kentucky were far more mobile than has been generally believed. One reason was that laws aimed at limiting slave movements were often loosely applied and unevenly enforced. Further, Kentucky was an overwhelmingly rural society with poor roads, and it was difficult to patrol counties thoroughly. Though many bondsmen had a limited knowledge of Kentucky's geography, most knew the rural roads and footpaths in their communities as well as the routines of their owners. Thus, many slaves found it relatively easy to move throughout their neighborhoods both day and night, with or without the approval of their owners, and to return safely to their cabins.

Slavery in Kentucky was not so confining that bondsmen were deprived of engaging in recreation. With little or no spending money, slaves usually found it necessary to exploit whatever talents they possessed for their own recreation. Bondsmen used their melodious voices, their physical dexterity, and even their work as a social event.

Slave recreation began at the cabin. Children played marbles outside the cabin door or games such as "Sheep-meat," which required the person who was "it" to hit the other players with a ball of yarn to make an "out." Pitching horseshoes was another popular game. The small amount of equipment needed existed on most farms, and it was not unusual for slaves to play games with their owners. At the end of a day's work, some parents told stories to their children; others played the banjo, guitar, or violin, and danced or sang songs.[15]

Most slaves could look forward to free time on the weekends. Usually, when bondsmen finished their assigned tasks on Saturday afternoon, they could do as they pleased for the remainder of the day and Sunday. This offered the men an opportunity to go fishing, for sport or to supplement the family's diet, and the women a chance to visit their neighbors or hold a quilting bee. Others had parties, dances, or sing-alongs.[16]

Saturday afternoon and Sunday provided slaves with an opportunity to "resort to the woods" for amusement and recreation of all kinds. They usually engaged in social recreation such as dancing, singing, or gathering to play and listen to musical instruments; but the competition at games was keen. Groups of slaves ran foot races, held jumping contests, and wrestled, sometimes butting heads like sheep or biting ears and fingers. Boxing was another favorite sport. Slaves formed a ring to contain the fighters. It was not unusual for liquor to flow during these recreational activities, and occasionally slaves received injuries.[17]

Saturday nights were a favorite time for slave frolics. Sometimes these social functions coincided with a dance of the white community, and before the night ended, the whites went over to watch their bondsmen enjoy themselves. At other times, slave dances were purely black affairs, unknown to the whites. Attending unauthorized slave frolics could be, of course, a risk for those without passes. During the dance attended by approximately 150 slaves at Fern Creek, the patrol suddenly appeared and demanded passes. The patrollers whipped about fifty who had no passes before Armstage Brisee refused to be punished. In the violence that followed, Brisee was wounded and another black injured. On another occasion during a snowy February night in 1831, as about fifty slaves danced in an old distillery building just outside Lexington, the patrol appeared unexpectedly. Without passes and fearing punishment, the slaves put out the lights and refused to surrender. A short standoff ended when someone fired "balls and buck shot" into the house. In the confusion that followed, slaves fled in all directions. The patrol later found one dead slave, "shot through the head," and several others lying wounded on the floor.[18]

While some slaves danced the "reels" and familiar period steps, others preferred the more highly individualistic dances favored by the black community. "We liked," Robert Anderson recalled, "the dances of our own particular race." Anderson believed that the "motion" of black dances—"shuffling of the feet, and swinging of the arms and shoulders in a particular rhythm"—expressed the mood of the slave's innermost being. If no music was available, black dancers could "play a tune with their feet," Anderson wrote, "dancing largely to an inward music," the "Double Shuffle," the "Heel and Toe," or the "Buck and Wing."

"Patting juba" was another favorite activity of slaves at dances and church meetings. Juba was an extension of mere handclapping, an intrinsic part of African music, to patting the knees rhythmically, then clapping the hands, followed by striking the left shoulder with right hand and the right shoulder with the left hand, all the while singing and keeping time with the feet. The practice probably began in the early 1800s, and was well known in Kentucky in the 1830s.[19]

Sunday also provided an opportunity for many slaves to leave the familiar surroundings of their farms to enjoy a day in the nearest town. Lexington provided a favorite gathering spot for bondsmen in the Bluegrass, but other nearby communities like Athens also drew crowds of blacks. On Sunday mornings, many slaves put on their best clothes and walked or rode the train to Lexington, where they spent the day relaxing with friends or relatives. Renting horse-drawn carriages and "junketting in every direction" or spending their extra money on pastry and soda drinks were other favorite Sunday afternoon pastimes. Whites occasionally pressured merchants not to sell to the blacks who thronged into town on the Sabbath, hoping to quell the weekly influx, but at least one merchant always preferred profits over boycotts.[20]

Aside from weekly diversions, slaves celebrated some holidays, with Christmas time the most extended one. Owners usually released their bondsmen from work during the period between Christmas and New Year's (though some slaves did not get the entire week off) and slaves generally received special food allotments at Christmas. Their children could look forward to a stick of hard candy, in addition to whatever gifts their parents provided. Adults on some farms also received extra portions of whiskey. On Christmas Day slaves often flocked into the nearest town, sporting their best clothes, hoping to spend their holidays in some kind of merrymaking.[21]

Music had been a vital part of the lives of bondsmen since before the time when Cato Watts played his violin as blacks and whites danced on Corn Island in the late 1770s. Slaves sang at home for enjoyment, on their way to the field or factory, to relieve the monotony of their jobs, or to communicate ideas. They improvised songs and expanded original melodies to devise a "peculiar music of their own," frequently set in a minor key and wrapped in religious themes. Songs were "word pictures" of their predicament, expressing the ecstasy and the despair of their daily lives. Stephen Foster did not compose his songs out of his "head," a former Bardstown slave recalled in the 1930s; he heard them in the songs of black people.[22]

Slaves particularly favored marching songs. Many times bondsmen marched to the tobacco patch and the hemp field singing a spirited air. Such songs helped get them through their tasks, and when the day ended, they sang their way back to the cabin. Favorite marching songs in the Bluegrass included:

> Heave away! Heave away!
> I'd radder co't a yaller gal,
> Dan work for Henry Clay,
> Heave away, yaller gal, I want to go.

or the ever popular "Eliza Jane":
> You go down de big road
>   An' I'll go down de lane,
> Ef you gits dar befo' I does,
>   Good bye, Liza Jane![23]

One Christmas season the hills east of Mount Sterling echoed with the melodic sounds of marching songs as bondsmen returned home from working in the iron furnaces of the region. Happy for the freedom of the holidays, the captain led his men in proclaiming their joy:
> Oh Lord have mercy on my soul,
> De hens and chickens I have stole.

The chorus of the jubilant singers followed, whereupon the captain improvised another verse. A week later, when the time arrived for the iron workers to return to their furnaces, they sang a tearful farewell, the captain once again improvising the lead:

> Fare ye well, ye white folks all!

followed by the melodic chorus,

> wo—o—o—o—o!
> And fare ye well, ye niggers too!
> wo—o—o—o—o!
> I holler dis time, I holler no mo!
> wo—o—o—o—o!

until the sound of their voices disappeared into the night.[24]

"Corn" songs provided slaves with some of their most famous

marching songs. On some of the larger Kentucky farms, slaves traditionally volunteered to help neighboring farmers shuck their corn during the fall harvest season. Although it sometimes meant a long walk and a night of hard work, a shucking party afforded slaves an opportunity to socialize, to engage in friendly competition, and to enjoy a good meal and a dram of whiskey with friends.

Shucking bees differed only by degree from one community to another. On the appointed evening, bondsmen gathered and marched to a farm, their corn songs reverberating through the countryside. Particularly beautiful harmony often identified a group to the waiting farmer and his slaves. From another direction, a splendid tenor voice or captain's solo sometimes signaled the approach of a neighbor's bondsmen. The arriving slaves sat on the grass, laughed and joked, or talked with friends until everyone appeared.

The visiting slaves knew what to expect. After greetings from the farmer, each man received a generous drink of whiskey or brandy. The bondsmen next divided into two groups, each choosing a "captain" or "general." Promises of special recognition for the best team and the best individual shuckers at the supper spurred men into the corn fields.

Madison Campbell remembered the corn songs of a central Kentucky bee during his youth. The slaves chose a "general of the corn pile" who lined out songs as the men shucked a long row of corn. The general sang that he

> got a letter from Tennessee
> That the Queen of Morocco had wrote to me,
> that the Negroes were all going to be free.[25]

At a Madison County farm the captains ordered the men to begin singing as they marched off toward the piles of corn. "Old Marster shot a wild goose," the solo lead began, and the men joined in the chorus:

> Ju-ran-zie, hio ho.
> It wuz seben years fallin'.
> Ju-ran-zie, hio ho.
> It was seben years cookin'.
> Ju-ran-zie, hio ho.
> A knife couldn't cut it.
> Ju-ran-zie, hio ho.
> A fork couldn't stick it.
> Ju-ran-zie, hio ho.

When shucking ended, the slaves gathered at the farmhouse, where they helped themselves to a huge spread of food including fried chicken, turkey, freshly baked bread, all kinds of vegetables, and delicious desserts.[26]

Accounts of bondsmen agree that corn shuckings represented some of the high points of their recreation. Francis Frederick described both the ecstasy and the depression that resulted from a corn shucking he attended as a lad. The corn pile, Frederick recalled, was about 180 yards long, and more than three hundred slaves gathered. Farmer Taylor greeted the men kindly and doled out brandy before the captains chose their men and began work. The laborers took their positions and the corn songs rang out.

>Captain: Fare you well, Miss Lucy.
>All: John come down de hollow.
>Captain: Fare you well, fare you well.
>All: Weell ho. Weell ho.
>Captain: Fare you well, young ladies all.
>All: Weell ho. Weell ho.
>Captain: Fare you well, I'm going away.
>All: Weell ho. Weell ho.
>Captain: I'm going away to Canada.
>All: Weell ho. Weell ho.

The men worked merrily until two o'clock in the morning, when one team finished. Reuben, the winning captain, and his men gathered together, holding their hats above their heads, singing, "Oh, oh! fie! for shame" to their vanquished opponents. Turning, the victors marched to farmer Taylor's house, where Reuben sang out: "Oh, where's Mr. Taylor? Oh, where's Mr. Taylor," the men answering "Oh, oh, oh!" each time. When Taylor appeared on the veranda, the captain sang:

>Captain: I've just come to let you know.
>All: Oh, oh, oh!
>Captain: The upper end has beat
>All: Oh, oh, oh!
>Captain: But isn't they sorry fellows?
>All: Oh, oh, oh!
>Captain: But isn't they sorry fellows?
>All: Oh, oh, oh!
>Captain: But I'm going back again,
>All: Oh, oh, oh!
>Captain: And where's Mr. Taylor?
>All: Oh, oh, oh!
>Captain: And where's Mr. Taylor?

All:     Oh, oh, oh!
Captain: I'll bid you, fare you well,
All:     Oh, oh, oh!
Captain: For I'm going back again.
All:     Oh, oh, oh!
Captain: I'll bid you, fare you well,
And a long fare you well.
All:     Oh, oh, oh!

The men returned to the field, their spirits high, to help their defeated friends finish the shucking, whereupon they marched to the farmhouse and sat down to a splendid supper prepared and served by the Taylor women. It was, Frederick recalled, one of the most joyous occasions of his youth. But within weeks, about thirty of the "happy band," including Reuben, the captain, were sold from the neighborhood.[27]

On another occasion, tragedy struck during a cornshucking. The bondsmen received their whiskey and went into the fields in a jovial mood, but before the night ended a "rumpus broke out." Two slaves began arguing, and one stabbed the other to death and ran into the woods. Captured shortly afterward and taken before the courts, the slave forfeited his life for his crime.[28]

Bondsmen became ill, and sometimes died, from the same diseases that attacked whites. Because slavery was a system of labor, it remained in the best interest of owners to provide adequate medical care for their bondsmen. But the paucity of physicians and the inability or unwillingness of slaveholders to defray medical costs sometimes subverted even the best intentions. Thus, the farm medicine cabinet proved the first line of defense against illness or debilitating disease. The slave owner or his wife generally treated everyone on the farm, but at times a slave administered the various patent medicines and home remedies to bondsmen, and slave parents usually maintained their own medicinal chest.

Typical apothecary supplies included "anti-bilious pills," medicinal "eye water," "worm destroying lozenges," "fever" powders and pills of all descriptions, "female pills," as well as trusted potions for "asthma," "phthisic," and "fits." Well-stocked medicine chests included "nerve ointments," "healing salves," "anti-dyspeptic pills," "calomel" purges, and "syrups of all kinds." Farmers supplemented the patent medicines with the traditional home remedies, consisting of a wide variety of roots, herbs, leaves, balms, broths, and asphytic bags.[29]

When patent or home remedies failed, it became necessary for slaveholders to seek help. In white physicians, bondsmen faced a poorly trained profession that almost universally believed certain devastating diseases attacked only blacks. Some doctors thought blacks subject to a strain of "Negro" consumption not prevalent in whites, while others who discounted the consumption theory believed respiratory diseases invaded blacks disproportionately. Lunsford P. Yandell, one of Louisville's most famous physicians, believed that blacks were best constituted for the torrid zone and concluded that their health problems generally stemmed from the change of seasons. Other physicians, probably closer to the truth, traced diseases ascribed solely to slaves to improper clothing or poor shelter.[30]

Nevertheless most Kentucky masters summoned doctors when their slaves were sick or seriously injured. George Conrad, Jr., remembered that on the Harrison County farm where he grew up, slaves got "very good" medical attention including visits from their owner's doctor. When the youthful Logan County slave, Black Mary, became ill in 1853, her owner summoned the local doctor. Unable to make a diagnosis, the physician prescribed a "physic." Black Mary's health deteriorated further, and in October the physician diagnosed her illness as being "like typhoid fever." Mary's owner continued the medicine prescribed by the doctor, but she did not improve. In April 1854 Mary's condition worsened, and her master sent for her father, a slave on another farm, for a final visit with his daughter. Mary lingered several days, attended by her owner, before dying "without a struggle" on April 11, 1854. During Mary's long illness, the physician also tended the physical problems of the other slaves on the farm.[31]

In the Bluegrass area, where slave holdings were generally larger, masters sometimes contracted with physicians on a yearly basis for medical care for a slaveholder's family and his bondsmen. Other physicians, when called to care for one inhabitant of a farm, often inspected all others from the main house to the cabins. Specific care provided slaves by Bluegrass doctors included dispensing "sundry" medicines and pills, extracting teeth, providing obstetrical services, caring for burns, nursing bruises, and reducing fractures.[32]

The meager statistics on Kentucky's slave population after 1820 reveal two fairly discernible trends. First, though women usually outnumbered men by a small margin, male and female slaves were remarkably equal in numbers for virtually every age period, with only two aberrations. The number of women declined rather sharply as they reached the childbearing years, probably indicating an increased incidence of death in childbirth. The large decrease in the number of male bondsmen came between ages thirty and thirty-nine. Hard work, dangerous jobs, and the southern slave trade furnish possible explanations. Second, it appears that life expectancy for Kentucky's slaves was slightly below that of whites. Between 1830 and 1860, about 6 percent of Kentucky bondsmen lived to be fifty or older and 3 percent lived past sixty. During that same period, almost 8 percent of the whites lived past fifty and about 3.5 percent beyond sixty. However, the gap between black and white life expectancy closed ever so slightly with each passing decade.[33]

State laws required that owners of infirm or aged slaves provide for their care, and public officials possessed the authority to enforce compliance. While it seems clear that most Kentucky slaveholders fulfilled their responsibility in this regard, some owners circumvented the law by selling seriously ill slaves south. Newspaper advertisements occasionally reminded Kentucky slaveholders of the voracious New Orleans market, where they might easily sell slaves rendered "unfit for labor by Yaws, Scrofula, Chronic Diarrhea, Negro Consumption, [and] Rheumatism."[34]

Slave owners also had to care for bondsmen with disabilities—those with sight, hearing, and speech impairment, the mentally retarded, and the mentally ill. Between 1830 and 1860, the only period for which statistics exist on any of these conditions, several patterns appear. In 1830 the incidence of hearing and speech impairment and blindness, the only categories listed, mirror the percentage of black and whites in the population, as do all categories of illness of 1850. Between 1850 and 1860 these impairments increased rather dramatically among whites and correspondingly declined among blacks. Viewed singularly from 1830 to 1860, hearing and speech impairments, mental retardation, and mental illness among blacks were reported lower, proportionally, than among whites. However, the percentage of blindness among blacks was much higher than that of whites between 1830 and 1840, and slightly higher in 1850 and 1860. The number of blacks reported as suffering from any of these disorders remained quite small.[35]

The most difficult health care problem for slaveholders concerned the mentally retarded and mentally ill. In severe cases, state law required their institutionalization at the owner's expense. Some slaveholders placed bondsmen with mental illness in state facilities and paid for their maintenance for years. The alternative care was "private charge," an apparently cheaper option chosen by almost three-fourths of slave owners.[36]

Though the health care provided for slaves seems clearly inadequate, the practical result was an apparently healthy black population. Foreign observers almost universally described Kentucky slaves, both male and female, as having the most healthy appearance of any they saw in the South. Civil War induction records later confirmed this impression.[37]

Most Kentuckians, black and white, believed during the pre-Civil War period that bondage was less harsh in the Bluegrass state than in the Deep South. This perception stemmed partially from the fact that Kentucky masters owned fewer slaves and generally worked side-by-side with their bondsmen, thus seemingly making their interaction much more personal than in the large gang system employed to the south. According to this scenario, the proximity of Kentucky to free soil also had an ameliorating effect on slaveholders. With a seven-hundred-mile border of free soil along the Ohio River, many concluded that unreasonable treatment of their bondsmen might force slaves to choose running away as their best option.[38]

Foreign visitors to the Lower South and the Commonwealth also concluded, almost unanimously, that Kentucky's slaves fared better than those on the cotton and sugar plantations, an opinion Harriet Beecher Stowe, the author of *Uncle Tom's Cabin*, shared. Though Kentucky's slaves had little good to say about bondage, they, too, believed the "peculiar institution" less oppressive in their native state. Some, of course, may have had such beliefs instilled by masters who wanted them to think that way. But, for whatever reason, fugitive Lewis Clarke, while traveling throughout the North telling his story to abolitionists, repeatedly asserted that slavery was "better" in his home state than anywhere else. William Webb, who earlier experienced slavery in the Deep South states of Georgia and Mississippi before moving to Kentucky, thought life immensely easier for slaves in Kentucky.[39]

Whether as a reaction against abolitionist denunciations or because of typical white southern sensitivity to criticism, post-Civil War Kentucky historians have continued to describe the state's "peculiar institution" as a benign form of bondsmanship. Emma Connelly, writing in 1890, spoke romantically of a system of paternalism where masters' main concerns were caring for and protecting their bondsmen in a manner that created little "serious discontent" among slaves. E. Polk Johnson, in his 1912 history of Kentucky, stated that because Commonwealth slaves were "allowed a great deal of liberty," such "pleasant relations" developed between the races that bondsmanship was "not a grievous burden" for blacks. William. E. Connelley and E.M. Coulter, in their 1922 work, described an equally benevolent system of bondsmanship where "the nature of the labor to be performed [by slaves] made their lot fairly easy." In 1918 the first monograph on slavery in the Commonwealth appeared when Ivan E.

McDougle, a professionally trained historian, published a rather brief work, *Slavery in Kentucky 1792-1865*. McDougle, convinced that a "true Kentuckian" always sought the welfare of his slaves, concluded, as those writing before him, that slavery in Kentucky was "a comparatively mild form of servitude." About twenty years later, amateur historian J. Winston Coleman, Jr., published the most complete study yet written on the Commonwealth's bondsmen, *Slavery Times in Kentucky*, which promptly became the standard work on the subject. Though a groundbreaking study which included a chapter on "The Darker Side" of the institution, Coleman, nevertheless, labeled Kentucky slavery "the mildest form that existed anywhere in the United States."[40]

Slavery in Kentucky was *not* a mild form of servitude, for, to the modern mind, no such condition existed. Slavery was a heinous evil for everyone it touched, regardless of the degree of degradation. But there are, of course, gradations within systems, even the "peculiar institution." It does not excuse those systems to explain such differentiations. To state that slaves fared better under Kentucky's slave system as compared to that of the Deep South does not exonerate the evil of both systems. Under slavery, generalizations are exceptionally hard to make and easily misunderstood, for exceptions are numerous. Yet to understand slavery, in all its cruel aspects, requires both generalizations and attempts at analysis of gradations. One generalization is easy: slavery was a system where one race controlled another, where psychological as well as physical restraints and wounds abounded. For, once a slave, you would always be a slave, subject to others. Of that fact, statements of degree of harshness pale into insignificance. For even if well treated, as many Kentuckians, black and white, claimed, slaves knew that freedom was a distant dream—and, for most only a dream. Of that they were sure.

As in other states, Kentucky law enjoined owners from abusive or inhumane behavior toward their bondsmen, and as Jonathan Thomas, a Lexington fugitive interviewed in Canada in 1847 phrased it, most treated their slaves "as well as the nature and condition of servitude permits." Treatment obviously depended, to a great extent, on the character and personality of the slaveholder, the response of a slave to his or her master's demands, and the bondsman's own expectations in life. The key to good treatment, as Edd Shirley, a former Tompkinsville slave, aptly put it, was for slaves to "do what their master told them to do." Most slaves did just that. They ascertained what their masters expected of them, developed a working relationship, and survived.[41]

Within an admittedly restrictive system, many Kentucky bondsmen told of reasonably good treatment by their owners. George Dunn remembered being whipped only once, and considered the slaves on his farm to be well treated. David Barrett, when interviewed in 1837, said he "could not complain of harsh treatment" at the hands of his Fayette County master, while Lewis Bibb, interviewed in Louisville in 1863, spoke of his former owner as a "rightly good man." Yet all three eventually fled the system as fugitives. Other bondsmen mentioned cases of unusually good treatment in slavery, and a few even prospered. Lewis Clarke said he had personal knowledge of slaves who were treated "exceedingly well" by their owners, and the "liberal treatment" Tabb Gross received kindled a desire for freedom that led him to purchase himself. Harry Smith, born a slave in Nelson County, praised one of his owners, describing him as a "kind and indulgent" man with a wife who had "few superiors." William Ruth highly complimented one of his owners, calling him "an extraordinary man" who was "in advance of all the county for kindness to his slaves." With a rudimentary education obtained from his owner's sons, Robert Harlan, who lived as though free, began a business career that led to his ownership of a barber shop in Harrodsburg and a grocery store in Lexington. Harlan's profits paid for travel to California, Canada, and England before he finally purchased his freedom and settled in Cincinnati.[42]

But even among the "good" masters the record could be inconsistent. While masters might not physically mistreat their slaves, they, like their bondsmen, were sometimes "flighty and unreasonable," resulting in bad relationships. Conflicts between masters and slaves frequently resulted in whippings, the most common punishment described by Kentucky bondsmen. Virtually all slaveholders kept whips to impose their authority, and in an era of corporal punishment most used them. Commonly-used whips varied from a strip of twisted, tapered, rigid cow hide, usually reserved for adults, to a fire-hardened hickory switch used on the legs of children. Since few arbiters existed to reduce tensions in slave-master relationships, it became, therefore, imperative for slaves to know when whipping threats were idle or real.[43]

Some bondsmen exhibited more success in fathoming their master's will than others. Smart Edward Walker, in an 1894 newspaper interview, bragged that he could "read" his master "like a book." His owner never whipped him, Walker told the reporter, because he "knew me pretty well" and realized that a scolding was more effective. There were, however, other ways to escape a whipping. Francis Frederick once avoided a whipping from his enraged master through the intercession of his mistress, as did Isaac Johnson, after promising never to run away again. Sometimes a slave threatened with a flogging could beg off. When Henry's owner tied his hands in preparation for a whipping, Henry admitted his waywardness and promised to stay home at night in the future. Believing Henry repentant, his owner decided not to whip him. Occasionally, slave owners concluded that continued punishment only made recalcitrant slaves worse. When Peter Bruner was caught after having run away, an offense he had committed several times, his owner decided to forego punishment since it had not worked in the past. Instead, he offered Peter a portion of the profit from the crops he raised. Peter remained faithful for the entire growing season and realized thirty dollars profit when the crops were sold.[44]

For most slaves, however, violation of their master's will resulted in a swift flogging, usually administered by the owner. Children often found themselves in double jeopardy since they received corporal punishment from both their parents and their owners. J.F. White, reflecting upon his youth in an 1855 interview in Canada, said that he was "brought up, or rather whipped up, in Kentucky." Peter Bruner remembered being whipped with a stirrup for failing to follow instructions when he was only ten and later for innocently selling a skinned cat, which he thought was a rabbit, to a white family. When quite young, Francis Frederick received a sound flogging for setting a ball of cotton on fire in his master's house.[45]

"Bucking" was one of the more punishing methods of whipping bondsmen, both children or adults. After tying a slave's hands together in front, his master forced him to sit down and draw his knees toward his chest. The slave's arms were then forced around his knees and pushed down far enough to allow a stick to slide under his knees but above his arms. A stick of three-and-one-half feet or longer, prevented rolling to either side, thus locking the bondsman in a position that completely exposed his back. Owners particularly upset with their slaves left them "bucked" after the whipping, prolonging the agony.[46]

The method used in whipping slaves—flogging was no respecter of sex—varied from farm to farm. One slave remembered being tied to the ground and whipped as he lay prostrate, and another recalled being whipped as she lay spread-eagled over a cedar chest. A slave owner in Monroe County flogged his slaves after tying them to a barn rafter, and a few farms even had whipping posts.[47]

Many slaves reported harsh whippings by their owners or those responsible for their conduct, and when a slaveholder was too weak to subdue particularly unruly bondsmen, it was not uncommon for neighbors to assist in inflicting punishment. Joana Owens remembered seeing male slaves tied up by their thumbs and whipped on the Hancock County farm where she grew up; and a white Kentuckian described a similar scene, where a slaveholder tied disobedient bondsmen by their wrists, hoisted them up until only their toes touched the ground, and beat them with a cowhide whip. On occasion these whippings were so severe that they left the slave with a cut and bleeding back. Edd Shirley saw a slave girl whipped until blood flowed down her back, and Robert Glenn carried into the 1930s the scars of a bloody beating he had received as a child for leaving a saddle outside the barn all night. The frequency of newspaper advertisements describing runaways as having "marks of the whip" on their backs, or as being "much scarred with the whip," confirm the regular use of the lash by Kentucky masters.[48]

Unfortunately, some slaveholders in the heat of anger were unconcerned if the blows with which they flogged their slaves were life threatening. A fugitive interviewed in Canada told of a Madison County master who, in a fit of rage, whipped a slave to death. Isaac Johnson reported seeing a slave whipped and then badly cut with a knife by his owner. The bondsman died five days after the abuse. Another slaveholder, while intoxicated, whipped a slave until she passed out from the blows before torturing her with hot tongs. The slave died.[49]

Instances of severe abuse, and even murder of slaves, did not always escape public notice or go unrecorded by newspapers. In a well-publicized 1839 case, authorities charged a Lexington couple and their son with harshly abusing a young, female slave. The charges levied by creditable witnesses ranged from seeing the bondswoman improperly dressed and without shoes during the winter to hearing her tormented screams from within the house. The testimony of a physician who visited the slave's owner proved far more damaging. Upon entering the home, the physician saw the bleeding slave being beaten on the back, face, and head. In another room he found blood splattered on the wall. Another witness described seeing the slaveholder's son strip the slave to her waist and whip her on the back and strike her in the face with the butt of his whip. When the slave, taken from her owner, arrived at the work-house, a physical examination revealed bruises, burns, and scars over much of her body.

Another famous court case covered by the newspapers occurred in the spring and summer of 1855. Martha, a twelve-year-old slave of Alpheus and Margaret Lewis of Bourbon County, arrived at the home of a neighbor, bleeding at the ears, after having been brutally beaten on the head and shoulders and burned on her neck, arms, hands, and legs. An investigation by county authorities revealed that another Lewis slave, Sally, the mother of several children, possessed large burn scars on her body. She testified that she had been tied with her feet off the ground, severely whipped, and then stoned. The county sold the abused slaves at auction, but under state law the proceeds, less court costs and commissions, went to the abusing Lewis family.

An equally brutal episode involved Caroline Turner of Lexington, a possibly demented, well-known slave abuser, who was the wife of a retired judge. In 1837 the powerfully built woman, while whipping a slave, threw him out a second story window onto a stone patio. The slave received a severe spinal injury and a broken arm and leg, crippling him for life. Nothing developed from a Fayette County investigation of the incident.[50]

The most shocking incident of premeditated, barbarous cruelty occurred in isolated Livingston County one Sunday night in December 1811. Lilburn and Isham Lewis, nephews of Thomas Jefferson, became incensed at George, an unruly slave, after he dropped a pitcher of water. Later, in a drunken rage, they seized the slave and tied him to the floor of the kitchen cabin. The brothers assembled their seven slaves and ordered them to build a large fire in the fireplace. Lilburn locked the door and informed his slaves that he intended to end their insolence once and for all. While the terrified slaves stood against the wall, Lilburn struck George in the neck with a single blow from an axe, probably killing him instantly.

The two brothers then compelled one of the slaves to dismember the body of the murdered bondsman. The remains of George's body were burned in the fireplace piecemeal until about 2:00 A.M. when an earthquake hit western Kentucky, causing the chimney to collapse and smother the fire. The next day, during aftershocks, the Lewis brothers forced their slaves to clean the remains of the body out of the fireplace and begin rebuilding it. They concealed the unburned portions of George's body among the rocks of the reconstructed chimney.

The demise of Lilburn and Isham began when new earthquakes struck Livingston County in early 1812. The rebuilt chimney fell, exposing the unburned remains of the body. A dog dragged the skull to the house of a neighbor who took it to county authorities. Rumors spread like wildfire, leading to an investigation, and within a few weeks a grand jury indicted Lilburn and Isham for murder. Released on bond, the brothers returned to their farm, but realizing that most whites in the county believed they were guilty, they decided upon a suicide pact. When Lilburn accidentally shot himself while demonstrating how the suicide would be carried out, Isham was unable to kill himself. Arrested and jailed, Isham escaped before the trial and disappeared. He was believed to have been killed in the Battle of New Orleans.[51]

Other slaves, if not given life-threatening punishment, still received harsh discipline. Some owners branded recalcitrant bondsmen, typically for running away. In describing a runaway slave named Jane, an advertisement in a Louisville newspaper stated that she could easily be identified by the letter "L" branded on her breast, and a McCracken County slaveholder advertised for his runaway, Mary, who had an "A" branded on her cheek and forehead. A Lexington slave pen owner advertised that he was holding a runaway, Callie, who had an "H" branded on her cheek, forehead, and breast, and Mose, a slave boy, who had an "X" burned into his buttock. Cropping ears provided another form of mutilation for slaveholders to identify bondsmen they considered to be troublesome.[52]

Masters also put iron rings on the feet or metal collars around the necks of what they saw as difficult-to-control bondsmen. A Lexington master asked local citizens to be on the lookout for Jim, who had a metal ring around his left foot, and a Fayette slaveholder advertised for a runaway, Elijah, who had an iron ring locked around one of his ankles. Cassius M. Clay wrote in his memoirs of seeing slaves with iron collars around their necks, sometimes with bells attached to them. Some collars were apparently round, with a hole for a lock or rivets on one side. Others were shaped like a "U"—Clay described them as like the "horns of a Texas steer"—with connections for a bar to be locked across the open end. Still other owners merely locked chains around the necks of slaves, making it easy for them to prevent an agitated slave from fleeing punishment or running away.[53]

Kentucky's slave code did not provide for penitentiary offenses for bondsmen. Slaves charged with a misdemeanor did not receive a jury trial, and conviction resulted in a penalty of up to thirty-nine stripes on the offender's bare back. Most towns and every county seat possessed a whipping post, where authorities exacted punishment and where citizens heard and saw such beatings. Slaves charged with felonies such as robbery, burglary, arson, rape of a white female, and murder received, upon conviction, the death penalty.[54]

There existed, however, a single punishment option to the death penalty, a seldom used law which allowed the substitution of corporal punishment in capital offenses. Until 1847, when the law was repealed, a slave might claim "benefit of clergy" which allowed, at the judge's discretion, an alternative punishment of branding the bondsman in the palm of the hand and a severe flogging. Rarely used, benefit of clergy provided, presumably, an option in cases where slaves were convicted of capital offenses in spite of the absence of evidence. When Preston, a Warren County slave claimed "benefit of clergy" after conviction for the difficult-to-prove crime of arson, the judge rejected the plea and implemented the sentence. But Bird, a Barren County slave convicted of the emotionally inflammatory crime of assaulting a white woman, received "benefit of clergy" from a judge who may have been skeptical of the slave's guilt.[55]

While Kentucky's slave code, like those of North Carolina, Tennessee, and Arkansas, was considerably more liberal regarding the rights of slaves accused of crimes than those of the Deep South states, the Commonwealth, nevertheless, dispensed a separate and decidedly unequal "justice." Though no grand jury was necessary for an indictment, a 1798 law did allow masters to engage in an informal defense of their slaves in a felony trial. Another law shortly thereafter admitted bail for accused slaves, and an 1806 enactment required the presence of a defense counsel. More crimes required capital punishment for bondsmen than for whites, however, and the law code strictly limited slave testimony to their own confessions, their own defense, or giving evidence in cases involving blacks, mulattoes, or Indians. Unfortunately, corroborating testimony by fellow slaves seldom had any influence in court decisions.[56]

Theoretically, a bondsman possessed the right to appeal a conviction, but the state's highest court, the Court of Appeals, failed to rule on any slave's appeal before 1859. Slaves giving testimony in court, unlike whites, swore a special oath which threatened them with "thirty-nine lashes" for giving false testimony. Regardless of the guilt or innocence of a bondsman legally convicted of a felony, the Kentucky slave code protected the master from financial loss. In each case the court determined the condemned slave's value and paid that amount to the owner from public funds, a system which doubtless led some slaveholders to accept more readily an unjust guilty verdict.[57]

In spite of the relatively humane laws of Kentucky, the slave's position before Commonwealth courts was so weak that a pioneer historian of the state's blacks labeled it a "legal fiction." Though some slaves charged with felonies freely confessed their crimes and others who denied wrongdoing were doubtless lying, many slaves punished with death were convicted on hearsay evidence, mere suspicion, or upon the flimsy testimony of whites.[58]

Several cases illustrate the precarious legal position of bondsmen. Jesse, a Christian County slave, reported finding the body of a white female in a wooded area. Local authorities promptly arrested the slave and charged him with murder. After a short trial and a "speedy verdict," Jesse went to the gallows. Officials charged Jacob with killing a white man with an ax. Jacob protested vigorously but vainly, claiming that he only defended himself when attacked by the white man. Jacob died shortly afterward "at the end of a rope." In Hopkinsville a jury convicted and hanged "Old Kemp" for shooting and wounding his master, a well-known citizen. Old Kemp's forgiving owner vigorously argued against the death penalty but without success.[59]

Fayette County authorities charged two bondsmen, Moses and Bill, with a felony offense in 1831. Moses insisted on his innocence; Bill admitted his guilt, stating he had acted alone. The court swiftly sentenced both men to death. In a final statement from the scaffold, each man "addressed the audience with composure & in an appropriate & sensible manner," but Moses's appeal fell on deaf ears and both men were hanged.[60]

Kentucky slaves, then, lived a fairly mobile, though limited life, but one in which they were constantly exposed to injury. It could come away from home, from the patrol, probably less successful as a regulator of slave mobility than as an instrument for harassment and oppression of individual blacks, or it could come in familiar territory through punishment by owners. Few owners abused their slaves by withholding medical care and, typically, did not engage in life-threatening punishments. Unfortunately, the institution of slavery was built upon the forceful subjugation of bondsmen to the will of their owners. Kentucky law placed few restraints on slaveholders while providing virtually no legal redresses for bondsmen. Such a system was open to abuse, and sadly, Kentucky experienced several cases of egregious mistreatment and virtual barbarity.

Yet, life had to go on for Kentucky's slaves. The remarkable fact of slavery is that slaves had the inner strength, given the hopelessness of their situation, to fashion a community, to raise children who grew to maturity with a slim vision that, one day, their world might be better, even free.

In one sense, it does not matter whether slavery was less harsh in one state, or one place, than in another. The system, no matter what form it took, by its very existence, degraded those held in servitude by the simple fact of its existence. Yet, it is true—as those who have studied slavery across state lines have noted—that differences did exist. Slavery in some plantation/agricultural systems was *much* harsher than in others. To understand slavery fully requires its exploration under all conditions. Slavery in Kentucky may not have been, typically, as harsh as in the Deep South states. Yet the examples of abuse in the Commonwealth doom the system to condemnation, demonstrating what an awful thing slavery was.

*Three*

# Resistance To Slavery

THE mind of the Kentucky slave was partially conditioned by the white man's concept of the place of blacks in society. Some bondsmen never voiced any thoughts of acquiring freedom, and many of those who did only chose the path that led to protest or freedom after years of slavery. When an Ohio River ferryboat captain objected to Elisha Green's boarding with an open-ended pass, suggesting that he intended to run away, Green replied in disgust: "I do not want freedom in that way." Henry Bibb, a man who possessed a strong, independent mind, admitted that he probably would have remained a slave for life if the mistreatment of his wife and daughter had not "blasted" whatever happiness he expected in bondage and "kindled a fire of liberty." Jonathan Thomas spoke of a desire to be free from childhood; yet, at age twenty-one he entered an arrangement to purchase his freedom over the next thirty-one years.[1]

In spite of their *idée fixe*, many Kentucky slaves ultimately rejected the institution of slavery. Indeed, when given the opportunity, numbers of slaves lived independently of their masters, successfully caring for the health and happiness of their families. Others would have chosen independence and freedom had they been presented a viable alternative during the antebellum period. Kentucky bondsmen believed that it was not an inherent weakness of blacks, but the brutalizing effect of slavery, that doomed them to an inferior position, preventing racial progress. "Slavery is the greatest curse on earth," Isaac Griffin, a Trimble County bondsman, told an interviewer in 1856. "Nothing exceeds it for wickedness." A Louisville servant described bondage as too "miserable" to be put into words, and a Madison County runaway, upon viewing a larger world, scathingly denounced slavery as "ruinous to the mind." Though the path to freedom remained extremely difficult for most Kentucky bondsmen, once they got the vision racial progress and upward mobility began.[2]

Emancipation remained the easiest way to acquire freedom. All of Kentucky's pre-Civil War constitutions allowed the legislature to pass laws providing for the legal emancipation of slaves, and a small but vocal white minority agitated throughout the antebellum period, calling for the end of slavery, usually employing religious, economic, moral, and humanitarian arguments. Though unsuccessful, they were influential for much of the antebellum period in maintaining a mechanism that facilitated manumission.[3]

Discussion of freedom between a master and a slave was an implicit criticism of bondage. Manumission involved a conscious decision on the owner's part that slavery, as an institution, was wrong, and on the slave's part that freedom, with all its potential problems, was right. Regardless of which party initiated emancipation, both the master who allowed freedom and the slave who accepted it went on record as opposing slavery to some degree.

Slaveholders promised emancipation, both idly and seriously, for a wide variety of reasons. The mere promise of freedom, however, had no authority in a court of law. Slaves only acquired freedom through a written legal statement, termed "free papers," or by a properly drawn last will and testament.[4]

Many owners never intended to emancipate a slave when they pledged eventual freedom. They usually made the promise to ensure the slave's continued service and good behavior. Such pledges had no immediate costs, though falsely raising a slave's hopes could prove troublesome in the long run. Nevertheless, masters had a habit, a former Kentucky bondsman remembered, of pledging freedom, but not following through with emancipation. Masters frequently made vague promises of "freedom in a few years" which were promptly forgotten before their words got "cold," another slave recalled, and many bondsmen who expected to be freed at their master's death found that they had, instead, become the property of his heirs or were to be sold as part of the estate.[5]

William Hayden's experience was not atypical. While he was quite young, his Lincoln County mistress assigned him the task of serving her daughter, Polly. If he performed his duty faithfully, William's mistress told him, he could expect emancipation when Polly married. Shortly after Polly's wedding William learned, to his dismay, he had been sold. William's new owner also held out the "prospect of freedom." If he worked hard for five years, his master said, he would acquire his freedom, along with a horse, a saddle, and a new suit of clothes. When the bondsman pressed his claim at the end of the five-year period, however, William's owner told him that if he wanted freedom he must purchase it. William spent forty years as a slave, much of it expecting to be emancipated. Occasionally, slaves concluded after years of waiting that the offer of freedom was only a ruse and finally ran away.[6]

On the other hand, some slaveholders honored their pledge of emancipation. Typically, emancipated slaves had a close relationship with their owners, and a paternalistic liaison usually continued between the freemen and their benefactors. In some instances, former owners guaranteed county officials that freemen would not become wards of the court, and occasionally, to implement promised emancipation, freemen would post bonds which they would forfeit upon failing to provide for themselves. Not uncommonly heirs contested wills emancipating slaves, prolonging servitude until the bondsmen proved their manumission in court. Obviously, emancipating slaves was not something to be entered into lightly by either party, and masters resorted to it infrequently.[7]

For many slaveholders, emancipation was an agonizing decision. Conditioned by their belief in the inferiority of blacks, slaveholders could not imagine the successful integration of a large, free black population into white society. For them, colonization seemed the only logical solution, especially after an 1851 law required that emancipated slaves leave the state. Kentucky built one of the most active colonization societies in the South, supported by numerous religious groups, important politicians, grants from the legislature, and some of the largest slaveholders. From its earliest activities in the late 1820s, the Kentucky Colonization Society operated from both a humanitarian and a racist impetus. Some, who genuinely believed slavery should end as quickly as possible, saw colonization as a method of encouraging masters to emancipate their bondsmen, while others, who did not like the example of free blacks living among their slaves, viewed colonization as a method of removing freemen from the state.[8]

Slaves emancipated specifically for emigration to the "Kentucky" settlement in Liberia, Africa, were sharply divided on the advisability of going there. For some, the offer of freedom held out great hope for the future. Spurred by letters of immigrants who spoke of unprecedented liberty for blacks on the African continent, a trickle of freemen flowed to Liberia in the 1830s and 1840s. Others, doubtless influenced by the negative rumors about life in Liberia, preferred remaining slaves in a society surrounded by friends and relatives to facing the uncertainty of isolation, poverty, disease, and death in a faraway land. To stem the unpleasant rumors, in 1834 the Kentucky Colonization Society sent a free black, Joseph Jones, to examine the quality of life in Liberia. Upon his return, Jones toured the Commonwealth with the society's agent, answering questions about Liberia.

The Fayette County Colonization Society sent Jeremiah Semple, a Louisville freeman, to Liberia, anticipating that a favorable report from a black man would stimulate emigration. Ultimately, however, Kentucky's efforts at colonization failed. Slaves were reluctant to go and free blacks suggested that a truly humanitarian policy would assist blacks in acquiring their just rewards within the Commonwealth. During more than thirty years of effort, the Kentucky Colonization Society sent fewer than 660 former slaves to Liberia.[9]

James G. Birney, a Danville native, was a typical Kentucky emancipator. Motivated by a growing belief that slavery violated both God's law and the Declaration of Independence, Birney first supported the colonization movement and gradual emancipation before deciding on abolition as the only answer. In October 1834, while in his early forties, Birney formally emancipated six slaves. A Muhlenberg County resident, Robert Wickliffe, freed his bondsmen at his death in 1850 and directed that money from the sale of one of his farms be used for their future health and happiness. Emancipations such as these occurred throughout the antebellum period.[10]

Deciding to accept freedom when the opportunity arose was a grueling experience for some slaves. When Kentucky's most famous abolitionist, John G. Fee, learned that his father intended to sell Julett, a faithful old bondswoman, Fee purchased the slave with borrowed money and issued her a "perpetual pass," telling her she was a "free woman." Unable to buy Add, Julett's husband, Fee remembered his saying: "I am glad you can free her; I can take care of myself better than she can." Later, when Fee's mother requested Julett's services, his father offered to repurchase the slave. The younger Fee refused and his father ordered Julett off his property, never to return. Distraught over the thought of never seeing her children again, Julett begged Fee to resell her to his father. Fee refused, saying: "We must simply abide the consequences." After a "day of agony" for Julett, Fee's father relented, allowing her to remain on his farm.

Julett remained on the Bracken County farm with her husband and bore three more children, all free-born. On the eve of the Civil War, Julett moved to Ohio with her free children. Learning that several of her children still held in bondage were to be sold south, Julett returned to Kentucky to help them escape. As she led her children and grandchildren toward the Ohio River, they were overtaken and captured. Julett went to prison and a slave trader took her entire family to the southern slave market.[11]

Purchasing one's freedom was a much more explicit criticism of slavery. When slaves bought their freedom, they did so within a "system" heavily dependent upon the good will of their owner. Slaveholders controlled almost everything involved in the transaction: the price, the interest rate, and the terms of the payments. Contracts were often informal, and bondsmen occasionally had different interpretations of the agreement from their owners. Yet, the fact that a master allowed a slave to purchase his or her freedom indicated a certain willingness to cooperate in aiding a slave's quest for freedom.

Raising the money to purchase freedom was an extremely difficult task, even for the most enterprising and fortunate slave. None but the hardest working, thriftiest, most responsible bondsmen had the remotest chance of success. It often meant working nights, weekends, and holidays to acquire the money, but many slaves demonstrated remarkable ingenuity in acquiring "pocket money." Some raised poultry or sold produce from their gardens and game trapped in the forests. Chopping wood or gathering bluegrass seed were ways of earning extra money in the fall. Bondsmen wove baskets, caned chairs, or made floor mats in their spare time, and there was an ever-present market for brooms. Some of the more skilled craftsmen made and sold shoes. Bondswomen sometimes sold cookies in the nearest town, worked as wet nurses, or practiced midwifery to supplement their incomes. In addition, many masters provided bondsmen with small financial incentives, allowing the frugal to save their earnings.[12]

William Hayden was an excellent example of an energetic young man determined to purchase his freedom. As a youth, Hayden fished the Kentucky River in his spare time, selling his catch. His dependability resulted in agreements with local innkeepers to buy all his fish and to employment on weekends and holidays. Hayden polished boots, washed dishes, and performed odd jobs, none of which encroached upon his "master's time."[13]

Arriving at a purchase price and terms of payment was an entirely individual matter. If a slave possessed particular skills, he or she often paid more. An Ohio River steamboat steward who earned his master $250 a year paid $2,100 because of his "good wages," and another slave worked six years to raise the $1,600 he contracted to pay. William Jackson's Louisville owner allowed his slave to retain anything he earned above $240 a year. "Laying by $50 a year" from his extra earnings over a twenty-year period, Jackson raised the necessary $1,005 required to purchase his freedom. Bondsmen often received favorable consideration in the price their masters charged them. Aby Jones, a Kentucky expatriate living in Canada, believed the seven hundred dollars his older brother had paid for the freedom of Aby and a younger brother was a bargain, and Richard Hawes was appreciative that his owner had set him free, accepting a promissory note for three hundred dollars and interest to be paid as Hawes was able. Charlotte Burris's husband bought her in the mid-1850s for only twenty-five dollars. Racked with physical infirmities, Charlotte believed the purchase price was about what she was "worth." Many instances occurred in which hard-working women ironed clothes, baked cakes, and tended the sick to raise money to purchase themselves and members of their family.[14]

Traditionally, male slaves purchased themselves before buying other members of their family, usually to preclude legal problems. A bondsman could not legally "own" a slave, and numerous difficulties might arise during the purchase period without the continued good will of the owner of one's wife or relatives. Purchasing one's wife first had at least one definite advantage—it assured that any future children of the marriage would be free. Also, it sometimes motivated the husband to accumulate the funds for his own purchase as soon as possible. For instance, Frank, a Pulaski County bondsman, worked for seven years to raise the eight hundred dollars needed to purchase his wife, Lucy. Remarkably, Frank was able to raise an additional eight hundred dollars to buy himself within two years.[15]

Slaves sometimes entered pacts to assist one another in obtaining their freedom. After working diligently for years to purchase himself and his family, Tabb Gross was reminded by Smith, a slave friend, of an agreement they had made twenty years earlier that whoever obtained freedom first would assist the other. Smith had already paid three hundred dollars toward his purchase price of one thousand dollars, but he had little prospect of raising the remainder. Gross, a minister, visited a number of churches north of the Ohio River where he raised the needed seven hundred dollars. Smith's family, however, still lived in bondage when the Civil War began.[16]

Some bondsmen bought their freedom at the urging of a white friend, and occasionally black churches purchased their slave ministers. The state legislature sometimes passed laws allowing specific slaves to contract for their freedom. Austin Hubbard left his entire estate to Narcissa, his bondswoman, in 1825, "provided she could obtain her freedom." The legislature authorized Narcissa to purchase her freedom so she could inherit the property.[17]

Reaching purchase agreements did not preclude failure of the bargain. Upon the advice of a local minister, Josiah Henson traveled to Maryland to negotiate a purchase price with his absentee master. Henson paid him $350 in cash and signed a promissory note for $100. When he returned to Kentucky, he learned that his master claimed he still owed him $650. Unable to read and unsure of the figures on his contract, Henson hid his manumission papers, believing he had been deceived by his owner. In a similar situation, a freeman paid all but $135 of the purchase price for his wife, before he was killed in a river accident. When his wife could not complete the agreed-upon payments, her owner sold her, and she remained in bondage six more years. Another bondsman entered into a long-term contract to purchase himself for $1,000. The slave had paid $400 when his owner died unexpectedly. Shortly thereafter, the bondsman learned of his impending sale.[18]

Slaves who could not expect emancipation and those without hope of purchasing their freedom expressed opposition to bondage in several ways, most of them non-violent. The typical protest was the work "slowdown." Utilized by all but a few slaves, the slowdown consisted of working at one's own pace, something most owners simply took for granted. Others disrupted farm operations by feigning illness or breaking equipment. A few engaged in more serious protests by resorting to sabotage such as arson, a crime punishable by death until 1851, when an alternative of two hundred stripes, no more than fifty at one time, became an option. Suspicion did not always fall upon bondsmen when a cabin, barn, smokehouse, outbuilding, or factory burned, but unexplained fires resulted in numerous convictions of blacks during the antebellum period.[19]

Many slaves harassed their masters by temporarily running away, usually to get out of a distasteful job or to postpone a whipping. Hall, a Madison County farm hostler, was probably typical. While sleeping in the hay loft, he heard his master shouting threats because hogs had gotten into the horse trough. Realizing that punishment was usually not far behind threats, Hall slipped off the farm and hid in the woods. Slaves who temporarily ran away usually lived in the woods a day or two, but some stayed away for months. Upon deciding to return home, they often sought out a minister, or a white farmer friend, to intercede with their master.[20]

Occasionally, bondsmen, frustrated by their situation, struck out blindly against the institution of slavery by engaging in violence against themselves, members of their family, or their masters. Distinguishing between authentic and apocryphal attempts at self-destruction, however, is extremely difficult. Peter Bruner admitted in his memoirs that when he was ten, he deliberately injured himself "for revenge" after a severe whipping, and later, at age seventeen, threatened to drown himself. Only a few other personal accounts of self-inflicted punishment exist. Israel Campbell reported hearing of a bondswoman who slit her throat rather than be sold to a slave trader, and an abolitionist wrote of a slave mother and father who murdered their children before taking their own lives to prevent being sold South. In perhaps the most infamous example of self-destruction, a captured fugitive killed one of her children rather than see her offspring returned to slavery.[21]

Slave violence against owners was slightly more common and took several forms. The principal motive for aggression against a master was revenge for harsh or brutal treatment. The absence of extensive source material often makes these episodes difficult to analyze. Poisoning was one of the most feared but probably least used methods of revenge employed by slaves against their masters. Realizing their vulnerability, slaveholders, from their earliest settlement in Kentucky, made poisoning a crime punishable by death. In 1858 several members of a Louisville family barely escaped serious injury when a ten-year-old slave girl, seeking to revenge a recent whipping, laced their food with arsenic. A Fayette County court sentenced Cassilly, a young bondswoman, to death in 1849 for putting broken glass in the food of her master's family, and Harriet, a house servant, received the death penalty for poisoning her owner's coffee. Masters frequently blamed bondsmen for poisonings following unexplained illnesses or deaths. When a family of eight became ill after eating their "usual morning meal," suspicion soon fell upon their slave cook, and the sudden death of a baby under the care of a young slave girl led to her prompt conviction for poisoning the child. Realizing their untenable position, slaves often fled the scene of a suspected poisoning, confirming their guilt in the minds of their white accusers.[22]

Bondsmen infrequently fought with and even murdered whites. Conviction for murder carried the death penalty, though at least thirty days had to elapse between the trial and the execution. Lewis Clarke reported an incident in which a slave retaliated against an abusive master by attacking and almost drowning him. Murdering a master was more likely an act of last resort or a spur-of-the-moment action resulting from unusual and sustained abuse. Slaves who murdered their masters realized that they had little chance of escaping punishment, regardless of extenuating circumstances. One famous 1844 case involved Richard Moore. An habitually abused bondsman, Moore, while being brutally beaten, turned on his mistress and choked her to death. He fled northward, but was quickly apprehended. Though virtually everyone in Lexington knew of Richard's abuse, no one came to his defense, and the county authorities afforded the unlucky slave only the "formality of a trial" before they publicly hanged him, a telling example for every bondsman who thought of revenge.[23]

Slaves occasionally took the life of an overseer. The most famous case occurred in Henderson County in 1862, when a slave or group of bondsmen seized their overseer, who had repeatedly flogged them, and strangled him with his own suspenders. County authorities brought six of the farm's bondsmen to trial for murder. The witnesses against the accused were all slaves. In an unusual decision, the jury acquitted all but Daniel, who paid with his life. Regional farmers publicized Daniel's execution, and in similar cases, owners took slaves to hangings, hoping to make an impression on them.[24]

Kentucky masters, like those of the Deep South, exhibited an almost paranoiac fear of slave rebellion. The slave code, at both the state and local levels, prevented the importation of bondsmen from "rebellious" areas, and promised corporal punishment for those participating in clandestine meetings or making "seditious speeches." Inciting a rebellion was a felony, but slaves convicted of conspiracy to rebel or raise an insurrection could receive the death penalty immediately.[25]

Ironically, Kentucky slaves never chose mass insurrection to protest bondage. Yet, rumors of insurrection periodically ran rampant, creating hysteria among Kentucky's whites which resulted in increased degradations for the black community. When insurrection scares occurred, the white community, almost unanimously, concluded that abolitionists were the major instigators. Whites believed that these so-called troublemakers moved secretly among the slave population circulating "bits" of abolitionist literature and inciting the slave population to rise against their masters.[26]

Kentucky's slave "rebellions" consisted, in actuality, of slave conspiracy "scares," none of which resulted in uprisings or left a trail of slaveholder blood in its wake. In 1810 Lexington authorities arrested and jailed a number of bondsmen thought to be planning a "dangerous conspiracy," but no rebellion occurred. Similarly, Henderson trustees "became alarmed" in 1838 at the number of weapons concealed by the black community, but the feared uprising never happened. Officials in Florence uncovered and foiled a runaway conspiracy in 1838. There was no bloodshed, though one of the suspected leaders escaped.[27]

The largest conspiracy scare in Kentucky began in Christian County in 1856. Citizens of Hopkinsville and Lafayette, a small town near the Tennessee border, became alarmed when stories reached them that the slaves at the iron works, just south of the Kentucky line, planned an uprising. The bondsmen, according to rumors, intended to fight their way across Kentucky to Indiana and freedom. Frantic, the inhabitants of Lafayette sent urgent pleas for help to neighboring towns, and began organizing a defense. In Hopkinsville the local authorities promptly arrested and jailed between thirty and fifty black suspects. Liberal applications of the lash produced confessions of a conspiracy scheduled for Christmas Day. About 150 Hopkinsvillians hurried off to defend Lafayette. When they arrived, they found the town in panic but no evidence of rebellious slaves. In Pembroke, southeast of Hopkinsville, where the wildest rumors had circulated, authorities jailed one black suspect, whom they expected to hang shortly, and planned to arrest others.[28]

Rumors of rebellion in southwestern Kentucky quickly spread throughout the Commonwealth, resulting in the rapid exposure of similar conspiracies. A vigilance committee in Cadiz, where a state of panic also existed, hanged a free black preacher, Solomon Young, whom they believed had originated the plot. Other slaves languished in jail, awaiting trial. At Volney, southwest of Russellville, Billy Smith and Peter Norton went to jail for conspiracy to kill a white family, and whites beat to death a slave employed at the iron works in a futile attempt to extract information. Officials in Henderson County began preparations to put down a rumored slave revolt, and in Taylor County a black youth warned officials of a plot planned for Christmas Day. The mayor of Louisville, fearing imminent "insurrection," ordered all bondsmen off the streets after 8:00 P.M. during the Christmas holidays. Rumors placed plots in Carroll County, where authorities arrested a black minister, William Anderson, and in Bath County, where forty armed slaves allegedly planned to revolt.

Slave rebellions in Kentucky were an aberration of the white mind, a side-effect of the paranoia slaveholding created. By systematic, brutal whippings, Kentucky whites extracted information confirming their preconceived fears. Under duress, slaves readily confessed conspiracy and insurrection where none existed. There were, in fact, no white victims of slave rebellions in Kentucky—only black ones. Although whites whipped, imprisoned, and even hanged slaves, force never ended a suspected slave rebellion. Only time, diminishing hysteria, and moderating emotions of whites terminated Kentucky's "rebellions." In Hopkinsville officials released those still in jail within a matter of weeks, and in Carrollton, Rev. William Anderson went free, but for those slaves hastily hanged, as the law allowed, there was no reprieve.[29]

Rumors of a slave "plot" had disastrous effects for the black community. With each scare, leading whites demanded new controls, and local officials strengthened the patrol system. Watchmen, looking for hidden weapons, barged into slave cabins with increasing ferocity, determined to subdue any "incendiary spirit" they found.

Rebellion scares provided the opportunity for vigilance committees to arrest or even hang suspected troublemakers, giving their activities a pale cast of "legality." Black ministers especially fell under suspicion during a slave plot scare. Officials frequently regulated their freedom of movement, and mobs disrupted black church services.[30]

The proximity of free soil made running away the most available avenue of acquiring freedom open to Kentucky bondsmen. Twenty-four Kentucky counties, stretching more than seven hundred miles along the Ohio River, bordered free soil, and seven of the state's largest towns were river ports. Though generally poor roads made travel difficult, fewer than a hundred miles separated the state's largest centers of slave population from free soil, with no location more than two hundred miles from the Ohio River. Lexington, the heart of the Bluegrass and the region with the largest slave population, was about sixty-five miles from the Ohio via either Louisville or Maysville. Covington, on the Ohio River across from Cincinnati, the city with the largest black population in Ohio, lay seventy-nine miles directly north of Lexington.

The heavily slave-populated counties of western Kentucky were even closer to the Ohio River. Though Hopkinsville was about seventy-five miles from Henderson, directly north on the Ohio, the river was only fifty miles away in northern Crittenden County. Madisonville was within thirty-five miles of the river at Owensboro, Henderson, and Crittenden County. Princeton was about twenty-eight miles from the river in Crittenden County and at Smithland, and Mayfield just twenty-one miles from Paducah. It was only seventy miles from Bowling Green to Owensboro, but the Ohio River was fifteen miles closer at Cloverport. Glasgow was within seventy miles of the river in Meade and Breckinridge counties.

Recognizing the potential for escaping to free soil, Kentucky's first slave code, passed in 1798, sought to discourage slaves from running away. It allowed any citizen to apprehend a "suspected" runaway and, upon meeting certain conditions, to receive a reward. Unclaimed runaways were hired out in order to pay the cost of their apprehension and incarceration, and in cases where an owner did not appear within a year, officials sold the slave to pay all expenses.[31]

Kentucky's early fugitive slave laws remained virtually unchanged until the 1830s, when increasing agitation of the slavery question at the national level led to new enactments. Over the next thirty years the legislature steadily increased the fees paid for apprehending fugitives and provided stiffer penalties for those convicted of enticing or assisting slaves to escape. In the two decades before the Civil War, Kentucky slaveholders joined the growing chorus of complaints about the problem of fugitive slaves, and called for new, vigorous federal regulations. The passage of the national Fugitive Slave Law in 1850 raised a renewed awareness of runaways throughout the Commonwealth, and Kentucky blacks, both slave and free, found their movements more restricted than ever before.[32]

The fugitive slave issue was, in reality, something of a tempest in a teapot. Though a greater problem for Kentucky than for Deep South states, the number of actual runaways still remained small. In the census year of 1850, Kentucky slaveholders reported only 96 fugitives from the state's 210,981 slaves. This amounted to only one fugitive for every 2,198 bondsmen, a figure representing under one-half of one percent. Ten years later, after a decade of agitation on the fugitive slave question, the percentage of runaways had increased slightly. Only 119 of the state's 225,483 slaves in 1860 were fugitives, slightly over one-half of one percent, or one runaway for each 1,895 slaves.[33]

As opposed to leaving a farm for a brief period, deciding to run away to seek total freedom was one of the most difficult choices bondsmen made. Experience, sophistication, and intelligence played an important role in the decision to flee, but hostility to the system, courage, and opportunity to escape often proved decisive. While not all bondsmen dreamed of liberty, a few independently concluded that they preferred liberty to bondage. Lewis Clarke, a slave who hired his time and provided for his own room and board, "dreamed" of freedom for years before escaping, and two Kentucky fugitives in Canada informed an interviewer that while no one told them that freedom was better than bondage they drew that conclusion on their own. Henry Bibb remembered standing, while still a lad, on the banks of the Ohio River, wondering if he would ever be able to escape to freedom. Fugitive George Williams, who grew up in Maysville, decided that "slavery was wrong" when he was only twelve years old, though he had to wait twenty-one years before the opportunity to flee appeared.[34]

For a few slaves, the decision to run away came during a period of uncertainty in their lives. Peter Bruner decided to flee following a bad week grinding corn, when "everything had gone wrong" and his master had become increasingly hostile. Milton Clarke's decision came in the summer of 1840, when his situation changed drastically. Dejected because he could not inherit the real estate his sister Delia had left him, Milton discussed his problems with three musician friends, and they all decided to "strike for liberty." A Frankfort slave found his life suddenly disrupted when his owner sold his livery stable business and announced he had no further need for a servant.

Told that he had a reasonable time to find a suitable buyer, but failing that, he would be sold to a slave trader, the bondsman used his pass to "find" Canada. After one of his owners died, Lewis Hayden of Lexington fled, believing that it was a matter of time before he would be standing on an auction block.[35]

Traveling in a free state sometimes provided bondsmen with an opportunity to learn about freedom or to escape. Josiah Henson first heard of Canada, and the potential for freedom there, while preaching in Ohio, though he did not immediately decide to flee. Milly, an eighteen-year-old bondswoman, grasped her freedom while traveling in the North. Writing her Kentucky master, Milly thanked him for his kindness and the love of his family, but confessed that the education he had given her taught her the "value of freedom," leaving her with no alternative but to escape at the first opportunity. When a Boone County master allowed nine of his slaves to visit some of their family members in Ohio whom he had previously freed, the slaves decided not to return to Kentucky. Writing their former owner, they informed him that he could recover his team and wagons, but that they had chosen freedom.[36]

Threatened or harsh punishment also led to the flight of slaves. When Eli Johnson asked for the money promised him, his owner threatened a severe lashing if he "mentioned money again." With each inquiry, his master's mood turned increasingly hostile. Johnson soon concluded that only running away could prevent an inevitable whipping. After David Barrett arrived home early one Monday morning following an all-night frolic, his owner promised punishment. Without changing from his good clothes, Barrett went directly to the field and began plowing. When his master appeared unexpectedly and ordered him to take the horse to the barn, Barrett surmised that his owner hoped to catch him in the barn and whip him. Barrett unhitched the horse and rode to a clump of trees where he hid until dark. That night he ran away. Francis Frederick, after contemplating running away for years, finally made the decision because of a severe flogging. His life under slavery, he believed, offered him little more than similar treatment in the future.[37]

A more frequent motivation for fleeing, however, proved to be the fear, real or imagined, of being sold south, or the actual sale of a family member or friend. Smart Edward Walker became concerned about his future after several of his relatives living on a nearby farm ran away. Shortly thereafter, Walker learned of his master's negotiations with a slave trader. Concluding that his owner did not trust him, Walker escaped to Canada at the first opportunity. Henry Morehead, a self-described "born and bred" bondsman, fled north with his family from Louisville when he became aware of the impending sale of his wife and children. A slave mother of eight who frequently sold her owner's produce at the Cincinnati market planned an escape when she learned that her northern Kentucky owner intended to sell some of her children. Several days later she packed her family's belongings in a wagon, covered them with vegetables, and left for market. The mother rendezvoused with her husband and children just south of Covington and hid them beneath the produce. Upon reaching the northern side of the Ohio, she unloaded her family in a black neighborhood and hired a local laborer to drive the wagon back to the Kentucky side of the river. Aided by abolitionists, the family of ten eventually reached Canada and freedom.[38]

Slaves desiring to run away faced almost insurmountable problems. Frequently husbands did not live on the same farms as their families, and occasionally, some of the younger children resided in owner's houses, making the logistics of escape difficult. Slaves running from threatened punishment or imminent sale seldom had the luxury of deciding the time or place of their departure. Being forced into a mid-week flight usually meant detection the next morning and lessened considerably the prospects of success. In planning escapes, bondsmen had to make the difficult decision of whether or not to inform friends and relatives, since doing so might result in an indiscretion or betrayal that would jeopardize success. Sometimes this meant the unannounced departure of one's closest relatives.[39]

The Ohio River presented one of the greatest obstacles escaping slaves faced. Those slaves who regularly traversed the river on errands for their owners and faithfully returned stood the best chance of crossing without suspicion. Dick Daily, a Carroll County slave, crossed the Ohio several times a week carrying his owner's produce to market. Considered a faithful bondsman, he was given the privilege of going to Madison, Indiana, whenever he desired. One Saturday night in 1857, Daily gathered his four children from a nearby farm, crossed the river in a skiff, and fled northward. Milton Clarke, who hired his time from his master, worked as a steward on an Ohio River steamboat. Once he resolved upon escaping, Milton simply slipped away from the boat while it was docked on the northern side of the river and traveled northward almost leisurely.[40]

Some bondsmen never solved the problem of crossing the Ohio. Lewis Talbert lived a few miles south of the river in Carroll County. He had planned his escape for years, eventually taking several trusted friends into his confidence. The conspirators periodically met late at night in the woods to discuss their preparations, but the question of passing over the Ohio River baffled the group. They intended to run away at night, but, unfamiliar with the river, they feared they would not find a boat in the darkness. Finally, Talbert and his friends decided to take tools with them to build a raft, an unfortunate decision that severely delayed their escape.

Talbert and twelve other fugitives arrived at the river late on the night of their flight. Using two logs found on the bank, the fugitives constructed a small raft which allowed only two people to cross at a time. After laboring all night, only six of the fugitives reached Indiana, forcing the runaways to hide on both sides of the Ohio during the day. Their owners discovered the flight the next morning and organized a large posse which raced north of the Ohio to block all avenues of escape. That night the remainder of the fugitives reached the northern shore, but their efforts to achieve freedom failed. Scattered and without food in a hostile environment, all the runaways, except Talbert and two others, were easily rounded up by the posse.[41]

Planning proved to be the key to successful escapes. When Josiah Henson finally decided to flee his master's Daviess County farm in 1830, he and his wife began elaborate preparations for their journey to Canada. Following a time-honored pattern, Henson planned his departure for a Saturday night. Sunday was a holiday and, in his capacity as an overseer, Henson scheduled himself to be away from his master's home for two additional days, hoping he would not be missed for several days. Realizing that his youngest children, ages two and three, would be too heavy to carry in their arms, Henson and his wife made backpacks with shoulder straps to ease their load. Getting his elder child, Tom, out of his master's house before they left required diplomacy and deception. With all his preparations completed, Henson went to his owner on Saturday at sundown and reported on his work. After taking a few steps toward home, Henson turned as if he had forgotten something and asked if he could keep Tom for several days so his wife could "fix him up a little." That night a fellow slave ferried Henson's family to the northern side of the Ohio River and their trek to freedom began.[42]

Henry Bibb and his wife completely disguised his flight from their Trimble County farm. They planned his escape for Christmas, when Bibb had a week's vacation and permission to work for extra money in a slaughterhouse near Bedford, and he wore a new suit of clothes, hoping to disguise his identity. After a sad farewell to his wife and daughter, Bibb easily crossed the Ohio River, landing in Madison, Indiana. There he hid until nightfall when he boldly boarded a steamer for Cincinnati.[43]

The well-known Ohio abolitionist and self-proclaimed "President of the Underground Railroad," Levi Coffin, told the story of a bondswoman in Boone County who adopted the ploy used by Cassie and Emmeline in *Uncle Tom's Cabin*. Realizing that she would be hotly pursued if she tried to cross the Ohio River immediately, the slave prepared a hiding place in a haystack on the farm and successfully avoided detection. Supplied with food by her friends, she waited six weeks before she slipped away to the river, paddled a skiff to the other side, and fled northward.[44]

Traditional stories of slaves' fleeing their Kentucky homes describe a well-defined "underground railroad" on which fugitives moved silently, inexorably northward from station to station without detection, until they reached freedom in a northern state or Canada. These accounts, however, are sometimes exaggerated. The vast majority of the slaves who escaped made the most difficult part of the journey to freedom—traversing Kentucky and crossing the Ohio River—on their own, usually going through countless hardships in the process. Most received no assistance from the underground railroad. They often traveled at night for weeks, catching whatever sleep they could during the day, and frequently went days without food. Many slaves with hearsay knowledge about free soil and Canada remained unsure of its direction or which road to take to get there. Peter Bruner, who made several unsuccessful attempts to escape, confirmed the problems runaways sometimes had with geography. "I always took the wrong direction," Bruner wrote in his memoirs, admitting that he often ended up "farther south."[45]

Nor did bondsmen know what to expect when they arrived north of the Ohio River. Kentucky's newspapers frequently reported the recapture of runaway slaves on free soil, indicating a hostile white population, and owners often confused their slaves with false stories about life in the North and in Canada and about the activities of abolitionists, making it difficult for fugitives to know whom to trust. Runaways also had to contend with black spies who operated along the Ohio River, waiting to betray them for a price.[46]

In spite of the perils, those fugitives reaching free soil knew that their best opportunity for escaping lay in contacting another black person. Sometimes this meant approaching a total stranger. A hotly pursued group of slaves fleeing from northern Kentucky, with no other alternative, approached a black man they saw chopping wood. He proved to be friendly, hiding them in the woods and supplying food until he arranged for their escape. One fugitive slave, completely without friends in Cincinnati, approached a group of black children and asked them if they knew "where that old colored man lives who saws wood." The children replied with the black man's name and address, allowing the fugitive to find help in the black community. Another closely pursued fugitive also ran for a black neighborhood in Cincinnati, hoping to hide until he could find help. He finally approached a black child who gave him food and pointed him to a place where he could gain assistance. Black churches provided another obvious contact for fugitives. Many black churches secretly aided fugitives, a work usually carried out by church members rather than the minister, thus protecting him from vulnerability.[47]

Slaves living in the vicinity of the Ohio River usually knew blacks residing on free soil, and fugitives often went to their homes seeking advice or refuge in their flight to freedom. When a Louisville slave and his wife fled upriver on a packet ship to Cincinnati, they went to the home of a former slave friend, who concealed them until they secured assistance for their trip to Canada. A group of Boone and Kenton county slaves, upon arriving in Cincinnati, went to the home of a former slave who had lived in their neighborhood. Their black friend hid the fugitives, but a band of slave catchers descended in force upon the black community, capturing the entire party.[48]

Finding fugitives did not always mean that they returned to slavery. A young Frankfort slave disappeared while on a trip with his mistress to Cincinnati. His master, accompanied by two officers, tracked the slave to the home of a woman on Sixth Street in the black community of Bucktown. The slaveholder persuaded the young man to return to Frankfort, but as they began walking away, the woman "raised a shout," causing many black people to pour into the streets. Within minutes the young fugitive disappeared in the crowd. John Hatfield, a free Cincinnati black, related an incident in which a slave catcher intercepted a group of Kentucky fugitives and by deception concealed them in a basement until his confederates arrived. When area blacks realized what was happening, they sneaked the fugitives out of the basement two at a time until all thirteen were free, then dispersed the runaways throughout the city. After hiding out in Cincinnati for about two weeks, the fugitives continued their journey to Canada. On another occasion, when a slaveholder retrieved three fugitives from a black neighborhood in Cincinnati, a local "colored man of property" agreed to purchase the slaves for $450, giving a real estate mortgage as collateral. The slaves went free.[49]

Historically, the activities of blacks as underground railroad "conductors" have received little notice, when in fact, blacks often initiated the entire process of escape. Knowing or meeting someone who had contact with free soil was very important for slaves who contemplated obtaining their freedom. John and Mary grasped their opportunity when several "colored friends" from Cincinnati visited Lexington. John asked them to arrange for someone to lead them out of bondage. Upon returning home, the Cincinnati visitors contacted abolitionists and eventually sent a "young white man" to assist them in their escape. In another instance Willis Lago, a Cincinnati black visiting Woodford County, met Charlotte, a local slave who desired freedom. Charlotte agreed to pay Lago fifty dollars to help her reach free soil. The twenty-seven-year-old black, known for her poise and beauty, later disappeared, never to be seen again. Kentuckian Horace Morris and Ohioan Elijah Anderson helped a number of fugitives make contact with the underground railroad. Unfortunately for Anderson, authorities arrested him during one of his forays into Kentucky, and he died in prison in 1857.[50]

Slaves living in communities near the Ohio River sometimes helped their friends escape. This was especially true in larger towns, such as Louisville, where fugitives could blend into the crowd. Washington Spradley, one of Louisville's wealthiest black freemen, took credit for aiding many fugitives along their journey to freedom. For some of the poorer, perhaps less cosmopolitan inhabitants, however, being involved with runaways was a very risky business. The mother of Joseph Cotter, later a well known black poet, told her son of the difficulties she faced when she, and the black couple for whom she worked, assisted a runaway. The fugitive appeared at her employer's door late one night seeking aid. The couple stored several of the woman's possessions and helped her cross the Ohio River. Unfortunately, authorities caught the fugitive and she turned informer. In the crisis that followed, the frightened couple lost their composure, but Mrs. Cotter seized the initiative and hastily disposed of the fugitive's possessions. Without evidence, the authorities did not press charges.[51]

Whites from Kentucky and the North played a prominent and often critical role in the underground railroad, but very few personally led slaves out of bondage. The abolitionist Levi Coffin wrote of a Louisville white who assisted runaways passing through that city when the opportunity arose. To allay suspicion, the Louisvillian generally hid the fugitives until they were given up for lost, whereupon he purchased stateroom tickets for them on a Cincinnati-bound packet. The Louisville abolitionist usually took the fugitives aboard and placed them safely in their stateroom before disembarking. Once in a while, he traveled with them to Cincinnati. Coffin credited the unnamed white Kentuckian with forwarding twenty-seven fugitives to Cincinnati during one spring and summer before he was arrested, convicted of aiding fugitives, and sentenced to two years' imprisonment. In other instances, a white "gentleman" first told Francis Frederick about Canada, saying: "If I promise to get you safely away from here, you must not mention a word of it to any one," and an anonymous white widow hid Sally, a fugitive from a northern Kentucky farm, and later contacted Cincinnati abolitionists, who smuggled the runaway to freedom.[52]

Such activities of whites, however, were atypical. Levi Coffin seemingly confirmed this fact when he wrote that fugitives "generally stopped among the colored people" once they got north of the Ohio River. Those fugitives who went through his home, Coffin wrote, distrusted him and initially refused to give their names, where they were from, or the name of their owners. Coffin's main contribution consisted of assisting local blacks, whom he believed lacked the contacts, sophistication, and expertise, to smuggle fugitives successfully northward and to provide food, clothing, shelter, money, and organizational ability. Fugitives often spent days or even weeks in the Cincinnati area before they became acquainted with white underground railroad leaders. A party of twelve slaves fleeing from northern Kentucky, pursued and scattered, wandered for three days before several members of the group, suffering from "hunger and exposure," arrived at Coffin's house. "Aunt Rachel" fled Kentucky and lived in a free black settlement outside Newport, Indiana, for an entire winter before her friends took her to Coffin's home for underground railroad connections.[53]

Analysis of the activities of most underground railroad leaders reveal the same story. "Conductors" on the underground railroad seldom helped slaves inside the state of Kentucky. When Mason County authorities tried the Reverend John B. Mahan, a Brown County, Ohio, abolitionist, and a well-known worker on the underground railroad, for enticing Kentucky slaves from their masters, they could not prove, even in a solidly proslavery courtroom, that Mahan had ever set foot on Kentucky soil, though there was no doubt that he had assisted slaves passing through his county. Allen Sidney, a Kentucky slave who worked as an engineer on a boat that plied the Ohio River, met Tom Dorum, a Cincinnati abolitionist, during one of his many trips to the Queen City. Over a period of two years Dorum and Sidney held numerous conversations during which the abolitionist offered the slave and his wife assistance on the journey to Canada, but Dorum always left the move out of Kentucky to the slaves. John Van Zandt, a Hamilton County, Ohio, abolitionist, participated in a plot to help nine slaves escape a Kenton County farm, but the runaways fled their neighborhood and crossed the river without Van Zandt's assistance. The abolitionist met the fugitives the morning after their flight and conducted them on the first leg of their journey, the closely watched Cincinnati route. Ruffians in the pay of slave owners captured Van Zandt and all but one of the fugitives. Taken to court, Van Zandt had to pay damages and a five-hundred-dollar fine for violating the 1793 Fugitive Slave Act.[54]

There were, however, a handful of brave, dedicated, northern white abolitionists who risked their own freedom by going to Kentucky to lead slaves to freedom. Quaker Laura S. Haviland, a Canadian-born worker on the underground railroad for thirty years, entered Boone County from Indiana disguised as a berry picker with a scheme to free the wife of fugitive John White. Haviland found White's wife and arranged for her escape, only to see the plans fail. Frustrated, White personally returned to rescue his family, but was captured and jailed. Her underground railroad activities thwarted, Haviland eventually purchased White's freedom from his owner. John Fairfield, a Virginian who had moved north because of his opposition to slavery, entered Kentucky several times to lead slaves to freedom. On one occasion while buying farm products in northern Kentucky, Fairfield learned that a large group of slaves intended to strike northward for freedom. Fairfield contacted the slaves and agreed to lead them out. The group struggled across the Ohio River in leaky boats, suffering from cold and hunger, before Fairfield put them in touch with members of a black Baptist church in Cincinnati and, later, Levi Coffin. Kentucky authorities eventually captured Fairfield, but he escaped to Ohio after spending a winter in prison.[55]

In the early 1850s abolitionist Thomas Brown moved with his family to Henderson, where he peddled millinery from a wagon along the Ohio River from Hancock to Union counties. White Kentuckians apparently viewed Brown with suspicion from the beginning, and when a slave woman and her child disappeared after Brown had sold goods in the area, they had him arrested. Pressured by several interested Kentucky slaveholders, Union County authorities promptly tried and convicted Brown for slave stealing, sentencing him to two years in prison.[56]

No abolitionist who ventured into Kentucky became more famous, or acted more recklessly, than Calvin Fairbank, and none worked as closely with black abolitionists associated with the underground railroad. Born in New York, Fairbank grew up believing slavery to be a sin. In 1837, at age twenty-one, he rescued his first Kentucky slave. While returning up the Ohio River after a trip to Cincinnati, Fairbank met a distressed slave girl during a stop in Maysville. He got the bondswoman aboard the steamer without incident and saw her safely to Pittsburgh. A year later Fairbank began his close association with William Casey, a Cincinnati freeman, when, using small boats, they rescued a slave family of fourteen. Casey and

Fairbank delivered the family to Henry Boyd, a prosperous Cincinnati black, who got them safely to Lawrenceburg, Indiana, where he put them on the underground railroad.

In 1839 Fairbank entered seminary and eventually graduated from Oberlin College in 1844. During those years Fairbank became acquainted with most of the leaders of the abolitionist movement and continued his forays into Kentucky. In 1842 Fairbank, with Casey at his side, rendezvoused at the barn of a free black family in northern Kentucky. Using a specially constructed hay wagon, they secreted a slave family of eight inside and drove them to Cincinnati and freedom. That same year Fairbank and John Hamilton, another Cincinnati black, smuggled a Kentucky escapee northward across the Ohio River on a log.

Fairbank did not limit his activities to rescuing slaves from their masters. In the spring of 1843, while "looking through" the Lexington jail, Fairbank found a young, intelligent, self-educated female slave of "exquisite figure and singular beauty" who was scheduled for sale at auction. The abolitionist told the young slave that he intended to "exert every effort" to prevent her sale to New Orleans. Fairbank went to Cincinnati, where he described the slave's plight to a "number of well-to-do" blacks and several prominent, wealthy whites. With contributions totaling $2,275 in his pocket and permission to draw up to $25,000 on the accounts of three wealthy whites, Fairbank returned to Lexington for the auction. In spirited bidding between Fairbank and a New Orleans "Frenchman," the abolitionist purchased the slave girl for $1,485. Following the final banging of the gavel, someone in the crowd of over two thousand asked: "What are you going to do with her?" Fairbank shouted: "Free her, sir."

By far the most dangerous, though not the most disastrous, episode for Fairbank occurred in the fall of 1844 when he secured the freedom of Lewis Hayden, his wife, and their ten-year-old son. While preaching in Lexington, Fairbank concocted a scheme whereby he and Delia A. Webster, a flighty young teacher from Vermont, would accompany the Hayden family from Lexington to Ohio. With a slave driving their rented hack, Fairbank, Webster, and the disguised Haydens faced numerous delays and hardships before making their underground railroad connections in Hopkins, Ohio. Naively hoping not to be connected with the Hayden family's disappearance, Fairbank and Webster returned to Kentucky, only to be arrested at Millersburg, about twenty-eight miles northeast of Lexington. As a result of incriminating evidence found in a letter in Fairbank's possession, Webster received a two-year prison sentence, but was soon freed after lenient treatment. Fairbank pleaded guilty and received a sentence of

## PUBLIC MEETING!

Since the law of 1833, prohibiting the importation of negroes into our state has been modified, and virtually repealed, and believing that the large importation of refuse negroes which will follow this virtual repeal of the law of 1833, will prove disasterous to the best interests of the State AND BELIEVING THAT SLAVERY IS, IN ITS BEST FORM, A SOCIAL AND POLITICAL CURSE TO THE COUNTRY, AND SHOULD NOT BE MADE PERPETUAL, but should be removed gradually, so as to least interfere with the rights of present slaveholders, we, the undersigned citizens of the County of Boyle, slaveholders and non-slaveholders, being in favor of some system of gradual emancipation with colonization, invite our fellow citizens, friendly to the cause of emancipation, to meet with us at the court-house, in Danville, on Saturday, 17th day of March, 1849, to consult together upon what course should be pursued by the friends of the Cause in the present emergency and to appoint delegates to the State Emancipation Convention, proposed to be held in Frankfort, on the 25th of April next.

University of Kentucky Special Collections

fifteen years imprisonment, serving more than four years before being pardoned by Governor John J. Crittenden. Hayden arrived safely in Amhurstburgh, Canada, and promptly wrote his former master explaining that his hatred for the institution of slavery had led him to "try freedom." Within a short period of time, Hayden became a leader among black abolitionists, eventually moving to Massachusetts, where he was involved with the Boston Vigilance Committee and in other community affairs, including service in the state legislature. In 1849 Hayden essentially "purchased" his freedom from his former owner to help get a pardon for Fairbank.

Fairbank's final downfall as an underground railroad conductor began in October 1851. Fairbank spirited a slave woman, Tamar, from Louisville to Salem, Indiana, where he left her with a friend. Fairbank returned to Jeffersonville, Indiana, where a week later a band of Kentuckians kidnapped him and took him to jail in Louisville. Convicted in a Kentucky court of aiding the escape of slaves, Fairbank received a fifteen-year sentence. He entered prison in March 1852 and remained there until pardoned in 1864.[57]

Though most white Kentuckians abhorred the activities of people like Fairbank, no one created the furor of E.J. "Patrick" Doyle, an abolitionist and Centre College student. In the summer of 1848, Doyle attempted to lead a group of slaves, variously estimated at between forty-two and seventy-five and said to be "a class of the finest" servants in Fayette and Bourbon counties, in a dash for freedom. Though armed, the slaves secretly fled their cabins on Saturday night without violence and were not missed until Sunday morning. A heavily armed, undisciplined posse, which increased in size as the chase progressed, tracked the fleeing slaves through Harrison and Bracken counties, harassing their movement. Doyle's band was within fifteen miles of the Ohio River before being surrounded. "As lovers of *Liberty* they fought bravely," a sympathetic white Kentuckian wrote, but numbers prevailed and though some scattered to the woods before the battle ended, most surrendered. Authorities housed the fugitives in several jails in the area, but, fearing a lynching, they took Doyle to Lexington, where a quick trial resulted in a verdict of twenty years at hard labor. He later died in prison. Bracken County officials selected seven suspected ringleaders from among the captured black fugitives and tried them for rebellion. Three Fayette County slaves named as ringleaders—Shadrack, Harry, and Prestley—received the death penalty. The others, totaling about forty, went south with slave traders. Whether or not any of the original fugitives reached free soil remains unknown.[58]

An equally famous episode of mass escape culminated in a series of bizarre events in Cincinnati. Seventeen slaves from Boone and Kenton counties slipped away under cover of darkness one Saturday in January 1856. With the women and children riding on a sled, the escapees arrived at the frozen Ohio River the next morning and crossed on foot. Upon reaching the northern bank, the fugitives went to the home of Elijah Kite, a former slave and previously their neighbor. That same morning, before more than a handful could escape farther north, the owners of the slaves arrived with several deputy marshals and surrounded Kite's house. A noisy mob soon gathered. Kite tried to negotiate with the authorities but ultimately decided to resist. An officer who broke open a window and attempted to enter the house was repelled with a gunshot wound in the arm. The authorities eventually battered the door down and rushed inside. Robert Garner fired several shots before the marshals overwhelmed him. His wife, Margaret, concluding that their children would be recaptured and returned to a life of slavery, cut the throat of one of her children and attempted to take the lives of the other three before being subdued. The case became nationally known as abolitionist lawyers attempted a strategy of getting her tried in Ohio for the murder of her child, but they failed to prevent the return of Margaret Garner to Kentucky and slavery. After languishing in a Covington jail for a short time, she was sold south.[59]

In attempting escape, simply traveling through Kentucky and the free states frequently proved to be one of the most difficult tasks in a fugitive's quest for freedom. An unusually detailed account of Andrew Jackson's escape illustrates the difficulty. After much planning, Andrew Jackson, a bondsman possessing the usual fears and trepidation, finally decided "to get started" one Saturday night. Hoping to confuse his owner, he tore up some of his old clothes, smeared them with blood, and left them conspicuously in nearby woods. From his farm near Bowling Green, Jackson walked toward "Shakertown" in Logan County, famous for its antislavery posture, posing as a turnpike worker going to his job. Finally forced to ask directions, Jackson faced questions about his identity from a man on horseback. When he smiled and fumbled through some papers searching for his nonexistent pass, the man rode on.

A few miles farther, another traveler demanded to see his pass. Jackson ran unpursued into the woods and then continued walking parallel to the road. About dusk, the fugitive returned to the road and walked all night. At daylight the "weary and hungry" Jackson went to sleep in a patch of woods. Awaking in the afternoon, he resumed his trip, following the fields and woods, until night approached. Unsure of the correct direction, Jackson returned to the road the next morning. But when he approached a house, and did not stop when hailed, Jackson found himself being chased by several armed men with dogs. Running into some woods, Jackson crossed and recrossed a stream several times in an attempt to confuse the dogs and then hid, only to be discovered by two unarmed men. Again he fled, but after running as long as he could, he realized that he was heading south. Returning to the road, Jackson walked all night, leaving the road only to let travelers pass or to find wild berries to eat. At dawn he sought the safety of the woods to sleep. During the early part of his journey, Jackson's spirits were extremely low. Alone, he appeared to be surrounded by enemies. Forced to traverse a virtual wilderness, he feared death by wild animals at night or capture and severe punishment by the patrol.

The next morning Jackson followed the road, only to be discovered and chased as he approached a house. Thinking he had eluded his pursuers, Jackson fell into an ambush where he received a glancing blow to his shoulder from a club. Pursued by a dog, a boy, and a man on a horse, Jackson ran for a clump of bushes. He disabled the dog with a stone and struck the horseman with a stick. The man pulled a gun, which misfired. Jackson threw a rock at his opponent and fled, losing his pursuers in a pasture. When everything was quiet, Jackson resumed his journey, resolving to stay away from the roads. He found going through the fields and woods very difficult, however, and returned occasionally to the roads to ensure that he was traveling northward.

The next day Jackson noticed a farmer watching him from a hilltop as he walked through a field. When he altered his course, hoping to place a large creek between himself and the farmer, the man gave chase, his dog bounding off toward the fugitive. Assuming that the farmer used the dog to herd cattle, Jackson turned and clapped his hands, saying, "s't-a-boy! s't-a-boy!" motioning the dog in the direction of several cattle in a nearby field. When the dog began running the cattle, the farmer had no alternative but to stop the dog. Jackson swam the creek and bathed his "bruised and swollen feet and limbs" in the water. After a much-needed nap Jackson found enough blackberries to soothe his stomach and remained at the creek for about twenty-four hours, sleeping and bathing his aching body.

The following day, after a pursuit by two men with dogs, Jackson resorted at last to a bit of ingenious subterfuge. He waited until a carriage passed and then followed it down the road. When he met someone coming toward him, Jackson inquired "how far ahead master's carriage was?" Using this procedure, Jackson reached the Ohio River at Union County, crossing at Barker's old ferry.

Once across the Ohio, Jackson rested his weary, bruised body for a night before continuing his journey. Though he had not known what to expect, he had anticipated a less hostile atmosphere, and the voice of a man shouting "stop!" caught him by surprise. When he did not stop, the man threw a stone that hit him in the leg. Jackson ran, pursued by several men who fired weapons at him at least twice. He escaped only by hiding in a ravine.

Continuing northward, Jackson finally met a friendly white man who put him to work plowing in his field. Before the day ended, however, a group of men, apparently slave catchers, surrounded Jackson, bound him with a rope, and took him to jail, where he remained for six weeks. Taken from one jail to another, forced to eat inferior food, and suffering with swollen, painful infections which caused the skin to peel from his feet and limbs, Jackson began to wonder if he would not have been better off remaining in Kentucky. When his health improved, Jackson's jailer auctioned off his services to pay his jail costs. The man who bought his labor treated him well, but, determined to be free, Jackson fled at the first opportunity. Traveling only at night, Jackson passed through Hillsborough and Carlisle before taking a job in Bloomington, Illinois, where he worked for about a year. With new clothes in his satchel and "considerable" money saved, Jackson went to Wisconsin, where he later found a brother he had not seen for nine years. Looking back over his life in 1847 at the age of thirty-one, Jackson believed only good had come from his decision to run away. He possessed a job and plenty of clothes, knew how to read and write, and believed that, given the chance, all Kentucky's slaves could improve themselves as he had done. His only regret, he wrote in his memoirs, was that so many remained in chains.[60]

Jacob D. Green made three attempts to flee Kentucky bondage before he gained success. In his first effort he got as far as Utica, New York, before being captured. On his way home, Green fled again, spending a week in Oberlin, Ohio, before going to Zanesville, where he resided four months. In Zanesville, police charged Green with breaking a store window and threw him in jail. While incarcerated, a Kentuckian claimed the fugitive and paid his fine. Green's new "owner" sold him in Louisville. Green spent the next year serving Silas Wheelbanks as a coachman and waiter while he planned his next escape.

Green saw his chance to flee one Monday morning when ordered to drive his owner's daughter to see her grandmother. Upon reaching a deserted area, Green ordered the girl out of the carriage and tied her to a tree with her shawl. The fugitive drove a short distance toward Lexington and then turned the horses loose. Arriving back in Louisville about 7:00 P.M., Green went straight to the riverfront, where he hoped to catch a boat to Cincinnati. After standing around watching for a while, Green picked up a white man's trunk and carried it on board. When nobody was looking, Green jumped into the ship's hold and stowed away. The boat arrived in Cincinnati about daybreak.

Green slipped away without detection, but had the misfortune of bumping into his owner's nephew. The two men struggled, but Green broke away, fleeing through the streets and across fences into the black neighborhood, where he found refuge in a cellar. Later, in desperation, the runaway approached a black child who introduced him to an agent of the underground railroad. Eventually, the fugitive, disguised as a female, rode the regular railroad to Cleveland. In Cleveland he took a boat to Buffalo, New York, and from there to Toronto, Canada.[61]

Lewis Clarke's successful escape did not occur on his first flight from his Madison County farm. On a Saturday in August 1841, only two weeks after his most recent failure, Clarke packed up his clothes in his seed bag, saddled his pony, and "set sail" by the north star with sixty-four dollars in his pocket. Though faced with the potential dangers other fugitives experienced, his escape, in the final analysis, was relatively easy.

To avoid suspicion, Clarke began his trip in old clothes, but changed to a better suit after traveling about twenty-five miles. He headed first for Lexington, the home of his brother Cyrus, where he could safely spend the night. Clarke's initial encounter with potential danger occurred when he met a Baptist minister who asked several probing questions but readily accepted his answers.

Clarke arrived at his brother's home about dark and remained through Sunday reminiscing about old times and discussing his escape plans with Cyrus. He left Lexington early Monday morning and covered the fifty miles to Mayslick by nightfall. Believing he could pass for white, Clarke decided to spend the night at a tavern. Wearing glasses as a disguise only called attention to himself, creating an anxiety that prevented his getting any sleep that night.

Clarke exited the tavern the next morning without incident. He crossed the Ohio River uneventfully and arrived in Aberdeen, Ohio, directly opposite Maysville, before noon. Though ecstatic at being on free soil, the fugitive, completely without friends, scarcely knew which direction to turn. Still traveling on his pony, Clarke faced repeated questioning by whites during the week it took to reach Cincinnati. There the runaway spent several days with old friends. On their advice, Clarke sold his pony and caught a boat to Portsmouth, Ohio, where he took a canal boat to Cleveland.

At Cleveland, Clarke faced several situations that caused him alarm. First ruffians accused him of having passed counterfeit money, and then he had difficulty securing a room in a tavern, but in each instance he averted serious trouble. Clarke remained in Cleveland for several days trying to find a way to get across Lake Erie. Afraid to ask directions, he finally decided that it was his only alternative. He booked passage on a steamer that sailed that night and stepped ashore the next morning in Canada, a free man. His flight to freedom had taken six weeks. He missed his friends, Clarke later wrote in his memoirs, and he missed the land of his birth, but with his only options being slavery in Kentucky or freedom in Canada, he believed he had made the only logical choice.[62]

No slave's flight to freedom received more attention than that of Josiah Henson. His well-laid plans put Henson, his wife, and their four children on the north side of the Ohio River without difficulty in September 1830. Fearful of being captured at any moment and totally without friends or knowledge of the roads, Henson began a two-week trek eastward to Cincinnati, where he expected to get help. Hiding deep in the woods during the day and traveling only at night, leaving the road at the approach of another traveler, Henson's family soon became exhausted. His weary, frightened wife heaped bitter recriminations upon him, wishing she had never left slavery, and his children sometimes cried all night. Ten days into their journey the fugitives ran out of food, forcing Henson to abandon his caution by searching for provisions during daylight. To allay suspicion, Henson headed south, stopping at two houses before a kind woman filled his handkerchief with bread and meat which he took back to his hungry family. That night Henson pushed harder than ever and two days later arrived on the outskirts of Cincinnati. With his family carefully hidden in the woods, Henson, who was familiar with the area, entered Cincinnati alone to contact his friends. They greeted him warmly and that evening escorted the rest of his family into town.

After a short period in Cincinnati, the Hensons began traversing Ohio. They walked at night until they reached the Scioto River, after which they traveled during the day along the "military" road which ran through an extensive wilderness. They soon ran low on food. Forced to drag themselves through briers and struggle over fallen trees, they were soon bruised and bleeding. The howls of wild animals terrified his wife and children at night, and during the day they constantly fell behind. The fugitives eventually came upon an Indian village where they received warm greetings, food, and a place to sleep.

Learning of the nearness of Lake Erie, the fugitives resumed their journey the next morning. After another night in the woods, the Hensons entered a great, treeless plain southwest of the village of Sandusky. As they neared the town, Henson hid his family in the woods and went to the shore, where he found several men, one of whom was black, loading a vessel. Hired to help load the ship, Henson carried several bags on board before he risked questioning the black about the distance to Canada. When the black man told him that they were going to Buffalo, which was across the river from Canada, Henson confessed that he was a runaway and that his family was hiding in the woods. The black laborer approached the captain, who, after hearing the fugitives' plight, invited Henson and his family to sail with them that night.

Knowing that there were slave catchers operating near Sandusky, the captain told Henson to work the remainder of the day before returning to get his family. The captain promised to sail to a nearby island, where he would stop. After dark he would send a john-boat to shore for the fugitives. That afternoon Henson's new black friend and two sailors accompanied him to retrieve his family. To Henson's chagrin his wife, fearing he had been captured because he had been gone so long, had moved the children. After a few moments of agony, Henson discovered one of his children hiding in the grass, and then found his frightened wife. With the aid of his friends, the exhausted band of fugitives rendezvoused with the boat and entered Buffalo the next evening. The captain of the vessel paid their way across the river on the ferry. After six weeks of trial and suffering, Henson's family stepped onto Canada's free soil.[63]

Kentucky runaways arriving in Canada did not find a "promised land." Canadians expected too much from them, untutored and unrefined as they were, one Kentuckian told an interviewer. A people born free did not appreciate the poverty and lack of education of some blacks reared in Kentucky slavery, another fugitive pointed out. Unscrupulous northern blacks also entered Canada, posing as fugitives solely for a handout, giving rise to rumors that all fugitives were lazy and unwilling to work, a situation that hindered acceptance of blacks in general. "The colored people have their inferior class as well as other people," a Kentuckian told a Colchester, Canada, interviewer in 1856. "We don't claim to be better than other people, but we claim to be as good." Given the chance, Kentucky fugitives believed, they would prosper as others had. Kentucky fugitives never received full equality in many areas of Canadian life, and a few felt the pangs of discrimination. Nevertheless, the "second-hand prejudice" they received in Canada, Kentucky fugitives and expatriates believed, was better treatment than they had experienced anywhere in the United States.[64]

Canada offered black Kentuckians many opportunities for self-improvement. Kentucky fugitives participated in self-help organizations, such as Henry Bibb's Refugee Home Society and his newspaper, *The Voice of the Fugitive*. Volunteers worked with new arrivals, thus easing cultural shock through adult education, established emergency funds, helped fugitives find land, and cared for the sick. Kentucky blacks sent their children to school, though they usually experienced segregation, and, where no schools existed, they created them. One Kentucky fugitive told interviewers of his belief in the efficacy of education: "Intelligent parents will raise up intelligent children."[65]

Kentucky fugitives found fertile soil and a tolerable climate in Canada. They usually worked initially as farm laborers, sometimes for successful blacks, and the cheap price of land allowed many to buy their own farms. Because Canada needed laborers, fugitives found jobs as mechanics, bricklayers, painters, and plasterers, and at least one, David Clay, formerly of Madison County, manufactured plows. Still others speculated successfully in real estate, and a few became prosperous. After twenty-five years in Canada, the Reverend William Ruth owned more than one hundred acres, fifty of it fenced and cultivated, and another portion in apple, pear, and peach orchards. George Ramsey, a self-employed blacksmith, saved money every year, accumulating over twenty thousand dollars during his thirty-one years in Canada.[66]

Though Kentucky slaves enjoyed their freedom in Canada, they forgot neither their loved ones nor their former owners. Several fugitives wrote their former masters, telling them where they lived and inquiring about their family and friends. They almost always expressed regret that they had not made their "feet feel for Canada" earlier. Letters to Kentuckians also carried word of former neighborhood fugitives they encountered upon their arrival in Canada, usually giving a report of their prosperity and good health. Henry Bibb was one of the most prolific letter writers. His correspondence with his former owners during the 1840s and 1850s condemned them for destroying his family, treating his mother harshly, and engaging in religious hypocrisy.

Upon reaching Canada, fugitives frequently tried to arrange for their families to join them. Jackson Whitney unsuccessfully urged his former master to make restitution for the harsh treatment he had received by freeing his wife and children and sending them to Canada. Robert Brown wrote a slave friend asking that she notify his former owner of his willingness to pay $750 for the freedom of his wife and child. After fleeing to Canada, Horace Hawkins purchased several members of his family. Concerned that he might be captured if he ever returned to the United States, Hawkins opened negotiations to purchase his own freedom. His owner insisted on a price of five hundred dollars but, in no position to bargain, eventually settled on two hundred dollars. Not every slave was so fortunate. Through an intermediary, Sally traced the small child she left behind to a Lexington purchaser, but the owner of her child refused to sell, making it impossible for the fugitive to unite her family.[67]

Some fugitives, unable to live in freedom while their families languished in bondage, returned to Kentucky to free their loved ones. A Mason County woman, who successfully escaped with her husband and youngest child, decided, against her husband's wishes, to return to Kentucky to rescue the children she had left behind. With the aid of "friends in Ohio" and dressed as a male, the fugitive crossed the river in a skiff and walked through the fields to her former neighborhood. Hiding near a spring where she knew her children would come for water, she waited. Her oldest daughter arrived and the two planned the escape. Late that night her daughter appeared, but without two smaller children who were sleeping in the owner's house. The fugitive had no alternative but to leave without them. She and her daughter crossed the Ohio that night and eventually reached Canada.[68]

Henry Bibb made one of the most heroic, though fruitless, efforts of any fugitive to rescue his wife, Malinda, and their daughter, Mary Frances, out of slavery. In the spring of 1838, after a winter in Canada, Bibb, against the advice of his friends, retraced his steps through Ohio toward Kentucky, peddling dry goods to pay his expenses. At Cincinnati he boarded a steamboat for Bedford, where he successfully contacted his family. They made plans for Malinda and Mary Frances to escape upriver by boat to Cincinnati, where they would find Bibb waiting.

After returning to Cincinnati, someone betrayed Bibb, and he was arrested and eventually jailed in Louisville. Miraculously, Bibb escaped and walked to Bedford where, with the assistance of a slave, he contacted his wife. She was watched by both blacks and whites, Malinda told him, and he should flee without them.

Bibb made a second attempt to rescue his family in the summer of 1839. When he contacted his mother, however, "a little slave girl" saw him and informed his owner. Bibb successfully hid in the area for a week, completing his plans to take out his family the next Saturday night, but another slave, thought to be a friend, betrayed him for a reward. An armed mob arrested Bibb, confiscated his Bible, Methodist church membership certificate, cash, watch, and pocket knife, placed him in irons, and confined him in jail. Several days later Bibb's owner sold him, his wife, and daughter to Louisville slave dealer Matthew Garrison. Garrison separated Bibb from his wife and child, and Bibb assumed they had been sold south. Garrison returned Malinda a few days later but without Mary Frances. The grieved parents believed their child had been sold, but to their surprise, the slave dealer returned Mary Frances after several weeks.

After three months in a Louisville slave pen, Bibb and his family went to New Orleans in chains. Bibb had several opportunities to escape, but could not abandon his loved ones. A Louisiana planter purchased Bibb and his family, taking them to a plantation where the slaves were "poor, ragged, stupid, and half-starved." About a year later, in December 1840, the planter sold Bibb's wife and daughter. Bibb never saw them again.

Bibb passed through the hands of several more owners before he escaped northward through Missouri. There he met a black riverboat steward who helped him reach Canada. After almost five years, Bibb resumed his search for his wife and daughter. Returning to his former neighborhood in Trimble County, Bibb learned that his wife had sent word to her friends in Kentucky that, never expecting to see her husband again, she had remarried. Bibb returned to Canada and his work in the antislavery movement.[69]

The racism that slavery implied required that blacks be taught from birth that they were inferior to whites. Indeed, by law and by custom whites reinforced "supposed" black inferiority in every relationship between the races. Blacks, however, rejected slavery as the "natural" state of their race, refusing to accept the position assigned them by the white majority, and most spent their lives seeking the basic human freedoms they believed they rightly deserved. The vast majority of bondsmen who protested their servitude engaged in passive resistance. They labored at their own pace or sabotaged operations to prevent overwork. A few undertook violent acts, burning barns or attacking masters or overseers. While most never acquired freedom, some, through emancipation, by purchasing themselves, or by running away, gained the right to enjoy the fruits of their own labor, if not total equality.

Running away was the chief freedom option for most slaves. Kentucky's geographic location and the proximity of large numbers of slaves to the Ohio River made running away inviting. The few who chose this path generally made the decision to flee on their own and traveled across Kentucky and the Ohio River with little or no help.

They frequently found a hostile white population north of the river and experienced great difficulty in getting assistance on their journey to Canada. Those who successfully escaped did not forget their families and friends who remained in bondage in Kentucky. That some risked recapture by returning for loved ones indicated just how much they wanted others to experience that new condition—freedom.

*Four*

# The Slave Trade

THE slave trade in Kentucky began with the first settlers. Virginia's slave surplus made it relatively easy for pioneers going to Kentucky to purchase bondsmen at favorable prices for labor on the frontier. After the initial period of settlement in which slaves assisted in clearing the land, building cabins and outbuildings, and erecting fences, many owners concluded that they had no need for large numbers of bondsmen. Selling unneeded slaves to other pioneers was, for many slaveholders, both a solution to labor surplus problems and a source of badly needed income. Thus, slave ownership in Kentucky continued in a state of flux from the earliest settlement.[1]

A slave's market value depended upon a number of factors, including health, age, sex, disposition toward work, and especially possession of a skill. Supply and demand also played an important part in fixing prices. During the pioneer and early national period, when the need for labor was greatest, slave prices remained steady and most sellers found buyers on the domestic market. Prices in isolated rural areas, however, lagged behind those of the cities and towns, even during periods when slaves were scarce.

Typically, buyers preferred slaves in their prime, usually between the ages of eighteen and thirty-five. In 1786 Daniel Boone purchased a Pennsylvania slave woman before she reached age twenty, paying "Ninety poundes Current Lawfull [sic] money," and eleven years later, when John Breckinridge needed a skilled hostler, he bought Johnny, a young Virginia bondsman for $250. After 1800, slave values rose only slightly for almost four decades. A newly arriving farmer, hoping to purchase slaves in their early prime years, could expect to pay $350 to $450 for a female and between $400 and $700 for a male.[2]

The economic collapse of the late 1830s depressed slave values, but with the growth of the southern market in the 1840s prices rebounded as slave traders canvassed the state for prime hands. The 1850s brought a rapid rise in slave prices and Kentuckians sold their surplus "down the river" in increasing numbers. By 1860 prime slaves of both sexes regularly brought between $1,500 and $2,000 from slave traders.[3]

In addition to prime slaves, there were three other categories on the market: children, the elderly, and the so-called "fancy girls." The value of children differed by region, but only slightly. Since work habits and behavior were not major considerations, the sale of children depended largely upon the status of their health, with males regularly bringing higher prices than females. Before 1850, when price increases were more modest, buyers paid between $150 and $350 for a preteen child, and $400 to $600 for youths in their mid-teens. During the 1850s, the value of children in the marketplace increased rather dramatically, with prices almost doubling during the decade.[4]

Bondsmen past their prime laboring years often proved to be of small value to slaveholders. During the first four decades of the nineteenth century, the prices of females tended to depreciate when they reached their mid-to-late thirties. This decline continued steadily until child-bearing ceased, usually about age fifty, when prices fell precipitously. One Nicholas County farmer, early in the nineteenth century, sold an "aged" woman for only $20, and in the mid-1830s a Bourbon County farmer offered for sale a thirty-eight-year-old female slave at $300 and asked only $245 for a forty-four-year-old woman. A Fayette County sales record in the mid-1840s revealed a 58 percent decline in prices for women between the ages of forty-five and sixty. After 1850, however, the market value of females between thirty-six and fifty began to climb, and by 1860 they showed roughly a 60 percent increase. Prices of women over fifty held steady at about $175 throughout the decade of the 1850s.[5]

The value of male slaves began to decline when they reached about age forty, after which prices dropped slowly but steadily, a phenomenon that continued through the first four decades of the nineteenth century. A thirty-five-year-old male sold for about $750 in 1845; a forty-year-old might bring no more than $250. In the decade of the 1840s, prices of men between the ages of forty and sixty dropped about 40 percent, and slaves over age sixty often sold for very small sums. A Nicholas County study revealed that the average price before 1830 of slaves over fifty was usually less than $125, and in 1842 a seventy-five-year-old Cumberland County slave sold for only $11. During the 1850s, the downward spiral in the prices of older slaves ended. Males between thirty-six and fifty, who might have sold for $550 at mid-century, brought prices as high as $1,000 in 1860. During the same decade, prices of slaves over age fifty rose about 50 percent, reaching values as high as $500 by 1860.[6]

The final category of Kentucky slaves consisted of the "choice stock" of "fancy girls" whose prices had a dynamic of their own. They were attractive, young, often genteel, usually mulatto females who were purchased to be mistresses or prostitutes. While some of these young women may have been imported into Kentucky to be sold at the Lexington slave market, acknowledged as one of the largest suppliers of fancy girls outside of New Orleans, the vast majority were Kentucky born and reared. Numerous Kentucky slaves spoke of beautiful slave girls on their farms who had been taken as mistresses by their owners, a fact which the number of mulattoes seemed to confirm. Slaves also wrote of sisters, mothers, and wives who rejected their master's sexual overtures, only to become a "fancy girl" to the next slave trader passing through the county. Eighteen-year-old Delia Clarke, described by her brothers as "virtually white," was typical of this group. When she resisted the sexual advances of her owner, he promptly sold her south. Those chosen for the role of a fancy girl usually had no alternative to their fate. Very few were as fortunate as Malinda Bibb, who was rejected for being uncooperative. Malinda was separated from Henry, her husband, after they had been placed in a Louisville slave jail. When returned several days later, she told her husband of fighting off the trader's advances in "a private house where he kept female slaves [for his customers] for the basest purposes."[7]

Buyers paid unusually high prices for fancy girls for reasons unconnected to the prices of other slaves. The health of these young women was, of course, important in determining their price, but the color of their skin, their youthful appearance, the beauty of their features, and the buyer's sexual attraction were often the determining factors. Prices for fancy girls ranged between $1,000 and $2,000 during the 1840s and 1850s, and rose even higher on the eve of the Civil War.[8]

Though some owners refused to sell slaves, most Kentuckians, white and black, accepted trading in slaves as a fact of life. There was very little public sentiment against the domestic slave trade, and in general, slave owners saw no difference between selling slaves and farm animals. Indeed, in a society where horse trading became a pastime, owners sometimes traded bondsmen for livestock. Some owners expressed regret at selling their slaves and many stipulated strict conditions which buyers must meet, but almost nothing prevented purchasers from disposing of bondsmen as they pleased. The one effort to limit the southern slave trade in Kentucky was the nonimportation act of 1833. More the result of a surplus of bondsmen

The Slave Trade / 87

# GREAT SALE of SLAVES

## JANUARY 10, 1855

THERE Will Be Offered For Sale at Public Auction at the SLAVE MARKET, CHEAPSIDE, LEXINGTON, All The SLAVES of JOHN CARTER, Esquire, of LEWIS COUNTY, KY. On Account of His Removal to Indiana, a Free State. The Slaves Listed Below Were All Raised on the CARTER PLANTATION at QUICK'S RUN, Lewis County, Kentucky

**3 Bucks** Aged from 20 to 26, Strong, Ablebodied
**1 Wench,** Sallie, Aged 42, Excellent Cook
**1 Wench,** Lize, Aged 23 with 6 mo. old Picinniny
**One Buck** Aged 52, good Kennel Man
**17 Bucks** Aged from twelve to twenty, Excellent

TERMS: Strictly CASH at Sale, as owner must realize cash, owing to his removal to W... Offers for the entire lot will be entertained previous to sale by addressing the undersigned.

### JOHN CARTER, Esq.
Po. Clarksburg         Lewis County, Kentucky

*Coleman Collection, University of Kentucky Special Collections*

than a growing antislavery movement, this law prohibited bringing slaves into Kentucky for resale south. Although the legislation succeeded in slowing the importation of slaves, it did not stop the practice. When the legislature repealed non-importation in 1849, it exculpated those who had violated the measure.[9]

Owners sold slaves for every imaginable reason. Sometimes a slave asked to be sold to be near a family member or to be separated from a spouse. Those who were viewed as "troublesome" slaves frequently wound up on the auction block—put in their owner's "pocket," as one former bondsman phrased it—when their owners could no longer tolerate their actions. Some owners sold fugitives to slave catchers for a fraction of their value, hoping to recover a portion of their loss, and sheriffs eventually sent unclaimed runaways to auction to pay their jail expenses. More common reasons for selling slaves were to pay debts, to settle estates, and to dispose of unneeded natural increases. Others, however, sold some or all of their slaves simply to make money. For whatever reason, the result was a thriving slave-trading business in Kentucky by the beginning of the nineteenth century.[10]

Until the mid-1840s, most Kentucky slaves placed on the market were sold locally or regionally. Typically, farmers sold surplus slaves to neighbors, or to someone in town; or sheriffs, county commissioners, or estate administrators auctioned off slaves at a courthouse door. Even after the dramatic growth of the southern market in the late 1840s, local trading in slaves remained brisk, but increasingly slave traders predominated at local auctions while their agents scoured backcountry farms looking for surplus slaves.[11]

Slave traders became the most publicly despised individuals in Kentucky, denounced by white and black inhabitants and by foreign visitors alike. In the early 1820s, a Bourbon County slave owner described "SOUL PEDLING" as the most despicable of crimes, and a decade later a Lexingtonian informed a newcomer that no amount of wealth could secure respectability for even a retired slave trader. Bondsmen, with real cause for contempt, viewed slave traders as dishonest, deceitful, and disrupters of families. Foreign travelers in Kentucky painted an even harsher picture. Slave traders possessed the "soul of a brute," one visitor wrote. They ate and drank too much and exhibited uncouth personal habits. Yet, the same traveler noted, they talked incessantly of their love of freedom. Another visitor decried traders' obvious ill-breeding, their unmistakable appearance, and their evil eyes.[12]

Although this assessment of the character of slave traders clearly revealed the genuine hostility of some, it had little effect on the volume of trading in human cargo. Buyers and sellers of slaves for both the domestic and southern markets thrived as businessmen in the Commonwealth throughout the antebellum period. City directories listed slave dealers alongside the most respectable businessmen, such as lawyers and bankers; and newspapers unhesitatingly ran their advertisements. Indeed, many of the largest slave traders kept standing advertisements in major newspapers, offering top prices for slaves. Many people viewed these dealings as socially acceptable, capitalistic practices.[13]

Lexington quickly became the slave-trading center of Kentucky. The reasons for this ascendancy included the availability of bondsmen in the surrounding counties, the flow of surplus slaves westward from Virginia and Maryland, and the mounting profits from the southern market. Lexington's early slave traders were largely commission agents for whom trading in slaves was just one part, but a respectable part, of their business activities. In the early 1830s, however, Pierce Griffin and Michael Hughes, two trading firms dealing exclusively in slaves, began sending bondsmen to the profitable Natchez, Mississippi, market. Soon thereafter Thomas B. Megowan filled his slave "jail" with surplus Kentucky chattel, waiting to be shipped to the Deep South. By the early 1840s, Lexington's slave traders were well established, highly visible businessmen. In 1843 Hughes and Downing took its first load of slaves to Natchez, making a handsome profit. After purchasing thirteen slaves for $5,292.50 in the central Bluegrass and expending $257.72 for expenses, the firm sold its human cargo in Natchez for $8,695.00, reaping a 57 percent return on its investment.[14]

Large profits lured an additional two dozen dealers into slave trading in Lexington during the 1840s and 1850s. Lewis C. Robards, the most unscrupulous of the traders, was the only Lexington slave dealer actively engaged in the business throughout the decade of the 1850s. In the late 1840s, Robards rented the "pens" formerly used as a slave "jail" by trader William A. Pullum. There Robards housed his common stock in damp, unhealthy, eight-foot-square "coops" with brick floors, seven-foot ceilings, and barred windows and doors. As his business expanded, Robards purchased additional space, including an old theater which he remodeled into a jail. Robards housed his "choice stock" of "fancy girls" on the second floor of a building next to the theater. An 1854 northern visitor to Lexington described the sharply contrasting living conditions of Robards's "fancy girls":

> After dinner visited a negro jail—a very large brick building with all the conveniences of comfortable life, including hospital. Tis a place where negroes are kept

for sale—Outer doors & windows all protected with iron gates, but inside the appointments are not only comfortable, but in many respects luxurious. Many of the rooms are well carpeted & furnished, & very neat, and the inmates whilst here are treated with great indulgence & humanity, but I confess it impressed me with the idea of decorating the ox for the sacrifice. In several of the rooms I found very handsome mulatto women, of fine persons and easy genteel manners, sitting at their needle work awaiting a purchaser. The proprietor made them get up & turn round to show to advantage their finely developed & graceful forms—and slaves as they were this I confess rather shocked my gallantry. I enquired the price of one girl which was $1,600.[15]

Robards seemed to embody the evil characteristics attributed to slave traders. He purchased slaves on the condition that they would not be sent south and shipped them to his Fayette County farm to allay suspicion, only to send them to Natchez at the first opportunity. He bought slaves and free blacks from kidnappers, and possibly engaged in kidnapping himself, practices that led to repeated court cases but no convictions. One 1851 kidnapping involved a free woman named Arian Belle and her four-year-old daughter, Melissa, whom Robards quickly sold to a Louisiana planter. White friends of Belle intercepted Robards's human cargo in Louisville and eventually secured the release of the woman and her child. On another occasion four years later, seven children kidnapped from Portsmouth, Ohio, turned up in Robards's Lexington jail. Robards also dealt in terminally ill slaves. To one customer, he guaranteed Delphia "sound in mind and body" after a physical examination at his jail. Delphia died of consumption before reaching her New Orleans purchaser.[16]

Louisville was the other great entrepôt for Kentucky slaves. The city's earliest slave traders consisted of small-time operators who often conducted sales on the streets. Stimulated by its riverport connections with the southern market, commission merchants, auctioneers, and general agents added trading in slaves to their other business endeavors. By the 1830s, Louisville had several jails and nearly fifty businesses that dealt in slaves. Few of these companies engaged exclusively in slave trading, and most did not advertise that aspect of their business.[17]

Louisville's small slave-trading firms continued operations throughout the antebellum period, but by the mid-1840s larger companies dealing exclusively in slaves began to appear. Soon William Kelly, Thomas Powell, the Arteburn brothers, William Talbott, and

Coleman Collection, University of Kentucky Special Collections

Matthew Garrison emerged as Louisville's most prominent traders. Spurred by state laws that made their business easier, slave traders began advertising openly and soon erected slave pens to house their purchases. The growth of these firms and citizen hostility to their unsightly slave pens prompted municipal regulation of the slave trade in the early 1850s. An 1851 Louisville ordinance required each slave vendor to purchase a three-hundred-dollar license and punished violators with a fine of between ten and twenty dollars a day. Two years later aldermen set the price of a slave-trading license at between one and three hundred dollars, but required applications to be accompanied by the written consent of a majority of the citizens residing within four hundred feet of an establishment. The fine for operating without a license increased to as much as a hundred dollars per diem. Public opposition to slave jails in residential areas continued in Louisville during the existence of slavery.[18]

Henry Bibb described the conditions he and his family endured in the fall of 1839 in the Louisville "work-house," where slave trader Matthew Garrison housed bondsmen he intended to ship to New Orleans. The large brick building, surrounded by a stone wall and patrolled by armed watchmen, appeared to Bibb much as he envisioned the state prison. As they entered the compound, Bibb was startled to see that about half the inmates were white. Both the whites, who were criminals, and the slaves, being held for "safe keeping," wore heavy chains and worked cutting or breaking stones. Some were singing, others crying or praying, and still others cursing. After his ankles were chained, Bibb labored sawing stones from sunup until sundown. At night the male prisoners returned to locked, insect-infested cells where they slept on cold, stone floors with "little bedding." The women, among whom were prostitutes and thieves, occupied the second floor. Meals, eaten without complaint, consisted of scanty helpings of corn bread, wormy beef shanks, and cows' heads in pot liquor. To the deeply religious Bibb, it seemed as if his family had descended into hell.[19]

The Louisville black community was Kentucky's most vigilant in trying to protect blacks from the illegal activities of kidnappers. Frank Cranshaw, a slave active in the Louisville religious community, attended the Fourth Street Methodist Church, later renamed Asbury Chapel. One Sunday morning word spread among Louisville blacks that Cranshaw had been kidnapped and incarcerated on a slave trader's ship heading south. Crowds of blacks, hoping that God would "stop the boat," marched on the canal through which the ship must pass. Their protest forced the sheriff to stop the vessel, and an investigation revealed that Cranshaw was, indeed, illegally detained on the boat. After his release, Cranshaw and many of his friends marched to their church where they held a "great prayer-meeting," praising God for the rescue.[20]

In addition to the city dealers, numerous small traders, often associated with Deep South firms, bought small numbers of slaves and held them on their farms until they amassed enough for a profitable trip south. In the early nineteenth century, Edward Stone, who lived north of Paris, began buying Bluegrass-area slaves, usually between the ages of ten and twenty-five, for sale south. Stone held his slaves in the fortified basement of his farm home. In Madison County, Bill Myers, a well-known slave speculator, kept regionally acquired slaves on his farm where, one slave later recalled, they were poorly housed, meagerly clothed, and fed "just like hogs." John Madinglay, a Nelson County trader, bought large numbers of area slaves. According to Isaac Johnson, a slave on Madinglay's farm for several years, the trader used them to tend his fields and clear new land. After gathering his fall crops each year, Madinglay marched all but a handful of bondsmen needed for the spring planting to Louisville for transshipment by water to the southern market. Slave-gathering farms also operated in the Bowling Green and Christian County areas, both centers of large slave populations.[21]

A slave trader's visit to a farm—any farm in the state—was a most unnerving event for bondsmen, since there was a constant fear of being sold. When bondsmen on the Mason County farm where Francis Frederick lived saw a slave trader arrive, each asked immediately, "Is it me?" That evening, while Frederick and his family ate in their cabin, their owner and the slave trader entered. "My master pointed first to one, and then to another, and three [men] were immediately handcuffed, and made to stand out in the yard," Frederick wrote in his memoirs. In another cabin the trader purchased two women who "were so terrified that they dared not say a word." The other slaves watched helplessly as their chained friends marched off "two and two." A Laurel County farmer acted more subtly. When he arranged the sale of a young slave or a spouse, he sent their loved ones to work away from the house for the entire day, making their separation a fait accompli. Not all slaves went so meekly, however. A Nicholas County slave woman refused to go with a slave trader, only to be struck on the head with the butt of a whip and knocked to the ground. The trader then seized the dazed woman, tied her hands, and "drove her off" to his slave prison.[22]

If slaveholders could not sell surplus bondsmen to a neighbor or successfully bargain with slave traders who visited their farms, public auction provided yet another alternative. Auctions constituted a regular monthly feature of county court day, the time when farmers streamed into most county seats and small towns to sell their farm products—horses, mules, cows, slaves—on the public square.[23]

Activities associated with auctions were notorious. Sellers often attempted to disguise whatever flaws their slaves might have. They instructed slaves to testify, when asked, to their willingness to work hard, to their honesty, and to their agreeable nature. Owners frequently covered graying hair with black shoe polish, rubbed oil on aging bodies to make them appear young and healthy, dressed bondsmen in their best clothes, and occasionally provided a drink of whiskey, hoping to make their bondsmen more agreeable. Anticipating such deceptions, prospective buyers carefully examined the merchandise, whether human beings or horses, before the sale began, checking teeth, feeling muscles, and inquiring about age.[24]

Most slaves placed on the auction block were routinely bid upon, struck off by the auctioneer, and taken to their new home, either in the neighborhood or the Deep South. Barring intervention by a white friend, a husband sold with his wife had no choice but to cooperate if he hoped to maintain the family unit. A woman, alone, pregnant, or with a small child, would seldom fight back. Occasionally, however, a slave auction failed to proceed as planned. When a Winchester slave named George, who had a reputation for resistance, went on the auction block, nobody locally wanted him, but slave traders took up the bid. Soon, however, George threw his head back, rolled his eyes, and began foaming at the mouth. The bidding ceased and George was dragged off to the jail, having thwarted his sale south.[25]

Traders constantly moved their slave coffles destined for market along Kentucky's roads, railroads, and rivers. Bondsmen in coffles traveled the roads handcuffed, usually two by two, with a heavy chain connecting the entire column. Women and children usually followed without restraints. Wagons carrying food, supplies, and those who became sick accompanied the larger caravans. Sometimes there were enough wagons in a slave caravan for the women and children to ride.[26]

Slave traders who marched their slaves overland to the southern market usually left Kentucky in the summer or early fall. Thus, their human cargo arrived just as planters were reaping the profits from their spring planting. The hard journey, some traders believed, helped prepare slaves for the kind of life they could expect in the cotton and cane fields of the Deep South. The day usually began about sunup for most slave coffles. Meals consisted mostly of bread, meat, and coffee. The bondsmen marched until early afternoon when the trader began looking for a night camp, thus avoiding the

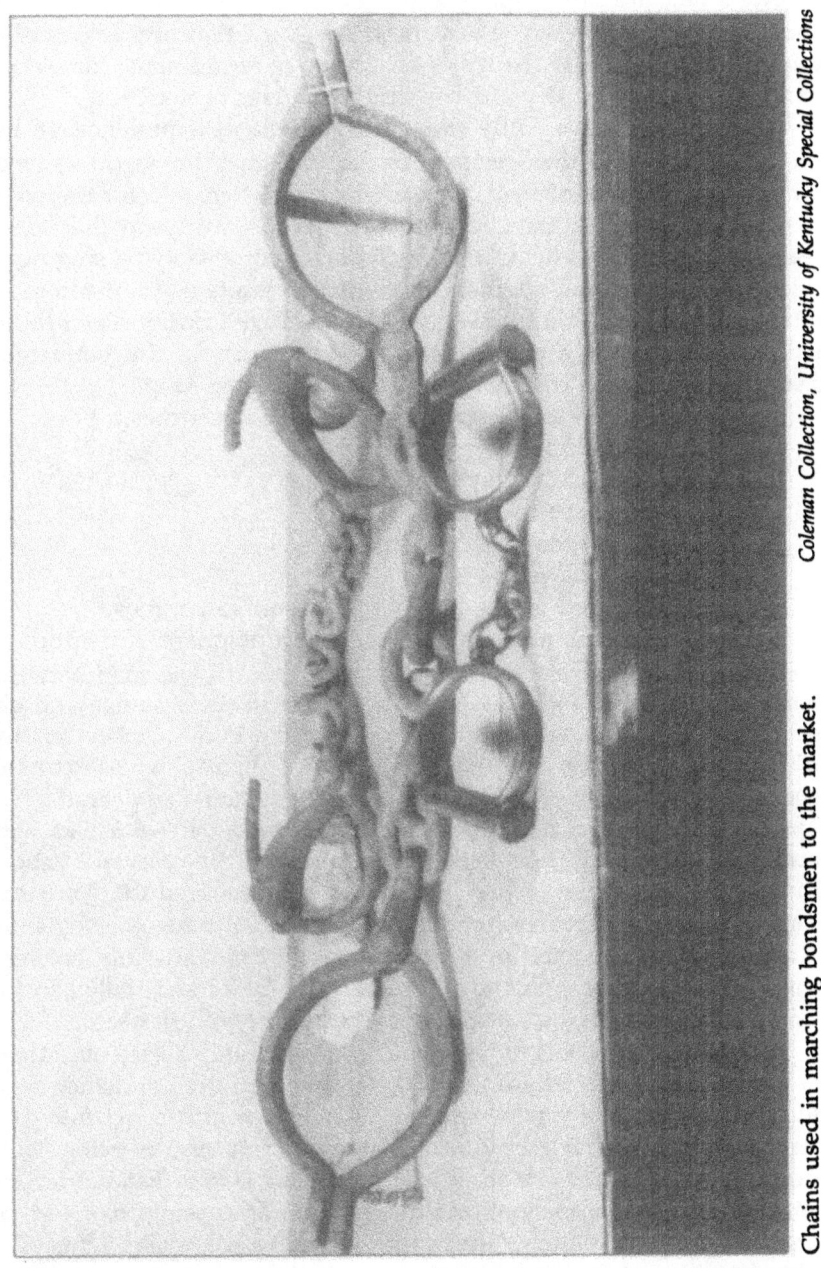

Chains used in marching bondsmen to the market. *Coleman Collection, University of Kentucky Special Collections*

worst of the summer heat. Whenever possible, traders halted their caravans near a farm, hoping to bed slaves in a barn or perhaps on some of the farmer's hay. Most traders realized that pushing a coffle too fast might cut into their profits, so it was not unusual for a caravan to rest an entire day after several hard days of marching.[27]

Observing a slave coffle was an unforgettable experience. In his old age a Hardin County resident could not forget the horrid scene of a chain-laden coffle of men, women, and children which camped at his father's farm. A traveler near Mt. Vernon surmised that a beleaguered caravan of heavily chained slaves could only be singing to "drown" their mental anguish. Peter Bruner wrote in his memoirs of a trader who hitched up newly purchased Clark County slaves to his coffle and ordered them to "start up a song." As the bondsmen marched away from their friends and family, they sang:

O come and let us go where pleasure never dies,
Jesus my all to Heaven is gone,
He who I fix my hopes upon.
His track I see and I'll pursue
The narrow road till him I view.
Oh come and let us go,
Oh come and let us go where pleasure never dies.[28]

James H. Dickey, a white minister, left a poignant description of a bizarre caravan of slaves he met trudging down the road between Paris and Lexington in 1822. Hearing music in the distance and observing a flag bobbing ever skyward beyond a knoll, Dickey hurried his carriage to the top of the rise, where he pulled aside, expecting to see a military parade. To his shock, a slave coffle appeared. Two violin-playing bondsmen led the way, followed by two slaves with cockades decorating their hats. In the midst of the caravan of about forty male bondsmen, a pair of chained hands waved the American flag. The slaves, securely handcuffed, were joined together by short chains which connected to a forty-foot-long chain that ran between them. About thirty women, tied together at one hand, followed the caravan. All marched in "solemn sadness," the minister wrote.[29]

Riverboats and barges were widely used to ship slaves, and there is little doubt, especially after 1850, that most of the bondsmen leaving Ohio River port towns were on their way south, a fact that gave rise to the phrase, used by both owners and slaves, of being "sold down the river." Boats loaded with Kentucky slaves, headed for the southern market, appeared on the Ohio and Mississippi rivers in the early nineteenth century, and soon towns like Maysville, Louisville, Henderson, and Paducah became points of departure for Kentucky's southern slave trade. River traffic to the New Orleans sales, heaviest during the winter months when overland travel was difficult, opened up additional opportunities when the boats docked at trading centers such as Natchez.[30]

The size of riverboats made them convenient for transporting large numbers of slaves south. Thomas Hughes, a northern Kentucky slave who complained of his harsh treatment, expressed surprise when his owner handcuffed him, tied him to a horse, and took him to Maysville. To his chagrin, Hughes soon found himself on a boat loaded with slaves, bound for Louisiana. Fugitive J.W. Lindsay described the departure from Louisville of a large number of slaves for the Deep South. One Sunday morning, a crowd of several hundred blacks gathered on the dock, waiting to bid farewell to friends and loved ones boarding the vessel. A "young girl" of about seventeen, with a "little bundle" of clothes, led the slaves as they approached the dock. The crowd moved in as the slaves passed. "Old gray-headed fathers and mothers" gave their children their "last farewell" as they walked by. One man peered in a window for a final glimpse of a friend, only to be rebuffed by one of the guards. Lindsay described the departure as "the most horrible scene" he had ever witnessed.[31]

Though not used extensively, Kentucky's railroads and stagecoaches also served as conduits for the movement of slaves. Foreigners reported traveling on trains with as many as a hundred slaves, chained together, headed for market, and Rev. Elisha Green, a frequent rail and stage passenger, reported sharing accommodations with small groups of handcuffed slaves, usually on their way south.[32]

Those engaged in transporting slaves had to guard against both escapes and slave stealers, especially while descending the Ohio River, where free soil was only a few hundred feet away. Henry Bibb described the conditions his family experienced when they were taken to New Orleans by steamboat in the fall of 1839. The boat was crowded with inquiring, gawking passengers, he remembered, and the slaves were handcuffed or chained almost day and night, making sleep difficult and privacy impossible. Abraham Lincoln gave a most penetrating description of manacled slaves being taken south in 1841 by a small Kentucky slave trader. "They were chained six and six together," Lincoln wrote a friend. "A small iron clevis was around the left wrist of each, and this fastened to the main chain by a shorter one at a convenient distance from, the others; so that the negroes were strung together precisely like so many fish upon a trot-line." Guards frequently patrolled these boats, protecting their cargo with revolvers and bowie knives, but upon reaching the Mississippi River many slave traders relied more on surveillance than chains, believing that the width and depth of the river discouraged escapes.[33]

The best opportunities for slaves to escape came while traveling through the Upper South. One of the most famous escape "conspiracies" occurred in 1829, when slaves purchased in Maryland by well-known trader Henry Gordon engaged in insurrection on the road between Greenup and Vanceburg. Gordon and two associates, G.T. Allen and William B. Petit, were driving ninety slaves of "all ages and sexes" overland to Mississippi. The slaves somehow acquired a file and eventually many, if not all, cut through their shackles. The plan called for two slaves to begin fighting. When the traders intervened, the other slaves would throw off their chains, turn on the drivers, and kill them. The conspiracy began as planned. When Petit attempted to separate the combatants, a number of slaves freed themselves and killed him. Another slave grabbed Petit's gun and shot Allen dead. Within minutes more slaves seized guns either from the men they had killed or from the wagons, and Gordon received two gunshot wounds before being beaten. Gordon's injuries were superficial, but he appeared to be dead. While the slaves ransacked the supply wagon, Gordon, with assistance of a slave woman, mounted a horse and escaped.

The conspirators had very little chance of getting away once Gordon sounded the alarm. Only sixteen slaves fled the scene of the revolt, and they were promptly captured. The so-called ring leaders, six men and a woman named Dinah, stood trial for murder. Five of the men and Dinah, who was pregnant, were convicted and sentenced to death. Greenup County authorities hanged the men immediately, but delayed carrying out Dinah's sentence until after the birth of her child.[34]

Another "conspiracy" occurred on September 17, 1826, on the Ohio River near Hardinsburg, about ninety miles below Louisville. As Edward Stone, a Bourbon County slave trader, floated down the Ohio with seventy-seven bondsmen for the New Orleans market, some of the slaves mutinied. The poorly organized revolt began about mid-morning when a small number of slaves, armed with "hatchets and brick bats," attacked and killed a passenger sitting near the flatboat's bow. The mutineers threw the body overboard, creating a commotion that attracted the attention of Stone and his nephew. The Stones and an employee, unaware of what was happening, began moving toward the stern without their weapons. The mutineers met the three men about midship, where hand-to-hand fighting broke out. Stone twice pulled free from his assailants. The second time a female slave handed him a gun, but a mutineer struck Stone's arm as he fired, and the bullet pierced the trader's head. The insurgent slaves prevailed, and in a matter of minutes the three slave traders were dead.

Once in control of the flatboat, the mutineers tied weights around the three corpses and sent them to the river bottom. Next, they ordered the steersman, who had remained at his post, to land them on the Indiana bank. Upon reaching free soil, the mutineers murdered the steersman and plundered the boat before sinking it. They then marched off aimlessly in sizeable groups into the inhospitable Indiana countryside with virtually no chance of escape. Authorities apprehended fifty-six in one group and sixteen in another. Ultimately, all slaves aboard the flatboat were captured and taken to Hardinsburg. Five, believed to be ringleaders, were tried, convicted of murder, and hanged. Seven others "strongly suspected" of conspiracy were "tried and cleared." Another forty-seven were sold south as punishment, and the remainder returned to Bourbon County.[35]

Those who did not, or could not, rebel, often found themselves offered for sale in the South. Kentucky slave dealers worked closely with traders in Natchez and New Orleans who frequently sought bondsmen without regard to their health. William Wells Brown, a Kentucky native, described one scene on board a ship shortly before it docked several miles north of Natchez. He and a few other slaves busily dyed the grey hair of old men and shaved their beards, making them appear ten years younger, while the traders instructed bondsmen on proper responses to questions about their health or age. A few slaves, Brown recalled, were sold immediately after disembarkation to eager buyers, but most were taken several days later to the pens outside Natchez—the famous "Forks of the Road" market. The next morning, Wells wrote, "swarms of planters" arrived, and the sales began. Another Kentuckian, Henry Bibb, described how he was prepared for the New Orleans market. The slaves were forced to wash in "greasy" water and to comb their hair so they would appear "slick and lively."[36]

The number of Kentucky slaves sold southward during the antebellum period has been estimated at between 2,000 and 8,500 annually. Calculating Bluegrass state slave exports to the Deep South is complicated by the paucity of reliable figures on the natural increase, emancipations, and the number of bondsmen imported into Kentucky. The best analysis, taking these variables into considerations, indicates that Kentucky exported about 2,300 slaves south each year in the 1830s, approximately 2,000 annually in the 1840s, and about 3,400 per annum in the 1850s, for a total of about 77,000 sent to the Deep South. Of those men, women, and children, most never saw their Kentucky homes, or loved ones left behind, ever again.[37]

The Kentucky slave trade began with the appearance of the first white settlers and continued uninterrupted into the Civil War. Most slaves before the mid-1840s were sold locally and probably remained in the region where they were born, a factor which led to increasing numbers of husbands, wives, and children living on separate farms. The growing demands of slave labor in the Old Southwest after about 1845 resulted in the sale of many thousands of black Kentuckians "down the river."

The slave trade was one of the most dreadful aspects of Kentucky slavery since trading in human flesh attacked the basic foundation of slave society—the family. Typically, Kentucky slaveholders praised the importance of the institution of marriage and of the family for both whites and blacks. In doing so they raised a howl against slave traders' destructive force upon the slave family, but, in the final analysis, their protests were mere lip-service. For, in fact, no one was safe from the trader, since a slaveholder's death or bankruptcy frequently placed slaves in the hands of new owners who were in a position to negate even the strongest instructions against separating families or selling slaves south. In truth, money ruled when a slave's value stood juxtaposed between profit or loss, and in the final analysis, all but a few whites accepted trading in bondsmen as a fact of life, as common in Kentucky as horse trading.

*Five*

# Slave Hiring and Free Blacks

SINCE Kentucky bondsmen usually performed the same kinds of labor as free workers, both owners and non-owners quickly realized the advantage of slave hiring. Renting slaves allowed small farmers without capital to use bondsmen, or, for those who preferred not to become slave owners, gave the opportunity to acquire labor, skilled and unskilled, as the need arose. For owners with a temporary or permanent labor surplus, hiring out bondsmen meant extra income with minimum risk. Though open to abuse, working as "free" laborers usually provided hired slaves a measure of independence and opportunities for self-improvement. As a result, the practice of slave hiring elevated the status of bondsmen in Kentucky society and became for some a step toward freedom.

There were basically three methods of slave hiring. Many small farmers rented slaves from neighbors on an informal basis. They were usually looking for slaves with particular skills to accomplish specific tasks. Hired slaves worked for a day, a week, or perhaps a month, constructing buildings, clearing land, or harvesting crops. Upon completing the job, the leased slaves returned to their master's farm. This informal system of slave hiring was especially common in the early years of the Commonwealth and continued in rural areas and small towns throughout the existence of slavery.[1]

Second, Kentucky slaveholders leased their slaves to neighbors or regional farmers on a more formal basis. They drew up written agreements stipulating all conditions, usually in the form of promissory notes. If neighbors failed to hire available bondsmen, owners might auction their services to the highest bidder. Every December, especially in the larger towns, newspapers contained numerous advertisements describing slaves available for hiring or notices seeking slaves with particular skills. On the first day of each year almost every sizeable town, from the mountains to the Mississippi River, held slave hiring auctions on the public square. Potential lessees flocked into town, and when the day ended, slaves of all ages and sexes went home with their new masters for the coming year.²

Placing bondsmen with commission agents and traders for leasing was a third form of renting out slaves, especially in Kentucky's larger cities. Representing themselves or clients, agents and slave traders advertised extensively. Some general agents and traders hired slaves for clients or for speculation. Others, anticipating the coming year's market, leased slaves hoping to place them for a percent of their annual wages or to sublease the bondsmen to local factories and businesses. One Louisville firm, preparing for a new year's demand for labor, advertised for "100 women and boys for brick-yards, draymen, etc., 40 men and boys for ropewalks, 40 men and boys for hotel waiters, and 50 Boys and Girls for tobacco stemmeries." An 1854 notice of an agent living near Lexington listed a large number of slaves for hire, including men, women, and fifty to sixty "small boys and girls," among whom were skilled blacksmiths, brick-moulders, rope spinners, and farm hands.³

A few slaves attempted to influence the conditions of their employment, either before or during the leasing process. When informed that they would be rented out, slaves sometimes canvassed the neighborhood in search of masters who might treat them kindly or who lived conveniently nearby in order to facilitate visiting families and relatives. Slaves seeking such arrangements had to have favorable reputations in the community, since their new masters required references attesting to their disposition and willingness to work. These arrangements frequently proved difficult for slaves because they operated in a hirer's market, especially during the first half of the nineteenth century. Slaves offered for hire at auctions occasionally attempted to dissuade potential renters by unfavorable comments or strange conduct. One male slave at a Mt. Sterling auction told several potential lessees that he was "spoilt" and as a hired slave would "be of no use to anybody," and a young woman who wanted her renter to believe that she could never please her new mistress was led off crying: "She won't like me."⁴

But eventually contracts were made and usually ran from January 1 to December 25. During the week following Christmas, owners renegotiated existing contracts, found new hirers, or made preparations for auctioning slaves' services to the highest bidder. Contracts typically specified the rental fee, working conditions, and benefits, if any, accruing to the slave. Owners generally opposed subleasing, expected adequate housing, and required the renter to provide health care for their slaves. Almost all contracts directed the lessee to provide bondsmen with suitable clothes, and some required cash payments to the slaves.[5]

The 1841 contract hiring Cynthiana and her two children required that she return to her owner with "a good new linsey frock, a good new flax linen shirt, a good new pair of shoes, a good new pair of yarn stockings, a two dollar and half blanket, a bonnet, and . . . two new linen shirts and frocks." Cynthiana's two children were to receive "new linsey shirts and frocks" immediately and "new tow linen slips" in the spring. The renter of Thomas agreed, in addition to promising good treatment, to "return him at the end of the year with a sufficient supply of good & reasonable clothing of all kinds." The 1853 contract of Sally stipulated that she would receive "two shirts, two summer dresses, one plaid linsey dress, two pairs of stockings, two pairs of shoes, one winter dress and one blanket."[6]

Leasing slaves sometimes meant large profits for owners. Wages steadily increased, with profits reaching their peak during the 1840s and 1850s, when hired slaves brought annually between 12 and 15 percent of their total value. With the annual cost for maintaining a bondsman about $170, any food, clothing, lodging, or health care provided to the slave by the lessee was money in the pocket of the slaveholder. A Louisville owner who rented out three skilled slaves in 1838 reaped a handsome profit of $636 while suffering no expenses and no losses.[7]

Nevertheless, hiring out bondsmen involved some risk. Slaves occasionally refused to work except under conditions they deemed favorable. Joe, an urban slave, would not labor in the country. "I threatened to sell him," his owner wrote, but Joe "said he would rather be sold" than reside outside of town. Some rented slaves ran away from their employers, causing days or even weeks of lost wages, and still others fled, never to return. Owners often found it difficult to collect fees when their leased slaves proved uncooperative, a situation that might result in litigation. Finally, there always existed the possibility of abuse, overwork, serious injury, or even the death of hired slaves.[8]

Hiring slaves as agricultural laborers began with the first settlers, and the practice steadily expanded during the nineteenth century. White farmers who needed additional hands during the busy seasons of planting and harvesting sometimes rented or "borrowed" slaves from their neighbors. As the number of farms grew and the economy expanded, more farmers began leasing slaves on a yearly basis. Though they sometimes paid in kind, especially during the early years of settlement, by 1850 the average cost of hiring slave laborers was $125 a year.[9]

Domestics were a major portion of the hired slave-labor force, serving white Kentuckians in both rural and urban areas. In addition to caring for children, rented slave women did much of the cooking, washing, ironing, and housekeeping. Older men and boys worked as house servants and carriage drivers, and slave children performed numerous chores around the kitchens.[10]

Slave hiring was not limited to agriculture and domestic service. Indeed, the most characteristic features of slave rentals were the variety of jobs performed by these slaves and the extension of the practice, with each passing decade, into new areas of the economy. Most of the deliveries in towns and villages were made by leased slaves toiling as draymen. They also served as mechanics of all descriptions, worked in railroad switch yards, constructed railroads and canals, and toiled at the salt licks. Hired slaves also labored in the building trade. Skilled slave carpenters, rented by the day or by the year, constructed homes and outbuildings in rural areas and in the cities, with lumber milled by hired bondsmen. Hired men and boys also worked in the brickyards.[11]

Rented bondsmen played a crucial role in Kentucky's service industries. Often indispensable to owners of hotels, restaurants, and taverns, they served as cooks in the kitchens, waiters and bartenders in the dining rooms, and housekeepers. They also chopped firewood, stoked fires, carried luggage, and ran errands for both the owners and their guests. Barbering was another profession where leased slaves provided an important service to the white community. In addition to assuring the slaveholder a good income, barbering taught the bondsman a valuable trade. Hired slave laborers frequently worked as janitors and handymen for businesses, stores, city governments, and white churches. Still other rented slaves were midwives and hospital attendants. The Kentucky, Ohio, and Mississippi rivers also claimed the services of hired bondsmen. In addition to handling cargoes, toiling in ships' galleys, and serving as engineers, waiters, and stewards, rented slaves provided much of the musical entertainment on passenger boats.[12]

Leased bondsmen were an important labor force in the state's manufacturing industry. Urban centers, where Kentucky's factories flourished, and rural areas, where natural resources sometimes determined factory locations, provided slaveholders with ample opportunities for leasing their slaves to manufacturers. Laborers usually worked on the task system, thus allowing them to make a few extra dollars for themselves by working overtime. The bonuses offered for a trouble-free year by some factory owners, when added to overtime, enabled a few workers to accumulate funds over the years to purchase their freedom. In numerous factories, skilled hired slave laborers worked with little supervision, lived on the premises in barracks, and ate their meals at a common table.[13]

Whites began placing their surplus bondsmen in these well-paying positions before 1800, and within a few years hundreds of hired slaves worked in hemp and ropemaking factories. By 1830 more than a hundred leased slaves worked at a single Lexington bagging factory, and a few of the cotton and woolen plants employed even larger numbers. Employment of hired bondsmen at the iron furnaces and tobacco factories located throughout the state was also extensive. Additional rented slaves worked in coal mines, nail factories, grist mills, woolen mills, and carding factories.[14]

Christmas vacation, with the payment of overtime and bonuses, was the most pleasant time of the year for leased industrial slaves. In one 1829 celebration about thirty hired bondsmen employed at a hemp factory paraded through Carlisle in Nicholas County on Christmas Day. The workers wore hats with plumes made of hemp and uniforms decorated with hemp and waved a large flag woven from hemp. A whistler, imitating a fife, and a drummer led the demonstration. After about four hours of marching, workers concluded their celebration with food and drink. Laborers marching home at Christmas from employment in eastern Kentucky iron furnaces in the 1850s were equally picturesque as they tramped through Mt. Sterling. Their captain led the way, lining out a song, followed by a chorus of over a hundred voices.[15]

Kentucky's first comprehensive slave code in 1798 and numerous town regulations made it illegal for owners to allow bondsmen to hire their own time and "trade as free" people. Nevertheless, many owners disregarded the law by permitting slaves, including entire families, to engage in whatever business they desired, provided they paid them a specified weekly or monthly sum. Slaves occasionally won the privilege of leasing themselves by demonstrating to their masters how profitable it was for them to permit bondsmen to accept outside employment offers. In an especially open-ended agreement, a Livingston County owner allowed his slave, Allen, to "bargain and trade for himself" and to travel at his pleasure from Smithland to Morgantown, Virginia.[16]

Allowing bondsmen to rent their own time provided them with their best opportunities in a slave society. Participating in a free-market economy by offering one's services for pay was, as Lewis Clarke said in 1842, a "taste of freedom." Consequently, slaves preferred to lease themselves because it gave them leverage for increasing their independence. Hiring one's own time frequently meant association with free blacks or even living in a free black community, situations that resulted in more than one slave's flight to freedom. Self-hiring could also enhance educational opportunities. For example, Elisha Green learned elementary arithmetic by working in a store where he weighed salt, hemp, and other items. He was also able to improve his reading ability in his spare time by perusing the books placed at his disposal by white friends. Another slave, forbidden education by his owner, nevertheless learned to read when taught by his lessee's children.[17]

More important, slaves who hired their own time and were willing to work long hours could significantly increase their income. William Hayden, an energetic, hard-working young man, fished in the Kentucky River when he was not working at a rope factory and peddled his catch to local whites. A deal to supply several Frankfort innkeepers with fresh fish eventually led to friendship with one innkeeper who gave Hayden a job shining shoes, washing dishes, and cleaning up on weekends and holidays. Hayden picked up additional cash by running errands, carrying messages, and playing his tambourine at parties and dances. Later, he learned barbering. By saving his extra income, Hayden purchased his freedom in 1824 at age thirty-nine.[18]

About 1810, Frank, a Pulaski County slave, began leasing his own time. After working all day on farm chores, Frank explored the caves of Pulaski and neighboring Rockcastle County by torchlight at night, digging niter with a pick and shovel. From the niter Frank manufactured saltpeter for which there was steady demand. By hard labor and personal determination, Frank, over a nine-year period, accumulated several thousand dollars.[19]

Milton Clarke began hiring his time in 1838, after he agreed to pay his owner two hundred dollars annually. With a pass allowing him to travel on the Ohio and Mississippi rivers, Clarke, a drum and bugle player, joined a company of hired-out black musicians who performed on a circuit. In the spring and summer, they played for dances and cotillions at the Harrodsburg Springs Hotel. During the fall and winter, they performed for dances and balls in Lexington, Louisville, and Cincinnati, and on Ohio River steamboats. After playing with the band for a short period and observing that money was "fast and easy" for men with their talents, Milton Clarke persuaded his new-found friends, George, Henry, and Reuben, to "strike for liberty." Following an engagement in Cincinnati, the band members fled northward to freedom.[20]

Occasionally, a leased slave demonstrated real entrepreneurship.

Jim, a Louisville carpenter who hired himself in 1845, paid his owner $25 a month during the spring, summer, and fall and $20 a month in winter, provided work was available. Jim prospered sufficiently to purchase several houses, which he rented to hired slaves and free blacks. As his income grew, Jim began placing "hired out slaves" in jobs throughout the city, taking a percent of their pay as commission. Eventually, the black entrepreneur achieved, unknown to his owner, income of more than two hundred dollars monthly while continuing to pay his owner at the agreed-upon rates. Jim's empire began to collapse, however, when one of his associates was picked up by the town patrol. The forged papers found on the worker led to an investigation of Jim's other employees, all of whom proved to be runaway slaves. Though Jim had to pay his owner a large financial settlement, he escaped prosecution and later purchased his freedom.[21]

The pay slaveholders required from bondsmen who leased themselves depended, to a great extent, upon the particular slave's talents and the cooperation of his or her owner. Most slaves possessed little actual bargaining power and simply made the best deal they could. The cost of hiring one's time remained relatively stable in the early nineteenth century. William Hayden paid $120 a year in the early 1800s, and Milton Clarke considered his owner a "miser" for charging him $200 a year in the 1830s. In the 1840s and 1850s as the demand for rental labor increased, owners raised prices. Isaac Throgmorton, a barber, paid his owner $240 annually for over twenty years, as did William Jackson. Another slave, who worked as a steward on the river, paid his owner $250 per annum, and Bartlett Taylor hired his time, working as a butcher, for $300 a year.[22]

Though hiring out slaves was a growing practice, it is difficult to estimate the number of bondsmen involved. One study of the 1833 tax rolls in Louisville revealed that about 20 percent of the city's slave population was leased. Another study, analyzing the incomplete censuses of 1850 and 1860, placed Louisville's hired slave population at about 16 percent and Lexington's at only 7 percent, a figure that appears too low.[23]

The journey from leased slave to hiring one's own time to acquiring freedom was usually long and difficult, but it was a road a small group of Kentucky slaves successfully traveled. Though freemen represented only .2 percent of the total population in 1790, and just 1.1 percent in 1860, their percentage of the black population demonstrated steady growth. From slightly under 1 percent in 1790, freemen increased to 4.52 percent of the black population in 1860. A slight percentage decline during the 1850s was the result of the national Fugitive Slave Law passed in 1850 and state legislation that required slaves emancipated after March 24, 1851, to leave the Commonwealth within thirty days.[24] [see Figure 1]

### Figure 1

### KENTUCKY'S FREE BLACK POPULATION 1790-1860

|      | free blacks | % of blacks | % of population | % of increase |
|------|-------------|-------------|-----------------|---------------|
| 1790 | 114         | .95         | .2              |               |
| 1800 | 741         | 1.8         | .3              | 550.0         |
| 1810 | 1,713       | 2.08        | .4              | 131.2         |
| 1820 | 2,759       | 2.13        | .5              | 61.0          |
| 1830 | 4,917       | 2.9         | .7              | 78.2          |
| 1840 | 7,317       | 3.85        | .9              | 48.8          |
| 1850 | 10,011      | 4.53        | 1.0             | 36.8          |
| 1860 | 10,684      | 4.52        | .9              | 6.7           |

[Source: 1790-1860 Census Reports]

The largest number of free blacks concentrated in the towns of the Bluegrass region. In 1860, for instance, nine out of ten urban freemen resided in Bluegrass towns, with more than one-half residing in Lexington and Louisville. Though a sizeable portion of urban blacks, freemen constituted a small percentage of the total black population of the region. Freemen also made up a small portion of the black population in the large slaveholding area of western Kentucky where, during the 1850s, their numbers either stagnated or declined. In the mountain counties, where few slaves resided, freemanship increased during the nineteenth century. Percentages of freemen among the black population there were frequently high, but the numbers were quite small. No town, for instance, contained more than eleven freemen, and Jackson County, with 75 percent freemen in 1860, had but twenty-eight blacks. Freemanship was even smaller in the Jackson Purchase.[25]

Kentucky's free blacks lived under difficult, but not impossible, conditions. White Kentuckians, like their counterparts in the Deep South, believed that blacks could not care for themselves as free people, insisting that freemen were lazy, worthless, and less fortunate than slaves. The difficulties of freemen, however, stemmed less from their personal inability to compete in an open market than from artificial disadvantages placed upon them by white society. Though the Kentucky Constitution of 1792 allowed free blacks to vote, the Constitution of 1799 sharply distinguished between free whites and black freemen, to the detriment of the latter, and much of the early slave code was applied to free blacks.[26]

Crimes which prescribed the death penalty for slaves—manslaughter, murder, rape of a white woman, arson, and rebellion—applied equally to freemen. Conviction for sabotaging or destroying bridges, dams, and canal locks, as in the case of slaves, also required the death penalty. For non-capital crimes, freemen received corporal punishment, fines, and imprisonment. Those convicted for participating in riots or unlawful assemblies received up to thirty-nine lashes, and punishment for attacking a white person was thirty stripes. Freemen who engaged in murder conspiracies might get as many as a hundred stripes, all "well laid on" the bare back. Conviction for carrying a gun in public resulted in a five-dollar fine, and harboring a slave was a fifteen-dollar fine or up to twenty lashes. Composing free papers or writing a pass for slaves was a penitentiary offense of up to five years.[27]

In court, free blacks operated from a distinctly inferior position. Though they generally held the same rights as whites in misdemeanor cases, where punishments for both races were typically the same after 1850, freemen could not testify against Caucasians in capital cases. Freemen possessed the right of trial by jury, could challenge juror selections in certain instances, and could give evidence in their own behalf. Free blacks occasionally exercised their right of appeal.[28]

The state of Kentucky relegated an important part of the regulation of freemen to local governments. Expanding the authority of cities and towns to regulate the activities of free blacks partially resulted from the gradual movement of free blacks into urban centers and partly from the belief that unbridled freemen exhibited a negative influence on slaves. Free blacks convicted of loitering or "misbehaving" in towns or of keeping a "disorderly house" were hired out for up to three months, and freemen manufacturing or selling alcoholic beverages were subject to fines of fifty to three hundred dollars. Like slaves, freemen suffered from the patrol system, which permitted night watchmen to enter their quarters without warrants.[29]

The free black family lived a precarious existence. Marriage between freemen was not legal until 1825. The Commonwealth refused to recognize wedlock between free blacks and slaves; progeny of these unions took the mother's status. With little variation, slaves who achieved financial success purchased themselves and then began buying members of their family. When conditions allowed, male slaves purchased the freedom of their wives first, to prevent having more children born into slavery, before buying their own freedom. A few freemen, chafing under their poor quality of life and their limited freedom, migrated to free soil at the first opportunity, but most remained, making a life for themselves and their families in Kentucky.[30]

Many of Kentucky's free blacks resided in rural settings where they carved out a place for their families in predominantly white communities. Success depended upon a host of variables, but achieving prosperity and maintaining an impeccable reputation were crucial. London Ferrill, the famous black preacher, built his reputation in the early 1830s, when he resided on the outskirts of Lexington. He lived faithfully with his wife, made regular payments on his rented house, adopted two children to whom he willed all his worldly possessions, and earned the good will of some of Lexington's prominent citizens during a life of service to both the black and white communities.[31]

Thousands of Kentucky's freemen resided in towns and cities where numbers made the approval of the white community less important. Though most free blacks believed it advisable to maintain good relations with the white community, free populations in towns like Maysville, Paris, Lexington, Louisville, Danville, Frankfort, and Paducah created, at least partially, a life unto themselves. For instance, in Louisville, free blacks, with domestic slaves intermingled, lived in urban, segregated enclaves where they developed a strong sense of community. Those who prospered usually rented or purchased homes in the predominantly black neighborhood that developed in a four-block area between Ninth, Chestnut, Eleventh, and Walnut streets. This area and the five adjoining blocks contained 25 percent of Louisville's freemen. The remaining free families were scattered across the other wards. More than one-half of Louisville's free black households were two-parent homes, with the overwhelming majority of fathers having an occupation.[32]

Lexington's free black population was also scattered, but a third resided in several enclaves or in the central business district in 1860. Houses in the enclaves were located in less desirable neighborhoods or adjacent to factories or businesses. Almost 30 percent of the free black enclave residents were homeowners, while about 46 percent of nonenclave freemen owned homes scattered among white residences. Approximately one-third of Lexington's freemen were homeowners. The remaining freemen lived in all sections of town.[33]

Free blacks had to compete with both slave and white labor in Kentucky's work force, and subsequently their wages were less than they might otherwise have been. In those few occupations avoided by whites or where labor shortages existed, their compensation sometimes equalled that of free labor. In fact, opportunities for freemen to apply whatever skills they possessed in a profession were much greater in Kentucky than in most areas of the North. Their success in the labor market, more than anything else, explains why most Kentucky freemen remained in the Commonwealth rather than migrating to free soil. In addition, a few Kentucky free blacks sought to improve their financial situations by expanding their trades into the Deep South despite the ever-present risk of being irretrievably kidnapped into slavery. A historian of the Louisville black community explained their choice as "the same instinct" that led "free men and women" everywhere to contest "for the right to make a living."[34]

In Kentucky, as elsewhere, the ministry was the most respected profession for free blacks and usually the most financially rewarding. In addition to providing spiritual guidance, ministers served as liaisons between the black and white communities. Ministers, especially those with small congregations, frequently held other full-time jobs. Though the pay was often unattractive, teaching stood next to the ministry in respectability. Most freemen taught at schools associated with black churches. Samuel L. White, one of the Louisville black community's most distinguished free residents, taught music to "the best classes of colored and white citizens." Barbering was another highly respected profession because of the potential income. In many towns, free black barbers often made a more than adequate living and frequently invested their surplus capital in property and other businesses. The most successful restricted their visible trade to white patrons. Freemen also succeeded as tailors, usually catering to whites only, and many free blacks enjoyed profitable careers as entertainers.[35]

Free blacks played a very important role in food services. Blacks owned grocery stores, sold vegetables, poultry, and other produce on the streets, and operated prosperous butcher shops with both black and white clientele. Others ran confectionery shops and ice cream parlors which thrived, especially on hot summer weekends. One catering operation built such a reputation in Louisville that it was the gathering spot for well-known citizens and Northern officers after the outbreak of the Civil War. As early as 1807, a freeman owned a central Kentucky inn where white travelers dined and slept. Many free black males made a living as hostlers and stablekeepers; free black women worked as domestic laborers and cooks in private homes, restaurants, and hotels.[36]

Commerce on the Ohio, Mississippi, and other rivers provided freemen many additional opportunities for employment as stewards, pilots, and stevedores, some of the better-paying jobs for free blacks. The building trades, where pay was also good, employed many freemen. They worked as laborers, carpenters, plasterers, and brick layers on building projects throughout Kentucky. Freemen also toiled as painters, and at least one free black paint contractor, Peter Lewis, kept a crew busy painting Louisville's buildings. By the eve of the Civil War, free blacks made up a sizeable proportion of the skilled tradesmen and mechanics in Kentucky.[37]

Freemen also filled positions in bagging and wagon factories, were shoemakers, and one freeman, Madison Smith, manufactured stoves which he marketed in the Louisville area. Though selling whiskey to slaves was illegal, free blacks owned and operated saloons where they sold alcohol to both blacks and whites. A number of blacks were involved in merchandising enterprises of various kinds, including secondhand stores, where they sold used furniture, carpets, and clothes to blacks and whites.[38]

Many free blacks prospered in Kentucky and lived full, meaningful lives. They won the respect and appreciation of both the black and white population and frequently left a mark on communities. Mason County's Henry Alexander opened a store and with the profits successfully branched out into several other business enterprises. Two of his daughters received their early education in Philadelphia, and ultimately, Alexander sent three of his children to Oberlin College. Rolla Blue was one of Lexington's most successful free blacks. Blue speculated in Lexington real estate, and at his death funds raised from the sale of his property purchased the freedom of many of his relatives. Lexington's Dennis Seal was equally well known. From a grocery store and stable business, Seal expanded into real estate and rental property. His business transactions with both blacks and whites enabled him to leave his children an extensive estate, including two brick houses.[39]

Pulaski County's Free Frank was also remarkably successful. Brought to Kentucky in 1795, Frank struggled in frontier Pulaski County for years before he accumulated the $1,600 necessary to purchase his wife in 1817 and his own freedom two years later. Over the next ten years, Free Frank demonstrated phenomenal entrepreneurial talent. While his wife, Lucy, engaged in household handicrafts, Free Frank expanded his saltpeter manufacturing, begun on a part-time basis while he was still a slave, by building a factory in Danville. With several prominent white friends and Free Zibe, another successful Pulaski County freeman, as partners, Free Frank purchased over four hundred acres of land, three hundred of which he owned outright. In 1830, Free Frank traded his saltpeter factory for the freedom of his son, "young" Frank, sold his land, and, with an affidavit attesting to his character and ingenuity signed by nineteen prominent Pulaski County citizens, emigrated with his family to Illinois.[40]

Louisville's Washington Spradling was a freeman with many talents. Free while still a teenager, Spradling was typical of successful black entrepreneurs in Kentucky. Starting as a barber, Spradling soon acquired a reputation as an expert shaver, but he made most of his money in real estate as a broker and investor. In addition to purchasing and leasing lots, Spradling built houses, both frame and brick veneer, which he sold or rented. Though without formal education, his intellectual acumen ultimately won him the respect of the entire black community. Because of his widespread knowledge in law, blacks with legal problems sought his counsel. By 1850 he had amassed thirty thousand dollars. Spradling was also a generous contributor to black charities and the Methodist church.[41]

But for the vast majority of Kentucky freemen, including those who achieved prosperity, life as a free black minority in a white-dominated slave society was not without its anxieties. While it was possible for freemen to achieve a "degree of respect," provided, one observer wrote, they behaved themselves, many never really felt free. Free blacks, because of their color, always had to prove their freemanship on demand. Thus, freemen had to keep "free papers" in their possession at all times. These certificates identified the freemen by name, age, description, county, and details of emancipation. The badly worn parchment carried by Perry, a Jessamine County freeman, was typical. It described Perry as "a negro man twenty-three years of age, five foot and one-half inch high, black complexion with a scar in his left eye-brow." Possession of this free paper, the county court stated, entitled Perry to "all the privileges of a freeman as full as if he were born free." Henry Nutter's Fayette County free papers, dated December 1, 1851, decreed that the thirty-four-year-old, five-foot-six-inch "free man of color," had proven himself free "to the satisfaction of the Court." Whites could challenge any black's claim of freemanship, and those who could not produce free papers usually wound up in jail. Kentucky authorities regularly jailed blacks who claimed to be free but who possessed no free papers, advertising them as runaways.[42]

The mobility of free blacks was restricted in several ways. Railroads frequently refused freemen passage, regardless of free papers, unless they were "identified as free" to railroad authorities by a "respectable white person." Many freemen also ran into problems on stagecoaches. One reported that he was "collared" by a drunken passenger who demanded, "Where are you going?" in spite of the fact that other whites on the stage identified him as free. Harassment of free blacks led Elisha Green to complain that he was actually less free to travel as a freeman than he had been as a slave. Green claimed that although he was a free resident of Maysville, suspicious ferrymen prevented him from crossing the Ohio River, and that whites commonly threatened him while traveling to visit his wife, a slave in Mayslick. Green told of one occasion, while passing through Washington, when a "negro trader" accused him of being a runaway, in spite of his identification. When the trader threatened to put him in jail, stating that he had heard similar answers from runaways before, the exasperated Green announced that he was tired, having walked eight miles, and time in jail would give him a needed "rest."[43]

Poor black freemen were constantly threatened with being arrested and hired out if they were found in a town with no visible employment. After 1825 poor freemen also faced having their children, at the discretion of local authorities, bound out as apprentices. The law allowed the apprenticing of "poor free children of colour" when officials provided county courts with "information" that their parents were "incapable" of rearing their children "in honest courses." Though the law required that apprenticed children be taught a profession, be properly fed and cared for, and be taught to read, its ambiguous language created a standing threat to the family. In 1843 the legislature removed the provision requiring that free black apprentices be taught to read.[44]

Kentucky law allowed free blacks to purchase slaves, provided they were members of their own family, but very few freemen possessed enough capital to buy their relatives. The fact that free black owners of slaves did not always emancipate bondsmen after purchasing them has led some critics to charge that blacks were no different from whites as slaveholders. Most freemen purchased relatives for philanthropic reasons and doubtless intended to emancipate them, but buying and emancipating slaves were not actions to be taken lightly by any freemen. Purchasing slave relatives may have rescued them from ownership by whites, but the threat of reenslavement by whites remained real. Few freemen could post the bonds some counties required to ensure that newly emancipated slaves would not become wards of the county, and for those black owners who fell into debt, there was the threat of having one's slaves confiscated and sold. Black slave owners, furthermore, found it difficult without the assistance and cooperation of whites to transport their slave relatives to free soil, a state requirement for emancipation after 1851. The experience of Garrard County freeman Steve Kyler illustrated the perils of black slaveholders. In the mid-1850s Kyler purchased his wife, Cynthia. He did not emancipate Cynthia because state law required that she leave the Commonwealth. Unfortunately for the couple, Kyler became mired in debt and his creditors seized his "slave" wife as payment. Kyler sued to retain Cynthia, claiming her as his wife and not his slave, but lost in both the county court and the Kentucky

Court of Appeals. Cynthia went to the auction block to pay her husband's debts.[45]

Kidnapping represented still another threat to free blacks. Selling free blacks into slavery became a crime after 1801, but rumors of corrupt patrollers who sold freemen to slave traders persisted throughout the antebellum period, and they were partially substantiated by several public incidents. Slave traders found it profitable not to ask questions about "slaves" brought to them in the dead of night or under suspicious circumstances. Free blacks who worked the rivers, especially those who traveled to the Lower Mississippi, reported incidents of intimidation and even of being shanghaied into slavery.[46]

Free blacks also suffered from white society's unwillingness to respect their legal rights. Rolla Blue, after the fashion of many freemen, appointed a white as executor of his will, believing that representation in court by a Caucasian might preserve its integrity. Free Frank and Lucy found that winning a case in court did not necessarily end their legal problems. When a questionable suit for a $212 debt was brought against Free Frank and Lucy, the Pulaski County Court promptly ordered them to pay. The free couple, without hiring a lawyer, appealed to the Kentucky Court of Appeals. In an 1824 decision, the state court ruled in favor of Free Frank and his wife, remanding the case to the lower court, "reversed with cost." The Pulaski County Court refused to comply for several terms before Free Frank hired an attorney who forced the court to act. The lower court ruled against Free Frank and Lucy a second time, only to be reversed a second time by the Kentucky Court of Appeals in 1827.[47]

While not always threatening their freedom, a large segment of the white population remained suspicious of, if not outright hostile to, free blacks. In 1818 state law forbade free blacks from other states to migrate to Kentucky, and whites sought to prevent freemen from mingling with slaves. Furthermore, when disruptions to the tranquility of a community occurred, suspicion usually fell as heavily upon freemen as slaves, resulting in periodic attempts to expel free blacks from the state. The occasional arrest of freemen charged with helping fugitive slaves served to confirm in the minds of whites that free blacks were involved in the operations of the underground railroad.[48]

White citizens harassed freemen on various fronts. One freeman, thought to have knowledge of fugitive activities, was threatened with ninety-nine stripes if he did not implicate a third party suspected of being an underground railroad leader, and a Louisville freeman described midnight raids on the homes of free families by the "iniquitous" patrol in search of blacks illegally visiting their Kentucky relatives and friends. Uncovering suspicious blacks in freemen's homes more often than not meant fines, imprisonment, or even expulsion from the state.

Harassment sometimes prevented free blacks from pursuing their vocation. Samuel L. White, a photographer, musician, and composer, was one of Louisville's most distinguished freemen. He taught studio classes to both blacks and whites in his home near the Jefferson Hotel. "Negro-haters" sometimes harassed White and his family by throwing rocks from the hotel windows onto the roof of his house. Others threw rocks through his windows which, on occasion, landed near members of his family and guests. When White complained to the authorities about the harassment, the police "advised him to leave the State." J.C. Brown was a successful Louisville mason who worked on jobs as far away as Shelbyville and Bardstown. His prosperity evoked the anger of white masons, who threatened to "break every bone" in his body if he did not leave Louisville.[49]

Suspicious whitefolk frequently took "the law" into their own hands, to the detriment of free blacks. When "some drunken wretches" began fighting at a religious camp meeting in Logan County and armed "desperados with whiskey" demonstrated menacingly nearby, the black "rumsellers," not the intoxicated "white scoundrels," were punished. County youths "organized themselves into a night & day police," a white minister wrote in his diary, and "whipped several negroes for selling whiskey." When whites in Lexington attacked the office of Cassius M. Clay's *True American* in 1845, the mob spilled over into the black community. A gang, "disguised as 'Black Indians,' " attacked "some peaceable and unoffending free negroes, beating them in a most cruel and inhuman manner," and one freeman was tarred and feathered on "the public square." Authorities, typically, failed to identify any member of the mob.[50]

False rumors of a slave rebellion in Frankfort in 1856 brought that city's large free black community under intense scrutiny. About a week after the scare began, a handbill signed by "Many Citizens" appeared announcing a "'Black List' of about a dozen free negroes who were notified to leave Town by 6 o'clock." The "pack of scoundrels" vanished, a white inhabitant wrote his son, leaving their loved ones behind in "tears." The developing crises between the North and the South also fueled panic in the free black community. The fear of anti-black legislation after the passage of the Fugitive Slave Law in 1850 caused many apprehensive free blacks to flee the state for safety, and anger at John Brown's raids generated a new wave of harassment of unoffending Kentucky freemen.[51]

Stages of freedom existed across Kentucky. Slave leasing, which fit perfectly into Kentucky's economic system of small farms and small slave holdings, provided flexibility for an archaic institution and typically worked to the benefit of owners. Rental slaves gained a slight degree of freedom only upon being allowed to hire their own time and, if economically successful, purchasing their freedom. Such a process frequently required many years, and the problems involved in the procedure were enormous, complicated by the fact that self-hiring was illegal in the Commonwealth.

Unfortunately for blacks, becoming freemen, by whatever means, carried with it few of the basic constitutional guarantees enjoyed by whites. Legal discriminations relegated freemen to a position inferior to that of whites at the workplace, in the courts, and before the government; and in the eyes of most of the white majority racial prejudice labeled free blacks failures, regardless of their accomplishments. In spite of their second-class existence, free blacks, who tended to reside in urban areas where numbers provided a feeling of security and a sense of independence, joined with slaves to create a black community. Under such constraints, the accomplishments of Kentucky's free blacks become truly amazing.

*Six*

# Religion and Education Before 1865

RELIGIOUS services provided the most integrated society that Kentucky blacks, slave or free, experienced. From the earliest settlement, blacks and whites worshipped in the same churches. Routinely, slaves joined the churches of their owners, although bondsmen were rarely forced to attend. Those masters who did insist upon slaves' attending their churches usually expected their bondsmen to take religion seriously. Indeed, owners sometimes agonized over the salvation of their slaves, and black Christians were occasionally instrumental in the conversion of their masters or of members of their families.[1]

In the minds of most blacks, however, whether slave or free, the white man's church, which preached without practicing the equality of all before God, proved unsatisfactory. Though attitudes differed by degree among local churches and denominations, white congregations maintained, blacks believed, "the order of master and slave in the church." Blacks and whites sat in the same churches, listened to the same sermons, worshipped together in song, and professed faith in the same Supreme Being, but never on a basis of true equality.[2]

Bondsmen did not have to be cynical non-believers to perceive the church as the servant of slaveowners' interests. Black members understood the symbolism of sitting in the back of the church, sometimes separated from whites by a gate, or of occupying only balcony seats, or of being relegated to overflow space. They knew why they were unable to make a complaint against "the white portion of the church" or against mistreatment by an owner-member except through a sympathetic white. Black members rarely voted on church business, except at the convenience of the white members, and they understood their role when the minister, after serving communion to the white congregation, said "now you black ones, if you wish to commune, come down."[3]

Slaves and freemen also comprehended the anomaly of the church's position with respect to the black family in contrast to its view of the white family. In an era of strict religious discipline, churches expelled slaves for abandoning their spouses, for adultery, and for fornication. Yet the congregation to which Rev. George Bibb belonged, and to whom he had preached on numerous occasions, raised no protest when his owner sold the black minister away from his family. Nor did whites complain when a member of another church advertised an elderly slave as "a Christian in good standing in my church" and then sold the slave away from his wife.[4]

Slaves also grasped the true meaning of "the message" preached to them by white ministers. For many masters, religion served as a method of social control, and preachers, especially after 1800 when antislavery sympathies among ministers declined, willingly obliged slaveholders with sermons stressing subordination of the black race. Sermons on peace, love, compassion, and redemption, many slaves recalled, were transformed into admonitions of honesty, hard work, and "servants obey your master" before their conclusion.[5]

Slaves also recognized their inferior position within white denominations by the different standards applied to blacks called into God's service. Whites sometimes questioned the sincerity of Protestant slave preachers, or openly doubted their ability to handle capably the duties of ministers, or repeatedly forced black ministers to prove themselves. White church leaders wrangled over the credentials of black preachers, raised questions about their right to perform ordinances such as baptism, and worried lest slave sermons possess some subversive meanings. Black Catholics fared little better than Protestants. The three young black novices in "The Little Society of the Friends of Mary, at the Foot of the Cross," begun in the 1820s at Loretto, were "set apart" by their different dress, rules, and offices. They "received nearly all the vows" of sisterhood before the experiment ended with their release from their obligations.[6]

Blacks sought their own ministers, separate churches, and control of their religious services. From the earliest settlement, blacks called to preach had ministered to slaves and freemen, filling a void left by the sermons of whites. Typically, black preachers demonstrated unusual qualities of character and leadership long before they entered the ministry. After experiencing a well-publicized conversion, they frequently exhibited their spiritual wisdom first in Sunday schools. Possessing strong personalities supplemented by a noticeable charisma, they usually won the respect of at least a portion of white religious leaders. Though frequently conservative and cautious in their relations with whites, black ministers stubbornly opposed compromise with white authorities on religious matters.[7]

Gaining acceptance by the white community was rarely easy for black preachers. Those called to the ministry sometimes learned their religion, and how to preach, at unauthorized religious services which slaves held in the forests, where they worshipped away from the white man's watchful eye. With kettles or washpots turned upside down on the floor, one side propped up to "catch" sounds of their meeting and a vine stretched across the road to hamper the patrol, these services sometimes lasted late into the night. Slave preachers were often simple farm hands who, through their ability with the spoken word, emerged as the black spiritual leaders on isolated farms. Others informally exhorted among black people from door to door on Sundays, praying for the sick and infirm, or conducted prayer meetings in their homes until they eventually gained recognition as ministers. Regardless of the path taken, once ministers received "the right hand of fellowship" from blacks, they usually achieved more formal recognition. Most slave ministers, after a suitable length of time, received a license to preach and were formally ordained. Ordination services usually featured a council of white ministers who questioned the candidate regarding theology. Upon being satisfied, the council commanded newly ordained black ministers, in the presence of other local black ministers, to "go forth and preach the gospel."[8]

Exercising the "gift" of preaching had important benefits for slave ministers. Owners with strong religious convictions, for instance, were more likely to emancipate slaves called to the ministry; and the perquisites enjoyed by black preachers, whether from individuals or from their own churches, made it easier for them to purchase their freedom. Slave preachers also enjoyed more mobility than did most blacks. White churches typically gave black ministers permission to preach wherever an opportunity arose, and many traveled extensively ministering to slaves and freemen, often in unsupervised services.

Increased opportunities for education were another benefit preachers enjoyed, though many black ministers never learned to read. Those who remained illiterate relied on their memories, sometimes quoting long passages of scripture and delivering memorized sermons. Most, however, realized the necessity of at least a rudimentary education for religious leaders who based their dogma on a written record, and they readily availed themselves of opportunities for improving their education. For some this meant spending nights and weekends improving skills, usually by reading and studying the Bible.[9]

Black preachers faced the difficult task of reconciling the spiritual world, about which they preached and where all were equal before God, to the harsh, temporal world of inequality where slaves and freemen lived. Thus, after ministering to the spiritual needs of congregations on Sunday, black preachers "look[ed] after the interests" of their parishioners during the week, frequently helping church members in economic distress or mending hostile relationships between slaves and their masters. When social aberrations occurred, such as attacks on black families or the kidnapping of freemen, ministers called their congregations to prayer and fasting before consoling the distressed or organizing demonstrations against unfair treatment, always being careful not to push too hard.[10]

While most blacks remained members of white churches until after the Civil War, those who could do so formed separate, all-black churches. Separate churches usually arose when blacks became a sufficiently large portion of the congregation to express displeasure with their subordination to the white members. In each instance, the mother church established a committee of whites to oversee the black congregation. The oversight committees usually attended black church services, acted as church clerks when necessary, and provided financial advice. Though these committees attempted to retain control of almost every aspect of the black churches, they succeeded only partially.[11]

Next to the family, separate churches were the most important black institution during slavery. For the religious, black churches offered an approach to God that promoted individual self-respect. Equality of worship in their own churches with fellow blacks ameliorated some of the more psychologically damaging aspects of slavery and allowed a spiritual release through sermons and songs that often included subtle attacks upon the slave system. Black churches also developed laymen who ultimately supplied the religious leadership the black community needed, proving that blacks could take care of their own religious concerns. But churches were more than religious institutions. They were the center of culture, where blacks, whether slaves or freemen, fashioned a degree of solidarity. Churches gave blacks their best opportunity for free speech, offered possibilities for formal economic cooperation, provided buildings for schools, and served as social centers. For the non-religious, the church afforded an opportunity for entertainment or for meeting with friends.[12]

Although some black churches claim an earlier origin, none was older, or more famous, than First African Baptist Church in Lexington. Its founder, a slave named Peter, popularly known as "Old Captain," is believed to have been the first black preacher in Kentucky. A member of the famous "Traveling Church" which entered Kentucky in 1781, Old Captain later joined the white Baptist church at the "Head of Boone's Creek" in Fayette County. After hiring his time, he moved to Lexington, where in the mid-1780s he began holding informal services in his cabin. As his ministry grew, Old Captain baptized converts in spite of the opposition of the white Baptists and formed the First African Baptist Church about 1801. Though there is no record of Old Captain's having been formally ordained, his church ultimately obtained partial recognition from the white Baptist association and grew to over three hundred members. Never totally independent, Old Captain's church maintained an uneasy alliance with the white Baptists throughout his tenure. Old Captain died in 1823 at age ninety.[13]

London Ferrill succeeded Old Captain as pastor of First African Baptist. Ferrill, a former slave with "remarkable natural gifts" for preaching, arrived from Virginia before 1817 and began ministering to blacks in the area. Almost everyone in Lexington recognized Ferrill's ability, and the First African Baptist Church invited him to join their fellowship, perhaps with the idea of eventually replacing Old Captain. Ferrill refused, citing the church's irregular relationship with white Baptists. But in 1820 when a majority of the members judged Old Captain too feeble to continue, Ferrill, encouraged by Lexington's town trustees, accepted the pastorate of First African Church. Vigorously opposed by a majority loyal to Old Captain, Ferrill, with 280 members, bolted the church and began meeting in a hall provided by white Baptists, thus splitting the church. The white Baptist church later ordained Ferrill, accepted First African members baptized by Old Captain, and in 1824 received the new black church into the Elkhorn Association. The conservative Ferrill dominated the black religious scene in Lexington for the next thirty years, during which the First African Baptist Church became the largest church in Kentucky with 1,828 members.[14]

At Ferrill's death in 1854, the First African Baptist Church called Frederick Braxton, a slave, as its minister. Under Braxton, who later acquired his freedom, the church continued to prosper, increasing to 2,223 members by 1861. A year later the church became embroiled in a controversy involving "political" questions, leading to another split. Braxton and five hundred members walked out, taking their church letters in a "coffee sack," and founded the Independent Baptist Church, later renamed Main Street Baptist, located on property owned by Mary Todd Lincoln.[15]

Pleasant Green Baptist Church was another influential black congregation in Lexington whose pastors left a mark on the city. After the split of 1820, Old Captain's church was known as the "African

Church" until about 1829, when it took the name Pleasant Green Baptist Church. After the death of Old Captain, "Brother January" became the minister for an undetermined period, followed by George Brents, a freeman. During those years, membership remained small. In 1855 the congregation selected George W. Dupee, a slave, as pastor, and under his leadership Pleasant Green experienced remarkable growth. Converted in 1842 and ordained in 1851, Dupee had served the black Baptist church in Georgetown before moving to Pleasant Green. Dupee built a reputation as an outstanding preacher who possessed a "strong intellect." He was responsible for starting several black Baptist churches during the 1850s, calling the first meeting of black ministers in the state in 1861, and organizing the first association of black churches in 1864. Perhaps the most notable episode in Dupee's life occurred in 1856 when the slave pastor went on the auction block. Dupee's distraught congregation persuaded the minister and deacons of the white First Baptist Church to purchase their pastor, repaying the white Baptists in small, weekly payments. Dupee served Pleasant Green until 1864, when he resigned to become pastor of the Washington Street Colored Baptist Church in Paducah.[16]

Lexington possessed several other black churches. St. Paul's African Methodist Episcopal Church began in a rented stable in 1820 under the leadership of Rev. William Smith. A brick sanctuary constructed ten years later had to be enlarged in 1850 because of St. Paul's rapid growth. Asbury Methodist Episcopal Church, founded in 1847, resulted from the hard work of Henry H. Lytle and a determined band of black Methodists. After meeting in rented buildings for several years, the congregation built a church in 1854. At the end of the Civil War, the church consisted of about five hundred members. Lexington's black Christian Church organized in 1851 when its members withdrew from the white Christian churches. Thomas Philips, a freeman and the driving force behind the church, began with only thirty-five members. William Davis, the second pastor, enlarged the congregation to about one hundred members in 1859. Alexander Campbell succeeded Davis in 1864. Under Campbell's leadership, the church grew to several hundred members by the end of the Civil War. Campbell, one of the more remarkable black ministers in central Kentucky, founded several Christian churches.[17]

Blacks in Louisville also preferred separate churches. The man primarily responsible for founding that city's first separate black church, Henry Adams, was born in Franklin County, Georgia, in 1802. Converted and baptized during his youth, Adams was licensed to preach at age eighteen and ordained October 29, 1825. After preaching for four years in Georgia and South Carolina, Adams journeyed westward to Louisville, where in 1829 he became pastor for the black members of the First Baptist Church. An intelligent, godly man, Adams devoted the early years of his ministry to zealous preaching and diligent study. Through hard work he became a "good English scholar" who demonstrated "considerable proficiency" in Biblical languages. Under Adams's guidance black membership at the white church steadily increased, comprising almost half of the congregation by 1841. In 1842 Adams successfully led the black members out of the white Baptist church and formed the "Colored" or "African" Baptist Church, later renamed Fifth Street Baptist Church. Over the next thirty years Adams dominated the black religious scene in Louisville. During that period he earned the support of Louisville's most respected citizens, one of whom described his influence within the black community at the beginning of the Civil War as "incalculable." Known for his protracted revivals, Adams was credited with 10,000 conversions and 1,300 baptisms. He died in 1872, still "anxious for the better Condition of his church, for the amelioration of his race, and for the Conversion of his Children."[18]

The founding of the Colored Baptist Church was an orderly affair. After black members informed the First Baptist Church that they preferred to meet separately, committees of blacks and whites met to draw up an agreement. Adams and the black committee members agreed upon articles of separation which contained the Baptist "Confession of Faith," a "Church Covenant," and "Rules of Decorum." A white "standing committee" promised to protect the black church and its members "from molestation in times of excitement," while "leaving them to manage their internal affairs in their own way." The Colored Baptist Church, composed of 475 charter members, officially called Henry Adams as pastor and began holding services in April 1842.[19]

Though never completely free from the influence of the white standing committee until after the Civil War, Louisville's Colored Baptist Church largely controlled its own destiny. The congregation willingly consulted with the white church when it needed advice in financial matters, but protested vigorously "when a difference of opinion" arose over the extent of the white church's oversight. The white standing committee existed for "protection alone," the black congregation informed the First Baptist Church, and could "*in no way whatever impair the independence and rights of the Colored Baptist Church.*"[20]

Next to worship services, the semi-monthly business meetings were the heart of the Colored Baptist Church. The rules of decorum were detailed and specific. The pastor moderated all business meetings except when he stepped aside to participate in debates. The church kept official records of business meetings, selecting its first black secretary, Solomon Patterson, after two years of white clerks. At business meetings members spent considerable time hearing charges against those who violated church doctrine or decorum. The Colored Baptist Church excluded members for fighting, intoxication, improper language, lying, attending horse races, playing cards, failure to pay debts, immorality, and "sundry things unbecoming a Christian." In most instances, the accused presented their cases, and the members either exonerated them on the basis of the evidence or forgave them after a full confession. Occasionally the church excluded members who had confessed and requested forgiveness, but seldom on a single hearing. Those who refused to attend hearings were always excluded.[21]

Church finances constituted another major consideration of business meetings. Long before establishing a separate church, black members of First Baptist apparently had been financially responsible for the "African" portion of the white church. As early as 1839 the black congregation worshipped in "a large new brick building put up by their own means" and paid Adams's yearly salary of five hundred dollars. As a religious body, they had three potential sources of income. The regular weekly church offerings provided most of the church's finances, and members gave generously. Contributions from August 1841 to September 1842, for instance, totaled $1,057.94. In times of need or during special building programs, the church placed an assessment on each member. In 1849 and again in 1851, the church asked some members to give five cents a week, and those better situated to pledge at least three dollars a month. The church also authorized "agents" to collect money. Agents were either paid by the month or given a percentage of what they collected. In 1855, for example, Adams, an agent throughout his ministry, received one-fourth of his collections, and agent-church member John Collins, Sr., was paid fifteen dollars a month and expenses. During times of financial crisis, Colored Baptist Church also sent "Brethren into Different States" to raise money. A seven-member business committee oversaw all financial matters after 1844.[22]

The pastor's salary was the largest yearly expense of the Colored Baptist Church. Upon separation from First Baptist, the church raised Adams's salary to $600 annually. Ten years later they offered him $800 per annum, but Adams announced he would accept only $700. Though possessing the best intentions, the church seldom paid the pastor his entire salary. By May 1844, for example, the church was already about $275 behind; and in July 1849, when the people had contributed all he believed they could give and church debts were still pressing, Adams decided to forgo his salary for the remainder of the year.[23]

Maintaining a suitable building was a second major expense for Colored Baptist. Upon separation, the congregation began looking for a permanent location and soon purchased a structure for five thousand dollars on Fifth Street between Walnut and Chestnut streets. Church members, whenever possible, made needed repairs; but major projects, such as raising the floor to create a basement or refurbishing the sanctuary, were contracted to professionals. By the late 1850s Colored Baptist possessed one of the finest church buildings owned by blacks in America. Other church expenses consisted of supplies, such as baptismal "gum" boots for the pastor, the church clerk's salary, and contributions to missions.[24]

The Second Colored Baptist Church of Louisville, renamed Green Street Baptist Church in 1860, began as a mission of the white First Baptist Church. About 1839 a small group of approximately twenty-five blacks, led by George Wells, began meeting in an old house on First Street. In 1844 they asked First Baptist for permission to start a second black church. A committee of blacks and whites drew up a church covenant and rules of decorum to form the Second Colored Baptist Church. The congregation called Wells, later described by his parishioners as "an able and useful preacher," as their pastor. Wells pastored the church until his death in 1850, when there were three hundred members. Charles Satchell succeeded Wells in September of that year. A native of Cincinnati, Satchell was better educated than Wells and was more sophisticated than his congregation. This difference, when combined with the church's financial problems, created considerable tension. Though the church voted to rehire him, Satchell bid the church "temporal & spiritual" farewell in a letter of resignation in November 1851. The church grew by twenty-eight members during Satchell's tenure. Orrin Shanks replaced Satchell in April 1852, but served for only five months before he died.[25]

In September 1852 Second Colored Baptist Church called Richard Sneethen as pastor. An ex-slave born in Virginia, Sneethen had served churches in St. Louis, Missouri, and Galena, Illinois, before arriving in Louisville. He found a ready acceptance at Second Colored Baptist, where he built a reputation among black Baptists as a sound preacher and able spiritual leader. In 1860 the church gave Sneethen a lifetime appointment, and under his leadership the congregation grew to 725 members before his death in 1872.[26]

Business meetings, moderated by the pastor, were an important part of the activities of Second Colored Baptist Church. Members, casting secret ballots, elected all church officers by a majority vote, received members from other churches, and expelled members for stealing, lying, cheating, playing cards, fussing, fighting, dancing, drinking, nonattendance, treating the church with contempt, and "flying in the face of the pastor." W.Y. Clinton became the church's first black clerk in 1849. The church kept formal minutes of all business meetings from its founding, but unfortunately, several years of records during Wells's ministry were lost.[27]

From its inception Second Colored Baptist Church experienced financial troubles. The congregation was unable to pay Wells a salary in the early years, but members supplemented his income as a laborer with gifts in kind. Upon the establishment of the Second Colored Baptist Church, Wells became its full-time minister, his salary consisting of an offering taken bimonthly. In 1846 the church voted Wells a yearly stipend of $250, but lowered it to $200 annually for the final four years of his pastorate. Much of Second Colored Baptist's financial distress arose from an 1847 decision to purchase a two-thousand-dollar building and pay for it in only four years. When donations from members proved insufficient and expected assistance from white Baptists failed to materialize, the church tried to raise funds through "fairs." Though not always successful, an 1849 fair raised $275 for payment on the church building.[28]

Financial problems persisted after the church invited Charles Satchell to become pastor at the higher salary of $400 annually. One reason for the church's difficulty in meeting its obligations became apparent in January 1851, only five months after Satchell became minister, when members learned that Wash Anderson, the church treasurer, had embezzled $661.32. In an attempted settlement, Anderson gave the church a $553 mortgage on a lot he owned and a note for $108.32. He eventually repaid the church $344.42 of the funds he had taken. After the embezzlement the church instituted an improved accounting system.[29]

During Richard Sneethen's ministry, the financial position of Second Colored Baptist improved. Offerings seldom fell below church expenses, averaging about $1,100 annually during one eight-year period. In 1854 the church hired a sexton at a salary of $150 a year and in the late 1850s increased Sneethen's salary to $480 annually. During Sneethen's ministry, the church built a new, brick edifice, valued at six thousand dollars.[30]

Blacks also participated actively in Louisville Methodist churches and by the 1830s outnumbered white members. The Center Street Methodist Church, which dates from around 1831, was the outgrowth of the desire of blacks to gain control of their worship services. In 1835 Washington Spradling leased a lot to the church and members erected a new building. Though under the auspices of the Methodist Episcopal Church, the Center Street congregation seemed to some whites to be too independent and a potentially dangerous "free church." White Methodists regained control in 1845 by moving the congregation to a new structure on Center Street, providing the historic church its final home. During the Civil War, when white Methodists seemed to have little time for supervision of the church, Center Street Methodist seceded from the Methodist Episcopal Church, South, and joined the African Methodist Episcopal Zion Church.[31]

Louisville's Quinn Chapel African Methodist Episcopal Church was equally famous. From its humble beginnings in a stable in 1840, the church moved to a partially finished brick building in 1854, worshiping in the basement for four years until completion of the sanctuary. During those years the pastor, Rev. Willis R. Revels, canvassed northern states, raising much of the cost of the building. Because of its large free black membership and its active educational program, Quinn Chapel was known as the "abolition" church in Louisville. As a result, some slaveholders refused to permit their slaves to attend Quinn Chapel.[32]

Fourth Street Methodist Church, later known as Asbury Chapel, was easily the most controversial black congregation in Louisville. A house of worship since 1829, the building was leased by the white Methodists in 1842 and purchased by James Harper, a free black Methodist minister, in 1845. At Harper's request, and contrary to usual practice, the judge handling the sale of the church appointed five black trustees. Four years after the Methodist Episcopal Church had split into northern and southern branches, Harper attempted to lead Asbury Chapel into the African Methodist Episcopal Church. White Methodist leaders objected, maintaining that the black members could leave the southern church but they could not take the church property with them. After a heated confrontation in the sanctuary between black and white Methodists, the contestants referred the dispute to the courts, which ultimately decided in favor of the blacks. The controversial Harper left Louisville, but returned in 1849 and led the schism in Asbury Chapel during Hiram R. Revels's pastorate. Each side claimed ownership of the sanctuary then under construction, precipitating a bitter court struggle which Harper's group eventually lost. After pastoring a small number of dissidents for a short period, Harper moved to Baltimore, Maryland.[33]

In the small towns and rural areas of Kentucky, where separate churches were less common, three types of black congregations developed. Most blacks who worshipped as a separate congregation did so in white sanctuaries. Typically, they petitioned white church leaders to hold separate services, either at night or on Sundays. The black members of the Forks of the Elkhorn Baptist Church in Woodford County worshipped separately, sometimes with no whites present, on Sunday afternoons. In 1839 the church appointed "four colored brethren to watch over the conduct" of the all-black services. The white minister preached to the black congregation about once a month, and black preachers filled the pulpit the other three Sundays. The African Baptist Church of Henderson, which traced its origins to informal meetings of slaves and freemen in log cabins, became part of the white church in 1840. In 1845 the African Baptist Church reorganized, called Rev. Willis Walker, a slave, as minister and resumed worshiping separately in the white church basement.[34]

While many black congregations continued meeting separately in white churches until after the Civil War, most hoped to acquire their own sanctuaries. The black members of First Baptist Church in Bowling Green conducted separate services in the white sanctuary on the first Sunday of each month for years before erecting their own building in 1845. Blacks at Stamping Ground Baptist Church began conducting autonomous services in the white Baptist church building in 1840. After raising money for fifteen years, the black congregation entered their newly completed sanctuary in 1855. Seeing the handwriting on the wall, the white church reluctantly recognized the African Baptist Church as a separate, if not equal, congregation.[35]

Those black denominations unable to afford separate sanctuaries sometimes joined together to construct a common meeting house. In Nicholasville black groups in a cooperative effort in 1843 constructed the "Union Church." The sanctuary served several small fellowships for years. In Madison County where "African" congregations had existed since the early nineteenth century, black ministers decided in 1845 to build "a church of their own." An ex-slave, Tom Robinson, donated land valued at sixty dollars, and local blacks constructed a sanctuary for use by Baptists, Methodists, and possibly other black groups.[36]

In towns and communities scattered throughout the Commonwealth, sufficiently prosperous blacks organized autonomous, separate churches, mostly after about 1840. The First African Baptist Church of Maysville, begun under the leadership of Elisha W. Green, was typical. Green, a member of the white church, became convinced in the 1840s that he should do "something for God." On his own initiative but with the approval of white Baptists, Green began holding prayer meetings in the home of a black church member. When the group became too large for home meetings, they rented a building where they worshiped for five years. By the end of the decade, Green was the recognized pastor of the black church members. In 1850 Green's First African Church gained admission into the white Baptist association. Later Green expanded his ministry into several counties of northern Kentucky, and in 1855 while preaching in Paris, the black members of the white Baptist church asked his assistance in establishing a separate congregation. The minister of the white Paris Baptist Church reluctantly agreed to the separation and drew up a statement of faith and rules of decorum for the First African Baptist Church of Paris. First African had the authority to call a minister, elect officers, and administer religious ordinances, but only with the advice and approval of the white Baptist church. First African would "cease to exist," the white Baptists informed the black congregation, if it broke "the rules and regulations" laid down by that church.[37]

During the 1840s both the black Presbyterians and Baptists began meeting separately from the white congregations in Danville. In 1841 with the permission of the First Presbyterian Church, blacks repaired the "old church" and began evening prayer meetings and Sunday afternoon services, probably with a white present. By the 1850s, a black three-man committee was supervising the services and maintaining proper decorum. Black Baptists organized a separate church in 1846. Rev. Jordan Meaux, known for his spiritual wisdom, provided leadership during the early years. Freeborn Rev. Henry Green became the next pastor, followed by Rev. Isaac Slaughter, a "great Bible student and a fearless defender of the faith," who served twenty-six years.[38]

In 1833 black Baptists in Frankfort organized an autonomous congregation, the Colored Baptist Church. The church acquired an outstanding pastor when James Monroe answered their call in 1845. Monroe remained nineteen years, gaining recognition as both a preacher and a leader among black Baptists. John G. Fee, a white Kentucky abolitionist and a visitor to Monroe's church in 1858, described him as a "portly, fine-looking" man who delivered a "very effective sermon," and George W. Dupee, for whom Monroe frequently preached revivals, called him "the best preacher he [had] ever heard." Monroe's church hosted the first meeting of black minister and deacons in Kentucky.[39]

Some traditional Protestant theologians have argued that black folkways tended to subvert religious canons in two ways. The first involved "conjuring"—the role of superstition, ghosts, fortune-telling, and so-called trick doctors, all of which commanded credence among the black population in general and among black Christians in particular. Since many Kentucky blacks believed in spirits, witches, haunted houses, and ghosts, some white critics contended that conjuring was innate to the race, and therefore present in the black church. It was held that only blacks practiced conjuring.

Conjuring was a pattern of belief that sought to give meaning to the inexplicable in life. Unlike Christianity, where evil was usually explained as God's judgment, the conjurer offered the believer a chance to implement his or her own judgment. To the believer, the conjurer, usually for a fee, could place an evil "hex" on one's enemies or "charm" a person to act in some desired manner.[40]

Some slaves did resort to conjuring. Henry Bibb sought the aid of a conjurer to secure better treatment from his master. One conjurer prescribed that Bibb mix "alum, salt and other stuff into a powder" and sprinkle it near his owner, and that he chew a "bitter root" and spit the juice toward his master. A second conjurer prescribed sprinkling a dust made from cow manure, red pepper, and "white people's hair" in his master's bedroom. In each instance the conjurer's remedies failed miserably. On another occasion, Bibb turned to a conjurer for advice on winning a young lady's love. Told that he should scratch her with a frog's bone and place a lock of her hair in his shoe, Bibb found, to his dismay, that his actions alienated the girl. Later, after becoming a minister, Bibb, embarrassed at his earlier succumbing to superstition, denounced the entire concept of conjuring and wrote that only education could eliminate such misguided ideas. George Conrad told of a jealous aunt whose conjuring resulted in the death of two of his younger brothers. Blacks could "conjure each other," Conrad told an interviewer in his old age, but he cynically remembered that conjuring had no effect on "whitefolks." These and other tales of conjuring, however, were the exception rather than the rule. Conjuring was, in fact, little relied upon by slaves, denounced by black religious leaders, and had diminished in influence by the 1860s.[41]

A second, and probably more controversial, question involves the role of African heritage in the lives and religious services of black Kentuckians. In the twentieth century, two views on the survival of African culture in the American South emerged. Anthropologist Melville J. Herskovits maintains that Africans possessed a strong system of religious beliefs, much of which survived in the American South in spite of a harsh slave system. He and his followers contend that many "Africanisms" were naturally incorporated into black religion, including the black preference for the more emotional services of Baptist and Methodist churches, black spirituals, hand-clapping during church services, and the custom of propping-up pots to catch and suppress the sounds of secret religious meetings.[42]

Black sociologist E. Franklin Frazier, on the other hand, concluded that slavery, as practiced in mainland British North America, stripped slaves of virtually all of their African heritage and culture, including religious beliefs. It remains "impossible," Frazier wrote, "to establish any continuity between African religious practices and the Negro church in the United States." Supporters of this view emphasize the process of acculturation, the accommodation of slaves to white culture. They maintain that blacks joined the more revivalistic Baptist and Methodist churches because their owners were members of those churches. Similarly, hand-clapping and black spirituals resulted from cultural parallelisms rather than from African memories.[43]

Both the views of Herskovits and Frazier carry complicated ideological baggage since adherents of each camp tend to interpret the other's view of the retention of Africanism as a statement on the condition of modern blacks in America. In approaching this difficult issue, one needs to keep in mind certain factors that shed light on the religious development of American blacks. It appears, for example, that the process of removing Africans to British North America had the effect of depriving the vast majority of any real African heritage in religion, especially when compared with the religious inclinations of Africans taken to the Caribbean and South America. This stems partially from the fact that fewer than 5 percent, about 427,000 of enslaved Africans, were shipped to the American South, almost all of them before 1808. Those 427,000 increased to about 4,000,000 by 1865. The remaining 9,000,000 went to the Caribbean and South America. In 1834 when slavery ended in the British West Indies, the 1,665,000 imported had declined to 781,000. A similar decline occurred in the enslaved population of Central and South America. Unlike the Caribbean region and South America, the black population in British North America rapidly became native-born, and those with memories of Africa diminished "with each passing generation."[44]

The absence of a sacred book of established orthodoxy also impeded the retention of African religious concepts. Since Africans could, therefore, hold opposing views without heresy or controversy, African religions became flexible, realistic, and pragmatic. Traditionally, Africans viewed God as the creator and sustainer of life in a man-centered universe. Theirs was a highly moral religion, much concerned with both personal and social conduct. That is, the African concerned himself not only with treatment of his own body, but also with a myriad of social relationships "since the individual exists only because others exist." In African society it was morally wrong to show disrespect, lie, steal, murder, or rape. Good morals included honesty, truthfulness, kindness, and hard work.[45]

Peculiarly African superstitions apparently played only a small role in the religion of black Kentuckians. Though blacks occasionally described a slave as being of pure African blood or of descending from a line of African kings, they never identified their religion as African. Indeed, every indication suggests that black religious organizations sought regularity—orthodox acceptability—in their relationships with white religious denominations while simultaneously demanding independence. Yet, African religious ideology contained much that enabled slaves to adapt readily to the Christianity of their enslavers, both on the Atlantic seaboard and later in Kentucky. The belief in a supreme God who gave comfort in time of trouble, the emphasis on social conduct, and the emotional message of both black and white ministers made the transition easy.[46]

Black church services, sermons, and theology varied in sophistication from one preacher to another, among congregations, and between cities and the countryside. Black theology was remarkably Biblical, highly personal, and incorporated both the Old and New Testaments. From the Old Testament ministers preached of a God who would punish in this life or at Judgment Day those who broke his laws. They identified with the children of Israel, God's chosen people, who were harshly enslaved in a distant country but ultimately delivered by divine intervention. From the New Testament, they preached about the suffering of Jesus, their personal savior, who atoned for their sins and set an example of forgiveness. In both testaments they found hope for a better life once their sufferings ended.[47]

Black church services were enthusiastic. The singing and preaching were sometimes loud, congregational testifying was common, and shouting and dancing frequently occurred. Black preachers, as one slave remembered, could really "whip" the devil in their sermons, as amens and shouts of agreement with the preacher's proclamations reverberated through the meeting house.[48]

Black sermons touched on a number of subjects and represented different ideas to church members. A sermon which told of God's personal interest in their day-to-day lives helped many slaves develop a feeling of self-worth. It gave others a sense of identity when they were "told and retold" that the "struggles of the Israelites" were ultimately successful. Sermons of hope sometimes gave meaning to a seemingly meaningless existence. For some slaves, religious services provided a moral and spiritual guide for life, a navigable path through an uncharted course. Others doubtless believed that if they accepted their condition in this world and applied Christ's teachings of humility, honesty, and integrity in their own lives, they would be rewarded for their faithfulness in their next life. Some gleaned from sermons suggestions for survival, especially when ministers promised protection by an active God who would personally intervene in their lives when danger approached. Few, however, interpreted ministers' sermons as a call for open rebellion, as indeed, they were not. Nevertheless, many communicants developed an "internalized" hatred for the "peculiar institution" because of sermons they heard.[49]

Some slaves became convinced that they had been "freed" by their religious experiences. Through religion they achieved a Christian victory over their masters which resulted in an attitude of moral superiority. They considered their own experiences to be genuine, as opposed to the obvious insincerity of whites who professed Christianity, yet enslaved fellow Christians. Black Christians, some slaves believed, observed their religion "more closely" than whites, making it, as Frederick Douglass once said, almost impossible for slaves to "have confidence in the piety of their masters." In the minds of some slaves, their masters' religion was different from theirs, and both knew it.[50]

Congregational singing was often the heart of black church services. Many churches used standard denominational hymnals, often handed down from the white mother church, but spirituals were far more important in black music. Spirituals, which possessed "African rhythms and tonal patterns," represent the clearest influence of the slaves' African heritage, and are a distinct contribution to American music. Spirituals were usually "low, plaintive symphonies" which expressed the suffering and sadness of slaves, and frequently sounded like a "rhythmical chant" sung in a minor key, but included many happier themes of joy and spiritual victory. Most spirituals were unwritten, but many were standard, well-known songs such as "Joshua Fit de Battle of Jericho" and "Go Down, Moses," which blacks had sung for years. On numerous occasions, however, the congregation improvised spirituals on the spur of the moment, inspired by an important event in the life of the church, a member, or a Biblical character. When singing spirituals, the choir and congregations usually swayed gently from side to side, clapped hands, and patted their feet.[51]

Whites who visited black churches or heard their preachers usually spoke favorably of the content of sermons. Respected Lexingtonians, after listening to London Ferrill while standing across the street from his church, concluded that "his views of the Scriptures were very correct." Rev. William Pratt praised several black preachers, and the historian of Clear Creek Baptist Church told of the good work of black ministers associated with that congregation. On one occasion Rev. George Browder of Logan County commented on the "fine ideas" contained in a sermon of George McLean, and on another he praised the spiritual "power" of a message delivered by Duncan Hines.[52]

Visitors from the North and England were equally complimentary. The sermon and congregational singing of a Louisville church in the 1850s impressed visiting northern abolitionists. In 1846 the famous British geologist Sir Charles Lyell praised the services of a Louisville black Methodist church he attended. The large, gas-lighted building seated four hundred, with the men occupying one side and the women the other. The minister "spoke good English," Lyell wrote in his diary, and "quoted Scripture well." Though the minister occasionally made "mysterious and metaphysical points of doctrine" which seemed beyond "human understanding," eliciting comments of support from the crowd, Lyell agreed with his contention that the human race devolved from a common ancestry. Lyell, however, remained unimpressed with a "very extravagant" prayer given by a lay-leader, and he thought the singing "wild" but "not unmusical."[53]

Black churches had a wide range of spiritual concerns which reached beyond their own congregations. Henry Adams's First Colored Baptist Church established several branch missions in Louisville, some of which grew into mature churches. Black churches also expressed a special concern for foreign missions in Africa. Adams's church and First African in Lexington contributed regularly to African missions, as did other black congregations. On rare occasions touring black missionaries preached in some of the state's black Methodist churches. A former Jessamine County slave, Rev. James Priest, began an illustrious career when he went to Liberia as a missionary for the Presbyterian Church. Priest pastored a church for almost three decades, served four years as vice-president and president of the Liberian senate, and ended his career as an associate justice of the supreme court.[54]

Black churches also took seriously their social responsibilities. Most of the larger churches created "sick committees" which visited and assisted ill members. Louisville's First Colored Baptist Church divided the city by wards and assigned a deacon to supervise visitation in each. The church expected monthly committee reports on the condition of sick members. At First African Baptist Church in Lexington, Rev. London Ferrill's care for the ill during the 1833 cholera epidemic not only won him the praise of blacks and whites, but also set an example for both races.[55]

Other church committees dealt with social responsibilities, such as assistance to the poor. Most decisions were made on an individual basis, such as providing a pair of shoes for a destitute member, but a general consensus existed that churches should be responsible for interment of all members without "means to bury themselves." At Louisville's First Colored Baptist, for instance, a standing committee received applications and dispensed funds for burying indigent members. In regions where churches were too small to meet financial requirements, the black community raised funds for burial of the poor. Since many congregations viewed alcohol abuse as a religious problem, they also supported local temperance movements. One major social organization, the Colored People's Union Benevolent Society of Lexington, assisted local churches in their charitable work. Begun in 1843 and composed of the city's most outstanding black leaders, the Benevolent Society "clothed the naked, fed the hungry, cheered the grief stricken, and brought joy and gladness to hundreds of desolate homes."[56]

Members of black churches proved to be no less susceptible to religious controversies and no more monolithic in their views than those of white congregations. Much controversy arose from strictly held church doctrines and vigorously enforced rules of decorum which, when combined with the strong personalities of most ministers and lay leaders, led to questions of propriety regarding numerous activities of church members. Several members of Louisville's Second Colored Baptist Church became irate in 1846, when the church resorted to a money-raising "fair" to solve financial problems, resulting in an argument that disrupted the congregation for weeks. Offended older members of Fourth Street Methodist Church in Louisville "declared that the officers had admitted the devil" when a member played a violin during a worship service in 1847; and when the choir director at Quinn Chapel installed an organ in that Louisville church, "the sister threatened to throw it into the street." Churches also carefully monitored the activities of their congregations under the assumption that responsible members should never participate in religious services at other churches without permission. One church threatened to dismiss those who attended unauthorized "prayer meetings," and another reproached a member who preached a sermon "without the authority of the church," forcing him to admit his bad judgment.[57]

Internal squabbles among church members, or between members and pastors, were problems many black congregations had to solve.

Though not always successful, most attempted to settle controversies in an orderly fashion. When one member of the First Colored Baptist Church in Louisville charged another with slander, the church set up a court-like procedure to evaluate evidence in the case. "After a carefull [sic] hearing of all the witnesses on both sides," the congregation voted that there was insufficient "Gospel evidence to sustain the report," clearing the accused. On other occasions when church members became embroiled in controversy but refused to attend a congregational hearing, the church sent a three-man committee to inform the members of the church's decision. Church leaders were perturbed most when controversies attracted the attention of the white community.[58]

Most black ministers and churches cooperated with each other in the name of religion. Ministers exchanged pulpits, assisted each other financially, and participated in ordination services. Churches shared information on members, the character and record of ministers, and supported each other in difficult times. Nevertheless, hostility occasionally arose between ministers and among churches. Rev. London Ferrill refused to associate with "Old Captain's" First African Baptist Church in Lexington, eventually contributing to a split in the pioneer's church. Shortly thereafter Ferrill drew criticism from a local black, Harry Quills, who claimed that Ferrill had not possessed a good reputation when he lived in Virginia. When the accusation proved frivolous, Quills charged Ferrill with violating the law which prevented freemen from immigrating into the Commonwealth. White Lexingtonians went to Ferrill's rescue, obtaining a special exemption from the legislature so that the preacher could remain in Kentucky. A similarly unfortunate relationship developed in Richmond between Rev. Madison Campbell and one of his close friends, Rev. John S. Irvine. When Campbell converted from Methodist to Baptist, Irvine became one of his earliest supporters, making Campbell his assistant. Eventually, the congregation decided that Campbell was the superior preacher and called him to be minister. A bitter struggle ensued and Irvine eventually abandoned the Baptist persuasion.[59]

Competition for membership also embroiled churches in controversy. When Louisville's First Colored Baptist Church learned that "a certain minister," later identified as Rev. George Wells, intended to start a second separate Baptist church in the city, the congregation denounced his actions as "mischief to the Baptist Cause among the Colored community." Wells successfully established Second Colored Baptist in 1844, but the First Colored congregation, which lost about a hundred members to the new ministry, refused to cooperate with the new church until after Wells's death in 1850. In explaining its rejection of a proper relationship with the Second church for six years, First Colored Baptist informed its sister institution that "the only cause of difficulty between the two churches was the improper conduct of Br George Wells." Since "God in his providence has seen fit to remove" Wells, First Colored Baptist announced, no impediment prevented a *"friendly & Christian"* relationship between the two churches. On another occasion, when the Beargrass black church split, First Colored Baptist offered fellowship to those quitting that church. When only a few moved their membership to First Colored Baptist, the congregation denounced those who failed to unite with a church as "disorderly persons."[60]

Religious dissension occasionally disrupted black churches, but the greatest threat to their tranquility arose from external pressures from the white community. Black pastors were sometimes harassed by local newspapers, by white ministers, and by local governmental officials. In the mid-1850s, Paris prohibited night services at black churches that lasted past 9:00 P.M. Only the importuning of a white citizen secured a change of the regulation, allowing blacks an additional hour to conclude services and arrive home before the night bell rang. Lexington's trustees, equally concerned about the activities of the town's black churches, appointed several white citizens to "superintend" meetings. On one occasion, when the mayor learned that Episcopal theological students were teaching slaves to read at Sunday school, he recommended that they cease, citing the likelihood of mob action against the seminary if the public learned of their actions.[61]

City ordinances in Louisville were slightly more liberal. The longstanding policy requiring that a white be present at religious services conducted by blacks was only loosely applied. Louisville allowed black services on weekends and Wednesday nights to run until 10:00 P.M., but required the night watchman to guard closely against noisy disturbances. Much of the hostility to black congregations in Louisville involved churches located near white residential areas. Whites repeatedly complained to the city's common council, describing the black services as a "nuisance."[62]

Occasionally, black ministers experienced harassment during church services. Rev. Elisha Green told of an 1855 incident when he preached at George Dupee's church in Georgetown. After reading from the scriptures and leading the congregation in prayer, Green announced his text, only to be interrupted when "a white man came in with a stick in his hand." The intruder walked halfway up the aisle, banged his stick on the floor, and asked if there were whites present. When Green answered "No," the man "shook his stick at" the minister and demanded that he vacate the pulpit. Green, fearing violence, abruptly ended the service. Whites threatened Rev. Madison Campbell on several occasions. In 1846 in Garrard County as the congregation enjoyed a picnic lunch following the preaching service, a white man rode up and asked to see the minister. The intruder demanded to know who authorized the service, and "threatened to kill" Campbell if he ever preached there again. A slave member of the congregation named Cash interceded, explaining that they had permission to have the service. The white man drew a knife and Cash picked up two rocks. Violence was averted when the white man rode off, but Cash was later arrested for his part in the incident. On another occasion, three white men entered the church at Waco during Campbell's sermon, taking seats near the back. Assuming they were there to hear the sermon, Campbell preached on "the fall of man, and his reconciliation to God." After the service the whites candidly told Campbell that they had come to the church to "break up" the meeting and "whip" the preacher, but upon hearing his sermon changed their minds.[63]

Black preachers and churches came under increasing scrutiny in all sections of Kentucky in the late 1850s. After John Brown's Harpers Ferry raid in 1859, rumors spread that authorities intended to round up "the leading negro preachers" and sell them "down the river." With the coming of the Civil War and military occupation of Kentucky, the positions of black clergymen and parishioners deteriorated, especially during 1861-62. Military rule greatly restricted mobility, both day and night, and some blacks found it dangerous or impossible to attend church. Louisville's church socials and youth singing groups ceased meeting in 1861, early victims of the war. Several of the city's churches closed temporarily in the spring of 1862, when the provost marshal ordered that blacks out at night must possess a pass, whether slave or free. Threats of violence forced the Green Street Baptist Church of Louisville, formerly Second Colored Baptist, to hire a watchman to guard the congregation during night services. Army occupation also created difficulties for churches in rural areas. The military appropriated a black church in Garrard County for a hospital at the beginning of the war, and Rev. George Dupee found the black Baptist church in Paducah occupied by Union soldiers at the war's end.[64]

In spite of these difficulties, black ministers spoke out increasingly during the Civil War, demanding freedom for their people and urging young men to join the Union army. With black troops passing through Louisville in large numbers during the last two years of the war, several black congregations formed Soldier's Aid Societies to assist the sick and wounded. These societies, run by the church women, nursed soldiers and cooked them "sumptuous" meals on holidays. The ladies raised money for their work through lectures and concerts. During the Civil War ministers made their first move to form a separate organization of black churches. In 1861 Rev. George Dupee issued a call for black ministers and deacons to meet at Rev. Armisted Steel's Versailles African Church. At that meeting Dupee, Steel, and Rev. James Monroe laid the groundwork for what later became the General Association of Colored Baptists.[65]

Churches were also the center of social and cultural activities within the black community. Sunday schools, a goal if not always an accomplishment of black churches, were more than an instrument of religious education. Much of the organized recreation of blacks consisted of Sunday-school-planned churchwide picnics on holidays or young people's sing-a-longs. Many of the church choirs, especially in the larger towns, presented Sunday afternoon concerts, attracting much attention among blacks. Louisville's Mozart Society was the direct result of a series of choir concerts. Organized in 1852 by W.H. Gibson, Sr., a talented musician and one of Louisville's outstanding blacks, its membership included Samuel White and Henry Williams, two of the city's best known black music teachers. Members of the Mozart Society performed concerts, occasionally with the instrumental support of several local German musicians, for charitable causes. The Mozart Society played a major role in introducing classical music to the black community. Black churches constituted the center of intellectual development as they increasingly opened their doors for informational speeches, exhibitions, and lectures in the two decades before the Civil War.[66]

Education was second only to religion as a goal of black churches. In contrast to states of the Deep South, Kentucky did not prohibit by law the education of slaves, though scattered white opposition existed to the idea of literate bondsmen. Several white religious denominations facilitated the work of black church schools by advocating slave education for religious and humanitarian purposes, a goal endorsed by individual Christian slaveholders. Finally, and most important, the desire of numerous slaves for self-improvement propelled many to learn to read and write.[67]

Slaves became literate in several ways, not all directly associated with churches. Many slaves gained rudimentary education on the farms where they grew up. Some owners instructed slaves in reading and writing to enable them to study the Bible, and still others hoped education might prepare their bondsmen for freedom. Many slaves became literate through makeshift classes taught by members of their masters' families. Those slaves who were hired out to a job where some knowledge of counting, reading, or even writing was necessary were provided opportunities for rudimentary instruction, and a few of the more industrious built on this beginning. Madison Campbell's desire for education became so strong that he hired his owner's son as a tutor, and the famous minister, George W. Dupee, taught himself to read, as did the mother of poet Joseph S. Cotter, who in turn taught her children.[68]

Some Kentucky slaves acquired an education at private schools in their neighborhoods, most of which had some religious affiliation. These schools, with both black and white teachers, taught black children individually or in small numbers, either on weekdays, nights, or Sunday afternoons. Most of the pupils were children of freemen or slaves with passes from their owners, but in some instances a few whites also attended these schools. A day school for black children opened in Frankfort in 1820, and Jane Washington, a pioneer black educator, ran another in Lexington before the Civil War. Elijah P. Marrs studied at night for about a year on his Shelby County farm under Ham Graves, a black man. Marrs acquired the basic skill of writing and increased his reading comprehension, which he later supplemented at Sunday school. Henry Morehead's desire for an education led him to pay for his lessons with his own money at a Louisville night school, where he studied reading and spelling. Isaac Curtis walked six miles on Sunday afternoons to study with a "person who gave lessons in reading and writing," eventually developing a strong interest in things scholarly.[69]

The saga of William Hayden was typical of bondsmen who desired to be literate. Hayden received his first instruction at age seventeen, when his hirer's children began teaching him. Later, as he moved from job to job, Hayden always found someone to teach him. While toiling as a wagonmaker in Lexington in 1804, Hayden chopped wood in his spare time to pay for evening and Sunday lessons in reading, writing, and spelling. He wrote his first words in sand and later practiced writing with homemade ink on scrap paper picked up from the Fayette County Courthouse floor. In 1807 Hayden became the assistant of Ned, a Lexington slave who taught a class of thirty at a night school, and soon succeeded to the teacher's position.[70]

Although Kentucky whites usually tolerated these schools and generally raised few objections to educating blacks, there always existed the likelihood that hostile whites might forcibly close them. In 1816 trustees in Greensburg, Green County, ordered a school stopped where Joe, a slave, taught a handful of bondsmen. The trustees threatened all participants with fifteen stripes if they persisted in holding class. According to Henry Bibb, "a Miss Davis, a poor white girl," opened a school for Trimble County slaves in 1833. When news spread that she gave books to slaves and was teaching them to read, Bibb recalled, the white community ordered the patrol to shut down the school. A white Quaker who taught blacks at a Louisville school suffered even worse harassment. Charged with writing passes for runaways, the Quaker soon found himself in jail on trumped-up charges. In Lexington threatened mob violence forced the closing of a school for blacks in the 1830s, and after John Brown's raid, the city council attempted to close all black schools.[71]

Most literate blacks probably received whatever education they acquired from church-related Sunday schools, where the religious nature of the information tended to lessen the hostility of the Caucasian community. Many white Christians viewed the conversion and teaching of blacks as a mission field to "the heathen at their own door," and thus regularly engaged in instructing blacks, both free and slave, to read, write, and spell. White churches frequently donated their discarded hymnals, religious books, maps of the Holy Land, and other teaching tools to black churches, thus making possession of school materials acceptable. The result was that thousands of blacks, both children and adults, received a rudimentary education, though they were not always literate, in the Sunday schools of mixed or all-black churches.[72]

Since many blacks, free and slave, hoped to give their children more than the meager education they received on Sunday, a number of the larger black churches established day schools. Rev. Henry Adams of First Colored Baptist Church pioneered in the education of black children in Louisville. The scholarly Adams apparently began teaching children on an individual basis shortly after his arrival in the city in 1829. By 1841 Adams operated on Woods Alley between Ninth and Tenth streets a school that eventually required the services of four teachers, including Annie Lee and Mary Jones Richardson. William H. Steward and Bartlett Taylor were two of Adams's most famous students. Before the end of the Civil War, Green Street Baptist, Jackson Street Methodist, Center Street Methodist, Ninth Street Methodist, and St. Mark's Episcopal churches had established schools for blacks in Louisville.[73]

William H. Gibson, Sr., was even more famous than Adams as a teacher. Freeborn in Baltimore, Maryland, Gibson received his education from private tutors who included the Rt. Rev. Daniel A. Payne, bishop of the African Methodist Episcopal Church, and other divines. Responding to a request for a qualified teacher from Rev. Harper, pastor of the Fourth Street Methodist Church, later called

## Religion and Education / 143

In 1855 the Berea ridge, which stands on the border of the mountains and the bluegrass, was a wilderness of tangled brush and forest trees. But the founders of Berea were men who believed that church and school needed each other for good living. Berea College began as an elementary one-room school, unpainted, unplastered, covered with rived boards. Mr. J. A. R. Rogers, a graduate of Oberlin College, was the first principal.

*Berea College Archives*

Asbury Chapel, Gibson arrived in Louisville in June 1847. After teaching six months at the school of Robert M. Lane, an Ohio native who had labored in Louisville for several years, Gibson started his own institution in the basement of the Fourth Street Church located at the corner of Fourth and Green streets. By moving the school to the center of Louisville, he created considerable hostility, but the untiring efforts of "Harper and his white friends" and the hard work of Gibson mollified critics. Between fifty and one hundred pupils, including slaves and freemen, attended the day and night classes of the Fourth Street Methodist school on a regular basis. Gibson's school emphasized the three R's and music, as well as some vocational training which was taught by his wife. Periodic "exhibitions" and concerts demonstrated to the public the progress of his pupils.

In the late 1850s Gibson's school added algebra, geometry, and Latin for older, more advanced students. When Rev. R.G. Mortimore, teacher of the advanced classes, later became head of the mathematics department of Wilberforce University, six of his top students, including W.H. Gibson, Jr., matriculated there. Gibson, Sr., also opened a branch school at Quinn Chapel, and in 1859 he ambitiously established grammar schools in Frankfort and Lexington, leaving his wife and George A. Schafer in charge in Louisville. Unfortunately, the "political excitement" caused by the outbreak of the Civil War forced the suspension of both new schools. During the hectic fall of 1862, when Confederate General Braxton Bragg's forces threatened Louisville, Gibson left for Indianapolis, Indiana, to head a school for contraband children, but he returned to the Falls City in 1866 and resumed his teaching career.[74]

First African Baptist Church of Lexington possessed the most successful educational program in central Kentucky. Ferrill's church began classes for members' children in the early 1830s, and within a few years about thirty pupils studied under an elderly Tennessee white man whose salary was paid from fees assessed the pupils. First African's educational program continued through the Civil War. Black communities in towns such as Richmond, Maysville, and Bowling Green also operated schools for their children from time to time. Fourteen counties, besides Jefferson and Fayette, reported blacks' attending school in 1850.[75]

Although the percentage of slaves benefiting from these opportunities remained low, reports of bondsmen who could read and write are fairly common. Ministers, it should be remembered, frequently knew how to read or write, and almost all slaves knew some literate black person. Slaves sometimes told of writing their own pass to freedom, a claim confirmed by advertisements for runaways which described the fugitive as "a pretty good scholar," or able to "read and write tolerably well." Court records of suits brought by bondsmen also indicate a degree of literacy.[76]

Educational statistics for freemen, who usually attended school with slaves, are somewhat more abundant. Among the 2,361 free blacks aged fourteen and under in 1850, a total of 288, or approximately 12 percent, attended school. Almost half, 141, were pupils in Jefferson County's black schools. In Boyle County, 76 freemen were in school, but just 38 freemen attended school in Fayette County. Seven pupils attended school in Morgan County and five in Franklin County. Of the free blacks over age nineteen in 1850, about 2,500, or approximately 45 percent, were literate. By 1860 the number of freemen receiving an education had declined to 209, or about 8 percent of the 2,611 children under age fifteen. The number of literate freemen, however, increased to slightly over 3,000, representing about 56 percent of those above age nineteen.[77]

Next to the family, churches were the most important institution in black society. By providing a link between the real world of oppression and racism in which they toiled for their daily bread and the spiritual world of fairness and equality which they hoped for beyond this life, religion helped many blacks endure the travail of slavery. Since they occupied in all respects, whether literate or not, an inferior status in white churches and since they believed, whatever their religious conviction, that the message whites preached was racist, blacks preferred separate religious services. Whether worshipping in an all-black service in a white sanctuary, in a meeting house shared by several denominations, or in an autonomous—if never completely free—congregation which had its own building, blacks wanted to control their churches. Though their separate services were typically orthodox from the perspective of whites, blacks, nevertheless, found opportunity to formulate their own expression of worship in both song and sermon. Ultimately, black churches became, in addition to a religious sanctuary, the nucleus around which blacks organized their own social, educational, and cultural activities.

*Seven*

# Kentucky Blacks in the Civil War

IN the late 1850s many of Kentucky's blacks were aware of the growing antagonism between the sections, the role of slavery in the controversy, and the potential impact upon their lives. A few, both free and slave, fearing the worst, fled north of the Ohio River at the first opportunity. By 1860 others, aware of the association of Abraham Lincoln's presidential campaign with the antislavery movement, eagerly waited for and talked openly of anticipated freedom. After the election, rumors of imminent emancipation continued to spread, and in one area of central Kentucky slaves became convinced that they would be freed on March 1, 1861.[1]

Gradually, as the Southern states seceded and hostilities began, news of the war spread throughout the black community. Even so, many bondsmen had difficulty interpreting the events engulfing them. Rumors abounded of one side's successes only to be contradicted shortly thereafter. All the while, masters assured their slaves that, whatever the outcome, they would remain bondsmen. Of those early war years, one slave later wrote, "we did not know what to believe." As the war progressed, contacts with Federal troops and the activities of educated blacks helped bondsmen become better informed. Shelby County's Elijah P. Marrs, for example, apprised slave friends of events by reading newspapers aloud to them "for hours."[2]

Life became more complicated and uncertain for most Kentucky blacks during the early stages of the Civil War. Many freemen complained that the war offered Negrophobes an opportunity to harass the black community. Whites threatened to enforce laws which authorized prison sentences for freemen who left the state and returned, and Northern freemen who ventured into the Commonwealth occasionally landed in jail, charged with being runaways. False arrests usually took months to rectify, and blacks objected to laws that restricted their employment while requiring them to pay taxes for services they could not enjoy.[3]

Harassment by law officers was a major problem for all blacks in the early days of the conflict. In some cities and counties authorities systematically searched the premises of blacks, confiscating weapons. Louisville blacks increasingly claimed that they had "no redress" against police officers who invaded their homes in the middle of the night, searching for stolen goods or fugitives. The "Home Guards" forced blacks off the streets, sometimes administering harsh punishments for those without passes. Independent or so-called "abolition" congregations occasionally fell under suspicion, especially when Confederate forces threatened Kentucky, resulting in the interruption of religious meetings. Authorities, including the military, frequently used vagrancy laws to retard the movement of blacks, and runaways arriving from the South or escaping northward from the Commonwealth experienced no relaxation of the fugitive slave laws. Meanwhile, bondsmanship, including hiring out and the slave trade, continued.[4]

Changing conditions caused by the hostilities created new opportunities for a few bondsmen. The war brought higher wages for skilled laborers, and several black entrepreneurs were credited with having "grown rich" during the conflict. In some areas of the economy, blacks also found whites more willing to labor alongside them, and there was a noticeable decline in white hostility toward black mechanics. Some black observers also noticed a reduction in cruel treatment, such as floggings, both in towns and in the countryside.[5]

Still other blacks took advantage of the volatile conditions to challenge the slave system. Those suspected of violating the slave code found it easier, especially in urban areas, to evade detection by hiding in the black community. Whites increasingly noticed a change in the work patterns of hired slaves and that bondsmen seemed less inclined to obey orders. One of the most unusual demonstrations of black hostility to the slave system occurred at New Castle in December 1861. After getting off work one night, a group of about fifty slaves marched through the streets, frequently tarrying in front of the homes of pro-Southern whites, "singing political songs and shouting for Lincoln." The demonstration lasted until midnight. Activities such as these, as well as perceived increases in the number of barn burnings and other acts of violence, mistakenly convinced many white Kentuckians that a black revolution was imminent.[6]

The arrival of Federal troops in Kentucky provided many slaves with their first real opportunity to challenge involuntary servitude. Troops had scarcely arrived before blacks entered the military camps.

Many went solely out of curiosity, but most were there to earn extra money by working for the soldiers or by providing what one Vermont enlistee called "truly wonderful" musical entertainment. Slaves usually returned to their cabins within hours, but the prolonged presence of Union soldiers in large numbers inevitably led to an influx of slaves into camps.[7]

Friendship with Federal troops and employment opportunities with the military further enticed slaves to flee their bondage. Some soldiers encouraged slaves to run away, while others, seeking to escape the hard work of camp duty, simply hired local bondsmen to perform tasks. Once troops and slaves mutually realized what each offered the other, bondsmen entered Federal camps in increasing numbers. What began as a trickle of slaves into Union camps during the summer of 1861 swelled to a steady stream by the year's end. In November there were rumors of a "general stampede" at Camp Nevin in Hart County as slaves entered at the rate of one an hour. Soon almost every regiment employed at least a half-dozen fugitives who lived in camp.[8]

This early flow of slaves into Union lines created enormous problems for the Federal army, both practical and political. Once troops filled their labor requirements, they had no use for additional slaves or their families. Unfortunately, the employment of a few bondsmen opened a floodgate the troops could not close. From the military's point of view, the presence of fugitives increased logistical problems and exacerbated relations with Kentucky's white leaders. This situation was complicated further during the first two years of war by the absence of a consistent Federal policy for handling fugitives who entered Union lines. Thus, generals reacted individually to the influx of blacks, a situation that resulted in difficult times for many fugitives. Upon taking command in Kentucky, Brigadier General William T. Sherman, for example, ordered his subordinates in October 1861 to surrender runaways according to Federal and Commonwealth laws, if owners claimed them. When his inquiries brought "no instructions" from Washington regarding policy, Sherman decided in November to ignore the issue of refugees. "We have nothing to do with them at all," he instructed a subordinate, "and you should not let them take refuge in camp." During 1861 only those slaves fleeing from seceded states, the so-called "contrabands," found refuge in Federal camps. Kentucky slaves, the legal property of people in a loyal state, received no such welcome.[9]

A year later officers operating in Kentucky still had no instructions regarding the increasing number of fugitives in camp. In August 1862 the commander at Columbus prohibited slave women from entering his lines while his counterpart at Bowling Green followed a policy which excluded all bondsmen. During 1862 some officers regularly allowed slaveowners to enter their camps to remove bondsmen, while other officers received severe reprimands for similar actions. Major General Gordon Granger, harassed by Kentuckians who hoped to retrieve fugitives, called the situation "embarrassing," and in November 1862 he begged Major General Henry W. Halleck to develop a "definite policy." Unfortunately, conflicting orders regarding the treatment of fugitives in Union camps continued through the summer of 1864.[10]

The attitudes of Federal troops toward fugitives' entering Union lines further complicated the situation. While few were abolitionists, most observed slavery for the first time upon entering Kentucky, and in general, they did not like what they saw. Slaves entering the camps related stories of severe abuse from "Rebel" owners and frequently won the sympathy of troops. Masters often alienated soldiers when they appeared at camps and threatened to whip or shoot fugitives who resisted returning to slavery. Such actions caused many lower-echelon officers and their troops, regardless of their attitude toward blacks, to become hesitant about returning runaways to their owners. Some officers released only those fugitives who expressed a desire to go home, while others used subterfuge to prevent the recapture of slaves in camp. Soldiers increasingly resisted orders to surrender fugitives to their owners and demonstrated a reluctance to expel slaves who joined their ranks as they marched through the state. As time passed, those owners of fugitives hiding in military encampments faced increasingly hostile troops who demonstrated a willingness to use force to prevent the recapture of slaves.[11]

During the summer and fall of 1862, as the number of slaves fleeing to Union lines increased dramatically, three conditions combined to transform this growing migration into a serious problem. The first was the impressment of large numbers of blacks, free and slave, by both the Confederate and Union armies for military labor. Wherever the two armies went, they impressed black laborers, disrupting families and creating refugees. During the occupation of southern Kentucky in late 1861, the Confederates impressed thousands of slaves to work on defensive positions from Columbus on the Mississippi River to Mill Springs in the east. By early 1862 fugitives entered Union lines with horror stories resulting from Confederate impressment. According to one runaway, the Confederates sometimes seized entire slave families "without respect to age or sex." Some built military fortifications, others worked as nurses in hospitals or washed clothes, and many became servants. Those lucky enough to escape usually fled northward to Union lines. The less fortunate were sold south. When impressed bondsmen belonged to Southern sympathizers, the Confederates usually compensated the owner for the work performed, but none of the money went to the slaves.[12]

As soon as the Federal army entered Kentucky, it began impressing slaves, initially seeking the slaves of those deemed disloyal. As the Union military effort intensified, Federal officers began impressing slaves without regard for ownership, a policy that evoked severe criticism from some Unionists. After March 1862 Union officers regularly impressed hundreds of slaves throughout the state to build roads, to cut timber for building new bridges and repairing old ones, to chop wood for fueling railway engines, and to labor on Federal river boats. The army compensated Unionist slaveowners for work performed by their bondsmen; in the case of disloyal owners, the Federal government paid wages and provided subsistence to the slaves. Some of these slaves never returned to their owners.[13]

The events surrounding the invasion of Kentucky by Confederate General Braxton Bragg and Major General Edmund Kirby Smith during the summer and fall of 1862 greatly increased impressment and the refugee problem. At least a thousand Tennessee contrabands moved northward into Kentucky with Union forces as they tracked the Southern army. Unsure of the destination of Confederate forces, authorities in Ohio River cities scrambled desperately to build fortifications. In Louisville officials drafted more than a thousand slaves and freemen for the "spade and shovel brigade," which worked around the clock. During the crisis the provost marshal combed the town for laborers, picking up blacks found on the streets, emptying the jails and workhouses, snatching them at all hours of the night from their homes, and patrolling the Ohio River for those attempting to flee. Not even black ministers were exempt. Estimates of the total number of blacks and whites working on the fortification ran as high as ten thousand.[14]

In northern Kentucky not enough blacks were available to dig the entrenchments needed to protect Cincinnati. Consequently, authorities impressed large numbers of Cincinnati free blacks. City police, who had a history of harassing freemen, rounded up blacks wherever they found them, dragging them without explanation from their homes, places of employment, and the streets. Policemen drove some eleven hundred freemen to a holding pen where they were caged like animals, unable to inform loved ones of their whereabouts. Upon reaching Kentucky, their harsh treatment continued. As the freemen dug entrenchments on the section of the line from

Alexandria Road to Newport Turnpike and Licking River, Union soldiers periodically appeared, selected workers from among the freemen, and marched them off at bayonet point to become regimental cooks and servants. Many wondered if they would ever see their homes again.

The circumstances were partially rectified when Major General Lew Wallace learned of these injustices and appointed Cincinnati Judge William M. Dickson to take command of the impressed workers. Dickson selected a staff, organized the "Black Brigade," freed those workers taken by Union regiments, and ordered his men back to their Cincinnati homes to secure clothes and supplies and to reassure their families. As the freemen entered their own neighborhoods, the police once again began rounding them up, arresting about four hundred. In spite of this continued harassment, more than seven hundred reported for duty the next morning and marched back into Kentucky. When the military crisis ended, Dickson gave the Cincinnati freemen credit for building most of northern Kentucky's defenses.[15]

In the midst of the Confederate invasion of Kentucky, President Abraham Lincoln of September 22, 1862, issued his preliminary Emancipation Proclamation, followed by the final notice on January 1, 1863. Even though the action legally did not affect Kentucky, Lincoln had created a second condition which encouraged slaves to flee from their owners and which gradually undermined slavery in the Commonwealth. White Kentuckians bitterly denounced the president, and the state legislature rejected the document. But once the proclamation was generally known, slaves became less hesitant to enter Federal lines, and many Union officers, in turn, became indifferent to whether an impressed slave's owner was a Union or Confederate sympathizer.[16]

Ultimately, impressed blacks and refugees performed most of the labor that supported the Federal war machine in Kentucky. From impressment it was also only a short step to recruiting blacks for the Federal army, the third and most important condition that resulted in the influx of slaves into Union lines. The Federal government had rejected offers of free blacks to enlist at the outbreak of the war, and Lincoln assured slaveholders in 1861 that the war would not affect the "peculiar institution." The need for troops, however, forced the president in December 1862 to authorize the use of black troops, but fearing the adverse reaction of Kentuckians, Lincoln exempted the Bluegrass state. Consequently, the first Kentucky blacks who served in the Federal army joined outside the Commonwealth. One of the earliest volunteers, James Stone, was a fugitive who had "settled down as a white man" in Ohio. Stone, who joined the Federal army at Oberlin in August 1861, more than a year before Lincoln authorized black troops, died from battle wounds in a Nashville, Tennessee, hospital on October 30, 1862. As soon as blacks became eligible to enlist in the Federal army, Kentucky blacks living in the North joined as opportunities arose. Isaac Johnson was typical of this group. Formerly a slave on the Beech Fork River, Johnson had fled northward with a discharged Michigan soldier. With freedom in Canada virtually in his grasp, Johnson abruptly changed his mind and joined a Michigan company of United States Colored Troops.[17]

By mid-1863, when the Federal government began actively recruiting blacks, but before Lincoln authorized recruitment in the Commonwealth, many Kentucky slaves enlisted at Union recruiting stations north of the Ohio River or in occupied Southern states. They hurried by the thousands to camps at Fort Donelson, Clarksville, Nashville, and Gallatin in Tennessee. Thousands of others crossed the Ohio River to join the army in southern Illinois, Indiana, and Ohio. Evansville, Indiana, located within a few miles of one of Kentucky's largest slave centers, was a convenient destination for slaves enlisting in the west, and Cincinnati, which offered a bounty of four hundred dollars, drew many recruits from the northern counties. In addition, Northern states from Michigan to Massachusetts sent recruiting agents into the Commonwealth to entice blacks into units from those states. Long after recruiting was legal in the Commonwealth, officials in southern Indiana reported that groups of "five to ten" Kentucky slaves regularly passed through their district on their way to fill draft quotas in Northern states.[18]

Though still concerned about the reaction of whites to black recruiting, Lincoln made his first move toward enrolling Kentucky blacks into the Union army when in early 1863 he authorized a census of blacks between the ages of eighteen and forty-five. The enumeration of freemen—there were only 1,650 of draft age—became public during the summer, eliciting protests from many whites and several Federal commanders. Lincoln continued to promise Governor Thomas E. Bramlette, as late as the fall of 1863, that no Commonwealth slaves would be recruited, but with a Federal manpower shortage and the availability of 40,285 draft-age Kentucky slaves, more discerning whites realized that the enlistment of blacks could no longer be delayed. Reluctantly, Bramlette in March 1864 acquiesced in the recruitment of blacks, but only to fill deficits created by the failure of whites to meet the state's draft quota. Bramlette's agreement with Lincoln was an obvious face-saving gesture, since recruiting had actually begun two months earlier west of the Cumberland

River in the counties administered by the Military Department of Tennessee.[19]

In March 1864 when the recruiting of blacks began in earnest, Kentucky continued to be a special case. The Federal government promised to maintain strict control over recruiting procedures by enrolling only those free blacks and slaves who applied. Loyal owners received certificates guaranteeing compensation of up to three hundred dollars a recruit and assurances that property taken by enlistees would be returned when their slaves joined the army. Slave recruits were to be taken to rendezvous camps "outside of the State." These concessions, the Lincoln administration hoped, would have an ameliorating effect on most whites.[20]

A few whites recognized that recruiting blacks was the death knell of slavery and tried to minimize their losses. Concluding that their slaves would ultimately enter the army, these owners decided to enroll their bondsmen to help fill Kentucky's draft quota and thereby establish a bounty claim. As owners, they received the bounties due slave enlistees until July 1864 when the government decided that bondsmen who volunteered would receive the bounty, a promise not always honored.[21]

Whites also used slave enlistments to escape the draft themselves. Many Kentuckians simply enlisted their slaves at the local recruiting office with little or no payment of money to the bondsmen, while others promised slave substitutes cash they never received. In some instances, however, owners paid slaves premium prices for taking their places in the military. During the final year of war, the practice of buying and selling blacks as substitutes for whites was common. Since Federal policy loosely defined "runaways" and "refugees" as eligible for induction, making it difficult for them to escape military service, black Kentuckians sometimes concluded that they had no choice but to become substitutes. Some bondsmen signed up with agents of wealthy Northerners who swarmed into Kentucky promising large bounties. These slaves frequently found that trusted "substitute brokers" were in reality "bounty scalpers" who took most of the money, leaving them with a pittance.[22]

Federal authorities mistakenly believed that their moderate policy would mollify white hostility to black recruiting. Echoing the attitude of the legislature, Colonel Frank L. Wolford, a Kentucky cavalry officer, protested so vehemently that he received a dishonorable discharge from the Union army. Recruiting officers in every district of the state encountered opposition from fellow recruiters and from large segments of the white population, virtually thwarting the March 1864 call for black troops.[23]

Faced with the failure of black recruitment in Kentucky, the Federal government during June and July 1864 initiated a vigorous effort to ensure its success. Adjutant General Lorenzo Thomas, charged with raising black troops for the Federal army, began enrolling all available, able-bodied slaves, "regardless of the wishes of their owners," a policy that excluded only the severely infirm and the physically handicapped. The government garrisoned military camps to receive and protect these recruits in Paducah, Owensboro, Bowling Green, Lebanon, Louisville, Covington, Camp Nelson, and Louisa. Anyone who interfered with black recruiting was promptly arrested.[24]

The offer of Federal protection for slave volunteers provided many Kentucky bondsmen with their first viable opportunity to flee slavery. They responded by the thousands in order to achieve their freedom. Volunteers frequently told company clerks at Federal camps that they enlisted "to be free" or "for liberty." Joining the army also provided an opportunity to make a statement regarding their manhood—their worth as human beings. As soldiers they might fight alongside whites as equals while simultaneously delivering a death blow to the hated system of involuntary servitude. Those who received volunteer bounties might also improve the potential for land ownership, independence, and a better life after the war. Others viewed the military as an adventure, and many Kentucky slaves experienced their first knowledge of the "outside world" in Federal blue.[25]

The large slaveholding region of central Kentucky—Fayette and surrounding counties—proved to be one of the best recruiting zones for the Union army in the Commonwealth. Volunteers flowed into Lexington from all directions during June 1864. They arrived from Bourbon County by the trainload, and one large Mercer County contingent of recruits, upon arriving in Lexington, marched through the streets shouting their support for the Union. Slave recruits quickly filled the draft quota of Jessamine County, and in nearby Madison County slaves ran off in droves to join the army. Boyle County slaves "thronged" into the Danville enlistment office the first day it opened. Upon being formed into squads, they marched off toward Camp Nelson, a recruiting center located on the Kentucky River in southern Jessamine County. Slaves in Marion County volunteered in such numbers that authorities closed the recruiting office until they had processed the mass of enlistees. Slaves completely filled the county's draft quota.[26]

By the end of May there were four hundred recruits at Camp Nelson and recruiters reported that slave volunteers came in by the "hour." Within two weeks two thousand black soldiers were training there; eventually, more than five thousand black troops entered the army at Camp Nelson. Hundreds of slaves from Bracken to Trimble counties turned northward to enlist at Covington. Further eastward along the Ohio River slaves flocked to Maysville and Greenupsburg, though in lesser numbers.[27]

In the western half of the state, slaves also volunteered in large numbers. "Cheerful" recruits, some no more than fifteen years old, journeyed to Louisville to enlist, often having walked long distances. Marching through the streets of Louisville, the new enlistees on one occasion demonstrated their hostility to slavery by singing songs such as "John Brown." Blacks entered the recruiting office at Bowling Green by the score, with three hundred arriving from surrounding counties in one month. When recruiting slowed in September 1864, the army opened additional recruiting offices in Cave City, Franklin, Allensville, and Hopkinsville, absorbing numbers of recruits from the large slaveholding counties of western Kentucky. Slaves also demonstrated "enthusiasm" for military service in the counties surrounding Owensboro and Henderson, joining in large numbers. Brisk enlistment also continued west of the Cumberland River. By July 1, about two hundred recruits had joined regiments at Paducah, and a "fine body of men" totaling six hundred drilled at Smithland and Columbus.[28]

Most slaves who ran off to join the military slipped quietly away from their cabins as opportunities arose. G.W. Buckner remembered being awakened late at night by his mother, who whispered for him to tell his uncles "good-bye." The startled child opened his eyes to see four of his uncles leaving to join the army, "the light of adventure shining" on their faces. George Conrad did not get to wish his father farewell. His father and thirteen other slaves disappeared one night shortly after the Federal army began recruiting blacks. Conrad's "old Master" found the men the next day at the Cynthiana recruiting office, and talked one slave, Arch, into returning to help with the crops. Of the group, only Conrad's father returned after the war.[29]

Many slaves who fled to join the army found their journeys filled with frustration and disappointment. Paul H. Kennedy ran away with the assistance of Federal troops stationed near his Elizabethtown home, only to be caught and returned to his owner. He was successful on his second attempt, walking all the way to Louisville to enlist. Peter Bruner's first attempt at joining the army proved equally unsuccessful. A gang of about six white men scattered the small party of volunteers, eventually capturing them all. More than a year passed before Bruner made good his escape.[30]

Some successful escapees enlisted only after days of fear and uncertainty. Twenty-four-year-old Elijah P. Marrs made up his mind one Sunday morning in September 1864 while walking to church in Simpsonville. On his way Marrs met a number of his slave "comrades" and told them of his decision. When several asked to join him, Marrs challenged those who desired to enlist "to roll [up] their sleeves" as a sign of solidarity. He soon attracted a force of twenty-seven men who elected him "captain." During the morning services, panic struck the church when false rumors spread that Confederate troops were in Simpsonville. The frightened Marrs eventually suppressed his self-doubts, rallied the men behind him, and called a "council of war." The slaves agreed to rendezvous that night at the black church for a farewell sermon from Rev. Sandy Bullitt, a recently drafted black preacher, and then to march to Louisville to fight for "the principle of freedom." That night Marrs and his men, armed with "twenty-six war clubs and one old rusty pistol," began their trek to Louisville. A 10:00 P.M. stop for food at the farm where Marrs's mother was a slave almost turned into disaster when, awakened in the dark, she "screamed at the top of her voice." The band resumed their march to Louisville without waiting for food. Tired and hungry, the volunteers arrived at the Louisville recruiting office about 8:00 A.M., September 26.[31]

Ironically, the first violence many black volunteers experienced came not from the Southern armies, but from local whites. Recruits leaving Boyle County were "pretty severely injured" by a mob of angry whites, and upon arriving "grievously dispirited" at Camp Nelson, the post commander "refused to accept them." In the Lebanon area "certain persons" detained a group of about seventeen recruits under false pretenses, releasing them after administering a hundred lashes to each man, and in Green, Taylor, and Adair counties gangs whipped volunteers whenever they caught them. In Marion County two blacks arrived at the recruiting office after whites had cut off their left ears, and eight volunteers were reportedly murdered in Nicholas County. On one occasion, Hancock County volunteers had to be locked in the jail to protect them from an angry mob, some of whom were Kentucky white recruits.[32]

Additional complications in recruiting blacks occurred when former owners appeared at recruiting offices and Federal camps shortly after the volunteers arrived, hoping to reclaim their slaves. Federal commanders, either hostile to black recruiting or unsure of government policy, frequently forced slaves to return to their masters. Some owners attempted to entice recruits into returning home by taking their wives or girl friends to Federal camps, alternately promising the enlistees a better life if they returned home or threatening retribution against loved ones if they refused. After a Bourbon

County slaveholder persuaded a Cynthiana recruiter that he should be allowed to converse with his slaves, the master talked one of the six into returning home, apparently to assure food for his family. Within four hours after Marrs and his band of recruits reached Louisville, their owners arrived, "hunting their slaves," and eventually reclaimed one under-age volunteer. The provost marshal of Boyle County, in cooperation with a number of slaveholders, personally went to Camp Nelson and attempted to persuade twenty recruits to return to slavery. The post commander intervened, but one recruit went home with his owner. On another occasion Boyle County's provost marshal lured three hundred volunteers outside Camp Nelson for a rendezvous with their owners, hoping to return them to slavery. Only the diligence of Thomas Butler, a Sanitary Commission official, foiled his plans.[33]

Not all blacks rushed to the Federal barricades. A few fled the state to avoid military service, and some free blacks bought substitutes. Most slaves who hesitated in enlisting expressed concern for their families' well-being, since many slaveholders threatened retaliation against loved ones of volunteers. The Federal government naively reassured potential enlistees by telling them that their masters were honor "bound" to take care of families of volunteers. Government policy was equally unrealistic regarding the fate of those slaves rejected for military service. Though a few entered "invalid" or labor regiments, in most instances the government forced those "unfit for service" to return to their masters. This, of course, placed many of these slaves in untenable positions.[34]

These and other circumstances combined in 1864 to turn the spring flood of recruits into a late summer trickle. Consequently, General Thomas concluded that it would require "armed parties passing through the counties," impressing slaves, to enroll the quantity of troops needed. Indeed, a policy of impressment of all available black males already existed in some areas of Kentucky. As early as February 1864, black troops operating out of Clarksville, Tennessee, began impressing slaves in southern Kentucky, and troops from west of the Cumberland River, where forcible induction of bondsmen had begun some months earlier, impressed slaves as far east as Henderson County in June 1864. The 120th U.S. Colored Infantry, commanded by white Lieutenant Colonel John Glenn, was especially zealous. In their June raid into Henderson County, soldiers of the 120th rounded up every black they could find. A similar raid into Union County by Colonel J. Cunningham impressed large numbers of slaves. By September units of black troops scoured the countryside, impressing blacks wherever they found them. The violence and bloodshed associated with the impressment of slaves caused bitter complaints from white Kentuckians.[35]

The forcible induction of blacks continued for the remainder of the Civil War. Squads of both black and white troops roamed Kentucky's cities and counties in search of recruits. While most slaves viewed recruiters as liberators, others saw them as press gangs. When a Henderson-area slave complained that, for health reasons, he did not want to enlist, Glenn reportedly shouted: "Take this damned nigger to the jail." Given that option, blacks usually concluded, as one former slave put it: "I would rather enlist than be put in jail." Since the army could induct "vagrants," most blacks never really had an option. "Colored folks here and elsewhere complain bitterly of their impressment," a correspondent wrote to the New York Times from Louisville in March 1865. Louisville blacks told stories of being seized by "recruiting" officers at recreational gatherings and of being dragged from "their beds" in the dead of night. Complaints about violence used in recruiting blacks eventually led to a condemnation of such practices, but it did not end the use of force.[36]

The trickle of slaves fleeing into Union lines that began in the summer and fall of 1862 grew steadily after 1863, and when slave recruits entered Federal lines, in many cases their families followed. "This morning Henry was missing and my favorite saddle horse Mack!" a Logan County minister wrote in July 1863. "I suppose he is aiming for some of the Yankee camps." Six months later the same observer reported that "thousands" of slaves were enlisting and "thousands more" were fleeing to Federal encampments. A Lexington slave disguised her disappearance in January 1864 by asking her mistress for permission to go to a church choir rehearsal. The next day the owner learned that her slave, and several others from the neighborhood, had fled to Union army lines, taking a carriage and three horses with them. In Warren County two slaves ran off in February 1864 while their master worshiped in church, and in nearby Logan County, a slave family escaped with their owner's mules and wagon. "So many negroes are running away & stealing horses," an itinerate preacher wrote in his diary, "that my family feels safer when I am at home."[37]

Increasingly, slaves fled in family groups. Susan, a Henry County slave, escaped with all her children in May 1864 after the men had run off. Abram, Bob, Jeff, George, Ellen, Dolly, William, Ida, Nicholas, and Lucy, all trusted Logan County slaves, fled a month later. With their few clothes, and a wagon, a carriage, two horses, and two mules belonging to their owner, the slaves, along with about twenty area bondsmen, set out for a Union camp in Clarksville, Tennessee.

Hotly pursued and overtaken, a few fugitives escaped by abandoning the caravan. Of those recaptured, several fell under the lash and others were hired out in Louisville. William Jones and his wife, Scott County slaves, started for Camp Nelson on March 11, 1865, taking only their clothes and their life savings of sixty-six dollars. Captured and robbed by the patrol in Lexington, Jones, who boasted that he "would rather die than go back," was back in his slave cabin within forty-eight hours. A second escape attempt without his wife was successful, but Jones never recovered his stolen money.[38]

In early March 1865, the promulgation of a Federal law freeing the wives and children of soldiers also increased the number of slave families entering Union camps. Mary Fields, whose husband was in the Union army, "left to-day" with her daughters, Eliza and Mildred, "being free under the law," a Louisville diarist wrote in March 1865, and a week later her slave Ed enlisted, freeing his wife Patsy and their sons Coleman and William. Lucinda, a Lexington slave of Rev. William Pratt, learned through a letter from her husband Henry, a Camp Nelson enlistee, that she was free. Henry advised Lucinda to hire herself to someone or to join him at Camp Nelson. Lucinda agreed to continue working three days a week for two dollars, but two weeks later Pratt awoke to find "the Kitchen cleaned up, the bread . . . ready for baking & kindling at hand to start a fire," but no Lucinda. An unknown number of female slaves married soldiers for the sole purpose of freeing themselves and their children.[39]

Taken altogether, the events beginning in 1862 with the impressment of slave labor and culminating in the forced induction of bondsmen into the army and the fleeing of their families to Federal camps during 1864-65 removed large numbers of slaves from Kentucky farms. Those who remained developed more independence, which caused their owners to view them as increasingly intractable. A Bourbon County master believed local slaves to be "insubordinate" and unwilling to work after 1863 and a year later, a Fayette County observer found the slaves "no longer humble," but "restless, impertinent, and discontented." In 1864 a Louisville newspaper lamented that slaves in many Ohio River counties could no longer "be controlled by their masters." A Logan County farmer observed that by 1865 many of the slaves in southern Kentucky were also "refusing to work." Those who offered slaves financial incentives usually fared better than those who tried to maintain the status quo. Slaves on a Lexington farm accepted their owner's 1863 offer of fifteen dollars a month wages and remained on the farm throughout the war. Peter Bruner worked for wages during one period of the war, demanding payment at the end of each day, and later, in 1863, agreed to farm and chop wood for his master for half the profits he produced.[40]

After 1863 the realization that slavery was doomed led thoughtful whites to contemplate the future without it. Robert Anderson's conversation with his owner was probably typical of thousands of exchanges between masters and slaves across Kentucky as the war drew to a close. After thinking "for some time" about fleeing to the army, the twenty-one-year-old Anderson made up his mind in 1864. "I went to my old master and talked it over with him. At first he was angry," Anderson wrote in his memoirs, but "then he told me I would have to decide for myself what I wanted to do. . . . He seemed to sense the fact that the slavery of the past was over, and that a new era was opening for all. We had quite a talk, and parted friends." Another owner, tormented over having to pursue his fleeing bondsmen, secretly hoped they would make good their escape, thus absolving him of any "responsibility." A few slaveholders attempted to ease the transition from slavery to freedom by giving their bondsmen land during the war.[41]

The Federal government estimated that 71 percent, or all but about sixty-five thousand, of Kentucky's slaves were legally freed by March 1865, though all had not left their former owners. The result of this decline in black laborers was the near collapse of Kentucky's agriculture by 1864-65. Tobacco production had dropped 57 percent, wheat 63 percent, barley 15 percent, and the hemp crop had declined by four-fifths. The assessed value of slaves, which stood at $107,494,527 in 1860, decreased to $34,179,246 in 1864, a decline of 68 percent. A year later, slave property was valued at only $7,224,851. Though slavery did not officially end until December 1865, it was essentially destroyed by March 1865.[42]

One of the saddest tragedies of this mass movement of slave families was that many suffered greatly after entering Union lines. Federal authorities were generally as unprepared and as unwilling to receive refugees after 1863 as they had been in 1861 and 1862. When hundreds of relatives followed recruits to Fort Anderson in Paducah, they soon encountered starvation and hostile military commanders who ordered that women, children, the ill, infirm, and aged be "returned to their masters." Only the direct disobedience of that order by Colonel H.W. Barry forced the government to reverse its policy. In late 1864 General Thomas officially approved Barry's policy of caring for refugees, but many continued to suffer from exposure and hunger for the duration of the war. Similar tribulations of hunger, poor housing, unsanitary conditions, and hatefulness greeted families of recruits at Bowling Green, Munfordville, and Louisa.[43]

The treatment of refugees at Camp Nelson was, unfortunately, all too typical. During the summer and fall of 1864 relatives of central Kentucky recruits lined the roads leading to Camp Nelson, swelling to thousands the number of black refugees from Kentucky and Southern states seeking refuge there. Upon arriving they found a hostile post commander, Brigadier General Speed S. Fry, who rejected any responsibility for feeding or sheltering refugees. Fry promptly ordered the return of all those unfit for military service—women, children, the elderly, the ill—to their owners, promising that "the lash" awaited any refugee who returned to Camp Nelson.[44]

Nevertheless, women and children, expelled from their homes by unfriendly owners or those urged to come to Camp Nelson by their soldier-husbands, continued to arrive, but Fry's policy of harassment did not abate. When three women expelled from camp returned, Fry had them bound and whipped as an example for all. Reports also spread of "men, women, and children, tied together," guarded by Union soldiers, waiting for their masters to claim them. Still others told of squads of soldiers "hunting slaves" throughout the camp, "returning them to their masters." A slave girl employed as a cook at the camp hospital, arrested and held for her master on Fry's orders, "begged" to be shot rather than sent back into slavery. A band of sympathetic soldiers who heard her pleas eventually rescued the girl, successfully preventing her return.[45]

The shortage of food, shelter, clothing, and health care among refugees at Camp Nelson created some of the worst living conditions of the Civil War. Many of the women were forced to compete for the few jobs available as cooks and washerwomen in order to keep their loved ones alive. Extended families lived in small tents, crude huts, and shanties built from scrap material. "Nowhere in the whole range of my observation of misfortune and misery occasioned by the war," a United States Sanitary Commission worker wrote, "have I seen any cases which appealed so strongly to the sympathies of the benevolent as those congregated in the contraband camp at Camp Nelson." Despite an appalling death rate, refugees continued to arrive and they continued to die. General Fry periodically swept the camp with troops, harassing refugees out of his lines, only to see them return. To solve the recurring problem, Fry decided to expel those refugees living inside Camp Nelson and destroy their shantytown in order to prevent their return. Early on the morning of November 23, 1864, a bitterly cold day when the temperature remained below freezing, the warmly clad soldiers of the provost guard drove four hundred raggedly clothed women and children, including the sick, from their huts into "the wintry blast."[46]

Joseph Miller, a Lincoln County recruit and former slave, described what happened to his wife and four children that day in an affidavit written November 26:

> About eight Oclock Wednesday morning November 23" a mounted guard came to my tent and ordered my wife and children out of Camp The morning was bitter cold. It was freezing hard. I was certain that it would kill my sick child to take him out in the cold. I told the man in charge of the guard that it would be the death of my boy I told him that my wife and children had no place to go and I told him that I was a soldier of the United States. He told me that it did not make any difference. he had orders to take all out of Camp. He told my wife and family that if they did not get up into the wagon . . . he would shoot the last one of them. On being thus threatened my wife and children went into the wagon My wife carried her sick child in her arms. When they left the tent the wind was blowing hard and cold and having had to leave much of our clothing when we left our master, my wife with her little one was poorly clad. I followed them as far as the lines. I had no Knowledge where they were taking them. At night I went in search of my family. I found them at Nicholasville about six miles from Camp. They were in an old meeting house belonging to the colored people. The building was very cold having only one fire. My wife and children could not get near the fire, because of the number of colored people huddled together. . . . I found my wife and children shivering with cold and famished with hunger. They had not received a morsel of food during the whole day. My boy was dead. He died directly after getting down from the wagon. I know he was Killed by exposure to the inclement weather. I had to return to camp that night so I left my family in the meeting house and walked back. . . . Next morning I walked to Nicholasville. I dug a grave myself and burried my own child. I left my family in the Meeting house—where they still remain.

One hundred and two of the four hundred refugees driven from Camp Nelson died from exposure.[47]

Only the efforts of religious humanitarians, such as John G. Fee, and Northern philanthropic organizations, like the Sanitary Commission, prevented Camp Nelson from becoming an even-greater disaster for refugees. These friends of the refugees worked for months to ameliorate some of the worst conditions, protesting the government's policy at every opportunity. It was not, however, until accounts of the Camp Nelson expulsion in November reached the Northern press that their protests had a significant impact. On December 15, 1864, General Lorenzo Thomas announced a new policy to provide shelter and rations for families of recruits in all rendezvous camps, easing, though not completely correcting, the harsh conditions.[48]

Major General S.G. Burbridge, commander of the District of Kentucky, appointed Captain T.E. Hall—both men were abolitionists—superintendent for refugees at Camp Nelson. Hall, with lumber furnished by the government and labor supplied by soldiers, constructed refugee homes similar to army barracks. Women and children, many of whom remained improperly clothed and fed, crowded into these barracks by the hundreds, resulting in disease and deprivation. Pneumonia became rampant, and by February 1865, with half the women and children at Camp Nelson sick, the death rate rose daily. Those admitted to the hospital "huddled together in rags and dirt," waiting for the hand of death to pass over them.[49]

From the beginning John G. Fee had stressed the need to consider the customs and habits of the refugees when constructing housing. "They have been *accustomed* to the fire place and cabin," he complained, not to wards haunted by disease. Fee urged the superintendent to separate the barracks into individual family rooms and build only cottages in the future. When some complained about the cost of firewood for cottages, Fee commented sardonically: "It is cheaper to buy additional fire wood than coffins and graves." Hall finally agreed and began building duplex cottages, 32 by 16 feet. Authorities expected each sixteen-foot-square apartment to house ten or twelve refugees. Carpenters completed about twenty-nine cottages by the end of the Civil War, easing slightly some of the worst housing problems.[50]

Refugees also flocked into Louisville. By the autumn of 1864 a large refugee camp, consisting mostly of women and children, occupied ten acres of land on Broadway near the outskirts of the city. Its inhabitants, as at other camps, survived the harsh conditions in abandoned buildings, shanties they constructed, and discarded army tents. Though Union authorities provided some sustenance for the refugees as early as 1862, and Northern freedmen's aid organizations donated clothes, fuel, and other assistance, women and children perished by the hundreds from pestilence and disease. City officials did nothing to alleviate the suffering of these poor or sick blacks, with the single exception of isolating those with contagious diseases.[51]

Louisville's black benevolent societies played a vital role in easing the plight of the city's refugees. During the war the Fifth Street Baptist Church established a "Colored Soldiers' Aid Society" to assist both recruits and their families. At society meetings, speakers, sometimes from the North, exhorted the people to raise recruits while contributing money to sustain their families. The black ladies of Louisville also sponsored fairs and benefits to raise money, clothes, fuel, and furniture for destitute refugees. Contributions from local black businessmen supplemented those from out-of-state donors. On one occasion the "Arlington's Minstrels" graciously staged a benefit for the ladies' society.[52]

In late 1864 when the Federal government began playing a more active role in assisting refugees, the Reverend Thomas James, a vigorous fifty-eight-year-old New York freeman who worked among Louisville's black soldiers and refugees for the American Missionary Association, assumed charge of the refugee camp. James built a refugee home which provided "temporary assistance" while he worked on the overall problem of permanent lodging for Louisville's black homeless. Under James's leadership, strict rules to govern the morals and movement of refugees were set up, and the first school established for their children.[53]

James, controversial from almost his first day in Louisville, clashed with the city's white leaders and with local ministers such as Henry Adams, who believed the Northerner pushed too hard. Proslavery whites were particularly hostile to James. During his first eighteen months in Louisville, death threats forced James to post nightly guards at his door. On one occasion, he narrowly escaped injury when his guards fled as a band of men attacked his apartment. Later, when he headed the refugee camp, James refused to light candles in his apartment, fearing bushwackers. Before his departure from Louisville, a blow from an assailant wielding a metal bar left James's right arm paralyzed.[54]

With the arrival of Major General John M. Palmer in February 1865 as military commander of Kentucky, James finally acquired a superior who supported his abolitionist views. James informed Palmer that hundreds of blacks remained incarcerated in slave pens throughout the city, and urged the use of military force to free them. Palmer attached James to the Provost Marshal's office and ordered him "to inquire" into the matter. James began a systematic survey of Louisville's old slave pens, freeing whomever he found. At Garrison's infamous jail, James freed 260 slaves, many confined in leg irons. After freeing blacks from all five Louisville slave jails, James began rescuing slaves held in less obvious places. A black waiter at the National Hotel informed James that nine slaves were secretly confined there by a slave trader. With a squad of troops, James pushed past an objecting hotel clerk, rescued the men, and promptly mustered them into the military. Because of the work of men like Thomas James and Federal laws freeing recruits and their families, Palmer told an overflow, cheering crowd of blacks at Center Street Church on March 20, 1865, that slavery had essentially ended in the Commonwealth.[55]

When slaves entered the Union army, recruiting officers completed an enlistment form which indicated their occupation, physical condition, and company assignment. At their enlistment, only 329 of the 20,905 black recruits failed to list an occupation. Though slaves went into camp with a variety of backgrounds, experiences, and skills, more than 97 percent listed their occupations as farmers or laborers. The remaining 3 percent were artisans, servants, draymen, wagoners, and teamsters. Only five recruits claimed the ministry as their profession and three had held jobs as clerks.[56]

The medical examinations indicated the physical and mental conditions of black recruits. In general, the white examiners found the black recruits to be remarkably healthy. The Paducah physician who examined slaves from fifteen western counties commented favorably on their muscular upper-body development, and an Owensboro doctor who examined slave recruits from eleven surrounding counties concurred, marveling at the strength of their "chest and arms." The physician in Lebanon who examined a "large number" of blacks from a triangle of counties—Meade to Adair to Anderson—believed them to be unsurpassed in "bone and sinew, muscle, chest measurement, and general physique." The doctor at London examined recruits from some of the most populous black belt counties, such as Garrard and Madison. Kentucky black recruits were "the stoutest and most muscular men I ever examined," the physician informed the Federal government, and for sheer strength and physical appearance, he did not believe they could be "surpassed by any people on earth." The examiner for the mountainous northeastern region placed the Commonwealth's blacks "among the very best" in the army, while the physician for the Bluegrass area categorized those he examined as "not inferior to the whites in physical organization." Only the Louisville examiner concluded that blacks suffered physically in comparison to whites.

Dr. E.P. Buckner, the army's physician in Covington, gave about 1,600 physicals to black Kentucky recruits, leaving the largest record of any examiner. He believed relatively "nutritious" diets had produced men with such "full" chests, "powerful" muscles, and "finely developed" physiques. During examinations the inductees expressed few complaints about their "livers, stomachs, bowels, kidneys, or bladders," Buckner reported, and he found tuberculosis "comparatively rare." There were few instances of "functional" heart disease among recruits and about five cases of "organic" heart disease. Evidence of fractures was *"uncommon,"* and Buckner found his subjects' teeth "nearly always *perfect."*

After examining Kentucky's black recruits for a period of about two years, Buckner reached several conclusions. The generally held view that blacks were more susceptible to scrofula than other races was erroneous. His disqualification of only 10 percent of the blacks examined led to the conclusion that they suffered from "fewer disabilities," proportionally, than other races. Furthermore, Buckner concluded that rheumatism affected the joints of blacks more adversely than whites and that their eyesight was definitely inferior to that of whites. But, overall, blacks entering the Union army were healthy and very fit for service.[57]

Kentucky's black troops were organized into all-black units—designated United States Colored Troops—commanded by whites and a small number of black noncommissioned officers. The rapid growth of these units—there were fifteen organized regiments by July 1864—forced a frantic search for officers. As quickly as whites passed officer examination boards in Lexington, Nashville, and elsewhere, they hurried off to command the newly created regiments. It is impossible to determine the exact number of black Kentuckians who joined the Union army, since some who enlisted outside the Commonwealth may not have been credited to the state. By July 1864 the government estimated sixteen thousand had volunteered, and anticipated an additional four thousand recruits within a month. Eventually, the army reported a total of 23,703 black Kentucky troops, an impressive 56.5 percent of the 41,935 eligible slaves and freemen between the ages of eighteen and forty-five. Kentucky provided about 13 percent of the 178,895 black Union troops. Only one state produced more black soldiers for the Federal forces than did Kentucky.[58]

Black regiments served in a number of theaters outside the Commonwealth. The 6th U.S.C. Cavalry Regiment and the 116th U.S.C. Infantry Regiment, both organized at Camp Nelson, took part in the siege of Petersburg, Virginia, and the 4th U.S.C. Heavy Artillery Regiment, organized at Columbus, saw duty in northwestern Tennessee. The 100th U.S.C. Infantry, a regular army regiment commanded by Colonel Reuben D. Massey, participated in the Nashville campaign. The 8th U.S.C. Heavy Artillery Regiment spent most of its tour of duty in the Paducah area, where it had organized in April 1864, and the 12th U.S.C. Heavy Artillery Regiment operated in southcentral Kentucky. Colonel Massey's 100th Infantry also campaigned in central Kentucky, and the 108th U.S.C. Infantry garrisoned Owensboro.

Kentucky mustered at least twenty-three regiments, but some were never at full strength.[59]

Many blacks found entering the military to be a traumatic experience. Elijah P. Marrs's first night in the barracks made him wish he "had never heard of the war." After induction, Marrs and his fellow recruits marched to Taylor Barracks on Third Street in Louisville, where they received uniforms, weapons, bunks, and company assignments. That night, as Marrs slept on the top bunk, the recruit in the middle, sleeping with a cocked revolver in his bed, accidentally discharged his weapon, killing the man on the lowest bunk. Recruits promptly descended upon the dead soldier, stealing the three-hundred-dollar substitute fee he had collected only hours before. During the few hours Marrs actually slept the remainder of that night, he experienced "horrible" dreams. Reveille awakened Marrs to a new day and soon to a new attitude. When an officer called his name and he stepped forward for his rations, Marrs "felt freedom" in his "bones," and he thought to himself, "Pshaw! . . . This is better than slavery."

Other recruits arriving at Camp Nelson were similarly perplexed. Only the work of the U.S. Sanitary Commission ameliorated the government's inertia in providing housing and food for black soldiers. Thomas Butler, Sanitary Commission representative, opened the previously all-white Soldiers' Home to black troops, at first allowing them into the washing and dining areas, but he eventually reserved the north wing for blacks, allowing them to share the facilities equally. In spite of their initial reception, recruits soon felt at home in Camp Nelson, and in later months tents and food awaited black troops when they arrived.

Kentucky's black recruits spent most of their time in camp engaged in purely routine activities. They did little marching to or from battle and even less fighting. Those who took few or no interests with them into the military suffered most from boredom, but for the energetic recruit, military life offered many opportunities. The deeply religious usually wasted little time in locating fellow believers, a place to worship, and a willing preacher. Rev. Sandy Bullitt preached to his Simpsonville friends on their third night in the Louisville barracks, and at Camp Nelson it seemed to one observer that preachers kept the dining hall busy almost nightly, and on Sundays from "sunrise to taps." The saintly Elijah P. Marrs found devout Christian friends wherever he went. On one occasion when stationed in Bowling Green, a soldier Marrs had never seen before walked up to him and said: "You look like a Christian." Marrs greeted the stranger warmly and expressed his concern over the absence of religious fervor among his fellow black soldiers. Shortly thereafter, with the permission of his captain, Marrs and his new friend, Swift Johnson, led "a glorious prayer meeting" in the barracks.

One of the first thoughts of many soldiers upon getting settled in camp was to inform their loved ones of the events which had transpired in their lives since leaving home. For many illiterate blacks this meant finding someone to write letters for them. Humphrey, a former Madison County slave stationed at Camp Nelson, found a friend to write letters for him on a weekly basis. Humphrey described the army as a better life than slavery, and the money he regularly sent his family impressed them. Eventually, friends and relatives arrived at Camp Nelson to observe for themselves. After several visits Humphrey's father, Alfred, concluded that his son was right, and he informed his owner of his intention to enlist at Camp Nelson. Letter-writing white ministers performed a very important service for black soldiers at Camp Nelson. One army chaplain wrote 150 letters to soldiers' families in a single month, and troops crowded around John G. Fee each evening with letter requests. Sanitary Commission authorities estimated that its associates at Camp Nelson wrote five thousand letters for black soldiers. Literate blacks were also besieged by requests for letter writing. Elijah P. Marrs was known as "that little fellow from Shelby County" who could write. He could be found, when off duty, "surrounded by a number of men, each waiting his turn to have a letter written home."

The military also provided opportunities for soldiers to make new friends and renew old acquaintances. When he shipped out of Louisville, Marrs met a pretty young woman named Emma in Lexington. She followed him to Camp Nelson and found a job near camp, where Marrs visited her on several occasions. After being transferred from Camp Nelson, Marrs learned later that Emma had died in a refugee camp. When stationed in Russellville, Marrs made a number of friends, one of whom was Henrietta Forees, who nursed him back to health when he became seriously ill. In Bowling Green Marrs's friends included Mary V. Cook, one of the state's leading women after the war, and he renewed his friendship with A. Robinson, the son of his former owner, who sought out Marrs while passing through Bowling Green. The two men had a "joyous time together." Marrs showed his white friend the camp, his company barracks, and the sights of interest in the town. "We talked freely of old slave times without a show of prejudice on either side," Marrs later wrote in his memoirs. When Robinson left, he presented Marrs with a box of cigars. The two men parted and never saw each other again. On another occasion, while shepherding refugees from Bowling Green to

Camp Nelson, Marrs met a number of his old friends at the Louisville railroad station, including "many young ladies," one of whom he later married. It was a time of celebration, and Marrs later recalled having done his "share of boasting that day."[60]

Military camp also offered black soldiers an opportunity to improve their minds, bodies, and occasionally their pocketbooks. Many black troops wanted to acquire an education, a desire not ignored by missionary associations. By November 1864 thirteen volunteer missionaries were teaching classes at Camp Nelson, and countless numbers of individual soldiers, both black and white, took it upon themselves to teach reading and writing to individuals and groups of blacks at Federal encampments. Black troops also attended classes to improve their musical talents. Camp Nelson authorities provided instruction in drums, the fife, and the bugle for members of the field marching band, and there were glee clubs for troops, with occasional classes in vocal music. Time always seemed to be available for recreation of various sorts around camp. Soldiers played games, engaged in wrestling matches, held regimental picnics, and, of course, used weekend passes to "visit the ladies." Soldiers could also make extra money in their spare time. When passing through Nicholasville, the men in Marrs's company earned a few dollars by guarding a circus.[61]

Black volunteer societies helped relieve the suffering of soldiers by supplementing the inadequate nursing services of the Federal government. The Soldiers' Aid Society of Louisville's Green Street Baptist Church, under the leadership of Misses Mary Lewis, Tally Fietus, and Fausie Pope cared for the sick and wounded black soldiers brought to hospitals in Louisville and New Albany, Indiana. Society members also visited the barracks of black troops, caring for the sick and providing for the needy. The Colored Soldiers' Aid Society of the Fifth Street Baptist Church engaged in similar work. The Louisville Colored Ladies' Soldiers' Aid Society, which held most of its meetings in Methodist churches, also raised money to assist sick and disabled black soldiers and their families. Other Louisville groups which aided wounded and disabled soldiers and assisted their families included the "Sons and Daughters of the Morning" and the "Daughters of Zion." These agencies supplemented the work of the U.S. Sanitary Commission in administering hospital care for Kentucky's black soldiers.[62]

Though assigned to artillery, cavalry, and infantry units, black troops were viewed by most white officers as primarily "hewers of wood and drawers of water." The Federal government recognized as early as June 1864 that abuse of blacks existed in Kentucky and ordered that black recruits receive only "their fair share" of labor assignments, but observers noted that regardless of the number of white troops available, blacks performed the hardest work. Four days after joining the army in Louisville, Elijah P. Marrs was ordered to take a squad of men to clear off several lots at Tenth and Broadway streets. Marrs's first thought upon receiving orders from a "white man" to perform manual labor was probably similar to that of thousands of black volunteers: "Is my condition any better now than before I entered the army?" Nevertheless, Marrs marched off with his labor detail, believing that the army provided a step toward freedom, but like so many of his black friends, he longed for the day when no one could order him to "come and go."[63]

Literate blacks, or those with special skills, possessed the best opportunities for assignment to leadership positions in the Federal army. When officers learned that Elijah P. Marrs could read and write, they made him third duty sergeant of Company L, 12th U.S.C. Heavy Artillery Regiment, and later, temporarily, regimental quartermaster sergeant. His brother, Henry C. Marrs, became orderly sergeant for another company, and eventually became sergeant major. Peter Bruner, attached to Company C, 12th U.S.C. Heavy Artillery Regiment, spent most of his time as a laborer, but he later served in the base hospital as a nurse, a position that usually went to troops recovering from illness. The vast majority of black troops in the field, in addition to recruiting slaves, served as pickets or as guards.[64]

Elijah P. Marrs's career in the 12th U.S.C. Heavy Artillery Regiment was typical. About three weeks after he enlisted in Louisville, Marrs and his friends shipped out for Camp Nelson. Though they were placed in an artillery unit, their training consisted mostly of close-order drill, with new men being added daily. In autumn 1864 with the first report of approaching Confederates, officers ordered the regiment to man the artillery. Company L got into position as best it could and awaited throughout the night for an attack. A few of the nervous cannoneers claimed they heard noises and approaching horses, but no attack occurred.

With only five weeks of training at Camp Nelson, the 12th U.S.C. Heavy Artillery received orders in late November to move to southcentral Kentucky. The heavily loaded recruits marched out of Camp Nelson toward Lexington, nineteen miles away. The unusually warm, dry weather soon produced a cloud of dust that clogged eyes, ears, noses, and mouths. Upon running short of water, many troops drank from stagnant pools found along the roadside, resulting in much sickness. The soldiers arrived in Lexington at sunset and learned that no provision had been made to feed them. That night, after dining on hardtack and water, Marrs slept in a "hog car" at the station and dreamed of his mother, his lost love Emma, and Rev. Bullett's farewell sermon.

The 12th regiment left Lexington the next morning and arrived in Louisville about 2:00 P.M., without having had lunch. Once again, to their dismay, no food awaited them. Without money, the troops looked covetously at the black and white food vendors who roamed the depot, selling baskets of ham sandwiches, fried chicken, and desserts. Finally, their frustrated captain nodded toward the vendors and said: "Press it." The soldiers promptly appropriated the food. Though convinced that such behavior was wrong, the hungry Marrs reluctantly confiscated some bread and meat; others "went the whole hog," taking entire baskets of food. The troops then marched to the Louisville and Nashville Depot, singing "I wish I was in Dixie's Land." From there they traveled in open freight cars to Bowling Green, arriving the next morning. About one-half the regiment took up garrison duty at Bowling Green forts, while the remainder went on to Russellville, where they found quarters in a stockyard. The men of the 12th regiment garrisoned three forts and engaged in recruiting black troops.

About two weeks later remnants of the 17th U.S. Kentucky Cavalry, after a clash with Confederate cavalry, arrived in Russellville, where they found the 12th regiment under orders to fall back before the approaching enemy toward Bowling Green. The men of the 12th regiment packed their gear and began a forced march. They covered twenty miles the first day and camped that night in an old schoolhouse. Their officers, expecting an attack at any moment, placed half the men on guard duty during the night. The force straggled into Bowling Green early the next afternoon. There they learned of Major General George H. Thomas's victory over the Confederates at Nashville and the unlikelihood of an attack on Bowling Green. The next few days were difficult ones for Company L. The cold fall wind drove the men into every available stable, outhouse, and abandoned building in the area. Overcrowding forced Marrs, as he phrased it, to take "an apartment." The soldier dug a hole in the ground, filled it with straw, covered it with boards and dirt, and lived there "comfortably" during his short stay in Bowling Green.

Marrs and his fellow troops expected to go to the military front, but when orders arrived, the regiment was again split. The men of Company C, U.S.C. Heavy Artillery Regiment, received orders to drive a thousand head of cattle to Nashville. The company carried rations for six days, eighty rounds of ammunition for each man, and tents. The drive went smoothly until the troops reached Franklin, about twenty miles south of Bowling Green. The weather suddenly worsened, they ran out of food, and Confederate bushwhackers shot into their camp each night when they lit fires. The soldiers foraged enough food to keep the drive going and eventually delivered the cattle in Nashville. Upon returning to Bowling Green, Company C garrisoned the forts and resumed recruiting black troops.[65]

About half of the 12th regiment, including Elijah P. Marrs, marched first to Munfordville and then a few days later to Glasgow. Upon hearing rumors of approaching Confederates, they moved toward Cave City. After going a few miles, they met another retreating Federal force. The two commanders decided to return to Glasgow to engage the enemy. The Union troops routed a small band of Confederates near Glasgow and entered the town on Christmas Day 1864. It seemed to Marrs that every black in the county greeted the victorious soldiers. When the Federal force occupied an abandoned fort outside Glasgow, the Rebels operating nearby cut off their retreat. Two nights later the Union troops silently slipped out of their exposed position at the fort and began a three-day "tramp" to Elizabethtown, where they found two companies of black troops doing garrison duty. From Elizabethtown the 12th regiment marched westward toward Hardinsburg, covering twenty-two miles the first day. The next day they entered Big Springs, pushing a small Rebel force out of the town without a fight.

Big Springs was the major engagement of the war for the men of the 12th U.S.C. Heavy Artillery Regiment. On January 5, 1865, the Federal troops camped at a white church on the outskirts of Big Springs. When two black soldiers went into town to ascertain the location of the Confederates, they were disarmed and told to make a run for the church. William Nichols reached the church safely; the other soldier fell dead in the churchyard as bullets splattered against the side of the building. Marrs and Henry Adcock led two squads of twenty men each on flanking movements to flush out the Confederates, but the enemy fled before the Union troops took their positions. That night the enemy made several demonstrations, only to be driven back each time. During the next two days the Confederate and Union soldiers exchanged fire on several occasions. During the lull in fighting, the Federals recruited black troops.

On Sunday, January 8, a large Confederate force unexpectedly appeared on a ridge as the Union troops prepared to induct their recruits into the army. When the Union troops began forming battle lines, the new recruits fled in every direction. After about two hours of glaring at each other, a Confederate officer rode forward and demanded the "unconditional surrender" of the Union forces. When they refused, the Confederates surrounded the black force and began to move forward. The Rebels demanded their capitulation two more times, promising "bloody consequences" if they refused, but the Union officer rejected each overture. The Confederates made one final surrender appeal as they prepared a hay-loaded wagon to burn the black troops out. Marrs's company commander, First Lieutenant Homer L. Love, quickly wrote out the surrender terms he would accept: his troops would turn over their arms in exchange for paroles and guaranteed safe return to their regiment. The Confederate commander, who clearly did not want a fight, promptly accepted Love's terms. Some of the black soldiers feared that the Rebels would not honor the terms of the surrender; one tore his stripes from his arm to conceal his rank and another attempted to flee, but cooler heads prevailed. When the black troops surrendered their arms, they were surprised by the friendliness of the Confederates who shook hands and "talked as if nothing unpleasant had happened."[66]

The black parolees, guarded by the Confederates, marched out of Big Springs by the light of their burning equipment. About midnight, they made camp at the home of a Union sympathizer who fed everyone a hearty meal. After eating, Marrs burrowed down into the snow and slept soundly. Following a good breakfast the next morning, they marched to Elizabethtown, where the Confederate officer turned the captured men over to the Union commander and then rode out of town. The next few weeks were terribly trying for Marrs and the men of Company L. After receiving new arms and going into camp at Muldraugh Hill, the men lived on half rations—hardtack, an ounce of meat, rye coffee, no sugar—for two weeks before returning to Bowling Green.

Life improved for the 12th regiment during the spring of 1865. The men of Company L found adequate quarters in barracks located below Fort Smith on Reservoir Hill. In February they manned Battery A at the fort, high above their barracks, and waited to ward off a rumored Confederate attack. With only thirty minutes of artillery drilling, the men loaded their cannon and waited throughout the night for an attack that never came. The next morning Marrs was astounded to find the grapeshot they had loaded lying on the ground in front of the cannon. The shot had slid out when the inexperienced troops tilted the cannon downward from the steep cliff. On another occasion, Marrs learned from a black soldier on furlough that his wife was being held against her will on a county farm. With the soldier as a guide, Marrs and ten men attempted to rescue the woman, but Rebel fire prevented the men from crossing the Barren River. Marrs, with a larger squad, located the farm the next day only to learn that the soldier's wife "had fled to parts unknown."

The troops of Company L received their biggest assignment when Marrs took charge of hundreds of black refugees who had congregated in Bowling Green, many of whom were living in wretched conditions. From his headquarters in an old Methodist church, Marrs distributed government rations, found clothes for the needy, and maintained order in the camp. When fights occurred, Marrs held courts-martial and dispensed justice. In the spring of 1865 Marrs received orders to transfer those refugees willing to go to Camp Nelson. Marrs gathered together about 750 refugees, ranging in age from six months to eighty years, including "some of the prettiest girls" he had ever seen, and with a squad of men from Companies C and L, under the command of Captain Cyrus O. Palmer, they began the trip to Camp Nelson.

The journey proved difficult. After a crowded all-night train ride, the party arrived in Louisville at 7:00 A.M. Against seemingly impossible odds, Marrs and his men moved the 750 refugees, mostly women and children, through the crowded railroad station and busy streets. Marrs became separated from Captain Palmer, who appears to have provided no leadership, and arrived in Lexington late that night. Marrs possessed no rations and Captain Palmer furnished no provisions for the "almost famished" refugees. Marrs spent what little money he had before locating General Burbridge, who provided "one ration" for each refugee. About 1:00 A.M. Marrs marched his charges to "Morgan's old negro pen," where they found more food and a place to sleep. There the "colored Ladies of Lexington" generously assisted the exhausted refugees by feeding and caring for the children. To the consternation of Marrs, some of the refugees, fearing their children would not survive the ordeal, left them the next morning with the Lexington aid society women.

The weary band entrained at Lexington for Nicholasville, where the tracks ended, and walked the final eight miles to Camp Nelson. By the time the unfortunate refugees reached Camp Nelson, Marrs had become disgusted by their treatment, but their triumphant entry into the compound eased his pain. As the refugees marched down the street, every door opened, and men with torches soon appeared to light their path. After feeding the refugees and assigning them tents in this "City of Refuge," Marrs delivered "a neat little speech," entrusting his charges in the "hands of the Lord." Marrs and his men went to the Soldier's Home, ate in "fine style," and then bedded down for their first sound sleep since the journey of mercy began.

Ten days later Marrs and his men left Camp Nelson for Bowling Green. In Louisville, where crowds had periodically harassed and attacked black soldiers and unruly youth gangs sometimes cursed and stoned blacks, they experienced their first trouble from whites. As Marrs and his men waited at the Louisville station to entrain for Bowling Green, police attempted to force them from the depot. Marrs's men fixed their bayonets and charged the police, scattering them in every direction. It was a splendid victory for Marrs in front of a number of his Louisville friends who were there to see him off.

Marrs's company was in Bowling Green when news of General Robert E. Lee's surrender arrived. The thoughts of the men turned to home, but another year passed before they were discharged. The regiment left Bowling Green in the fall of 1865 for Columbus, where many of the men took ill. Everyone rejoiced when they were transferred to Paducah. With few work assignments, Marrs used his spare time at Paducah to earn three hundred dollars, which he saved. Marrs's military career ended with his discharge April 20, 1866.[67]

Wherever they served in Kentucky black troops more often than not encountered hostility from whites, both civilians and soldiers. Treatment of the 5th and 6th U.S.C. Cavalry Regiments was typical. Harassment of these units began at Camp Nelson as they were being formed. Racial epithets were commonly hurled at black soldiers, but they were also victims of beatings and murder. One officer at Camp Nelson, commenting on the longstanding hostility directed at black troops, stated that "rarely a day passed" without a violent attack on one of his men.[68]

The 5th and 6th U.S.C. cavalries were part of a larger force which marched eastward out of Camp Nelson in late 1864 to attack the Confederates at Saltville, Virginia. The insults, taunts, and ridicule from their fellow white soldiers began almost immediately. Along the march black soldiers quietly endured the humiliation of having their hats knocked off, their horses stolen, and verbal charges that they were cowards who would run away at the first sound of enemy fire. On the day of the attack, October 2, 1864, the Union commander put into battle only 2,500 men, 400 of whom were from the black regiments, of his 4,000 troops. The Rebels defended a mountainside position, strongly protected by log and rock breastworks. The Union soldiers fought to within fifty yards of the first Confederate line when the order to charge was given. The black troops "rushed upon the works with a yell and after a desperate struggle carried the entire line killing and wounding a large number of the enemy and capturing some prisoners." Unable to penetrate the second Confederate line, and hampered by heavy casualties, the Union forces withdrew. In an engagement which gained nothing, 114 black troops and 4 of their officers fell dead or wounded and most remained overnight on the battlefield. The next morning, in one of the more horrifying atrocities of the Civil War, Confederate soldiers systematically executed about a hundred of the wounded and captured Federal troops, most of whom were black. Those wounded black troops who had reached Federal lines after the battle suffered grievously during the Federal army's retreat, since no one wanted to be left behind. But according to their commanding officer, none scoffed at the black troops as they returned to Kentucky.[69]

Most whites went into the Civil War with the assumption that blacks were incapable of becoming soldiers. This concept stemmed from the widely held view that blacks were, in every way, inferior. Though blacks had a long history of standing by their Kentucky owners in the Indian wars, and though tales of their heroism were well-known, the nineteenth-century white mind found it difficult—indeed impossible—to transfer such heroism to black troops fighting an organized battle in the Civil War.

Though few whites changed their opinions regarding black equality during the war, black troops produced a mild revolution in the thinking of some. One physician, after observing blacks in combat, declared that the black man "possesses courage sufficient to make him an effective soldier, no person acquainted with him can deny. Let his officers inform him that he has a right to do a thing desired, and that the officers want it done, and he will do it if it be possible for bravery, determination, and physical manhood to accomplish."[70]

White officers who fought with black troops in Kentucky, however grudgingly, usually came to respect their willingness to fight and die for the Union cause. Stephen Jocelyn, first lieutenant in the 115th U.S.C. Infantry Regiment stationed in Bowling Green, admitted that Kentucky's black troops "fight well." A battalion commander with the 6th U.S.C. Cavalry Regiment was slightly more liberal in his praise. His battalion, about 300 men, attacked about 350 Confederate cavalrymen near Marion in January 1865. The black troops, in their first engagement of the war, "charged over open ground and did not fire a gun until within thirty yards of the rebels," driving the enemy back about one-half mile, the officer reported. The officers who led the black troops into battle at Saltville, Virginia, also had praise for their soldiering. General Burbridge spoke highly of the gallantry of the 5th U.S.C. Cavalry Regiment, stating that it performed "better" than any of the other troops on the battlefield while absorbing the "principal loss." Finally, the rate of volunteering among blacks of military age in Kentucky, a standard which will probably never be surpassed, testifies to both their desire for freedom and their courage.[71]

The Civil War further complicated the lives of Kentucky blacks. Harassment and harsh treatment increased, but most slaves eventually realized how much they stood to benefit from a Union victory and bided their time. It is significant that when the first viable opportunity occurred for large numbers to escape slavery, Kentucky's bondsmen left their masters by the thousands, entering Union camps and volunteering for the Federal army. Unfortunately, those seeking refugee status within Union lines frequently met with rebuff, or upon entering Federal camps, discrimination and abuse. Those who became soldiers sometimes watched helplessly as their families suffered and died in refugee camps, while they themselves frequently endured the indignity of discrimination within the military as they fought to end slavery. Nevertheless, black civilians and soldiers, convinced that their new status was better than slavery, contributed more than their share of the physical labor and much of the military power that ran the Federal war machine in Kentucky. Out of their effort came victory and, eventually, freedom of a sort. For those blacks who survived the horrors of slavery and Civil War, many battles were yet to be fought and won before they would enjoy the most basic freedoms guaranteed by the Federal Constitution that Kentucky whites had so long possessed.

*Eight*

# Freedom's Pains: Life in the Immediate Postwar Era

AFTER Appomattox, blacks in Kentucky found themselves in a unique and bewildering situation with respect to their status. The legislature and state courts rejected federal measures that freed either black soldiers or their families, leaving about sixty-five thousand blacks in slavery until the ratification of the Thirteenth Amendment in December 1865. To the chagrin of local officials, thousands of displaced black refugees flocked into cities and towns, seeking the protection of federal authorities. In rural areas where some were expelled from their cabins and others were unwilling to accept the authority of their owners, blacks ranged through the countryside seeking food, shelter, and employment.[1]

Whatever their status, Kentucky's black population received contradictory advice. Federal officials proclaimed their freedom; slaveholders considered them fugitives. Generals urged blacks to seek employment to ensure their economic survival; slave owners threatened to prosecute those hiring their slaves. Reformers urged blacks to migrate to regions where opportunities were greater; railroad conductors refused to transport them without passes from their masters; and urban officials tried to have them arrested as vagrants.[2]

Recognizing this desperate situation, Major General John M. Palmer, federal commander for Kentucky after February 1865, decided to use his military authority either to end slavery in the Commonwealth immediately or to facilitate the movement of Kentucky slaves north of the Ohio River. Utilizing martial law which had existed in Kentucky since July 1864, Palmer issued Order No. 32 on May 11, 1865, granting Louisville blacks, including slaves, the right to move freely within the Commonwealth or across the Ohio. A supplemental Order, No. 49, of July 20, extended this policy, allowing refugees to leave the crowded, often unhealthy, refugee camps throughout the state. Palmer's proclamations remained in effect until martial law ended in mid-October 1865.[3]

"Palmer's passes," sometimes called "free papers" by those still in slavery, drastically increased the movement of blacks which began during the Civil War. Upon securing a pass from virtually any army officer, blacks moved about freely seeking employment, riding trains or riverboats wherever they desired. It is difficult to assess the impact of this dispersion on Kentucky's blacks. What one black Kentucky observer described as "chaos" for former slaves, another considered a "most wonderful shifting" of the black population in every direction. As one black later put it: "Better a thousand fold liberty with poverty than plenty with slavery."[4]

Taking advantage of Palmer's passes, blacks crossed the Ohio River by the thousands, often through Louisville, where the army assisted them with ferry service. Blacks in Bourbon County jammed the roads to Paris in late July, seeking "free papers" from the provost marshal, and proclaiming Cincinnati as their destination. The military or various reformers assisted even greater crowds at Camp Nelson. One missionary there eventually helped 350 refugees reach Ohio, personally financing their transportation and living expenses. In other instances squads of Union troops rescued slaves held on farms and assisted them across the Ohio River. Palmer estimated that 5,000 freedmen had crossed the Ohio River at Louisville by mid-July, and more than 10,000 by November, beginning a trend of black out-migration which continued through 1890 [see Table 1 & Figure 1]. The greatest number emigrated during the turbulent 1860s when the state's black residents declined by 14,000. The pace slowed during the next decade when the black population increased by fifty thousand, almost equaling the white growth rate. Emigration resumed at a moderate level during the 1880s when the black population declined by 3,380 [see Table 2 & Figure 2].[5]

## Table 1

### Population Statistics 1860 - 1900

| Year | Black | White | Percent Black |
|------|-------|-------|---------------|
| 1860 | 236,167 | 919,517 | 20.4 |
| 1870 | 222,210 | 1,098,692 | 16.8 |
| 1880 | 271,451 | 1,377,179 | 16.5 |
| 1890 | 268,071 | 1,590,462 | 14.4 |
| 1900 | 284,706 | 1,862,309 | 13.3 |

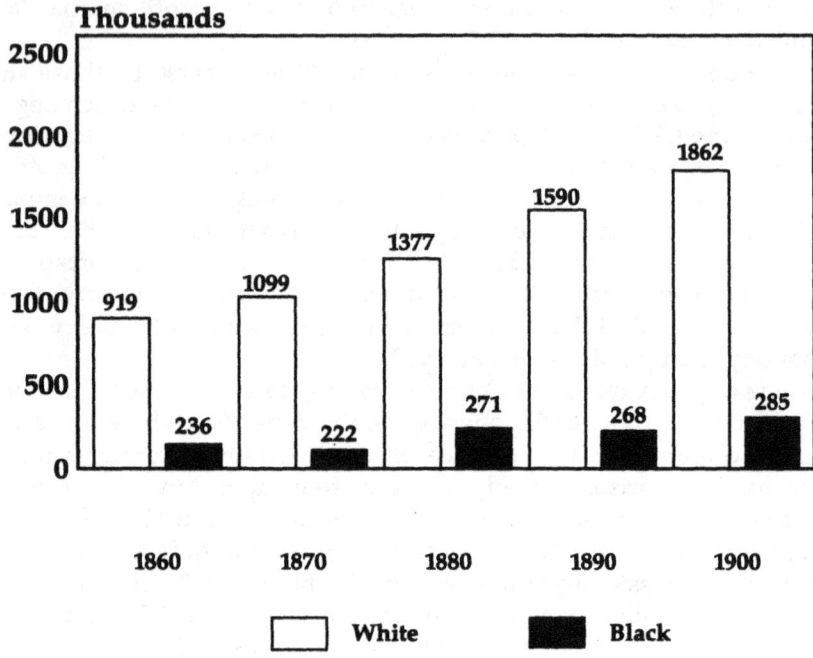

Figure 1: White and Black Populations, 1860-1900

| Table 2 | | | |
|---|---|---|---|
| Percentage Growth or Decline in Black and White Populations 1860 - 1900 | | | |
| **Black** | | **White** | |
| 1860-1870 | -5.9% | 1860-1870 | +19.5% |
| 1870-1880 | +22.2% | 1870-1880 | +25.3% |
| 1880-1890 | -1.2% | 1880-1890 | +18.4% |
| 1890-1900 | +6.2% | 1890-1900 | +13.4% |

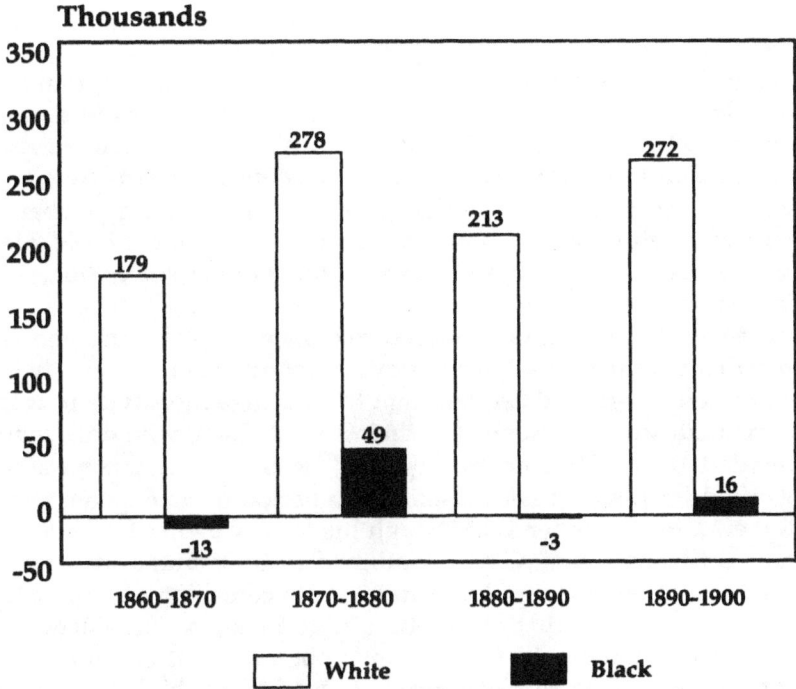

Figure 2: Changes in Population, 1860-1900

Black Kentuckians, using Palmer's passes during the spring and summer of 1865, also crowded into cities and federal military camps— Bowling Green, Camp Nelson, Covington, Lexington, Louisville, Munfordville, Paducah, and others—often moving on to other locations when conditions became intolerable. Multiple families sometimes lived in a space unsuitable for a single family, occupying abandoned buildings, barns, and stables. Ravished by poverty and disease both in the cities and the countryside, working when possible, some resorted to stealing to stay alive. Although extensive suffering existed during this transition period, most slaves preferred their freedom, and the responsibilities that went with it, to slavery. Individuals clearly suffered demoralization and death, but as a whole, Kentucky's former bondsmen accepted their condition, as one white observer later wrote, with a "becoming grace," behaving "like men of sense and character" as they went to work building a new life.[6]

Blacks were on the move for a number of reasons in the immediate post-Civil War period. Many, exhibiting a love for their "Old Kentucky Home," returned to their slave communities to visit friends and families. Isaac Johnson felt a "strong desire" to visit his former master in Nelson County. Johnson found his old owner in desperate physical and financial straits, but not unfriendly. When offered a fair wage to return to work on the farm, the freedman, remembering a past of harsh treatment, politely refused. Johnson found old friends and relatives of his father still in the area, but learned nothing of his immediate family.[7]

Many former masters offered freedmen employment, and some pleaded with their ex-slaves to stay. Many freedmen, especially those advanced in age or those reluctant to challenge the advice of whites, remained, some for the rest of their lives. Others, who only comprehended their "freedom by degrees," as one freedman phrased it, worked for their former masters for a period of time before leaving. Robert Glenn was typical. Though his former owner told him, "You are as free as I am," Glenn continued to be haunted by a nagging feeling that he must ask for permission to come and go. As he lay in bed at night those first few months after emancipation, Glenn "built air castles" contemplating freedom's potential, but his thoughts before going to sleep always returned to his friends, his kind treatment, and his steady income. Then one morning when he overslept, the farm manager "spanked" Glenn on the head and demanded that he get to work. Glenn sprang from his bed and began his morning chores as though still a slave. "I almost forgot I was free," he told an interviewer. Later that morning, when given another order, Glenn stood for a few minutes in silence without responding. Called in and asked why he was not working, Glenn said frankly, "I do not know," but within minutes he decided he could never truly feel free living on the same farm where the memories of slavery remained so vivid. Glenn left his old master immediately and never returned.[8]

Blacks were also on the move freeing relatives and friends still held in slavery. Parents who had not lived on the same farm as their offspring, mothers who had followed their husbands to military camps without their children, and fathers who had been soldiers reclaimed their loved ones before migrating to other areas. In some cases where parents were deceased or their whereabouts unknown, grandparents attempted to acquire their grandchildren, though they sometimes failed. When Catherine Riley of Logan County demanded her child still held in slavery, her former owner beat her with a club and left her beside the road "covered with blood." Thomas McDougal, on furlough from Virginia, returned to Larue County in October 1865, hoping to reunite his family. Upon arrival in Hodgenville, McDougal freed his family, but inadvertently took with him clothes not belonging to his children. His wife's former owner had McDougal arrested and incarcerated where he languished for weeks, unable to post bail. One soldier from the 118th U.S. Colored Infantry returned to his home county in September 1865 to free his family. The slave owner refused to allow the veteran to see his family and threatened to kill him if he ever returned to the farm.[9]

Rev. Elisha Green's struggle to free his daughters illustrated the dilemma of many families. Green had three daughters owned by different whites in the Maysville area. When Amanda fled to Green's home with a Palmer pass, Green was arrested for "harboring slaves." In court the judge pronounced him guilty and fined him thirty dollars, refusing to hear his lawyer's argument. Green at first refused to pay the fine, but eventually compromised and paid seven dollars court costs when Amanda's owner decided he could no longer retain her as a slave. Maria's owner threatened similar action when she ran away to her father. When Green refused to return the girl, the slaveholder acquiesced to Maria's freedom, but only if she left the state. Green quickly found a safe place for her in Ohio. Because fear kept Caroline, a third daughter, from leaving her owner, Green arranged for a squad of troops to rescue her and to rendezvous with him north of the Ohio River, thus assuring her freedom.[10]

Another reason for the mass movement of blacks was the rumor which spread in the summer of 1865 that those still held as slaves would be freed on Independence Day. Thus, thousands of blacks flocked into army camps and towns to participate in the celebrations. In Louisville a committee of blacks led by the redoubtable Thomas James, with the support of Palmer, planned a great celebration for July 4. "The sable sons and daughters of Ham," as Danville black Malcolm Ayers phrased it, began arriving days before the celebration. Local black families opened their homes and tables to the pilgrims, and on the morning of July 4 "colored bands" played as men, women, and children crowded the streets with flags and banners. When the parade began, the 123rd U.S.C. Infantry Regiment led the way, followed by a martial band. As they marched past the black churches—Asbury and Quinn chapels, Fifth Street Baptist, Jackson Street Methodist, Green Street Baptist, York Street Baptist, Center Street Methodist—more than six hundred Sabbath school children and brass bands playing patriotic music joined the parade. Next came about 150 government employees with a large banner, followed by the uniformed male benevolent societies—Sons of Union, West Union Sons, Independent Sons of Honor, United Brothers of Friendship, United Fellows—and then the ladies' aid societies and their tastefully decorated floats of singing girls. After the workingmen's float, with laborers "plying the saw, the plane, hammer, and mallet," came the 125th U.S.C. Infantry Regiment and more martial bands. The parade of perhaps ten thousand marched up Second Street and then southwest about two miles to Johnson's Woods. By early afternoon the crowd had swelled to nearly twenty thousand. Three regiments of troops stood guard to prevent interference with the meeting.

After a "great" dinner for the entire crowd, Rev. Thomas Strother, pastor of Quinn Chapel, called the meeting to order. Rev. Thomas James, described by one observer as a "whole team" by himself, began the ceremonies with a "very nice short speech." Some of the early speakers reviewed the racial progress of American blacks and their exploits during the Civil War, but the speech of John M. Langston of Oberlin, Ohio, proved the most inspiring to many listeners. Rising to thunderous applause, Langston proceeded with "stirring strains of eloquence, interspersed with anecdotes and side-splitting yarns," to give a history of the United States and the role blacks played. "He seemed to understand all things pertaining to our race, and what is best to be done for them," the Danville visitor wrote.

Late in the afternoon General Palmer, who had been attending a circus in Louisville, learned that he was expected to speak at the great gathering of blacks at Johnson's Woods. Using a "chariot and horses" borrowed from circus friends, the general arrived at the meeting about 5:00 P.M. to a "deafening" applause. When it proved virtually impossible to get through the throng, those near the front lifted Palmer "over their heads" to the platform. In a long, rambling speech, Palmer repeatedly stated that slavery, in effect, no longer existed in Kentucky, to which his listeners responded with "loud, long, and continued applause." There is little doubt that those still claimed as slaves under existing Kentucky law left the celebration believing they were free.[11]

Thousands from surrounding counties also participated in a July 4 celebration at Camp Nelson, planned by a committee of black men and women. With "hundreds of dollars" in contributions from visitors and soldiers, the committee purchased foodstuffs later prepared by the camp's women. After a "grand review" of soldiers which lasted until noon, the crowd gathered at a grove of trees near the refugee home to listen to martial music and patriotic speeches. The celebration opened with prayer, followed by songs from a children's choir and music from a military band. After a soldier read the Declaration of Independence, Sergeant Knox, in the first of several addresses by blacks, reviewed the role blacks had played in American and Biblical history. Then the integrated crowd sat down to a magnificent dinner of breads, meats, vegetables, and a variety of desserts. Later in the afternoon, there were more speeches and martial music, and songs by a quartet of black soldiers from Chicago, Illinois.[12]

Given the circumstances of blacks following the Civil War, many people realized that they could not make much progress in "pulling themselves up by their own bootstraps." It was even less likely that white Kentuckians would rush to their aid. By the end of 1865 everyone but the most prejudiced agreed that if blacks were going to be successful, they needed more than the assistance of volunteer agencies. Black self-help groups and northern philanthropic societies worked to meet the essential needs of destitute freedmen, but such efforts were insufficient. John G. Fee and others like him wanted to make sure that Kentucky's former slaves did not become a subclass of "boot blacks." The federal government, Fee argued, must adopt a policy of bold action. As a minimum, blacks should be allowed to acquire land and achieve economic success, thereby assuring independence "in their own eyes and in the eyes of others."[13]

Several federal officials served in positions where they could recommend, if not fund, the kind of assistance for former slaves that John G. Fee envisioned. Major General Oliver O. Howard, the head of the Bureau of Refugees, Freedmen, and Abandoned Lands, commonly called the Freedmen's Bureau, and that agency's director for Tennessee, Major General Clinton B. Fisk, both ardent abolitionists, expressed concern about the problems facing Kentucky's blacks after the war. Though Kentucky legally lay beyond the jurisdiction of the Freedmen's Bureau, as early as June 1865 Howard directed Fisk to begin extending his influence, if not authority, to the Commonwealth. With the adoption of the Thirteenth Amendment, Fisk formally announced on December 26, 1865, that the bureau would exercise supervision over Kentucky's former slaves.[14]

The goal of the Freedmen's Bureau under Fisk was to assist former slaves in their transition to freedom by guaranteeing impartial justice, and by promoting "industry, peace, good order, and education" for Kentucky's blacks. By March 1866 Fisk, who headed Kentucky's bureau from June 26, 1865, until June 13, 1866, had divided the state into three subdistricts, with headquarters at Lexington, Louisville, and Paducah. Major General Jefferson C. Davis succeeded Fisk on June 13, 1866, and created a southern subdistrict with headquarters at Bowling Green. Brigadier General Sidney Burbank replaced Davis on March 1, 1867, and remained in charge of the bureau for a year and a half. Subdistrict headquarters quickly expanded to six under Burbank, with new offices in Danville and Henderson, but before the end of 1867 the government reversed Burbank's policy and began closing bureau operations in Kentucky. By June 1868 Kentucky's bureau consisted of the three original subdistricts, but even those offices were closed by the end of the year. On January 7, 1869, Major Benjamin P. Runkle became head, and he presided over the agency's termination. The bureau's educational activities ended in the summer of 1870, although the veterans' claim offices remained open through June 1872.[15]

Though its officials made a valiant effort, the agency failed to achieve the reforms desired by men like Fee, primarily because of inadequate funding. Congress did not fund Kentucky's bureau until July 1866, forcing officials to finance the first six months of their work by fines, fees, and forfeitures. Later federal appropriations proved inadequate for the task in Kentucky. During one five-month period in 1866, the bureau fed, clothed, sheltered, protected, and nursed destitute and sick freedmen on a daily appropriation that averaged only thirty cents per person.[16]

The small corps of officials assigned to the Freedmen's Bureau was another problem. Fisk's plan for each district called for a chief superintendent, an acting assistant adjutant general, and a clerk. He divided Kentucky's 110 counties, 80 of which he believed required bureau supervision, into eleven districts, each headed by a superintendent with three agents. Of this total of fifty-seven Freedmen's Bureau officials, twenty-one had supervisory or clerical duties, leaving only thirty-six for field service. In November 1866 Jefferson C. Davis reported just twenty-five civilians employed by the bureau—thirteen superintendents and twelve agents. A year later Sidney Burbank reported sixteen clerks on duty, but only one agent.[17]

To ensure good will, bureau superintendents appointed local whites as agents. Their salaries, which ranged from fifty to one hundred dollars a month, did not always attract the best men, and for those who took their jobs seriously, the heavy work load was a thankless task. Harassment and death threats prevented many agents from performing their duties, and some proved to be poor administrators who neither followed instructions nor maintained proper records. Others were either paternalistic or unconcerned about problems of the freedmen, and a few were abusive. Freedmen complained that some agents charged exorbitant fees for routine paper work, refused payment for services received, and resorted to corporal punishment or imprisonment of blacks who did not follow orders.[18]

The effectiveness of the Freedmen's Bureau was diminished further by the inadequate number of federal troops posted in Kentucky.

This shortage resulted from the greater demand for troops in the Deep South, and the policy of quick demobilization of black troops in Kentucky. Though the army continued to recruit blacks into June 1865, the number of new recruits failed to keep pace with the rapid discharge of veteran black troops. The ten thousand black troops in the Commonwealth at the end of the war were reduced to six thousand by October 1865, virtually all of whom were discharged by the middle of 1866.[19]

To be successful, bureau agents required the presence of troops. Agents kept busy adjudicating contract disputes, investigating reports of violence against freedmen, handling complaints about relatives illegally bound in apprenticeships or held against their will, drawing up school reports, and burying the dead, all duties that drew the ire of many white Kentuckians. Though the total size of the troop force assigned to the Kentucky bureau is unknown, the number of officers indicates a small contingency. Jefferson C. Davis reported twenty-one army officers, only two of whom ranked as high as colonel, available for duty with the Freedmen's Bureau in November 1866. In mid-October 1867 Sidney Burbank had just eight officers, the same number available to Benjamin P. Runkle a year later. In the spring of 1869 the government severed all relationship between the army and the bureau. The lack of troops, considering the size of the Commonwealth, restricted the military to reacting to events.[20]

A final reason for the bureau's limited success stemmed from the general hostility of white Kentuckians at the war's end. Whites, like blacks, were bewildered by the emancipation process. They were informed that the Emancipation Proclamation did not apply to the Commonwealth; yet they witnessed the steady freeing of slaves by the army and Congress. The Constitution, whites believed, guaranteed state rights; yet, the flouting of state authority by General Palmer made newspaper headlines daily. White hostility to federal actions during the war was quickly transferred to Freedmen's Bureau officials and the social revolution they sought to achieve between 1866 and 1870. Taken altogether, the end of slavery and the implementation of the Freedmen's Bureau resulted in a level of violence that made the years 1866-70 among the most lawless in Commonwealth history.[21]

Much of the violence that gripped Kentucky in the years immediately following the Civil War stemmed from the prevalent belief of whites in the inferiority of blacks. The desire of the majority of white Kentuckians to keep freedmen "in their place" allowed a minority to engage in "dark and bloody deeds," creating a "system of terrorism" in the Commonwealth. Within a short period of time after the introduction of the Freedmen's Bureau, a hard core of terrorists earned the reputation of being "some of the *meanest unsubjugated* and *unreconstructed, rascally rebellious revolutionists*" in the entire South. These terrorists would not stop, one bureau agent believed, until they forced all freedmen to bow before their white "Master." Terroristic actions ultimately forced most freedmen, however reluctantly, to view all whites as their enemies. On one occasion when a bureau official called intimidated freedmen together and asked them to point out those who might harm them, "an old man answered 'Tell me Dear Sir who there is in this locality that wouldn't kick a nigger if he had a chance.' "[22]

Mob violence posed one of the biggest problems facing the new freedmen during the life of the Freedmen's Bureau. Gangs roamed at will throughout much of Kentucky, especially in rural areas, intimidating, beating, and murdering freedmen. In some counties these terrorists were labeled "moderators" and in other regions "regulators," "guerillas," or the Ku Klux Klan. They varied in size from small bands of four or five to gangs of fifty or more and represented, as one bureau official phrased it, "the pulse" of the white community. Usually operating at night and often in disguise, these self-proclaimed disciples of law and order presented blacks and Union whites with "notices" from "Judge Lynch" threatening whippings, burnings, and death.[23]

While it is impossible to ascertain the origins or identity of night riders, some were doubtless bands of outlaws thriving on the uncertain times. Others were returned Confederate soldiers who were unhappy with black emancipation or federal assumption of state authority. The Ku Klux Klan, though its membership was surely exaggerated, also engaged in attacks on blacks and Union whites. Other acts of violence were perpetrated by individuals or members of a single family who "took the law into their own hands" to justify a perceived wrong.

Some of the incidents in which blacks were intimidated, threatened, whipped, beaten, raped, burned out, or murdered occurred in isolated areas and were never reported, making it impossible to catalog all episodes of violence. Extant records, however, reveal a callous disregard for the humanity and property of blacks previously unseen in the state's history. An early 1866 report recounted fifty-eight incidents including more than two dozen whippings and beatings of men and women, three rapes, eight attempted murders, nine murders, and one case of burning a freedman alive. The 1866-67 bureau report listed twenty murders, eighteen shootings, and eleven rapes in 319 cases of maltreatment of blacks. The monthly reports for 1867 reveal a steady level of violence for the entire year. The thirty-seven "outrages" of January grew to sixty-eight in December and included six murders and five shootings. The bureau report for 1867-68 included twenty murders among its 324 "outrages." The bureau's final report, 1868-69, detailed twenty-six murders, three rapes, and thirty shootings among 327 incidents of violence and maltreatment.[24]

Three other sources of information concerning violence in Kentucky between 1866 and 1870 describe the horror more vividly. One, a Frankfort newspaper account, listed 115 hangings, shootings, and whippings between 1867 and 1871. The second, a petition to Congress from the "colored citizens of Frankfort and vicinity," described episodes of violence from November 1867 through May 1870. This stark document listed more than one hundred cases of violence growing out of seventy-nine incidents. It included twenty-four mob lynchings, the murder of twenty-one men and three women during mob violence, and numerous beatings and whippings. The third, a catalog of violence committed against blacks compiled by George C. Wright, enumerates sixty-seven lynchings between 1866 and 1870.[25]

Whatever the number or identity of people engaged in harassing blacks, it proved extremely difficult for freedmen to receive justice in Kentucky. The system of intimidation and terror, the prohibition of black testimony against whites in state courts until 1872, and the hostility of most whites toward federal involvement, made it difficult to arrest, and virtually impossible to convict, those charged with crimes against blacks. The monthly reports of outrages against blacks revealed the futility of the federal effort. There were only two arrests stemming from thirty-seven outrages in December 1866; four arrests from eighteen outrages in February 1867; and fifteen arrests from thirty-four outrages in October 1867. During the year July 1, 1867, to June 30, 1868, there were no arrests in ten of the twenty murders of blacks; in the other ten cases, four were acquitted, the court took no action in one case, and three remained before various courts.[26]

The principal reason for this dismal record of justice was that whites, both citizens and officials, protected the accused regardless of the evidence. In some areas of Kentucky armed men served as bodyguards for those charged with crimes against blacks, and in others those accused of attacks on blacks walked the streets without fear of arrest. In Marion County local officials used state law to shield regulators from the bureau and in Warren and Logan counties local courts refused to act against the accused. Columbus officials made no serious investigations in three cases of murder in 1867, and when the body of a black man "whose skull had been broken by parties unknown" was brought into town, "the corpse was quietly buried by the negroes, and nothing more said about the occurrence." It was not unusual for county officials to conduct a cursory inquest with no serious "attempt to learn any facts," and those county prosecutors who interpreted the law as applying equally to both races were usually ostracized from society.[27]

Nevertheless, Freedmen's Bureau officials made a sincere, if futile, attempt to arrest and prosecute those charged with crimes against freedmen, and achieved limited successes. Most of these convictions occurred when the federal government, over the objections of state officials, assumed jurisdiction under the 1866 Civil Rights Act in cases involving freedmen. Where evidence of wrongdoing existed, bureau officials took the complainant and witnesses to a United States commissioner who issued a warrant for the arrest of the offender. If arrested and indicted, the accused faced trial in the United States district court. While this procedure greatly facilitated convictions and perhaps deterred some of those contemplating violence against blacks, convictions were few because of the difficulty of arrests.[28]

The families of black soldiers were particular objects of hatred and suffered horribly from postwar violence. They were especially vulnerable since some troops were not discharged until 1867. Clarissa Burdette received unmerciful whippings at the hands of her former owner before her husband, Elijah, returned from serving in the artillery, and an Estill County soldier's wife told of being repeatedly brutalized. On one occasion after being knocked down with a chair, her former owner's son ripped off her clothes, tied her spread-eagled on the floor, and whipped her until she became "insensible." When Jane Coward, the wife of a soldier, tried to move off a Green County farm, her owner beat her "nearly to death" and threatened to kill anyone who attempted to rescue her.[29]

On other occasions, slaveowners and Confederate veterans violently drove the wives and children of soldiers from their homes. With their husbands unable to assist them, the less fortunate hovered without adequate food or shelter in the neighborhood where they had been slaves, praying their husbands would return soon. A gang of ex-Confederates invaded Jordan Finney's home in Walton, Kentucky, three times. Finney, who had previously been beaten with "clubs and stones" when he attempted to free a daughter still held in slavery, lived with his wife and daughters, two of whom were married to soldiers. After repeated abuse of the women and children, the attackers destroyed the family's clothing and furniture and eventually forced the black homeowner out of the county.[30]

In some instances discharged soldiers were attacked before they reached home. A gang of "rowdies" surrounded a soldier mustered out in Louisville in 1866 and stole his money, clothes, and weapon. When told to run for his life, the veteran fled with only a shirt on his back. A bullet fired by the thieves struck the unfortunate soldier in the hand. Out in the countryside bands of rogues went from farm to farm beating and robbing black veterans. Reuben Atkins, a veteran of the 123rd U.S.C. Infantry, was robbed of fifty dollars shortly after he returned to Jessamine County in 1866, and many discharged soldiers reported severe beatings by former owners in Woodford and Scott counties. Shortly after Henry Gaines took a job with his former master, he found a note on his door warning him to leave Kentucky within three days. With the support of his employer, Gaines remained, but several days later an armed gang entered his home and whipped him severely "in the presence of his family." Gaines felt he had no alternative but to leave Kentucky. Numbers of returned soldiers were "shamefully" beaten in the vicinity of Camp Nelson, and in Mercer County a white man shot Peter Branford, a recently returned soldier, "without cause or provocation."[31]

Many Kentucky whites were deeply offended by the sight of former black soldiers walking the streets with guns. In some western Kentucky towns authorities levied fines on blacks for carrying weapons, imprisoning those who persisted. Local courts in some areas ruled that any white man could disarm blacks, and guerillas and ex-Confederates regularly confiscated firearms from former black soldiers. The most notorious gangs of killers sought out black veterans and marked them for death. Whites also attacked soldiers on furlough because they carried weapons. Shortly before Elijah P. Marrs arrived in Shelbyville on furlough in 1866, a soldier warned: "Sergeant, I pity your case to night." That evening, when a fire broke out in town, Marrs rushed to the scene. After the fire was out, someone shouted: "Yonder is a negro officer of the army," and three men with knives jumped Marrs. The soldier picked up a stick and fought off the attackers as he retreated the one-half mile to his parents' home. Once in the house, Marrs began firing his revolver at the assailants, who fled. A few nights later a white man confronted Marrs as he escorted his girlfriend through Shelbyville. Marrs drew his pistol and the would-be attacker withdrew. Others on furlough were less fortunate. A Camp Nelson soldier received severe head and facial lacerations when he attempted to visit his wife, and a soldier visiting his home in Auburn died when someone burst in and shot him in his sleep.[32]

On a number of occasions violence against blacks took the form of lynchings. Rape of white females was the common charge against lynched blacks. In March 1866 Paris "citizens" lynched two blacks for the alleged rape and murder of two white females, one of whom was ten years old. Another lynching occurred in Franklin County in May 1866 when authorities arrested Charles, "a colored boy," for allegedly assaulting a seven-year-old white girl. After his arrest "a mob" took Charles from the jail, and "without any excitement or disorder," administered the "merited punishment," a historian of Franklin County wrote. Tom, a Daviess County freedman accused of raping a white woman in May 1866, was lynched on the courthouse square. "[While] on his way to the jail," a county historian wrote, "an unknown party placed one end of a rope over his head, and threw the other end over a limb of a tree in the court-house yard." Tom strangled when hoisted off his feet by the mob. A lynch mob containing a number of prominent Franklin County citizens in January 1868 took Jim Macklin from the jail cell where he had been lodged for the alleged rape and murder of a white girl. The mob ceremoniously hanged Macklin at the scene of the crime. Shortly after the lynching, bureau officials collected enough evidence on the case "to establish the fact that . . . [Macklin] was innocent." In January 1869 a mob removed an accused black rapist from the Daviess County jail and hanged him near the courthouse. Lynch mobs killed two blacks in 1870, one charged with rape in Fleming County and the other with attempted assault in Cynthiana.[33]

Blacks were also lynched for violent acts against whites. Al McRoberts met his death on Christmas Eve 1866 after a Boyle County constable named Harris, who had threatened to kill the freedman, attempted to disarm him. An argument ensued, and McRoberts shot at Harris three times. Danville police, who because of Harris's previous threats had given McRoberts permission to carry a weapon, nevertheless arrested the freedman. As officers led McRoberts to jail, they failed to prevent Harris from severely beating their prisoner with a cane. Upon arriving at the jail, the enraged Harris shot and "seriously" wounded McRoberts. That night a mob took McRoberts from the jail and hanged him.[34]

In Nicholasville Adam Smith shot and killed a white man. Boz, another black at the scene, was "accidentally" wounded in the fray. County officials lodged Smith in the Nicholasville jail, where a mob broke in and mortally wounded him. The mob then sought out Boz, dragged him from his bed, and hanged him. Smith lived long enough to identify five of his assailants, all later arrested by federal authorities.[35]

Blacks were also the targets of much random violence in the period following the war. Whites, for real or imagined reasons, sometimes struck out blindly at blacks, committing offenses that ranged from the most trivial to the most odious of crimes, almost "because they were there." For some, blacks served as a convenient scapegoat for all their problems, personal or financial. Others easily vented their hatreds and passions on an "inferior" without fear of recriminations. Wherever blacks lived in Kentucky, they faced the possibility of random violence because of their proximity to hostile whites.[36]

Communities of blacks which arose after the Civil War, such as Camp Nelson in Jessamine County, were special targets of random violence. Those who flocked into Camp Nelson during the war, seeking protection and assistance from federal authorities, did not anticipate the haste with which the government withdrew its support in 1865 and 1866. With no place to go, many blacks remained in Camp Nelson, looking to a small band of white northern missionaries for leadership. What had been a "City of Refuge" to desperate refugees in 1864 became to white "regulators" living in the area a "Niggers [sic] nest" in 1866, and they vowed to break up the mostly black community. Early in 1866 before the government closed the camp, gangs of whites began beating black soldiers caught alone outside the perimeter, and as soon as federal authorities abandoned Camp Nelson in June 1866, regulators began threatening those who remained. Bands of armed ruffians frequently moved through camp at night, entering cabins and robbing blacks of their money, watches, and weapons.[37]

By late 1866 the outlaws regularly harassed the missionaries, apparently believing that if the white leaders left, the blacks would follow. In October a gang armed with revolvers and shotguns entered the home of Rev. Abisha Scofield, threatening death if he did not leave. The black community rallied to Scofield's support, organizing pickets to guard the camp at night. But when the regulators failed to return during the next two weeks, the guards, all of whom worked daily, ended the vigil even though the soldiers promised by the Freedmen's Bureau to protect the Camp Nelson community had never arrived.[38]

On November 19, 1866, at about 1:00 A.M., thirty regulators returned, easily capturing the missionaries. Many blacks fled into the night at the appearance of the regulators, but one man, John Burnside, refused to leave his house. Burnside fought off the attackers, wounding one severely and another mortally, but the mob eventually stormed his house and beat him mercilessly, leaving him for dead. After threatening the missionaries with death if they stayed, the attackers left. The next morning the small black community at Camp Nelson again became an armed camp. For eight days and nights the freedmen and their missionary friends stood guard, awaiting the arrival of bureau troops. The soldiers finally appeared on Saturday night but left in search of regulators a day later. Upon capturing two suspects, the troops returned to Lexington, leaving Camp Nelson blacks to fend for themselves. The regulators promptly returned and rode up and down the streets swearing revenge if harm came to their friends. The missionaries, with the aid of Gabriel Burdett, a black preacher, fled for their lives. Regulators continued to harass and attack Camp Nelson blacks and their white friends for years.[39]

Many individual blacks became the victims of random intimidation, abuse, and even murder. A white attacked a black cart driver in the streets of Paducah for refusing to hand over his whip. The drayman suffered life-threatening stab wounds in his back and abdomen. After severely whipping a nine-year-old black child, a Louisville woman forced her to sleep in an outhouse on a bitterly cold night. The child suffered severe frostbite, resulting in the amputation of her toes. Regulators in Columbus attacked the home of an "old woman." When she refused to surrender, the ruffians set the house afire, seized the freedwoman as she ran out, and viciously whipped her. "An old colored man" was shot in Fayette County for refusing to allow a white man into his house, and in western Kentucky an eighteen-year-old shot and killed "an old negro" because he ran from a whipping. A white approached a young black man in Louisville and, for no known reason, stabbed him to death "in broad daylight." A gang of whites attacked Joseph Balls, a resident of the black community in Bath County, beating and kicking him until his stomach cavity ruptured, spilling his intestines on the ground. Balls, a freeman for many years, suffered for two days before dying. A Danville bully badgered an elderly black man, took his cane, and then shot him to death in a store. In another incident in the same town, a white, allegedly without provocation, murdered a mentally retarded black in the city streets. An intoxicated man in Garrard County, "wishing to try his pistol," deliberately aimed and fired at a black man building a fence. The freedman fell dead. And on the outskirts of Lexington, two white teenagers murdered a twelve-year-old black, brutally cutting his throat before severing his genitals.[40]

Many of the gangs inflicting punishment on freedmen consisted of Negrophobes who wanted to rid Kentucky of all blacks by preventing their leasing, buying, or living on the land of others. Regulators near Hall's Gap issued a threatening "Notice" to anyone selling land to blacks, and in Henry County "Black *Injeon*" posted a "Notice" listing the names of blacks who would be burned out if they did not move "north of the Ohio River without delay." In western Kentucky a mob of rowdies gave a Daviess County farmer one day to expel blacks working on his farm. If he refused, they promised to burn every house on the farm. Regulators visited numerous white farmers in Daviess County, warning them not to rent or lease land to blacks. In Nelson County officials reluctantly advised freedmen in 1868 not to build homes because the bureau could not prevent regulators from burning them.[41]

Freedmen who lived in counties bordering the Ohio River frequently found it better to move across the river than face constant harassment. In Meade County the notorious Shacklett family gang threatened to kill any black who refused to cross into Indiana. A mob of about five hundred regulators stalked Gallatin County, forcing blacks to flee north of the Ohio. One Freedmen's Bureau official stated that two hundred blacks, fearing "the lash and other abuses," crossed into Indiana from Warsaw in a single day. In the western Kentucky counties gangs of whites threatened freedmen in December 1867, warning them to be out of the Commonwealth by February 20, 1868. These threats, the results of a premature announcement of the bureau's closing, "produced terror and consternation" among blacks, causing them to flee by the hundreds to Ohio River towns. In several sections of the Jackson Purchase, freedmen fled "masked bands" en masse, many north of the Ohio River. Henderson was the only location in western Kentucky where civil officials provided assistance to black refugees fleeing violence.[42]

While some blacks fled from almost every county and many left the Commonwealth, most freedmen went to other parts of the same county or to nearby counties. Whether fleeing an immediate threat of violence, wanting to get "beyond the reach of their masters" in a place where they were "unknown," looking for the security in numbers an urban environment offered, or simply seeking better economic conditions, former slaves deserted rural areas. Scarcely a town or city failed to experience rapid growth. In the eastern part of the state blacks in Greenupsburg, Mt. Sterling, and Maysville refused to return to the countryside in spite of their harsh living conditions. Fear drove them from northern Kentucky counties into Covington, away from the farms where labor opportunities were actually greater. "Outrages and maltreatment" forced massive numbers of freedmen into Louisville and other central Kentucky towns. Lexington's black population tripled by 1870 with the addition of about 4,600 freedmen, making the town about one-half black. Hundreds of freedmen crowded into Owensboro and Henderson, and families from the Jackson Purchase counties flooded into Paducah, where they sought employment. The black communities in Bowling Green and Russellville in southcentral Kentucky experienced similar growth.[43]

The vast majority of the freedmen who fled to Kentucky's villages, towns, and cities took any available housing. Leaving slavery with little or no money or possessions, they lacked adequate food, clothing, shelter, or fuel. In Covington freedmen packed like "sardines" into "wretched old dilapidated ware houses [sic], cellars, garrets and miserable shanties," usually located in the most unsanitary sections of the city. Poorly clad and starving, emaciated and "marked" by disease, and unable to afford medical care, they lived in squalor, stalked by death.[44]

Refugees arriving in Lexington settled in "ill ventilated cabins and dilapidated houses." Multiple families crowded into a single room as freedmen clustered into shanties on poorly drained streets and alleys near the railroad or the stockyard. Others settled on the outskirts of Lexington on land previously thought uninhabitable as opportunistic whites built all-black subdivisions of shotgun shacks on narrow strips of poorly drained land. One of the earliest of these segregated black communities was on bottomland used for mule stalls during the Civil War. With decaying garbage and animal waste everywhere, disease spread, exacerbated by a shortage of clothing and fuel.[45]

Federal officials struggled to force refugees to leave Camp Nelson. Despite their efforts 2,477 women and children were within the perimeter in September 1865, and about 1,000 six months later. Those without adequate housing or money occupied huts and cabins recently abandoned by discharged soldiers or squatted in government buildings earmarked for sale. A few of the more fortunate managed to rent parts of occupied buildings or three acres of land for a few dollars a month. Some suffered daily for want of food or clothing, and many of the "utterly destitute" turned to begging, stealing, or prostitution to stay alive. With disease rampant, an appalling death rate gripped the camp. By March 1866 the 1,300 refugee graves at Camp Nelson reflected a death rate of almost 50 percent for the previous fifteen months.[46]

Freedmen fleeing to Louisville "huddled" like "cattle" into shacks, shanties, cellars, and outbuildings in "Smoketown," located on Preston, Floyd, and Jackson streets south of Broadway. Inhabitants of these poorly constructed buildings on inadequately drained lots suffered the "cold blasts" of winter and the stench of decaying filth, garbage, and stagnant water during summer. Others settled on McAlister's, Grey's, and O'Neal's alleys and on 9th Street near the railroad tracks, where poor drainage, waste, and the sheer press of humanity made life miserable. Blacks unable to find shelter, starving

Housing for freedmen at Camp Nelson.

and sick with smallpox, walked the streets, begging food and clothing. The lack of food, clothing, housing, and medical care, exacerbated by rising prices and coal shortages, greatly increased diseases and death. One hundred and thirty-five blacks died in Louisville in February 1866, a 16 percent per annum death rate. Though black community leaders quickly realized the need for better living conditions for freedmen, years passed before significant improvements occurred.[47]

Further west, blacks flooded into Owensboro, filling "ill ventilated" buildings, frequently surrounded by stagnant water, in the worst sections of town. In winter poorly clad, hungry freedmen suffered for want of fuel and clothing. Measles, scarlet fever, and other diseases ran rampant through the black community, and during hot weather many fell victim to "typho-malarial fever." Russellville freedmen congregated into old stables, abandoned buildings, and outhouses where they lived in unhealthy conditions, trying to elude disease and death. Blacks in Bowling Green were short of every kind of clothing. Housing was in short supply and diseases rampant. It was much the same in Paducah, where destitute freedmen, unable to purchase food, clothes, or pay for medical care, died on the streets.[48]

In eastern Kentucky destitution and disease were diminished only by the smaller number of blacks living there. Refugees in Catlettsburg and other Big Sandy River communities could not find suitable shelter or sufficient food. Without proper clothing or money to buy fuel, many suffered horribly during the winters. In Maysville, the old and young, many of them half-starved, lacked sufficient clothes or fuel, and Mt. Sterling freedmen endured inadequate medical care and food.[49]

Kentucky whites, saying "the Yankees freed them, now let them take care of them," refused state funds for sick and destitute freedmen. A February 1866 law which called for dividing the funds from a two-dollar poll tax on adult blacks equally between paupers and education was long delayed and raised little money, much of which never reached the needy. Following a massive protest by freedmen, the legislature amended the law, allocating all the tax revenue collected from blacks to the care of paupers, but with no better results. State officials proved equally reluctant to assume care of aged, deaf, blind, or insane freedmen.[50]

City and county governments and private physicians were only slightly more willing to assist sick and destitute freedmen. Louisville officials argued that they did not control the pauper fund, thereby refusing responsibility for poor blacks, and private physicians often required a two-dollar to five-dollar fee in advance before treating freedmen. Bureau officials eventually concluded that as long as the federal government assisted freedmen, Louisville officials would do nothing, and events proved that interpretation reasonably correct. Only in cases involving communicable diseases, such as smallpox, would Louisville authorities cooperate with the bureau by receiving freedmen into the city's "pest house," thus protecting the general public.[51]

Physicians in Bowling Green usually refused to treat sick freedmen, and blacks in Mt. Sterling often found it impossible to secure a doctor's service. Blacks were no more fortunate in Gallatin County, where officials bluntly informed the bureau agent that issues of hygiene and medicine among freedmen were not government business and that local blacks must pay for medical care like everyone else. In Covington neither city officials nor local physicians, who required prepayment, expressed concern for the destitute sick, though the city provided coffins for poor freedmen. In 1868 when state pauper funds finally became available, Covington designated eight hundred dollars for "taking care of negro paupers." Claims filed by whites for assisting "old family servants" and requests by newly arrived freedmen from other counties, however, were rejected. The remaining $2,700 from the black pauper fund went toward building "negro huts on the poor farm." The absence of local black charitable organizations made postwar adjustment for Covington freedmen especially difficult.[52]

Black paupers fared slightly better in some central and western Kentucky towns. County officials in Lexington maintained a small aid program for freedmen. In Owensboro where disease raged among the freedmen, physicians accepted charity cases, but they could not provide all the care needed, and city authorities refused responsibility. The city government of Paducah collected the poll tax on freedmen, and officials appropriated small sums for the destitute, sick, and insane. In western Kentucky, where large numbers of blacks resided, local officials probably made the greatest attempt to assist the poor. The efforts of Larue's county judge were slowed only by the limited money available, and the county court in Madisonville aided a modest number of black poor. In early 1866 civil authorities in Henderson willingly adopted sanitary measures designed to prohibit the spread of disease in the black community. As part of their program, they established a hospital for freedmen funded from the poll tax on blacks. During 1867 and 1868 Henderson officials went on record, more than any other town in Kentucky, for opposing abuse of freedmen.[53]

While the white population seemed to wait for "the poor, sick, infirm, aged, and children . . . to starve and die," the black community struggled to alleviate suffering and sickness. In Louisville where blacks possessed a long history of assisting the poor and infirm, churches and leading citizens established several relief organizations by early 1866. Fifth Street Baptist Church began a movement for a hospital for freedmen in February 1866, raising $180 at its initial meeting. Other churches made similar pledges, and leaders soon selected a location. A month later another group of blacks began raising funds for an orphans' home. A Freedmen's Sanitary Commission grew out of a citizens' meeting in April 1866. Led by John Fowles and a board of directors which included Washington Spradling, the commission and a few of their white "friends" began raising money for the sick and homeless. Working with the churches, the Sanitary Commission established a hospital at the corner of Seventeenth and Broadway. Within a short period of time, the hospital had about thirty-five patients nursed by four attendants, but a lack of funds hampered efforts to provide adequate health care. An inspection in June 1866 revealed clean floors and a ward in good order, but half the windows were broken out and a shortage of bed linens allowed only one change a week.[54]

Freedmen in other parts of the state began similar charitable projects. In the fall of 1865 Paducah blacks organized a Freedmen's Aid Society to support orphans, the aged, and the infirm. A second philanthropic organization, the Freedmen's Sanitary Commission, evolved in April 1866. By June Paducah's Sanitary Commission had collected $204, but the general poverty of the black population and the high cost of burying the dead quickly depleted their funds. In June 1868 freedmen at Columbus, following the leadership of black ministers, organized a Freedmen's Aid Association, and a Hopkinsville Benevolent Society, operating with "scanty resources" in 1868, assisted local blacks in feeding the starving and burying the dead.[55]

A number of white organizations in other states assisted Kentucky freedmen by collecting clothes for the needy, thereby alleviating some of the worst poverty. The Northwestern Freedmen's Aid Commission of Chicago, Illinois, worked with freedmen in Paducah, and the Cincinnati-based Western Freedmen's Aid Commission assisted the poor at Columbus. The Freedmen's Aid Society of the Methodist Episcopal Church operated missions in several southcentral Kentucky towns, and the Friends Association of Pennsylvania worked in Louisville.[56]

Other individuals and groups also contributed to the well-being of Kentucky freedmen. During late 1865 northerners and Union soldiers contributed about six thousand dollars toward assisting the indigent at Camp Nelson. General Fisk hoped to use the money to buy land for blacks and to care for the poor, aged, orphans, and black soldiers. In some areas of Kentucky the quartermaster's department distributed clothes to men, leaving apparel for women and children in short supply. The Friends Association filled the gap on several occasions in 1866 by contributing shirts, pants, underwear, and shoes for children and dresses and skirts for women. New York citizens, on a number of occasions, sent boxes of clothes for distribution to freedmen, and on at least one occasion a Lexington shoe merchant donated 150 pairs of shoes.[57]

While black philanthropists and their white friends eased the plight of small numbers of freedmen, the Freedmen's Bureau provided most of the humanitarian relief for black Kentuckians. This aid came primarily in the forms of food, clothing, fuel, and health care. Yet, the Freedmen's Bureau, lacking money, manpower, and vision at all levels, never intended to be the sole supplier of relief for poor, sick, indigent blacks. Indeed, bureau officials urged former slaveowners to keep freedmen, especially the aged, on their farms and to provide for their needs there. They also appealed to the charity of "humane white people" to assist freedmen and urged local and state government officials to appropriate relief funds. And finally, these officials constantly called upon the already beleaguered black population to do more to ease the suffering of their own people. The failure of white Kentuckians to accept responsibility for the human needs of freedmen led to the bureau's humanitarian intervention in the Commonwealth.[58]

Preventing starvation among Kentucky freedmen was the most immediate problem the bureau faced. In 1866 the government began supplying meals for needy freedmen, but from the outset it operated with a limited scope and purpose. While bureau agents realized that many freedmen were perishing from hunger, higher officials feared that free rations would destroy their initiative, making them "idle and profligate." Thus, bureau administrators decided that food could "only be issued to prevent starvation." The agency ordered a thorough investigation of each freedman requesting assistance and required that a "clerk or orderly" visit freedmen to ascertain those "worthy of aid." Furthermore, meals supplied to freedmen were not the equal in amount or in nutrition of an "army ration" issued soldiers, and those given to children and the elderly were even smaller. Always cost conscious, bureau officials carefully instructed agents on the selection of meals in order to make them "go farther." Bluntly stated, rations given to freedmen were, at best, bare subsistence.[59]

The bureau also limited its major efforts to urban areas during winter months. Most rations distributed by the bureau went to Louisville's destitute and those confined in the Refugee's and Freedmen's

Hospital. In March 1868, for instance, the government supplied 7,898 rations to 256 hospital patients and 1,058 to Louisville's indigent. The remainder of Kentucky's poor received 1,296 meals, all at a total cost of $2,074.80. These meager appropriations meant that each hospital patient received the equivalent of only one meal a day, that 353 of Louisville's indigent were fed the equivalent of three meals for one day, and that 432 people from across Kentucky got the equivalent of three meals for one day. The next month the hospital served 6,200 meals. Louisville's destitute received 600, or 27 percent of those issued in the entire state. Lexington apparently received most of the rations distributed outside Louisville. In November 1867, for instance, 480 meals went to Lexington freedmen, with the remainder going to Louisville. In early 1868 the bureau distributed about 500 rations in Lexington and 800 in Covington and Newport. Most nutrition assistance was given during 1867 and 1868 when the bureau issued 72,592 meals to patients at the Refugee's and Freedmen's Hospital, 8,569 rations to destitute blacks, and 1,174 to indigent whites, all at a total cost of $17,714.07. Soup kitchens for indigent freedmen might have eased suffering, but bureau officials repeatedly rejected the idea.[60]

Helping indigent freedmen acquire clothing and fuel to shield them from the winter's cold was another immediate goal of the bureau. Considering the suffering of freedmen and the limited funds, some agents believed that supplying the indigent with clothing and fuel was the most feasible goal. During the harsh winters of 1867 through 1869, the bureau gathered and distributed hundreds of shirts, coats, blouses, hats, hoods, and blankets. Agents also issued hundreds of pairs of shoes, trousers, hose, underwear, and stockings, and dozens of yards of flannel, linsey, and other kinds of cheap cloth. The bureau possessed only limited capital to purchase coal for destitute freedmen, a program hindered by a rise in coal prices during the winter of 1866-67. Once again the bureau made its major effort in cities and towns. In Louisville, Lexington, Lebanon, and Paducah, bureau agents purchased for distribution "limited" amounts of coal during the winter of 1867-68 and in Covington they provided freedmen with two hundred bushels. While the bureau's efforts in both clothing and fuel doubtless saved a few lives, the amount of aid was far less than the suffering required.[61]

The programs of blacks to establish medical and hospital care for freedmen immediately after the war were commendable, but failure to acquire local and state support for their projects made it imperative that the Freedmen's Bureau step in. As in other programs, however, the bureau's medical efforts were little more than an afterthought.

Medical care was slow in arriving, of short duration, and limited to urban areas. Probably no more than five bureau dispensaries—a medical doctor's office with attached druggist facilities—operated within the Commonwealth at any one time between 1866 and 1869. Though the bureau termed any facility with a bed and attending physician a "hospital," in fact Kentucky freedmen had only one hospital, the Refugee's and Freedmen's Hospital which operated in Louisville from July 1866 until about August 1868. Finally, bureau policy allowed treatment of only the truly indigent, and those deemed unlikely to survive were not admitted.[62]

The bureau's first medical assistance program began in January 1866 when a dispensary for freedmen opened in Louisville at the corner of Center and Green streets. The staff physician, Dr. John A. Octerlony, received patients for three hours during the day and made house calls throughout the black community. All freedmen received free vaccinations. The dispensary charged fifty cents for an office visit and medicine, seventy-five cents for a house call, and four dollars to deliver a baby, but few actually paid the fees. Dr. Octerlony, well respected in the black community, treated 2,405 freedmen during his first five months. At the end of June 1866 the bureau transferred Octerlony to the New Refugee's and Freedmen's Hospital at Fifteenth and Broadway streets. The bureau abandoned the dispensary and turned it over to former Confederate army physicians, whom blacks distrusted, and it soon closed. The bureau opened another dispensary on Third Street between Walnut and Chestnut in August 1866. In 1868 bureau officials divided the city into three districts, with the Third Street location serving central Louisville, an East Market Street dispensary for the eastern section, and a dispensary at the Home for the Destitute in the western district. Physicians at these dispensaries treated hundreds of patients and gave out drugs, but within three months they were all closed.[63]

By late 1866 bureau dispensaries operated in several other cities. At Covington the physician saw only twenty-two patients the first month and dispensed no drugs, but once freedmen learned of its existence, they found the doctor, J.G. Temple, to be a good "friend and advisor" and began using his services. During the first six months after it opened, the Covington physician issued 493 prescriptions, but the bureau closed the facility October 15, 1868, despite Temple's warning that many women and children would suffer. Lexington's dispensary opened in December 1866. The "attentive and faithful" physician there treated more than a hundred patients monthly, but the bureau began curtailing services in July 1868 and terminated operation in October.[64]

Mt. Sterling's dispensary got off to a poor start with no patients during the first month, but in February 1867 the doctor dispensed medicine to 150 people. The number of freedmen visiting the dispensary declined sharply thereafter, as complaints grew about the doctor's hesitancy to treat blacks, and in May 1868, the government transferred the facility to Owensboro. Unfortunately for the freedmen in Owensboro, where a need for free medical service genuinely existed, the bureau discontinued the dispensary after only five and one-half months. In April 1867 the bureau hired Dr. Fred Hassig to head Paducah's dispensary. Hassig, who treated blacks in his private practice without regard to their ability to pay, served without complaint, but his alcoholism and the fact that the bureau was already curtailing medical service in a drive toward "economy" led to termination of his services after eight months. Paducah authorities initially agreed to continued medical assistance for freedmen if the bureau furnished free medicine, but the plan collapsed, leaving Hassig, and a doctor still under contract to the bureau, to treat indigent freedmen.[65]

Louisville's Refugee's and Freedmen's Hospital at Fifteenth and Broadway was by far the most important medical facility of the bureau. As the bureau's only hospital, it served patients sent there from all parts of the state. The hospital began in July 1866 with 144 admissions, some of whom had been transferred from the failing black hospital. The number of patients increased steadily and within six months the hospital served over 200 patients a month, reaching a high of 308 in February 1868. During the period of its operation, about ten patients died each month. Between October 1867 and October 1868, the busiest time of the hospital's existence, the death rate rose to 14 percent a month.[66]

The Refugee's and Freedmen's Hospital suffered insurmountable problems from its beginning. In addition to its very limited meals, which seldom included "eggs, milk, [or] vegetables," the hospital experienced shortages of almost all necessities. Candle allowances for ten days proved insufficient to light wards for one night, and the soap supply was not enough to launder a fraction of the linen. Pilfering posed a serious problem. Patients and employees walked out with blankets, sheets, pillowcases, and other items which the hospital could not replace. Administrators also struggled with other matters, such as the housing, if not the care, of the mentally ill, as well as moral concerns about unwed pregnancies, treatment of venereal diseases, and legal problems growing out of the sale of cadavers to medical schools.[67]

Kentucky bureau officials began reducing hospital services at

Louisville in the fall of 1867, just as the period of greatest occupancy began. The number of patients declined from a high of 240 in January 1868 to a low of 104 in July, when instructions arrived to admit no more patients. Aware of the continuing need for a hospital for freedmen, bureau officials began unilateral negotiations with city officials, hoping they would assume operation of the Refugee's and Freedmen's Hospital. On several occasions the bureau offered the hospital and all medical stores, valued at $6,208.30, to the city without charge. The mayor and aldermen responded evasively to each offer, but they clearly did not want to fund a hospital for blacks. When no decision had been made by December 10, 1868, the government sold the property. The seventy patients still in the hospital remained until April 10, 1869, when they were transferred to Taylor Barracks. Twenty days later those still recuperating, along with twenty-one orphans entrained for Washington, D.C., ending all of the bureau's medical activities in Kentucky.[68]

One of the most important legacies of the bureau was its assistance programs for orphans, the handicapped, and the physically and mentally ill. With almost no state support in these areas before 1870, blacks were left to their own initiative and to the largesse of the federal government. The bureau combined a "Home for the Destitute" and an "Orphan Asylum" in a building at Fourteenth and Broadway in Louisville where they cared for orphans and those unable to provide for themselves, including the aged, the poor, and the insane. In addition to supplying food and shelter, the bureau paid the salaries of attendants. J.S. Atwell, later a famous minister at St. Stephen's Episcopal Church in Petersburg, Virginia, became the first director of the Louisville orphan asylum. The bureau assisted the orphan asylum in Lexington until it also was forced to close when local blacks proved unable to take over the institution, and the orphans were transferred to Louisville. All efforts to interest local and state officials in continuing these services after the bureau's termination failed, with the single exception of placing the insane in the segregated state asylum in 1868.[69]

Health and economic concerns were only some of the matters which placed enormous stress upon the black family. Subjected to various forms of humiliation, black fathers were frequently attacked, dragged from their beds, tortured, and their homes destroyed as other members of the family watched helplessly. The mob which entered the home of one black preacher forced him to watch as they "ravished his wife," and a Nicholas County rabble, after breaking into a man's house, repeatedly violated his wife "in his presence." A gang in the same county raped a young black girl not quite twelve years old on a "public" street, threatening to kill her "if she told."[70]

Many blacks could not unite their families, even after the Thirteenth Amendment. In early 1866 a Louisville newspaper encouraged whites not to release former slaves by treating lightly the shooting of a sheriff assisting a freedman attempting to claim his wife. Shortly after Freedmen's Bureau officials arrived in Kentucky, agents received several complaints of family members still being held as slaves. In April 1866 William H. Boyd, whose parents were deceased, called upon the bureau agent in Paducah to free his sister, twelve-year-old Ann E. Boyd, who was kept in slavery by her former owners. A month later bureau agents heard reports of freedmen held as slaves in southern Boone County, and George Givens testified in September 1866 that two Webster County whites still held his children in bondage, refusing to release them to him. The bureau agent for Trigg and Lyon counties reported that a "rebellious" element in western Kentucky continued to hold slaves in June 1866, and only the threat of court action forced a Webster County white to deliver "Mark" to his father. In a more unusual case, Mary Brown returned in late 1867 from Canada to claim two children she had left behind when she fled slavery. One daughter, Dinah, still lived as a slave in Nicholasville, and the other, Mary Jane, was being held in Fleming County. In each instance, the former slaveholders refused to give up the children, forcing the black woman to seek redress through the Freedmen's Bureau. Slavery died hard in Kentucky.[71]

Black parents also experienced disruption of the family when the county took away their children or relatives without their consent and bound them to long-term apprenticeships. Basing their decisions on the poverty or supposed moral laxity of parents or relatives, or upon the absence of a guardian, county courts used an 1866 state law to apprentice black children to whites, giving former masters preference. In the minds of most blacks and some bureau officials, apprenticeships were a subterfuge to provide whites with cheap labor by reestablishing slavery legally. Parents and relatives vigorously protested the illegal indenture of children and sought in numerous instances to recover their loved ones through the bureau and the courts. Margaret Baker, a Cincinnati freedwoman seeking custody of her nephew, was typical of relatives hoping to reunite families. "I am married and have a good home," she wrote bureau officials in Covington, "and [I] would like to have him with me. . . . Please do all in your power to get him for me and I will remember you in my prayers."[72]

Others sought family members displaced by slavery, the conflict, or postwar violence. Elisha Green searched for his young son who had disappeared during the war from his Mason County owner. Because Federal soldiers were in the area when his son disappeared, Green suspected that the lad had run away and was still alive. Green mailed letters to various ministers describing the missing child, asking them to announce his search in their churches and schools. In May 1866, Elder Ward Clay, a minister in Xenia, Ohio, located Green's son about six miles from Columbus. Clay sent the lad home by rail. Mary Stowers, an Owensboro slave, was separated from her four-year-old son, Willis, in 1846. The child had eventually been sold to an Alabama cotton farmer. After the war, Willis, who did not know of his mother's whereabouts, moved to Evansville, Indiana. In 1874 "an old woman" arrived in town and began asking about Willis. Mary eventually found her son, proving her identity by describing events that only his mother could know. Many family members sought records on sons and fathers, trying to establish whether or not they had survived the war; some thought to be dead returned to the delight of their parents. When Peter Bruner arrived in the Winchester area to visit his mother in 1866, she did not immediately recognize him, having heard he was dead. Peter did not remain in Kentucky long, but before leaving he attempted, unsuccessfully, to free a sister still held on a nearby farm. His sister later took matters into her own hands, setting fire to her belongings and fleeing to Ohio.[73]

Establishing the legality of the family unit posed very real problems for the black family in the immediate postwar years. State laws prohibiting legal marriages for blacks and mulattoes remained in effect until February 14, 1866. Then an 1866 law declared cohabitating blacks legally married and their children legitimate if they paid a fifty-cent fee and recorded with a county clerk their intention to remain husband and wife. Those paying the court clerk an additional twenty-five-cent fee received a marriage certificate. The act proclaimed future marriages of blacks and mulattoes legal if performed by a "minister in good standing" with a "recognized church of colored persons." Unfortunately, some county clerks refused to perform the services described in the law. In these instances, the Freedmen's Bureau, for slightly higher fees, issued marriage licenses and certificates. That almost-penniless blacks across Kentucky paid the fees and recorded past unions as well as new marriages indicates the importance they placed on the family unit.[74]

But during and after the war, slavery, poverty, poor housing, and violence all adversely affected marital relationships. Some freedmen, perhaps forced into an unwanted marriage by an owner before the war, saw the end of slavery as an opportunity to terminate an unfortunate relationship. Others, experiencing freedom for the first time, decided to start over in life unburdened by the responsibility of a wife, husband, or family. Still others, free after years of harsh control of their lives, lapsed into promiscuity. Bureau agent reports exaggerated the number of freedmen "taking up," or cohabitating with each other in many areas of the Commonwealth, since many blacks did not possess the wherewithal to purchase marriage certificates. Nevertheless, an alarming number of fathers, lovers, or husbands deserted their children and young mothers. Sarah Fields of Woodford County was typical. She and her husband, Jackson Fields, had one child before he joined the army and another was born after he left home. Upon his discharge, Jackson, instead of returning to his family, remained in Louisville where he married another woman. Sarah eventually found Jackson, but he refused to "recognize her as his wife," citing her unfaithfulness in his absence. Sarah sought the help of the Freedmen's Bureau in getting "her husband back to help her make a living for herself and [her] two children." The bureau ordered Jackson to pay Sarah fifty dollars, but left Sarah to fend for her children alone.[75]

A few women without public assistance or an income simply abandoned their children, hoping someone would feed them. In one instance a bureau agent found three nearly starved, abandoned children "in a Cabin in the woods in Garrard County." Other mothers, believing it impossible to feed their children, voluntarily indentured them. On occasion unemployed or irresponsible parents hired out their children and lived on the money they earned. Desperate mothers sometimes turned to prostitution to survive. Numbers of prostitutes walked city streets or occupied brothels near military bases. Some prostitutes managed to retain and care for their children but others could not. Harriet Smith stated that she turned to prostitution, under the "protection" of James Bridwell, because she was unable to feed her child after her husband, Harrison Smith, had entered the army. After the war her husband sought custody of the child through the Freedmen's Bureau, citing his wife's cohabitation with Bridwell.[76]

In spite of unfavorable conditions, the family and family values were strong enough to survive the impact of slavery, the Civil War, and its aftermath. Fathers and mothers repeatedly demonstrated a determination to acquire their freedom while simultaneously maintaining family unity. Most couples reaffirmed marriage vows made during slavery, either before county or bureau officials. Freedmen hunted for lost relatives, and parents struggled for custody of their children in an effort to preserve their family. If Louisville was typical, the vast majority of black households in 1870 and 1880 were not only headed by a male but were two-parent families. Indeed, the trend after the Civil War was toward an increasingly stronger nuclear family. The number of children living with both parents in Louisville increased from 70.8 percent in 1870 to 75.8 percent in 1880. During the same period the number of matriarchal families declined, as did the number of orphans.[77]

Blacks emerged from the Civil War into an atmosphere of confusion and uncertainty. Poverty stricken, frequently the object of harassment or violence, and without basic, state-supported human services, they suffered horribly during the immediate postwar years. Generally speaking, they believed themselves to be as capable of success as white Kentuckians, given an equal opportunity. But asking a people only recently held as slaves to begin freedom without the basic necessities of life—food, clothing, shelter, and health care—as did most former owners, the state government, and many within the federal government, was shameful and unjust. How could anyone expect black Kentuckians without boots to pull themselves up by their own bootstraps? The harsh conditions, however, did not dull the belief of blacks that freedom was better than slavery and that, given a fair chance, they would eventually progress to the point of partaking of the good life they associated with freedom. To ease their painful entry into free society, blacks organized self-help groups which brought relief to a few, but only the guidance, protection, and assistance of the Freedmen's Bureau, limited though it was, prevented starvation and death on a large scale. The black family, the rock of slave society, withstood the trials and tribulations of the immediate postwar years to become the foundation of postwar black society. And though equality still eluded them, black society could look forward to perfecting their religious institutions as they fought for a system of public education.

*Nine*

# Post-Civil War Religion, 1865-1891

THE most significant development in black religion after the Civil War was the gradual transition from racially mixed to all-black churches, especially in towns and rural areas where blacks were small in numbers. To some extent continuing membership in white congregations resulted from the lack of black church buildings, but for most worshipers, the decision not to leave white churches was an individual one. Oftentimes black Christians remained in the white-dominated churches for sentimental or emotional reasons. They associated a sanctuary with their own religious conversion, or desired to be buried beside loved ones in the "black portion" of the church graveyard. They were also reluctant to give up their status as legal members in good standing. In 1866 a white church in Franklin still had forty-six black members, and although most of them transferred to black congregations within a few years, the last black did not leave the church until 1895. In 1867, a year after the formation of a separate black church in Somerset, thirty-four blacks continued to worship with the whites, and in Lewisburg the last black member did not leave the white congregation until 1907.[1]

In a few churches where blacks remained as members, whites virtually removed them by informing them that they were not wanted. The New Salem Baptist Church in Nelson County began to discourage blacks from joining after 1880 and suggested to the few members left that they also resign. In 1892 it essentially ordered black members to leave the church. Other white churches revealed their latent hostility for black members by promptly excluding those who withdrew to prevent their return. The desire of white denominations to exclude black members became even more obvious when, shortly after the war, most gave up "evangelizing the colored people," leaving their souls to the care of black ministers.[2]

Churches continued to be the most important institution in shaping the black community, and the movement begun by religious leaders during the Civil War to establish separate churches and organizations continued at a rapid pace. Baptists, the largest and most aggressive denomination, led the way. Rev. Henry Adams, pastor of the Fifth Street Baptist Church in Louisville, called together ministers and laymen from twelve black churches in August 1865 to form the State Convention of Colored Baptists. The ministers, representing mostly central Kentucky Baptists who had separated from white churches before the war, elected Adams president. The convention framed a constitution and created committees on education, missions, and membership. Following this lead, black Baptists throughout Kentucky bolted white institutions in record numbers and formed separate congregations and regional organizations.[3]

The State Convention of Colored Baptists held three more annual meetings. The second convened in August 1866 at the Frankfort Baptist Church, where Rev. James Monroe gave the keynote address. The membership committee reported rapid growth, and a number of new churches joined the association. The black First Baptist Church in Lexington hosted the 1867 convention, and Rev. Richard Sneethen, pastor of Louisville's Green Street Baptist, delivered the opening address to an enthusiastic audience. In 1868 the convention returned to the Fifth Street church in Louisville, and it began on a positive note. Richard DeBaptist, a prominent minister in Chicago, Illinois, delivered a stirring main address and the first official census indicated a membership of 6,260, but dissension soon developed. Sneethen, feeling slighted because the organization had not selected his church for the 1868 Louisville meeting, had already withdrawn Green Street Baptist from the convention, and opposition mounted to the "Hill" location in Frankfort for the proposed Baptist college, probably because of the prohibitive cost of building a road to the site. To forestall growing dissension, the convention chose a committee to recommend a new organization. The State Convention reemerged in 1869 as the General Association of Colored Baptists.[4]

Education of ministers, more than any other issue, had dominated the four meetings of the State Convention of Colored Baptists. Even before the first meeting, Henry Adams and others decided that ministerial training was the top priority. When the convention met in August 1865, several leading Baptists who had already agreed to purchase the "Hill" property in Frankfort for two thousand dollars as the site for the college turned the project over to convention trustees. The delegates, aware that raising that sum of money from a people emerging from slavery would be a monumental task, voted to ask churches to assess each member five cents monthly. Though several churches and individuals quickly made generous donations, the delegates realized that they would need the assistance of white Baptists.

Contacts with the white Baptist association led the two state organizations to exchange observers. The first white observer attended the black convention in 1866. In turn, the black organization sent Rev. Adams to the white association meeting, beginning a dialogue between the two Baptist groups which lasted for years. At the convention in Lexington in 1867, Rev. William Pratt, a white man in whom most black ministers had confidence, promised to assist in securing white financial aid. At the 1868 convention Adams announced that he had secured from the white association promises of assistance for the education of black ministers.

The August 1869 General Association of Colored Baptists convened at the black First Baptist Church in Lexington amidst growing enthusiasm. Total membership had jumped to 12,620 as the association absorbed new churches and Baptist organizations. The delegates chose the venerable Adams as moderator and began the process of perfecting their organization. After framing and adopting a constitution, officers established a state Sunday School Board, endorsed plans for a church newspaper, and renewed their commitment to founding a college.

Following the death of Henry Adams, Rev. George W. Dupee, pastor of the Washington Street Baptist Church in Paducah, became the association's dominant leader. Elected moderator in 1871, Dupee held that position for the next eleven years. During Dupee's tenure the association grew to 239 churches and almost 42,000 members. The repeated selection of Dupee as moderator eventually led to "unrest," resulting in the election of Rev. Peter Johnson to that position in 1882. During Johnson's four years as moderator the association added 5,000 members and 48 churches. Other outstanding moderators included Rev. Daniel A. Gaddie, Rev. S.P. Young, and Rev. J.K. Polk. In 1891 the association had 346 churches and 57,285 members.[5]

In 1875 the association accomplished one of its objectives when it took over Dupee's *Baptist Herald*, which he had published in Paducah since 1873, as the denominational newspaper. A monthly, the *Baptist Herald* contained news and sermons of leading ministers from Kentucky and contiguous states. In 1879 the association changed the paper's name to the *American Baptist*. During Dupee's tenure as moderator, the association also continued its liaison with white church leaders. Representatives of white Baptists attended almost every convention, and in 1877 John G. Fee of Berea College addressed the association on the subject of education. Surprisingly, the General

Association made little use of Berea College for training ministers, probably because of its interdenominational orientation, preferring instead to send students to Roger Williams University in Nashville, Tennessee.[6]

During the 1870s under Dupee's leadership, the General Association of Colored Baptists achieved, after initial failure, its major goal of establishing a college. At the first meeting of the association, delegates voted, by a slim majority of one, to build their college in Louisville. In November 1874 Elder A. Barry opened a "temporary" theological school in the Olivet Baptist Church located at West and Walnut streets in Louisville. Poorly funded and attended, the theological school enrolled only eighteen students and lasted but five months. Upon its failure, the General Association and its affiliated churches reverted to sending ministerial students to Roger Williams University.[7]

In the late 1870s with H.C. Marrs as the catalyst, a series of events culminated in the founding of Baptist Normal and Theological Institute in Louisville. In May 1878 Marrs, a layman from the Central Baptist Association, appeared before the General Association seeking endorsement as a fund raiser for the proposed college. In that capacity he persuaded the white Baptist association to lend support and shortly thereafter contributions from several northern philanthropic and religious organizations began to arrive. By the time the institute opened, black Baptists had raised $1,800.[8]

In 1879 the General Association sold the "Hill" site in Frankfort, retrieving its investment, and purchased the "Zane" property in Louisville for $13,800, paying $300 down toward a ten-year note. The fenced lot of about two and one-half acres consisted of one square block between Kentucky and Zane streets and Seventh and Eighth streets. A large brick house suitable for use as a college occupied the center of the property. A "second," or main floor, consisting of four large rooms and three small ones separated by a wide hall stood above an eight-room basement. The third floor contained six rooms and the fourth consisted of one large room suitable for chapel services. The association later had the roof raised, adding eight much-needed rooms.[9]

Everything seemed to be in place, but association leaders, gripped by indecision, failed to act. At that point H.C. Marrs again seized the initiative. Summoning his brother, Elijah P. Marrs, a grade-school teacher in Shelbyville, to assist him, the two men won the support of the school's board of trustees and the General Association for their plan to open the Baptist Normal and Theological Institute. Under the agreement Elijah P. Marrs would hire teachers and serve as manager. The institute, with Professor W.R. Davis as principal and Gertie Hutchinson as a teacher, opened inauspiciously on November 24, 1879, with Elijah P. Marrs lamenting that the Baptist leaders who "should have been there were absent." Among the forty students who took classes that first term were E.J. Anderson, T.M. Faulkner, John Thompson, George Patterson, E.P. Adams, and M.P. Berry, all of whom later became well-known preachers or teachers.

Neither H.C. nor Elijah P. Marrs, both of whom realized their lack of qualifications, wanted to manage the institute once its success was assured. When Elijah P. Marrs and members of the board heard Rev. William J. Simmons's address on the importance of an educated ministry at the first closing exercises in June 1880, they had found the man to head the school. The trustees offered Simmons the position of principal, changed to president shortly thereafter, and he assumed the leadership in September 1880.[10]

Simmons had already accomplished much in his first thirty-one years. Born a slave in South Carolina, he had escaped with his mother and sisters to Philadelphia, Pennsylvania, just before the Civil War. After studying privately with an uncle, he was apprenticed to a dentist. In 1864 Simmons, only fifteen years old, joined the army and fought from Petersburg to Appomattox Court House. At the war's end he studied at Madison University in New York, eventually graduating from Howard University in 1873 with a B.A. degree. After teaching school and engaging in several economic ventures in the South, Simmons decided upon the ministry. Ordained in 1878, he answered a call a year later to the black First Baptist Church in Lexington.[11]

To a people long deprived of education, the opening of Baptist Normal and Theological Institute under its new president in the fall of 1880 occurred under "favorable circumstances." But as President Simmons surveyed the campus, his task seemed almost insurmountable. Besides the obvious need of funds, the grounds of the college, though adorned with shrubs and trees, were unkempt, the front gate had fallen down, the building was dirty, and the need for repairs was everywhere apparent. Living quarters for the president—two small rooms—were inadequate; no desks existed for the teachers; only rough benches served the students; and soot from the kerosene lamps had blackened the windowpanes.[12]

The school suffered, further, from a lack of quality. Only two teachers and probably no more than thirteen full-time students opened the fall 1880 term. Simmons had to locate additional instructors for the 111 students who enrolled before the academic year ended. Whenever possible, Simmons hired professors with college or advanced degrees, but that proved extremely difficult, especially in the early years. The school had several women teachers, usually the wives of local ministers or of male faculty. Several promising students who taught part-time while working toward degrees later joined the faculty. Professor Charles S. Dinkins, who arrived in 1880, was the only faculty member before 1884 besides Simmons who had a college degree. There was, however, a steady improvement in faculty with degrees, especially as student teachers graduated. In 1884 Simmons added William R. Granger, who possessed a bachelor's degree, and E.S. Porter, a trained physician, to the faculty. Charles H. Parrish, Sr., Charles F. Sneed, Ione E. Wood, and Mary V. Cook, all outstanding student teachers, completed B.A. programs in the late 1880s and became regular members of the faculty. By 1891 more than half of the full-time faculty held degrees. J.W. Hoffman, principal of the Normal Department, held a Ph.D., while three teachers—Charles F. Sneed, who taught mathematics and government, his wife, Lavinia B. Sneed, an English and Latin teacher, and Miss A.G. Gilbert, instructor of English and Greek—had master's degrees. R.S. Wilkinson, professor of language and political science, was the only other college graduate on the all-black faculty.[13]

The faculty suffered from poor salaries. Too often, Simmons lamented, faculty received little more than "food and clothing" for their efforts and without the funds donated by northern philanthropists and missionary societies, some might not have been paid. Because of the low pay, faculty often supplemented their salaries as ministers or writers. Despite such difficulties, there appears to have been no lack of dedication to the cause of education. Although a white visitor to the college in 1881 criticized the appearance of the grounds and the lack of faculty with baccalaureate degrees, a conversation with Elijah P. Marrs made him forget those shortcomings, and he was in awe at the dedication of Kentucky's black Baptists. The officials of the institute—board of trustees, executive board, and board of visitors—consisted of outstanding leaders of the black Baptist church and the black community, but few had a college education or special knowledge for administering an institution of higher learning. As a result, policy differences which occasionally harmed the quality and impeded the progress of the school developed.[14]

Most students arrived academically unprepared for college. The school accepted students at whatever level they found them but pushed them as far as they could go intellectually. Some took remedial work, often a single class per term, hoping for eventual entry into college classes. A few local ministers signed up for classes for self-enrichment, never expecting to compete a program. Even with low fees of about fifty dollars a term, most students were too poor to attend without also holding a job. Growth was slow. During the 1881-82 school year, ten students studied in the academic program. Ten years later the college program still enrolled only nineteen students. Though only about three students graduated from the college program each year, the total number of students taking classes grew from 192 in 1882 to 250 in 1891.[15]

Acceptance to the Baptist Normal and Theologial Institute depended more upon religious proclivities than academic achievement. The school accepted only those with "good moral character." When students were unknown to the administration, officials sometimes required "testimonials" in their behalf "from persons of good standing." Very rigid rules regulated their behavior at all times. Students must attend church, be punctual, keep themselves and their rooms clean, refrain from swearing and gambling, avoid socializing with the opposite sex, and secure the president's permission to leave town. "Verbal orders" from a person in authority were "as binding as the printed 'Rules and Regulations.' " Students were required to attend chapel services each morning as well as daily prayer meetings and occasional missionary meetings. The institute was, as the catalog stated, "no place for the lazy and indifferent."[16]

In spite of the problems, Simmons plunged diligently into the task of upgrading and diversifying the Institute's program. In 1883 he engineered a new state charter changing the school's name to State University. The College Department program placed heavy emphasis on English, literature, mathematics, Latin, Greek, history, science, and modern foreign languages. Convinced that proficiency in the "Three R's" was the greatest need of blacks, whatever their level of labor, Simmons loaded the first two years of the Normal Department program with courses in reading, writing, grammar, arithmetic, general science, and history. In the third and fourth years, students took elementary Latin and Greek, advanced science and mathematics, government, and bookkeeping. Throughout all these courses, students participated in numerous rhetorical and literary exercises, Bible classes, and vocal music programs. State University also had a two-year Theological Department with a program leading to a B.D. degree for those already possessing a college education. Based heavily on theology, church history, homiletics, and moral philosophy, the program was also open to ministers without college degrees who wanted self-improvement. For pastors unable to come to the campus, the university offered a Literary and Theological Course through extension classes. While requiring courses on theology and church history, the extension program emphasized literature. Those completing this program also received the B.D. degree.[17]

Simmons's years of dealing with pastors in outreach programs convinced him that black Baptists needed a national organization to unify, inform, and improve ministers. He believed, further, that such an organization might provide the guidance pastors needed to improve their people, since developing the intellectual, cultural, and artistic potential of blacks often began in local churches. In the mid-1880s Simmons called a meeting in St. Louis, Missouri, to organize black clergy into a nationwide denomination, and in August 1886 more than six hundred black ministers chose Simmons as president of the newly created American National Baptist Convention. State University became the center of ANBC activities, and Simmons served as president of the ministerial group until 1890.[18]

Simmons believed that black economic difficulties as mechanics and artisans resulted from lack of education. Frequently unable to read, write, or perform basic arithmetic, black skilled workers seldom became "Boss workmen," thus making the training of blacks as apprentices impossible. Like Booker T. Washington, Simmons saw the solution in an industrial education which would teach tradesmen the basic skills necessary to be successful in the arena where most blacks actually lived. By establishing an industrial department at State University, Simmons hoped to train "enlightened, educated men and women," to be "leaders" in their trades and "examples" to the black community. In programs designed to prepare the "hand as well as [the] head and heart," State University taught sewing, cooking, printing, photography, telegraphy, shoemaking, blacksmithing, drawing, masonry, and carpentry. Industrial classes, usually taught upon demand, lasted from a few weeks to six months. Some programs, such as the "cook school," consisted of no more than a few self-enrichment lessons and lectures for young women, and the blacksmith course did not require actual practical experience. The sewing class dealt mostly with hand-crafting clothes, though the catalog promised some instruction in sewing machines. According to the university's literature, the printing and telegraphy programs were among the most rigorous courses in the industrial curriculum.

Simmons was at his best when publicizing the importance of education. Each year the university gave prizes to outstanding students in a host of categories. Named after faculty, trustees, leading black Baptists, and American heroes, these awards honored outstanding students in Bible, spelling, geography, class notetaking, deportment, and overall academic achievement. For those in the industrial division, there were "certificates" for excellence in cooking, sewing, drawing, and typesetting. Simmons also publicized the university through the work of its students, sending samples of their achievements in industrial education to the "World Exposition" in New Orleans.[19]

The Baptist school also engaged in a number of religious "service" activities, all of which publicized the importance of education. For pastors in the Louisville area, the university offered special lectures featuring outstanding ministers from Kentucky and nearby states. Speeches covered a wide variety of topics, ranging from church doctrine to "How to read the Scriptures well in Public Worship." University singers and musicians regularly performed at regional black celebrations, and on one occasion Simmons sponsored a "tournament" of singers during which forty musicians performed before a crowd of two thousand people at Louisville's Liederkranz Hall. The event gained wide publicity for the college.[20]

State University could not have succeeded without the indefatigable fund-raising efforts of school officials and the financial support of black churches, the black and white communities, and northern philanthropic and missionary associations. As president, Simmons spent much of his time raising money. He traveled throughout the Commonwealth and into the North, frequently taking State's "jubilee singers" with him, thus advertising the university's music department as he sought contributions. In Louisville, State received staunch support from Fifth Street Baptist Church, which opened its sanctuary to university services and, on occasion, borrowed money to see the school through financial crises. The church's "University Society" played a dual role of increasing awareness in education while simultaneously raising money. Occasionally, Louisville's black Baptist churches united in citywide fund-raising projects for the school, and the Baptist Women's Educational Convention, organized in 1883, became a vocal advocate of State University, raising hundreds of dollars annually. The white Baptist association, especially during State's early years, donated regularly to the university, as did local white churches and religious organizations.[21]

Northern philanthropists, more than any others, sustained State University financially. Shortly after the college opened in 1880, Elijah P. Marrs appealed to northerners for support in a letter in the New York *Witness*. Readers of the *Witness* responded with desperately needed capital to assist the school through its first year. The American Baptist Home Missionary Society, which matched in 1880 the money raised by the black community the previous year, continued making large gifts critical to the college's success. The society contributed $1,500 in 1881 to pay teachers' salaries and $2,500 a year later. The amount of money donated annually by the society varied, but was never small. In 1888 the society agreed to pay off the $7,800 mortgage still owed on the property, provided the General Association retired the school's "floating debt." The association agreed, but failed to raise the money. The society generously waived the requirement and paid the loan, in addition to making a contribution of two thousand dollars. The society also helped the college with donations of equipment, and the American Baptist Women's Home Missionary Society made regular contributions toward teachers' salaries. President William J. Simmons, who tirelessly presented the needs of State University to philanthropic organizations, also obtained grants of five hundred dollars from John D. Rockefeller in 1884 and a thousand dollars from the Slater Fund in 1885.[22]

In 1890 Simmons abruptly resigned from State University to found, at the behest of influential white Louisvillians, Eckstein Norton Institute, a black school which emphasized industrial education, located at Cane Springs in Bullitt County. Charles H. Parrish, Sr., Mary V. Cook, and Ione E. Wood also resigned to join the Eckstein Norton faculty, leaving a decimated State University faculty. Within weeks after the new school opened, however, Simmons died from a heart attack. Negotiations with Professor C.S. Dinkins, then teaching in Alabama, to replace Simmons at State University failed, and the school began the 1890-91 academic year without a president. During the fall, while Charles F. Sneed served as interim president, the board of trustees chose Rev. J.H. Garnett, a principal in the Seguin, Texas, schools as the new president. A graduate of Oberlin College, Garnett had earned the B.D. degree from Baptist Union Theological Seminary in Chicago. Garrett brought with him several years' experience as a college president. Inaugurated in Fifth Street Baptist Church, Garrett served as president until 1894. Though less well known than Simmons, Garrett enjoyed success in finding degree-holding teachers to replace departed faculty, and the college experienced continued growth.[23]

Pre-Civil War independent black churches and their ministers dominated the General Association of Colored Baptists. In Louisville the great ministers from slavery days usually "died in the harness," and assistant ministers groomed for the position or preachers closely associated with the church usually replaced them. The venerated Henry Adams pastored the Fifth Street Baptist Church until his retirement in 1871. Rev. Andrew Heath, his assistant minister and "a Man of fair literary attainments," succeeded Adams and pastored the church until 1887. Heath's assistant and successor, Rev. John H. Frank, served the church as minister until the late 1930s.[24]

Richard Sneethen, the able pastor of Green Street Baptist

Church, led that congregation until his death in 1872. His successor, Rev. Daniel A. Gaddie, described as "a fine scholar" who always took a "bold stand," became one of the most controversial black ministers in Louisville. A former member, Gaddie had been ordained at Green Street in 1865, and he remained closely associated with its ministry. He pastored Green Street church until 1911. Rev. W.W. Taylor, pastor of Louisville's influential York Street Baptist Church since 1845, remained until his death in 1882. His successor, Rev. C.S. Dinkins, began the church's long association with State University faculty. Under Dinkins's leadership, the church changed its name to Calvary Baptist in 1883, and two years later Rev. Charles H. Parrish, another professor at State University, became pastor and continued well into the twentieth century.[25]

In 1880 Rev. Elijah P. Marrs, the popular co-founder of State University, became pastor of Bear Grass Baptist Church. A year later Marrs, a strong leader who possessed a better than average education, received a lifetime appointment, and he served until his death in 1910. Ex-slave Elisha Green remained a dynamic force within the Baptist churches of Maysville and Paris until he died in 1889, and Rev. Reuben Lee, a "pious and discreet" leader, served the Georgetown and Versailles churches and exerted a strong regional influence until his death in 1876. The black Baptist churches in Cynthiana and Danville had but two pastors each between the end of the Civil War and 1891, and in Richmond, the beloved Madison Campbell, who began preaching while a slave, remained in his pulpit until his death in 1903. The great revivalist and founder of churches, Rev. G.W. Dupee, pastored the Washington Street Baptist Church in Paducah from the end of the Civil War until he died in 1897. A dominant force within the General Association, Dupee reportedly baptized ten thousand converts.[26]

Freedom significantly increased the mobility of Baptist ministers. For the first time, preachers were able to leave pulpits for new churches wherever they chose. The result was a tremendously mobile black ministry that enabled the more talented pastors to move steadily up the ladder of success. The politically active Rev. Q.B. Jones, present at the creation of the General Association, accepted the call to the black First Baptist Church of Frankfort in 1864 when Rev. James Monroe moved to Lexington's First church. Several years later Rev. Robert Martin began twenty years of ministry at the Frankfort church. The Reverends George Patterson and Eugene Evans followed Martin. Frankfort's Independent or Corinthian Baptist Church, organized in 1876, claimed three of Kentucky's outstanding preachers before 1891: James H. Parrish, C.C. Stumm, and William A. Creditt.[27]

In 1875 Rev. J.F. Thomas, D.D., succeeded James Monroe at the influential First Baptist Church in Lexington. Five years later he moved to Ebenezer Baptist in Chicago. Dr. William J. Simmons followed Thomas, but left after one year for the presidency of State University in Louisville. Rev. S.P. Young succeeded Simmons and served into the twentieth century. Rev. Frederick Braxton, who pastored Lexington's Main Street Baptist Church until his death in 1876, was also the church's most famous minister, but other postwar pastors included Rev. Robert Mitchell and Rev. Eugene Evans. The great slave preacher, Rev. Nelson Loving, led State Street Baptist Church in Bowling Green until 1867. Postwar ministers such as J.F. Thomas, C.C. Stumm, and Allen Allensworth made State Street one of the most influential in the Commonwealth.[28]

Allen Allensworth proved typical of the talented, upwardly mobile, post-Civil War Baptist ministers. After achieving the rank of petty officer in the Union navy, Allensworth returned to Louisville where, following his conversion at Fifth Street Baptist Church, he worked as a sexton while taking classes at the American Missionary Association's Ely Normal School. Upon leaving Ely, Allensworth taught several years for the Freedmen's Bureau before entering Roger Williams University in Nashville to prepare for the ministry. Though he left without graduating, Allensworth experienced immediate success among Baptists. In addition to serving as the financial agent of the General Association, Allensworth pastored several churches, building a reputation for being an outstanding lecturer and "teaching" minister. He later worked as a field representative for the American Baptist Home Missionary Society, before accepting the pastorate of Union Baptist Church in Cincinnati, Ohio, where he served until appointed Chaplain to the Twenty-Fourth U.S. Colored Infantry Regiment in 1886. Allensworth, known for his humanitarian projects during the Spanish-American War, rose to the rank of lieutenant colonel before retiring in California, where he established an all-black settlement.[29]

Whether in small, poor churches in rural Kentucky, as most were, or in large, urban, influential congregations, black Baptist ministers preached a conservative theology. After the Civil War, ministers required members to legalize their marriages promptly and continued the strict policy of excluding from church services those who attended the theater, circuses, minstrel shows, and dances. Participating in games of chance, visiting houses of ill fame, or being found in a "Delicate Situation," also meant loss of membership. Ministers paternalistically extolled the virtues of good citizenship and hard work, while denouncing activities which cast a bad reflection on the entire race. Church membership required attendance at all services, including Wednesday prayer meetings and special events. It was not enough, one preacher phrased it, to preach salvation only. Christianity required a higher moral standard for life, a "transformation of character." Blacks, he continued, should "live cleaner and honester [sic] lives" as an example for all. As the twentieth century neared and older preachers lost control of the General Association, many lamented the liberalizing tendencies and growing secularism of younger ministers and Christians.[30]

If the records of Louisville's large Baptist churches are typical, blacks dug deeply into their pockets when the collection plate passed. Fifth Street and Green Street congregations contributed between two and three thousand dollars annually during the postwar era. In both churches, pastors' salaries ranged between nine and twelve hundred dollars a year, while assistant ministers made about one-third as much. Typically, these churches spent about one-half of their income in ministerial salaries. Other salaries included those of sextons, organists and their assistants, treasurers, clerks, and night watchmen. Additional expenses involved maintenance of church plants and equipment and funds for education and African missions. In the area of social programs, Fifth Street and Green Street congregations maintained "poor funds" for health care and burial of the indigent, and members of both churches sat on the boards of the Old Folks Home and the Orphan Home Society.[31]

Baptist ministers and their congregations engaged actively in community service. Church choirs frequently provided the music for dedication ceremonies for black public schools, and church sanctuaries often served as "public" auditoriums for the black community. State University used Louisville churches to inaugurate new presidents and to hold graduation services and fund-raising events featuring the school's jubilee singers. Churches also hosted benefits for black social organizations and events featuring individuals or groups with morally uplifting programs.[32]

Baptists usually preferred to avoid political involvements. Ministers often warned their members not to press for civil rights, and congregations occasionally protested vehemently when ministers publicly endorsed political candidates. One Louisville church considered preventing its minister and deacons from electioneering on pain of expulsion. Even so, individual Baptist churches used their auditoriums for educational conferences and political meetings, and in 1886 Green Street Baptist in Louisville hosted a countywide conference whose delegates petitioned the Kentucky General Assembly to enact civil rights legislation for the benefit of the Commonwealth's black population.[33]

Methodists constituted the second-largest denomination among Kentucky's blacks though they were outnumbered by Baptists, one Methodist pastor estimated, about nine to one. Unlike Baptists, black Methodists split into several branches. In 1866 the Methodist Episcopal Church, South, organized recently emancipated black preachers into the "Colored Mission District," essentially the Colored Methodist Episcopal Church, South, under the authority of a white man, and appointed the black ministers to churches throughout Kentucky. A year later Methodist officials divided the state into two districts centered around Asbury Church in Lexington and Jackson Street Methodist in Louisville, with Hanson Tolbot, a black minister, as leader. In 1868 white officials added another black administrator, H.H. Lytle, but the demand for a separate organization forced the Methodist Church in 1869 to establish an all-black "Lexington Conference" with a black bishop, Rev. Edward Thomson.[34]

Other Kentucky churches affiliated with the African Methodist Episcopal Church. Louisville's Quinn Chapel, a small Methodist congregation during slavery times, made significant gains after the Civil War, capitalizing on its "abolition" reputation. Famous for its outstanding choir under the direction of William H. Ditson, and ministers known for their intellectually stimulating sermons, Quinn Chapel provided strong leadership for the entire black community. Another well-known Louisville church, Asbury Chapel, survived antebellum court strife and post-Civil War destruction by fire, but remained a center of controversies which occasionally led to congregational splits. Though several outstanding ministers occupied its pulpit, the church never achieved its potential for influence.[35]

The African Methodist Episcopal Zion Church formed its "Kentucky Conference" in 1866 at the Center Street Church in Louisville, which had seceded from the Methodist Church, South, during the war. A number of court battles over property developed between black Methodists who wanted to remain with the southern church and those who preferred affiliation with the AME Zion Church. After a court decision in 1868 returned the Center Street Church property to the Methodist Church, South, most of the congregation left and formed the Fifteenth Street AME Zion Church. A year later some of the more prosperous members of Fifteenth Street church withdrew to establish "Curry Chapel" Zion church, pastored by Rev. E.H. Curry. Several years later this congregation purchased land on Jacob Street where it eventually built Jacob Street Tabernacle, one of the largest, most respected Zion churches in Louisville. Its choir, directed by N.R. Harper, was among the city's best.[36]

The AME Zion Church produced one of Kentucky's greatest

preachers, Rev. Alexander Walters. A native of Bardstown, Walters had attended a private school before the Civil War ended. Sent to Louisville in 1868 to continue his education, the serious-minded Walters studied for four years and graduated valedictorian of his class. Converted at the age of twelve, Walters acquired his license to preach in 1877 while living in Indiana. He joined the Kentucky Conference a year later and received an appointment to the Corydon Circuit, teaching in the local black school to augment his income. In 1881 the bishop assigned Walters to the Cloverport Circuit where he established five churches among black Methodists. Again Walters supplemented his income by teaching in the black school, where he had a profound influence on the youthful Joseph Cotter, later Kentucky's best known black poet. When the Fifteenth Street congregation in Louisville abandoned its building in 1881 for a beautiful new edifice on Twelfth Street, Walters became pastor of a remnant group of about twenty-five which refused to leave the old sanctuary. Walters's meteoric rise in the AME Zion Church began when he left Fifteenth Street to pastor a congregation in San Francisco, California. His success in erecting an eighty-thousand-dollar sanctuary in that city resulted in appointments to several important positions in the denominational hierarchy before he was elected bishop in 1892 at the age of thirty-four.[37]

The factionalism of black Methodists did not prevent establishment of a number of thriving, prosperous churches throughout the Commonwealth following the Civil War. The construction of houses of worship was testimony to their stewardship. By 1871 black Methodists in Cynthiana possessed a parsonage and a five-hundred-seat brick sanctuary valued at six thousand dollars, and Wesley Chapel congregation in Georgetown built a five-thousand-dollar brick house of worship shortly thereafter. Third Street AME Church in Owensboro erected a large auditorium in 1873 at the cost of sixteen thousand dollars, and observers of Freeman's Chapel Methodist Church in Hopkinsville, completed in 1880, labeled it one of the most beautiful in the town.[38]

While the Methodist Church remained after emancipation an old-fashioned, revivalistic denomination with a strong emphasis on personal salvation, it did not neglect the social and political problems facing the black community. Churches in Louisville supported the orphanage and Old Folks Home, and their sanctuaries served as community auditoriums. Quinn Chapel hosted the state black teachers' convention in 1870, and was also the scene of several meetings protesting the absence of impartiality for blacks in Kentucky courts. Several Quinn Chapel members played prominent roles in the streetcar segregation demonstrations of 1870, and Rev. J.C. Waters, Asbury Chapel's pastor, led several protest rallies at his church.[39]

Other denominations followed Baptists and Methodists in establishing separate churches, though black congregations usually remained within the white organizational structure. The first efforts of Presbyterians came in the form of educational assistance for training black ministers. There were apparently no separate Presbyterian churches for blacks until the late 1870s. In 1868 black Cumberland Presbyterians met in convention at Henderson, where they began their own ecclesiastical organization, though they possessed no separate houses of worship. From this small beginning, black Cumberland Presbyterians in 1874 finally organized a separate General Assembly. Blacks persistently sought help and advice from the white association, sending delegations to their synod meetings for years. Concerned about educational opportunities for their ministerial students, black Cumberland Presbyterians requested assistance for their "poor young preachers" on several occasions. Finally, in the early 1880s, black Cumberland Presbyterians, with the support of whites, opened the Bowling Green Institute to educate blacks in general and ministers in particular. The institute enrolled about seventy-five students by the mid-1880s, but failure to prosper led to the school's removal to Springfield, Missouri, in the early 1890s.[40]

The Episcopal Church gained few followers among blacks. In 1861 an Episcopal missionary, Rev. William I. Waller, organized St. Mark's Episcopal Mission, a "separate and distinct congregation" for Louisville blacks. The congregation purchased the German Lutheran Church building on Green Street between Ninth and Tenth streets. In 1867 the parishioners became the St. Mark's Episcopal Church, Colored, under the leadership of Rev. Joseph S. Atwell. A talented preacher, Atwell quickly built a thriving church program, including a school praised by the white community, but he resigned in 1868 to pastor a church in Petersburg, Virginia, after which St. Marks ceased to exist. Several years later white Episcopalians assisted in organizing for blacks the Church of Our Merciful Savior on Madison Street between Ninth and Tenth streets. Though small, the church was influential in the black community into the twentieth century.[41]

Black Disciples of Christ churches owed much to the support of Rev. W.H. Hopson, pastor of the white church in Louisville. After the Civil War Hopson worked with blacks in organizing and building a strong church in Louisville, which was pastored in the 1870s by Rev. J.D. Smith. Acutely aware of the need for an educated ministry throughout the South, the white minister, with the aid of the Missionary Board in Indianapolis, spearheaded the founding of Louisville Bible School. Located on Seventh Street, the school opened in 1873 with about twenty-one in attendance. Students arriving in Louisville in the early, difficult years of the school were fortunate to have Smith and Hopson as teachers. Working together, these men helped ministerial students find boarding homes and part-time employment. Graduates from Louisville Bible School soon filled Disciples pulpits in Carlisle, Millersburg, Paris, Louisville, and Mt. Sterling, as well as several midwestern cities.[42]

In 1884 black entrepreneur Preston Taylor, apparently with the support of other black leaders, moved the Louisville Bible School to New Castle in Henry County, renaming it Christian Bible College. Taylor had worked as a stone cutter, railway porter, and contractor before entering the ministry. After studying at the Louisville Bible School, Taylor became a successful minister in Mt. Sterling, building the largest Disciples of Christ church in the Commonwealth. The new Bible college, originally valued at eighteen thousand dollars, with facilities for 150 boarding students located on seven acres of property, struggled for several years under the leadership of its president and professor of Biblical literature, T. Augustus Reid. Benefit concerts in Louisville by the Grand Encore Concert Troupe in 1886, and by the Excelsior Jubilee Singers in 1887, both Nashville groups, failed to save the beleaguered school, and it closed in 1892. That same year, the Disciples reopened the Louisville Bible School.[43]

The small number of black Catholics in Kentucky continued to worship in white churches in rural areas such as Nelson, Washington, and Marion counties. In Louisville in 1868 Father J. Lancaster Spalding began holding separate services for blacks in the basement of the Cathedral of the Assumption. A year later about seventy-five blacks began worshiping at St. Augustine Church, built on Fourteenth Street near Broadway, the site of Civil War barracks and the hospital. Spalding served the church until 1873, followed by several Cathedral assistants. A Josephite, Father John White, served as priest from 1885 until 1893. During the early years several prominent Baptists, including W.H. Gibson, Sr., and Mary V. Smith, served as choir directors. St. Augustine maintained small assistance programs for indigent and elderly members.[44]

Kentucky also possessed a small but dedicated movement of independent black churches following the Civil War. These churches, congregational in polity, grew out of the general activities of the American Missionary Association in Kentucky and from the specific efforts of John G. Fee at Camp Nelson. While preaching among refugees and soldiers at Camp Nelson, Fee met Gabriel Burdett, a thirty-four-year-old slave from Garrard County. Burdett, who strongly denounced his home church for sanctioning slavery in 1862, fled to Camp Nelson to join the army two years later. There he quickly impressed the white missionaries as "a noble and extraordinary man" who worked tirelessly for the salvation and survival of black refugees.[45]

While still a soldier, Burdett, with Fee's assistance, acquired an AMA commission, beginning a special relationship between them that lasted twelve years. Burdett evangelized and taught school until unexpectedly transferred by the Union army to Nashville, Tennessee, in May 1865, and later to Texas. Returning to Kentucky in September 1866, Burdett contemplated becoming an evangelist, but changed his mind when given a home and three acres of land at Camp Nelson. The Camp Nelson "Church of Christ" with its one hundred worshipers became the center of Burdett's religious activities in March 1867 when he assumed its pastorate.[46]

Over the next ten years Burdett served as minister of the Camp Nelson church and regional revivalist with most of his salary coming from the AMA. Believing that the "chains of Slavery" could never truly be broken until blacks left white-controlled churches, Burdett founded separate congregational churches, usually with associated schools, in the counties around Camp Nelson. To fill these new pulpits, Burdett, during his evangelizing, recruited talented black preachers and young men interested in studying for the ministry. As he passed through the countryside "gathering souls," Burdett found whites increasingly receptive to him personally and to his religious message. In his former home, Garrard County, where he was well received, he organized several churches. In addition to attending his revivals, whites occasionally invited Burdett to speak to their congregations, and several counties offered their courthouses to the evangelist for religious services. A man of considerable organizational ability, Burdett soon formed an "association" of anti-caste, black churches in central Kentucky.[47]

Burdett's years of service at Camp Nelson were not without difficulties. From the beginning the established denominations opposed his efforts to create separate black congregations, resulting occasionally in bitter religious disputes. More pressing, however, were his personal financial problems. For years Burdett had to support not only a wife and children but also his sister-in-law and her nine children. His pay from the AMA was both irregular and inadequate for his needs. Remuneration from his church, whose members were also poor, was a pittance, and his employed children earned negligible amounts. Yet Burdett agreed to provide the local school teacher with board at no charge when the revenue from student tuition failed to pay his salary, and could not resist contributing to the AMA when special needs arose. And when he took time off from his religious work for political activities, Burdett scrupulously refused his salary, though members of his family were sometimes without adequate clothing. All the while he lamented that he was short of fuel and late in paying his grocery bill. When the AMA, on one occasion, fell behind in his salary and asked him to live off his savings, Burdett's reply was typical of the freedman's dilemma. "I have been a slave all my life," he stated, "and I have no savings."[48]

After Burdett moved his family to Kansas in 1877, the AMA continued its work. The small Plymouth Congregational Church in Louisville prospered through the 1880s. After moving into a new building, Plymouth evolved during the early 1890s into one of the most influential religious institutions within the black community. But AMA support of black ministers steadily declined as its emphasis shifted to education. Many of the independent congregations, like the Camp Nelson Church of Christ, did not prosper in the 1880s. The Camp Nelson Church was without a pastor in 1881 and again in 1890. Shortly thereafter, the church's trustees asked the Disciples of Christ to assume control of the institution, an offer they declined.[49]

Still, across Kentucky, the church remained, next to the family, the most important institution in the lives of blacks during the postwar years. Most black church members quickly decided to establish separate congregations and though prosperity sometimes eluded them, churches represented for blacks the one sphere of their lives where they successfully controlled their own institutions. Whether as a hiding place during racial aberrations or as a meeting place for those agitating for public schools, state-supported social programs, or political rights, churches were the center of black life. With the new opportunities freedom afforded, church leaders took up new causes. Every denomination preferred an educated ministry and most made strides in education, but the Baptists led the way by founding State University. In an effort to solve some of the problems posed by the poverty which gripped the black community, churches also expanded their social activities. In doing so, they became even more the center of black activity.

*Ten*

# Post-Civil War Education, 1865-1891

AS the Civil War drew to a close, Kentucky blacks expressed a strong desire for a system of public education. "The Colored people are Sending for us from Every Direction," a black federal official wrote in January 1865; "they want Schools Started." In Maysville, a "deep interest in the education of their children" led freedmen to open a school even before the war's end, and missionaries at Camp Nelson reported that refugees were daily "calling for instruction." Louisville mothers began raising money in early 1865 as black leaders held strategy meetings on procedure for establishing a school system, and in January 1866 prominent Louisville blacks petitioned the Kentucky legislature for public schools "controlled by the colored people." In Lexington parents held public meetings in the black community to discuss the possibility of free public schools for their children. At the end of 1866 newly arriving Freedmen's Bureau officials to their amazement found an almost universal "disposition among the Freedmen to Educate their children."[1]

Teachers and missionaries with experience in instructing Kentucky blacks were confident of their potential for education. One teacher, after visiting a refugee school at Camp Nelson in 1864, wrote that he had "never seen more rapid progress" among pupils, and Rev. John G. Fee described Kentucky's blacks as "among the brightest and best" in the country, capable of the "highest development." A missionary found the children in her class "bright, animated, and intent to learn," and a young black, after teaching for a few months in a Lexington school, concluded that her pupils possessed "natural mental endowments" comparable to those "of white children." Such testimony confirmed what newly arriving bureau officials soon concluded, that the progress of children in black schools differed little from that of children in Kentucky's white schools.[2]

From the beginning, though, blacks advocating education encountered a number of obstacles. In a few cases blacks themselves were responsible for the problem. Some freedmen did not appreciate the value of education, and in a few communities leaders devoted to public schools failed to emerge because of ignorance or inertia. In rare instances mobs of blacks hostile to education closed down schools or refused to accept females as teachers. Personality conflicts also led to wrangling. Northern black ministers sometimes regarded their Kentucky counterparts as too conservative for friendly cooperation, and the issue of who was in charge repeatedly arose. A power struggle between church leaders and bureau officials in Louisville over selection of teachers, for instance, closed one school for several days, sending 125 children home until bureau representatives capitulated. Sectarian quarrels over school locations, especially between Baptists and Methodists, caused bitter controversies, and some argued about the teaching of church doctrines.[3]

A more important impediment to the development of public education for blacks was the indifference, if not hostility, of the white community. The absence of a tradition of education in Kentucky was partially responsible for the indifference, but many whites distrusted the motives of northerners who were already teaching blacks in several urban areas and were afraid that education would result in social equality, higher taxes, and the destruction of a cheap labor supply. A few cynical whites attempted to convince unlettered blacks that education would drive them "crazy." The situation was exacerbated because many prominent whites opposed black education, and because those who appreciated the necessity of educating freedmen refused to speak out publicly. In a few communities, whites prevented schools by merely refusing to sell land to blacks.[4]

As troublesome as these problems were, poverty represented the greatest obstacle to black education. Suddenly released from slavery, the vast majority of freedmen faced the difficult task of simply supporting themselves, much less supporting schools. While many were willing to sacrifice for their children's education, they also recognized the need for outside assistance. Building on the foundation of church schools established during slavery, the black community, with the aid of missionary and philanthropic associations, as well as contributions from the Freedmen's Bureau and individual whites, and belatedly, with some local and state aid, created Kentucky's post-Civil War black educational system.[5]

Several missionary and philanthropic associations launched educational endeavors among Kentucky's blacks before the Civil War ended. The most energetic, the American Missionary Association, made its greatest contributions during 1867-68. Other religious groups included the Friends Association of Pennsylvania, the Free Baptist Mission of Providence, the Protestant Episcopal Aid Society, and several independent Methodist and Baptist organizations. Among the benevolent societies involved in the education of Kentucky blacks were the Cincinnati Branch of the Western Freedmen's Aid Commission, the Northwestern Freedmen's Aid Commission of Chicago, and the National Freedmen's Relief Association. A few private individuals began schools before developing liaisons with the various agencies. These organizations engaged in a host of complementary activities. They recruited teachers, provided transportation, paid salaries, purchased land, constructed and furnished schools, and donated textbooks. Although the total contributions of these agencies are unknown, a report in 1868 placed the yearly expenditures of two societies, the AMA and WFAC, at $12,220.98, and these figures were probably representative.[6]

While the undertakings of these societies with their limited funds were admirable, they could not, in the words of a realistic bureau official, "supply a hundredth part" of black educational requirements in Kentucky. The education of children and adults and the preparation of black teachers in the Commonwealth required a mass infusion of funds. Only the state of Kentucky and the federal government could adequately fund a statewide system of public education for blacks.[7]

The Commonwealth's initial contribution to the education of freedmen was meager because legislators took the position that blacks must pull themselves up by their own bootstraps. Two laws, approved in 1866 and 1867, provided that proceeds from taxes paid by blacks be split between education and care for paupers. These measures also authorized common school trustees to create a separate educational system for blacks if so inclined. The more extensive 1867 law placed control of black school systems under county governments and allowed an expenditure of $2.50 for each pupil attending school for three months, but neither measure permitted any supervision by blacks or provided for school buildings. In 1868 the legislature gutted the earlier laws by decreeing that all paupers must be cared for from the black tax fund before monies could be spent for education.[8]

Scandal attended the supervision of the black tax fund. The fund contained $5,656.01 in March 1867, only half of which might be used to educate 41,804 eligible children. Thus, by taxing blacks, Kentucky officially raised about six cents annually per pupil, but the law was changed before the money actually reached school districts. While some money ultimately trickled down to black schools, county officials claimed that most went for paupers, leaving little or nothing for education. In addition, state education officials had difficulty ascertaining how counties actually spent the funds. The state superintendent of public instruction suspected white malfeasance in a "majority" of the counties. County officials constantly delayed dispersing education funds, and when revenues finally arrived at schools, officials received less than they expected. Further confusion arose because the law did not require that public schools be established for blacks, and no one could compel the state or the counties to disburse funds for education. When appropriations were not forthcoming, blacks felt cheated, and some understandably tried to evade taxes. In February 1871, the legislature repealed the 1867 school law, divorcing the black pauper and school funds, but essentially leaving blacks without a public school system until 1874.[9]

The Freedmen's Bureau, working with black educational leaders and mostly northern humanitarians, provided much of the initial impetus for black education in Kentucky. Unfortunately, the bureau arrived late and exited early, never meeting actual educational needs. The superintendent of bureau schools, army chaplain T.K. Noble, was not appointed until December 1866, a full year after the bureau's establishment in Kentucky. Noble scarcely took his job before the government announced plans to terminate bureau operations in Kentucky, including educational activities. Protests from dedicated bureau officials led to reconsideration of the decision, but in April 1869, Noble's job ended. The new superintendent, Benjamin P. Runkle, and his caretaker staff, presided over the dispersal of remnant funds and bureau school closings. Runkle completed his task in the summer of 1870.[10]

In spite of weaknesses and shortcomings, those who directed the bureau possessed a mission and determination to succeed. If they had been given the proper financial support and authority, they might have achieved much more. Philosophically, these men hoped to recreate in Kentucky "the common school system of the North." The freedmen's schools, they believed, should be "exponents of higher civilization, the stepping stones to *right thinking* and *right living*" as blacks struggled toward "respectability." Only education, they were convinced, would provide freedmen "*a fair chance*" in life. In working toward their goals, bureau officials were, in general, convinced that they, not the black community, should make most decisions.[11]

Upon arrival in Kentucky, bureau officials began organizing boards of trustees from among black leaders in order to achieve the goal of a board in every school district in the state. They instructed agents to determine the number of school-age pupils in their districts, ascertain the need for teachers, estimate possible local financing, and check on the availability of schoolhouses. Eventually, the bureau drew up a model contract for all communities. Three trustees, elected by local blacks, would find living facilities for teachers and pay their salaries, set and collect tuition, and finance the education of indigent children. Teachers had to file monthly progress reports with the bureau. The bureau superintendent and agents gave speeches and promoted meetings in the black community emphasizing the importance of education, worked consistently to expand the school term, and advertised for teachers. They also pressured state officials to support public schools for blacks.[12]

Though constantly short of money, the bureau made its greatest contribution to black education in Kentucky through a financial assistance program. Most of the freedmen schools charged twenty cents to $1.50 a month tuition to pay teachers, sums thousands of parents could not pay. The bureau partially solved the problem of providing education for indigent black pupils by passing out "admission" tickets, usually working through black churches. Since the bureau could not legally hire teachers, it "paid" for the tickets by renting black churches, or other buildings owned by blacks, as schoolhouses, with the understanding that the rent would be used to pay the teacher. The amount disbursed for schoolhouses usually ranged between $25 and $35 a month, but costs were considerably higher for a few of the larger schools, and yearly bureau expenditures were impressive. The bureau paid $20,496.26 rent on school buildings in 1867 and at least $11,788.56 in 1868.[13]

Other expenditures of the bureau illustrated the diversity of its financial support. The general arrangement among the agencies working in Kentucky called for the bureau to pay rent, for the benevolent societies to pay for transporting teachers to the field, and for freedmen to incur the cost of board. Where shortages existed and direct requests were made, however, the bureau on occasion contributed funds to transport and board teachers, purchase school lots, buy buildings, and complete construction of schools begun by freedmen. At other times the bureau dispersed "rent" money to help with general school expenses, made loans to schools, appropriated cash to purchase desks and other furniture, and in one instance, offered a thousand dollars to a Lexington school, provided city officials raised five thousand dollars. The largest bureau expenditures went toward building and repairing schoolhouses. Although far short of need, the expenditures were still substantial, including $18,629.18 on construction in 1867-68 and $33,150.41 in 1868-69. A September 1868 report showed an expenditure of $41,415.97 for construction of new buildings. In the last year of the bureau's operation, ending July 1870, Superintendent Runkle spent almost $49,000 on all aspects of education, the single largest yearly expenditure. Bureau officials estimated that before 1871 they provided 50 percent of the total expenditures on black schools.[14]

It is difficult to determine the exact number of black schools operating in Kentucky between the end of the Civil War and 1871. When federal officials arrived, they found schools already in session in some urban black churches and at army camps. By the spring of 1866, thirty-five black schools existed with 4,122 mostly tuition-paying pupils, taught by 58 teachers, 33 of whom were black. These schools were "sustained almost entirely" by the black community; only five received aid from benevolent societies.[15]

From that small base, the bureau, working with the black community and benevolent groups, rapidly expanded educational opportunities. In the spring of 1867, after one year of bureau activities, there were ninety-six schools, forty-three supported "entirely by the freedmen" through pupil tuition or patron subscriptions. Enrollment increased to 5,921 students taught by 122 teachers, three-fourths of whom were black. As the academic year closed in June 1868, about 8,000 students attended 172 day and six evening schools taught by 190 teachers. In 1867-68 freedmen paid $10,000 in tuition, donated more than $17,000 for teachers' salaries, and raised another $14,000 for school construction. Contributions by freedmen supported "wholly or in part" 158 schools in 1867-68. Blacks comprised 148 of the 184 teachers. Only 136 schools existed in the fall of 1868, and pupils declined to about 6,000, but the number of teachers remained constant. By December, however, schools mushroomed to 249, teachers to 268, and pupils to over 10,000. By early spring 1869 there were 267 schools—87 completely supported by freedmen—284 teachers, and almost 13,000 pupils. During the school year of 1868-69, black children paid more than $26,000 in tuition. A year later, as bureau doors closed and blacks braced against declining financial support, almost 10,500 pupils still attended 219 schools. Tuition payments declined drastically during the fall of 1869 but were the highest of any six-month period for the spring of 1870, rising to almost $17,000. Overall, Kentucky blacks contributed larger sums for education of their children than did those of any southern state except Louisiana.[16]

Teachers in freedmen schools were predominantly black, something their communities preferred. Some, who arrived from the North, had studied at Oberlin College in Ohio. A few began teaching after studying a term or two at Berea Literary Institute, but that school's major contribution lay in the future. Most were prewar freemen or former bondsmen who became literate during slavery. The quality of black schools depended upon the observer. As one bureau official phrased it, some consisted of little more than "huddling a few hundred children and adults together in some old shed or barn, or worn out Government building and calling it a school." Such characterizations were more apropos to the period immediately after the war, but criticism of "almost totally incompetent" teachers who could neither read nor write persisted. Fortunately, many of the earlier, underqualified teachers left as more competent instructors came on the scene. Some attributed the poor quality of teachers to low pay, but bureau teacher salaries, about $31 a month, one-half of which usually went for board, were actually higher than those paid at white public schools. Others, evaluating the same schools and teachers, marveled at their progress.[17]

Most freedmen schools met in black churches, usually restricted to single rooms that sometimes lacked stoves or windows. Teachers were often church pastors or their wives. Schools and attendance followed a general pattern. A small number of schools began their school year in August or September each year. After harvest and the approach of winter, the number of schools and pupils increased rapidly, peaking in November and again in March. The number of schools and attendance declined again as spring planting neared. Geared to the work season, schools began at irregular times, and some lasted no more than a month or two. Urban schools had the longest terms, and a few even continued through the summer, often staffed by students from Oberlin College and Lincoln University in Pennsylvania, or by teachers from black public schools in northern cities.[18]

Large classes predominated. Almost all the monthly reports listed more than fifty students per room, with a much smaller average attendance. A school in Smithland, for example, reported fifty enrollees, but only thirty-five attended regularly, and a Paducah school of 125 pupils had only seventy-five attending daily. A June 1867 report gave a 14 percent absentee rate, but only 66 percent, 3,928 of the 5,921 students enrolled in the state, were "always present," indicating that many students may have attended for only a few days or weeks. The number of pupils "always present" rose to 69 percent for the school year 1868-69, but declined sharply in the fall of 1869 to 44 percent. Student attendance returned to normal, 68 percent, in the spring of 1870 when 6,475 of the 9,422 enrollees were "always present." The overall average attendance at bureau schools was about

80 percent, but only a fraction of the potential students took advantage of educational opportunities. Superintendent Noble estimated in October 1868 that no more than eight thousand of the twenty thousand who attended bureau schools were present in any single month and that perhaps thirty-two thousand children received no education at all. A similar estimate in June 1869 indicated that thirty thousand pupils attended during the year, with a one-month peak of 12,702.[19]

More than half of the pupils, who ranged in age from six to seventeen, progressed into the "easy lesson" reading and spelling level, and about one-third became "advanced readers." About 40 percent studied geography and arithmetic. The number of "graded" schools fluctuated wildly, indicating a serious quality problem. There were thirty-nine graded schools in the spring of 1867 with no classes higher than the fourth grade, and just 368 students studied in the "higher branches." Though the number of "graded" schools increased to sixty-nine in June 1868, and the number of pupils in those classes grew to 481, no students progressed beyond the third grade. By the spring of 1869 "graded" schools declined to twelve, with 629 in the advanced classes. In the spring of 1870 report, there were no graded schools, although 885 pupils were enrolled in the "higher branches." Most schools lacked basic essentials such as desks, textbooks, and classroom supplies. The American Tract Society furnished many of the texts, some of which contained short biographies of well-known blacks and moralistic lessons on self-help.[20]

Despite the plethora of problems, the accomplishments of freedmen schools were impressive. Even with their shortcomings, bureau officials ranked them as one of the most successful endeavors of the Reconstruction period. And, ironically, more blacks probably attended bureau-supported schools in Kentucky in 1869 than whites attended public institutions. By 1870 about twenty-two thousand blacks between ages ten and twenty-one, roughly 30 percent, were literate; among all blacks ten or older, the figure rose to about thirty thousand.[21]

Achievements in black schools would have been even greater without hostility from the white community. Since it was virtually impossible for whites to teach in rural black schools without the support of army troops, they usually taught in the less hostile, urban areas. In the countryside white mobs broke up, bombed, and burned schools. In small towns white gangs harassed, threatened, attacked, and drove out teachers.[22]

As a result, the drive for education by Kentucky's black community began in the cities, with Louisville leading the way. The fervent interest in education during the spring of 1865 blossomed into a host of schools over the next several months, with the Fifth Street Baptist School emerging as the leading institution. At Fifth Street church-chosen trustees had enrolled 250 pupils by July, with an average daily attendance of 227. For five and one-half hours each weekday Rev. Henry Adams, one of his daughters, and a Miss Roxborough, all salaried by the church, taught reading, spelling, arithmetic, geography, and writing. In April 1865 Green Street Baptist voted to reopen its school in the church basement, to fence in a lot behind the church for a playground, and to empower trustees to hire a teacher. When a month passed without action, the church dismissed all trustees, chose a new board, and opened the school with their pastor, Richard Sneethen, as superintendent. Green Street School had 105 pupils in July 1865 with 90 attending regularly.[23]

Methodist churches eagerly joined the early struggle for public education in Louisville. Center Street School reopened before the war's end with the "highly respected" Peter Lewis as head trustee. By early summer Laura Wilson and Alice Woodson were teaching 130 pupils in the church basement. A monthly tuition of one dollar per student paid the teachers. The schoolroom, unlike many, had chalk boards, maps, and charts. A white teacher employed by the AMA joined the staff for the 1865-66 year, and enrollment soon climbed to capacity at 230. For weeks after the school opened in 1866, about forty children appeared at the door daily to inquire about vacancies. Quinn Chapel began a school in April 1865 with only forty-five students taught by J.H. Cook, an Oberlin graduate, but eighty-six were in regular attendance by midsummer. In early 1866 W.H. Gibson, Sr., returned to Louisville and resumed teaching at Quinn Chapel, making the school one of the city's best. Asbury Chapel school enrolled 111 students and regular attendance stood at ninety-seven. Ninth Street Methodist, with about sixty pupils taught by Rev. Thomas Brooks and his wife, and Jackson Street Methodist, where Henry Miller's class had forty-seven pupils, were the two smallest schools.[24]

One of the most successful Louisville schools, St. Mark's Episcopal, opened in February 1865 when Kentucky's white Bishop B.B. Smith purchased a small building and brought in D.D. Dennehy, a white Bostonian, as teacher and a young black woman as an assistant. St. Mark's soon had about forty-six day pupils and between sixty and eighty studying at night, all paying about one dollar monthly tuition. This school apparently became part of the newly created black Episcopal Church on the corner of Ninth and Green streets in early 1867. The school, located in a building behind the church, seated fifty pupils comfortably. Under the direction of the new rector of St. Mark's church, Rev. Joseph S. Atwell, the school received about nine hundred dollars per annum from the Protestant Episcopal Aid Society and $180 from the Freedmen's Bureau, with the remainder of its budget coming from pupil tuition. Atwell employed Cornelia A. Jennings, a graduate of the Philadelphia Institute, as teacher. During the next eighteen months St. Mark's School built a solid reputation as an educational institution. In late 1868, however, Atwell married Jennings and the couple moved to Virginia. The school found worthy successors in D.A. Straker, a native of Barbados, and his female assistant, but when they left after two years, the school declined.[25]

From the beginning of their work in Kentucky, educational leaders faced a dearth of qualified black teachers. Allocating a thousand dollars to train a hundred black teachers "will do vastly more towards educating the Freedmen," one bureau official commented, "than three times that sum expended in supporting northern teachers." In early 1868 they took the first step in solving the teacher shortage by establishing Ely Normal School in Louisville. Named for Major General John Ely, a strong advocate of education for blacks, the school began as a twenty-five-thousand-dollar venture of the AMA, the WFAC, and the Freedmen's Bureau. In July 1867 the AMA and WFAC jointly purchased a lot fronting one hundred feet on Broadway and 250 feet on Fourteenth Street. The bureau constructed a large, two-story building, fifty by seventy feet. The ground floor consisted of four rooms, all well-lighted and ventilated, each capable of seating seventy-five students. The second floor contained an auditorium, two recreation rooms that became part of the auditorium when sliding doors were opened, and an office for the principal and teachers.

The dedication of Ely Normal School in April 1868 was a festive affair. While the Falls City Band played, Louisville blacks gathered in the new building, eventually overflowing into the streets. The program began with music from a fifty-voice children's choir. Though black leaders were present, white ministers, bureau officials, representatives of the benevolent societies, and white politicians dominated the ceremonies. Local Unitarian and Presbyterian ministers offered prayers and Rev. T.K. Noble, bureau superintendent of education, gave the major address. Other speakers included Judge Bland Ballard, James Speed, Rev. E.W. Cravath of the AMA, Episcopal Bishop B.B. Smith, and Colonels J.S. Catlin and Benjamin P. Runkle of the bureau. The crowd of freedmen made its contribution when, upon returning "to their homes, . . . they thanked God and took fresh courage."[26]

Though founded to train teachers, Ely Normal School was little different from most schools in Louisville. The "normal department" consisted of "special instructions" for 40 of the 396 pupils. John Hamilton and O.H. Robins, both white graduates of Oberlin, were the first two principals at Ely. The school had seven teachers the first year and six the second, all but one white. Allen Allensworth was typical of normal department students. He began his first "regular" education upon entering Ely Normal. Allensworth achieved quick promotion into the normal department but left before graduation to teach in a bureau school.[27]

The Lexington black community enthusiastically supported education. Discussions regarding formation of schools began before the war ended, and by the fall of 1865 five tuition schools teaching about three hundred pupils were underway. But always more wanted to attend than could pay the tuition. Concern for the large number of poor children led to a September "mass convention" of blacks who favored the establishment of a "free school," and the black school board immediately began work on the problem.[28]

The black First Baptist Church of Lexington, pastored by Rev. James Monroe, opened a school in the fall of 1865 with a well-qualified teacher, E. Belle Mitchell, instructing twenty-seven pupils. Within days Mitchell's class increased to an average of fifty-one. The school lacked supplies, but all children had soon mastered the alphabet. By November attendance averaged sixty-nine, but only ten had reached the "First Reader" and just six were able to study "Primary Arithmetic." When cold weather approached, attendance declined as poorly clothed children stayed home. When school resumed after the Christmas recess, only thirty-five pupils returned, but the average attendance grew to fifty-seven within three weeks. By early March Mitchell had ninety-five enrolled and a regular attendance of seventy-eight, all but two of whom were between six and sixteen. Mitchell's success with her students gave her "reasonable hope" that blacks might climb out of their "untutored state." The AMA paid Mitchell's salary of twenty dollars a month and board. Other schools were located at Pleasant Green Baptist Church, Main Street Baptist Church, Asbury CME Church, and the Christian Church.[29]

After a year of fund raising by the black women of Lexington, Howard School, a free school for the poor named after Freedmen's Bureau director O.O. Howard, opened in September 1866. The school occupied a large brick building on Church Street known as "Ladies' Hall," which James Turner and other local black leaders purchased for $3,500. Howard School opened with three black teachers and five hundred enrollees. The school was able partially to furnish classrooms with chalk boards and seats with contributions from the bureau and the AMA as well as a sum of three hundred dollars from Lexington's black public school fund, but only one class had desks, and the oversize rooms needed partitioning to be functional.[30]

In October 1866 S.C. Hale, the AMA "Superintendent of Education" for Lexington, arrived and assumed direction of Howard School. Hale immediately recruited several local teachers and imported others, but the year ended with six white teachers, all northerners. By November Howard had grown to almost seven hundred pupils, but attendance declined during the winter months, only to rise again in the spring. During the 1866-67 school year, 1,121 different pupils attended Howard School, an indication of the practice of some students to move periodically among schools. The average daily attendance the first year was about 350, or approximately fifty students per class. Teachers who also taught in the evening school, which enrolled about forty-five pupils, had a staggering class load. Most children studied in the primary classes, but 207 took the intermediate course and 276 the advanced classes. In 1871 thirty-four students pursued the normal school program. About 1869 as the bureau ended its activities in Kentucky, several Lexington schools were consolidated with Howard School, which moved into a new six-thousand-dollar building on Corrall Street. The AMA remained until 1874.[31]

During the last year of the Civil War, another center of education developed at Camp Nelson in Jessamine County. In 1864 while working among black troops and refugees, John G. Fee formulated plans for the education of soldiers and their families. A soldiers' school opened in the summer of 1864 with small classes of short duration meeting in tents. Prospects appeared more promising when classes moved to a government building in August, but the school disbanded when newly arriving black soldiers occupied the structure. In early 1865 Fee conducted several regimental schools, usually at night in the barracks. By August about fifty soldiers were "under instruction," and within a few months there were more than a hundred. Fee and his missionary friends discovered a number of "young, bright" students whom they viewed as "men of promise" among Kentucky's black soldiers.[32]

In early 1865 separate schools for boys and girls opened in the Refugee Home, with interested mothers attending classes with their daughters. By late summer 1865 over four hundred women and children attended school and another 150 awaited the arrival of additional teachers. Soon more than six hundred pupils were reading from the New Testaments distributed by their twelve teachers.[33]

The most memorable event in the history of the children's school occurred in August 1865 when Fee hired E. Belle Mitchell, an eighteen-year-old black woman, as a teacher. Fee, who wanted the schools and faculty integrated, believed it was essential to have at least one black teacher to serve as a role model for the pupils. He met Mitchell during a visit to Danville and learned of her education in the public schools of Xenia, Ohio. Impressed with her credentials, Fee invited the "genteel" young lady to teach at Camp Nelson. When Mitchell arrived at Camp Nelson, she attracted little attention until she tried to eat in the dining hall. Military officers and all but two of the white teachers walked out, refusing to dine with her. Fee rejected all protests from the white teachers, but when he was absent briefly, the camp superintendent forced Mitchell to leave. She had been at Camp Nelson for only three weeks.[34]

After the government had terminated its operations at Camp Nelson, Gabriel Burdett, the missionary Abisha Scofield, and Fee's son Howard, with $1,520 from the bureau, purchased two government buildings and established Ariel Academy. One large two-story, twelve-room building served as a boarding house, and a second contained five classrooms and a chapel. An eight-hundred-dollar grant from the bureau paid for necessary improvements, and the school, though poorly furnished, opened under AMA auspices. In the fall of 1868 Isaac M. Newton and his wife joined the teacher corps at Ariel, and a year later the academy had thirty-seven pupils.[35]

Educational interest was equally keen in other central Kentucky towns and counties. By the fall of 1866 three schools, totaling 120 pupils, held sessions in Danville and Boyle County. With many still unschooled, Danville blacks met in 1868, selected trustees, and began raising money for another school. Rev. Madison Campbell helped organize a black board of trustees in Madison County, and four schools, with bureau support, soon opened. Richmond's two schools, with several teachers who had been educated in Ohio, ranked among the best in the region by 1870. In Paris a white man donated a schoolhouse, and with additional support from the bureau, four schools were soon "flourishing." The board of trustees in Cynthiana enrolled fifty-one pupils in its schools, and others opened in Grant and Gallatin counties. Freedmen in Nicholas County purchased a school building and began repairs but fell three hundred dollars short of the amount needed. They then looked to the bureau for funds to complete the renovation.[36]

Although blacks in northern and eastern counties were just as anxious for their children's education, poverty frequently prevented success. In Covington blacks chose a school board in mid-1865 and immediately began raising funds. Within a short period of time, two free schools, assisted by benevolent societies and the bureau, began operation. In Maysville freedmen supported three schools without assistance, but in Mayslick and Flemingsburg bureau capital finished school building projects begun by the black community. Two churches in Mt. Sterling raised $975 for schools and the bureau contributed an additional $450. Catlettsburg blacks possessed two schools, both underfunded. Only the efforts of the bureau and of Alexander Batts, the town's most prosperous freeman, kept one school going. At the other, W.E. Kilgore, a former black soldier, won praise from bureau officials as a dedicated teacher. Blacks in the mountain counties, whom bureau officials believed to be "some of the most intelligent and best informed" in Kentucky, received little assistance from the government, and the small number of widely scattered school-age children made it impossible for them to support their own schools.[37]

In Simpsonville the black board of trustees opened a school in September 1866 and hired Elijah P. Marrs as teacher at a salary of twenty-five dollars a month. About 125 children paid tuition of one dollar monthly, thus permitting operation without bureau assistance. Marrs later taught in similar schools under black boards of education at Newcastle and at LaGrange. Rev. Bartlett Taylor's "free" school at Shelbyville had seventy-five pupils in regular attendance. Those who were financially able paid tuition, with the bureau contributing twenty-five dollars a month to assist the poor. In Breckinridge County Marshall W. Taylor, a freeman who had gained a rudimentary education as a child before the war, taught at the "Noble School" at Hardinsburg. The bureau contributed $250 toward the school's construction and provided fifteen dollars monthly.[38]

Blacks in Daviess County were among the most energetic in western Kentucky in pursuing education for their children. Shortly after the war, the Owensboro Freedmen School Committee acquired land and began raising money through benefits. When their money ran out, the committee borrowed three hundred dollars from a white citizen, and the school opened in October 1866 with 150 children. Later, under the direction of the bureau, the community elected a board of trustees, and with four hundred dollars assistance, built the "Ely School," a large brick structure. By the fall of 1867 almost seventy pupils sat in two grades at Ely, paying a total of $33.50 tuition a month. The bureau contributed forty dollars monthly. Though racked by controversy during the fall of 1867 over the morals of their teacher, William Sykes, bureau officials were satisfied with the progress of Ely School. In 1867 Owensboro's black community made one of the first protests against Kentucky's failure to educate their children.[39]

Blacks, with the aid of the bureau, also actively engaged in the support of education in southcentral Kentucky. In most areas freedmen supplied fuel, lights, and textbooks for their schools. Cave City blacks with government supplies built a school on land donated by an educational booster, Ned Triggs. Thirty children were soon ready to pay fifty cents monthly tuition, but leaders could not locate a black teacher. Two teachers recruited by the bureau taught seventy-five pupils in a black-owned school in Glasgow. Robert Young donated the land and, with $130 from the bureau, the freedmen of Cumberland County constructed their own schoolhouse. Oberlin-educated Nathaniel Price soon taught fifty tuition-paying students. Blacks in Franklin made extensive plans for a school and raised two hundred dollars, but needed assistance from the bureau to complete the project.[40]

With support primarily from the black community, three Warren County schools opened shortly after the war. In Bowling Green a white citizen purchased a government building used as a hospital during the war and moved it to a lot donated for black education. The large school, "properly fitted" at a cost of five hundred dollars, opened in mid-1867 with two black teachers, Linton Slaughter and James B. Wallace, sent by a missionary association. Even so, these schools fared poorly the first year. One school closed in early 1868 because pupils could not pay tuition, and A.D. Jones, the black teacher in another school, resigned in the spring of 1868 after struggling through much of the school year without pay. A white teacher who arrived from Cleveland in the fall of 1868 endured threats and ostracism, surviving only with military protection. Another group of Warren County blacks established a tuition school at Drakes Creek, near Bristow Station. Three black trustees, Leroy Trigg, George W. Hackney, and Wiley Bly, all landowners, raised money for a building and brought in a white teacher, P.J. Thompson, from Ohio. The trustees agreed to pay the tuition of the poor and orphans. Twenty-one pupils entered the school, but most could not pay tuition, and the trustees quickly fell behind in paying Thompson's salary.[41]

Logan County had several schools in 1867 and 1868, none of which lasted. One 1867 report indicated that eighty pupils attended a school in a black church in Russellville, but suffered from inadequate texts and no teacher. During 1868 Laura Johnson and her mother taught a few students in a rented building. Those unable to pay tuition attended Martha Morton's school for the "poor." Rev. Thomas Penick, a vigorous advocate of education in Gordonsville, signed up sixty children for his church's school. Pupil tuition paid the teacher, and ten dollars a month from the bureau assisted indigent pupils. In Todd County Moses T. Weir taught a small tuition school at Elkton in a building rented by the bureau, and Henry Bibb instructed a class of about fifty in Allensville. Bibb's supporters purchased a lot and built a classroom which they were unable to furnish.[42]

Blacks quickly saw the need for a school in Madisonville. The first had black teachers but lasted only three months. Another opened in the summer of 1867 with Roxe Clarke as the teacher. Though unqualified, Clarke agreed to teach until a competent teacher could be found. Blacks selected their own board of education in Hopkins County, and white school officials eventually expended small amounts of money for Madisonville's black schools.[43]

Three small centers of education existed in the Jackson Purchase. Two white missionaries, supported by the NFAC, taught classes of black children in Paducah during 1865 and 1866. The school grew rapidly, reaching about 160 by the time of the pupil exhibition of January 31, 1866. One student, a teacher from Michigan reported, had "really superior ability." The ten-year-old began reading in the primer in June 1865. By exhibition time he had progressed to the fourth reader and had completed the primary geography and arithmetic books. A year later two additional schools, each with a black male teacher, opened, and bureau leaders began preparations for a large new building. Plans called for construction of a two-thousand-dollar schoolhouse, with a 250-pupil capacity on a lot donated by a white citizen. The bureau eventually invested almost three thousand dollars before completing the school in 1868. Paducah Baptists also had a tuition school of 125 students in 1868. At Columbus in 1865 four missionaries taught 115 pupils in a school sponsored by the WFAC. A year later two white missionaries, Linda and Rose Brower, began instructing about eighty pupils, including a few adults, in a schoolhouse built by the freemen. The school lasted for several years. Blacks in Hickman bought a lot and lumber to build a school, and Warren Thomas, a local black carpenter, contributed fifty dollars and agreed to superintend the project, but they ran short of funds and required two hundred dollars from the bureau to complete it. Unable to find a black teacher, the three black trustees hired an Ohio white woman as instructor.[44]

As commendable as these educational efforts were all across Kentucky, black leaders realized that support offered by the benevolent societies and the Freedmen's Bureau were only temporary. If they hoped to overcome the poverty and conquer the ignorance that engulfed them, blacks believed that they must have a state-supported system of education. As the first major statewide black convention assembled in December 1867 at the AME Church in Lexington, reports from delegates throughout the Commonwealth painted a gloomy picture of black education. Each passing month and succeeding convention witnessed declining outside support and continued opposition of state officials to an educational system for blacks. When the great "Colored Educational Convention" called by bureau chief Runkle and black educational leaders met in Louisville in July 1869, the gala atmosphere of the marching bands and colorful uniforms of local benevolent societies could not conceal the bleak future of black education in Kentucky. In his address Runkle announced that bureau support would end by the summer of 1870 and passed the educational torch to Kentucky blacks. The message was clear: blacks must assume responsibility for whatever educational progress they hoped to make.

The 250 delegates attending the 1869 convention represented the best black educational leadership in the Commonwealth. The convention chose H.J. Young of Louisville president and selected fifteen vice-presidents. Well-known participants from across the state included Allen Allensworth, George W. Dupee, John H. Jackson, A.A. Burleigh, Elijah P. and H.C. Marrs, Jordan C. Jackson, James Turner, and Daniel A. Gaddie. Having acquired at least rudimentary instruction during slavery, most delegates realized the importance of education, and they believed that a state system of black public schools was the key to achieving equality. In a spirit of good will, they called upon members of the legislature to "rise above any prejudices. . . and find it in your hearts to be just, because we are human beings, the children of a common parent, creatures of a common destiny, and should be instructed alike in all that pertains to humanity."

As part of a wide range of concerns, the convention demanded "equal taxation and equal education" for black citizens. But responding to reality and a desire to control their own affairs, they organized their own "Kentucky State Board of Education," as a prerequisite to creating a system of black schools. Delegates drafted a constitution and by-laws, authorized annual meetings, and chose William H. Gibson, Sr., and Q.B. Jones, both of Jefferson County, president and vice-president of the seven-member board. They charged the board with encouraging local school boards, creating a system of record keeping, and developing a program of teacher certification. Finally, they selected Rev. R.G. Mortimer of Louisville to head a five-man "Board of Examiners."[45]

When the 1870 convention met at Quinn Chapel in Louisville, black educational leaders were on their own. The fifty assembled delegates, some of whom were prominent in the 1869 convention, debated problems in black education but adjourned with no prospect of resolving them. During the next four years many of the schools established under the Freedmen's Bureau closed for lack of funds. Private schools relying on black congregations and benevolent societies experienced declining revenues, and many closed their doors. Public support remained sporadic and inadequate at best and nonexistent at worst, making the years from 1870 to 1874 the nadir of black education in Kentucky.[46]

The movement for publicly supported school systems for blacks began in urban areas. In Louisville initial signs of a change among white leaders occurred in March 1870 when the city adopted a new charter creating separate funds for black and white schools. The next month, in response to a petition drive spearheaded by Marshall Woodson, the city school board appointed a committee to investigate the need for black schools. The white "Committee on Colored Schools," chaired by J.D. Pope, a "champion" of black education in Louisville, recommended in September 1870 that the $3,659.32 blacks had paid in taxes between 1866 and 1870 and the $729.53 due from the state be placed in "the colored school fund," along with a city appropriation of $3,500. The committee recommended opening two schools in October, one in Fifth Street Baptist Church, a second in the Center Street Methodist Church, and selecting a site for a third school as quickly as possible. Each school should have a principal and two teachers, with monthly salaries of $40, $30, and $25 respectively. The school board concurred.

In October 1870 the board established a school at Fifth Street Baptist Church, designated No. 1, with principal Susie Adams and teachers Elvira C. Green and Ada Miller and another at Center Street Methodist, No. 2, with Lottie Adams as principal and Martha A. Morton and Julia Arthur as teachers. The board shortly designated a third at Jackson Street Methodist School, with Mrs. E. Stansberry as its principal and Mary A. Johnson and a white woman, Florence Murrow, as teachers. During the first year the three schools operated on a total budget of under a thousand dollars.[47]

In July 1871, the school board appointed a black "Board of Visitors" consisting of Horace Morris, Marshall Woodson, Jesse Merriwether, G.W. Brown, Washington Watson, A.J. Bibb, Napoleon Bonaparte, John Morris, and J.R. Riley. In view of the inadequacy of existing schools, the school board in November 1871 urged city officials to seek permission to place in their school fund all taxes paid by blacks for a period of five years. To ease their situation temporarily, the Board of Visitors recommended leasing Ely Normal School, still operated by the AMA, as a public school. Horace Morris began the negotiations between the school board and the AMA in 1871, eventually agreeing on an annual rent of $900. Though not centrally located and situated near the railroad tracks, the consolidated school began enrolling Louisville black children in September 1872. Professor Joseph M. Ferguson of Cincinnati assumed the principalship at an annual salary of five hundred dollars. Most of the teachers transferred from the church schools. The lease arrangement, unfortunately, lasted only one year, after which the building fell into disrepair.[48]

The next year, 1873, pupils entered four new schools in Louisville. Eastern School opened in a rented building (in the East End until completion of a three-story brick building) at the corner of Jackson and Breckinridge streets. The new building contained three classrooms on each of the first two floors and a chapel on the third. The well-lighted, gas-heated structure, with an office for the principal and meeting rooms for the two teachers, cost seven thousand dollars. Horace Morris gave the dedicatory address to a large group of black and white dignitaries in September 1874, and the Fifth Street Baptist Church choir provided music. Morris told his audience that blacks appreciated the progress they had made through the efforts of the white school board, but they still expected full equality in order to enjoy all rights guaranteed under the U.S. Constitution. Western School also began in a rented building while awaiting completion of a new structure on Magazine Street between Fifteenth and Sixteenth streets. The new school opened in 1875 with five teachers. Portland School rented a somewhat dilapidated building, employed one teacher, and enrolled thirty pupils. Within two months attendance jumped to more than fifty.[49]

Central School, located on the southeast corner of Sixth and Kentucky streets, was the crowning achievement of early black public education in Louisville. Erected at a cost of twenty-five thousand dollars, the three-story brick structure contained, in addition to a basement, ten recitation rooms, a large chapel, and a principal's office. The October 7, 1873, dedication ceremony was one of the grandest events ever held in the black community. In addition to leading white politicians from the city and state, dignitaries included Bishop Daniel A. Payne of the AME Church and a number of local black ministers and educational leaders. The president of the school board presented the keys to the new building to the chairman of the black board of visitors, Horace Morris, who addressed the large crowd. Morris then handed the keys to J.M. Maxwell, the school principal. Music by the Fifth Street Baptist choir opened and closed the ceremony. Maxwell, a high school graduate from Xenia, Ohio, resigned almost immediately to accept a position in Washington. Lottie Adams became acting principal, but she shortly relinquished the post to P.M. Waring. In 1875 Maxwell returned as principal to Central School and remained for more than twenty years.[50]

Louisville's public black school system increased in numbers dramatically. Central grew from 457 the first year to more than a thousand in 1874. The entire city system expanded from 712 pupils in 1870 to 1,847 by the fall of 1873, and teachers from nine to nineteen. The average teacher taught about sixty pupils in 1873.[51]

In Lexington, small amounts of tax money periodically trickled into black schools as early as 1866, but the impetus for a system of public education began in 1872 when Rev. James Turner met with the city council. Turner pleaded for aid, explaining that the black community alone could not fund teacher salaries and property mortgages. The city council responded by appropriating $750 from the white school fund to be applied to the debt on the Fourth Street School, six hundred dollars from the capitation tax, and a promise of one-half of the revenue from the 1872 railroad tax. These desperately needed appropriations funded rapid improvements in Lexington's black schools.

Pressure from black educational leaders and the newly appointed superintendent of city schools forced the city to develop a program of public education for its 1,500 school-age blacks. In a plan implemented in January 1874, the city agreed to pay the salaries of teachers at three schools if the black "Advisory Board," created at the behest of the white school board and chaired by Turner, provided the buildings and paid the costs of furnishings, heat, and school supplies. The city set principals' salaries at forty dollars a month; teachers received thirty-five dollars. Thus, in an unequal arrangement, the "Ladies' Hall" School on Church Street, Howard School on Corrall Street, and Fourth Street School became, at least partially, the public system for blacks.[52]

Little interest in public-supported schools for blacks developed in other areas of the state. An 1871 act of the legislature created public schools for Owensboro, but it specifically prohibited admission of blacks. The legislature permitted black trustees in Bowling Green to sell their building and construct a centrally located school in 1873, but provided no funds. The city of Henderson began its first tax-supported public school program for blacks in 1871 and Covington followed two years later. Among the public school systems created by the legislature, Hancock County's were the most detailed. The act delineated district lines, appointed trustees, including at least one black, and authorized the paying of teachers' salaries with tax money. Unfortunately, Hancock's black schools existed only on paper.[53]

In this difficult time for black education, some churches and communities were able to keep their schools alive into the early 1870s.

Elijah P. Marrs, who taught at LaGrange during 1871-72, was typical of the more successful teachers. When he arrived in that city with his new wife, parents of his students contributed a three-months' supply of coffee, sugar, and other foodstuffs. Marrs raised a hundred dollars toward his salary from ticket sales to his spring school exhibition. The next year Marrs taught at New Castle where he had about one hundred pupils. Once again his exhibition raised much of his salary. The young teacher spent the 1874 fall term studying at Roger Williams University in Nashville, returning in January 1875 to teach about 125 scholars at New Castle. During his years of teaching, parents sometimes paid tuition in chickens, geese, hogs, and produce from their gardens. Henry Weeden, later a chronicler of Louisville blacks, was one of several outstanding students Marrs taught in the early 1870s. After 1874 the more successful church schools usually became part of the public school system.[54]

One of the more unique private institutions that helped fill the void left by the departure of the Freedmen's Bureau was Mattie E. Anderson's Frankfort Female High School. Anderson, a white northern idealist with a strong sense of noblesse oblige, arrived in Frankfort in the fall of 1871. With six hundred dollars of her own money and without connection to any benevolent societies, Anderson purchased a schoolroom which she furnished and later enlarged as money became available. Several teachers from northern high schools, including a handful of blacks, joined Anderson during the 1870s, and Female High eventually offered primary, intermediate, and high school classes. Anderson financed Female High through a monthly tuition of one dollar, though she did not reject the indigent. Anderson's school contributed significantly to education in the Bluegrass. Her visits with parents raised educational awareness, and Female High became an important supplier of black teachers for the first public schools in Franklin, Fayette, and Woodford counties. Anderson's school continued as a private venture throughout the 1870s, and she eventually became a principal in the Frankfort black public system.[55]

Catholic schools played a small but important role in educating freedmen. The first black Catholic school began in mid-1868 when the priest at Lebanon built a schoolroom next to the church. Later in the year, Father Francis De Meulder became concerned about the education of blacks and founded St. Catherine's School in his residence in New Haven. The Sisters of Loretto supplied the teachers for both schools. St. Monica's was the first Catholic school in Bardstown, established in 1871 under the administration of the Sisters of Charity of Nazareth. The first teacher, Josie Smith, was black, as was her replacement, Mandy Hynes. Later, the Sisters of Loretto assumed teaching responsibilities. Catholics in Louisville founded St. Augustine's School in 1871, the first black school directly connected with a Catholic church. Catholics also founded schools at Springfield in 1877 and at Raywick in 1885. Catholic schools, with the exception of the one in Louisville, eventually functioned as part of the public schools after the mid-1870s.[56]

Several of the benevolent societies continued their educational activities in Kentucky during the critical period of the early 1870s. The Methodist Episcopal Church's Freedmen's Aid Society supported schools in Leitchfield, Cloverport, and Hardinsburg in 1871 and 1872, and the AMA paid teacher's salaries at schools in Lexington, Versailles, Danville, and Camp Nelson. The Camp Nelson school, Ariel Academy, under the leadership of Gabriel Burdett and Howard Fee, continued in operation into the mid-1870s. The AMA sent Enoch Seales to Camp Nelson for the 1870-71 school year. During 1871-72 an Oberlin College student, B.A. Imes, taught at Ariel with two of John Fee's sons. In 1874 a white Ohio Quaker and his wife taught at the academy.

Gabriel Burdett hoped Ariel Academy would fulfill two major needs. He wanted a quality school at Ariel—Burdett used the term "regular Academy"—for training teachers, making it a center for educating blacks. To accomplish that end, he worked to lengthen the school year from three to nine months, and by 1874 Ariel had adopted a six-month school year. Second, Burdett wanted to train teachers for schools he hoped to open in neighboring counties. By March 1873, seven students were ready to assume teaching positions, and Burdett expected to prepare ten or twelve more by the spring of 1874. Unfortunately, the decline of outside financing led to the academy's closing.[57]

In the late 1860s and 1870s, there was only one white-controlled educational institution where black Kentuckians could participate equally. While laboring at Camp Nelson, John G. Fee had perfected his idea of founding an "anti-caste," interracial, educational institution in an integrated Christian community. Fee chose Berea, a Madison County community which had been the location of his pre-Civil War school. Berea Literary Institute, which allowed admission of anyone with "good moral character," opened in January 1866 with only white students.

Shortly after the war's termination, over forty black families migrated to Berea, where they purchased land from Fee's supporters and enjoyed educational opportunities for their children. During the summer and fall of 1865, Fee recruited additional students from among the thousands of black soldiers stationed at Louisville and Camp Nelson. A.A. Burleigh, Berea's first black graduate, recalled meeting Fee during one of his recruiting trips. While awaiting discharge at Camp Nelson, Burleigh learned that someone wanted to see him at the chaplain's office. When Burleigh arrived, Fee introduced himself and asked the young sergeant his plans. Burleigh replied that he anticipated attending school in Massachusetts. Fee announced that he was recruiting "young men and women" to attend Berea Literary Institute and took a notebook from his pocket. "I have here forty-one names and yours will make the forty-second," Fee told Burleigh. "Will you come?" Burleigh replied, "Yes, sir," and Fee added his name.

In preparation for admitting the first blacks into the Institute, Rev. W.W. Wheeler and his wife, Ellen, began tutoring a small class of black pupils in early 1866. On March 6 the institute integrated when four of the tutorial class enrolled. Eighteen of the forty-three whites walked out, causing considerable excitement, but most returned shortly. Within a month Berea had eighteen black students, enrolled in literally "all grades" from primary to college.[58]

The enrollment of Berea increased to about seventy blacks as ex-soldiers began arriving in the spring of 1866. A.A. Burleigh, already literate, arrived in April and entered the "Academic" department, causing a second "exodus" of white students. Burleigh, who recalled being the only adult in the class, though not the only black, was an excellent example of the kind of student Fee attracted to Berea. Fee felt that qualified blacks should aspire to a college education. Anticipating W.E.B. DuBois's idea of the "talented tenth," he believed that men like Burleigh must provide the intellectual leadership blacks needed and that they should not be limited to vocational education. Within a short time, T.K. Noble wrote, the academic curriculum at Berea compared "favorably with the schools in the East," and in the early 1870s Berea's teachers took pride in requiring their Latin students, half of whom were black, to take the same examination as students entering Harvard University. Though Burleigh progressed rapidly, remedial work and semesters away from school earning expense money prevented his graduation until 1875, almost ten years after he began study. Burleigh was one of four graduates in the class of 1875 and the only black. Increasingly, blacks in central Kentucky, hearing of Berea, decided that if they "wished to get knowledge [,] there was the spot."[59]

Berea's leaders realized the need to be imaginative while assisting blacks in acquiring an education. Fee contacted black ministers, urging them to inform their congregations about opportunities at Berea,

Howard Hall, named in honor of General O.O. Howard, was constructed on the Berea campus in 1869 with funds provided by the Freedmen's Bureau.

*Berea College Archives*

and the school sent out its best black scholars as student recruiters. In addition to keeping costs to a minimum, Berea provided employment which allowed students to earn most of their expenses. Many male students labored clearing away the forest or on crews constructing buildings at the institute, and females worked in the kitchen and dining hall. Fee personally encouraged students to complete their education, promising everyone financial assistance when it became "really necessary." School officials contacted organizations which administered scholarship funds, worked with the Freedmen's Bureau in awarding grants, gave free tuition to all black children living in the school district, and inaugurated an endowment fund.[60]

The racial atmosphere at Berea Literary Institute was truly unique. Black students, who outnumbered whites every year but one between 1866 and 1894, occupied a position of equality in every aspect of campus society. They sat interspersed with whites in class, in chapel, and in the dining room. They were members of all college social, scholarly, and recreational organizations, holding about one-half the elected offices. In 1872 school officials essentially accepted interracial dating, a policy which remained in effect until 1892. When dissatisfied, black students felt secure enough to request changes at Berea. Frank L. Williams, an outstanding Kentucky educator, recalled instances of "racial antagonism," but believed that they occurred because some students were "very sensitive" and others occasionally exercised "poor judgment." On one occasion, A.A. Burleigh protested conditions so vehemently that the faculty charged him with "repeated insubordination, . . . insolence, . . . [and] violent and disorderly talk and conduct among the students." Alumni association president John J. Jackson objected to regulations regarding the "social privileges of the two races," probably the most racially liberal on any college campus, as too strict, and throughout the 1870s and 1880s students repeatedly decried the college's failure to promote James Hathaway to professor and to recruit additional black faculty.[61]

Blacks were an important part of Berea in other ways. Julia Britton, a pianist and vocalist, taught music for two years, 1870-72, and James Hathaway became an instructor in Latin and mathematics after graduating in 1884. Gabriel Burdett sat on Berea's board of trustees for twelve years until succeeded in 1879 by Jordan C. Jackson, a Lexington businessman and community leader, who served for sixteen years. Black ministers spoke at Berea chapel services, and commencements were thoroughly integrated affairs in which crowds of two thousand, including former Union and Confederate soldiers, gathered to hear speeches and student recitations. The program usually included regional black ministers, and Rev. William J. Simmons, president of State University in Louisville, gave frequent addresses. Other speakers included successful black educators such as Peter H. Clark, principal of Cincinnati's black high school.[62]

Thomas Burton, who went to Berea in 1881 when there were 280 black and 122 white enrollees, was probably typical of the school's early students. Converted after hearing a sermon preached by Rev. Madison Campbell, Burton, an illiterate, decided to "get an education." At age twenty-one and with $9.75 in his pocket, he walked the fifteen miles from Richmond to Berea. Burton obtained a job cooking for students who lived at Howard Hall, and the next day entered the "primary department." After attending one term, he worked all summer on a farm, returning to the "intermediate department" in the fall. Forced to leave school during the spring term, Burton went to Maysville, where he first worked as a laborer before becoming a roustabout on the river. He entered the "normal preparatory department" in the fall, but a lack of money forced him to work as a steel driver on a railroad during the spring semester. Burton eventually entered the "college preparatory department," passed Kentucky's teacher examination, and taught school before studying medicine in Indiana.[63]

One of Berea's greatest contributions came in training teachers for Kentucky's black schools. Of the first thirteen graduates, all but two of whom were men, eleven became teachers. Beginning in the early 1870s, many of Kentucky's black school teachers were Berea students who attended classes for one or two terms and then taught for the remainder of the year to pay expenses. Berea's "corps of teachers" increased each year, and when public schools finally began, Berea placed many of its most qualified students as teachers, especially in central Kentucky. During 1877-78, for instance, more than a hundred blacks who had been educated at Berea taught in the public schools, and another one hundred of those enrolled as students at Berea had already qualified to teach. Other Berea graduates became outstanding ministers, lawyers, and other professionals.[64]

During the years 1870-74, as blacks struggled almost alone to educate their children, the call for a system of public education grew stronger. In January 1873, a delegation of black educational leaders met with the superintendent of public instruction to urge support for public schools. A series of regional educational conventions in 1873 and 1874 called upon the legislature to establish equal schools for the state's blacks. By the end of 1873, black leaders made it apparent that if the legislature which assembled in February 1874 did not create a system of public schools, they intended to force the issue through state and federal courts.[65]

Blacks found an ally in some of Kentucky's superintendents of public instruction. As early as 1869 Superintendent Z.F. Smith pointed out the moral failure of the white majority to educate its black minority. "It will not exonerate us to say . . . [that failure to educate blacks] affects no one except negroes," Smith reported to the legislature in 1870, "and [that] it therefore matters little what may be the result of it. The moral quality of an action is not to be determined by the insignificance of the person or persons against whom it may be directed, but by the motives and intent of the author." Later, when blacks acquired the ballot, Superintendent H.A.M. Henderson, taking a more practical approach, reminded the legislature that democracy is based on the idea of an educated electorate, making black public schools essential. Failure to act, Henderson argued further, might prevent the Commonwealth from acquiring its share, about fifty-nine thousand dollars, of proposed federal appropriations for improvement of black public schools in the South.[66]

Responding to these pressures, the Kentucky legislature in February 1874 created a separately maintained, segregated, unequal system of black public schools. The law instructed white county school commissioners to draw educational districts and to appoint three black trustees with nominal administrative powers in each district, but it left "final" authority with county officials. The trustees were to locate schoolhouses a suitable distance from white schools, hire qualified teachers to teach six hours a day, and maintain adequate records. The standard school term lasted three months, but districts with fewer than sixty pupils might limit school to eight weeks; the law required at least one school in each county.[67]

Funding for the black system came from property taxes, the one-dollar tax on males over age twenty-one, and all fees, fines, and forfeitures assessed on the black population. Legislators, anticipating financial shortfalls in a system based solely on taxing blacks, expected additional funds from the black population and from the city, county, and federal governments. Some cities and towns supplemented state funds, but federal appropriations did not materialize and funding for black schools remained low. Between 1875 and 1882, before the equalization of school funding, the number of pupils and black school districts doubled, along with appropriations. Yet state funds for the same period averaged only forty-nine cents per pupil, with a low of thirty cents in 1876 and a high of fifty-eight cents in 1881. The black school fund totaled $18,707 in 1875, but declined to $15,180 in 1876. The fund averaged about $31,000 for the next four years before rising to $40,733 in 1881. In the last year before equalization, the fund dropped to $37,216, about one-third the amount spent for white schools.[68]

In 1875, the first year of operation, about 600 black public schools opened in ninety-three counties, instructing 18,000 pupils, slightly under one-half of the eligible children between six and sixteen. Two years later 18,107 of the 53,126 eligible students enrolled in 532 schools in 108 counties. About 13,000 pupils attended regularly. The number of children eligible for public education increased about 4,000 annually thereafter, reaching 74,432 in 1882, when 30,000 enrolled in and 20,000 regularly attended the 844 schools located in 110 counties.[69]

Equalization of the black and white school funds in 1882, to be discussed later, resulted in a significant increase in state support for the black school system [see Table 1]. State appropriations immediately rose threefold, and a total of fifty thousand dollars over the next three years. In 1889 state appropriations for the first time surpassed $2.00 per child and two years later reached $2.15. In the years after 1883, interested blacks, assisted by some city and county governments, continued raising additional monies for black public schools.[70]

Table 1

PUBLIC FUNDING OF KENTUCKY BLACK SCHOOLS 1875–1891

| Year | Pupils | School Fund | Per Child |
|---|---|---|---|
| 1875 | 37,414 | $ 18,707.00 | $0.50 |
| 1876 | 50,602 | 15,180.60 | 0.30 |
| 1877 | 53,176 | 29,219.30 | 0.55 |
| 1878 | 59,839 | 31,116.28 | 0.52 |
| 1879 | 62,973 | 31,486.50 | 0.50 |
| 1880 | 66,564 | 31,950.72 | 0.48 |
| 1881 | 70,234 | 40,733.98 | 0.58 |
| 1882 | 74,432 | 37,216.00 | 0.50 |
| 1883 | 87,640 | 113,932.00 | 1.30 |
| 1884 | 92,530 | 129,542.00 | 1.40 |
| 1885 | 97,894 | 151,735.70 | 1.55 |
| 1886 | 99,799 | 164,668.35 | 1.65 |
| 1887 | 102,754 | 169,544.10 | 1.65 |
| 1888 | 107,170 | 203,623.00 | 1.90 |
| 1889 | 109,158 | 223,773.90 | 2.05 |
| 1890 | 111,400 | 239,510.00 | 2.15 |
| 1891 | 112,818 | 253,840.50 | 2.25 |

Source: *Ky. Doc.* (1891-92), No. 34, 146.

With equalization, which included extension of the school age for blacks to twenty, a tremendous increase in eligible students and available money occurred. In 1883 about 32,000 of the 88,000 eligible black pupils enrolled, but only 22,000—one-fourth of those eligible—attended the 536 black schools regularly. The infusion of new funds and the construction of additional schoolhouses quickly improved black educational opportunities. By 1886, 41 percent of the 100,000 eligible pupils had enrolled, and regular attendance increased to 64 percent, a figure slightly higher than that of whites. In 1889 one-half of the 110,000 black school-age children enrolled and 31,000 attended regularly. The number of school buildings increased to 809. School population figures increased slightly to 113,000 in 1890-91. Just under one-half of those students enrolled in 860 schools and approximately 32,000 attended regularly.[71]

Creation of public schools and subsequent improvements in funding provided an enormous stimulus to the education of blacks in Kentucky, but equal educational opportunity remained little more than a dream. Buildings, furnishings, and other equipment were usually inadequate and frequently inferior in quality. Most county schoolhouses were frame or log buildings; brick structures were limited to the cities. In the late 1880s almost one-fifth of the public schools were actually held in black churches. The superintendent of public instruction estimated that only 57 percent of the school buildings were in good condition and that one-third should be condemned. Henry Allen Laine described the Madison County school where he eagerly sought education in 1880-81 as a leaky "old slave cabin" heated by a large fireplace. Pupils sat on split-log benches and wrote on slates. When the fire dimmed, Allen recalled, students ran into the yard and "gathered sticks" for fuel. In 1891 the total value of black school buildings across the whole state was only $295,000, and the furnishings in them were worth just $25,000.[72]

Though a few whites, usually associated with the AMA, continued teaching after the establishment of public education, most teachers were black. The law creating black public schools required teachers to pass an examination in spelling, reading, writing, and common arithmetic for certification. In the late 1880s about 71 percent of the twelve hundred black teachers held first-, second-, or third-class teaching certificates; the remainder taught without certification. Fewer than one hundred possessed normal school degrees, and approximately 13 percent had no previous teaching experience when hired. In 1891, 18 percent of the certificates held by black teachers were first-class; 50 percent were third-class. During the 1880s about 110 blacks served on examination boards, and more than 2,000 were common school trustees.[73]

Low salaries for teachers presented a major problem for black public education throughout the 1870s. In 1879 John H. Jackson, a leading educator, estimated that the annual salary of the average black teacher was about fifty dollars. Salary improvement for black teachers in the early 1880s allowed favorable comparison of their monthly remuneration with white teachers, but the short school terms made dependence upon teaching for one's livelihood impractical. The constant shortage of qualified teachers would have been more serious had not many ministers supplemented their income by teaching. During the 1880s elementary teachers earned between thirty-seven and forty-seven dollars a month. Those teaching in the few high schools made between eighty-three and ninety-five dollars monthly. Males drew higher salaries than females, and those teaching in cities and towns earned considerably more than those out in the counties.[74]

Black educational opportunities were inadequate in many ways. The school year was short, the program of study limited, and the quality of instruction low, especially in the rural areas. In the early 1880s about 85 percent of black schools had terms of sixty-six days or fewer. Henry Allen Laine recalled attending in 1879 a three-month school where *Webster's Speller* was the only text and the teacher used whatever "she could find" for instructional materials. A year later, Laine remembered, the county began its first planned program of instruction for black pupils and increased the term to five months. By the late 1880s the average term for black schools officially became six months, and in 1891 it rose to eight. Unfortunately, in more than a hundred districts the school term, in fact, remained three months. The pupil-teacher ratio throughout the period averaged about 50 to 1.[75]

Educational leaders and sympathetic whites became acutely aware of the inadequate financing of black public schools as soon as they were in operation, and they began agitation for equal funding. In 1875 Rev. E.H. Fairchild, president of Berea College, and a group of black ministers met to discuss their options. They decided upon an educational convention to protest the inadequacies of black public schools. In response to this call, delegates from across the Commonwealth gathered at the Fayette County courthouse on November 10, 1875, to develop a plan of action. In his keynote address Fairchild denounced the "wholly inadequate" public school law and laid out a set of goals. The first step, he told his audience, was for the black community to become more involved in the education of their children. It was important for individuals to "stimulate each other" by organizing educational meetings. Ministers must "present the subject . . . [of] equal school advantages" to their parishioners at every opportunity. Fairchild called upon newspapers, such as the *American*

Biracial education at Berea College, 1887.

*Citizen,* edited by Henry Scroggins of Lexington and several Berea faculty, to run editorials and articles on the problems blacks faced in obtaining an adequate education. Further, Fairchild urged the delegates themselves to petition the legislature for equal funding and facilities for black children and circulated among them a sample petition to be distributed throughout the counties. Finally, Fairchild urged white leaders to support equal school systems, pointing out the problems society faced when it failed to educate its citizens.[76]

Implementing Fairchild's proposals proved to be no small chore. While the black community possessed adequate avenues of communication through church associations, they had no single organization dedicated solely to educational improvement. That problem was largely solved when state superintendent of public instruction H.A.M. Henderson, at a meeting of black teachers in 1877, called for creation of the Colored Teachers' State Association. If his purpose in establishing the teachers' association was to ensure white control over the mounting agitation of blacks for equal education, as some believed, the effort failed. The association chose the outspoken John H. Jackson as president, and at its first meeting in August 1878 the delegates named a committee of five, with Jackson as chairman and J.M. Maxwell as its most prominent member, to draw up a memorial to the legislature setting "forth the educational wants of the colored people."[77]

The memorial committee's report, which established a reform agenda for the 1880s, dominated the proceedings at the association's 1879 meeting in Louisville. After methodically pointing out the inequities of the existing black educational system, the report called upon the legislature to: (1) fund the black and white schools equally, on a per capita basis; (2) increase school age eligibility from sixteen to twenty, as in the case of white children; and (3) establish a state-supported normal school for training black teachers. The association selected a committee, led by John H. Jackson, J.M. Maxwell, and Horace Morris, to present the memorial to the legislature. To improve chances for a hearing of their grievances, the teachers' group urged blacks throughout the Commonwealth to "hold mass meetings" in support of its program.[78]

At the next legislative session the association's memorial committee received encouragement at a meeting with the Joint Committee on Education, but the General Assembly failed to take up the matter. Subsequent teachers' conventions reaffirmed support for the memorial, promising continued agitation through petitions and mass meetings, but when the legislature had not acted by September 1881, the association decided to take the issue into the federal courts. Shortly after blacks filed a suit to force the equalization of black and white school funding and possibly to integrate the public schools, the legislature officially received the association's memorials and began consideration of a bill that called for equality in taxation, school funds, and age eligibility.

In the end, blacks successfully secured a school equalization law largely because of pressure from federal court cases. A month after the introduction of the equalization bill in the legislature an Ohio case, *U.S.* v. *Buntin*, decided in February 1882, placed the state's separate school financing system in jeopardy. As a result of a challenge to the poll tax levied on blacks but not on whites for education, which had been brought by Paducah blacks under the Fourteenth Amendment, the federal court in *Kentucky* v. *Jesse Ellis* ruled unconstitutional on April 4, 1882, the state's separate funding system. In light of these developments, the only choices open to the Kentucky legislature were to integrate the schools, close them down, or equalize funding. It chose the third option but, by requiring a referendum on the bill, attempted to make the decision appear to be that of the people, not of the general assembly. The April 24, 1882, law authorized equal funding for segregated school systems, repeal of the school capitation tax on blacks, and a small increase in the school property tax.

Black voters faced a dilemma. By voting for the referendum, they would eliminate the despised school capitation tax, but they would appear to favor segregated schools. If they opposed the bill, they would be voting against equal funding as well as segregation. If they helped to defeat the law and the state schools closed, as seemed likely, they could be blamed for destroying their own schools. The mass meetings held during the summer to discuss the issue reflected their uncertainty. More often than not, black speakers straddled the issue by simultaneously condemning segregation and praising the benefits to be derived by the black community. Ultimately, black citizens were left to their own devices, and most supported the new law.[79]

Unfortunately, the passage of the referendum in August 1882 did not prevent expenditure discrimination against blacks, since local boards of education remained in a position to manipulate funds unfairly. In fact, only the Paducah and Louisville boards of education equalized funds for the academic year 1882-83. Blacks were forced, once again, to resort to the federal courts. Owensboro, where black schools struggled under 1871 and 1880 discriminatory state laws, led the way. At a July 18, 1882, meeting, black community leaders petitioned Owensboro officials to remedy the city's unfair, unconstitutional system of taxation and distribution of school funds. When city officials did not respond to their petition, Owensboro blacks resolved at a meeting held on August 24 to enroll their children in the white schools. If refused admittance, they agreed to sue for admission to the white schools in the federal courts.

When schools opened on September 18, 1882, Edward Claybrook and several black leaders escorted three children into the Lower Ward white school. Upon being denied admittance as they anticipated, local blacks challenged in federal court the unequal distribution of Owensboro school funds, which had resulted in inferior black schools. In April 1883 the court declared that state laws which allowed municipal corporations to discriminate in the collection and distribution of funds in a manner that resulted in substandard schools for blacks were in violation of the Fourteenth Amendment. Owensboro and other municipalities grudgingly accepted the decision, although discrimination against blacks in school funding continued into the twentieth century.[80]

Upon achieving at least a limited victory in the equalization of school funding, black educational leaders turned their attention toward acquiring a normal school. The agitation of the teachers' association that began in 1878 reached a crescendo at a November 1885 statewide conference in Lexington. After formulating a list of grievances not limited to educational matters, the convention selected a committee of twenty, with William J. Simmons as chairman, to present their petition to the legislature. In January 1886 blacks from throughout the Commonwealth convened in Frankfort, and with the support of the superintendent of public instruction, presented their petition to the governor. Later, the committee of twenty, with Simmons as spokesman, presented a "strong, logical, and convincing appeal" for a normal school to the legislature's Joint Committee on Grievances and Propositions. As a result of these actions and the support they generated, the legislature created State Normal School in May 1886, appropriating seven thousand dollars for a building and pledging an annual budget of three thousand dollars. Students who qualified for admission would pay no tuition if they agreed to teach two years in the public schools for each year they attended classes.[81]

In October 1887 State Normal School opened in Frankfort on "Normal Hill." John H. Jackson, one of Berea's first black graduates, was chosen president. Early faculty included C.C. Monroe, his wife Mary B. Monroe, and Ida Joyce (who later married President Jackson). During the first three years students received instruction in teacher preparation programs at the common and high school levels. In 1890 State Normal School entered a period of rapid growth by adding departments in agriculture and mechanics in order to qualify for federal funds under the Morrill Act. C.C. Monroe became professor of agriculture, Moses A. Davis professor of mechanics, Ida Joyce instructor in the "Domestic Economy" department, and Rev. William A. Creditt joined the normal department. The first class of fifty-five students grew to seventy-seven in 1891, quickly overcrowding the five classrooms. In spite of early problems, including inadequate space, State Normal's graduates partially alleviated the shortage of black teachers.[82]

Providing pupils with a quality education became the principal challenge facing black teachers following the establishment of public schools. In the early years teacher enrichment depended largely upon individual initiative. Formation of the black teachers' association provided an opportunity to set up structured programs to achieve cultural enrichment, to improve teacher performance, and to advance the cause of public education. Starting with the first meeting, some of the better-educated members began giving lectures, delivering papers, and participating in panel discussions on subjects designed to assist inadequately prepared teachers. Topics included orthography, grammar, reading, mathematics, hygiene, the "Upgraded School," "How Best to Promote the Cause of Education," and the "Literary Culture of the Teacher." A reading circle committee helped teachers share books at a reduced cost. By the 1880s "How to teach" papers dominated the programs, but controversial topics such as compulsory education, school integration, and woman suffrage also received attention. Though women held important positions on committees, none was elected to an office until 1889.[83]

Teachers also learned new classroom techniques by attending teachers' institutes, most of which lasted for two or three days. Before the founding of State Normal School, Berea College contributed greatly to the quality of black public education by holding institutes for central Kentucky teachers. In addition to speeches by Berea faculty, black teachers presented papers or gave demonstrations on how to teach the three Rs, music, history, and other subjects. After the establishment of State Normal School, instructors from there began to conduct weekend and summer institutes throughout Kentucky. Soon communities from the Bluegrass to the Mississippi River benefitted from teachers' institutes, leading the superintendent of public instruction to announce in 1887 that black public education was "no longer an experiment." President Jackson estimated that one-fourth of the state's black teachers attended State Normal institutes during the first four years of the school's existence.[84]

Even after creation of the public school system, blacks continued to receive their best educational opportunities in urban areas. Louisville's black advisory committee presided over some seven schools that increased in enrollment between 1877 and 1891 from three thousand pupils to five thousand. During those years the average daily attendance doubled from 1,732 to 3,509, and the number of teachers increased from forty to eighty-four. The average teacher taught about forty-five pupils, but overcrowding existed everywhere. At some schools more than one hundred students jammed into a single room, forcing them to take turns sitting at the desks. The number of students attending grades one through four was small, but enrollment increased sharply in the fifth grade, reaching a peak in grade eight. In 1876 Louisville added an "A" Grade class, beginning with five superior students. The "A" class, which numbered fifteen in 1880, became part of the high school when it opened in 1882. Though unable to keep pace with the needs, the school board opened Fulton and Portland Elementary schools in the late 1870s, followed in 1882 by California Elementary on Kentucky Street and in 1884 by Main Street Elementary. Maiden Lane School began holding classes in 1890 with the controversial A.E. Meyzeek, a graduate of Indiana State Normal College, as principal.[85]

Though Louisville's black public school teachers suffered from frequent, irrational transfers, contracts with officious morality clauses, and salaries inferior to those of whites, the system nevertheless boasted a number of outstanding, dedicated instructors. J.M. Maxwell, a former Howard University student, served as principal at Central School for more than twenty years. In 1882 when Central Elementary added a three-year high school program, C.W. Houser, a graduate of Minnesota's normal school and James E. Simpson, a University of Pennsylvania graduate, joined the faculty. The curriculum included English, American literature, history, and philosophy, in addition to a rigorous program of science and Latin. William H. Perry, a native of Terre Haute, Indiana, and an early graduate of Central's "A" Grade, was principal at Eastern School for ten years before transferring to Western School. W.T. Peyton, a Cincinnati, Ohio, high school graduate, held the principalship of several schools, including Western.[86]

Louisville blacks were especially proud of their night schools. Shortly after the establishment of public schools, leaders began calling for night schools for children and adults. Many working children could not attend during daytime, a problem they shared with numerous adults who desired an education. In response to this demand, the school board opened night schools at Eastern and Western. Blacks made greatest use of night school programs in the late 1870s, when at times enrollments exceeded five hundred at each location. Visitors reported observing children in grammar school studying side-by-side with men of forty, all motivated by a desire for education. Joseph Seamon Cotter, later a recognized poet and principal of one of Louisville's elementary schools, received much of his education in night classes. By the late 1880s when strong opposition to the evening program developed on the school board, enrollments had declined. In January 1886 the school board expelled all pupils over age twenty, but immediate opposition to the action forced a compromise. Any pupil who had entered school before age twenty might remain until age twenty-five.[87]

Black schools in Lexington made less progress after the creation of the public system. Apart from the general problem of low support by the state, Lexington blacks fell into quarreling among themselves. About 1876 school officials opened a new four-room school on Patterson Street near the railroad to accommodate pupils leaving church schools. Inadequate financial support reduced the number of Lexington's black public schools to two by 1882 and led to severe overcrowding, a problem that eased slightly in 1885 when the school board constructed a new, four-room brick school. Unfortunately, improvements sometimes occurred at the expense of older schools. By the late 1870s Howard School was in dire need of repairs, partially because of the uncertain relationship between the AMA, the former proprietors, and the city. County schools were especially poor, frequently meeting in improperly heated, dilapidated buildings. As in other areas, equalization of educational funds did little to correct these problems.

Teaching in Lexington's overcrowded public schools was, as Howard School principal John H. Jackson phrased it, a "thankless mission." There was a general shortage of qualified teachers, and efforts to establish a normal program to train instructors repeatedly met with hostility from white administrators. In 1878 Jackson, on his own initiative, created an "A" Grade class with normal instruction for advanced students whom he hoped to place in teaching positions. When city officials refused to fund the program, Jackson petitioned the AMA for the needed money.[88]

Responding to Jackson's request, the AMA in 1882 resumed its educational work in Lexington, repairing and assuming control of Howard School, offering the first and second grades and a high school. When the school opened with northern white teachers, none of the students was performing below the fourth reader, but it was unable to maintain that standard for long. During the first few years, the school enrolled 140 pupils, with an average attendance of about

100. Continued growth and deterioration of the neighborhood led school officials to seek new quarters in the late 1880s. With a grant of seventeen thousand dollars from Phebe Chandler of Massachusetts, the AMA built a three-story brick structure, Chandler Normal School, about one mile from the center of Lexington. Within a year Chandler Normal encompassed grades four through twelve and established a satellite institution, Hand Primary School, for grades one through three.[89]

Outside these two urban areas, public education between 1874 and 1891 differed widely in quality. Always at the mercy of the white majority, blacks struggled to maintain whatever level their schools reached. In 1881 Bourbon County had more than a thousand children attending fifteen schools, some located in churches but taught by public school teachers. Though facilities were cramped and badly furnished and parents were too poor to improve them, black trustees carried out their duties energetically, raising what funds they could to supplement teacher salaries. In 1875 a public school, taught by the daughter of Gabriel Burdett, opened at Camp Nelson. Ariel Normal School reopened in 1882 with white teachers from the North who lived among local blacks. Ariel, which had primary and normal programs, hoped to train teachers for schools in central Kentucky. Beset by financial and internal problems from the onset, Ariel remained an important, if feeble, institution until the turn of the century. In Franklin County there were five schools, all of which were in good condition, and in Frankfort William Mayo of Cincinnati assumed the principalship of Clinton Street High School in 1882 and built a solid reputation as an educator.[90]

In 1879 blacks in Owensboro occupied a newly constructed brick school on Poplar Street where, in the first few years, three teachers taught about two hundred pupils daily. With the equalization of school finances and the subsequent increase in funding, officials acquired another building, improved the interior furnishings, and hired several teachers from Louisville and Cincinnati. A third school building constructed in the upper ward burned before it could be occupied, forcing city officials to rent the AME Church on Third Street. The percentage of eligible blacks in school grew from 20 percent in the mid-1880s to 37 percent in 1891 when the total enrollment reached 754. For unknown reasons city officials replaced black teachers with whites for a period of ten years after 1887, an issue which deeply divided the black community.[91]

Blacks in the Bowling Green area enjoyed some of the better schools. The city school, newly built at the cost of thirty thousand dollars, had four hundred pupils in 1885. The county schools, where some buildings were in poor condition, possessed better than average teachers, a factor that encouraged county blacks, eager for public education for their children, to raise money to supplement teacher salaries.[92]

In 1875 in Christian County, where the black community united behind public education, 500 pupils enrolled in five inadequately staffed schools. By the mid-1880s the county funded over twenty schools with a total of fifty black teachers, and as a result of individual and organized study, compared favorably with the white system. Henderson's black school, with John Mason and his wife Martha as teachers, added another room in 1878 and hired one of its graduates, Virgie Harris, as teacher. By 1882 the school possessed four teachers, a ten-month term, and enrolled 386 pupils. Henderson had two black schools by 1891.[93]

Upon acquiring freedom, black Kentuckians had begun an unprecedented movement for educational improvement. Quick action on the part of state government would have helped blacks take their rightful place in Kentucky society, since education could have eased their transition to freedom. Unfortunately, whites tended to look with disfavor upon educated blacks. Without state funding and beset by poverty, the only alternative open to blacks lay in creating private schools by marshalling public support within their own community, by drawing upon the resources and know-how of northern benevolent societies, and by utilizing federal support through the Freedmen's Bureau. Sadly, most of these early schools atrophied with the termination of outside funding. A publicly supported state system of education, always the goal of black leaders, became their only hope. Black movers and shakers began a prolonged period of agitation, carefully pointing out to the legislature the absence of both wisdom and fairness in their refusal to establish public education for some children because of their color. In 1874 the legislature finally established public schools for blacks, but they were segregated and poorly funded. Black leaders immediately began calling for equal funding for their schools and for a teacher training college, both of which they won in the 1880s, but with mixed results. The parsimonious legislature proved reluctant in the support of education for black children in almost every instance, a policy that tended to hold blacks in the position of an underclass, resulting in a legacy of poverty and suffering that haunts Kentucky to this day.

*Eleven*

# Labor, Living Conditions, and Recreation, 1865-1891

BLACKS faced severe economic handicaps in the years immediately following the Civil War. Those who migrated to the cities frequently found jobs scarce, competition keen, and unemployment widespread. In addition, most lacked the skills for the few jobs available. A large number faced a choice between standing idle on the streets or seeking work as strikebreakers, and either alternative provoked the white community to criticism. In the countryside where most blacks lived, the situation was equally bleak. Farmhands preferred to move away from their old "masters," but most continued to work in agriculture. Unfortunately, slaveholders, applying state laws still in force, threatened prosecution of those who hired their "slaves," thus preventing potential workers from earning a livelihood. As one black phrased it in his autobiography, "things were pretty much in chaos."[1]

The enormity of the economic problems facing black Kentuckians required bold and innovative solutions. In central Kentucky Rev. John G. Fee urged the federal government at the war's end to establish employment agencies to find jobs for blacks. The agents, Fee advised, should travel throughout the Commonwealth, ascertain locations of jobs, and help blacks relocate there. He suggested, further, that the government contact northern entrepreneurs who wanted to exploit the timber, coal, and iron deposits of the state and urge them to hire freedmen to clear the forests, saw the lumber, and work the mines. In Louisville the board of aldermen discussed an equally innovative plan calling for white mechanics and artisans to teach their trades to young blacks through apprenticeships. Unfortunately, neither plan received support.[2]

In 1869 black Civil War veterans in Lexington assumed the lead in finding work for the unemployed of that city by calling a public meeting to discuss the issue. Recognizing that many blacks were under pressure from vagrancy laws applied by the white community, black leaders urged those without jobs to enter into labor contracts with white farmers. To facilitate contract negotiations, they established an employment agency, and within a few months it had placed over three thousand workers, mostly in agricultural jobs. In 1869 blacks in Louisville, hoping to reduce unemployment, called a convention. The meeting urged blacks throughout the state to improve their economic condition by becoming artisans or agricultural workers. Blacks convening in Frankfort in 1870 tried to dispel rumors that they were undependable workers. Participants assured regional employers that, if treated fairly, they would adhere to contracts faithfully, and they denounced proposals, circulating in regional newspapers, to supplant black workers with Chinese laborers.[3]

Despite their efforts, most blacks, especially those in urban areas, had to solve the problem of employment on an individual basis. Opportunities and ingenuity were frequently the determining factors. Elisha Green, a minister with minimal education, was typical of those who gained employment as a handyman. Convinced that he must have a "trade," Green accepted whatever jobs were offered. While working for a white woman, she asked if he could whitewash. When Green admitted that he "knew nothing about whitewashing," she instructed him to buy some lime and she would explain the process. From that beginning Green developed a successful whitewashing business. He also learned how to cane chairs, a skill he later taught his children. They were soon caning chairs for fifty cents each. In time he purchased tools to repair his children's shoes. In the process he learned shoe repair, opening another new source of income. Carpenter's tools came next, and soon Green advertised himself as a "jack of all trades."[4]

Others simply found outlets in business. After returning from military service, Elijah P. Marrs and his brother H.C. formed a partnership consisting of a drayage business and a farm. Both men arose each day before dawn and tended the horses. At daylight H.C. managed two wagons, keeping them busy at eight dollars a day. Elijah tilled twenty-five acres of rented land. The brothers continued their enterprises until each had accumulated enough money to begin his education. Seventeen-year-old Joseph Cotter, a brickyard laborer, began his upward mobility when he bought a horse, paying a small amount each week from his meager wages. A deal to help cultivate an eight-acre farm in return for feed for his horse went sour, but Cotter persisted and soon owned the horse, as well as a bridle and a wagon. For the next four years Cotter toiled all day hauling goods through the streets of Louisville; after work he attended night school and eventually became a teacher.[5]

Most blacks, relegated to agricultural labor in the countryside, were less fortunate. Emerging landless from slavery, agricultural laborers suffered in the workplace from the lingering shadow of slavery, artificially depressed wages, and an unpredictable business cycle. White determination to control their labor force further complicated working conditions. An 1866 state law which restricted the witnessing of contracts to whites stipulated that a contract, to be valid, must be fulfilled in its entirety. But for some blacks, contracts which bound them for a full year's service were painfully reminiscent of slavery, and those who left "without good cause" before official termination of the agreement, even if they had worked eleven months, forfeited all wages for the time employed.[6]

Without effective bargaining power, most blacks reluctantly entered into individual labor agreements with white landowners. The appearance of the Freedmen's Bureau of Kentucky in 1866 tempered slightly the dependent position of blacks in contract negotiations. Bureau officials sought to achieve "fair and just" agreements for freedmen, but they assured white landowners of their intention to enforce the terms of contracts on both parties. Unfortunately, both the landowner and the freedmen to some extent were able to thwart these efforts because the bureau lacked both manpower and influence to regulate contract making. Whites were reluctant to enter into contracts with blacks who insisted upon registering them with the bureau. Since contracts could be agreed upon without the approval of the bureau, those blacks desperate for work usually accepted an agreement on the landowner's terms. Frequently, contracts were verbal agreements, with only white witnesses, a condition which placed an extraordinary burden on blacks who later sought to challenge the terms. In spite of a widespread myth that blacks were unwilling to work, it appears that the overwhelming majority became "self-supporting" within a year of the war's termination.[7]

Black laborers made three types of working agreements with white landowners: sharecropping, contracting for wages, and apprenticeships. The share system, though easily arranged, was more likely to result in disputes. Contracts for sharecropping generally listed the responsibilities of farmhands and described the portions of the crops they were to receive for their labor. Under a one-year contract with a Burkesville farmer, Ruben Murphy was provided a house, land for a garden, tobacco plants, and waste wood for fuel. For his part, Murphy had to repair and re-roof the tobacco house, to provide his own team and tools, and to furnish all labor for working the land. At harvest he would receive two-thirds of the corn and tobacco. Elias Alexander's agreement required the services of his entire family for a year. The Alexander family received a house, a garden spot, firewood, tools, teams and their feed, and one-half of the crop. Elias provided the farm labor, and his wife performed domestic duties in the white household. Occasionally, contracts called for laborers to work on shares for one crop, such as tobacco, and for wages on other crops.[8]

While some blacks received an equitable share of crops they raised, others claimed that they got less than their fair portion, and bureau officials usually agreed. Several developments made sharecropping a disagreeable arrangement. Because of poor management, laborers sometimes fell into debt to landowners and learned only after the harvest that they had been advanced their entire share during the year in the form of provisions. For others, differences arose over the division of crops, and compromise settlements frequently proved ruinous to the sharecroppers. In the worst situations threats of violence forced sharecroppers to flee farms, thus abrogating agreements before dividing the harvest. The intervention of the bureau into disputes, an all-too-infrequent occurrence, was one of the few options sharecroppers had to secure reasonably just resolutions. Controversies over shares led to a decline in sharecropping in the late 1860s.[9]

Contracting for wages was a second option available to black farm laborers. They preferred the wage system for psychological and economic reasons. It bore few similarities to slavery, and the shortage of farm workers gave them leverage when making agreements. Some contracts consisted of elaborately drawn, handwritten documents which anticipated most eventualities. Others were short, fill-in-the-blank forms. Salaries might be specified as a lump sum for an entire family or wages might be spelled out for each family member. Employers almost always furnished room and board. While some laborers favored short-term contracts, most preferred the security of a yearly agreement. Average monthly wages for males under the contract system increased from about $14 in 1866 to approximately $17.50 in 1868. Wages for females averaged slightly over one-half that of males. Although the pay scale fluctuated, it was highest during the summer agricultural season.[10]

Lilborn Lilly agreed in May 1868 to work as a farm laborer "for the crop season" for $18 monthly, payable at the end of each month. Richard Blair contracted in 1866 to work for the entire year on a Shelby County farm. Blair had to furnish his own clothes and pay health-care costs, but his employer promised to supply food and lodging and to advance him $5 a month toward his $125 annual salary. Blair would receive the remainder of his wages when the contract terminated on December 25, 1866. Time lost because of sickness came out of Blair's salary. Elias and Mary Wilson contracted themselves and their two children for $160 for 1866. Their Bullitt County employer promised, in addition to "wholesome food and comfortable quarters," to pay all medical expenses. The Wilsons would draw one-half of their salary monthly, and the remainder on Christmas Day 1866.[11]

Contracts resulted in frequent disputes. Some employers accused laborers of indolence, disobedience, or theft and simply dismissed them, refusing to make final payments. Laborers sometimes made multiple contracts, choosing the highest bidder at the last moment, never accomplished the work they agreed to perform, or walked out on contracts at harvesting time. Mobs occasionally drove farmhands from their homes, preventing them from fulfilling their contracts and acquiring "the legitimate fruits of their labor."[12]

In handling contract disputes, the Freedmen's Bureau frequently sent ambiguous signals to black laborers, some of whom believed the agency should stand behind them whether their positions were right or wrong. Usually, agents settled difficulties amicably. Notification of the bureau's concern was enough to cause most landowners to reach quick settlements or to submit disputes to arbitration. When employers refused to cooperate with bureau investigations, agents sometimes assisted laborers in lawsuits to recover back wages. But in cases where hands violated their contracts, agents sometimes reverted to a judgment reminiscent of slavery, namely, corporal punishment. Since most blacks possessed no money to pay fines, a few agents reasoned that flogging contract breakers was the only punishment available to them, a policy blacks vigorously resisted.[13]

Apprenticeships were a third type of labor agreement utilized in Kentucky after the Civil War. Although closely linked with slavery in the minds of many blacks, apprenticeship contracts became the standard procedure for preparing children, whether orphaned, abandoned, or poverty stricken, to enter a trade. Usually, they were apprenticed until they reached the age of eighteen or twenty-one. The Freedmen's Bureau expected black children who met the required conditions to be apprenticed without race discrimination, and they usually enforced this policy when state officials refused to cooperate. Kentucky revised its apprenticeship law in 1866 and 1868 to include provisions for blacks, and many of the basic features applied equally to both races. The law required that apprentices receive humane treatment, proper medical care, adequate food, clothes, and shelter, and that they be taught a trade. Upon completion of an agreement, the apprentice also expected to receive a new suit of clothes.[14]

However, several features of the statutes applied only to black apprentices, and freedmen and bureau officials raised a howl of protest when state officials enforced them. The most offensive was the law that gave preference to former owners when apprenticing black children, a provision that blacks and bureau officials vehemently denounced. Another section authorized county court clerks to sign apprenticeship contracts on behalf of minors. These features placed control of apprenticeships into the hands of powerful whites and made it difficult, if not impossible, for blacks to influence the apprenticing of their children or relatives. Finally, freedmen and their friends decried the provision of the law which allowed masters to pay a cash payment to black apprentices—fifty dollars to females and a hundred dollars to males—in lieu of teaching them to read, write, and execute general arithmetic, as a scheme to maintain an illiterate, submissive work force.[15]

While the actual number of apprentices remained relatively small and the period of illegal indentures short, apprenticeships constituted a major source of litigation involving whites and blacks that came before Freedmen's Bureau courts. Criticism of apprentice masters included hiring out apprentices and confiscating the wages, physical abuse, and failure to teach a trade. Most complaints, however, centered around apprenticing children without the consent of parents or relatives, regardless of their ability to provide for them. Masters of apprenticed children frequently resisted attempts of parents to recover them, and blacks, often too poor to contest contracts legally, looked to the bureau for support. Bureau agents worked diligently to end discrimination in apprenticeships, achieving some of its most meaningful successes in this area. Their extensive review of apprenticeship contracts usually forced compliance with bureau standards or resulted in termination of the apprenticeship, a practice that returned hundreds of children to their parents.[16]

The more fortunate blacks acquired their own land, a goal vigorously supported by John G. Fee. Fee's idea of helping blacks acquire land and farm machinery met with slightly more success than his employment agency plan. Leaders associated with Berea College believed that blacks must own property to achieve independence, a goal complicated because many whites refused to sell land to them. Fee's solution called for sympathetic whites—Kentuckians and northerners—to form companies to purchase land for resale at favorable prices to blacks.[17]

This strategy partially reached fruition at Camp Nelson, where a few blacks built cottages on small parcels of land purchased outside of town. Eventually, Fee bought 130 acres for lots, farms, and schools from the two thousand dollars he raised. By 1891 more than forty black families resided on the segregated tract. Fee's plan for the "interspersion" of black homesteaders among white property holders became a reality only at Berea, where he and his friends willingly sold land to blacks. Offering generous terms, the reformers helped settle more than forty black families in Berea during the five years following the war, and by 1876 black and white homesteads were thoroughly integrated in the area.[18]

Blacks also acquired small plots of land in central Kentucky, usually in the vicinity of where they had been slaves. Some white landowners, recognizing the benefit of having a ready labor force at hand, divided small tracts of marginal land into lots which they gave or sold to freedmen, creating street-front settlements. Blacks built their own houses, drew water from a community well, tilled small garden plots to supplement their incomes, and worked for wages on the nearby estates on the white man's terms. In a few instances white entrepreneurs sold land to blacks, creating segregated settlements. Additional communities emerged from unknown origins or as blacks purchased land abandoned by whites, and by the 1890s dozens of "freetown" hamlets dotted the central Kentucky countryside.[19]

Though most blacks who flooded into Kentucky's towns and cities after the war rented houses, a growing number found ways to purchase their own homes. In Paris the socially minded Rev. Elisha Green and a white landowner cooperated in building an all-black community in a field originally intended for use as a "shipping pen," an indication of its marginal quality. The landowner agreed to subdivide the property into lots seventy-five by sixty feet and to build a one-door cottage with a chimney on each plot. For five hundred dollars cash or one hundred dollars down and the remainder at 6 percent interest, more than fifty black families in Paris acquired a home.

In Lexington, where the black population had increased dramatically, postwar settlers found homes in urban clusters in the interiors of blocks located largely on the city's periphery. As in other towns, new black communities usually developed on poorly drained bottomland near railroads, industries, or stockyards. By the early 1870s recognizable streets existed in several adjacent urban clusters, and by the 1880s Goodlowtown became the largest black residential community in Lexington. In a few instances white entrepreneurs subdivided marginal land for sale to blacks, often lending their names to the residential clusters that developed. Lots in Brucetown, located near a hemp factory, went on sale in 1865. Pralltown, a bottomland tract near a railroad, developed between 1868 and 1877. In 1869 another landowner offered blacks one hundred low-lying lots, probably Lee's Row community, for homes. Those with acceptable references could pay one-third down and the remainder on time. Taylortown and Smithtown clusters developed between the late 1860s and the late 1880s, and twenty families moved into poorly drained Kinkeadtown during the 1870s.[20]

Lexington's developing residential patterns produced several major results. Those blacks who lived downtown in the immediate postwar years, whether freemen from antebellum days or newly arrived countryside immigrants, were steadily pushed from the streets and alleys of inner Lexington to segregated clusters on the periphery of the city. By 1880 Lexington was a segregated city with the homes of blacks isolated from the white community and largely hidden from the view of whites. Further, few black institutions followed the people to the urban clusters. Most schools, stores, churches, and benevolent organizations remained on "black 'main street' " in the city's central business district, depriving black neighborhoods of badly needed social centers. And finally, the number of blacks who acquired property remained quite small. Blacks owning city lots in Lexington grew from 73 in 1865 to 420 in 1869 when their holdings represented 4.3 percent of the city's total assessed property value. Over the next decade the number of blacks owning lots climbed to 666, improving their share to 6 percent. This seemingly impressive achievement, considering the boom and bust economy of the 1870s, lost its luster when compared with the fact that blacks comprised 45 percent of Lexington's inhabitants.[21]

Louisville blacks were some of the most determined in seeking solutions to housing problems resulting from the city's mushrooming black population during the postwar decades. In 1866 a group of leading citizens formed a joint-stock company to purchase land and construct cottages in the California district near Sixteenth Street, already the location of a number of black-owned homes. The company anticipated enough construction to allow a few nonmembers to participate in the venture. Another group of blacks began leasing lots in Smoketown. "Neat" cottages soon sprang up on Breckinridge Street in an area from Preston to Jackson, from Jackson to Caldwell, and back to Preston. Blacks also moved into another region of new home construction known as Brownstown on Second Street between Magnolia and Shipp streets. In the 1880s blacks began purchasing lots on Orleans and Virginia avenues, between Thirty-sixth and Thirty-seventh streets. By the early 1890s so many blacks lived in that neighborhood that whites called it "Little Africa." Many located housing over the years by occupying older structures which became available throughout the city as whites left them to purchase new homes in better neighborhoods. As a result of these developments, Louisville's black housing, though concentrated into several neighborhoods, was remarkably integrated.[22]

By mid-1873 the *Courier-Journal* commented on the progress of blacks in Louisville. It pointed out that in several sections of the city blacks, through hard work and enterprise, had acquired "large amounts of real estate." In the first five years after the war, they had spent more than twenty-five thousand dollars from their savings to purchase homes. Unfortunately, progress for many was short-lived. The financial panic of 1873 and subsequent economic fluctuations took a terrible toll. Residents of Smoketown and Brownstown found that the availability of easy credit had lured them beyond their capacity to make payments, and many suffered foreclosure. In March 1874 leading blacks formed the Louisville Real Estate and Mutual Relief Association with a capital stock of thirty thousand dollars to assist homeowners with advice, planning, and purchases, but hard times intervened before they realized much success. In the years that followed, blacks increasingly denounced "exorbitant rents," and many doubted that they would "ever obtain a home."[23]

During the decade of the 1880s, black Louisvillians faced the prospect of segregated housing as they found themselves pushed increasingly into mostly all-black neighborhoods. In 1885 the Louisville *Times* boldly discussed the wisdom of confining blacks to a "colored district." One writer, who believed that whites were about twenty years too late in resolving the question of integrated housing, proposed "colonization" of the city's blacks in an area south of Bank Street and west of Twenty-sixth Street. The old "houses and rookeries" of blacks, he proposed, should be razed and replaced with "substantial two-story residences" for "white citizens."[24]

Finally, whether owners or renters, Louisville's blacks usually lived in inferior housing. They described even their newly constructed homes as "not the finest" and "not modernly built." Most consisted of three-room, poorly insulated, frame, shotgun houses. Some communities without wells hauled in their water. Thousands of renters spent their lives in "basements and ill-ventilated cellars." Multiple families lived in two- or three-room dilapidated shacks in conditions "impossible for human beings to exist." Whether owners or renters, blacks' homes were without modern bathroom facilities, and the residents lacked access to the free public bathhouses constructed for poor white families.[25]

Blacks also purchased farm homesteads in Jefferson and surrounding counties. Between 1865 and 1870 farmers with accounts in the Freedmen's Savings Bank spent an impressive amount of money for farms, supplies, and equipment. They put $416,000 alone into land, with thirty of the largest purchases averaging seventy-five acres. They spent an additional $75,000 for seeds, farm animals, agricultural implements, tools, and shop equipment.[26]

Acquisition of property by blacks, though minuscule when compared to that of whites, was impressive. In 1866 blacks possessed urban and rural property valued at $976,956. While only a handful accumulated more than a hundred acres over the next two years, farmers in many parts of the Commonwealth acquired thirty, forty, and even fifty acres of land, and by 1869 the value of property in black hands had more than doubled, totaling $2,016,784. A slow but steady accumulation of property continued, but tax valuation declined rather sharply during the late 1870s as a result of the economic dislocations caused by the panic of 1873. In 1878 when the tax valuation stood at $.45 per $100, blacks owned 5,995 city lots with a tax value of $1,288,155. Farmers paid a land tax of $1,275,300 on 181,139 acres, and an additional $641,000 on horses and mares, mules, jennies, and cattle. In 1878 black farmers produced about 10,000,000 pounds of tobacco, 210,000 pounds of hemp, 546 tons of hay, 1,500,000 bushels of corn, 147,000 bushels of wheat, and 1,500 bushels of barley. By 1885 taxable property of blacks increased to $4,000,000.[27]

For domestic workers, whether in rural or urban areas, the transition to free labor was the least abrupt. Where relationships with owners had been personal if not always friendly, black women usually remained with their old masters who appreciated their skills in cooking, cleaning, washing, ironing, and nursing the children. Others sought employment in urban areas. Regardless of location, wages were poor—between $25 and $125 a year depending on the number of different tasks performed—and hours were long. Servants in urban areas often lived in the homes of their employers. In the 1870s, however, many domestics, complaining about poor rooms and food, moved into their own housing. Newcomers to Kentucky's cities readily found jobs as domestics, personal servants, gardeners, carriage drivers, and handymen, but they complained about a lack of job security, "eight"-day weeks, and harsh treatment. The loudest outcry, however, stemmed from low wages. Domestics constantly complained of inadequate pay, frequent wage cuts, and inability to live on their salaries. Indeed, low pay, scarcely above subsistence, meant that those who remained domestic servants seldom prospered.[28]

Blacks also dominated those areas of the work force which depended solely on physical labor. Common or day laborers occupied the lowest rung of the economic ladder, frequently working in unhealthy and unsanitary conditions. At the bottom of the wage scale, they toiled by the hour, day, or week, at jobs shunned by most whites, with no assurance of steady employment. Jobs such as lifting, digging, or cleaning provided the unskilled with the bare necessities of life. More aggressive blacks began their own cartage businesses. In Lexington where blacks quickly came to dominate drayage, Edward Alexander achieved immediate success, amassing $2,200 worth of property by 1870. Visitors in 1890 noted that virtually nothing moved in Lexington except on the wagons of black draymen. The same was true of Louisville, where by the mid-1870s over 150 black draymen operated teams. Two of the most prosperous, James Seay Brown and George Buckner, built a reputation as dependable businessmen and each soon owned and managed four teams and wagons.[29]

Physical strength and a willingness to work hard opened up many opportunities for blacks in the building trades. A few skilled carpenters achieved early success in building schools for the Freedmen's Bureau. Soon hundreds of black carpenters worked on construction projects throughout the state, and as early as the mid-1870s, Louisville alone possessed sixteen black contractors who each employed from four to twenty men. One Louisville builder, Willis Tolbot, achieved distinction as a master stair-builder. Others acquired skills as plasterers, ceiling whiteners, and painters, and soon large numbers of blacks were successful in these professions throughout the Commonwealth. Blacks almost monopolized the hod carriers trade—carrying bricks and mortar—and there were a number of successful bricklayers, some of whom won large contracts in the 1890s.[30]

One of the largest black construction companies, under the leadership of Rev. Preston Taylor of Mt. Sterling, arose out of the refusal of contractors to hire blacks on a railroad project. To demonstrate that blacks could perform the work, Taylor organized a company and secured a contract to lay a two-mile section of track out of Mt. Sterling. Taylor built a commissary and quarters for the 150 men he hired, acquired horses, mules, carts, wagons, and other equipment needed for the project, and completed the job on time. Unfortunately for black business enterprise, Taylor declined other contract offers, preferring to return full-time to his ministry.[31]

Several trades offered an opportunity for some advancement, especially for those blacks who owned their own businesses. Tinsmiths, blacksmiths, and livery stable employees could count on steady work, as well as the few who toiled as pressmen, coopers, soap makers, hat makers, and tailors. Those who worked for railroads or in maintenance for hotels, sawmills, and foundries also prospered. Blacks also achieved success in boot and shoemaking. In 1880 blacks owned eight shoeshops in Lexington alone; they made similar gains in Louisville. Work in hemp and bagging factories was relatively extensive immediately after the war, but declined rapidly in the early 1870s. More blacks worked as cigar makers, at various jobs in the tobacco factories, and on the docks, warehouses, and rivers.[32]

A few blacks owned small manufacturing establishments in the postwar era. Ferdinand Robinson ran a modestly successful mattress factory in Lexington, accumulating by 1870 property valued at $1,300. In 1872 John L. Wheat incorporated the Union Cement & Lime Company in Louisville. By the 1890s Wheat had built his firm into one of the "larger industries" in the city. Page, Yancy & Company, a brick manufacturing firm, prospered in the 1880s and achieved annual sales of $45,000 by 1890. The company, unfortunately, fell upon hard times because of keen competition from white firms and was nearly bankrupt by the early 1890s. In the mid-1870s black businesses in Louisville included eight wagon and carriage makers, at least one black mechanic who made pumps, and stove manufacturer Madison Smith, who accumulated a small fortune.

Blacks were most active in the ownership of urban retail businesses. Bakeries, lunch counters, restaurants, and boarding houses, usually located in the central business district, offered blacks some of their better opportunities. George and Dan's Restaurant, popular with Federal officers during the war, became one of Louisville's most successful dining spots after Appomattox. Frank Gray and Thornton Thompson made a comfortable living as caterers, and Eugene DeGruy, known as a "French cook," ran a restaurant on Green Street. There were also a few black-owned grocery stores. Some of the smaller enterprises operated out of private homes, and most were located within black communities, indicative of an all-black clientele. Some, however, were more substantial. Willis Adams's grocery, one of about eight owned by blacks in Louisville in 1885, occupied a large brick building. Adams delivered groceries to his patrons throughout the black community. The New Eureka Grocery Company, founded in 1891, increased its stock from one hundred dollars to one thousand dollars in the early 1890s. Almost every town had a black-owned saloon.[33]

Blacks owned furniture stores, usually one of the more lucrative retail enterprises, in most of the larger towns. They sold new and used furniture and some traded in other secondhand goods. Throughout the 1870s and 1880s blacks operated several centrally located furniture stores on the same block in Louisville. They offered the "latest designs" in home furniture, carpets, and accessories to patrons of both races. Upholstery repair was often a part of these businesses. Lexington's most successful black businessman was a secondhand furniture dealer named Moses Spencer. A freeman, Spencer began building his fortune before the Civil War, and by the 1870s he possessed personal and real property valued at about twenty thousand dollars. At least two black real estate companies existed in Louisville during the 1870s and 1880s, and in 1887 blacks in Paris founded the Bourbon Colored Mutual Savings and Loan Association with John Spears as president.[34]

The best opportunity for blacks to prosper was in service-related occupations. Among those professions, barbering provided the quickest route to success. In addition to the job security which this skill afforded, barbers were able to invest their profits and spare time in other moneymaking ventures. Black barbers usually located their shops in central business districts, and the more successful ones in Louisville and Lexington rented space in the finest hotels and served only white customers. Black barbers who restricted their business to prosperous white customers realized that the best way to keep them was not to serve blacks. A few barbers apparently challenged the color line successfully. According to the New York *Freeman*, white customers frequented Nelson Neal's shop, reputed to be one of the most elegant in Louisville, although his clientele continued to be largely black. Nevertheless, black barbers, more powerful in Lexington than in Louisville, constantly felt pressure from white shopowners who coveted their patrons.[35]

A small group of blacks had successful careers as undertakers. J.H. Taylor, Louisville's first black mortician, arrived in the city in 1865 and worked two years as a carpenter before becoming a funeral director in partnership with Rev. Yarmouth Carr. Self-educated, Taylor soon built a respectable business and eventually merged with another undertaker, R.C. Fox. In the 1870s Fox left Taylor and formed a new undertaking firm, R.C. Fox & Brothers. When R.C. Fox died, his wife apparently ran the business. Louisville's earliest undertakers faced strong competition from white funeral directors, and they realized only modest profits. In 1887 William Watson opened a third undertaking company, just as white undertakers began refusing to conduct funerals for blacks. Employing sound business acumen, Watson reinvested his profits in quality equipment and soon outdistanced his black competitors to become, reputedly, Louisville's wealthiest black. Jordan C. Jackson was the first black undertaker in Lexington. Joining with Will Porter, a Cincinnati funeral director to found Porter & Jackson, Undertakers, Jackson began with only a team of horses and one wagon. Several years later Jackson bought out his partner, and with the increased profits, he expanded his operations, constructed a new funeral home, and diversified his business interests to become one of Lexington's most prosperous black citizens.[36]

In the postbellum years blacks also came to dominate the potentially lucrative job of waiting tables. Moving to one of Kentucky's towns to become a waiter became so common that one scholar labeled it a "rite of passage" for young blacks. Many remained waiters for years, rising to the secure positions of head waiter or second waiter at hotels or in railroad dining cars. Others were young men on the way up. Some worked only summers, attending school during the winter months, or until better-paying jobs came along. Many outstanding blacks, such as Methodist Bishop Alexander Walters, began their careers waiting tables in Lexington and Louisville hotels. Even more desirable were the so-called "positions of Trust," such as porters, messengers, stewards, and janitors. These jobs went only to blacks who possessed the "right" attitude. Once acquired, these positions frequently offered life tenure. On the other hand, jobs in retail sales in the white community remained extremely difficult to find, but ten blacks worked as salesmen and two as saleswomen in Louisville businesses in 1888.[37]

The handful of blacks who worked as horse trainers and jockeys were particularly fortunate for they had an opportunity to earn large incomes. Owners of fast horses could make a few hundred dollars annually at county fairs, but opportunities were far greater at the major race tracks in Louisville, Lexington, or Covington. Malcolm Ayres, who as a lad worked in the stables in Lexington, was the exercise boy for the first Kentucky Derby winner and later became a successful trainer. Abe Perry trained Joe Cotton, the Derby winner in 1885, and Dudley Allen trained Kingman, a horse he had once owned, into a Derby winner six years later. Edward Brown, known to the public as Brown Dick, trained and raced horses, a few of which he owned, at tracks throughout the country. One of his horses, Ben-Brush, became a famous stud.[38]

Blacks proved even more successful as jockeys. Fifteen black jockeys, several of whom were multiple winners, won the Kentucky Derby during its first twenty-eight years. Lexington's Isaac B. Murphy, Kentucky's most famous black jockey, dominated the sport during the 1880s. Murphy, who began his career as an exercise boy, had difficulty getting his first ride. But when opportunity finally beckoned, Murphy rode home a winner, and he never again had trouble finding a mount. Murphy became the first triple Kentucky Derby winner—1884, 1890, 1891—and finished in the money in three others. He won the Latonia Derby at Covington five times and four of the first five American derbies at Chicago. By 1885 he received an annual retainer of four thousand dollars and, in addition to his regular pay per race, special payoffs and bonuses for winning certain races. On several occasions Murphy made a thousand dollars in a single day, and by 1885 his annual earnings were estimated at ten thousand dollars. When he retired in 1892, he possessed an amazing lifetime record of 628 wins in 1,412 races.[39]

Other outstanding black jockeys carved out great careers which included Kentucky Derby victories. Oliver Lewis rode Aristides to victory in the first Kentucky Derby in 1875, and William Walker, who later became a successful trainer, won in 1877. Isaac Lewis was the winner in the 1880 Derby, and two years later Babe Hurd rode home to victory. Erskin Henderson won the Derby in 1885, and in 1887 Isaac Lewis won for a second time.[40]

One of the most prestigious positions held by blacks in Kentucky in the decade following the war was working in the federally chartered National Freedmen's Savings and Trust Bank. In September 1865 the freedmen's bank opened its third branch in Louisville. Shortly thereafter planning began for a branch in Lexington, but five years passed before it opened. Blacks served on the advisory boards and as cashiers of both banks. A major goal of the bank's founders, in addition to providing banking services for blacks, was to encourage freedmen to be thrifty and to save their money. Believing that the freedmen's bank reflected, to some extent, on their progress as a free people, Kentucky blacks preferred that it project the proper image. The Louisville branch moved four times, finally settling in a "neat and inviting" building in the white business district. The Lexington office occupied a building which had previously served as the Fayette National Bank.[41]

The Louisville freedmen's bank was one of the nation's most stable branch institutions. Its advisory board, heavily dominated by blacks, participated in all policy decisions and continually attracted quality leaders. W.H. Gibson, Sr., was the first black to serve as an assistant to the white cashiers, but in December 1868 the board selected Horace Morris as the first black cashier. Morris, "an accomplished accountant," remained head cashier until the bank's demise in 1874. At that time bureau officials and bank examiners found Morris's books in "perfect order," but efforts to reorganize the branch as a private bank failed.[42]

Blacks who deposited funds in the Louisville freedmen's bank represented several types of citizens. The overwhelming majority consisted of working-class people, many of whom deposited as little as five cents at a time. For most of these depositors, the freedmen's bank constituted a great experiment in racial improvement. Local black organizations, such as the Sanitary Commission and other self-help groups, also utilized the services of the freedmen's bank. One other early group of patrons, black Kentucky soldiers still serving in the military, deposited substantial sums. Indeed, the secretary of the freedmen's bank worked in conjunction with government officials, army paymasters, and branch cashiers to insure that soldiers deposited their money into the bank. Army officers and chaplains collected money from soldiers in the field, deposited it in the nearest freedmen's bank which in turn transferred the funds to the branch nearest each soldier's home. Following this procedure, Kentucky black soldiers between 1865 and 1867 sent thousands of dollars to their families. In 1870 the average depositor had $74.41 in the Louisville freedmen's bank. During the bank's ten-year history, accounts ranged from $5 to $825.[43]

Within three months after the Louisville bank opened, patrons had placed more than thirty thousand dollars in it, and by late 1869 deposits surpassed eighty thousand dollars. Under the leadership of Morris, the bank, beginning in December 1868, experienced spectacular growth as "a new era dawned." Morris, who understood the importance of "cultivating and maintaining credit," found new methods of expanding the bank's assets, such as assisting in the collection of Civil War soldiers' bounties, and by July 1870 deposits exceeded one hundred thousand dollars. Depositors increased from 709 when Morris became cashier, to 1,166 in January 1870, and finally to 2,959 in June 1874.[44]

Bank and bureau officials, convinced that the large Lexington black community was one of the most prosperous in the South, eagerly opened a branch there in November 1870. Founded late, when unprofitable banks were already going under, the Lexington branch got off to a shaky start. The white cashier, Oberlin graduate J.G. Hamilton, was already heavily burdened directing AMA schools in the city, and he proved to be an incompetent administrator. Though the bank offered financial services desperately needed by the black community, such as helping finance improvements at the Independent Baptist Church, it was doomed by mismanagement. By 1873 Hamilton had handed most of the bank's operation to Jordan C. Jackson, his assistant, but all efforts to save the institution failed, and it closed in June 1874. Shortages discovered at the Lexington branch were traced to Hamilton.[45]

The failure of the Freedmen's Savings Bank had an incalculable economic effect on the black community. While some overcame the jolt of losing their life's savings, others never recovered psychologically, and little doubt exists that the bank's failure resulted in a distrust of financial institutions among blacks and discouraged many who might otherwise have become more frugal. Shortly after the institution's failure, Louisville blacks organized and petitioned bank officials and Congress for payment of deposits that had been placed in the bank. Horace Morris informed depositors of the procedure for applying for their money, but it was 1881 before any dispersal of funds occurred. Eventually, depositors received four dividends, totaling about 60 percent of original balances, but Louisville depositors continued to pressure the government into the 1890s, hoping to achieve full restitution.[46]

Government jobs were also coveted, but they went to few blacks. The most numerous of federal positions, those of collector, storekeeper, and gauger, were handed out to prominent blacks when Republicans won the presidency and withdrawn when Democrats were victorious. Leaders such as Henry Scroggins and Jordan C. Jackson of Lexington, W.H. Gibson and H.C. Weeden of Louisville, and Richard Varian of Owensboro were among the best-known blacks to hold these positions. Blacks also received a few appointive positions in the Post Office Department, and by the mid-1880s an increasing number qualified and secured jobs as postmen.[47]

Several problems slowed the progress of black working classes and prevented their success in the labor market. Racial prejudice was the most burdensome. The dominant white population believed, in general, that blacks were indolent and lazy. To this charge there was no defense since, to the prejudiced, one idle black was sufficient to confirm the theory. Nevertheless, black leaders constantly exhorted the laboring classes to work harder, naively expecting that the elimination of all idleness would end discrimination in the marketplace. In addition, state and local legal restrictions limited black access even to the poorer-paying public jobs and systematically excluded them from positions of authority. Blacks fought against these restrictions but with little success.[48]

One of the early efforts to break through these restrictions and to acquire public jobs occurred in Louisville, where blacks sought appointments to the police force. During the 1870s and 1880s, Louisville's black community was the scene of increased crime. Residents complained that armed groups of men victimized them and charged white policemen who entered their neighborhoods with brutality. In 1873 blacks and whites living in the vicinity of the fairgrounds created a neighborhood crime-prevention watch and selected several men to serve as patrolmen, among them two blacks. A county judge confirmed the appointments in an apparent attempt to reduce crime in the area. In December 1873 one of the black patrolmen arrested a white man, the first such arrest in the city. The following July Jefferson County officials appointed seventeen blacks as "special police," possibly to ensure order at Independence Day celebrations.[49]

Pressure on city government for civil service jobs continued, and an 1883 resolution to hire blacks as policemen and firemen reached a board of aldermen committee but died there. In 1885 when a self-professed reformer won the mayoral election with the aid of black votes, a committee of blacks visited his office requesting jobs "in all the departments" of city government, reminding the mayor that he had promised justice for all minorities. The mayor, citing the state constitution and the city charter which barred black employment in municipal government, rejected the petition, claiming "the time . . . [was] not ripe." Blacks sought to remove the discriminatory prohibitions and continued to agitate for civil service positions into the late 1880s, but in 1891 there still were no blacks in the Louisville fire or police departments.[50]

Hostility from whites and segregation in the marketplace posed perennial problems for black workers. Because of white resistance, blacks had difficulty competing for jobs or for control of the workplace. Attacks and threats against W.H. Gibson, Sr., the first black railroad mail agent, forced him to retire from the position after several months, and a band of white citizens gave a black minister who organized "a labor protective union" to improve wages and job conditions of farm workers in Trigg County one day to leave. Whites in skilled trades generally refused to work with blacks, and, more importantly, they excluded them from their unions. The Knights of Labor was the only national labor union to espouse integration, and blacks associated with it in increased numbers during the 1880s. Nevertheless, in Kentucky the Knights were segregated at the local level, with separate organizations for the same trade. On occasion, Knights of both races held joint meetings but solidarity usually went no further than integrated demonstrations.[51]

Difficulties with white labor organizations led blacks to form their own unions, some of which chose names such as Lincoln or Hope, an indication that their influence may have been more symbolic than real. Louisville's Hod Carriers Union, one of the largest dominated by blacks, illustrates the impotence of these unions. In 1886 the hod carriers, with a strike fund of $1,250, struck the white bricklayer's union for whom they worked, hoping to increase wages by twenty-five cents a day. The white union easily hired replacement workers, and the strike failed. The Barber's Union, though unable to control the market, became powerful enough to force white barbers to cooperate with them on setting shop hours. Other black unions included waiters, coachmen, teamsters, porters, and brickyard laborers. Blacks in Winchester, publishers of the *Kentucky Industrialist*, the official organ of the Knights of Labor, also created a farmer-laborer organization which lasted into the 1890s.[52]

Blacks reacted in several different ways to the hardships caused by economic depression and discrimination in the marketplace. Their typical response was to rally together and try harder, usually through some form of self-help. They organized relief committees with the task of caring for the poor and unemployed among them, and they opened cooperative stores, hoping to lower the cost of living. To house the homeless, blacks joined together in a nationwide movement to "create homes."[53]

A few concluded, however, that Kentucky held no economic or political future for them and emigrated to Kansas. The first trickle of migrants to Kansas began about 1874 when Rev. John Dudley persuaded a dozen families to leave Hart County. Most of this party became permanently stranded in the Louisville area, but the next year James Rowlett and his family successfully resumed the trek and began a new life in Wichita. At least one other family from Hart County followed Rowlett. Hard times following the panic of 1873 and the antiblack violence and intimidation surrounding the disputed presidential election of 1876-77 gave further impetus to the Kansas migration. In Louisville a cheerless group of black leaders met in July 1877 and organized a colonization society to assist members of their race in migrating to Kansas.[54]

Gabriel Burdett, the AMA representative at Camp Nelson, was typical of those who became despondent about the future. After years of working tirelessly and optimistically to uplift and Christianize fellow blacks, Burdett reluctantly concluded that his people would never be more than a "hopeless minority" in Kentucky. Too many impediments blocked the path of progress, and conversations with his "best informed" friends in the mid-1870s convinced him that Kentucky blacks were "going down as a people" and would never be more than "partially free." In the end, Burdett's love for his family and his belief in freedom of thought forced his hand. Why, he reasoned, should he rear his children in this atmosphere when "free institutions" and "freedom of thought and actions" prevailed in Kansas? In the spring of 1877 he informed the AMA of his decision: "It would be a curse if I were to keep my children here in this condition, . . ." he wrote, "crushed down under the slow progress of this dull state." In July 1877 Burdett, with fifty dollars in his pocket and the blessings of the AMA, moved his family to Kansas, where he died in 1914.

During 1877 and 1878 several groups of black Kentuckians in Fayette, Garrard, Scott, Boyle, and Jefferson counties also migrated to Kansas, often under the leadership of Kansas recruiters. The colonists usually went by way of Topeka, from where they scattered into several communities, but most went to Nicodemus. The journey to Kansas was frequently difficult. Migrants struggled through bad weather, suffered from sickness and delays, and some dropped out along the way. Starting over was difficult for the Kentuckians, but they built homes, found jobs, and cleared their own land. A surprising number of the approximately one thousand migrants from Kentucky prospered.[55]

As Kentucky blacks struggled with the problems inherent in their transition from slavery to freedom, they found some release in the growing number of recreational opportunities available to them after 1865. The church remained an important center for socials, picnics, and festivals, though its role in organized family recreation steadily declined. Two favorite, if not new, activities were picnics and excursions. On Thursday, November 25, 1880, Louisville's black Baptist churches organized a great dinner to raise money for the Baptist Normal and Theological Institute while celebrating the newly designated Thanksgiving holiday. Riverboat excursions were also popular with churches. Excursions offered an opportunity for the membership to socialize, sightsee, and visit other towns, and for ministers to entertain denominational leaders.[56]

Increasingly, picnics and excursions took on a secular image, so much so that a few leaders feared that blacks were wasting their money on too much entertainment. For those who lived and labored in a city or who were unable to travel, these outings offered a bucolic afternoon on a nature trail or the sights of another city. Picnics associated with political campaigns and holidays drew huge crowds who often heard stirring patriotic addresses by black leaders and Republican candidates. Labor unions seeking solidarity held outings for members and their families, and lodges used picnics to display their drill teams. Many public schools rewarded the children with supervised recreational picnics at the end of the school year, and several women's clubs entertained their families at summer outings or raised money for charity by organizing excursions.[57]

Railroad excursions were particularly popular. Announcements in black newspapers gave sponsors, destinations, schedules, and costs. During the 1870s and 1880s, the demand for space forced railway lines to add special weekend runs to carry blacks to nearby towns or to destinations in other states. An 1886 excursion from Louisville to the Nelson County fair was a typical regional trip. The chartered L & N train—one engine, a baggage car, and five coaches for five hundred passengers—left for Bardstown on Saturday morning and returned late that night. Longer trips required an all-night ride, and these excursion groups packed stations late in the evening. After spending much of the next day in Indianapolis, Indiana, or Chicago, Illinois, they returned by train that night. More extended trips carried Kentucky blacks to Republican presidential inaugurations.[58]

Another popular postwar activity consisted of attending agricultural and mechanical fairs, usually in the fall of the year. Excluded from white fairs but eager to participate in such activities, blacks organized their own A & M fairs. This idea "caught the fancy" of the black community, and several counties throughout the Commonwealth began hosting A & M fairs. In addition to a recreational break from the boredom of everyday life, fairs provided entertainment, a chance to see old friends, and above all, an opportunity to display their accomplishments. The display booths, livestock shows, prizes, and sporting events served to demonstrate black achievement, thereby enhancing racial pride. These fairs were also financially beneficial for the entire community.[59]

Elijah P. Marrs, a cofounder of the Baptist Normal and Theological Institute in Louisville, described the spontaneous organization of the Shelby County A & M Fair. While contemplating one evening the progress made by black Kentuckians, he and his brother, H.C. Marrs, decided to organize a fair as a display of racial achievement. They formed a company, with H.C. as president and Elijah as secretary, raised $750 from fifty investors, and purchased a fairground. The fair netted $3,000 in 1871, the first year, but profits declined steadily over the next several years. Elijah Marrs sold out his interest in 1874, but the fair continued for years. Enthusiasts created similar associations in Louisville, and in Franklin, Bourbon, Nicholas, Clark, Boyle, and Nelson counties, most of which had a modicum of success.[60]

One fair, run by the Lexington Colored Agricultural and Mechanical Association, achieved greater fame than the others. At the behest of Henry King, several well known black leaders, including Henry Scroggins and James Turner, met at Ladies' Hall in 1869 and created a company which formed the A & M Association. Nearly twenty investors purchased about fifty shares of stock in the company at ten dollars per share. The association elected officers annually, and King, the first president, continued in that post during the early years. King's financial and administrative decisions placed the association on a sound basis from the beginning. By mid-1870 the company had a state charter, a constitution, and by-laws. In addition to highly respected officers who ran professional business meetings, the association built confidence by opening its books to the public. Its stock climbed to fifty dollars a share in 1891, and when the company reorganized in 1897, each share was worth more than a hundred dollars.

The Lexington association's fairs were a financial success from the beginning. The first fair, held in 1869, netted $1,368, and after a profit of $1,157 at the second fair, the association declared a ten-dollar stock dividend. Following record-breaking crowds and receipts in 1872, the company leased a new location on the Georgetown Pike where they erected a $3,500 exhibition building and constructed a 2,500-seat amphitheater and a race track. Attendance for the four-day event improved annually over the next fifteen years, and in 1887 the association, seeking larger facilities, moved to the white fairgrounds.

Excellent organization and attention to detail kept the Lexington fair running smoothly throughout its existence. Officials advertised widely, arranged transportation, hired plenty of ticket sellers and takers, appointed a sufficient number of marshals, watchmen, and policemen, and kept refreshment stands well-stocked with food and ice. The large premiums paid to winning contestants and the continual addition of new activities, such as the introduction of horse racing in 1872, spread the fair's fame throughout Kentucky and contiguous states. A report placed the 1891 fair's attendance at more than forty thousand, with excursion trains from as far away as Indiana and Ohio.

The association awarded prizes in dozens of categories. Children were eligible for premiums in three educational classifications—essays, penmanship, and painting—and in four activities—sewing, baking, canning, and livestock displays. Adults won prizes from one dollar to fifteen dollars in poultry and livestock competition, displaying skills in workmanship and manufacturing, and winning races. There were premiums for production of grain, fruits, vegetables, wines, cordials, honeys, and hams. Women competed in sewing, needlework, baking, preserving, and food displays. Aesthetic awards, such as the coveted gold medal which went to the person winning the largest number of premiums for floral displays, drew widespread public attention. The horse races, however, were the most popular events of the fair, probably because of premiums that ranged up to one hundred dollars. In 1891 the A & M Association awarded prizes totaling three thousand dollars.[61]

The growing spectator sport of baseball became very popular in Kentucky after the war. Black baseball first attracted attention in Louisville when the Mutuals and the Globes played an exciting game as part of the A & M Fair in September 1874. They probably consisted of local amateur or semiprofessional teams using names of better known eastern clubs. Competition probably remained at that level in the urban areas of the Commonwealth for about ten years.[62]

Louisville's first black professional team, the Falls Citys, organized in 1886. The team, apparently managed by C.H. Ennis, constructed a roofed stadium at Sixteenth Street and Magnolia Avenue on the streetcar line and began challenging other clubs. Popular players included Frank Garrett, the team's captain, and William Thompson, the catcher. In June the Falls Citys played the Major Hughes Club, a local white team, before a large crowd, and in July it held a three-game series with the Gordon Baseball Club of Chicago. The first Chicago game was marred by repeated disputes between Gordon's catcher and the umpire. The Louisville team next made a two-game road trip against the Memphis Eclipse Club, with the Falls Citys winning both games. After returning home, the Falls Citys again played the Major Hughes club before a crowd of about five hundred.

At a reception after the season ended, the Falls Citys' management announced that the club intended "to swing the willow throughout the Union" in 1887 by joining the Eastern Association. During the winter C.W. Hines, Louisville's correspondent for the New York *Freeman*, took over the team's management, and he secured a franchise for the Falls Citys in the League of Colored Base Ball Clubs. Hines boasted that the Falls Citys had the best stadium in the eight-team league that included the Washington Capital Citys, Pittsburgh Keystones, the Lord Baltimores of Baltimore, the Philadelphia Pythians, the Boston Resolutes, and the New York Gothams. In February 1887 the Falls Citys began selling a special group of tickets for one dollar good for six league games and seeking games "with any club" to fill open dates. After several exhibition games with local teams in April, the Falls Citys began the season as part of the new league. Repeated financial losses, however, doomed the league before the season ended, and the demise of the Falls Citys and the loss of their stadium followed.[63]

Chaos and confusion gripped blacks in the labor market at the Civil War's end. Bold actions were required to prevent their becoming a permanent underclass. But the suggestions of men like Thomas James, Elisha Green, and John G. Fee that blacks needed to become landowners, to enjoy equality in the marketplace, and to share the constitutional protections state government should provide, received scant support from those who possessed the potential to implement innovative solutions. It remained, therefore, for freedmen, laboring within a system where legal barriers and racial prejudice forced them to start from a disadvantaged position, to pull themselves up by their own bootstraps. While most blacks found jobs within a year of the war's end, the fruits of their labor usually meant subsistence wages and paltry living conditions. Hard work and frugality enabled a few to purchase land, including their own homes, but the modest successes of most precluded property ownership, and they remained poorly housed for generations following the Civil War. Freedom and employment resulted in new recreational opportunities for the black community, but whether at work, at home, or at leisure, Kentucky blacks lived in a segregated world enforced by the power of state government. The great tragedy of the post-Civil War years in Kentucky was that the white-controlled government did virtually nothing to ease the transition of blacks from slavery to freedom. Indeed, a large majority of white citizens and state government officials perceived blacks to be economic and social enemies who did not deserve the equal protection of the law, either at work or at play.

*Twelve*

# Civil Rights, Politics, and Society, 1865-1891

THE Kentucky legislature that adjourned in early 1866 reflected the opinion of the state's white majority by indicating that it had no intention of elevating blacks to a status of equality. Whether out of spite or merely to keep alive claims for compensation, conservative politicians, rather than eliminating all traces of slavery from state law, simply revised the old slave code, leaving much of it intact. Thus, those sections of Kentucky law defining slaves and mulattoes, articles describing emancipation procedures, regulations limiting the activities of free blacks, and measures dealing with runaways, though irrelevant, remained on the books. By adopting this approach, the legislature legitimized second-class citizenship in the minds of whites and ensured the lingering shadow of slavery for blacks.

After passing a number of measures which elevated freedmen to approximately the same position as that held by free blacks before the Civil War, the legislature fastened second-class citizenship on blacks by prohibiting them from giving court testimony against whites, sitting on juries, and voting. In other actions, the legislature laid the foundation for a segregated society. One law exempted physically impaired Civil War veterans from state and county taxation, and another prohibited the sale of homesteads for debt, but both laws applied only to whites. The legislature also mandated that tax rolls, taxes, and schools were to be divided by race, that treatment of apprentices might differ because of color, and that only whites could witness contracts. The antebellum law that provided harsher punishment for the rape of a white woman than for the same offense against black females remained intact. Another statute which declared interracial marriages a felony also required county officials to keep separate marriage records based on color.[1]

Kentucky's 1866 legal code contributed significantly to continuation of an atmosphere of intimidation and violence prevalent at the end of the Civil War. In the late 1860s unsympathetic state law enforcers paid scant attention to ensuring blacks the "full and equal benefit of all laws" and the protection "of person and property" guaranteed under the federal Civil Rights Act of March 1866. Nor were state officials enthusiastic about blacks' attaining "the full and equal enjoyment" of public transportation, inns, hotels, restaurants, theaters, and public amusements mandated by the Civil Rights Act of 1875. The failure of Kentucky to extend these and other basic constitutional guarantees to its black minority and the willingness of state officials to condone violence had the effect of fostering the abuse and harassment that characterized the 1870s and 1880s.[2]

The worst forms of violence inflicted on blacks were physical abuse and wanton murder. Beatings, murders, and lynchings, often attributed to the Ku Klux Klan, continued, though at slightly diminishing rates, for two decades after the Civil War. Blacks in the Fayette County town of Athens reported that racial violence made it "almost impossible for colored people to live" in the area. Emboldened klansmen periodically rode into town and indiscriminately "whipped and slashed" blacks. In Estill and Madison counties, klansmen roamed the countryside beating blacks and whites who befriended them. Blacks were driven from their jobs at the Red River Iron Company, and in Richmond klansmen took two blacks from jail and brutally beat one and lynched the other.

Blacks who survived these ordeals frequently related gruesome stories. John Sims, of Henry County, received a midnight visit from five masked men, one of whom he recognized. The intruders separated Sims and his wife and took them from their home in different directions. After going about four miles, the captors forced Sims to walk ahead and then began shooting at him. Wounded in the arm and hand, Sims fell, pretending to be dead. As he lay prostrate the attackers fired several more shots at his body. When Sims later returned home, he found his wife's lifeless body about three hundred yards from the house. She had been strangled and shot. Fearing for his life, Sims walked thirty miles to Louisville to get help.[3]

Other victims, unfortunately, did not survive to tell their story. Sam Bascom was one of these. When authorities found a "large quantity of highly inflammable material" under a store in Owingsville in Bath County, suspicion fell on Bascom. Though at a loss to explain why combustible material had been placed under the building and no fire set, authorities nonetheless jailed Bascom and charged him with attempted arson. Before the grand jury met, however, a mob of masked men took Bascom from the jail and hanged him. In Flemingsburg a "very orderly" midnight mob "broke down the door" of the jail and "knocked down" the jailer to get at nineteen-year-old Charles Coleman who had been accused of raping three white women. The mob took Coleman, reportedly calm throughout the ordeal, to a railroad trestle outside town and hanged him. The number of blacks who met violent deaths in this manner cannot be determined, but George C. Wright's study, *Racial Violence in Kentucky*, indicates that at least 138 died from lynchings between 1866 and 1891, and probably many more. The black-owned New York *Freeman*, reviewing the shorter period from 1869 to 1885 but covering all types of violence, listed 1,405 blacks murdered between those years.[4]

Brutality from law enforcement officers was another form of intimidation blacks experienced in the 1870s and 1880s. Blacks in Louisville, for instance, believed that police were quick to arrest members of their race in a greater proportion to their numbers than whites, especially for the petty crimes of theft, drunkenness, and disorderly conduct. During arrests, they believed, the police frequently used the billy club and the pistol, resulting in injury and death. Once in court, whether in urban or rural areas, they found justice to be elusive, even when witnesses testified in their behalf. This persistent mistreatment dismayed blacks. How long, many wondered, would it take for their "desire to conduct themselves properly" and their "habits of industry" to earn them equal justice?[5]

During the postwar decades, blacks faced discrimination from white efforts to create a segregated society. Whites increasingly went out of their way to deprive blacks from enjoying equal facilities. In one of the earliest episodes of blatant discrimination, the local hotel owner at Mt. Vernon, a town about forty-five miles south of Lexington, hastily removed his signs to prevent W.H. Gibson, Sr., the black railroad mail agent, from taking a room. Similar hostility drove black patrons from most of Kentucky's hotels by the late 1870s. They also incurred increasing difficulty getting "respectable" service in white-owned restaurants and saloons. Declining service and refusal to permit them inside establishments resulted, over the years, in relegating blacks to separate, carry-out windows. They fared little better in stores and shops because clerks and managers were sometimes inattentive or rude.[6]

Blacks also objected to their treatment at theaters, both as performers and as patrons. Posters and handbills advertising the minstrel shows in Kentucky theaters, many believed, depicted unfavorable images which ridiculed their race. When they purchased theater tickets, increasingly they were, unlike white patrons, "pointed upstairs." By the mid-1880s the color line in theaters solidified to the point that audiences were segregated, even when the entertainers were black. For instance, in 1886 when the famous Fisk Jubilee Singers performed at Louisville's Masonic Temple to raise money for the university, white managers of the concert reserved the large ground floor for a handful of white patrons and packed blacks into the gallery.[7]

Segregation and harassment at ball parks and race tracks was especially notorious. White baseball teams could play black clubs, but whites objected to integrated teams. When the first black "major leaguer," Moses Fleetwood Walker, arrived in Louisville, playing on an otherwise all-white Toledo, Ohio, club, the white crowd protested so vehemently that the Toledo manager decided not to play Walker. On the Toledo team's return to Louisville, Walker played, but whites hurled a steady barrage of insults at the black catcher throughout the game, adversely affecting his play. As in other areas of society, by the mid-1880s owners of Louisville's white baseball team excluded blacks from the grandstand and stopped offering complimentary tickets to black newsmen covering white baseball games. Blacks experienced similar prejudice and segregation at race tracks, but some public parks in Louisville remained integrated into the twentieth century.[8]

Blacks also encountered harassment and discrimination in public transportation. Permitted to sit where they desired in antebellum days, members of the black community, loath to be restricted to "second-class and disagreeable" accommodations, successfully appealed to the Freedmen's Bureau for relief in the late 1860s. During the 1870s and 1880s, without state or federal protection from discrimination, most blacks experienced harassment, segregation, and even physical violence at every stage of a journey. Increasingly, railroads resorted to "white" and "colored" ticket windows and further humiliated black patrons by assigning them to a "Colored Waiting Room." Some companies refused to sell blacks first-class tickets; others sold them first-class passage but restricted them to second-class accommodations or to the men's smoking car. Traveling long distances proved even more difficult since conductors refused to rent berths to blacks.[9]

Far worse was the growing trend toward intimidation and force to achieve railway segregation. A few companies permitted black females to purchase first-class tickets and sit in the ladies' car. But the experience of a Louisville woman was more typical. Possessing a first-class ticket, she sought entrance into the ladies' car, but the conductor locked the door and "ordered her into the smoking car." When she objected, displaying a first-class ticket, the conductor stopped the train and bodily removed her. A Berea college student, described as "an intelligent, cultured, neatly-dressed amiable young lady," received even ruder treatment when she traveled by rail from Lexington to Frankfort. After purchasing a first-class ticket, she was refused admission into the ladies' coach. Directed to the "men only" car, she objected and demanded a refund. At that point, the brakeman, with the assistance of a burly white man, forced her into the men's car.[10]

An 1883 attack on Rev. Elisha Green was even more violent. Green was traveling by rail from Maysville to Paris when a white minister and head of a girl's school, G.T. Gould, boarded at Millersburg with several faculty and students. When two members of the party could not find a seat, a white friend of Green's offered his place. Gould rejected that seat and either he or one of the professors, pointing to Green, said: "I'll make this nigger [sic] get up." Green refused to move, telling Gould that if he had been asked "politely" he would have gladly given up his seat, but before he would "be pulled out like a dog" he would die in his "tracks." Gould grabbed Green's arm and began pulling him out of his seat. Someone else pinned Green from behind, holding him while Professor E.L. Bristow struck the black minister with a brass-cornered valise. Green suffered lacerations on his head and one hand. The conductor and several other passengers broke up the altercation. Green eventually won a damage suit judgment of twenty-four dollars against his attackers, but the award had no effect in slowing the march of segregation in public transportation. By the late 1880s virtually all railroads serving the Commonwealth were segregated, and in December 1891 the general assembly began discussing a bill that called for "separate coaches or cars" for blacks. The struggle to stop the measure in the legislature, and later to have it struck down in court, proved to be one of the finest hours of Kentucky's black community.[11]

One of the few successes blacks achieved over segregation in public transportation occurred in the Louisville streetcar demonstrations of 1870-71. After formation of the streetcar lines in Louisville, the city developed a curious pattern for black seating. All three lines allowed black women to sit inside the streetcars, but they relegated males to standing on the front platforms on every route but two. The Main and Fourth Street excursion route reserved the rear seats of the car for blacks and the Market Street car accepted no black passengers. These rules were never popular with Louisville's blacks, frequent streetcar patrons, and by 1870 they seethed at the orders of Market Street drivers: "Get out; you can't ride in here. . . . [We] don't carry niggers [sic]." After months of discussing alternatives to streetcar segregation, a united protest began in October 1870 under the leadership of several black ministers.

The first demonstrations began on Sunday, October 30. Following morning worship at Quinn Chapel, a crowd gathered and by midafternoon about three hundred blacks marched to the streetcar stop at Tenth and Walnut streets. As previously planned, Horace Pearce and Robert and Samuel Fox boarded, paid fares, and took seats. First a white passenger and then the driver demanded that the three blacks leave the car, but they refused. After a short but heated discussion, the driver, assisted by other drivers who had arrived, physically ejected them from the car. Several demonstrators threw rocks at the streetcar, and with the crowd's encouragement, the three men picked up rocks and reentered the car. The line's superintendent soon arrived and offered to return their fares, but he insisted that the men leave the car. They refused. Eventually, the police arrested and jailed them for disorderly conduct.

At the trial two white lawyers presented a carefully reasoned defense of the actions of the three men, but if the blacks who packed the courtroom expected justice, they were disappointed. The judge, declaring that the case involved only the charge of disorderly conduct against the defendants, refused to admit their testimony against whites or to consider the arguments of their lawyers. Each received a five-dollar fine.

Thwarted by the state court, Robert Fox brought suit against the streetcar company in the United States District Court. During the winter of 1870-71 the black community remained calm as they awaited the federal court's decision, but as spring approached tempers flared. William Smith's attempt on May 1 to ride the Market Street line, which ended in violence, signaled an ominously aggressive attitude. The May 11, 1871, court decision in favor of Fox was a relief. Fox received a fifteen-dollar award, and blacks won the right to ride the streetcars.

On Friday, May 12, the day after the judge's decision, blacks began a systematic "ride-in" on every streetcar line. Although whites forcefully ejected a few black passengers, others boarded and sat down without incident. That night crowds of both races gathered, and a white mob attempted to drag Carey Duncan, a black youth, from a car in front of the Willard Hotel before the police rescued him. In this increasingly tense atmosphere, the streetcar owners proposed segregated streetcars, a solution promptly rejected by black leaders. With the prospect of more violence and loss of equipment, the owners capitulated, agreeing that blacks could ride all streetcars. "The new order of things" went into effect on Sunday with no major incidents, but it did not represent a changed attitude for whites. With the passage of times, whites steadily pushed blacks to the rear seats and by the mid-1880s seating in Louisville's streetcars was rigidly segregated.[12]

Kentucky's blacks realized that they would have to challenge the system of segregation, second-class citizenship, and harassment if they hoped to improve their situation in society. They were also aware that they could not stand as individuals against a policy dictated by the white majority. They must, as in slavery days, organize if they hoped to protest successfully against restrictions of their rights. As early as 1866 blacks throughout the Commonwealth had begun to call protest conventions to express their dissatisfaction. A mid-January convention in Louisville deplored the atmosphere of violence that prevailed in the state and petitioned the legislature for the removal of all discriminatory laws, thus paving the way for full civil rights. In a similar meeting in Lexington, leading blacks, after claiming the franchise as one of their rights, sensed the need for greater unity and issued a call for a statewide convention to consider their "anomalous political condition." Great excitement spread through the black community as they chose delegates for the convention.[13]

As the first great black convention assembled in Lexington on March 22, 1866, black leaders and their white friends arrived from all regions of the state. Rev. George W. Dupee of Paducah, Horace Morris of Louisville, and A.H. Hubbard of Lexington led the convention in a forthright discussion of issues facing blacks, including the right to vote. Though the convention adopted a mild resolution stating that they expected to acquire all rights enjoyed by whites, including the franchise, they decided not to press for those rights immediately. Instead, they urged blacks to take the first step to improve their condition themselves through self-help and moral uplift. Another major discussion of the conference was a state central committee to coordinate future meetings.[14]

In response to a circular letter from the state central committee calling for another statewide convention in Lexington in November 1867, blacks began holding local meetings during the summer and fall to choose delegates. As participants debated the issues, several speakers, referring to their war record and to the guarantees of the Constitution, forcefully demanded full civil rights. During the debate, two major concerns gradually emerged above the hue and cry. Blacks especially wanted the right to vote and the right to testify in state courts against whites.

When the second great protest conference convened in Lexington on November 26, 1867, more than ninety delegates representing over forty counties attended, the greatest assemblage of black leaders in Kentucky to that time. The convention selected W.F. Butler of Jefferson County as president, and Henry King of Lexington, Gabriel Burdett of Camp Nelson, and Rev. Elisha Green as three of the five vice-presidents. Shelby County's Bartlett Taylor was chosen treasurer. President Butler's opening speech set the tone of the meeting. "We had the cartridge box," Butler told his audience. "Now we want the ballot box, and soon we'll get the jury box. . . . We went out and fought the battles of our country, and gained our liberties," he continued, "but we were left without means of protecting ourselves in the employment of that liberty. We need and must have the ballot for that purpose."

The next day delegates to the convention adopted a "Declaration of Sentiment," representing a wide range of interests. They demanded the right of peaceable assembly, fair taxation, freedom from segregation and harassment during travel, and protection from violence. Not surprisingly, the two issues dominating the debates were the right to vote and the right to testify in state courts against whites. The convention eventually presented its case in two petitions. The first, a forceful polemic from a "poor and oppressed" people, urged the state legislature to grant blacks the right to testify against whites in state courts. The second, a cogent assessment of the conditions of Kentucky blacks, petitioned the Congress for the franchise and the right to testify against whites in court.[15]

Blacks continued meeting and voicing their demands in various parts of the Commonwealth during 1868 and 1869. By the time the February 1870 black statewide political conference convened in Frankfort, ratification of the Fifteenth Amendment was imminent. In mid-1870 Kentucky blacks acquired the right to vote, one of their most sought-after goals. Thereafter, their meetings usually centered on local or specific issues. An 1871 meeting in Bowling Green denounced the dismissal of an indictment against a state judge who had refused to accept black testimony, and an 1879 Louisville convention concentrated on equal rights issues. The 1882 state convention assessed the general "condition of the colored people," and an 1885 Lexington conference pushed for establishment of a black agricultural and mechanical college.[16]

Blacks also used celebrations of days with special historical significance in their communities to protest segregation, harassment, and violence. Each January 1, Jubilee or Emancipation Day, offered an excellent opportunity to demonstrate and give speeches. Emancipation Day in urban areas usually consisted of parades with banners and marching bands, frequently augmented by blacks from outlying districts. At day's end, leaders delivered highly political speeches to the black community. Interest in these celebrations waned after the 1870s.

Activities in Louisville and Lexington were the most elaborate of the larger celebrations. Louisville's Emancipation Day celebrations were strongly political. Following the celebration on January 1, 1866, participants gathered at an evening convocation and unanimously petitioned the legislature for full civil rights. A year later, 1867, following a great procession through the city's streets, the day's festivities ended at Center Street Methodist Church with speeches calling for political rights. The 1868 celebration terminated with a moderate speech which eschewed politics and emphasized self-help, but participants in the two-hour parade of 1869 convened at Asbury Methodist Church where they heard a reading of the Emancipation Proclamation and an oration by Rev. Henry J. Young demanding the franchise for blacks.

Lexington's January 1, 1866, Emancipation Day celebration was particularly memorable. Blacks from surrounding counties flooded into town. At mid-morning a gigantic parade, led by a dozen brightly dressed men riding on horseback, began moving down Broadway. Several bands playing patriotic songs were next in line, followed by uniformed soldiers. Then came what one observer called an almost "interminable" line of well-dressed black men, four or five abreast, broken from time to time by bands and groups of colorful flag-bearers. Several hundred children followed. As the procession wound its way through town, occasional shouts and cheers for liberty rang out. The parade route took the marchers to the fairgrounds, where the day ended with political addresses.

July 4 celebrations provided another occasion for blacks to protest the failure of Kentucky's legislature to give them full civil rights. These celebrations often consisted of huge crowds at a picnic or barbecue and an afternoon of speeches by blacks and whites. At an 1867 celebration in Lexington, several white speakers, including John G. Fee—who linked equality and civil rights with God's will—assured a large and receptive audience at the "Colored People's Barbecue" that Congress would soon extend them equal rights. In 1872 thousands of blacks from Jefferson and Shelby counties held a joint July 4 celebration at Anchorage. During the morning a young woman read the Declaration of Independence, and Captain Barrett's cornet band serenaded the crowd throughout the day. Numerous speakers urged members of the black community to cast their votes for the Republican party.

Adoption of the Fifteenth Amendment briefly gave Kentucky blacks a third historic day appropriate for rejoicing and protests. Although confined for the most part to 1870, these celebrations produced some of the most memorable gatherings for Kentucky blacks.

The Fifteenth Amendment celebrations of 1870 occurred in virtually every part of the state. The Mt. Sterling ceremony was one of the most notable for smaller towns. The black community chose a president, secretary, and marshals to organize the celebration, and on the morning of April 30 a parade formed at the United Brothers of Friendship Hall and marched through the town before terminating at a campground. Though the "president of the day" had hoped to engage well-known speakers, the crowd settled for a number of short speeches by local leaders. One address, by a white-haired man in the "evening" of his years, struck a cord of response for those who had spent most of their lives in slavery. His life had been "worn" out by slavery, and "his time was short," the old freedman told his audience, but he had one more goal. He intended "to go to the polls to vote . . . [for the] Radical party," he said, even if he had "to crawl." Late in the evening the crowd marched back to the town square for more speeches and cheers for the Fifteenth Amendment.

The largest Fifteenth Amendment celebration occurred in Louisville. Planners invited blacks from surrounding counties to participate, and for weeks before the ceremony volunteer committees from Louisville's black churches worked on arrangements for the grand celebration. On the morning of the parade, more than ten thousand blacks gathered in the city. The huge procession included several bands, and the participants carried banners of every color, size, and shape that praised freedom and deprecated slavery. Paraders marched through the streets of Louisville until they reached the Courthouse Square, a place where blacks had once been auctioned as slaves. There the honored guests, including Laura Claget, the "Goddess of Liberty," mounted a platform erected for the occasion. After an oration by Rev. Henry J. Young, the entire crowd sang "The Fifteenth Amendment," a song composed by W.H. Gibson, Sr.:

> Colored citizens, prepare ye; your manhood's complete,
> God grant that "we all may have peace."
> The ballot-box is open to all of our race,
> Put in your snowy flakes;
> For the Republican party will vote in a mass,
> For they have guarded well "Thermopylae's Pass."
> Vote for them long, vote for them strong,
> Vote for the brave and true.[17]

Though they possessed neither political rights nor power at the Civil War's end, blacks used politics to protest their subordinate condition and to pressure for an improved status in society. In their struggle to participate freely and openly in politics, they encountered opposition from every quarter. Conservative blacks cautioned their leaders to proceed slowly in exercising demands for both the franchise and the right to hold office. Further, Kentucky's Democratic party adamantly opposed the participation of blacks in politics, and the Republican party, with whom fate had tied blacks, proved to be a reluctant ally.

In spite of these problems, most members of the black community never doubted that political influence was paramount in acquiring full civil rights and, ultimately, a better life; and few doubted that whatever gains they made would come through the Republican party. During the 1866 elections, with black leaders calling for the franchise, they demonstrated full support for the Republican party. In Lexington one observer reported that blacks "hung like a cloud around the polls, eager and solicitous" for a Republican victory. Over the next several years, a number of organizations agitated for the franchise and attempted to prepare blacks for voting. Lexington's Colored Union Benevolent Society, a self-help organization with a long record of achievement, and the black Benevolent Society of Winchester provided regular forums for white speakers who informed audiences of the political issues and instructed them in voting procedures. Another important black pressure group, Louisville's Law League, spent much of its energy lobbying for enfranchisement, and the Soldiers League of Lexington, ostensibly a social organization, worked for political goals and enthusiastically endorsed U.S. Grant for president in 1868. Blacks also formed Republican clubs which recruited and instructed potential voters and served as liaisons with white party leaders.[18]

Few whites supported black participation in politics. An exception were Berea's leaders who for years had fought for civil rights for blacks, and had used their influence in behalf of freedmen throughout the postwar decades. Additional backing for black political rights came from the predominantly white, Unionist, Republican mountain counties. By early 1869 state representatives from eastern Kentucky, where blacks were traditionally few in number, demonstrated a willingness to vote in favor of measures that aided freedmen. Mountain whites verified their solidarity when they remained in the Republican party after blacks received the right to vote. Benjamin Bristow and John M. Harlan were two of several state and national leaders who worked for equal rights for blacks. While serving in federal positions, these men labored tirelessly to ensure equal protection under the law. William H. Randall and Sam McKee, two representatives of eastern Kentucky congressional districts, also spoke out in behalf of black rights. Randall was an early advocate of the Fourteenth Amendment and equal political rights for blacks, a position McKee adopted in mid-1867. Several state Republican leaders, such as James Speed, eventually adopted similar views.

Unfortunately for blacks, Kentucky's Republican party was a white organization at the war's end, and most of the leadership and membership intended to keep it that way. During 1866 and 1867 Republican leaders, their representatives in the general assembly, and party newspapers maintained that the franchise was a state matter, a position tantamount to opposing black voting. During 1866 and 1867 the issue of black party membership remained volatile. A few former opponents, like James Speed, changed their positions to favor black participation, but in 1868 when the state Republican party met in convention, it made its position official: black Republicans were not seated.[19]

Blacks had few alternatives. They began organizing their own party apparatus through local meetings while simultaneously mounting pressure on white Republican leaders to change their policy. Their efforts reached a crescendo in January 1870 when, in anticipation of the adoption of the Fifteenth Amendment, state black leaders met in Frankfort to organize their own Republican convention. After a frank discussion of political issues, they called for blacks to elect delegates to a February convention in Frankfort. At meetings throughout the Commonwealth, blacks pledged their support to the Republican party as they selected delegates. On February 23 representatives from almost a hundred counties arrived at the Colored Men's State Convention. With Louisville's H.J. Young presiding, this convention essentially formed a Black Republican party and laid plans for a statewide organization. In a series of resolutions, the convention denounced Kentucky's Democratic party for harassment of blacks, praised the federal government for defending minority rights, and pledged support for the Republican party as long as it continued its "liberal spirit and enlightened legislation."[20]

These actions doubtless affected white Republicans, but outside pressure forced them to accept black voting and party membership. By early 1870 they became aware that the national movement for the Fifteenth Amendment, enfranchising blacks, would be successful. White Republicans, having gone down in resounding defeats in previous contests with Democrats, belatedly recognized that black votes were their only hope for victory. When Kentucky's white Republican leaders met in May 1870, they began a rapprochement with blacks by placing Horace Morris on a committee to choose those who would explain voting procedures to the black electorate. The committee chose George A. Griffith, J.B. Stansberry, and H.C. Marrs to canvass the state.[21]

When the state Republican convention met in 1872, they seated black delegates for the first time and named J.B. Stansberry as temporary secretary. But by this time the issue of party participation had evolved into a demand by blacks for a share in the spoils. Recent party canvasses revealed that blacks constituted a large portion of the Republican electorate—a majority in many counties—and they wanted their share of nominees. Most white Republicans, who joined the party to preserve the Union rather than achieve racial equality, vigorously opposed officeholding by blacks. In the heated debates over this issue, three blacks, George Scroggins, Jeff Porter, and George A. Griffith, insisted that the firm support of the party by blacks should be rewarded. Delegates finally referred the divisive question to a racially balanced, six-man committee which reached an ineffective compromise. The sharing of political spoils remained a nagging issue which continued to divide the two races in the Republican party.

The thin veneer of unity veiled a deep political distrust between black and white Republicans. Most black leaders, regardless of white Republican duplicity, were true believers; they would not, under any circumstances, contemplate deserting the party that had given them freedom. Less dedicated blacks, who viewed Republican hypocrisy with disgust and who might have switched parties, really had few political options. With the passage of time, however, some concluded, as one disillusioned speaker told a Boyle County Republican rally: "Our vote is all they want," and a slow but small defection began as early as 1872. In that year a handful of blacks joined the Liberal Republican party and held a convention in Louisville. During the campaign, several black speakers stumped the state in behalf of its unsuccessful candidate, Horace Greeley. Those few who gravitated toward minor parties, such as the Prohibitionists, found them equally lily-white.[22]

A small number of blacks joined the Democratic party. The Democratic approach to freedmen alternated between outright hostility, designed to get out the white vote, and a campaign to convince blacks that Democrats were "their best friends," an appeal clearly aimed at dividing the Republican party. But the Democratic party offered them even less in tangible rewards. Like white Republicans, Democrats seemed only interested in blacks at election time. Patronage was even scarcer under Democrats, and the inauguration of a national Democratic administration frequently meant that blacks lost even their federal jobs. As early as 1871 several Lexington blacks bolted the Republican party and accepted seats at the Democratic convention, and shortly thereafter they organized a local black Democratic party. J. Allen Ross of Frankfort was one of the few important black Democrats who remained friends with black Republicans. As a state party organizer, Ross frequently canvassed Kentucky for Democratic candidates, and in 1888 he attended the National Negro Democratic Conference and served as secretary. Although black voters in a few elections turned out by the hundreds in support of proven Democratic friends, they were generally hostile or indifferent to the Democratic party, and there were even a few instances when black Republicans mobbed members of their race who voted Democratic.[23]

Acquiring the franchise did not make voting easy for blacks. White Kentuckians began obstructionist tactics immediately after passage of the Fifteenth Amendment to discourage or prevent blacks from exercising the franchise. Several cities—Louisville, Lexington, and Frankfort among them—altered their charters in order to hold elections before the amendment took effect. Lexington's charter also lengthened the terms of officeholding so as to delay black electoral influence. In another instance, the state postponed congressional elections in a futile effort to minimize the black vote. In Paris and Nicholasville officials redrew town boundaries, excluding black neighborhoods and preventing their participation in city elections. An elaborate manipulation of the electorate in Danville was even more devious. After securing a charter revision from the legislature extending residency requirements for voting from one to three years, town officials announced that county residents who owned lots in the Danville cemetery or who possessed local bank stock were city property holders and therefore eligible to vote in town elections. When the Kentucky Court of Appeals struck down the "property holders" restriction, Democrats bought a city lot which they divided into four-inch-wide strips and sold to white county residents, thus "qualifying" them to vote in Danville.[24]

Upon arriving at the polls, blacks found additional impediments that took various forms. Some timid black voters simply turned away when they were told that they were not qualified or were ineligible because they had not paid their taxes. Others were needlessly harassed by questions from election officials, or delayed because of an insufficient number of polling stations. Some voters received fake ballots—ballots with a well-known Republican at the top of a Democratic slate—in an effort to trick them into voting Democratic. When none of these devices worked, officials sometimes refused to accept ballots from blacks or simply "counted out" their votes.[25]

Election violence was the most serious form of intimidation. On this matter, blacks received a confused message from federal authorities. Washington assured those who felt threatened at election time that they would be protected at the polls. In actuality, federal authorities in Kentucky lacked manpower and resources to guarantee safety at the polls, and they made only modest efforts to protect black voters. Physical intimidation took essentially two forms. In rural areas, white gangs visited blacks prior to elections and threatened injury or even death if they voted. Such threats were effective, especially in heavily Democratic counties, and doubtless disfranchised thousands. In Ballard County, for instance, none of the 1,477 eligible blacks voted in a local election in the fall of 1870. In Franklin County random whippings and shootings reduced the number voting, and in one precinct a single eligible black voter remained on election day. In nearby Woodford County where tension between the races had been intense following an election, whites formed a "militia company" and hunted down and assassinated James Parker and Rev. William Turpin, "two influential Republicans." An inquest attributed the murders to "parties unknown."

In urban areas racial clashes frequently occurred at the polls. In Lexington, for instance, the racial tension that developed as blacks gathered to cast their first ballots in August 1870 was inflamed by the treatment they received at the polls. Election judges repeatedly questioned black voters, often about irrelevant matters, and harassed them throughout the day. The delays soon caused lines of blacks to form at several polling stations. Requests for additional voting booths were refused. At 7:00 P.M., when the polls closed, more than five hundred blacks still waiting to vote were turned away. Disgruntled leaders immediately circulated protest petitions and called for a city-wide meeting.

A large crowd convened the next Saturday night at a Baptist church to discuss the problems they had experienced on election day. After listening to several speakers, most of whom counseled caution, a group of black musicians gathered in front of the church at about 11:00 P.M. and urged those departing the rally to join in a protest march. Some advised against the march, but most joined a huge procession that began winding through Lexington's streets. The marchers shouted, sang "John Brown," and upon reaching the Phoenix Hotel, fired pistols in the air. Up to this point, the only injury occurred when a black was wounded in the arm as the procession passed the hotel. Though "not a single white man was distributed," Lexington's whites sounded the alarm bell. By the time the militia and policemen arrived on the scene, the procession had already disbanded, and people were on their way home. The police arrested two marchers, Claude Harvey and Rand Johnson, and as they were led away, a fight broke out. One black was wounded, and a part-time policeman was killed.[26]

In the August 1870 election in Harrodsburg, a mob of "rebels . . . took possession of the polls and intimidated" black voters. During the day more than two hundred shots were fired, wounding or killing seven or eight people. Before the day ended, the Republican candidate for county court clerk, after dodging several shots, was beaten with a baseball bat. A white Republican who assisted black voters was pummeled and told "to run for his life," and an estimated three hundred "Union men" were driven from the polls before they were able to vote. In 1871 firing between blacks and whites broke out just after the polls closed in Frankfort, Paris, and Lexington. In 1882 an altercation between two blacks at the polls in Frankfort resulted in a gunfight. When one of the blacks returned to the polls with a shotgun and wounded a white man, "the crowd" gunned down the black man in a hail of bullets.[27]

In spite of the problems experienced at the polls, blacks became, as one historian phrased it, "the linchpin" of Republican political hopes after 1870. Prior to the Fifteenth Amendment, Republican strength had been largely centered in eastern Kentucky. With the migration of large numbers of blacks into towns and cities, Republicans occasionally became the majority party in some precincts and counties. Demographic changes in many southcentral and Pennyrile counties even improved the party's chances in these two rural areas. The combined impact of black and white Republican voters became apparent in the gubernatorial contest of 1871. Republicans won twenty-seven counties, and their popular candidate, John M. Harlan, received ninety thousand votes, or 41 percent of the vote, including thirty-five thousand from blacks. Harlan's 56 percent increase over the 1868 Republican vote was more than half the total cast in any previous Kentucky election, and would normally have been enough for victory. Republicans correctly blamed their loss on a campaign of racism and Democratic election fraud. Over the next twenty-one years Republican candidates for governor never received under 39 percent of the vote.[28]

In local and county elections, blacks' votes brought occasional victories from eastern Kentucky to the Jackson Purchase. Republicans were elected councilmen, judges, magistrates, and sheriffs in a number of towns, including Danville, Cynthiana, and Hopkinsville. In central Kentucky Republican candidates were successful in Garrard, Jessamine, Washington, and Fayette counties. Black voters in Madison and Pulaski counties helped Republicans win the eighth congressional district while Clinton, Martin, and Lee counties voted GOP for the first time. Though Republicans were a substantial minority in the legislature, black votes made them a viable party statewide. In the years between 1871 and 1891, blacks almost always worked through the Republican party. At the national level they served as delegates to Republican conventions, endorsed nominees, and campaigned for party candidates. At the state and local levels from 1871 to 1891, they displayed loyalty and hard work on behalf of Republican candidates, while simultaneously struggling for equality within the party.[29]

Elijah P. Marrs was typical of Kentucky's dedicated black Republicans. His war experiences sparked his interest in politics. Marrs attended his first Republican rally in the Shelby County courthouse before blacks possessed the franchise, only to be accosted by the sheriff and escorted from the building. In 1869 Marrs helped found and became first president of the Oldham County Republican Club and shortly thereafter, with the adoption of the Fifteenth Amendment, he proposed a county celebration which won him fame.

An early stump speaker for GOP candidates, Marrs reminded audiences that they should vote the way they had shot. On the occasion of the first electoral participation of blacks in 1870, he tutored his friends on how they should vote in a letter to the Louisville *Commercial*. The Democrats, he wrote, did not have the interests of blacks at heart, regardless of their claims. The Republicans, he argued, were the "party of progress," of "justice and liberty," and of the Declaration of Independence. "Cast your vote," he concluded, for "the Republican party." Over the next two decades, Marrs was an omnipresent speaker for Republican candidates throughout the Commonwealth and a fixture at black political conventions.[30]

Marrs's devotion to the Republican party was matched by Gabriel Burdett, a preacher and gifted political leader. Burdett reared his children "to respect the Republican party," and equated God's will with GOP principles. From his base of operations at Camp Nelson, where he kept his flock informed on political issues, Burdett roamed the countryside in behalf of Republicans at election time. A good orator, Burdett had political astuteness which sometimes "astonished" Democrats, and he established a reputation for speaking his mind.

In addition to stump speaking, Burdett served the party in other ways. Though he refused, because of his ministerial responsibilities, to complete the term of a Republican state senator who had died while in office, the party chose him in 1872 as an elector for the seventh district, and his campaign speeches on behalf of Grant attracted favorable comments. Burdett's last and most active political involvement was as a delegate to the Republican state conventions of 1875 and 1876. During the 1876 campaign when widespread Democratic intimidation existed, his itinerary took him to the more populated areas of the state. In Louisville he explained to a large audience that the election was a "contest between right and wrong," and in northern Kentucky, he campaigned for the Republican candidate for Congress. For Burdett this campaign was a watershed. As a result, he came to question the Republican party's interest in the welfare of blacks and its hostility toward black candidates. By the time the disputed election of 1876 had been resolved, he had decided to emigrate to Kansas.[31]

The 1870s provided Kentucky blacks with the best opportunity to share political power with white Republicans, especially in urban areas. Where blacks existed in superior numbers, they were able to influence party decisions, but white Republicans seldom conceded them the right to hold office as they did in Scott County. More typical was the situation in Boyle and Fayette counties where racially equal party committees gave them an important voice in the selection of candidates but never allowed them to run for office. When early party conferences refused to select black candidates for Fayette County offices, Lexington blacks set forth their demands in a separate county meeting.

After repeated failures to win nominations, Fayette blacks in 1874 put up their own candidate, Henry Scroggins, for jailer. At the Republican convention they arranged for Jordan C. Jackson to nominate Scroggins, a popular deputy sheriff who had compiled an excellent record of service to both his race and to the party. Whites objected, hoping to run a black for the lower office of coroner. After leading on three separate voice votes, Scroggins lost in a written ballot. Illiterate black delegates, who were forced to ask others to write Scroggins's name on their ballots, believed that they were tricked. Whites, who jealously guarded the right of blacks to vote if not to hold important offices, nominated Horace P. Gains for assessor as an act of appeasement, but diehard blacks pressured Scroggins to run for jailer as an independent. Scroggins, a solid party man, refused, urging his supporters to unite behind Republican candidates.[32]

Louisville blacks came out of the Civil War staunchly Republican, but their small numbers in proportion to the white population limited their political influence. As in other regions of the state, white Republicans cultivated a black electorate who would adhere to the party principle of voting Republican but not seeking office. Democrats quickly attempted to exploit this situation by their policy of divide and conquer. Traditionally independent, Louisville's black GOP leaders refused almost from the beginning to acquiesce in this unequal party membership. When the Republican convention met to choose candidates for the 1870 election, Isaac Curtis nominated W.H. Ward for jailer. Ward did not receive the nomination, but blacks made their point.

The Republican Louisville *Commercial* carefully schooled blacks in voting procedure before the election. Go to the polls early, they were told, to avoid being excluded in the evening rush. The paper described the Republican ballot and the exact procedure for casting it. Voting went smoothly in most precincts except for several minor impediments designed by white officials to slow black voting. The outcome confirmed the distinctly minority position of the Republican party and reaffirmed its policy of no black candidates. Nevertheless, black candidates continued to seek office in Louisville. In 1872 W.H. Lawson, a paint contractor, unsuccessfully ran for marshal of the city court, and a year later a man named Drake was a candidate for the state legislature. Drake, an honest, impressive businessman, was opposed by white Republican leaders. His only public white support came in a few disingenuous compliments in the Louisville *Commercial*. Lawson and Drake both lost.

In 1875 Louisville black leaders met amid rumors of defection from the party to protest their inequality within the GOP. Speaker after speaker, though pledging support to the Republican party, asked when the leadership intended to honor the party's commitments to the black community. White Republican leaders responded with bribes, personal appeals, and promises of jobs to hold black leaders in line. These efforts, however, brought diminishing returns as the black community increasingly pursued a policy of enlightened self-interest, voting only for those candidates who supported programs they desired. A few, in spite of party pressure, continued to seek elective positions. In 1878 W.H. Ward made another race for public office, this time for marshal of the city court, and shortly thereafter Dr. Henry Fitzbutler submitted his name for various positions. Though Fitzbutler probably had little prospect of election to public office, attacks on him by white Republicans made his disappointment greater than it might otherwise have been.[33]

In 1886 the threat of independent political action by Louisville blacks finally brought dividends. They demanded the selection of black delegates to the Republican state convention, and whites capitulated. At this convention, whites broke the color line by nominating Horace Morris for county court clerk and W.H. Gibson, Sr., for coroner. Louisville's blacks responded to these nominations with an enthusiastic endorsement of the entire ticket. As election day drew near, they realized that Morris was in a tough fight but expected Gibson to be a "sure winner." On election day Morris ran far behind Gibson, and when both men lost, observers cried fraud. The black community then decided to run W.H. Gibson, Sr., as an independent candidate for Congress. The crowded field enhanced Gibson's chances, but as one newspaperman pointed out, Louisville's blacks would have to turn out in force. On the eve of the election, Gibson, doubtless under pressure from white Republican leaders, withdrew, again destroying hopes for a black elected official. Following the election, blacks expressed bitterness about their treatment by both Republicans and Democrats, and some argued that their only hope lay in embracing a third party. By the spring of 1887, however, they had returned to the GOP fold and resumed their old tactics of pressuring the party for concessions. When the Republican convention met in May, blacks nominated the popular Rev. Eugene Evans of Frankfort for superintendent of public instruction, claiming that he would add "strength to the ticket." Whites promptly voted Evans down.

In other regions of the state, black Republicans suffered essentially the same fate. In Paris they felt betrayed when white Republicans assured the defeat of J.M. Porter by running their own candidate for constable against him. This duplicity led to a vigorous debate when black Republicans next met in convention. Erasmus Wells argued the conservative, "go slow" position; J.B. Stansberry led those who demanded that blacks be given a share of the offices. The convention endorsed a policy of electing blacks to public office, but it had no apparent impact on white Republicans. By the mid-1880s young leaders meeting in convention in Paris, concerned about their political future, listed twenty topics of discussion, including, "Do the colored people owe any obligation to the Republican party?"

Every debate among blacks over the value of the two parties arrived at the same two conclusions. The Republican party was superior to the Democratic, except for its refusal to welcome blacks as equal partners. In protest of their inability to achieve equality within the party of Lincoln, blacks in Paris held a second important town meeting in 1887. With about six hundred in attendance, they formed the Independent Party of the Colored Race through which they hoped to achieve their "fullest rights as free American citizens." The new party, claiming to be neither Democrat nor Republican, promised to support the party which would "not only pledge itself, but prove by its works that it is a friend of the colored race." Some months later, in 1887, when the Republican party failed to nominate Rev. Eugene Evans for office, disgruntled blacks talked of holding another convention in Paris in July to select Evans as an independent candidate for governor.[34]

Black political successes after 1871 were few. They occurred most often in those districts where blacks were in a clear majority and ran one of their own, or where they were able to wring concessions with threats to enter their own candidates or to withhold support from white candidates. Their other successes, which were not always apparent, came when they were able to negotiate political deals with white Republican leaders. Some blacks used political payoffs to benefit the entire black community; others viewed them as a quid pro quo to line their own pockets.[35]

Blacks had already acquired the vote and were being seated at Republican conventions when they won the first of two important victories in their struggle for equality in Kentucky's courts. At both the state and local level, politicians and judges were remarkably conservative on the issues of the rights of blacks to give testimony against whites and to sit on juries. In 1867 the legislature had refused to grant them equal testimony rights, and the state's highest tribunal, the Court of Appeals, ruled that Kentucky's law prohibiting black testimony against whites was in conflict with the Civil Rights Act of 1866.[36]

Most protests about this system of justice emanated from individuals and small groups of blacks. After the disappearance of the Freedmen's Bureau courts, blacks formed self-help agencies, such as Louisville's Law League and the Fayette County Justice Association, to provide legal aid for freedmen facing complicated court procedures and to assist them in transferring their cases to federal courts. Though the practical problem of appealing cases to federal courts proved burdensome for a poverty-stricken people, it was, in reality, their only hope for securing justice.[37]

A few members of white bar associations also played a role in pressuring for equal rights for blacks in the courts. The state's refusal to allow blacks equal testimony rights had embarrassed some lawyers, but only the Lexington circuit court offered redress against whites as early as 1866. Pressure from the legal profession began in late 1868 when the Louisville Bar Association announced its support for an equal testimony bill then before the legislature. In the weeks that followed, prominent lawyers and judges rallied behind the legislation. When the bill failed, other county bar associations endorsed a law guaranteeing equal testimony, and in 1871 the Kentucky Bar Association joined in the chorus. The decision of the federal government to prosecute state judges for violating the Civil Rights Act of 1866 when they refused to admit black testimony against whites proved decisive. Under threat of indictment, state circuit judges admitted black testimony in most areas of the Commonwealth by late 1871. Thus, black testimony against whites was a fait accompli before the legislature legalized it in early 1872. Sadly, outside pressure and the loss of control over state courts in cases involving blacks, rather than genuine concern for their civil rights, were responsible for the legislature's action.[38]

Unfortunately, winning the right to testify against whites in state courts was a hollow victory. Ten years passed before blacks received the right to serve on state juries, and once again, the legislature responded only to pressure from a federal court which threatened to overturn indictments of grand juries from which blacks had been excluded. Finally, in 1882, the legislature removed the qualifying word "white" from eligibility for jury duty. Even then, several years elapsed before blacks actually sat on state juries. In Louisville, for instance, where blacks had served on federal juries for years, only the legal maneuverings of Nathaniel R. Harper forced the state to admit black jurors.[39]

Rev. Henry J. Young's comment that black men, once they acquired civil and political rights, "will be like white men—some will be radical and some [will be] conservative," was prophetic. During the 1870s and 1880s, blacks quarreled and differed on religious, economic, and political issues. Yet, the black community, consumed by a developing racial pride, possessed a certain solidarity. The postwar decades, especially in urban areas, were years of energy, of movement, and of a myriad of activities as new groups joined with older leaders in a remarkable drive for improvement. During these years, blacks were organizers, joiners, and social reformers. They were also givers. At almost all levels and in spite of generally grinding poverty, they generously contributed money and time in an effort to improve their race.[40]

The task of providing adequate social service for blacks was monumental following the termination of the Freedmen's Bureau. A parsimonious legislature and white demands for separation of the races guaranteed that any social services provided by the state and local governments would be an afterthought and that all institutions created would be segregated. The legislature chartered the "Southern Institution" for care of the deaf, mute, and blind in 1867, but it did not appropriate funds for the project. As a result, for about twenty years following the Civil War, handicapped blacks, except those who depended on the generosity of families, churches, or friends, had little alternative to begging. The breakthrough came in 1884 when the legislature chartered and funded segregated facilities for blacks at the Kentucky Institute for the Education of the Blind. The black section of the school opened in October 1886 in Louisville in a newly constructed, three-story building. Blind children received instruction in English, music, and industrial arts. Black facilities at the school for the deaf in Danville opened in 1885.[41]

Mentally ill blacks did not receive any official treatment in state facilities until 1868 when the general assembly directed that they be temporarily housed in segregated facilities at Eastern Asylum in Lexington. With the opening of new asylums in 1873, the state moved all black patients to the old, smaller hospital in Lexington. A year later the black asylum was overflowing, and some patients were assigned to segregated facilities at other hospitals. In 1876 the legislature decided to house blacks at all asylums, but in segregated buildings.[42]

The penitentiary was the state's atypical institution. Blacks and whites, both female and male, inhabited the same prison. The female prison population, though never large, usually contained slightly more blacks than whites. The number of black males, however, was always disproportionately larger than the white prison population. In 1868 blacks constituted about 39 percent of the state's inmates. Over the next ten years the number of black convicts increased precipitously, and thereafter they were always more than 50 percent of the prison population. Conditions for convicts, whether at work or in their cells, were unhealthy. To relieve overcrowdedness, the state resorted to convict leasing, a system that allowed corporations to employ prisoners for a period of months or years. Life under this system was much harder for blacks than for whites. More than 60 percent of those leased outside the prison were black, and one annual report listed twenty-four deaths—all blacks.[43]

Care for its poor and unapprenticed orphans fell almost entirely upon the black community. Churches and concerned citizens united, creating numerous organizations which cared for the indigent until local and state governments could be persuaded to accept at least partial responsibility. These mostly urban black institutions bore names like United Relief Committee and Christian Mutual Association, but the favorite organization was the Union Benevolent Societies founded in towns and villages across the Commonwealth during the 1870s and 1880s. Some societies were permanent organizations associated with churches or attached to lodges. Others, merely stopgap organizations, blossomed during severe economic crises, only to disappear when conditions improved. Most became carbon copies of Lexington's Union Benevolent Society which had served needy blacks since 1843. An early success in getting the government to assume responsibility for indigent blacks occurred when moral pressure from relief agencies in Louisville forced the city to construct a new segregated wing at the City Alms House in late 1868, the first of its kind in Kentucky.[44]

Another major problem involved assistance to fatherless and orphaned children. Louisville blacks, building on the meager foundation begun by the Freedmen's Bureau, organized a school for orphans. Originally located on Madison Street between East and Floyd streets, Polytechnic Preparatory School enrolled about 250 pupils by

1872. Backers of the school included well-known ministers representing several denominations. Rev. W.W. Taylor, pastor of York Street Baptist Church, directed the program which stressed industrial arts. Hard-pressed to serve so many children, the school board in 1872 appealed to northern philanthropists for financial assistance, laying out elaborate plans that included a national care facility for orphans and indigent children to be called The Children's Home and Polytechnic Academy at the Falls of the Ohio. Labeling their ideas "an original movement" and describing the school as a "pioneer of its kind," backers anticipated a capacity of eight thousand to ten thousand "inmates" and contemplated expanding care to the handicapped. It would be more profitable to train children "to choose habits of industry, morality, temperance and honesty," the brochure told prospective philanthropists, than to pay the costs of "houses of correction and state prisons." A lack of response doomed both the existing school and the planned expansion.[45]

In 1877 under the leadership of Peter Lewis and Shelby Gillespie, Louisville blacks began their final push for an orphanage. Lewis and Gillespie organized a committee of citizens of both races who soon formed a permanent organization and began raising money. Contributions from black churches, benevolent societies, the AMA, and interested whites enabled the committee to rent a house, and the first patron, Eliza Smith, entered the orphanage on January 12, 1878. Shortly thereafter the legislature chartered the Orphans' Home Society, an integrated organization whose governing body was chaired by a white president and a black vice-president. In mid-1879 the society purchased for three thousand dollars a nine-room brick home and three acres of land as a permanent location. Contributions by individuals and organizations such as the Ladies' Sewing Circle eventually established an endowment of $6,500 for the orphanage, but operating expenses always exceeded the budget. The institution housed eighteen orphans in the late 1890s. Blacks in Lexington were without an orphanage until 1892.[46]

Success in establishing an orphans' home stimulated a movement in Louisville to deal with the problem of black street urchins, a constant irritation to the police. City officials first addressed the issue of juvenile delinquency in 1871 when they built an industrial home, but limited its use to white males. With no home for black delinquents, the city was forced to place them in the penitentiary with adults. Blacks protested and petitioned city government, urging construction of facilities for black juvenile delinquents. They received support from the chairman of the white industrial school, who used both practical and humanitarian arguments in his call for a black department. His reports to the city indicated that ample room for expansion existed on the white grounds and that a modest appropriation could erect the needed building. The mayor agreed, but an 1874 bill for an industrial home for black males was held up for almost two years by a parliamentary maneuver before a compromise cleared the way for construction.[47]

In the fall of 1877 twenty-one male delinquents entered the black industrial home. A few of the children were orphans left to fend for themselves on Louisville's streets. The remainder were there because of irresponsible parents, or were genuine juvenile delinquents. During the late 1880s the home averaged about 111 residents with a 25 percent annual turnover. About one-fourth of the children assigned to the home were illiterate. In addition to industrial training, approximately three-fourths also received basic instruction in grades one through four. Although the industrial home program suffered from inadequate funding, it still addressed a serious need. A similar effort by black Louisvillians resulted in the construction of an industrial home for delinquent black girls in 1893.[48]

Louisville possessed one major volunteer organization designed to assist in solving the problems of black juvenile delinquents. Founded in 1885 by Albert Mack, the Young Men's Christian Association won the aid and support of some of the city's best-known black religious leaders. In an attempt to rescue wayward boys, Mack preached in black community churches and on the streets near gambling houses and pool halls. To keep boys off the streets once they had joined his movement, Mack opened reading rooms and organized recreational activities. Flushed with early successes, Mack began a movement for a national YMCA organization, an effort that slowed his progress at home. Louisville blacks finally acquired a YMCA building in 1892.[49]

Louisville's black community established two additional charitable institutions. In the late 1880s a committee of leading blacks purchased a building in Portland to serve as St. James Old Folks' Home. Despite assistance from several local churches and individuals, supporters could not fund the mortgage. St. James survived in rented buildings until new leadership revitalized the organization and purchased a home in the late 1890s. In 1891 a Louisville black lodge, the United Brothers of Friendship, built the Widows' and Orphans' Home for its membership. Valued at four thousand dollars, it consisted of two houses and several barns located on 230 acres of land.[50]

Burial space and funeral costs were constant, if not new, irritants for blacks after the Civil War. Black churches and benevolent organizations had a long history of assisting with burial costs. Objection to the burial of blacks in white cemeteries, however, raised an issue that involved considerable sums of money. By the 1880s black communities across the Commonwealth formed their own cemetery associations to solve this problem. The most famous was the Louisville Cemetery Association. In 1866 five hundred interested people successfully petitioned the legislature for a charter, and the new association immediately sold shares and purchased thirty-three acres of land on Goss Avenue. Landscaping, walkways, and monuments soon gave the cemetery an attractive appearance.[51]

Three new professional groups—physicians, lawyers, and newspaper publishers—furnished the post-Civil War black community with important new intellectual leadership. Although they made significant contributions to the progress of their race, practitioners of these professions usually found financial success elusive. Consequently, physicians, lawyers, and publishers frequently followed two or even three professions. Some combined being a physician with publishing a newspaper, and others were lawyers who also toiled as ministers or church musicians. Others taught school or worked at the post office to supplement meager earnings from their chosen professions.[52]

Black physicians had to play the major role in community health care, since white hospitals refused to admit blacks. Kentucky's first black physician, Dr. Henry Fitzbutler, a native of Canada, studied medicine at the University of Michigan and became its first black graduate. Fitzbutler and his wife, Sarah, arrived in Louisville in the summer of 1872. After setting up his practice, Fitzbutler began instructing a small group of promising students, but before he could prepare them for admission to one of Louisville's medical colleges, the schools adopted a segregated policy.[53]

Several other black physicians, who also became preceptors, soon joined Fitzbutler in Louisville. Dr. W.A. Burney extended his practice from New Albany, Indiana, into Louisville, and Dr. Rufus Conrad, a native, completed his study and set up practice in homeopathy. Dr. E.S. Porter, an 1878 graduate of Long Island College Hospital in New York and the first black member of the Louisville Board of Health, was the next to arrive, followed by Dr. B.F. Porter from South Carolina. These men, along with one white physician, Dr. John A. Octerlony, served the black community for years. Shut out of white-controlled medical facilities, Fitzbutler and his colleagues decided in 1886 to found their own medical college and free dispensary.[54]

Louisville National Medical School (LNMS) opened in the fall of 1888 with a state charter and three teachers—Fitzbutler, Burney, and Conrad. During the first year classes met in a fraternal lodge building. Six students who had been studying with the physicians for several years graduated in the spring of 1889. In the fall the school's founders purchased the old Louisville School of Pharmacy building and with an expanded faculty moved to the new, improved facilities. The three-year program of study attracted about thirty students annually, mostly from Kentucky, Indiana, and Tennessee. Many graduates from LNMS remained in Louisville, and by 1890 thirteen black doctors practiced in the city. In 1891 LNMS entered into a working agreement with State University, and a year later established its own hospital and nurse-training program.[55]

No other Kentucky community had a medical establishment equivalent to that of Louisville, but a few trained physicians practiced in Lexington and smaller towns during the 1880s and 1890s. Dr. Edward E. Underwood, a recent graduate from Western Reserve University, opened a practice in Frankfort in 1891 and quickly assumed a position of leadership. In 1881 Dr. Peter Allison became the first black physician in Lexington. In 1889 another Western Reserve graduate, Dr. John E. Hunter, arrived in Lexington, the same year as Dr. Perry D. Robinson, a graduate of Howard University. Hunter and Robinson shortly merged their practices and enjoyed instant success, both as physicians and as community leaders. Shortly thereafter, Dr. N.J. Ridley, a Meharry Medical College graduate, set up practice in Lexington. Dr. W.T. Dinwiddie, one of Kentucky's first black dentists, also practiced in Lexington.[56]

Black lawyers constituted a second important new professional class after the Civil War. The first black lawyers, N.R. Harper and George A. Griffith, received their licenses to practice in the fall of 1871. Griffith, described as "a fluent and logical speaker," returned to Owensboro, his home, to practice. Charles Morris joined the state bar a year later when he began practice in Lexington, and in 1891 James A. Chiles, a graduate of the University of Michigan, set up practice in the same city. In 1887 Robert Lander passed the bar and opened a law office in Hopkinsville after studying with a white lawyer. B.E. Smith had a law office in Bowling Green before moving to Lexington in 1893, and in 1891 Samuel Curtis, I.E. Black, and J.H. Lawson joined the Louisville black legal fraternity.

The career of N.R. Harper of Louisville illustrated the potential for problems as well as successes of black lawyers. Harper, a native of Indianapolis, Indiana, grew up in Detroit, Michigan. He acquired a public school education and studied in a law office before moving in 1869 to Louisville where he continued his legal preparation. Upon qualifying for the bar, Harper quickly became the state's best known black lawyer.[57]

Harper earned a modest living at his chosen profession. With court machinery "entirely in the hands of the whites," Harper experienced difficulty attracting clients, since many blacks concluded that it would be impossible for a black lawyer to win cases in front of white judges and juries. During trials he often endured, in addition to ever-present racial prejudice, frequent interruptions and "ungentlemanly" comments. Nevertheless, his persistence and hard work eventually paid off. In 1885 he became the first black to preside as a judge in Louisville city courts, and in an important constitutional case he won blacks the right to sit on Kentucky juries. During years of struggle, Harper steadily built his clientele, eventually becoming counselor for individuals, for organizations such as Louisville Real Estate and Mutual Relief Association, and for the city's black Methodist churches.[58]

Writers and newspaper publishers comprised a third important group of black intellectuals. In the postwar years black Kentuckians published at least nineteen secular and religious papers, mostly short-lived weeklies, and one magazine of national prominence. Most were highly partisan. Editors usually had an obvious agenda, and they engaged in frequent quarrels with each other over methods and procedures. They were strong advocates of human, civil, and political rights for blacks, and most saw the Republican party as the vehicle for achieving their goals. These positions embroiled them in constant controversy with white publishers. Editors also kept their readers informed on issues of particular interest to the black community, instructing them where to register, how to vote, and what actions would most likely influence the legislature. Papers carried news of local social activities, of lodge meetings, and of organizations in other regions of the state. Religious news, travel information, and the latest developments in public schools were other important news items. A few papers with literary sections published short stories and poetry written by blacks.[59]

Small circulations made revenue from advertisements critical to their survival. A number of white businesses and professions, both local and out-of-state, advertised in black papers. These included brewers, manufacturers, drug companies, tobacco shops, jewelers, dry goods stores, building supply companies, theaters, physicians, and lawyers. Most advertisements, however, came from black firms or institutions such as retail stores, restaurants, saloons, pool halls, lodges, undertakers, physicians, and lawyers. Black colleges and theology schools from various parts of the United States also purchased newspaper advertisements, and there were a few personal ads.[60]

Then as now, most newspapers were located in urban areas. The *Ohio Falls Express*, a weekly edited by Dr. Henry Fitzbutler, lasted from 1879 to 1904, when it was Louisville's most prominent black newspaper. Always controversial, Fitzbutler served as an advocate of the black community and engaged in a continuing feud with Henry Watterson, famous white editor of the Louisville *Courier-Journal*. The *Bulletin*, published from about 1879 until its demise in 1885 by John and Cyrus Adams, sons of the famous minister, Henry Adams, was equally controversial, if less successful. Edited by J.J.C. McKinley after 1880, the *Bulletin* took an uncompromising stand on behalf of equal rights for blacks, a position that frequently put the newspaper at odds with more accommodating black leaders. A moderate but highly political faction of Louisville's leaders, led by Horace Morris, published the *Kentuckian* for a short period in the 1870s and the *Champion* from 1890 until 1893. N.R. Harper edited short-lived papers in 1873 and 1885, and the *Planet*, copublished by Dr. Alfred Froman and Fitzbutler, survived for a few months in 1874. Dates for the *Informer*, "a spicy little sheet," are unknown.[61]

Louisville was also the home of several black religious papers. The *American Baptist*, edited by W.H. Steward, became the official organ of that denomination after 1879. The paper carried sermons and denominational news, in addition to special departments of interest to women and children. Steward remained aloof from politics, preferring instead to emphasize race improvement through moral uplift. During the 1870s Worden Churchill edited the *Christian Index* and Marshall Taylor the *Monthly Methodist*, two denominational papers, and H.C. Weeden edited another religious organ, *Zion's Banner*, for a short period in 1881.[62]

There were two important, if short-lived, papers published in Lexington. In the 1870s the *American Citizen*, a joint venture by several Berea College faculty members and Lexington black leaders, played an important role in elevating the condition of freedmen, especially in the area of education. Under the leadership of managing editor Henry Scroggins, the paper attracted a number of outstanding blacks as correspondents, including J.J.C. McKinley, Elijah P. Marrs, and Jordan C. Jackson. W.D. Johnson edited Lexington's other black paper, the *Standard*, in the 1890s. Johnson, with the support of James S. Hathaway, bitterly attacked "class legislation" with a "fearless pen." Another central Kentucky paper, the *Tribune*, published in Danville in the early 1880s, was known for its partisan Republican opinions.[63]

There were several black newspapers in western Kentucky. C.C. Stumm and C.R. McDowell published the Bowling Green *Watchman*, but little is known of the Bowling Green *Democrat*. Blacks in Hopkinsville published the *Baptist Monitor* in the 1880s, edited by James L. Allensworth. After its failure, a group of blacks acquired the press and began printing the *Kentucky News*. In August 1892 E.W. Glass, Rev. E. Williams, and Peter Boyd established the *Indicator* which lasted for several years. Rev. George W. Dupee's *Baptist Herald* was published in Paducah from 1873 to about 1878.

*Our Women and Children*, begun in 1888 and edited by William J. Simmons, was Kentucky's premier black magazine. Dedicated to the family, *Our Women and Children* offered female writers their best opportunity to demonstrate their talent. Mary V. Cook, a Bowling Green native, headed the magazine's educational department. A brilliant student, Cook graduated with honors from State University and joined the faculty as Latin professor. Shortly thereafter, she began reading papers at educational conventions and contributing articles to black newspapers under the pen name of Grace Ermine. In 1887 in Louisville Cook was one of the first females to read a paper before the black National Press Convention. Ione E. Wood also won praise as an outstanding writer. A New Jersey native and niece of William J. Simmons, Wood began publishing newspaper articles shortly after graduating from State University and joining the faculty as professor of Greek. Woman suffrage was one of her favorite topics, and beginning with the inaugural issue of *Our Women and Children*, Wood wrote a column promoting temperance.

Lucy W. Smith penned a column entitled "Women and Women's Work" in *Our Women and Children*. A Lexingtonian, Smith began teaching at age sixteen. She later graduated from the normal department at State University and served for many years as Simmons's private secretary. While still a college student, her articles on women's and children's rights began appearing in eastern newspapers, but her reputation as a writer rested on her magazine articles. Mary E. Britton also wrote for *Our Women and Children*. After attending Berea College, Britton taught school in Lexington. She published her first literary piece, an article that explored relationships among teachers, pupils, and their parents, in the *American Citizen*. Her unique ability for comparative analysis led to informative articles in newspapers throughout the East. Her reputation rose after she became a regular contributor to the women's column in the Lexington *Herald* under the nom de plume of "Meb." Other well-known contributors to Simmons's *Our Women and Children* included Lucretia Newman Coleman, Georgia Mable De Baptiste, and Ida B. Wells.[64]

The 1870s and 1880s were years of intellectual and cultural ferment for Kentucky's black community. With unfettered mobility, many blacks took advantage of new opportunities. Ministers, ex-military officers, and politicians on the lecture circuit toured the country during those years, speaking to large black audiences, mostly in urban areas and usually in black churches. Transportation facilities made Louisville and Lexington regular stops on the circuits, and informational lectures on the "Past, Present, and Future" of blacks or "Examples for Good within the Race," detailing racial pride and progress, were ever-popular. Educational lectures on science, or topics such as Africa, also delighted audiences, and speeches on "The Real Danger of the Republic," especially during controversial elections, drew crowds. Several Kentucky blacks won minor fame for their inspirational speeches on topics like "Shams," "Humbugs," "Masters of the Situation," and "The Cost of Leadership," and interest in the temperance movement filled church sanctuaries in all parts of the Commonwealth.[65]

Postwar urban blacks were also energetic club organizers. Louisville's Frederick Douglass Lyceum, formed in 1870, was typical of several chautauqua-type clubs. Its membership included many of the best-known community leaders, and its programs, held at the Fifth Street Baptist Church, included music, speeches, and debates. Several groups took their names from famous blacks. The Nat Turner Club, a relatively small group representing a cross section of Louisville's black community, met at the homes of members. At the famous 1889 celebration of Nat Turner's birthday, Dr. Henry Fitzbutler hosted twenty-six members at a banquet in his home. Following toasts to "Nat Turner," "Abraham Lincoln," "John Brown," and "Africa," Fitzbutler and several others delivered speeches. The Dumas Literary Club, named in honor of the black French writer Alexandre Dumas, staged plays as charity projects, raising money for institutions such as Louisville's orphan home. There were a number of women's organizations, like the Lunwood Club, which raised money for needy causes, while the Starlight Club was open only to young people between the ages of sixteen and nineteen.

A few Louisville clubs limited membership to black social leaders. The Elite, Fantasma, and the Quid Nunc clubs admitted only the best-educated, successful blacks whose wealth allowed them, more than the masses, to emulate wealthy white society. These groups enjoyed enormous prestige in the black community, and their large weddings, impressive receptions, and gala parties were thoroughly covered in the black press.[66]

Their largest and most popular social organizations were lodges and fraternal orders which began forming immediately after the Civil War. Lodges were secret organizations located in most urban areas, and many possessed separate orders for males, females, and juveniles. Lodges often established benevolent institutions, such as insurance companies, and most engaged in public service, including assistance to widows and orphans or rehabilitation of juvenile delinquents. Masons, Odd Fellows, and the United Brothers of Friendship were the dominant societies, but a number of unaffiliated groups such as the Independent Order of Good Samaritans, Independent Sons of Honor, and Daughters of Samona had large memberships.[67]

Blacks in Louisville were the most active in fraternal organizations. The Masons, organized before the Civil War, resumed their activities in 1866, and by the mid-1870s possessed three lodges with a total membership of over four hundred. The movement expanded rapidly, increasing to fifteen lodges by the early 1880s. The Odd Fellows grew from a small prewar organization to become Louisville's largest lodge by the mid-1870s, with fifteen hundred members. In 1880 they built their first lodge hall, valued at twenty-five hundred dollars, and five years later entered a new ten-thousand-dollar building. In 1861 Marshall Taylor, William Hazelton, Charles Morgan, and Charles Coates founded the United Brothers of Friendship. Originally open to both freemen and slaves, the UBF reorganized after the Civil War with W.H. Gibson, Sr., as state Grand Master. Under a succession of capable leaders, the UBF became a national and later an international lodge, with headquarters in Louisville. Its female auxiliary, the Sisters of the Mysterious Ten, was also based in Louisville.[68]

Music was an important part of social and cultural activities in the decades after the war, and blacks joined music societies in large numbers. Cities, especially Louisville, had a long tradition of talented musicians as both teachers and performers. W.H. Gibson, Sr., began teaching piano and guitar to young black artists before the Civil War, and his students performed in many local churches for decades. Mamie E. Steward and Andrew Bell also earned reputations as outstanding teachers of piano and organ. They were joined in 1870 by the brilliant pianist from Lexington, Julia Britton, who quickly established a reputation as an excellent performer and teacher. Nellie L. Frey and N.R. Harper were the city's principal instructors of vocal music. The Treble Clef Club, a Louisville organization of female artists under the direction of Eliza Davenport, worked toward a common goal of mutual improvement.[69]

Church choirs, glee clubs, and bands also offered talented blacks a measure of musical training in addition to opportunities for performances. W.H. Gibson, Sr., and N.R. Harper led outstanding choirs in local Methodist churches for years, and Madison Minnis and W.H. Steward built a great choir, with excellent accompaniment from outstanding organists, at Fifth Street Baptist Church. These and other choirs performed regularly at ceremonies and celebrations throughout the city. Some of the most talented members from these choirs also sang in local glee clubs, such as the thirty-member Mendelssohn Singing Association and the larger Louisville Choral Society, directed by N.R. Harper.[70]

Bands, an important component of most black parades and celebrations, were another popular form of musical entertainment. Many towns had boys' brass bands, such as the one led by David Crutcher in Henderson, and most urban areas possessed adult bands, such as Bowling Green's Excelsior Cornet Band. Some of the larger towns, like Louisville, had several bands and an orchestra.

Finally, there were several famous musical exhibitions in Louisville in the 1880s. Blacks organized the Colored Musical Association, with W.H. Gibson, Sr., as president and N.R. Harper as music director, and launched plans for a music festival in May 1880. The weekend of festivities included an orchestra from Detroit, Michigan, and a soprano soloist, Eliza Cowan, of Chicago, Illinois, but the members of the two-hundred-voice choral group, conducted by Harper and accompanied by organists Mary V. Smith and C.M. Bryant, were Louisvillians. In May 1881 the CMA held its second festival under the same leadership. Miss A.L. Tilghman of Washington, D.C., was the guest soprano soloist, but dozens of Louisville-area black artists also performed. The Cincinnati Choral Association presented a cantata, "Esther, the Beautiful Queen," accompanied by J.R. Cunningham's orchestra. In 1887 blacks staged a third exhibition, a "Cantata of Eight Nations," at Louisville's Liederkranz Hall. The two-evening program consisted of forty songs performed by local artists. A year later, 1888, Madame Seleka, "queen of staccato," and S.W. Williams, baritone, staged a highly successful concert in Louisville.[71]

At war's end, Kentucky's legislature had solidified second-class citizenship for black residents by legally creating a two-color society. This refusal to protect the rights of blacks endorsed and continued a lamentable tradition of harassment and violence that had existed during slavery. The natural result was a segregated society in which color assured a subordinate status for blacks in both the city and the countryside. In protest of their relegation to an inferior legal and social position, Kentucky's blacks began a crusade to achieve equality before the law. Working with reluctant white Republicans, blacks, after years of agitation, acquired the right to vote, to sit on juries, and to testify against whites in all courts. These hard-won victories were significant, but they, in fact, did little to change the actual position of inequality which blacks occupied before the state government and in white Kentucky society. Excluded from most state-supported institutions for the physically and mentally handicapped, blacks sponsored whatever social services their community enjoyed until their broad movement for reform eventually won unenthusiastic state support. The major achievement of postwar blacks was the emergence of a distinct society and culture, with black professionals in medicine, law, journalism, and religion providing the leadership. By 1890 neighborhoods in Louisville, Lexington, and other communities could point with pride to their achievements as a people freed from slavery, if not from racism.

# *Epilogue*

BLACKS played an important but largely unacknowledged role in the founding and development of Kentucky. Most slaves labored alongside their masters, contributing significantly to Kentucky's prosperity. But for the majority of slaves, day-to-day existence typically meant unrelieved poverty, limited movement, and subjugation to the will of owners with virtually no recourse in the law. Kentucky slaves wanted to be free, and many owners used the prospect of freedom as a reward for hard work and good behavior. The most fortunate Kentucky slaves were those emancipated by owners or those who purchased their freedom with money earned after hiring their own time. But before 1860 free blacks were never over 1 percent of the population, and racial prejudice condemned even freemen to an inferior status in society. Kentucky's least fortunate slaves were those sold south, away from loved ones. A few slaves acquired precarious freedom, though perhaps not equality, by running away to free soil. Those condemned to remain slaves found comfort in their families and hope through their religion, the two strongest institutions in Kentucky's slave community.

The Civil War was the first viable opportunity for large numbers of bondsmen to run away. In spite of the hardships and discriminations that greeted them, whether as refugees in Union camps or as soldiers in the Federal army, overwhelmingly blacks chose freedom, regardless of its perils. However, *true* freedom proved elusive because of the reluctance of white society to allow blacks fair, equal opportunities. Thus, the uncertainty that had characterized slavery continued as bewildering confusion gripped freedmen's lives at the war's end. Poverty-stricken, the object of widespread violence, and without basic, state-supported social programs, many survived the immediate post-Civil War years only through the aid of the Freedmen's Bureau. Though technically free, they were in reality relegated to second-class citizenship, without fundamental legal protections in a segregated society. As in the days of slavery, blacks turned to their churches for solace, and in the end their religious organizations were largely responsible for whatever unity and power they achieved. Fueled by the mistaken belief that the dominant white class would ultimately give them a fair portion of the power structure and forced to rely on their own self-help programs, post-Civil War black leaders initiated a broad movement of reform which they hoped would culminate in acceptance and equality. Through sheer determination and while occupying the bottom rung of the economic ladder, by 1891 they had acquired expanded political and legal rights, a system of public schools, and inclusion in most state social service programs, though always on a segregated basis.

Despite their slow progress, blacks were hopeful about the future in 1891. In general, those who had suffered under slavery and experienced the revolution brought about by emancipation believed that great progress as a people and as a society had occurred. They were proud of their accomplishments. They had survived the darkness of slavery and the destruction of Civil War, and many believed that given the right approach, their secondary position in Kentucky would end. But to the less hopeful, their progress had come at terrible physical and spiritual costs. Along with the minimal benefits that arrived with freedom came much suffering. White society had fought every advancement, and a terrible burden of violence, ignorance, and unrelieved poverty had fallen pitilessly upon the black family. For most, the ideals of equality expressed in the Declaration of Independence and the rewards of hard work and self-reliance inherent in the American Dream seemed more elusive than ever. Indeed, by 1891 white social mores had fashioned an ever-tightening position of inferiority upon Kentucky blacks which proved stronger than constitutional guarantees.

With declining support from white liberals and diminishing national concern over their fate, black Kentucky leaders possessed few options in 1891. As in the past, leaders placed their hope for future equality in the false premise that full acceptance in Kentucky society only required that they build respect for their race by becoming responsible, hard-working citizens. Such good citizenship in a democracy should win favorable response from the white community, they reasoned. The future would provide the answer.

# NOTES

### Abbreviations

| | |
|---|---|
| CWH | Civil War History |
| FCHQ | Filson Club History Quarterly |
| JNH | Journal of Negro History |
| JSH | The Journal of Southern History |
| MVHR | Mississippi Valley Historical Review |
| Register | The Register of the Kentucky Historical Society |
| | |
| AMA | American Missionary Association Manuscripts, Microfilm, Amistad Research Center, Dillard University, New Orleans, Louisiana |
| BC | Berea College Archives, Berea, Kentucky |
| Draper MSS | Draper Manuscript Collection, Wisconsin Historical Society, Madison, Wisconsin; microfilm copy at Western Kentucky University |
| FC | Manuscript Division, Filson Club, Louisville, Kentucky |
| KDLA | Kentucky Department for Libraries and Archives, Frankfort, Kentucky |
| KHS | Kentucky Historical Society, Frankfort, Kentucky |
| LC | Manuscript Division, Library of Congress, Washington, D.C. |
| NA | National Archives, Washington, D.C. |
| UK | Special Collections, University of Kentucky, Lexington, Kentucky |
| UL | University of Louisville Archives and Records Center, Louisville, Kentucky |
| WKU | Kentucky Library, Western Kentucky University, Bowling Green, Kentucky |
| RG | Record Group |

### Prologue

1. William M. Darlington, ed., *Christopher Gist's Journals* . . . (Pittsburgh, 1893), 31, 43-44, 58; J.A. Richards, *A History of Bath County, Kentucky* (Yuma, Arizona, 1961), 11-12.

2. John Bakeless, *Master of the Wilderness, Daniel Boone* (New York, 1939), 32, 66-72; Otis K. Rice, *Frontier Kentucky* (Lexington, Ky., 1975), 59-60.

3. George W. Ranck, *Boonesborough* . . . (Louisville, Ky., 1901), 10-11, 161-64; Bakeless, *Boone*, 90-91.

4. Life of Boone Papers, Draper MSS, 4 B 145-257; Daniel Boone Papers, *ibid.*, 11 C 28, 56, 62, 76-78; George Rogers Clark Papers, *ibid.*, 48 J 34; Bakeless, *Boone*, 131, 160-67, 182-86, 204, 213, 216, 218; Jonathan Truman Dorris, ed., "Early History of Madison County," *Register* 30 (1932): 131-32.

5. Ranck, *Boonesborough*, 116.

6. William Whitley Papers, Kentucky Papers, Draper MSS, 9 CC 30-37; J. Winston Coleman, Jr., *Slavery Times in Kentucky* (Chapel Hill, N.C., 1940), 10-11.

7. Emma M. Connelly, *The Story of Kentucky* (Boston, 1890), 110-12.

8. Coleman, *Slavery*, 6-8; *Kentucky's Black Heritage* . . . (Frankfort, Ky., 1971), 4-5.

9. Helen T. Catterall, *Judicial Cases Concerning American Slavery and the Negro*, 5 vols. (Washington, D.C., 1926-37), 1:269; William Littell, ed., *The Statute Law of Kentucky* . . . , 5 vols. (Frankfort, Ky., 1809-19), 2:113-23; Bennett H. Young, *History and Texts of the Three Constitutions of Kentucky* . . . (Louisville, Ky., 1890), Part 2:27; John B. Boles, *Religion in Antebellum Kentucky* (Lexington, Ky., 1976), 102-4. See also Joan Wells Coward, *Kentucky in the New Republic: The Process of Constitution Making* (Lexington, Ky., 1979), 37-43. For a discussion of the origins and development of racism, see George M. Fredrickson, *The Black Image in the White Mind: The Debate on Afro-American Character and Destiny, 1817-1914* (New York, 1971), 321-23; John B. Boles, *Black Southerners, 1619-1869* (Lexington, Ky., 1983), 13; David Brion Davis, *The Problem of Slavery in Western Culture* (Ithaca, N.Y., 1966), 23-24; Winthrop D. Jordan, *White Over Black: American Attitudes Toward the Negro, 1550-1812* (Chapel Hill, N.C., 1968), 80, 101, 115, 134, 257-59.

10. Charles Embury Hedrick, *Social and Economic Aspects of Slavery in the Transmontane Prior to 1850* (Nashville, Tenn., 1927), 16-17; Coleman, *Slavery*, 6; Harry Toulmin, *The Western Country in 1793: Reports on Kentucky and Virginia* (San Marino, Calif., 1948), 68; Chester Raymond Young, ed., *Westward Into Kentucky: The Narrative of Daniel Trabue* (Lexington, Ky., 1981), 125, 134-35.

11. McAfee Papers, Kentucky Papers, Draper MSS, 4 CC 30; Coleman, *Slavery*, 3.

12. John Filson, *The Discovery, Settlement And Present State of Kentucke* . . . (Wilmington, Del., 1784), 28-29.

13. Pratt Byrd, "The Kentucky Frontier in 1792: Slavery, Land Holding and the State Constitution" (M.A. thesis, University of Wisconsin, 1947), 49; Ivan E. McDougle, *Slavery in Kentucky, 1792-1865* (Lancaster, Pa., 1918), 4.

14. U.S., *Second Census of the United States, 1800* (Washington, D.C., 1801), 2; Coward, *Kentucky in the New Republic*, 37, 63.

15. U.S., *Seventh Census of the United States, 1850* (Washington, D.C., 1853), 615. See figure 1.

16. Lowell H. Harrison, *The Antislavery Movement in Kentucky* (Lexington, Ky., 1978), 2-3; McDougle, *Slavery*, 9-10.

17. *Seventh Census, 1850*, 615; U.S. Department of Education, *Report of the Commissioner of Education* . . . *1868* (Washington, D.C., 1868), 100. Calculations by author. Twenty-eight percent of white families owned slaves in 1850. See Harrison, *Antislavery*, 3.

18. *Seventh Census, 1850*, 615; U.S., *Statistical View of the United States* . . . (Washington, D.C., 1854), 85. All calculations are by the author.

19. Richard L. Troutman, "The Social and Economic Structure of Kentucky Agriculture, 1850-1860" (Ph.D. diss., University of Kentucky, 1958), 15; Thomas D. Clark, *A History of Kentucky* (New York, 1937), 3-4. See figure 2.

20. All county descriptions are based on an 1860 map of Kentucky counties produced by the author from changes described in Wendell H. Rone, Sr., *An Historical Atlas of Kentucky and Her Counties* (Owensboro, Ky., 1965). See figure 2.

21. Unless otherwise cited, calculations by the author are from census reports. See U.S., *First Census of the United States, 1791* (Philadelphia, 1791); *Second Census, 1800*; U.S., *Third Census of the United States, 1810* (Washington, D.C., 1967; orig. pub. 1811); *Fourth Census of the United States, 1820* (Washington, D.C., 1821); *Fifth Census of the United States, 1830* (New York, 1965; orig. pub. 1832); *Sixth Census of the United States, 1840* (Washington, D.C., 1841); *Seventh Census, 1850*; U.S., *Eighth Census of the United States, 1860* (Washington, D.C., 1864). Statistics for urban areas are very sparse. Kentucky counties increased from 42 in 1800 to 109 in 1860, with most of the growth occurring outside the central Bluegrass region. See figure 2.

22. Troutman, "Kentucky Agriculture," 12; Thomas D. Clark, *Kentucky*, 2-3.

23. Troutman, "Kentucky Agriculture," 10-12; Thomas D. Clark, *Kentucky*, 2-3; Steve A. Channing, *Kentucky: A Bicentennial History* (New York, 1977), 39.

24. Troutman, "Kentucky Agriculture," 17-19; Thomas D. Clark, *Kentucky*, 6-7; Arthur C. McFarlan, *Geology of Kentucky* (Lexington, 1943), 185-86, 203. See figure 2.

25. Troutman, "Kentucky Agriculture," 20-21; Thomas D. Clark, *Kentucky*, 8; McFarlan, *Geology*, 204-5. See figure 2.

## 1. Labor, Living Conditions, and the Family

1. Francis Frederick, *Autobiography of Rev. Francis Frederick, of Virginia* (Baltimore, 1869), 5, 8-9.

2. William Webb, *The History of William Webb, Composed by Himself* (Detroit, 1873), 6-7.

3. Josiah Henson, *An Autobiography of Reverend Josiah Henson* (Reading, Mass., 1969; orig. pub. 1849), 33-36, 38, in Robin W. Winks, ed., *Four Fugitive Slave Narratives* (Reading, Mass., 1969).

4. Kate E.R. Pickard, *The Kidnapped and the Ransomed* . . . (New York and Auburn, 1856), 25-28.

5. Lexington *Kentucky Reporter*, September 9, 1829; John D. Barnhart, "Frontiersmen and Planters in the Formation of Kentucky," *JSH* 7 (1941): 19.

6. *Statistical View of the United States*, 95; Harrison, *Antislavery*, 3; McDougle, *Slavery*, 10-13; James C. Klotter, *The Breckinridges of Kentucky, 1760-1981* (Lexington, Ky., 1986), 63; Troutman, "Kentucky Agriculture," 117-19; Ulrich Bonnell Phillips, *Life and Labor in the Old South* (New York, 1929), 80. J. Winston Coleman, Jr., contends that the term "farm" replaced "plantation" in Kentucky after about 1835, *Slavery*, 45. Very few of the holdings in Kentucky would have been labeled plantations by planters in the Deep South or in Latin America. See Eugene D. Genovese, *Roll, Jordon, Roll: The World The Slaves Made* (New York, 1972), 7.

7. Frederick, *Autobiography*, 9, 26; Phillips, *Life and Labor*, 80; Benjamin Drew, *A North-Side View of Slavery* . . . (New York, 1968; orig. pub. 1856), 379; Lewis Clarke, *Narrative of the Sufferings* . . . (Boston, 1845), 69; Andrew Jackson, *Narratives and Writings* . . . (Miami, Fla., 1969; orig. pub. 1847), 8; Coleman, *Slavery*, 64. Twenty-eight percent of white families held slaves in 1850. See Harrison, *Antislavery*, 3.

8. Coleman, *Slavery*, 53; Drew, *North-Side View of Slavery*, 248; Channing, *Kentucky*, 101; Genovese, *Roll, Jordan, Roll*, 330-31.

9. John W. Blassingame, ed., *Slave Testimony: Two Centuries of Letters, Speeches, Interviews, and Autobiographies* (Baton Rouge, La., 1977), 430; Isaac Johnson, *Slavery Days in Old Kentucky* (Ogdensburg, N.Y., 1901), 22.

10. George P. Rawick, ed., *The American Slave: A Composite Autobiography*, 19 vols. (Westport, Conn., 1972), 16:14.

11. Willard Rouse Jillson, *Kentucky Hemp* . . . (Versailles, Ky., 1942), 3-5; Coleman, *Slavery*, 44, 80; Peter C. Smith and Karl B. Raitz, "Negro Hamlets and Agricultural Estates in Kentucky's Inner Bluegrass," *The Geographical Review* 64 (1974): 225; James F. Hopkins, *A History of the Hemp Industry in Kentucky* (Lexington, Ky., 1951), 25, 45-46, 51-55, 58, 61-62.

12. Klotter, *Breckinridges*, 63; Coleman, *Slavery*, 42-43; W.F. Axton, *Tobacco and Kentucky* (Lexington, Ky., 1975), 28-30, 43, 46-49.

13. Clement Eaton, *Henry Clay and the Art of American Politics* (Boston, 1957), 64, 122; James F. Hopkins et al., eds., *The Papers of Henry Clay*, 11 vols. (Lexington, Ky., 1959-92), 10:176-77.

14. Orlan Kay Armstrong, *Old Massa's People: The Old Slaves Tell their Story* (Indianapolis, Ind., 1931), 112-13. For an apologetic view of Kentucky slavery, see James Lane Allen, *The Blue-Grass Region of Kentucky* (New York, 1892), 45-83.

15. Blassingame, *Slave Testimony*, 211-12; Hopkins, *Papers of Henry Clay*, 10:614-15, 620. Clay concluded somewhat philosophically that, like Levi, he would have fled had he been a slave with an opportunity to escape. Leon F. Litwack, *Been in the Storm So Long: The Aftermath of Slavery* (New York, 1979), 55, 105-6, suggests that house servants, thought to be the most loyal, were frequently the first to flee during the Civil War, and Joel Williamson, *After Slavery* . . . (Chapel Hill, N.C., 1965), 34-35, says the same was true after emancipation in South Carolina.

16. Lexington *Observer & Reporter*, December 2, 1846; Lexington *Intelligencer*, June 21, 1839; Coleman, *Slavery*, 140; Jesse Kennedy to [George Waugh], September 3, 1837, Jesse Kennedy, Small Collection No. 744 (WKU). Alfred Spalding, a Civil War inducting physician, stated that "very few" of the Kentucky black males he examined had been "house-servants . . . confined exclusively to indoor work," in J.H. Baxter, comp., *Statistics, Medical and Anthropological* . . . , 2 vols. (Washington, D.C., 1875), 1:386. A study of Kentucky recruits by Leslie Rowland cited in Herbert Gutman, *The Black Family in Slavery and Freedom, 1750-1925* (New York, 1976), 72-74, indicates that more than 97 percent of the enrollees considered themselves to be farmers and laborers. Deborah Gray White's *Ar'n't I A Woman?: Female Slaves in the Plantation South* (New York, 1985), 49, indicates that the Kentucky household slave performed work little different from those of the Lower South.

17. Rawick, *The American Slave*, 16:9; Richard L. Troutman, ed., *The Heavens Are Weeping: The Diaries of George Richard Browder, 1852-1886* (Grand Rapids, Mich., 1987), 59; Charles Mayfield Meacham, *A History of Christian County Kentucky from Oxcart to Airplane* (Nashville, Tenn., 1930), 79.

18. Coleman, *Slavery*, 264-66. State law mandated the death penalty for administering poison. See Littell, *Statute Law*, 4:223.

19. Henry Bibb, *Narrative of the Life and Adventures of Henry Bibb* . . . (New York, 1849), 65-66, 71, in *Puttin' On Ole Massa: The Slave Narratives of Henry Bibb, William Wells Brown, and Solomon Northrup*, ed. Gilbert Osofsky (New York, 1969).

20. Gutman, *Black Family*, 73; Lowell H. Harrison, ed., "John Breckinridge's Bluegrass Plantation, Agreement to Operate, 1806," *FCHQ* 31 (1957): 108, 111-12; idem, "John Breckinridge of Kentucky: Planter, Speculator, and Businessman," *FCHQ* 34 (1960): 210, 224n. Johnny, purchased in Virginia, traveled to Kentucky alone.

21. William Hayden, *Narrative of William Hayden* . . . (Cincinnati, 1846), 35; Paris *Western Citizen*, November 30, 1838; Rawick, *The American Slave*, 7:39; Toulmin, *Western Country*, 86-87.

22. Hayden, *Narrative*, 43, 45-46; Lewis and Milton Clarke, *Narratives of the Sufferings of Lewis and Milton Clarke* . . . (Boston, 1846), 76-77.

23. Coleman, *Slavery*, 64; F[ortesque] Cuming, *Sketches of a Tour to the Western Country* . . . (Pittsburgh, 1810), 154; Richard C. Wade, *The Urban Frontier: The Rise of Western Cities, 1790-1830* (Cambridge, Mass., 1959), 126; Hanford Dozier Stafford, "Slavery in a Border City: Louisville, 1790-1860" (Ph.D. diss., University of Kentucky, 1982), 32; Toulmin, *Western Country*, 99; Rawick, *The American Slave*, 16:110.

24. Wade, *Urban Frontier*, 52; Channing, *Kentucky*, 96; E.S. Abdy, *Journal of a Residence and Tour in the United States* . . . , 3 vols. (London, 1835), 2:349; Jillson, *Kentucky Hemp*, 5-6; Louisville *Daily Journal*, November 29, 1830; Lexington *Kentucky Reporter*, September 1, 1830. According to Robert S. Starobin, *Industrial Slavery in the Old South* (New York, 1970), 18, about three thousand blacks toiled in 159 hemp factories by 1850. Manufacturers often owned some slaves and hired others. Bondsmen usually worked under the task system, allowing those who strove hardest to earn extra money. See Hopkins, *Hemp*, 135.

25. Wade, *Urban Frontier*, 125; Andrew Reed and James Matheson, *A Narrative of the Visit to the American Churches* . . . , 2 vols. (New York, 1835), 1:121; Drew, *North-Side View of Slavery*, 284-85; *Kentucky's Black Heritage*, 13.

26. Henson, *Autobiography*, 55-58; Blassingame, *Slave Testimony*, 690-95.

27. Wade, *Urban Frontier*, 125; Francis Pulszky and Theresa Pulszky, *White, Red, Black* . . . , 2 vols. (New York, 1853), 2:18; Cuming, *Tour*, 161; Peter Bruner, *A Slave's Adventures Toward Freedom* . . . (Oxford, Ohio, 1918), 19; William J. Simmons, *Men of Mark: Eminent, Progressive, and Rising* (Chicago, 1970; orig. pub. 1887), 430; John B. Cade, "Out of the Mouths of Ex-Slaves," *JNH* 20 (1935): 310; Charles Stewart, "My Life As A Slave," *Harper's New Monthly Magazine* 69 (1884): 735; *Kentucky's Black Heritage*, 13.

28. Isabella Trotter, *First Impressions of the New World* . . . (London, 1858), 244-45; Coleman, *Slavery*, 64; *Kentucky's Black Heritage*, iv.

29. Joseph Halbersham to Edmund Taylor, April 4, 1807, Microfilm File 388 (KHS); Coleman, *Slavery*, 127.

30. Blassingame, *Slave Testimony*, 162, 516; W.D. Johnson, *Biographical Sketches of Prominent Negro Men and Women of Kentucky* . . . (Lexington, Ky., 1897), 74, claims that Lewis George Clarke was "George Harris," widely known as "Uncle Tom," in Harriet Beecher Stowe's *Uncle Tom's Cabin*.

31. Frederick, *Autobiography*, 9; Robert Anderson, *From Slavery To Affluence* . . . (Hemingford, Neb., 1927), 9.

32. Frederick, *Autobiography*, 9-10, 15.

33. Anderson, *From Slavery To Affluence*, 11; Isaac Johnson, *Slavery Days*, 15, 18; Madison Campbell, *Autobiography* . . . (Richmond, Ky., 1895), 9.

34. Simmons, *Men of Mark*, 595; Lewis Clarke, *Narrative*, 24; Rawick, *The American Slave*, 16:13-14; Coleman, *Slavery*, 80. The amount of work expected from children varied among owners.

35. Victor S. Clark, *History of Manufacturing in the United States*, 2 vols. (New York, 1929), 1:341; Bruner, *A Slave's Adventures*, 21.

36. Louisville *Daily Journal*, November 29, 1830.

37. Pickard, *Kidnapped*, 35.

38. Frank Furlong Mathias, "Slave Days," in *History of Nicholas County*, ed. Joan Weissinger (Carlisle, Ky., 1976), 227; George W. Williams, *History of the Negro Race in America* . . . , 2 vols. (New York, 1883), 2:138-39.

39. Drew, *North-Side View of Slavery*, 328-30.

40. Coleman, *Slavery*, photographs opposite 50; Harrison, "Breckinridge's Bluegrass Plantation," 110. British traveler John Melish in *Travels in the United States* . . . , 2 vols. (Philadelphia, 1812), 2:207, stated that Kentucky slaves were "better lodged . . . than many of the peasantry in Britain." See Genovese, *Roll, Jordon, Roll*, 59-62, for a discussion of the number of hours in a typical working day.

41. Lewis Clarke, *Narrative*, 74; Thomas William Burton, *What Experience Has Taught Me: An Autobiography* . . . (Cincinnati, 1910), 18.

42. Lewis Clarke, *Narrative*, 74; Rawick, *The American Slave*, 16:1; Burton, *Autobiography*, 18; Harry Smith, *Fifty Years of Slavery in the United States of America* (Grand Rapids, Mich., 1891), 34. In post-Civil War interviews, slaves generally spoke favorably of their housing; autobiographers tended to be critical. See David Thomas Bailey, "A Divided Prism: Two Sources of Black Testimony on Slavery," *JSH* 46 (1980): 390.

43. Anderson, *From Slavery to Affluence*, 3; Rawick, *The American Slave*, 6:27, 98; Coleman, *Slavery*, 66. The 1798 slave code (Littell, *Statute Law*, 2:113-14) prohibited all blacks, except those living "at any frontier plantation," from possessing guns. The 1851 revision (Kentucky *Acts* [1850-1851], 1:296), which completely forbade blacks from owning weapons, did not prevent some bondsmen from acquiring firearms.

44. John Kellogg, "The Evolution of Black Residential Areas in Lexington, Kentucky, 1865-1887," *JSH* 48 (1982): 29-30; Wade, *Urban Frontier*, 124-25, 221; Stafford, "Slavery in a Border City," 105; Mary L. O'Brien, "Slavery in Louisville During the Antebellum Period: 1820-1860; A Study of the Effects of Urbanization on the Institution of Slavery as it Existed in Louisville, Kentucky" (M.A. thesis, University of Louisville, 1979), 18-22; James C. Klotter, "Slavery in Louisville, Ky.," in *Dictionary of Afro-American Slavery*, ed. Randall M. Miller and John David Smith (New York, 1988), 419-20.

45. Blassingame, *Slave Testimony*, 165; Rawick, *The American Slave*, 16:1, 5, 13-14; Anderson, *From Slavery To Affluence*, 3; Hayden, *Narrative*, 34; Thomas Burton, *Autobiography*, 18; Troutman, *The Heavens Are Weeping*, 178.

46. Frederick, *Autobiography*, 9; Rawick, *The American Slave*, 16:9; Coleman, *Slavery*, 53; Blassingame, *Slave Testimony*, 165; Cade, "Out of the Mouths of Ex-Slaves," 300-301. A study of slave testimony indicates (Bailey, "Two Sources of Black Testimony," 388-89) that interviewees maintained that diets were plentiful, while autobiographers spoke disparagingly of food allotments. For a discussion of slave diet, see Richard Sutch, "The Care and Feeding of Slaves" in *Reckoning with Slavery: A Critical Study in the Quantitative History of American Negro Slavery*, ed. Paul A. David et al. (New York, 1976), 231-82; William Dosite Postell, *The Health of Slaves on Southern Plantations* (Gloucester, Mass., 1970; orig. pub. 1951), 85-86; Kenneth F. and Virginia H. Kiple, "Slave Child Mortality: Some Nutritional Answers to A Perennial Puzzle," *Journal of Social History* 10 (1977): 284-309; idem, "Black Tongue and Black Men: Pellagra and Slavery in the Antebellum South," *JSH* 43 (1977): 411-28; and Robert A. Margo and Richard H. Steckel, "The Heights of American Slaves: New Evidence on Slave Nutrition and Health," *Social Science History* 6 (1982): 516-38.

47. Rawick, *The American Slave*, 16:2, 21, 25; Lewis Clarke, *Narrative*, 25; Bruner, *A Slave's Adventures*, 13; Norman R. Yetman, ed., *Voices from Slavery* (New York, 1970), 137; Frederick, *Autobiography*, 26-27.

48. Isaac Johnson, *Slavery Days*, 13; Bruner, *A Slave's Adventures*, 13; Lewis Clarke, *Narrative*, 25; Blassingame, *Slave Testimony*, 165; Rawick, *The American Slave*, 16:5-6; Coleman, *Slavery*, 53; Madison Campbell, *Autobiography*, 22; Cuming, *Tour*, 161. Foreign visitor James Flint described Kentucky slaves as being "well fed" and having "a healthy appearance" in his *Letters from America* . . . (New York, 1970; orig. pub. 1822), 116; and Englishman J.S. Buckingham, in *The Eastern and Western States of America*, 3 vols. (London, 1842), 3:8, concluded that Kentucky bondsmen had better diets than in the lower South. Civil War inducting physicians drew similar conclusions. See John David Smith, "Kentucky Civil War Recruits: A Medical Profile," *Medical History* 24 (1980): 194.

49. Rawick, *The American Slave*, 16:2, 5, 25; ibid., 6:10.

50. Lewis Clarke, *Narrative*, 25-26. One 1849 estimate placed the average pilfering

loss at ten dollars per annum. See Coleman, *Slavery*, 66.

51. Bruner, *A Slave's Adventures*, 19; Bibb, *Narrative*, 166; Lewis Clarke, *Narrative*, 25.

52. Coleman, *Slavery*, 63-64, 66. An 1849 estimate of twenty dollars a year to clothe a "field hand" was probably too high. The clothing of white common folk differed from that of slaves only by degree. See Thomas D. Clark, *Kentucky*, 96, 99.

53. Coleman, *Slavery*, 63-64; Rawick, *The American Slave*, 16:13; Virginia Papers, Draper MSS, 5 ZZ 89, September 3, 1792.

54. Rawick, *The American Slave*, 16:9, 18; Lewis Clarke, *Narrative*, 74; Coleman, *Slavery*, 64n. In the *Narrative of Richard Lee Mason in the Pioneer West 1819* (New York, 1915), 27, one traveler through Maysville in 1819 described the clothes slaves wore as "miserable," but two foreign visitors, Flint, *Letters from America*, 116, in 1818 and Buckingham, *Eastern and Western States*, 3:8, in 1842 described adequately dressed bondsmen.

55. Paul D. Escott, *Slavery Remembered: A Record of Twentieth-Century Slave Narratives* (Chapel Hill, 1979), 39; Yetman, *Voices from Slavery*, 137; Bibb, *Narrative*, 65.

56. Henson, *Life*, 17; Bibb, *Narrative*, 65; Blassingame, *Slave Testimony*, 390. Former bondsmen agreed in both the interviews and the autobiographies that slave children were poorly clothed. See Bailey, "Two Sources of Black Testimony," 390.

57. Littell, *Statute Law*, 2:113, 120; Kentucky Acts (1850-51), 1:291; Mary Sudman Donovan, "Kentucky Law Regarding The Negro 1865-1877" (M.A. thesis, University of Louisville, 1967), 8; Catterall, *Judicial Cases*, 1:269; Flint, *Letters from America*, 116.

58. Bibb, *Narrative*, 78. For an enlightening comparison with slave families of the Deep South, see Orville Vernon Burton, *In My Father's House are Many Mansions . . .* (Chapel Hill, N.C., 1985), 148-90.

59. Armstrong, *Slaves Tell Their Story*, 160; Rawick, *The American Slave*, 6:98; Bibb, *Narrative*, 79-80; Madison Campbell, *Autobiography*, 23; Anderson, *From Slavery To Affluence*, 4.

60. Bibb, *Narrative*, 74-80; Juliet E.K. Walker, *Free Frank: A Black Pioneer on the Antebellum Frontier* (Lexington, Ky., 1983), 23.

61. Madison Campbell, *Autobiography*, 25-30.

62. Coleman, *Slavery*, 57-59; J.H. Spencer, *History of Kentucky Baptists*, 2 vols. (Cincinnati, 1885), 2:657. The institution of slave marriages was a dilemma for much of the white community. Religious leaders urged teaching slaves the "sacredness and perpetuity" of marriage, something that might be accomplished, they argued, by having ministers perform all marriages. The success of these efforts is seen in an 1851 report which indicated that three Kentucky counties issued marriage licenses to blacks and ministers performed the ceremonies. These goals, in a system that did not allow legal marriages for blacks, posed obvious problems for anyone dedicated to Christian principles. William McElroy, a white minister, recorded his dilemma in an 1856 diary entry. Thom Ivins, a free black, purchased Amanda "for the express purpose of making a wife of her." McElroy agreed to perform the wedding, and a number of Ivins's white and black friends attended the ceremony. Shortly before the exchange of vows, McElroy learned that Amanda was the "wife" of another freeman at the time Thom purchased her. Concerned about the propriety of the marriage, McElroy sought the advice of prominent whites. They assured the minister that "all would be right" if he performed the ceremony. After the wedding, the whites served dinner for Ivins, his new wife, and their black and white friends. See Blassingame, *Slave Testimony*, 186; Walter Brownlow Posey, *Frontier Mission: A History of Religion West of the Southern Appalachians to 1861* (Lexington, Ky., 1966), 214-15; William Thomas McElroy Journal, March 12, 1857 (FC); and Blassingame, *The Slave Community: Plantation Life in the Antebellum South*, 2d ed. (New York, 1979), 165-66. Michael Tadman, in *Speculators and Slaves:*

Masters, Traders, and Slaves in the Old South (Madison, Wisc., 1989), 211, estimates that in the Upper South one of every five slave marriages ended with the sale of one partner.

63. Madison Campbell, *Autobiography*, 6.

64. Frederick, *Autobiography*, 28-31. Jerry's prayer was fulfilled. Frederick described the couple as "happy" and living with their "dutiful family of sons and daughters" twenty years after their marriage.

65. Frederick Law Olmsted, *A Journey in the Seaboard Slave States, With Remarks on their Economy* (New York, 1856), 55n; Bailey, "Two Sources of Black Testimony," 398; Andrew Jackson, *Narrative*, 8; Coleman, *Slavery*, 149-50. One foreign visitor took it for granted that a "breeding system" existed in Kentucky. See Adby, *Journal*, 349. In discussions of slave "breeding" for the southern market, leading scholars include Kentucky with border and Atlantic coast states and assume that the practice existed in the Commonwealth. See Frederic Bancroft, *Slave-Trading in the Old South* (Baltimore, 1931), 67-87, and Kenneth M. Stampp, *The Peculiar Institution: Slavery in the Ante-Bellum South* (New York, 1956), 244-51. Alfred H. Conrad and John R. Meyer in their influential article, "The Economics of Slavery in the Ante-Bellum South," *Journal of Political Economics* 66 (1958): 106-30, are convinced that breeding was an important part of slavery in the border states, but they gave no illustration of its existence in Kentucky. In a largely statistical study based on "circumstantial" evidence, Richard Sutch's "The Breeding of Slaves for Sale and the Westward Expansion of Slavery, 1850-1860" in *Race and Slavery in the Western Hemisphere: Quantitative Studies*, ed. Stanley L. Engerman and Eugene D. Genovese (Princeton, N.J., 1975), 173-210, without specific sources on Kentucky, concluded that border state slaveholders "systematically bred slaves for sale." However, Tadman, in *Speculators and Slaves*, 124, found the "sketchy" evidence cited to substantiate slave breeding to be "unconvincing."

66. Rawick, *The American Slave*, 16:18; Drew, *North-Side View of Slavery*, 328-29; Bruner, *A Slave's Adventures*, 11; E. Franklin Frazier, *The Negro Church in America* (New York, 1963), 31-32; Bibb, *Narrative*, 64.

67. Simmons, *Men of Mark*, 595.

68. Alexander Walters, *My Life and Work* (New York, 1917), 22-25. Blassingame, *Slave Community*, 183-85, described a similar childhood for many youths reared on Deep South plantations.

69. Madison Campbell, *Autobiography*, 5-12. Bailey, in "Two Sources of Black Testimony," 398, found that former slaves described a happier childhood when interviewed than when writing autobiographies.

70. Madison Campbell, *Autobiography*, 11-12, 22-24, 28.

71. Elisha W. Green, *Life of the Rev. Elisha W. Green . . .* (Maysville, Ky., 1888), 3, 10.

72. Lewis Clarke, *Narrative*, 14, 17-18, 22, 65-70, 74.

73. Pickard, *Kidnapped*, 56-59, 65, 68-69.

74. Gutman, *Black Family*, 30; Robert Dale Owen, *The Wrong of Slavery the Right of Emancipation . . .* (New York, 1969; orig. pub. 1864), 121; Bibb, *Narrative*, 65; Pickard, *Kidnapped*, 52-55.

75. Lexington *Observer & Reporter*, June 28, 1838; Louisville *Commercial*, May 1, 1874; Anderson, *From Slavery To Affluence*, 4-5; Darold D. Wax, "Robert Ball Anderson, A Kentucky Slave, 1843-1864," *Register* 81 (1983): 258.

76. Lexington *Observer & Reporter*, August 13, 1834; Lexington *Intelligencer*, June 21, 1839; Paris *Western Citizen*, September 24, 1831; Karl Bernhard, *Travels through North America . . .*, 2 vols. (Philadelphia, 1828), 2:133-34; Henry Timberlake Duncan to Henry Duncan, October 21, 1858, Duncan Family Papers (UK).

77. Wallace B. Turner, "Kentucky In A Decade of Change, 1850-1860" (Ph.D.

diss., University of Kentucky, 1954), 96; McDougle, *Slavery*, 17-18; Paris *Western Citizen*, September 24, 1831; Robert McMikell to James Piper, Bill of Sale, June 1831, James Piper Papers (UK); Coleman, *Slavery*, 119. Abolitionist Charles Elliott, *Sinfulness of American Slavery* . . . , 2 vols. (Cincinnati, 1850), 1:287-88, described three occasions when Kentucky slave traders sold infants, separating them from their mothers, and a fourth involving a child of about five.

78. Isaac Johnson, *Slavery Days*, 10-11.

79. Rawick, *The American Slave*, 6:9-10.

80. William Pratt Diary, January 1, 1856 (5 vols., UK); all references are to vol. 2. See also William Bruce Strother, "Negro Culture in Lexington, Kentucky" (M.A. thesis, University of Kentucky, 1939), 11; Simmons, *Men of Mark*, 605.

81. Pratt Diary, February 13, 1860.

82. Troutman, *The Heavens Are Weeping*, 94; S.J. Conkwright, *History of the Churches of Boone's Creek Baptist Association of Kentucky* (Winchester, Ky., 1923), 71-72; Trotter, *First Impressions*, 243, 252.

83. Blassingame, *Slave Testimony*, 48-49; Bell I. Wiley, ed., *Slaves No More: Letters from Liberia, 1833-1869* (Lexington, Ky., 1980), 257-59, 262, 266; "Gooley" to "Dear Mistresses," November 30, 1807, Duke Marion Godbey Papers, Reel 1, Microfilm 620 (UK).

84. George R. Browder Diary, October 7, 1853, photo and typescript copies (WKU); Henson, *Autobiography*, 51; Lewis and Milton Clarke, *Narratives of Sufferings*, 81-82.

85. Lexington *Observer & Reporter*, September 26, 1838, January 1, 1840, August 7, 1844; Lexington *Kentucky Gazette*, September 12, 1839.

86. Lexington *Observer & Reporter*, June 28, 1838, September 5, 1838; J. Winston Coleman, Jr., "Lexington's Slave Dealers and Their Southern Trade," *FCHQ* 12 (1938): 18-19; Coleman, *Slavery*, 189-90.

## 2. Slave Mobility, Recreation, Health, and Treatment

1. Littell, *Statute Law*, 2:113-14; Kentucky *Acts* (1849-50), 48; (1850-51), 1:301-2.

2. Minutes of the Bardstown Trustees, May 30, 1806, from the scrapbook of Ella Kourvenberg (?), reprinted in the Bardstown *Kentucky Standard*, September 17, 1936; J. Stoddard Johnston, ed., *Memorial History of Louisville From Its First Settlement to the Year 1896*, 2 vols. (Chicago, 1896), 1:67; Legislative Records of Louisville, Kentucky, November 5, 1853, Ordinance and Resolution Book 1, August 1, 1851, Book 2, November 5, 1853, Microfilm Project 10, Reel 45 (235 vols., UL). The curfew did not apply to a "slave found at the home of his wife" between 10:30 P.M. and daylight. During any given crisis, however, city authorities reserved the right to alter curfew regulations. See Baltimore *Sun*, December 26, 1856.

3. E.L. Starling, *History of Henderson and Henderson County, Ky.* (Henderson, Ky., 1887), 279; Coleman, *Slavery*, 104, 107; Minutes of the Trustees for the City of Bowling Green, June 7, 1825 (typescript, 3 vols., WKU), 1:18; Kentucky *Acts* (1825), 66. While writers used terms such as "town watch," "watchmen," and "patrols," they refer to the same type of activities whether urban or rural.

4. Wade, *Urban Frontier*, 88; Trustees Minute Book, Lexington, Kentucky, July 7, 1800, September 25, 1801, February 13, 1812, June 17, 1813, December 7, 1854, Microfilm 224 (UK).

5. Kentucky *Acts* (1850-51), 1:309-10; *The Revised Statutes of Kentucky . . . 1851 and 1852* (Frankfort, Ky., 1852), 520-21; Coleman, *Slavery*, 95-96. In the Ohio River counties, where potential for escape was the greatest and state requirements for county

diligence were strictest, patrols were limited to only thirty members.

6. McDougle, *Slavery*, 53; J. Winston Coleman, Jr., *Stage-Coach Days in the Bluegrass* . . . (Louisville, Ky., 1935), 196-97; Lexington *Kentucky Statesman*, March 29, 1853.

7. "Article of Agreement" in "Business Papers, 1830," May 23, 1830, Box 6, Brutus Janius Clay Papers (UK); Coleman, *Slavery*, 99, 101n; Harrison, "Breckinridge's Bluegrass Plantation," 106.

8. Coleman, *Slavery*, 100; Lewis and Milton Clarke, *Narratives of the Sufferings*, 81-83; Henson, *Autobiography*, 41-45. Slaves allowed extensive travel occasionally had passes signed by their owners and several other prominent whites.

9. Catterall, *Judicial Cases*, 1:308-9; Elisha Green *Life*, 6-7.

10. Lexington *Kentucky Gazette*, March 6, 1878; Walter H. Riley, *Forty Years in the Lap of Methodism: History of Lexington Conference of Methodist Episcopal Church* (Louisville, Ky., 1915), 29; Minutes of the Fifth Street Baptist Church (4 vols., Fifth Street Baptist Church Safe, Louisville, Kentucky, microfilm copies currently located at UL), 1: September 27, 1842, December 8, 1842, February 26, 1843, June 25, 1843, February 25, 1844, March 24, 1844, May 26, 1844, August 25, 1844, September 21, 1844, December 27, 1846, September 9, 1847; Minutes of the Green Street Baptist Church, Reel 1, Microfilm Project 92 (6 vols., UL), 1: January 12, 1845, April 18, 1845, May 11, 1845, June 8, 1845, July 13, 1845, October 14, 1849.

11. Buckingham, *Eastern and Western States*, 3:7-8; Trotter, *First Impressions*, 243-44.

12. Yetman, *Voices from Slavery*, 137; Rawick, *The American Slave*, 7:40-41.

13. Coleman, *Slavery*, 96-97, 113; Theodore Dwight Weld, *American Slavery As It Is: Testimony of a Thousand Witnesses* (New York, 1969; orig. pub. 1839), 92; Trustees Minute Book, Lexington, Kentucky, June 17, 1813; Lexington *Intelligencer*, October 12, 1838; Lexington *Observer & Reporter*, September 15, 1838.

14. Bibb, *Narrative*, 68; Coleman, *Slavery*, 102-3; Blassingame, *Slave Testimony*, 156-57; W.H. Gibson, *Historical Sketch of the Progress of the Colored Race, in Louisville, Ky.* (Louisville, Ky., 1897), 36.

15. John B. Boles, *Black Southerners, 1619-1869* (Lexington, Ky., 1983), 44; Rawick, *The American Slave*, 16:15, 18, 23; Blassingame, *Slave Testimony*, 518; Anderson, *From Slavery To Affluence*, 24-25.

16. Rawick, *The American Slave*, 16:3, 23; Wax, "Robert Ball Anderson," 259.

17. Bibb, *Narrative*, 68.

18. Harry Smith, *Fifty Years of Slavery*, 22-24; Bosworth v. Brand, Kentucky Reports, 1 Dana 377, Fall Term 1833; Coleman, *Slavery*, 101-3.

19. Anderson, *From Slavery To Affluence*, 30-31; Dena Epstein, *Sinful Tunes and Spirituals: Black Folk Music to the Civil War* (Urbana, Ill., 1977), 141.

20. Trotter, *First Impressions*, 243; Henry Caswell, *America and the American Church* (London, 1839), 223; Fred Marryat, *A Diary in America* . . . , 3 vols. (London, 1839), 2:200; Petition to Fayette County Court, May 1850, "Documents and Letters, Nov. 28, 1936-Jan. 29, 1940," Box 1, J. Winston Coleman Papers on Slavery, 1780-1940 (UK).

21. Bibb, *Narrative*, 56; Francis Fedric, *Slave Life in Virginia and Kentucky* . . . (London, 1863), 28; W.H. Venable, "Down South Before the War: Record of a ramble to New Orleans in 1858," *Ohio Archaeological and Historical Quarterly* 2 (1889): 461.

22. Johnston, *History of Louisville*, 1:41, 2:85; Anderson, *From Slavery To Affluence*, 24-25; Epstein, *Black Folk Music*, 179; Armstrong, *Slaves Tell Their Story*, 107. Appropriating folk themes is, of course, a time-honored practice of many classic composers.

23. Anderson, *From Slavery To Affluence*, 26; Coleman, *Slavery*, 76.

24. Venable, "Down South Before the War," 462-63.

25. Jonathan Truman Dorris and John Cabell Chenault, *Old Cane Springs* . . . (Louisville, Ky., 1937), 43-45, 47; Rawick, *The American Slave*, 16:3; Fedric, *Slave Life*, 47-49; Madison Campbell, *Autobiography*, 69-70.

26. Dorris and Chenault, *Old Cane Springs*, 47, 50.

27. Fedric, *Slave Life*, 47-50.

28. Quoted in Coleman, *Slavery*, 74. Execution was a less likely punishment for murder of another black than being sold south.

29. Coleman, *Slavery*, 32; John H. Ellis, *Medicine in Kentucky* (Lexington, Ky., 1977), 27; Lowell H. Harrison, *John Breckinridge: Jeffersonian Republican* (Louisville, Ky., 1969), 120-21; *idem*, "The Folklore of Some Kentucky Slaves," *Kentucky Folklore Record* 17 (1971): 26.

30. John H. Ellis, *Medicine*, 25-26; F. Garvin Davenport, *Ante-Bellum Kentucky: A Social History, 1800-1860* (Oxford, Ohio, 1943), 80-83; Lunsford P. Yandell Diary, January 15, 1830, Yandell Family Papers (FC). Yandell drew up a list of characteristics that he believed revealed blacks to be inferior to whites. Though convinced of their inferiority, Kentucky physicians eagerly sought the bodies of blacks for medical research. See Kentucky *House Journal* (1833-34), 107, 177-78; Charles Messmer, "Louisville on the Eve of the Civil War," *FCHQ* 50 (1976): 264; Meacham, *Christian County*, 82. For a survey of the medical profession's analysis of black health problems in the antebellum period, see Todd L. Savitt, *Medicine and Slavery: The Diseases and Health Care of Blacks in Antebellum Virginia* (Urbana, Ill., 1978), 7-47.

31. Rawick, *The American Slave*, 7:41; Troutman, *The Heavens Are Weeping*, 62, 71, 77.

32. Coleman, *Slavery*, 29-31; Harrison, *John Breckinridge*, 120; Account Sheet 1829-1830, Box 6, "Business Papers, 1830," Brutus J. Clay Papers; Postell, *Health of Slaves*, 108.

33. Statistical calculations are by the author and taken from the census reports, 1820 to 1860. See *Fourth Census, 1820; Fifth Census, 1830; Sixth Census, 1840; Seventh Census, 1850; Eighth Census, 1860*. Data from David C. Green, comp., "1860 Madison County, Kentucky Mortality Records," *Heritage Highlights* 2 (Spring 1990): [6-7], varies sharply from the 1860 census figures, revealing that blacks under age ten died at a significantly higher percentage rate than whites, while a much lower percentage of blacks than whites lived past age eighty. According to Richard Sutch, "The Breeding of Slaves for Sale," 185, Kentucky, like other border states, had a "significantly higher rate of slave births" than the states of the lower Mississippi valley.

34. Kentucky *Acts* (1850-51), 1:296-97. It was illegal to emancipate elderly, infirm, or ill slaves after 1850 unless they were provided one year's support and transported to another state, *ibid*., 305. J. Winston Coleman, Jr., "Lexington's Slave Dealers and Their Southern Trade," *FCHQ* 12 (1938): 17-18; Lexington *Kentucky Gazette*, July 4, 1839. See Weld, *Slavery As It Is*, 38-40, for accounts of old or sick Kentucky slaves sold south.

35. Kentucky *Acts* (1850-51), 1:296-97. The census reports did not separate statistics on the hearing and speech impaired. Statistics for the mentally ill and mentally retarded exist only for the period 1840 to 1860. All conclusions have been drawn from a statistical analysis made by the author. See *Fifth Census, 1830*, 116-17; *Sixth Census, 1840*, 288; *Seventh Census, 1850*, 615; *Eighth Census, 1860*, 171, 175, 179, 624-25, 631-33, 639-41, 647-49; *Statistical View of the United States*, 77. Though considered to be innovative, and perhaps the first modern census, the vital statistics of the seventh census were drawn from imperfect returns. See Carroll D. Wright, *The History and Growth of the United States Census* . . . (Washington, D.C., 1900), 47.

36. Donovan, "Kentucky Law Regarding The Negro," 34. Statistics on the institutional care for black mentally ill or mentally deficient exist for 1840 only. See *Sixth Census, 1840*, 288. Smallpox was the only other illness that required the mandatory institutionalization of blacks. See Leonard P. Curry, *The Free Black in Urban America 1800-1850: The Shadow of the Dream* (Chicago, 1981), 90. Savitt, *Medicine and Slavery*, 247-48, 251, described treatment of the mentally ill in Virginia as very similar to that in Kentucky.

37. Melish, *Travels*, 2:207; Flint, *Letters from America*, 116; Buckingham, *The Eastern and Western States*, 3:8; Trotter, *First Impressions*, 244. See Leslie Howard Owens, *This Species of Property: Slave Life and Culture in the Old South* (New York, 1976), 23-49, for a survey of slave health care in the Lower South.

38. Boles, *Religion*, 101; Genovese, *Roll, Jordan, Roll*, 53-54. One interpreter of slavery in Kentucky, Channing, *Kentucky*, 101, concluded that the benefits of more personal relationships were sometimes negated by closer "surveillance and supervision."

39. Melish, *Travels*, 2:206-7; Buckingham, *Eastern and Western States*, 3:7-8; Flint, *Letters from America*, 116; James Stirling, *Letters from the Slave States* (London, 1857), 51; Harriet Beecher Stowe, *Uncle Tom's Cabin; or, Life Among the Lowly*, 2 vols. (Boston, 1852), 1:23; Blassingame, *Slave Testimony*, 158; Webb, *William Webb*, 7, 9. For a discussion of slave working conditions on Deep South plantations see Genovese, *Roll, Jordan, Roll*, 59-62, and Owens, *This Species of Property*, 21-22.

40. Emma Connelly, *Kentucky*, 173-74, 188; E. Polk Johnson, *A History of Kentucky and Kentuckians: The Leaders and Representative Men in Commerce, Industry and Modern Activities*, 3 vols. (Chicago and New York, 1912), 2:171, 181-82; William Elsey Connelley and E.M. Coulter, *History of Kentucky*, 5 vols. (Chicago and New York, 1922), 2:797; McDougle, *Slavery*, 27, 93; Coleman, *Slavery*, 218.

41. *Kentucky Acts* (1850-51), 1:297; Blassingame, *Slave Testimony*, 250; Rawick, *The American Slave*, 16:23; Drew, *North-Side View of Slavery*, 358.

42. Blassingame, *Slave Testimony*, 159, 189, 348, 386, 430, 438, 520, 523; Drew, *North-Side View of Slavery*, 149, 376; Lewis and Milton Clarke, *Narratives of Sufferings*, 90; Rawick, *The American Slave*, 6:10, 16:16; Harry Smith, *Fifty Years of Slavery*, 9, 26; Simmons, *Men of Mark*, 421-22. Robert Harlan was, until he purchased his freedom, the slave of James Harlan, the father of later Supreme Court Justice John Harlan.

43. Blassingame, *Slave Testimony*, 516; Flint, *Letters from America*, 116; Lewis Clarke, *Narrative*, 18.

44. Blassingame, *Slave Testimony*, 517; Frederick, *Autobiography*, 14; Isaac Johnson, *Slavery Days*, 34; Troutman, *Heavens Are Weeping*, 140-41; Bruner, *A Slave's Adventures*, 34.

45. Drew, *North-Side View of Slavery*, 339; Bibb, *Narrative*, 64; Bruner, *A Slave's Adventures*, 13, 24; Frederick, *Autobiography*, 10.

46. Bruner, *A Slave's Adventures*, 30; Pickard, *Kidnapped*, 40.

47. Gabriel Burdett to E.P. Smith, May 24, 1867 (AMA); Rawick, *The American Slave*, 16:23, 57-58.

48. Fedric, *Slave Life*, 30-31; Rawick, *The American Slave*, 16:23, 47; Weld, *Slavery As It Is*, 50, 180; Owen, *The Wrong of Slavery*, 121; Yetman, *Voices from Slavery*, 137; Lexington *Kentucky Reporter*, September 1, 1830; Lexington *Kentucky Gazette*, January 18, 1838. See also Coleman, *Slavery*, 246-47.

49. Weld, *Slavery As It Is*, 90-93; Blassingame, *Slave Testimony*, 430; Isaac Johnson, *Slavery Days*, 31. See also William E. Ellis, H.E. Everman, and Richard D. Sears, *Madison County: Two Hundred Years in Retrospect* (Richmond, Ky., 1985), 116. Genovese's descriptions in *Roll, Jordan, Roll*, 63-68, reveal that Lower South punishments differed only by degree.

50. Weld, *Slavery As It Is*, 67, 87; Coleman, *Slavery*, 250-55.

51. Boynton Merrill, Jr., *Jefferson's Nephews: A Frontier Tragedy*, 2nd ed. (Lexington, Ky., 1987), x-xi, 215, 256-58, 267, 289, 291-97, 300-302; Lexington *Kentucky Gazette*, May 12, 1812.

52. Coleman, *Slavery*, 247-48; W.H. Townsend, *Lincoln and His Wife's Home Town* (Indianapolis, Ind., 1929), 95-96.

53. Coleman, *Slavery*, 248-49; Cassius Marcellus Clay, *The Life of Cassius Marcellus Clay* . . . (Cincinnati, 1886), 28; Bruner, *A Slave's Adventures*, 33.

54. William Littell and Jacob Swigert, eds., *A Digest of the Statute Laws of Kentucky*

... (Frankfort, Ky., 1822), 2:1160; Coleman, *Slavery*, 247; Townsend, *Lincoln*, 81; Littell, *Statute Law*, 2:117.

55. Littell, *Statute Law*, 2:117-18; Coleman, *Slavery*, 161-62; Commonwealth v. Bird (a slave), Barren Circuit Court, March 14, 1846, Order Books, vols. 12-13 (1845-48), 225; McDougle, *Slavery*, 37.

56. Littell, *Statute Law*, 2:117-18; Littell and Swigert, *Digest*, 2:1159; Bennett H. Young, *Three Constitutions*, Part 2:50, 84; McDougle, *Slavery*, 36, 38; Genovese, *Roll, Jordan, Roll*, 32; Stampp, *Peculiar Institution*, 206; Orville W. Taylor, *Negro Slavery in Arkansas* (Durham, N.C., 1958), 208-11, 213-15, 232-35; A.E. Keir Nash, "Slave Trials," in Miller and Smith, *Dictionary of Afro-American Slavery*, 742. There were a few instances where grand juries met to consider crimes of blacks. See Grand Jury Report, Bracken Circuit Court, 1848, typescript, "Documents and Letters, November 28, 1936- January 29, 1940," box 1, Coleman Papers. Virginia's slave criminal code was slightly harsher than that of Kentucky. See James Curtis Ballagh, *A History of Slavery in Virginia* (Baltimore, 1902), 82-89.

57. Daniel J. Flanigan, "Criminal Procedure in Slave Trials in the Antebellum South," *JSH* 40 (1974): 545; Littell, *Statute Law*, 2:118; Kentucky Acts (1850-51), 1:303; McDougle, *Slavery*, 37. Courts usually undervalued condemned slaves.

58. Quoted in Coleman, *Slavery*, 255. For an interesting, but this author believes questionable, contrast see Arthur F. Howington, *What Sayeth The Law: The Treatment of Slaves and Free Blacks in the State and Local Courts of Tennessee* (New York & London, 1986), which describes stronger legal rights for blacks in Tennessee.

59. Hopkinsville *Semi-Weekly South Kentuckian*, June 26, 1885; Meacham, *Christian County*, 79, 82-83.

60. Paris *Western Citizen*, August 20, 1831.

### 3. Resistance to Slavery

1. Larry Gara, *The Liberty Line: The Legend of the Underground Railroad* (Lexington, Ky., 1961), 40; Elisha Green, *Life*, 5-6; Bibb, *Narrative*, 66, 80-81; Blassingame, *Slave Testimony*, 49-50, 250-51.

2. Bowles, *Black Southerners*, 49-50; Drew, *North-Side View of Slavery*, 151, 199; Blassingame, *Slave Testimony*, 211. Henry Bibb, cited in Osofsky, *Puttin' On Ole Massa*, 18, called slavery "the graveyard of the mind." For a debate on the effect of slavery on blacks, see Bailey, "Two Sources of Black Testimony," 399-401.

3. Bennett H. Young, *Constitutions of Kentucky*, Part 2:28, 50, 83; Edward M. Post, "Kentucky Law Concerning Emancipation or Freedom of Slaves," *FCHQ* 59 (1985): 344-45; Bowles, *Religion*, 102-4, 107-10, 113-14, 118; Daniel Boone Papers, Draper MSS, 27 C 119-20; Clement Eaton, *The Freedom-of-Thought Struggle in the Old South*, 2d ed. (New York, 1964), 177-78; Robert William Fogel and Stanley L. Engerman, *Time on the Cross: The Economics of American Negro Slavery*, 2 vols. (Boston, 1974), 1:159-60; Gara, *Liberty Line*, 72; McDougle, *Slavery*, 64-65.

4. Catterall, *Judicial Cases*, 1:281; Robert M. Ireland, *The County Courts in Antebellum Kentucky* (Lexington, Ky., 1972), 30; Littell, *Statute Law*, 2:119; Post, "Kentucky Law Concerning Emancipation," 346.

5. Drew, *North-Side View of Slavery*, 270, 376; Andrew Jackson, *Narratives*, 8. State courts generally interpreted documents awarding emancipation "in strict accord with the provisions of the statutes authorizing emancipation." See Post, "Kentucky Law Concerning Emancipation," 357-58.

6. Hayden, *Narrative*, preface, 38, 41; Levi Coffin, *Reminiscences* . . . (London and Cincinnati, 1879), 312-13.

7. Ira Berlin, "The Structure of the Free Negro Caste in the Antebellum United States," Edward Magdol and Jon L. Wakelyn, eds., *The Southern Common People: Studies in Nineteenth-Century Social History* (Westport, Conn., 1980), 111; Ireland, *County Courts*, 30; McDougle, *Slavery*, 66-67, 69; Post, "Kentucky Law Concerning Emancipation," 347. Kentucky owners manumitted 152 slaves during 1849-50, about 10 percent of all slaves freed in the United States. See *Statistical View of the United States*, 64. Though the number of slaves freed in Kentucky in 1860 increased to 176, the state's percentage of all slaves manumitted dropped nationally to 6. See also *Statistics of the United States in 1860* . . . (Washington, D.C., 1866), 337. The 1851 law which stiffened requirements for emancipation apparently had little effect on actual emancipation. See *Kentucky Acts* (1850-51), 1:306.

8. Eaton, *Henry Clay*, 118; Early Lee Fox, *The American Colonization Society 1817-1840* (Baltimore, 1919), 39, 79; Boles, *Religion*, 121; Lewis and Richard H. Collins, *History of Kentucky* . . . , 2 vols. (Frankfort, Ky., 1966; orig. pub. 1874), 1:52, 76; Turner, "Kentucky In A Decade of Change," 103-4. For a rebuttal of the racist charge against those advocating colonization, see Jeffrey Brooke Allen, "Were Southern White Critics of Slavery Racist? Kentucky and the Upper South, 1794-1824," *JSH* 44 (1978): 169-90.

9. Lexington *Observer & Reporter*, August 13, 1834; Robert Johnson to "Respected Friend" [Thomas Dolan], August 20, 1846, typescript, "Documents and Letters, 1780-1860," Coleman Papers; Wiley, *Slaves No More*, 257-58, 261; Paris *Western Citizen*, January 23, 1846; Coleman, *Slavery*, 275-77, 285, 287, 289n; Luther Stephens, Will Book Q, December 19, 1845, Fayette County Records, Microfilm 127 (UK); Charles Raymond Bennett, "All Things To All People: The American Colonization Society in Kentucky, 1829-1860" (Ph.D. diss., University of Kentucky, 1980), 99-100, 170.

10. James G. Birney, Emancipation Document, Deed Book 19, October 1934, Mercer County Court, Microfilm 191820 (KDLA); Robert Wickliffe, Will Book 3, March 20, 1850, Muhlenberg County Court, Microfilm 556492, *ibid*. This was not the Robert Wickliffe of Fayette County, the largest slaveholder in Kentucky, known as "Old Duke."

11. John G. Fee, *Autobiography of John G. Fee, Berea, Kentucky* (Chicago, 1891), 61-67. Fee visited Julett in the prison at Frankfort during the Civil War, *ibid.*, 143-45.

12. Buckingham, *Eastern and Western States*, 3:7; Coleman, *Slavery*, 79-80; Thomas Speed, *Records and Memorials of the Speed Family* . . . (Louisville, Ky., 1892), 191; Madison Campbell, *Autobiography*, 12; Cade, "Out of the Mouths of Ex-Slaves," 310; Trotter, *First Impressions*, 244.

13. Hayden, *Narrative*, 25-26.

14. Blassingame, *Slave Testimony*, 389-90, 440; Gara, *Liberty Line*, 33; Drew, *North-Side View of Slavery*, 150; Manumission Document, September 1840, typescript, "Documents and Letters, 1780-1860," Coleman Papers; Freedom Purchase Agreement, May 1850, *ibid.*; Gutman, *Black Family*, 29; Cade, "Out of the Mouths of Ex-Slaves," 310; Calvin D. Wilson, *Negroes Who Owned Slaves* ([New York], 1912), 488.

15. *Kentucky Acts* (1850-51), 1:292; Walker, *Free Frank*, 41, 46, 48.

16. Blassingame, *Slave Testimony*, 348-52.

17. Henson, *Autobiography*, 44-45; Blassingame, *Slave Testimony*, 391; Strother, "Negro Culture in Lexington," 11; *Kentucky Acts* (1825), 73.

18. Henson, *Autobiography*, 41, 44-47.

19. *Kentucky Acts* (1850-51), 1:301. See also Lexington *Kentucky Gazette*, January 14, 21, 1812; Lexington *Observer & Reporter*, September 15, 1838; Lexington *Intelligencer*, October 12, 1838; Mrs. William C. Bullitt to "My Dear Boys," May 19, 1840, typescript, Bullitt Family Letters (UK); Herbert Aptheker, *American Negro Slave Revolts* (New York, 1943), 94, 252. Owens, *This Species of Property*, 70-105, has an excellent account of resistance in the Deep South.

20. Lewis Clarke, *Narrative*, 27-28; Fedric, *Slave Life*, 83-84.

21. Bruner, *A Slave's Adventures*, 13, 29; Israel Campbell, *Bond and Free: or, Yearnings for Freedom* . . . (Philadelphia, 1861), 18; George W. Carleton, *The Suppressed Book About Slavery!* (New York, 1864), 138; Cincinnati *Daily Gazette*, January 29, 1856.

22. Littell and Swigert, *Digest*, 2:1161; *Kentucky Acts* (1850-51), 1:301; Coleman, *Slavery*, 263-64; Hopkinsville *Semi-Weekly South Kentuckian*, June 26, 1885; Lexington *Kentucky Statesman*, January 2, 1857; Lexington *Observer & Reporter*, October 6, 1838. See Charles E. Hedrick, "Negro Slavery in Kentucky Before 1850" (M.A. thesis, University of Chicago, 1915), 34, for the origin of anti-poisoning legislation.

23. Littell and Swigert, *Digest*, 2:1164; *Kentucky Acts* (1850-51), 1:301, 303; Blassingame, *Slave Testimony*, 163; *American Missionary* 3 (1859): 161; Coleman, *Slavery*, 88, 249-51; Joel Lyle to John Lyle, May 23, 1837, Lyle Family Papers (UK); Weld, *Slavery As It Is*, 87; *Chicago Tribune*, January 29, 1893.

24. Meacham, *Christian County*, 82; Coleman, *Slavery*, 267-68; George L. Ridenour, *Early Times in Meade County Kentucky* (Louisville, Ky., 1929), 78. See also Miscellaneous Court Records, "Documents and Letters, November 28, 1936-January 29, 1940," typescript, Coleman Papers.

25. Eaton, *Freedom-of-Thought Struggle*, 194; Littell, *Statute Law*, 2:114, 117, 119; *Kentucky Acts* (1850-51), 1:293, 298, 303; Trustees Minute Book, Lexington, June 22, 1802; Lexington *Kentucky Gazette*, June 25, 1802.

26. Starling, *Henderson County*, 194-95.

27. Aptheker, *Slave Revolts*, 248, 331; Starling, *Henderson County*, 289; Lexington *Observer & Reporter*, November 7, 1838; Paris *Western Citizen*, November 16, 1838; Anna Dicken to Henry, January 26, 1861, Dicken-Troutman-Balke Family Papers (UK).

28. Charles B. Dew, "Black Ironworkers and the Slave Insurrection Panic of 1856," *JSH* 41 (1975): 332; Troutman, *The Heavens Are Weeping*, 94.

29. Baltimore *Sun*, December 22, 1856; Troutman, *The Heavens Are Weeping*, 94; Boston *Liberator*, January 2, 1857; Coleman, *Slavery*, 108-9. Chase C. Mooney's *Slavery in Tennessee* (Bloomington, Ind., 1957), 61-63, paints a similar picture of slave rebellion in Tennessee.

30. Blassingame, *Slave Testimony*, 156-57; Gibson, *Historical Sketch*, 36; Lexington *Intelligencer*, October 12, 1838; Troutman, *The Heavens Are Weeping*, 94; Pratt Diary, August 20, 1848. All references to the latter are to vol. 1.

31. Littell, *Statute Law*, 2:5-6.

32. McDougle, *Slavery*, 52-53; Wilbur H. Siebert, *The Underground Railroad from Slavery to Freedom* (New York, 1967; orig. pub. 1898), 311; Elisha Green, *Life*, 5; Gibson, *Historical Sketch*, 34; Gara, *Liberty Line*, 127-28.

33. *Statistical View of the United States*, 65; *Statistics of the United States in 1860*, 338. For a discussion of the claims and the facts regarding fugitive slaves, see Wallace B. Turner, "Kentucky Slavery in the Last Ante Bellum Decade," *Register* 58 (1960): 301-2; *Congressional Globe*, 36 Cong., 2 Sess. (January 14, 1861), 356; Gara, *Liberty Line*, 153. George W. Williams, *History*, 2:59, suggests that running away allowed the most militant bondsmen to flee slavery, thus preventing the inevitable "massacre [that] would have swept the South" had there been no "safety-valve."

34. Gara, *Liberty Line*, 40-41, 43; Boles, *Religion*, 98; James Freeman Clarke, *Anti-Slavery Days* (New York, 1883), 86; Blassingame, *Slave Testimony*, 49, 434-35; Lexington *Kentucky Reporter*, September 1, 1830; Lewis Clarke, *Narrative*, 30-31; Bibb, *Narrative*, 72; Drew, *North-Side View of Slavery*, 343. Most of the Kentucky fugitives went to Canada, possibly because of the effective application of the fugitive slave law. See Stanley W. Campbell, *The Slave Catchers: Enforcement of the Fugitive Slave Law, 1850-1860* (Chapel Hill, N.C., 1968), 114-15, 133-34, 136.

35. Bruner, *A Slave's Adventures*, 26; Lewis and Milton Clarke, *Narratives of Sufferings*, 81-83; Sandwich, Canada, *The Voice of the Fugitive*, December 17, 1851; Lewis

[Hayden] Grant to Mr. Baxter, October 27, 1844, photocopy, Coleman Papers.

36. Henson, *Autobiography*, 59; James F. Clarke, *Anti-Slavery Days*, 86; Sandwich, Canada, *The Voice of the Fugitive*, August 13, 1851.

37. Drew, *North-Side View of Slavery*, 361-62, 385-86; Blassingame, *Slave Testimony*, 189; Frederick, *Autobiography*, 32; Fedric, *Slave Life*, 75-76. Far more men than women became fugitives.

38. Blassingame, *Slave Testimony*, 518; Drew, *North-Side View of Slavery*, 180-81; Coffin, *Reminiscences*, 312-16.

39. Blassingame, *Slave Testimony*, 520; Frederick, *Autobiography*, 32-33.

40. Coffin, *Reminiscences*, 471; Louisville *Daily Democrat*, October 27, 1857; Lewis Clarke, *Narrative*, 45.

41. Coffin, *Reminiscences*, 206-9.

42. Henson, *Autobiography*, 60-62.

43. Sandwich, Canada, *The Voice of the Fugitive*, June 1, 1851. Laura S. Haviland, *A Woman's Life Work* . . . (Grand Rapids, Mich., 1881), 112-20, told a very similar story set in Northern Kentucky about a slave named George.

44. Coffin, *Reminiscences*, 203-4.

45. Gara, *Liberty Line*, 60-61; Blassingame, *Slave Testimony*, 189, 440; Bruner, *A Slave's Adventures*, 34.

46. Gara, *Liberty Line*, 160; Henson, *Autobiography*, 62; Coffin, *Reminiscences*, 208, 343; Louisville *Daily Courier*, August 20, 1852; Coleman, *Slavery*, 209-10.

47. Coffin, *Reminiscences*, 180, 306-7; Bibb, *Narrative*, 84-85; Jacob D. Green, *Narrative* . . . (Huddersfield, England, 1864), 34-35.

48. Lewis Clarke, *Narrative*, 36; Coffin, *Reminiscences*, 319, 458, 558; Cincinnati *Daily Gazette*, January 29, 1856.

49. Frankfort *Commonwealth*, December 11, 1849; Drew, *North-Side View of Slavery*, 363-64; Sandwich, Canada, *The Voice of the Fugitive*, August 27, 1851.

50. Gara, *Liberty Line*, 175-78; Coffin, *Reminiscences*, 447-48; Coleman, *Slavery*, 212-13; H.C. Weeden, *Weeden's History of the Colored People of Louisville* (Louisville, Ky., 1897), 42; Siebert, *Underground Railroad*, 183. Morris, a native of Louisville, worked on the underground railroad while a student in Ohio.

51. Stafford, "Slavery in a Border City," 118-19; *Kentucky's Black Heritage*, 25; Lucien V. Rule, *The Light Bearers* (Louisville, 1926), 168.

52. Coffin, *Reminiscences*, 347, 398-401; Frederick, *Autobiography*, 32.

53. Coffin, *Reminiscences*, 107-8, 114, 167, 208, 297-98. Coffin objected strongly to whites' entering Kentucky to assist slaves in escaping.

54. Coleman, *Slavery*, 214-15, 235-37; Blassingame, *Slave Testimony*, 525-26.

55. Haviland, *A Woman's Life*, 97-110; Coffin, *Reminiscences*, 304-7, 436.

56. Thomas Brown, *Brown's Three Years in the Kentucky Prisons* . . . (Indianapolis, Ind., 1857), 5-11, 13-15; Coleman, *Slavery*, 216.

57. Calvin Fairbank, *Rev. Calvin Fairbank, During Slavery Times* (Chicago, 1890), 3, 11, 24-25, 48-50, 53, 85, 103; Chicago *Tribune*, January 29, 1893; J. Winston Coleman, Jr., "Delia Webster and Calvin Fairbank, Underground Railroad Agents," *FCHQ* 17 (1943): 135; Blassingame, *Slave Testimony*, 695n. Fairbank reported that he received 35,105 stripes as punishment during his twelve years in prison.

58. Lexington *Observer & Reporter*, August 9, 1848; Pratt Diary, August 20, 1848; E.H. Goulding to [?], August 11, 1848, E.H. Goulding Letter (UK); Coleman, *Slavery*, 90-92.

59. Cincinnati *Daily Gazette*, January 29, 1856; Coffin, *Reminiscences*, 557-67. Stanley Campbell, *Slave Catchers*, 144-47. For a complete account, including the legal wrangling, see Julius Yanuck, "The Garner Fugitive Slave Case," *MVHR* 40 (1953): 47-66. Toni Morrison's *Beloved: A Novel* (New York, 1987) was based on the Garner incident.

60. Andrew Jackson, *Narrative*, 9-23.
61. Jacob D. Green, *Narrative*, 32-35.
62. Lewis Clarke, *Narrative*, 32-39, 42.
63. Henson, *Autobiography*, 61-69.

64. Drew, *North-Side View of Slavery*, 152, 327, 373, 376; Blassingame, *Slave Testimony*, 115, 443-44; Jason H. Silverman, *Unwelcome Guests: Canada West's Response to American Fugitive Slaves, 1800-1865* (Millwood, N.Y., 1985), 128, 145; William H. Pease and Jane H. Pease, *Black Utopia: Negro Communal Experiments in America* (Madison, Wisc., 1963), 9-10, 12, 63; Peter Carlesimo, "The Refugee Home Society: Its Origin, Operation and Results, 1851-1876" (M.A. thesis, University of Windsor, Canada, 1973), 4-29. There were a few instances in which fugitives asked to return to Kentucky and slavery. See Gara, *Liberty Line*, 150, and Coleman, *Slavery*, 55.

65. Blassingame, *Slave Testimony*, 48n, 52, 386; Drew, *North-Side View of Slavery*, 150-51, 247-48, 327, 339; Silverman, *Unwelcome Guests*, 58-59; Clara Merritt De Boer, "The Role of Afro-Americans in the Origin and Work of the American Missionary Association: 1839-1877" (Ph.D. diss., Rutgers University, 1973), 206. For the activities of Henry Bibb, see Robert C. Dick, *Black Protest: Issues and Tactics* (Westport, Conn., 1974), 219-23; Robin W. Winks, *The Blacks in Canada: A History* (New Haven, Conn., 1971), 396-97; Fred Landon, "Henry Bibb, A Colonizer," *JNH* 5 (1920): 442-44; Pease and Pease, *Black Utopia*, 110, 112, 116, 121.

66. Blassingame, *Slave Testimony*, 56-57, 88, 114-15, 441; Drew, *North-Side View of Slavery*, 151, 247, 370, 376, 381.

67. Blassingame, *Slave Testimony*, 29, 49-57, 114-15, 443; Coffin, *Reminiscences*, 350-51.

68. Sandwich, Canada, *The Voice of the Fugitive*, June 1, 1851; Blassingame, *Slave Testimony*, 436; Coffin, *Reminiscences*, 262-64.

69. Bibb, *Narrative*, 87-92, 96-106, 108, 111-13, 116-19, 138-52, 162-63. See Roger W. Hite, "Voice of the Fugitive: Henry Bibb and Ante-bellum Black Separatism," *Journal of Black Studies* 4 (1974): 273-82, for an account of Bibb's refugee and antislavery activities.

## 4. The Slave Trade

1. Virginia Papers, Draper MSS, 15 ZZ 46; Frontier Wars Papers, *ibid.*, 1 U 14; Brady and Whetzel Papers, *ibid.*, 1 E 87.

2. Simon Kenton Papers, Draper MSS, 13 BB 7; Nathan Heald Frontier War Papers, *ibid.*, 8 U 57; Harrison, *John Breckinridge*, 119; "Inventory of Slaves" in "Correspondence and Legal Papers, 1834," box 6, Brutus J. Clay Papers; "Inventory of Slaves" in "Correspondence and Business Papers, 1835," box 7, *ibid.*; Bills of Sale, October 7, 1811, April 19, 1814, October 3, 1814, January 23, 1819, January 1824, James Piper Papers; Meacham, *Christian County*, 80; Catterall, *Judicial Cases*, 1:287. For a different but essentially supporting comparison of slave ages and values in the Lower South see Fogel and Engerman, *Time on the Cross*, 1:72-75.

3. Channing, *Kentucky*, 102-3; Lewis W. McKee and Lydia K. Bond, *A History of Anderson County* (Frankfort, Ky., 1936), 217; Coleman, *Slavery*, 123; Eloise Conner, "The Slave Market in Lexington, Kentucky, 1850-1860" (M.A. thesis, University of Kentucky, 1931), 103. Slaveholders restricting their sales to their own region regularly sold their bondsmen at a discount. See Henry Timberlake Duncan to Henry Duncan, Jr., October 21, 1858, Duncan Family Papers.

4. "Inventory of Slaves" in "Correspondence and Legal Papers, 1834," box 6, Brutus J. Clay Papers; "Inventory of Slaves" in "Correspondence and Business Papers, 1835," box 7, *ibid.*; Elizabeth C. Underwood to Joseph Rogers Underwood, January 2,

1850, Series 1, box 1, folder 7, Underwood Collection (WKU); Coleman, *Slavery*, 121; Connor, "Slave Market in Lexington," 103.

5. "Inventory of Slaves" in "Correspondence and Legal Papers, 1834," box 6, Brutus J. Clay Papers; "Inventory of Slaves" in "Correspondence and Business Papers, 1835," box 7, *ibid.*; Coleman, *Slavery*, 121; Mathias, "Slave Days," 226; Conner, "Slave Market in Lexington," 103.

6. Coleman, *Slavery*, 121, 123; Mathias, "Slave Days," 226; J.W. Wells, *History of Cumberland County* (Louisville, Ky., 1947), 103; McDougle, *Slavery*, 24-25; Conner, "Slave Market in Lexington," 103; Fogel and Engerman, *Time on the Cross*, 1:74-75.

7. Bancroft, *Slave Trading*, 131; Coleman, *Slavery*, 157, 159; Harrison, *Antislavery*, 6-7; Lewis Clarke, *Narrative*, 67; Lewis and Milton Clarke, *Narratives of Sufferings*, 74, 81; Theodore Calvin Pease and James G. Randall, eds., *The Diary of Orville Hickman Browning*, 2 vols. (Springfield, Ill., 1925), 1:139; Bibb, *Narrative*, 112.

8. Pease and Randall, *Diary of Orville Browning*, 1:139; Bancroft, *Slave Trading*, 131; Coleman, *Slavery*, 121, 158-59.

9. Coleman, *Slavery*, 149, 154-55; Thomas D. Clark, "The Slave Trade Between Kentucky and the Cotton Kingdom," *MVHR* 21 (1934): 333; Blassingame, *Slave Testimony*, 696; Conner, "Slave Market in Lexington," 23; William Fontaine Bullock to Isaac P. Shelby, December 21, 1850, Shelby Family Papers (UK); Clark, "Slave Trade," 336; Harrison, *Antislavery*, 3; Channing, *Kentucky*, 102; *Kentucky Acts* (1848-49), 21-22, 35-36. Kentucky was atypical of Upper South states in that its prohibition against importation of slaves was short when compared with the bans of Delaware, Maryland, and Virginia which lasted from 1820 to 1860. Deep South states, including Georgia, Alabama, Mississippi, and Louisiana also periodically prohibited importation of slaves, usually for short periods, but Georgia's restrictions remained on the books for thirty-seven years and Tennessee's for twenty-six. Deep South bans seem to have been more ineffective than those in the border states. See Tadman, *Speculators and Slaves*, 83-86.

10. Troutman, *The Heavens Are Weeping*, 95; Thomas Buckner to Fountain Perry, January 3, 1823, Fountain and Rodrick Perry Papers (UK); Rawick, *The American Slave*, 16:38; Coleman, *Slavery*, 62, 118, 191-92; *Kentucky Acts* (1850-51), 1:291; Simmons, *Men of Mark*, 430.

11. Coleman, *Slavery*, 118, 170-71; McDougle, *Slavery*, 15-16; Bancroft, *Slave Trading*, 133; Roy P. Basler, ed., *The Collected Works of Abraham Lincoln*, 8 vols. (New Brunswick, N.J., 1953), 1:260.

12. Coleman, *Slavery*, 146; James Freeman Clarke, *James Freeman Clarke: Autobiography, Diary and Correspondence* (Boston, 1899), 103; Bibb, *Narrative*, 108, 112-14, 116; Thomas Hamilton, *Men and Manners in America* (New York, 1968; orig. pub. 1833), 304; D.R. Hundley, *Social Relations in Our Southern States* (New York, 1860), 139-42; Marryat, *America*, 2:144; Tadman, *Speculators and Slaves*, 192. Apologists for Kentucky slavery such as Nathaniel S. Shaler, *The Autobiography of Nathaniel S. Shaler* (Boston, 1909), 36, verbally abused traders while proclaiming the benignity of slavery in the Commonwealth, but Kentucky critics never subjected traders to the personal abuse employed in other border states. See William Calderhead, "The Role of the Professional Slave Trader in a Slave Economy: Austin Woolfolk, A Case Study," *Civil War History* 23 (1977): 205-6.

13. Bancroft, *Slave Trading*, 131-32; Coleman, *Slavery*, 164-66. The acceptability of slave traders is apparent in the business activities of the well-respected Lexington businessman, John Hunt Morgan. Morgan and his brothers speculated in slaves, utilizing the services of Lewis Robards and his agents in their dealings, and on one occasion loaned Robards $6,100. See James A. Ramage, *Rebel Raider: The Life of General John Hunt Morgan* (Lexington, Ky., 1986), 33. Michael Tadman, in an assessment of slave traders in the border states in *Speculators and Slaves*, 179-210, concluded that traders, rather

than being socially ostracized, were readily accepted as businessmen in southern society.

14. Coleman, *Slavery*, 150-56; Lexington *Kentucky Gazette*, August 23, 1838; Clark, "Slave Trade," 333. The profits of Kentucky slave traders compare favorably with those of some of the largest border state Atlantic coast dealers who had the option of shipping slaves by sea. See Calderhead, "Professional Slave Trader," 201-2.

15. Clark, "Slave Trade," 335-36; Coleman, *Slavery*, 157-58; Pease and Randall, *Diary of Orville Browning*, 1:139.

16. Clark, "Slave Trade," 335-36; Coleman, *Slavery*, 159, 210-12; Conner, "Slave Market in Lexington," 66-67. Kidnapped blacks placed in slave jails or on board ships heading south had a low probability of rescue.

17. *Niles' Weekly Register* 20 (June 9, 1821): 240; O'Brien, "Slavery in Louisville," 41; Bancroft, *Slave Trading*, 125.

18. O'Brien, "Slavery in Louisville," 41-42; *The Liberator*, November 7, 1851; Bancroft, *Slave Trading*, 125; Legislative Records of Louisville, Kentucky, Ordinance and Resolution Book 1, September 27, 1851, Book 2, October 17, 1853; Legislative Records of Louisville, Board of Aldermen Minutes, August 8, 29, September 5, 1853, Reel 11, Microfilm Project 10 (UL). In 1860 Louisville possessed about three hundred firms that offered services in slave trading.

19. Bibb, *Narrative*, 108-9; Sandwich, Canada, *The Voice of the Fugitive*, February 26, 1851.

20. Gibson, *Historical Sketch*, 36-37. The size of the Louisville black population and its proximity to free soil helps explain why that community's blacks were more vigorous in protecting their rights than any other in the state.

21. Frederick Law Olmsted, *Cotton Kingdom* . . . , ed. Arthur M. Schlesinger (New York, 1953), 326-27; Coleman, *Slavery*, 144, 173-74; Blassingame, *Slave Testimony*, 163; Isaac Johnson, *Slavery Days*, 21-22, 24; William Webb, *Webb*, 7-8; Bancroft, *Slave Trading*, 130.

22. Coleman, *Slavery*, 186-87; Fedric, *Slave Life*, 42-43; Rawick, *The American Slave*, 16:38-39; Lexington *Western Luminary*, October 4, 1826.

23. Clark, "Slave Trade," 333-34; Coleman, *Slavery*, 115-16.

24. Coleman, *Slavery*, 174; Norman B. Wood, *The White Side of A Black Subject* . . . (Cincinnati, 1894), 303.

25. Bibb, *Narrative*, 112-13; Gibson, *Historical Sketch*, 39; Allen, *Chronicles of Oldfields*, 89-91; Chicago *Tribune*, January 29, 1893.

26. Weld, *Slavery As It Is*, 76; Elisha Green, *Life*, 2-3; Bancroft, *Slave Trading*, 287-88.

27. Coleman, *Slavery*, 183-84, 187-88.

28. *Ibid.*, 187-88; Epstein, *Black Folk Music*, 177; Bruner, *A Slave's Adventures*, 11.

29. Lexington *Western Luminary*, October 4, 1826.

30. Rawick, *The American Slave*, 6:9-10; Coleman, *Slavery*, 144-45, 183-84; Channing, *Kentucky*, 102; Coleman, "Lexington's Slave Dealers," 7-8.

31. Blassingame, *Slave Testimony*, 211, 403-4.

32. Trotter, *First Impressions*, 252; Bancroft, *Slave Trading*, 131; Elisha Green, *Life*, 13-14.

33. Horace Brand to Henry Duncan, Jr., December 15, 1854, Duncan Family Papers; Bibb, *Narrative*, 112-13; Basler, *Abraham Lincoln*, 260; Coleman, "Lexington's Slave Dealers," 7.

34. Lexington *Kentucky Reporter*, September 9, 1829; Coleman, *Slavery*, 178. Though placed in Alabama, novelist Sherley Anne Williams based the main character in *Dessa Rose* (New York, 1986) on Dinah.

35. Lexington *Western Luminary*, October 4, 11, 1826; Coleman, *Slavery*, 176; *Niles' Weekly Register* 31 (November 18, 1826): 192. One or two slaves *may* have escaped, and

Lewis, Stone's personal servant who fought in behalf of his master, later received freedom.

36. Olmsted, *Cotton Kingdom*, 326-27; Lexington *Kentucky Gazette*, July 4, 1839; Coleman, "Lexington's Slave Dealers," 17-18; Coleman, *Slavery*, 186; William W. Brown, *Narrative of William W. Brown* . . . , ed. Larry Gara (Reading, Mass., 1969); Bibb, *Narrative*, 115.

37. Bancroft, *Slave Trading*, 272, 388-92; Turner, "Decade of Change," 299-300; Channing, *Kentucky*, 103; Coleman, *Slavery*, 194; Coleman, "Lexington's Slave Dealers," 4; Stampp, *Peculiar Institution*, 238; Michael Tadman, "Slave Trading in the Ante-Bellum South: An Estimate of the Extent of the Inter-regional Slave Trade," *Journal of American Studies* 13 (1979): 219-20. A recent study of Maryland's sales to the Lower South by William Calderhead, "How Extensive Was the Border State Slave Trade? A New Look," *Civil War History* 18 (1972): 42-55, suggests that Bancroft's figures, upon whose research statistics for that state are built, were too large by about 75 percent. Fogel and Engerman, *Time on the Cross*, 1:47-52, suggest that 85 percent of the slaves leaving the Atlantic coast states migrated with their masters.

## 5. Slave Hiring and Free Blacks

1. Harrison, "John Breckinridge," 211; Venable, "Down South Before the War," 461. For a general account of slave hiring for the entire South, see Orville Vernon Burton, "Hiring Out," in Miller and Smith, *Dictionary of Afro-American Slavery*, 321-26.

2. Coleman, *Slavery*, 123-25; Lexington *Observer & Reporter*, December 9, 1835; Louisville *Daily Courier*, December 24, 1854, January 3, 1855; Lexington *Kentucky Gazette*, January 1, 8, 1811; Venable, "Down South Before the War," 461-62; Isaac Johnson, *Slavery Days*, 18-19.

3. Coleman, *Slavery*, 125n; O'Brien, "Slavery in Louisville," 51; Conner, "Slave Market in Lexington," 43.

4. Clement Eaton, "Slave Hiring in the Upper South," *MVHR* 46 (1960): 669; Venable, "Down South Before the War," 461-62; Madison Campbell, *Autobiography*, 23; Elizabeth C. Underwood to Joseph Rogers Underwood, December 1, 1849, Series 1, box 1, folder 7, January 2, 1851, Series 1, box 1, folder 8, Underwood Collection; O'Brien, "Slavery in Louisville," 51-52.

5. O'Brien, "Slavery in Louisville," 23-24; Coleman, *Slavery*, 125; Elizabeth C. Underwood to J.R. Underwood, Series 1, box 1, folder 7, Underwood Collection; McKee and Bond, *Anderson County*, 217-18. Little difference existed between hiring contracts in Kentucky and those of the Lower South. See Starobin, *Industrial Slavery*, 128-29.

6. McKee and Bond, *Anderson County*, 217-18; Coleman, *Slavery*, 125; Misc., contract, December 25, 1854, "Documents and Letters," Coleman Papers.

7. Eaton, "Slave Hiring," 663; Coleman, *Slavery*, 66; Stafford, "Slavery in a Border City," 111. Figures for the annual expenses for a slave were for 1848.

8. Pratt Diary, 2: January 22, 1855; Pickard, *Kidnapped*, 54; Lewis and Milton Clarke, *Narratives of the Sufferings*, 82-83; Lexington *Kentucky Reporter*, September 1, 1830; Coleman, *Slavery*, 126-27; Catterall, *Judicial Cases*, 1:427.

9. Eaton, "Slave Hiring," 668, 673, 676; Dorris, "Early History of Madison County," 143; Harrison, *John Breckinridge*, 33; Elizabeth C. Underwood to J.R. Underwood, January 2, 1850, Series 1, box 1, folder 7, Underwood Collection. Eaton believed that renting slaves for work in agriculture had declined significantly by the 1850s.

10. O'Brien, "Slavery in Louisville," 29-31; Coleman, *Slavery*, 124; Louisville *Daily Courier*, December 24, 1854, January 3, 1855; Harrison, "John Breckinridge," 211.

11. Coleman, *Slavery*, 124-25; Catterall, *Judicial Cases*, 1:427; Eaton, "Slave Hiring," 663, 671; Martin J. Spalding, *Sketches of Early Catholic Missions of Kentucky* . . . (New York, 1972; orig. pub. 1844), 116; Gibson, *Historical Sketch*, 66; Conner, "Slave Market in Lexington," 43; O'Brien, "Slavery in Louisville," 51. For a microcosmic study revealing a flexibility in the institution of slavery similar to that in Kentucky, see Sarah S. Hughes, "Slaves for Hire: The Allocation of Black Labor in Elizabeth City County, Virginia, 1782-1810," *William and Mary Quarterly*, 3rd ser., 35 (1978): 260-86.

12. O'Brien, "Slavery in Louisville," 29-31; Misc., contract, December 25, 1854, "Documents and Letters," Coleman Papers; Mathias, "Slave Days," 229; Coleman, *Slavery*, 123-25; Blassingame, *Slave Testimony*, 389-90, 432; Hayden, *Narrative*, 43-46; Isaac Johnson, *Slavery Days*, 18-19; Elisha Green, *Life*, 9; Pratt Diary, 2: January 1, 1856; Cade, "Out of the Mouths of Ex-Slaves," 310; Stafford, "Slavery in a Border City," 111; Eaton, "Slave Hiring," 663; Lewis and Milton Clarke, *Narratives of Sufferings*, 77, 82-83; J. Winston Coleman, Jr., *The Springs of Kentucky* . . . (Lexington, Ky., 1955), 43-45.

13. Wade, *Urban Frontier*, 52; Abdy, *Journal*, 349; Eaton, "Slave Hiring," 671; Louisville *Daily Journal*, November 29, 1830; Kellogg, "Black Residential Areas in Lexington," 29.

14. Harrison, *John Breckinridge*, 120; Wade, *Urban Frontier*, 52; Louisville *Daily Journal*, November 29, 1830; Troutman, *The Heavens Are Weeping*, 74; Venable, "Down South Before the War," 462-63; Daniel K. Weis, "Reminiscences of Eastern Kentucky," 16-17, microfilm 544 (UK); Pickard, *Kidnapped*, 43-44; Eaton, "Slave Hiring," 663; Rawick, *The American Slave*, 16:110; Mathias, "Slave Days," 229; Conner, "Slave Market in Kentucky," 44. Industrial slavery in Kentucky experienced the same growth in the decade before the Civil War exhibited by the South in general. See Starobin, *Industrial Slavery*, 135.

15. Mathias, "Slave Days," 229; Venable, "Down South Before the War," 462-63; Weis, "Reminiscences of Eastern Kentucky," 16-17.

16. Littell, *Statute Law of Kentucky*, 2:116; Kentucky Acts (1825), 82; Stafford, "Slavery in a Border City," 117; Blassingame, *Slave Testimony*, 152, 394, 438; Hayden, *Narrative*, 43; Lewis and Milton Clarke, *Narratives of Sufferings*, 76-77; Jacob D. Wheeler, *A Practical Treatise on the Law of Slavery* (New York, 1968; orig. pub. 1837), 268-69; Catterall, *Judicial Cases*, 1:308-9. Kentucky's laws and attitudes toward self-hiring differed little from those applied in the Deep South. See Clarence L. Mohr, *On the Threshold of Freedom: Masters and Slaves in Civil War Georgia* (Athens, Ga., 1986), 44.

17. Blassingame, *Slave Testimony*, 152, 432-33, 441, 518-19; James Davidson to Leslie Combs, November 18, 1833, James Davidson letter (UK); O'Brien, "Slavery in Louisville," 23; Eaton, "Slave Hiring," 669, 678; Lexington *Kentucky Reporter*, September 1, 1830; Elisha Green, *Life*, 9; Hayden, *Narrative*, 25. According to Richard B. Morris, "Measure of Bondage in the Slave States," *MVHR* 41 (1954): 235, self-hiring was also a major step toward purchasing one's self in the Deep South.

18. Hayden, *Narrative*, 25-26, 38, 43, 45, 52.

19. Walker, *Free Frank*, 32, 35-36, 41, 46.

20. Lewis and Milton Clarke, *Narratives of Sufferings*, 76-77, 81-83; Coleman, *Springs of Kentucky*, 41-45.

21. Stafford, "Slavery in a Border City," 118-19.

22. Hayden, *Narrative*, 43; O'Brien, "Slavery in Louisville," 53, 55; Eaton, "Slave Hiring," 676; Madison Campbell, *Autobiography*, 24; Lewis and Milton Clarke, *Narratives of Sufferings*, 77; Blassingame, *Slave Testimony*, 385, 389, 440; Stafford, "Slavery in a Border City," 112.

23. O'Brien, "Slavery in Louisville," 55; Eaton, "Slave Hiring," 673-74. Genovese, *Roll, Jordan, Roll*, 390, estimates that owners rented out 5 to 10 percent of all southern slaves in the last decades before the Civil War.

24. *Statistical View of the United States*, 65-66, 85; *Report of the Commissioner of Education 1868*, 100; *Seventh Census, 1850*, 615; Collins, *History*, 1:61; Turner, "Decade of Change," 103; Kentucky *Acts* (1850-51), 1:308-9. While the percentage of free blacks in the total population rose slightly and while real numbers showed considerable growth, the percentage of increase in free blacks in the whole population declined dramatically except for the decade 1821 to 1830 which showed a 17 percent increase. Barbara Jeanne Fields, *Slavery and Freedom on the Middle Ground: Maryland during the Nineteenth Century* (New Haven, Conn., 1985), 2, 36, says that with regard to free blacks, Kentucky resembled the Lower South rather than the border states of Delaware and Maryland. For an excellent comparison of Kentucky freemen with those of the Deep South, see Genovese, *Roll, Jordan, Roll*, 398-413.

25. See the first seven census reports of the United States, 1791-1860.

26. Genovese, *Roll, Jordan, Roll*, 404; *African Repository* 6 (March 1830): 12; Young, *Three Constitutions*, Part 2:23, 37, 44. See also Winthrop D. Jordan, *White over Black*, 412. For an account of the laws regarding free blacks after 1798, see Juliet E.K. Walker, "The Legal Status of Free Blacks in Early Kentucky, 1792-1825," *FCHQ* 57 (1983): 382-95. Caleb Perry Patterson's often quoted statement in his *Negro in Tennessee* (Austin, Texas, 1922), 174, that a free black was "a sort of inmate on parole," aptly defined freemen's status in Kentucky. To compare Kentucky freemen with a Lower South state, see Orville Burton, *In My Father's House*, 203-24.

27. Littell, *Statute Law*, 2:113-16, 4:223-24; Littell and Swigert, *Digest*, 2:1160-61;. Kentucky *Acts* (1850-51), 1:296, 301-2. In certain instances of murder or acts of arson, options of two to ten years in prison or up to two hundred lashes, "not more than fifty at a time," existed. See Kentucky *Acts* (1850-51), 1:301-2.

28. Littell, *Statute Law*, 2:113-16, 4:223-24; Kentucky *Acts* (1834), 2:790-91, (1850-51), 1:302, 305.

29. Wade, *Urban Frontier*, 223; Madison Campbell, *Autobiography*, 66-67; Julia Neal, *By Their Fruits: The Story of Shakerism in South Union, Kentucky* (Chapel Hill, N.C., 1947), 61; Kentucky *Acts* (1834), 2:790, 792; ibid. (1850-51), 1:304-9; Littell, *Statute Law*, 4:224.

30. Walker, "Free Blacks," 384, 392; idem, *Free Frank*, 41, 46, 50-51; McKee and Bond, *Anderson County*, 62; Blassingame, *Slave Testimony*, 348-49, 385, 394; McElroy Journal, March 12, 1857; Gara, *Liberty Line*, 33; *Kentucky's Black Heritage*, 13.

31. Lexington *Kentucky Gazette*, March 6, 1878.

32. Gibson, *Historical Sketch*, 31-32; Blassingame, *Slave Testimony*, 390; Cyrus Baldwin King, "Ante-bellum Free Negroes as Race Leaders in Kentucky and Virginia during Reconstruction" (M.A. thesis, University of Kentucky, 1949), 81; Simmons, *Men of Mark*, 431-32; Paul J. Lammermeier, "The Urban Black Family of the Nineteenth Century: A Study of Black Family Structure in the Ohio Valley, 1850-1880," *Journal of Marriage and The Family* 35 (1973): 440, 443-45, 449, 451, 455; Curry, *The Free Black in Urban America*, 63, 65.

33. Kellogg, "Black Residential Areas in Lexington," 28-29.

34. Walker, *Free Frank*, 31; Ira Berlin, "Free Negro," 113-14; Gibson, *Historical Sketch*, 30-32.

35. John Taylor, *A History of Ten Baptist Churches* . . . (Bloomfield, Ky., 1827), 108; Legislative Records of Louisville, Common Council Minutes, August 15, 1853, Reel 27; Minutes, Fifth Street Baptist Church, 1: December 16, 1850; Gibson, *Historical Sketch*, 3-4, 13, 25, 29, 31-32, 40-41; Stafford, "Slavery in a Border City," 119-20.

36. Herbert A. Thomas, Jr., "Victims of Circumstance: Negroes in a Southern Town, 1865-1880," *Register* 71 (1973): 267; Buckingham, *Eastern and Western States*, 3:7; Gibson, *Historical Sketch*, 27, 29; Cuming, *Sketches of a Tour*, 168-69, 176-77; Elizabeth C. Underwood to Joseph Rogers Underwood, January 2, 1850, Series 1, box 1, folder 7,

December 29, 1850, Series 1, box 1, folder 8, Underwood Collection.

37. Blassingame, *Slave Testimony*, 389-90; Gibson, *Historical Sketch*, 26-32; Thomas, "Victims of Circumstance," 267; Drew, *North-Side View of Slavery*, 240-41; Berlin, "Free Negro," 106.

38. Abdy, *Journal*, 2:349; Ramage, *Rebel Raider*, 32; Gibson, *Historical Sketch*, 26-28; Thomas, "Victims of Circumstance," 267-68; Troutman, *The Heavens Are Weeping*, 58; Kentucky *Acts* (1834), 2:792.

39. Buckingham, *Eastern and Western States*, 3:7; King, "Free Negroes," 138; Strother, "Negro Culture in Lexington," 72-76; Rolla Blue, Deed Book 22, March 8, 1845, Deed Book 26, March 26, 1850, Deed Book 29, March 26, 1850, Fayette County Records, Microfilm 174 (UK); Dennis Seal, Will Book Y, March 1863, Fayette County Records, Microfilm 127 (UK).

40. Walker, *Free Frank*, 44, 53-54, 58-59, 61, 68.

41. Stafford, "Slavery in a Border City," 119-20; Gibson, *Historical Sketch*, 25-26; Weeden, *History*, 56-57.

42. Drew, *North-Side View of Slavery*, 150; Abdy, *Journal*, 2:348; Littell, *Statute Law*, 2:120; Coleman, *Slavery*, 101, 105-6; Henry Nutter Free Papers, December 1, 1851, "Documents and Letters, 1780-1860," Coleman Papers; Lexington *Kentucky Gazette*, January 3, 1809. Some counties required that freemen possess, in addition to their free papers, testimonials of their good behavior signed by well-known whites.

43. Conner, "Slave Market in Lexington," 97; Elisha Green, *Life*, 13-16.

44. Kentucky *Acts* (1809-10), 94-95, (1811-12), 160, (1825), 137-39, (1834), 2:790; Walker, "Free Blacks," 392. According to Gibson, *Historical Sketch*, 34-35, free blacks considered the threat of forcibly apprenticing their children one of the worst assaults on their families.

45. Kentucky *Acts* (1850-51), 1:292; Carter G. Woodson, ed., *Free Negro Owners of Slaves in the United States in 1830* . . . (Washington, D.C., 1924), v-vi; Calvin D. Wilson, *Negroes Who Owned Slaves*, 488; Conner, "Slave Market in Lexington," 47-48; Strother, "Negro Culture in Lexington," 72-74; Ireland, *County Courts*, 29-30; Kentucky *Acts* (1850-51), 1:306, 308; *Kyler and Wife* v. *Dunlap, Kentucky Reports*, 18 B. Monroe 561 (1857); Coleman, *Slavery*, 59-61. Woodson, 4-6, reported that black Kentuckians owned 575 slaves in 1830.

46. C.S. Morehead and Mason Brown, eds., *Digest of the Statute Laws of Kentucky* . . . , 2 vols. (Frankfort, Ky., 1834), 2:1268; Coleman, "Lexington's Slave Dealers," 22; Gibson, *Historical Sketch*, 36-37; Coleman, *Slavery*, 210-12; Conner, "Slave Market in Lexington," 66-67; Blassingame, *Slave Testimony*, 690-93.

47. Strother, "Negro Culture in Lexington," 74; Walker, *Free Frank*, 49-52; Catterall, *Judicial Cases*, 1:304, 307; *Free Frank and Lucy* v. *Denham's Administrator*, 5 Littell 330 (1824).

48. Morehed and Brown, *Digest*, 2:1219-20; Stafford, "Slavery in a Border City," 26-27; Wade, *Urban Frontier*, 223; Trustees Minute Book, Lexington, July 1, 1841, August 29, 1842; Louisville *Daily Courier*, January 21, 1859; Lexington *Observer & Reporter*, May 14, 1851.

49. Drew, *North-Side View of Slavery*, 240-48; Gibson, *Historical Sketch*, 36, 40-41. Freemen who were successful in Kentucky usually proved to be successful on free soil. See Wendell P. Dabney, *Cincinnati's Colored Citizens* . . . (New York, 1970; orig. pub. 1926), 46-47.

50. Troutman, *The Heavens Are Weeping*, 58; Paris *Western Citizen*, August 29, 1845; Frankfort *Commonwealth*, August 26, 1845.

51. Orlando Brown to "My Dear Son," September 23, 1856, Orlando Brown Papers (FC); Gibson, *Historical Sketch*, 34-35, 43. In *The Free Black in Urban America*, 111, Curry maintains that "antiblack mob violence" in Louisville was declining, as in other south-

ern cities such as New Orleans, Baltimore, and St. Louis, in the 1840s.

### 6. Religion and Education before 1865

1. Boles, *Religion*, 83-85; Madison Campbell, *Autobiography*, 17-19; Starling, *Henderson County*, 296; Rawick, *The American Slave*, 16:15; Thomas L. Webber, *Deep Like the Rivers: Education in the Slave Quarter Community 1831-1865* (New York, 1978), 52; J.J. Polk, *Autobiography* . . . (Louisville, Ky., 1867), 27; Lexington *Kentucky Gazette*, March 6, 1878.

2. Elisha Green, *Life*, 11; Boles, *Religion*, 83-84; Forrest Calico, *History of Garrard County Kentucky and its Churches* (New York, 1947), 512.

3. Boles, *Religion*, 83-84; Rawick, *The American Slave*, 16:3; J.W. Singer, ed., *The Negro Members of the Stamping Ground Baptist Church* (Stamping Ground, Ky., 1967), 3; Albert J. Raboteau, *Slave Religion: The "Invisible Institution" in the Antebellum South* (New York, 1978), 182; Fee, *Autobiography*, 60-61.

4. William Warren Sweet, *Religion on the American Frontier: The Baptists, 1783-1830* (New York, 1931), 421, 423, 437; Boles, *Religion*, 84; Blassingame, *Slave Community*, 168; idem, *Slave Testimony*, 54, 56; McElroy Journal, March 12, 1857; Bibb, *Narrative*, 169-70.

5. Boles, *Religion*, 80-81, 85-88, 93, 107-10, 113, 115-16, 118; Calico, *Garrard County*, 512; Bruner, *A Slave's Adventures*, 22.

6. Elisha Green, *Life*, 9, 11, 18; C.H. Parrish, ed., *Golden Jubilee of the General Association of Colored Baptists in Kentucky* . . . (Louisville, Ky. 1915), 188, 251; Spencer, *Baptists*, 2:656; Anna C. Minogue, *Loretto: Annals of the Century* (New York, 1912), 95-97; John T. Gillard, *Colored Catholics in the United States* . . . (Baltimore, 1941), 71, 197.

7. Troutman, *The Heavens Are Weeping*, 113; William Irvine Papers, Draper MSS, 1 Z 19; Robert H. Bishop, *An Outline History of the Church in the State of Kentucky* . . . (Lexington, Ky., 1824), 230-31; Frederick, *Autobiography*, 18-19; Elisha Green, *Life*, 3, 18-19; Lexington *Kentucky Gazette*, March 6, 1878; Boles, *Religion*, 89; John Taylor, *Baptist Churches*, 108; Minutes, Fifth Street Baptist Church, 1: February 25, 1844.

8. Boles, *Religion*, 91, 93-94; Raboteau, *Slave Religion*, 318; Rawick, *The American Slave*, 16:16; Elisha Green, *Life*, 2; Anderson, *From Slavery To Affluence*, 22-23; Calico, *Garrard County*, 313, 317-18, 362; Parrish, *Golden Jubilee*, 188, 193, 200-203, 251, 269; Madison Campbell, *Autobiography*, 18-20; Lexington *Kentucky Gazette*, March 6, 1878; Simmons, *Men of Mark*, 604.

9. *94th Anniversary Program, Oct. 17-21, 1945* (Lexington, Ky., [1945]), 1; Starling, *Henderson County*, 477; John Taylor, *Baptist Churches*, 108; Pratt Diary, 2: January 1, 1856; Boles, *Religion*, 89-90; Elisha Green, *Life*, 5, 9-10; Lexington *Kentucky Gazette*, March 6, 1878; Simmons, *Men of Mark*, 604; Coleman, *Slavery*, 56-57; Frederick, *Autobiography*, 18-19; Madison Campbell, *Autobiography*, 19; Minutes, Green Street Baptist Church, 1: November 17, 1851; Parrish, *Golden Jubilee*, 251.

10. Gayraud S. Wilmore, *Black Religion and Black Radicalism* (New York, 1972), 106; Elisha Green, *Life*, 25; Charles Lyell, *A Second Visit to the United States of North America*, 2 vols. (New York, 1849), 2:215; Gibson, *Historical Sketch*, 36-37.

11. Singer, *Stamping Ground Baptist*, 3; Minutes, Fifth Street Baptist Church, 1: April 1842; Minutes, Green Street Baptist Church, 1: September 29, 1844, January 23, 1851; Boles, *Religion*, 92; Elisha Green, *Life*, 11-13, 29; Weeden, *History*, 45. Lyell wrote (*Visit*, 2:213) that his "party were the only whites" present the night he visited a black Louisville Methodist church.

12. Peter J. Paris, *Social Teaching of the Black Churches* (Philadelphia, 1985), 9; Boles, *Religion*, 85, 99-100; Wilmore, *Black Religion*, v-vi; Raboteau, *Slave Religion*, ix.

13. Lewis G. Jordan, *Negro Baptist History U.S.A., 1750-1930* (Nashville, Tenn.,

1930), 111; George W. Ranck, *"The Traveling Church": An Account of the Baptist Exodus from Virginia* . . . (Louisville, Ky., 1910), 22-23; Spencer, *Baptists,* 2:654-55; Mechal Sobel, *"Trablin' On" The Slave Journey to an Afro-Baptist Faith* (Westport, Conn., 1979), 203, 335.

14. Robert Peter, *History of Fayette County* . . . , ed. W. Henry Perrin (Chicago, 1882), 471; Spencer, *Baptists,* 2:655-56; Lexington *Kentucky Gazette,* March 6, 1878; Sobel, "Trablin' On," 203-4, 336; Microfilm *Minutes of the Elkhorn Association of Baptists, Kentucky, 1824* (n.p., n.d.), 2 (hereafter cited *Minutes, Elkhorn Assn.,* with date); *ibid., 1846* (Georgetown, Ky., 1846), 6; *ibid., 1854* (Lexington, Ky., n.d.), 1.

15. King, "Free Negroes," 82; *Minutes, Elkhorn Assn., 1855,* 2; Spencer, *Baptists,* 2:657; Parrish, *Golden Jubilee,* 244-45, 271.

16. Parrish, *Golden Jubilee,* 186-87, 249-51; Sobel, "Trablin' On," 337; *Minutes, Elkhorn Assn., 1845* (n.p., n.d.), 1; *ibid., 1846,* 3; *ibid., 1848* (Lexington, Ky., n.d.), 1; *ibid., 1849* (n.p., n.d.), 1; *ibid., 1852* (Georgetown, n.d.), 1; *ibid., 1855,* 1; Spencer, *Baptists,* 2:659-60; Pratt Diary, 2: January 1, 1856; Strother, "Negro Culture in Lexington," 11.

17. Peter, *Fayette County,* 472-74; Posey, *Frontier Mission,* 218.

18. Fifth Street Choir Record, January 1, 1870-June 22, 1877, Fifth Street Baptist Church, November 1872 (Fifth Street Baptist Church Safe, Louisville, Kentucky, microfilm copy currently located at UL); Parrish, *Golden Jubilee,* 196; Spencer, *Baptists,* 2:657-58; Sobel, "Trablin' On," 197; New York *National Anti-Slavery Standard,* April 8, 1865; O'Brien, "Slavery in Louisville," 121; Gibson, *Historical Sketch,* 17; Parrish, *Golden Jubilee,* 196-97; Fifth Street Choir Record, November 1872; Minutes, Fifth Street Baptist Church, 2: November 13, 1872. The microfilm *Minutes of the Long Run Association of Baptists, 1803-1894,* 2 vols. (Louisville, Ky., 1803-94), titled Adams's church "Colored" 1842-49, "African" 1850-58, and "Colored" 1859-67. See also Ira S. Birdwhistell, *Gathered at the River: A Narrative History of Long Run Association* (Louisville, Ky., 1978), 44-46.

19. Minutes, Fifth Street Baptist Church, 1: April 3, 1842.

20. *Ibid.,* September 25, 1843, February 25, 1844, March 24, 1844; Minutes, First [Walnut Street] Baptist Church, February 17, 1844, March 11, 1844 (Walnut Street Baptist Church, Louisville, Kentucky); Birdwhistell, *History,* 44-46.

21. Minutes, Fifth Street Baptist Church, 1: April 3, 23, May 22, June 26, September 28, October 23, November 27, December 8, 1842, January 22, February 26, March 26, April 23, May 11, June 25, July 13, August 27, September 24, October 22, November 30, December 14, 24, 1843, February 25, March 24, August 25, September 21, 1844, December 27, 1846; Weeden, *History,* 45. Activities regarding membership differed little from those of white Baptist churches. See Ray H. and Elsie S. Wright, *History of Cox's Creek Baptist Church* (Cox's Creek, Ky., 1935).

22. Homer E. Wickenden, "History of the Churches of Louisville with Special Reference to Slavery" (M.A. thesis, University of Louisville, 1921), 19-20; Minutes, Fifth Street Baptist Church, 1: August 1, 1841-September 18, 1842, June 23, 1844, December 7, 1849, November 10, 1851, July 14, July 19, 1855.

23. Minutes, Fifth Street Baptist Church, 1: April 24, 1842, May 26, 1844, July 22, 1849.

24. B.T. Kimbrough, *The History of the Walnut Street Baptist Church, Louisville, Kentucky* (Louisville, 1949), 44; William J. Hodge, *Historical Sketch of the Fifth Street Baptist Church* (Louisville, 1969); Minutes, Fifth Street Baptist Church, 1: September 28, 1842, May 10, December 7, 1849, January ?, 1850, November 10, December 16, 1851; Sobel, "Trablin' On," 338; Ira Berlin, *Slaves Without Masters: The Free Negro in the Antebellum South* (New York, 1974), 345; *Minutes, Long Run Assn., 1858* (n.p., 1858), 2:15. During 1843 the congregation of Colored Baptist donated $115.50 for foreign missions. See

Birdwhistell, *History,* 46.

25. Minutes, Green Street Baptist Church, 1: undated 1844 entry, September 29, November 10, 1844, entry following December 1847, entry between July 14 and August 11, September 8, 1850, February 22, April 24, November 17, 1851, April 1, 1852, November 9, 1860; Sobel, *"Trablin' On,"* 339; Weeden, *History,* 14.

26. Minutes, Green Street Baptist Church, 1: September 12, 1852; King, "Free Negroes," 81; Sobel, *"Trablin' On,"* 339; Gibson, *Historical Sketch,* 18; Spencer, *Baptists,* 2:658; Weeden, *History,* 14.

27. Minutes, Green Street Baptist Church, 1: January 12, April 18, May 11, June 8, July 13, 1845, February 14, entry following December 1847, February 11, May 13, June 10, October 14, 1849, January 13, July 14, 1850, April 13, 1851, May 4, December 11, 1860; 2: January 8, 1874; 3: March 31, 1882, May 22, 1885, August 3, 1887, October 23, 1888, October 16, 1891; Weeden, *History,* 14.

28. Weeden, *History,* 14, 16; Minutes, Green Street Baptist Church, 1: November 10, 1844, July 13, September 14, 1845, September 13, November 8, 1846, January 10, March 2, 1847, January 14, July 8, October 14, 1849.

29. Minutes, Green Street Baptist Church, 1: September 8, October 3, 1850, January 23, 26, March 9, 1851, April 1, 1852. No record exists of Anderson's having paid the entire debt.

30. Minutes, Green Street Baptist Church, 1: February 9, 1854, October 9, 1857-November 10, 1865, undated 1858 "Money Matters" entry; Owen, *The Wrong of Slavery,* 208. The origin of Louisville's third major black church, the Fifth and York Street Baptist Church, remains obscure. After the First Colored congregation moved to a new building in 1845, leaving their old structure empty, it appears that a small group of members gravitated back to the old sanctuary along with a few disgruntled members of the Second Colored Baptist Church. Formally constituted in 1857, the congregation of forty-six members changed its name to York Street Church in 1861. Under the leadership of Rev. W.W. Taylor, the congregation became one of the leading churches in the city. In 1883 the congregation adopted Calvary Baptist Church as its name. The minutes of the church, dating from the antebellum period, were lost in the 1937 flood. See Parrish, *Golden Jubilee,* 272-73; Gibson, *Historical Sketch,* 19; Weeden, *History,* 16; John L. Miles, Jr., ed., *Calvary Baptist Church: A Century and Forty, 1829-1969* (Louisville, Ky., 1969), no page; *Minutes, Long Run Assn.,* 1858, 2:2, 15; *Louisville Commercial,* February 23, 1871.

31. David Morris Jordan, Sr., "The Lexington Conference and Negro Migration," mimeograph (n.p., n.d.), 6; Weeden, *History,* 56; Gibson, *Historical Sketch,* 14-15.

32. Gibson, *Historical Sketch,* 11-12; Weeden, *History,* 18; Daniel A. Payne, *History of the African Methodist Episcopal Church* (New York, 1969; orig. pub. 1891), 171. Quinn Chapel's most famous pastor, Hiram R. Revels, later served as the first black United States senator, filling the unexpired term of Mississippi's Jefferson Davis. See Vernon Lane Wharton, *The Negro in Mississippi, 1865-1890* (New York, 1965; orig. pub. 1947), 159.

33. Weeden, *History,* 49; Gibson, *Historical Sketch,* 5-10; Catterall, *Judicial Cases,* 1:407-8.

34. Ermina Jett Darnell, *Forks of Elkhorn Church* (Louisville, Ky., 1946), 39-40; Starling, *Henderson County,* 476-77.

35. Mingo Scott, Jr., *History of the State Street Baptist Church, 1838-1973* (Bowling Green, Ky., [1973]), 13, 15; Boles, *Religion,* 86-87; Singer, *Stamping Ground Baptist,* 3; *Minutes, Elkhorn Assn.,* 1861 (Lexington, Ky., n.d.), 8. The autonomous black Baptist Church at Shelbyville experienced essentially the same history: years of worship in the white sanctuary before acquiring one of its own. Sobel, *"Trablin' On,"* 340; Parrish, *Golden Jubilee,* 235-36.

36. Bennett H. Young and S.M. Duncan, *A History of Jessamine County, From Its Earliest Settlement to 1898* (Louisville, Ky., 1898), 199; Lewis G. Jordan, *Negro Baptist History*, 111; Sobel, "Trablin' On," 340; Madison Campbell, *Autobiography*, 32-33.

37. Elisha Green, *Life*, 5, 9-12; Sobel, "Trablin' On," 340, 342; *Minutes, Elkhorn Assn., 1861*, 8.

38. Calvin Morgan Fackler, *A Chronicle of the Old First* (Louisville, Ky., 1946), 65-66; Parrish, *Golden Jubilee*, 254; Sobel, "Trablin' On," 333.

39. E.E. Underwood, *A Brief History of the Colored Churches of Frankfort, Kentucky* (Frankfort, Ky., 1906), 4; Fee, *Autobiography*, 143; Simmons, *Men of Mark*, 604-5. Other separate black churches existed. The black Baptist churches of Owensboro and Georgetown dated from the early nineteenth century, and the Simpsonville church began conducting services in its own building in the 1830s. Autonomous black Baptist and Methodist churches in Nicholasville, Elizabethtown, Richmond, and possibly Versailles, began in the 1840s. In Cynthiana, black Methodists and Baptists, and in Paducah black Baptists met in their own sanctuaries during the 1850s. See Anonymous, *History of Daviess County, Kentucky* . . . (Chicago, 1883), 376-77; Sobel, "Trablin' On," 334; Parrish, *Golden Jubilee*, 186, 208-9; Frank M. Masters, *A History of Baptists in Kentucky* (Louisville, Ky., 1953), 134; Young and Duncan, *Jessamine County*, 198-99; Madison Campbell, *Autobiography*, 32-33, 38-39; *Minutes, Elkhorn Assn., 1849*, 1; ibid., *1861*, 8; Ella Cofer, *History of Severn's Valley Baptist Church* ([Elizabethtown], Ky., 1931), 15-16; William Henry Perrin, ed., *History of Bourbon, Scott, Harrison and Nicholas Counties, Kentucky* . . . (Chicago, 1882), 298; Masters, *Baptists*, 346; Simmons, *Men of Mark*, 605-6.

40. Raboteau, *Slave Religion*, 275-77. For a more complete discussion of conjuring, see Charles Joyner, *Down by the Riverside: A South Carolina Slave Community* (Urbana and Chicago, 1984) and Lawrence E. Levine, *Black Culture and Black Consciousness: Afro-American Folk Thought from Slavery to Freedom* (New York, 1977).

41. Bibb, *Narrative*, 70-73; Rawick, *The American Slave*, 7:40; Baxter, *Statistics, Medical and Anthropological*, 1:369; Lexington *Intelligencer*, November 9, 1838; Boles, *Religion*, 99.

42. Melville J. Herskovits, *The Myth of the Negro Past* (Boston, 1958; orig. pub. 1941), 6-9, 15-17, 137-38, 141, 207-13; Boles, *Religion*, 99. Raboteau, *Slave Religion*, 47-49, 92. For a thorough discussion of Africanisms, see Leonard E. Barrett, *Soul-Force: African Heritage in Afro-American Religion* (Garden City, N.Y., 1974); Joyner, *Down By the Riverside*; Genovese, *Roll, Jordan, Roll*; and Levine, *Black Culture and Black Consciousness*.

43. E. Franklin Frazier, *Negro Church*, 5-6; Raboteau, *Slave Religion*, 47-49; Boles, *Religion*, 80-81; Milton C. Sernett, *Black Religion and American Evangelicalism* . . . (Metuchen, N.J., 1975), 104-5.

44. Raboteau, *Slave Religion*, 44-45, 88-92.

45. John S. Mbiti, *Introduction to African Religion* (New York, 1975), 15, 35, 175, 178. See also Paul Bohannan and Philip Curtin, *Africa and Africans* (Garden City, N.Y., 1971; orig. pub. 1964), 173-87.

46. Bailey, "Two Sources of Black Testimony," 394; Boles, *Religion*, 81-82; Mbiti, *African Religion*, 15-17, 35, 175. The role of oral tradition in black religion in Kentucky remains a mystery.

47. Frazier, *Negro Church*, 11; *Minutes, Fifth Street Baptist Church*, 1: April 3, 1842; Boles, *Religion*, 94; Anderson, *From Slavery To Affluence*, 23-24.

48. Philo Tower, *Slavery Unmasked* . . . (Rochester, N.Y., 1856), 251-52; Boles, *Religion*, 90-91; Anderson, *From Slavery To Affluence*, 23; John Taylor, *Baptist Churches*, 108; Browder Diary, March 5, 1854, March 15, 1863; Raboteau, *Slave Religion*, 318; Armstrong, *Slaves Tell Their Story*, 231; Lyell, *Visit*, 2:213.

49. Anderson, *From Slavery To Affluence*, 23; Raboteau, *Slave Religion*, 317-18; Bailey, "Two Sources of Black Testimony," 392-93; Frazier, *Negro Church*, 11-12; Boles, *Religion*,

94-98; Lyell, *Visit*, 2:214; Benjamin Quarles, *The Negro in the Civil War* (New York, 1968; orig. pub. 1953), 165.

50. Sernett, *Black Religion*, 90, 92; Anderson, *From Slavery To Affluence*, 23; Boles, *Religion*, 95; Armstrong, *Slaves Tell Their Story*, 231.

51. Boles, *Religion*, 96-99; Raboteau, *Slave Religion*, 92, 244-45; Bruce Jackson, ed., *The Negro and His Folklore in Nineteenth-Century Periodicals* (Austin, Texas, 1967), 328-29; Fee, *Autobiography*, 143; Anderson, *From Slavery To Affluence*, 24.

52. Lexington *Kentucky Gazette*, March 6, 1878; King, "Free Negroes," 82; Parrish, *Golden Jubilee*, 271; John Taylor, *Baptist Churches*, 108; Troutman, *The Heavens Are Weeping*, 76, 126.

53. Tower, *Slavery Unmasked*, 252; Lyell, *Visit*, 2:213-14. The scientist remembered the service as less emotional than a white Methodist church he attended in Montgomery, Alabama.

54. Minutes, Fifth Street Baptist Church, 1: March 12, May 10, June 14, 1849, November 14, December 16, 1850, December 16, 1857; Parrish, *Golden Jubilee*, 228; *Minutes, Elkhorn Assn., 1856* (Lexington, Ky., 1856), 2; *ibid., 1857* (n.p., n.d.), 8; *ibid., 1860* (n.p., n.d.), 16; *ibid., 1861*, 6; Philadelphia *AME Christian Recorder*, April 5, 1862; Young and Duncan, *Jessamine County*, 191; Wiley, *Slaves No More*, 325.

55. Minutes, Green Street Baptist Church, 1: December 7, 1860; Lexington *Kentucky Gazette*, March 6, 1878; Simmons, *Men of Mark*, 207.

56. Minutes, Green Street Baptist Chruch, 1: February 14, 1847; Minutes, Fifth Street Baptist Church, 1: March 14, 1844, March 10, 1848; Blassingame, *Slave Testimony*, 385; *Constitution and By-Laws of the Colored People's Union Benevolent Society, No. 1, of Lexington, Ky., Organized May 1, 1843* (Lexington, Ky., 1877), 15.

57. David Benedict, *A General History of the Baptist Denomination in America and Other Parts of the World* (New York, 1848), 831; Minutes, Green Street Baptist Church, 1: November 8, December 11, 1846, October 30, 1861; Gibson, *Historical Sketch*, 56; Minutes, Fifth Street Baptist Church, 1: December 26, 1847.

58. Minutes, Fifth Street Baptist Church, 1: June 8, 9, 19, July 13, 23, September 24, October 22, November 30, 1843, May 26, June 13, 1844, October 1850 entry.

59. Elisha Green, *Life*, 6, 26; Minutes, Fifth Street Baptist Church, 1: November 30, 1843, September 9, 1847, December 16, 1850, May 11, 1853; Minutes, Green Street Baptist Church, 1: April 8, December 20, 1849; Sobel, "Trablin' On," 335; Simmons, *Men of Mark*, 206-8; Lexington *Kentucky Gazette*, March 6, 1878; Madison Campbell, *Autobiography*, 37-40.

60. Minutes, Fifth Street Baptist Church, 1: February 25, April 28, 1844, November 14, 1850; Benedict, *Baptist Denomination*, 815n.

61. Minutes, Fifth Street Baptist Church, 1: April 22, 1853; Elisha Green, *Life*, 13, 18-19; Trustees Minute Book, Lexington, July 1, 1841; Posey, *Frontier Mission*, 201-2.

62. Legislative Records of Louisville, Common Council Minutes, December 28, 1835, Reel 14; *ibid.*, July 28, August 8, 15, 22, 1853, Reel 27; *ibid.*, Ordinances and Resolution Book 2, October 17, 1853, Reel 45; Gibson, *Historical Sketch*, 12.

63. Elisha Green, *Life*, 6; Madison Campbell, *Autobiography*, 35, 43, 59-65.

64. Madison Campbell, *Autobiography*, 47-48; Troutman, *The Heavens Are Weeping*, 94, 175; Gibson, *Historical Sketch*, 24; *AME Christian Recorder*, April 5, 1862; Blassingame, *Slave Testimony*, 385; Minutes, Green Street Baptist Church, 1: October 10, 1862; Calico, *Garrard County*, 317; Simmons, *Men of Mark*, 606. The minutes of Fifth Street Baptist Church make no mention of the Civil War until February 1865.

65. Calico, *Garrard County*, 317-18; Minutes, Green Street Baptist Church, 1: November 23, 1864; Louisville *Daily Union Press*, January 7, 17, 19, 1865; Parrish, *Golden Jubilee*, 187; Spencer, *Baptists*, 2:660.

66. Minutes, Green Street Baptist Church, 1: February 6, 1862; Gibson, *Historical*

Sketch, 13, 24, 40, 55-56, 66; William Irvine Papers, Draper MSS, 1 Z 19; Weeden, *History*, 49; *AME Christian Recorder*, March 25, 1865; Minutes, Fifth Street Baptist Church, 1: October 8, 1851.

67. Coleman, *Slavery*, 78; William Henry Fouse, "Educational History of the Negroes of Lexington, Kentucky" (M.A. thesis, University of Cincinnati, 1937), 41; Boles, *Religion*, 104-6; Hedrick, "Slavery in Kentucky," 22; Posey, *Frontier Mission*, 212; Elijah P. Marrs, *Life and History of the Rev. Elijah P. Marrs, First Pastor of Beargrass Baptist Church, and Author* (Louisville, Ky., 1885), 15; Weeden, *History*, 54; Simmons, *Men of Mark*, 595.

68. Parrish, *Golden Jubilee*, 186, 194; Rawick, *The American Slave*, 7:41, 16:15; Riley, *Methodism*, 29; Henry Allen Laine, "My Life," typescript autobiography, 9 (Museum, Eastern Kentucky University); Mathias, "Slave Days," 227; Simmons, *Men of Mark*, 421, 601; Fouse, "Educational History," 22-23; Coleman, *Slavery*, 78-79; Frederick, *Autobiography*, 19; Elisha Green, *Life*, 9, 11; Madison Campbell, *Autobiography*, 12.

69. Simmons, *Men of Mark*, 662; Indianapolis *Freeman*, March 9, 1889; Gibson, *Historical Sketch*, 38; Pickard, *Kidnapped*, 40; Neal, *By Their Fruits*, 45; Richard D. Sears, *The Day of Small Things: Abolitionism in the Midst of Slavery, Berea, Kentucky, 1854-1864* (New York, 1986), 359-62; Margaretta Brown to Orlando Brown, April 13, 1820, Orlando Brown Family Papers; Fouse, "Educational History," 41; Marrs, *Life*, 12, 15; Drew, *North-Side View of Slavery*, 180-81; Weeden, *History*, 54.

70. Hayden, *Narrative*, 25-26, 28, 31-35.

71. "To Stop A School," *Green County Review* 2 (1979): 59; Bibb, *Narrative*, 68; Drew, *North-Side View of Slavery*, 241-42; Posey, *Frontier Mission*, 201-2; Thomas, "Victims of Circumstance," 255.

72. Gibson, *Historical Sketch*, 23; Fouse, "Educational History," 22; Lexington *Kentucky Gazette*, October 17, 1798; William Irvine Papers, Draper MSS 1 Z 19.

73. Simmons, *Men of Mark*, 431; Louisville Library Collection, collected mimeograph writing relating to Louisville, Kentucky, Institutions, 5 vols. (Louisville Free Public Library, Louisville, Kentucky), vol. 1; George D. Wilson, "A Century of Negro Education in Louisville, Kentucky," typescript report, Works Progress Administration (Louisville, Ky., n.d.) 8, appendix; S.E. Smith, ed., *History of the Anti-Separate Coach Movement* . . . (Evansville, Ind., [1894]), 145; Weeden, *History*, 47; Minutes, Green Street Baptist Church, 1: February 6, 1862; Louisville *Daily Union Press*, February 7, April 15, 1865; *Kentucky's Black Heritage*, 39.

74. Gibson, *Historical Sketch*, 3-5, 13, 38, 47, 69-70; Simmons, *Men of Mark*, 369-70.

75. Abdy, *Journal*, 347; James Monroe to Edward P. Smith, November 18, 1865, AMA; Philip Clyde Kimball, "Freedom's Harvest: Freedmen's Schools in Kentucky After the Civil War," *FCHQ* 54 (1980): 283; *Seventh Census, 1850*, 620.

76. John Taylor, *Baptist Churches*, 108; Riley, *Methodism*, 29; Bruner, *A Slave's Adventures*, 19; Coffin, *Reminiscences*, 352; Blassingame, *Slave Testimony*, 431-32; Lexington *Observer & Reporter*, October 28, 1835; Coleman, "Lexington's Slave Dealers," 19; Coleman, *Slavery*, 251, 263. Lewis Clarke, *Narrative*, 70, said that he had seen only three or four slaves who could "properly read" and none who could write, but McDougle's study of 350 randomly gathered advertisements for runaways that indicated that 108 could either read or write, led that author to conclude (*Slavery*, 79), that 10 percent of slaves could read and write and that 20 percent could read. This writer believes that Clarke's estimates were too low, and McDougle's far too high. The quick success in teaching black soldiers to read at Camp Nelson, Jessamine County, seems to indicate that many might have possessed some elementary training upon their arrival. One missionary's report indicated that 185 of about 1,000 soldiers in one regiment and 132 of another were reading from the *Bible* within a matter of weeks. See Louisville *Sanitary Reporter* 2 (September 1864): 61.

77. *Seventh Census, 1850*, xliii, 606-7, 620, 622-23; *Statistics of the United States in 1860*, 507-8. By contrast, 80 percent of whites over age twenty could read in 1850 and 84 percent in 1860. Approximately 60 percent of whites under age fifteen attended school in 1850 and almost 73 percent a decade later. See *Eighth Census, 1860*, 170-71, 174-75.

## 7. Kentucky Blacks in the Civil War

1. Gibson, *Historical Sketch*, 41-42; Victor B. Howard, *Black Liberation in Kentucky: Emancipation and Freedom, 1862-1884* (Lexington, Ky., 1983), 4; Harry Smith, *Fifty Years of Slavery*, 116; Isaac Johnson, *Slavery Days*, 36; Anna Dicken to Henry, February 10, 1861, Dicken-Troutman-Balke Family Papers.

2. Harry Smith, *Fifty Years of Slavery*, 116; Robert Anderson, *From Slavery To Affluence*, 42; Isaac Johnson, *Slavery Days*, 36; Yetman, *Voices from Slavery*, 137-38; James William Massie, *America: The Origin of Her Present Conflict* . . . (Miami, Fla., 1969); orig. pub. 1864), 266; Marrs, *Life*, 17.

3. Blassingame, *Slave Testimony*, 385-86; *National Anti-Slavery Standard*, March 19, 1864; Berlin, "Free Negro," 65.

4. McKee and Bond, *Anderson County*, 63; Blassingame, *Slave Testimony*, 385, 387; Gibson, *Historical Sketch*, 49; Troutman, *The Heavens Are Weeping*, 175; *AME Christian Recorder*, April 5, 1862; *National Anti-Slavery Standard*, March 19, 1864; *Lexington Observer & Reporter*, April 2, 1864; Gutman, *Black Family*, 378; *The War of the Rebellion: A Compilation of the Official Records of the Union and Confederate Armies*, 128 vols. (Washington, D.C., 1880-1911), ser. 1, vol. 20, pt. 2, 68 (hereafter cited as *OR*); Howard, *Black Liberation*, 44.

5. Blassingame, *Slave Testimony*, 390, 632; *National Anti-Slavery Standard*, April 8, 1865; Berlin, "Free Negro," 65; Gibson, *Historical Sketch*, 49; Howard, *Black Liberation*, 91.

6. Blassingame, *Slave Testimony*, 385; *AME Christian Recorder*, June 3, 1865; Anna Dicken Troutman to Henry, January 26, 1861, to Mother, April 3, 1863, Dicken-Troutman-Balke Family Papers; Troutman, *The Heavens Are Weeping*, 141, 171; *New York Tribune*, January 23, 1862; *Cincinnati Daily Gazette*, November 23, 1861.

7. Howard, *Black Liberation*, 5, 12; Thomas H. Parker, *History of the 51st Regiment* . . . (Philadelphia, 1869), 301-3.

8. Howard, *Black Liberation*, 5, 14; *OR*, ser. 2, vol. 1, 776.

9. General Orders, No. 9, October 22, 1862, The Negro in the Military Service of the United States, 1639-1886 (hereafter cited NIMS), microfilm 858, roll 1, frames 428, 431, 455, 699 (5 rolls, NA); *OR*, ser. 2, vol. 1, 777. Eventually all slaves who entered Union lines were labeled "contraband."

10. Howard, *Black Liberation*, 108-9, 114; *Paris Western Citizen*, March 28, 1862; *OR*, ser. 1, vol. 20, pt. 2, 91, ser. 2, vol. 1, 809, ser. 3, vol. 4, 501-2; General Orders, No. 27, March 21, 1862, No. 9, October 22, 1862, Brig. Gen. Q.A. Gillmore to Maj. Gen. Gordon Grainger, December 11, 1862, NIMS, roll 1, frames 480, 696-97, 699; Adj. Gen. Lorenzo Thomas to Col. S.G. Hicks, July 25, 1864, *ibid.*, roll 3, frame 432; Ira Berlin et al., eds., *Freedom: A Documentary History of Emanciaption, 1861-1867. Selected from the Holdings of the Naitonal Archives. Series 2: The Black Military Experience* (Cambridge, England, 1982), 263.

11. Howard, *Black Liberation*, 13-14, 16, 17, 23, 39.

12. *New York Tribune*, January 23, 1862; M.B. Morton, *Kentuckians are Different* (Louisville, Ky., 1938), 16-17.

13. Howard, *Black Liberation*, 45-46, 50; Mary Julia Neal, ed., *The Journal of Eldress*

Nancy . . . (Nashville, Tenn., 1963), 186; *National Anti-Slavery Standard,* July 11, 1863; Frances Dallam Peter Diary, October 10, 1863, Evans Family Papers (UK); Troutman, *The Heavens Are Weeping,* 169-70.

14. Howard, *Black Liberation,* 44; Gibson, *Historical Sketch,* 47; Robert Emmett McDowell, *City of Conflict: Louisville in the Civil War, 1861-1865* (Louisville, Ky., 1962), 83-84; *AME Christian Recorder,* September 27, 1862. W.H. Gibson, one of Louisville's leading blacks, was caught in the dragnet and labored on the fortification for a short time before obtaining a release through his physician.

15. Edgar A. Toppin, "Humbly They Served: The Black Brigade in the Defense of Cincinnati," *JNH* 48 (1963): 84-88; Vernon L. Volpe, "Squirrel Hunting for the Union: The Defense of Cincinnati in 1862," *CWH* 33 (1987): 244-45.

16. Howard, *Black Liberation,* 34, 36, 46, 50.

17. *National Anti-Slavery Standard,* July 11, 1863; Peter Diary, October 10, 1863; *OR,* ser. 3, vol. 4, 921-22; John David Smith and William Cooper, Jr., eds., *Window on the War: Frances Dallam Peter's Lexington Civil War Diary* (Lexington, Ky., 1976), 43; John David Smith, "The Recruitment of Negro Soldiers in Kentucky, 1863-1865," *Register* 72 (1974): 374; M.A. Harris to Riley Handy, January 2, 1973, Harris Small Collection (WKU); Isaac Johnson, *Slavery Days,* 36-38.

18. Gutman, *Black Family,* 368; Howard, *Black Liberation,* 51-52, 66-67; *OR,* ser. 3, vol. 4, 59-60, 559, 733, 768; Gibson, *Historical Sketch,* 47-48; Federal Writers Project, Works Progress Administration, *Military History of Kentucky,* 203-4. The federal government estimated that nine hundred black Kentuckians enlisted at Gallatin and one thousand at Evansville. The often-quoted figure in Collins, *History,* 1:136, placing Kentucky black enlistees in other states at twelve thousand seems too high.

19. Supt. of Census Joseph C.G. Kennedy to Sec. of Interior J.P. Usher, February 11, 1863, NIMS, roll 2, frame 37; Maj. W.H. Sidell to Col. James B. Fry, March 14, 1864; *ibid.,* roll 3, frames 135-36; *OR,* ser. 3, vol. 3, 416, 418-19, vol. 4, 177; John David Smith, "Negro Soldiers in Kentucky," 383-84; Howard, *Black Liberation,* 57. Federal draft problems in Kentucky were complicated by the number of residents who joined the Confederate army.

20. *OR,* ser. 3, vol. 3, 1174-75, 1178-79, vol. 4, 233-34, 248-49; General Orders, No. 34, April 18, 1864, District of Kentucky, Records of the U.S. Army Continental Commands, Record Group 393 (NA), hereafter cited USACC, RG 393.

21. Capt. William C. Grier to Fry, April 10, 1864, Records of the Provost Marshal General's Bureau, 1863-66, RG 110 (NA), hereafter cited PMGB, RG 110; Prov. Mar. to Sidell, March 16, 1864, NIMS, roll 3, frame 145; Howard, *Black Liberation,* 58, 64n, 68; Gutman, *Black Family,* 368; *New York Times,* March 13, 1865; Ira Berlin et al., eds., *Freedom: A Documentary History of Emancipation, 1861-1867. Selected From the Holdings of The National Archives of The United States. Series 1. Volume 1: The Destruction of Slavery* (New York and Cambridge, England, 1985), 616.

22. Gutman, *Black Family,* 368; Dorris and Chenault, *Old Cane Springs,* 122; Louisville *Daily Courier,* March 3, 1866; Stephen Jocelyn, *Mostly Alkali: A Biography* (Caldwell, Idaho, 1963), 34; Howard, *Black Liberation,* 68, 73; *New York Times,* March 13, 1865; Fry to Sidell, May 14, 1864, telegrams received, Asst. Prov. Mar. for Kentucky, PMGB, RG 110; John David Smith, "Negro Soldiers in Kentucky," 387; *OR,* ser. 3, vol. 4, 559. According to Baxter, *Statitics, Medical and Anthropological,* 372, slaveowners sometimes attempted to enroll elderly or ill slaves as substitutes.

23. E. Merton Coulter, *The Civil War and Readjustment In Kentucky* (Gloucester, Mass., 1966; orig. pub. 1926), 199-200, 206-7; *Kentucky House Journal* (1863-64), 397, 466, 579; *OR,* ser. 3, vol. 4, 177-79; John W. Blassingame, "The Recruitment of Colored Troops in Kentucky, Maryland and Missouri, 1863-1865," *Historian* 29 (1967): 542-43.

24. *OR,* ser. 3, vol. 4, 429-30, 548; Maj. Gen. S.G. Burbridge to Sidell, May 13,

1864, telegrams received, Asst. Prov. Mar. for Kentucky, PMGB, RG 110.

25. Isaac Johnson, *Slavery Days*, 36; *American Missionary* 9 (1865): 121; John David Smith, "Negro Soldiers in Kentucky," 390; Blassingame, "Colored Troops," 544.

26. Collins, *History*, 1:134; Gutman, *Black Family*, 368-69; John David Smith, "Negro Soldiers in Kentucky," 384-85; Capt. Thomas H. Moore to Sidell, May 12, 24, 1864, Capt. James M. Fidler to Sidell, May 16, 1864, telegrams received, Asst. Pro. Mar. for Kentucky, PMGB, RG 110; Dorris and Chenault, *Old Cane Springs*, 123; Howard, *Black Liberation*, 63; Col. R.D. Mussey to C.W. Foster, June 2, 1864, letters received, Colored Troops Division, Records of the Adjutant General's Office, RG 94 (NA), hereafter cited CTD, RAGO, RG 94; J.S. Newberry, *The U.S. Sanitary Commission in the Valley of the Mississippi, During the War of the Rebellion, 1861-1866* (Cleveland, 1871), 520; Tri-Monthly Report of Business and General Transactions, May 1864, Asst. Prov. Mar. for Kentucky, PMGB, RG 110; Ira Berlin et. al., *The Destruction of Slavery*, 607.

27. Capt. T.E. Hall to Sidell, May 25, 1864, Thomas D. Sedgewick to Sidell, June 7, 1864, telegrams received, Asst. Prov. Mar. for Kentucky, PMGB, RG 110; Newberry, *Sanitary Commission*, 520-21; Gutman, *Black Family*, 370-71; *Louisviille Daily Journal*, June 3, 1864; Grier to Sidell, April 7, 1864, letters received, Greenupsburg Prov. Mar. Office, PMGB, RG 110; Adj. Gen. Thomas to Brig. Gen. E.D. Townsend, April 25, 1865, NIMS, roll 4, frames 118-19.

28. S.E. Smith, *Anti-Separate Coach Movement*, 173; J.W. Gibson and W.H. Crogman, *The Colored American: From Slavery to Honorable Citizenship* (Atlanta, Ga., 1906), 552; *National Anti-Slavery Standard*, June 18, 1864; Thomas to Townsend, April 25, 1865, NIMS, roll 4, frame 118; Kate Ford and Henry A. Ford, *History of the Ohio Falls Cities and their Counties, with Illustrations and Biographical Sketches*, 2 vols. (Cleveland, 1882), 1:329; S.M. Starling to daughters [Mary and Anna], June 19, 1864, Lewis-Starling Collection (WKU); Capt. A.G. Hobson to Brig. Gen. James B. Fry, August 4, 1864, NIMS, roll 3, frame 458; Jocelyn, *Biography*, 30-34; Capt. J.R. Grissom to Fry, June 1, 1865, NIMS, roll 4, frame 151; John David Smith, "Negro Soldiers in Kentucky," 384-85; Anonymous, *Daviess County*, 168-69; *OR*, ser. 3, vol. 4, 501; Col. C.H. Adams to Brig. Gen. J.P. Hawkins, September 28, 1863, NIMS, roll 2, frame 584; Thomas to Townsend, April 25, 1865, NIMS, roll 4, frame 118.

29. Rawick, *The American Slave*, 6:30, 7:39-41.

30. Gibson and Crogman, *Colored American*, 552; Bruner, *A Slave's Adventures*, 32-33, 42-43.

31. Marrs, *Life*, 17-20.

32. Mussey to Foster, June 2, 1864, letters received, CTD, RAGO, RG 94; Newberry, *Sanitary Commission*, 520; *National Anti-Slavery Standard*, July 9, 1864; Fidler to Fry, May 31, 1864, NIMS, roll 3, frame 314; Fidler to Sidell, June 15, 1865, NIMS, roll 4, frames 161-64; Berlin et al., *Black Military Experience*, 259.

33. Lexington *Observer & Reporter*, July 16, 1864; *OR*, ser. 3, vol. 4, 501; *Senate Ex. Doc.*, No. 28, 38 Cong., 2 Sess. (ser. 1209), 17; Newberry, *Sanitary Commission*, 521-24; Rawick, *The American Slave*, 7:40; Marrs, *Life*, 20; Berlin et al., *The Destruction of Slavery*, 610.

34. *OR*, ser. 3, vol. 4, 210, 422, 474; Troutman, *The Heavens Are Weeping*, 186; Howard, *Black Liberation*, 79, 111, 116; Blassingame, "Colored Troops," 539; Lexington *Observer & Reporter*, July 16, 1864.

35. John David Smith, "Negro Soldiers in Kentucky," 385; *OR*, ser. 3, vol. 4, 429, 501; Browder Diary, February 27, September 5, 1864; Starling, *Henderson County*, 227-31; *Military History of Kentucky*, 209; *National Anti-Slavery Standard*, June 18, 1864. George Browder recorded as early as September 11, 1862, that Federal troops had "seized" a Logan County slave, "strapped a gun on him," and ridden off.

36. *National Anti-Slavery Standard*, June 18, 1864; Troutman, *The Heavens Are Weep-*

ing, 170, 184, 189; John David Smith, "Negro Soldiers in Kentucky," 385-86; Berlin et al., *Black Military Experience*, 273-74; Howard, *Black Liberation*, 73; *New York Times*, March 1, 1865; Ford and Ford, *Ohio Falls Cities*, 329; Gutman, *Black Family*, 368.

37. Troutman, *The Heavens Are Weeping*, 160, 171, 174; Neal, *Eldress Nancy*, 186.

38. Gutman, *Black Family*, 370; George D. Dicken to Anna and Frank [Troutman], May 24, 1864, Dicken-Troutman-Balke Family Papers; *Senate Ex. Doc.*, No. 28, 30 Cong., 2 Sess. (ser. 1209), 17; *National Anti-Slavery Standard*, June 18, 1864; Troutman, *The Heavens Are Weeping*, 179; Berlin et al., *Black Military Experience*, 276.

39. Berlin et al., *Black Military Experience*, 275; Henry Miller Diary, March 20, 1865 (FC); Pratt Diary, 3: April 1, 1865; Thomas James, *The Autobiography of Rev. Thomas James* (Rochester, N.Y., 1975; orig. pub. 1887), 24; John M. Palmer, *Personal Recollections of John M. Palmer . . .* (Cincinnati, 1901), 233; *New York Times*, March 13, 1865.

40. Troutman, *The Heavens Are Weeping*, 131, 156, 194; Howard, *Black Liberation*, 16, 91, 93; Anna Dicken Troutman to mother, April 3, 1863, Dicken-Troutman-Balke Family Papers; Peter Diary, January 27, 1864; Bruner, *A Slave's Adventures*, 41; *National Anti-Slavery Standard*, June 18, 1864.

41. Troutman, *The Heavens Are Weeping*, 171, 179; Neal, *Eldress Nancy*, 199; Peter Diary, January 27, 1864; Robert Anderson, *From Slavery To Affluence*, 43; John Egerton, *Generations: An American Family* (Lexington, Ky., 1983), 54, 57.

42. Ross A. Webb, *Kentucky in the Reconstruction Era* (Lexington, Ky., 1979), 39; Frankfort *Commonwealth*, April 28, 1865; Howard, *Black Liberation*, 71, 79, 82; Donovan, "Kentucky Law Regarding The Negro," 13. Lowell H. Harrison, *The Civil War in Kentucky* (Lexington, Ky., 1975), 101-2, points out that a rise in prices partially offset some of the losses in production.

43. Berlin et al., *Black Military Experience*, 262; *National Anti-Slavery Standard*, March 28, 1863; Howard, *Black Liberation*, 113, 117.

44. Pratt Diary, 3: July 4, 1864; Newberry, *Sanitary Commission*, 385; *National Anti-Slavery Standard*, June 18, 1864.

45. Berlin et al., *Black Military Experience*, 270; Newberry, *Sanitary Commission*, 527; *National Anti-Slavery Standard*, June 18, 1864; *The Liberator*, June 24, December 9, 1864.

46. Newberry, *Sanitary Commission*, 527-28; Gutman, *Black Family*, 372; *The Liberator*, December 9, 1864.

47. Berlin et al., *Black Military Experience*, 270-71; *American Missionary* 9 (1865): 85.

48. *Sanitary Reporter* 2 (September 1864): 61; General Orders, No. 29, December 15, 1864, NIMS, roll 3, frame 567.

49. John G. Fee to George Whipple, February 8, 1865, AMA; Howard, *Black Liberation*, 115-16; *American Missionary* 9 (1865): 85; Newberry, *Sanitary Commission*, 528.

50. *American Missionary* 9 (1865): 85; Elnathan Davis to M.E. Strieby, April 12, 1865, AMA.

51. Louisville *Daily Union Press*, January 28, 1865; James, *Autobiography*, 21; Howard, *Black Liberation*, 110; Blassingame, *Slave Testimony*, 385.

52. Minutes, Fifth Street Baptist Church, 1: February 7, 1865; Louisville *Daily Union Press*, January 7, 16, 1865.

53. James, *Autobiography*, 21, 32; Gutman, *Black Family*, 376n.

54. James, *Autobiography*, 22-23, 26-28. James claimed that ministers like Adams "were ready to do the bidding of their [white] masters," but Adams and his friends no doubt believed that the northerner would one day depart Louisville, as he eventually did, leaving them to an unpleasant fate James helped create.

55. Palmer, *Recollections*, 234; Louisville *Daily Union Press*, March 6, 22, 1865; Ross Webb, *Reconstruction*, 37; James, *Autobiography*, 21-22; *AME Christian Recorder*, April 1, 1865.

56. Gutman, *Black Family*, 367-68. For a sample of slave enlistment declarations, see

"Coleman Family Business Transactions and Correspondence," folder 162, Catherine and Howard Evans Papers (UK).

57. J.H. Baxter, *Statistics, Medical and Anthropological*, 364, 368-70, 372, 379, 382, 384, 386, 505, 510. Physicians who examined blacks entering the military in Kentucky summarized their findings in reports written between May and August 1865. The reports, between one and nine pages each, are generally couched in racist terms, but they contain an extremely valuable historical record. For a complete analysis of the physical condition of the Commonwealth's black soldiers, see John David Smith, "Kentucky Civil War Recruits," 185-96, and the more general work of Michael Anthony Cooke, "The Health of Blacks During Reconstruction, 1862-1870" (Ph.D. diss., University of Maryland, 1983), 37-43, 50-51, 123-25.

58. *OR*, ser. 3, vol. 4, 542, 733, 921, 1018, 1270; Kennedy to Usher, February 11, 1863, NIMS, roll 2, frame 37; John David Smith, "Negro Soldiers in Kentucky," 389. The 1867 report of the Kentucky Adjutant General placed 25,438 black enlistees in fifteen infantry, two cavalry, and four artillery regiments. See *Kentucky's Black Heritage*, 30.

59. *Official Army Register of the Volunteer Force of the United States Army for the Years 1861, '62, '63, '64, '65*, 8 vols. (Washington, D.C., 1865-67), 8:332, 338, 341; Joseph T. Wilson, *The Black Phalanx: A History of the Negro Soldiers of the United States in the Wars of 1775-1812, 1861-'65* (Hartford, Conn., 1888), 464-65, 476-78; Special War Order, No. 29, May 3, 1865, NIMS, roll 4, frame 132; *OR*, ser. 3, vol. 4, 1017-18.

60. Marrs, *Life*, 21-26, 32, 59, 60, 66, 68; Newberry, *Sanitary Commission*, 381, 387, 520, 524-26; Dorris and Chenault, *Old Cane Springs*, 122-23; Berlin et al., *Black Military Experience*, 630; Howard, *Black Liberation*, 111-12.

61. *American Missionary* 8 (1864): 262-63; Fee to Strieby, March 7, 1865, AMA; Marrs, *Life*, 28, 33, 65-66; *OR*, ser. 3, vol. 4, 460; Howard, *Black Liberation*, 65.

62. Minutes, Green Street Baptist Church, 1: November 23, 1864; Louisville *Daily Union Press*, January 7, 9, 17, 19, February 7, 1865; Thomas James to Whipple, February 10, 1865, AMA; New York *Times*, March 13, 1865; *Sanitary Reporter* 2 (September 1864): 61.

63. *OR*, ser. 3. vol. 4, 431, 921-22; Marrs, *Life*, 25.

64. Marrs, *Life*, 23, 27, 37, 61-63, 67, 73, 75; *Official Army Register*, 304; Weeden, *History*, 10; Newberry, *Sanitary Commission*, 526; Bruner, *A Slave's Adventures*, 43-44; *OR*, ser. 3, vol. 4, 451, 469; Troutman, *The Heavens Are Weeping*, 184; Mussey to Foster, June 12, 1864, NIMS, roll 3, frame 893.

65. Marrs, *Life*, 25, 27-31, 35-37; Bruner, *A Slave's Adventures*, 43-45; Jocelyn, *Biography*, 29.

66. Marrs, *Life*, 37-51; *Official Army Register*, 161. According to Quarles, *Negro in the Civil War*, 87, black spy Henry Blake operated in the Glasgow area in 1862; and the Louisville *Daily Union Press*, April 5, 1865, indicated the presence of a black infantry unit in Glasgow at war's end.

67. Marrs, *Life*, 51-57, 61-67, 69-71, 73; *Official Army Register*, 161; Bruner, *A Slave's Adventures*, 45-46; *National Anti-Slavery Standard*, February 28, 1863; John David Smith, "Negro Soldiers in Kentucky," 388.

68. John David Smith, "Negro Soldiers in Kentucky," 388; Newberry, *Sanitary Commission*, 521; Louisville *Daily Union Press*, April 11, 1865.

69. Thomas to Sec. of War E.M. Stanton, October 10, 1864, Col. James S. Brisbin to Thomas, October 20, 1864, NIMS, roll 3, frames 1097, 1099-1101; Klotter, *Breckinridges*, 127-28.

70. Baxter, *Statistics, Medical and Anthropological*, 368.

71. Jocelyn, *Biography*, 27-28, 45; Thomas to Stanton, October 10, 1864, January 1, 1865, NIMS, roll 3, frames 1097, 1200.

## 8. Freedom's Pains: Life in the Immediate Post-War Era

1. Mary Sudman Donovan, "Kentucky Law Regarding the Negro," 11-12; Ross Webb, *Reconstruction*, 37, 39; Palmer, *Recollections*, 239; Gutman, *Black Family*, 375.

2. *New York Times*, March 13, 1865; *AME Christian Recorder*, June 3, 1865; *Louisville Daily Union Press*, March 22, 1865; Gutman, *Black Family*, 382; *American Missionary* 10 (1866): 18; *National Anti-Slavery Standard*, November 11, 1865; Palmer, *Recollections*, 237-38; Berlin et al., *The Destruction of Slavery*, 53-54, 636-37.

3. *The Liberator*, August 11, 1865; Palmer, *Recollections*, 253; Ross Webb, *Reconstruction*, 38; *OR*, ser. 3, vol. 5, 125; Berlin et al., *The Destruction of Slavery*, 619-21.

4. *The Liberator*, August 11, 1865; Howard, *Black Liberation*, 80; Robert Anderson, *From Slavery To Affluence*, 48; *AME Christian Recorder*, June 3, 1865; Wood, *White Side of A Black Subject*, 307.

5. Howard, *Black Liberation*, 83; Gutman, *Black Family*, 381-82; Maj. Gen. Clinton B. Fisk to Maj. Gen. O.O. Howard, November 3, 1865, Press Copies, Letters Sent Assistant Commissioner's Office (hereafter cited PC, LSACO), Tenn., vol. 15, Records of the Bureau of Refugees, Freedmen, and Abandoned Lands, Record Group 105, NA (hereafter cited BRFAL, RG 105); Annie Hager to Fisk, January 12, 1866, Letters Received Assistant Commissioner's Office (hereafter cited LRACO), Tenn., *ibid.*; Elisha Green, *Life*, 21; Palmer, *Recollections*, 253; Ross Webb, *Reconstruction*, 38; U.S., *Statistics of the Population of the United States at the Tenth Census (June 1, 1880)* . . . (Washington, D.C., 1883), 392; U.S., *Eleventh Census of the United States, 1890*, 25 vols. (Washington, D.C., 1895), 1: part 1, 487; U.S., *Ninth Census of the United States, 1870*, (Washington, D.C., 1875), 1:31-32. Eighteen, or 31 percent, of the fifty-eight black Kentuckians who wrote "slave narratives" had left the Commonwealth. See Escott, *Slavery Remembered*, 146-47. Unless stated, all references to BRFAL, RG 105, are for Kentucky.

6. *AME Christian Recorder*, June 3, 1865; J.R. Lewis to Fisk, May 15, 1866, Inspection Reports (hereafter cited IR), Assistant Commissioner's Office (hereafter cited ACO), Tenn., box 23, BRFAL, RG 105; Coulter, *Civil War*, 263; Morton, *Kentuckians*, 27; Wood, *White Side of A Black Subject*, 307; Starling, *Henderson County*, 238; L. Boyd, *Chronicles of Cynthiana and other Chronicles* (Cincinnati, 1894), 209.

7. Gibson, *Historical Sketch*, 52; Isaac Johnson, *Slavery Days*, 39; Robert Anderson, *From Slavery To Affluence*, 48. Another migrating group included refugees stranded in Kentucky by war. They included wives and children who had followed soldiers to Kentucky and discharged black troops who desired to return to the southern states to reunite with families or to find work. S.A. Porter to Maj. J.H. Cochrane, August 4, 1865, PC, Letters Sent (hereafter LS), Louisville, vol. 139, BRFAL, RG 105; John W. Adams to Fisk, August 8, 1865, Cochrane to Col. H.A. McCaleb, Mary Baker to McCaleb, August 10, 1865, Letters Received (hereafter cited LR), Louisville, box 53, *ibid.*; R.E. Farwell to Fisk, December 21, 1865, LRACO, Tenn., box 2, *ibid.*

8. Rawick, *The American Slave*, 6:99; Nathaniel E. Green, *The Silent Believers*, 23; W.R. Roume to Col. R.E. Johnson, September 25, 1866, LS, Danville, no. 102, BRFAL, RG 105; Yetman, *Voices from Slavery*, 138-39.

9. Berlin et al., *Black Military Experience*, 269, 705-6, 750-51; Howard, *Black Liberation*, 125; *House Ex. Doc.* No. 70, 39 Cong., 1 Sess. (ser. 1256), 234-35.

10. Elisha Green, *Life*, 19-21.

11. James, *Autobiography*, 27-28; Palmer, *Recollections*, 240-42; *AME Christian Recorder*, July 22, 1865; *The Liberator*, July 21, 1865; New York *National Freedman* 1 (1865): 189. Much noise and confusion existed during his speech, but it seems irrefutable that Palmer told the crowd that "you are free—there is no more slavery."

12. Louisville *Daily Union Press*, July 7, 1865. For a look at freedom celebrations throughout the South, see William H. Wiggins, Jr., *O Freedom!: Afro-American Emanci-*

pation Celebrations (Knoxville, Tenn., 1988).

13. John F. Smith to J.H. Donovan, June 19, 1866, LS, Paducah, no. 79, BRFAL, RG 105; C.J. True to R.E. Johnson, September 30, 1866, LS, Maysville, no. 157, *ibid.*; A.W. Lawwill to Maj. Gen. John Ely, December 31, 1867, LRACO, box 12, *ibid.*; Donovan to Ely, May 4, 1866, LRACO, box 1, *ibid.*; John Fowles to Ely, April 6, 1866, LRACO, box 2, *ibid.*; William T. Buckner to H.A. Hunter, March 18, 1868, LR, Russellville, box 61, *ibid.*; *Third Annual Report of the Freedmen's Aid Society of the Methodist Episcopal Church* (Cincinnati, 1869), 6 (hereafter cited *FASMEC*); *Fourth Annual Report, FASMEC* (Cincinnati, 1871), 5; *Fifth Annual Report, FASMEC* (Cincinnati, 1872), 13; *American Freedman* 1 (May 1866): 25-26; John G. Fee to M.E. Strieby, November 30, 1866, AMA; Fee to Fisk, July 18, 1865, Registered Letters Received (hereafter cited RLR), ACO, Tenn., Microfilm 999, roll 7, frames 75, 78.

14. Howard, *Black Liberation*, 96-97; Ross Webb, *Reconstruction*, 41; George R. Bentley, *A History of the Freedmen's Bureau* (New York, 1970; orig. pub. 1955), 215; *Senate Ex. Doc.* No. 27, 39 Cong., 1 Sess. (ser. 1238), 2:3-4.

15. Louisville *Daily Courier*, February 22, 1866; Bentley, *Freedmen's Bureau*, 215; Ross Webb, *Reconstruction*, 41, 51; Ross A. Webb, " 'The Past Is Never Dead, It's Not Even Past': Benjamin P. Runkle and the Freedmen's Bureau in Kentucky, 1866-1870," *Register* 84 (1986): 347-48, 350; Ely to Jefferson C. Davis, August 15, 1866, LSACO, box 14, BRFAL, RG 105; J.S. Catlin to Benjamin P. Runkle, December 30, 1867, LRACO, box 7, *ibid.*; Lawwill to Runkle, December 28, 1868, LRACO, box 19, *ibid.*; Sidney Burbank to Howard, June 23, 1868, LSACO, *ibid.*; *General Orders, Circulars, Etc. Asst.-Commissioner, Bu. R., F., & A. L. Kentucky. 1866-68* (Louisville, Ky., 1869), No. 1, February 16, 1868.

16. Bentley, *Freedmen's Bureau*, 74; Ross Webb, *Reconstruction*, 47.

17. Ely to Fisk, May 15, 1866, LRACO, Tenn., box 6, BRFAL, RG 105; True to R.E. Johnson, February 25, 1868, LR, Lexington, box 48, *ibid.*; Davis to Howard, November 5, 1866, LSACO, vol. 15, *ibid.*; Burbank to Howard, October 14, 1867, LSACO, vol. 19, *ibid.*; Runkle to Edwin Whittlesey, July 20, 1869, LSACO, vol. 21, *ibid.*

18. Louisville *Daily Courier*, February 22, 1866; Ross A. Webb, "Kentucky: 'Pariah Among the Elect,' " in *Radicalism, Racism and Party Realignment: The Border States during Reconstruction*, ed. Richard O. Curry (Baltimore, 1969), 119; Donovan to Ely, May 4, November 13, 1866, LRACO, box 1, BRFAL, RG 105; James H. Rice to Gen. ? Fitch, February 19, 1866, LR, Lexington, box 46, *ibid.*; A.L. Robinson to Ely, May 24, 1866, Samuel McKee to Ely, July 20, 1866, Lawwill to Ely, December 14, 1866, LRACO, box 5, *ibid.*; R. Vance to Fisk, January 31, 1866, LRACO, Tenn., box 9, *ibid.* Fleeing slaves motivated Federal recruiting more than providing troops for the Freedmen's Bureau.

19. Howard, *Black Liberation*, 81; *OR*, ser. 3, vol. 5, 13; Coulter, *Civil War*, 265; Donovan, "Kentucky Law Regarding the Negro," 15.

20. Davis to Howard, November 5, 1866, LSACO, vol. 15, BRFAL, RG 105; Burbank to Howard, October 14, 1867, LSACO, vol. 19, *ibid.*; Howard to Runkle, March 5, 1869, LRACO, box 21, *ibid.*; Berlin et al., *Black Military Experience*, 706.

21. Louisville *Daily Democrat*, August 20, 1865; *Kentucky Senate Journal* (1866), 134-35; Louisville *Daily Journal*, February 21, 1866; *Senate Doc.* No. 49, 42 Cong., 2 Sess. (ser. 1467), 1.

22. Ely to Davis, August 15, 1866, LSACO, vol. 14, BRFAL, RG 105; Lawwill to Ely, August 9, 1867, LRACO, box 12, *ibid.*; Runkle to Burbank, November 15, 1867, LSACO, vol. 18, *ibid.*; *Senate Doc.* No. 49, 1; *House Ex. Doc.* No. 70, 39 Cong., 1 Sess., 230.

23. *Senate Doc.* No. 49, 1-3; J.J. Landrum to Ely, August 13, 1866, LRACO, box 5, BRFAL, RG 105; Lawwill to Ely, January 31, 1867, LRACO, box 12, *ibid.*; "Notice," March 1, 1867, LSACO, vol. 16, *ibid.*; J.H. Bridgewater to R.E. Johnson, June 8, 1867, LRACO, box 11, *ibid.*; James M. Fidler to Ely, July 1, 1867, LRACO, box 8, *ibid.*; *House*

Ex. Doc. No. 70, 207, 237-38; Starling, *Henderson County*, 338.

24. *House Ex. Doc. No. 70*, 201-2, 236-37; C.F. Johnson to Ely, July 28, 1866, LRACO, box 3, BRFAL, RG 105; Runkle to Burbank, December 12, 1867, LSACO, vol. 18, *ibid.*; Burbank to Howard, October 14, 1868, LSACO, vol. 19, *ibid.*; Starling, *Henderson County*, 338; George C. Wright, *Racial Violence in Kentucky, 1865-1940: Lynchings, Mob Rule, and "Legal Lynchings"* (Baton Rouge and London, 1990), 307-11; *House Ex. Doc. No. 1*, 40 Cong., 3 Sess. (ser. 1367), 1: 191-92, 1056. Document No. 1 lists murders from July 1867 to July 1868. All deaths of blacks except one were attributed to whites or parties unknown. The twenty-eight whites murdered were reportedly killed by whites.

25. William Gillette, "Anatomy of a Failure: Federal Enforcement of the Right to Vote in the Border States during Reconstruction," in *Radicalism, Racism and Party Realignment*, 272-73; *Senate Doc. No. 49*, 1-3.

26. *House Ex. Doc. No. 70*, 206; Ely to Davis, January 20, 1867, LSACO, vol. 15, BRFAL, RG 105; Ely to Burbank, March 13, 1867, LSACO, vol. 16, *ibid.*; Runkle to Burbank, November 15, 1867, LSACO, vol. 18, *ibid.*; Brig. Gen. H.G. Thomas to Runkle, March 31, 1868, LRACO, box 20, *ibid.*; Louisville *Daily Democrat*, May 2, 1866; Ross Webb, *Reconstruction*, 77; *House Ex. Doc. No. 1*, 1:191-92, 1056; Victor B. Howard, "The Black Testimony Controversy in Kentucky, 1866-1872," *JNH* 58 (1973): 150-51.

27. *House Ex. Doc. No. 1*, 1:1056; *ibid.*, No. 70, 203; Louisville *Daily Journal*, October 26, 1866; W.H. Merrill to Ely, July 28, 1866, LRACO, box 5, BRFAL, RG 105; Ely to Davis, November 5, 1866, LSACO, vol. 15, *ibid.*; Roume to R.E. Johnson, January 5, 1867, LS, Danville, no. 102, *ibid.*; Lexington *Kentucky Statesman*, July 9, 1867; L.F. Johnson, *History of Franklin County, Ky.* (Frankfort, Ky., 1912), 164-65.

28. R.E. Johnson to Runkle, November 30, 1867, LS, Lexington, no. 124, BRFAL, RG 105; Louisville *Daily Journal*, June 24, October 12, 1867; *House Ex. Doc. No. 329*, 40 Cong., 2 Sess. (ser. 1346), 24; *ibid.*, No. 1, 1:1056; Ross A. Webb, *Benjamin Helm Bristow: Border State Politician* (Lexington, Ky., 1969), 54-55, 60. Bristow successfully prosecuted twenty-nine cases.

29. *House Ex. Doc. No. 70*, 203; Berlin et al., *Black Military Experience*, 697.

30. *House Ex. Doc. No. 70*, 204, 237-38; Berlin et al., *Black Military Experience*, 683-84; anonymous black soldiers to E.M. Stanton, October 22, 1865, LR, CTD, box 112, RAGO, RG 94; Capt. G.E. Stanford and others to the president and secretary of war, May 30, 1866, *ibid.*

31. *Senate Ex. Doc. No. 27*, 2:10-11; Starling, *Henderson County*, 238; *House Ex. Doc. No. 70*, 205; Fee to "the officers of the Bureau," March 25, 1868, LR, Lexington, box 48, BRFAL, RG 105.

32. *House Ex. Doc. No. 70*, 203, 238; Petition of Daniel W. Higdon and others to Freedmen's Bureau, June 20, 1866, Unregistered Letters Received (hereafter cited ULR), Bowling Green, box 42, BRFAL, RG 105; Donovan to Ely, May 4, 1866, LRACO, box 1, *ibid.*; J.W. Finnie to Ely, October 1, 1866, LRACO, box 2, *ibid.*; *Senate Ex. Doc. No. 27*, 2:8; Marrs, *Life*, 73-75.

33. Collins, *History*, 1:170, 206, 208; L.F. Johnson, *Franklin County*, 164-65; Anonymous, *Daviess County*, 419-21; *House Ex. Doc. No. 329*, 4. According to L.F. Johnson, no black charged with "criminal assault" in Franklin County between 1865 and 1900 escaped the lynch mob. While sex crimes were the most common offense cited as a cause for lynching, statistics indicate that the majority of victims were in fact arrested for or charged with murder. See John Samuel Ezell, *The South Since 1865* (New York, 1963), 361.

34. Roume to R.E. Johnson, January 5, 1867, LS, Danville, no. 102, BRFAL, RG 105; Collins, *History*, 1:174.

35. R.E. Johnson to Ely, May 25, 1867, LRACO, box 10, BRFAL, RG 105; Ely to R.E. Johnson, May 1, 1867, James H. Rice to R.E. Johnson, May 1, 1867, LR, Lexington, box 47, *ibid.*

36. Collins, *History*, 1:192.

37. *House Ex. Doc.* No. 70, 233; Fisk to Howard, September 3, 1865, PC, LSACO, Tenn., vol. 15, BRFAL, RG 105; Farwell to Fisk, October 18, 1865, LRACO, Tenn., box 2, *ibid.*; Farwell to Fisk, January 26, 1866, LRACO, Tenn., box 6, *ibid.*; W.G. Rice to Levi F. Burnett, June 6, 1866, LRACO, box 5, *ibid.*; Abisha Scofield to R.E. Johnson, September 10, 1866, W.G. Rice to James H. Rice, September 18, 1866, LR, Lexington, box 49, *ibid.*; Marrs, *Life*, 64; Scofield to M.E. Strieby and George Whipple, December 14, 1866, AMA.

38. Scofield to Whipple, October 4, 1866, Fee to Whipple, December 12, 1866, Scofield to Strieby and Whipple, December 14, 1866, AMA; Merrill to Ely, December 20, 1866, LRACO, box 5, BRFAL, RG 105.

39. J.G. Nain to James H. Rice, November 23, 1866, LS, Nicholasville, no. 168, BRFAL, RG 105; Fee to the Freedmen's Bureau, March 25, 1868, LR, Lexington, box 48, *ibid.*; Scofield to Strieby and Whipple, December 14, 1866, AMA; Richard D. Sears, "A Practical Recognition of the Brotherhood of Man": *John G. Fee and the Camp Nelson Experience* (Berea, Ky., 1986), 67.

40. *House Ex. Doc.* No. 329, 4, 23; *ibid.*, No. 70, 202, 204, 206, 237; Hannah Carlisle to "Dear Husband," April 7, 1866, Carlisle Family Papers (Michigan Historical Collections, Bentley Historical Library, University of Michigan, Ann Arbor, Michigan); Louisville *Daily Journal*, February 8, 10, 1866; R.E. Johnson to Runkle, December 9, 1868, LR, Lexington, no. 125, BRFAL, RG 105.

41. J.J. Landrum to A. Benson Brown, September 1, 1867, LRACO, box 11, BRFAL, RG 105; "Notice," March 1, 1867, LSACO, vol. 16, *ibid.*; Lawwill to Ely, January 31, February 12, 1867, LRACO, box 12, *ibid.*; ? Ramsdell to Catlin, January 9, 1868, LRACO, box 16, *ibid.*

42. *House Ex. Doc.* No. 70, 237; *ibid.*, No. 329, 2-3; J.J. Landrum to Freedmen's Bureau, August 3, 1866, LS, Covington, no. 92, BRFAL, RG 105; A.B. Brown to Runkle, September 30, 1868, LRACO, box 15, *ibid.*

43. Gutman, *Black Family*, 378; York A. Woodward to Ely, December 31, 1866, LRACO, box 14, BRFAL, RG 105; Burbank to Howard, October 14, 1868, LSACO, vol. 19, *ibid.*; Lieut. W.H. Merrill to Ely, March 4, 1867, LRACO, box 13, *ibid.*; R.E. Johnson to Ely, August 31, 1867, LRACO, box 11, *ibid.*; R.W. Roberts to Ely, July 29, 1867, LRACO, box 7, *ibid.*; W. James Kay to Ely, April 3, 1867, LRACO, box 12, *ibid.*; *House Ex. Doc.* No. 329, 2-3, 7; Thomas, "Victims of Circumstance," 255; Morton, *Kentuckians*, 27.

44. R.A. Bell to Runkle, March 12, 1868, LRACO, box 15, BRFAL, RG 105; John L. Graham to R.E. Johnson, February 1, 1867, LS, Covington, no. 93, *ibid.*; Alan Raphael, "Health and Social Welfare of Kentucky Black People, 1865-1870," *Societas: A Review of Social History* 2 (1972): 146-47.

45. Bell to Runkle, March 12, 1868, LRACO, box 15, BRFAL, RG 105; R.E. Johnson to Runkle, July 31, 1868, December 9, 1868, LRACO, box 18, *ibid.*; Kellogg, "Black Residential Areas in Lexington," 35, 37; Thomas, "Victims of Circumstance," 259.

46. Scofield to Strieby, June 15, 1865, April 22, 1866, AMA; E.P. Smith to Col. Maxwell Woodhull, March 8, 1866, ULR, Louisville, box 54, BRFAL, RG 105; Merrill to Burnett, May 4, 1866, LRACO, box 5, *ibid.*; *American Missionary* 11 (1867): 85-86.

47. Louisville *Daily Courier*, January 4, 1866; C.H. Frederick to Ely, April 30, 1866, LRACO, box 2, BRFAL, RG 105; Bell to S.A. Edwards, December 10, 1868, LS, Medical Department (hereafter cited MD), vol. 55, *ibid.*; Burnett to R.M. Roberts, June 27, 1867, LR, Louisville, box 53, *ibid.*; H.M. Bullitt to Dr. M. Goldsmith, March 14, 1866, LRACO, Tenn., box 6, *ibid.*; Louisville *Daily Democrat*, January 20, February 3, 1866; Louisville *Daily Journal*, September 25, 1866, December 9, 1867; Weeden, *History*, 28, 58.

48. A.B. Brown to Runkle, February 29, 1868, Bell to Runkle, April 23, 1868, LRACO, box 15, BRFAL, RG 105; Merrill to Ely, April 1, 1866, LRACO, Tenn., box 7, *ibid.*; Fee to Fisk, July 17, 1865, LRACO, Tenn., box 2, *ibid.*; John F. Smith to Donovan, June 19, 1866, LS, Paducah, no. 179, *ibid.*; Raphael, "Health of Kentucky Black People," 147, 152-53; *House Ex. Doc.* No. 329, 17; Morton, *Kentuckians*, 27.

49. True to Ely, May 31, 1867, True to R.E. Johnson, March 26, 1868, LS, Maysville, no. 158, BRFAL, RG 105; R.E. Johnson to Runkle, December 31, 1867, LRACO, box 17, *ibid.*; P.G. Reeves to R.E. Johnson, December 31, 1867, LR, Lexington, box 48, *ibid.*; R.E. Johnson to Runkle, December 9, 1868, LRACO, box 18, *ibid.*; Raphael, "Health of Kentucky Black People," 147-48.

50. Kay to Ely, September 30, 1867, LRACO, box 12, BRFAL, RG 105; Ely to H.A. Dickey, August 11, 1866, LSACO, vol. 14, *ibid.*; Ely to Burbank, April 20, 1867, LSACO, vol. 16, *ibid.*; Runkle to Burbank, November 15, 1867, January 13, 1868, LSACO, vol. 18, *ibid.*; T.K. Noble to J.W. Alvord, January 13, 1869, LSACO, vol. 21, *ibid.*; Kentucky *Acts* (1865-66), 51; *ibid.*, (1867-68), 1:4; *House Ex. Doc.* No. 1, 1056; Donovan, "Kentucky Law Regarding the Negro," 57-59.

51. Burbank to Bvt. Brig. Gen. F.D. Genall, December 9, 1868, Runkle to Burbank, December 15, 1868, LSACO, vol. 19, BRFAL, RG 105; Catlin to Runkle, March 2, 1868, LRACO, box 16, *ibid.*; Bullitt to Runkle, December 9, 1868, LRACO, box 15, *ibid.*; Runkle to Burbank, September 19, 1868, LRACO, box 17, *ibid.*; Bell to Edwards, December 10, 1868, LSMD, vol. 55, *ibid.*; Louisville *Daily Courier*, January 24, February 1, 1866; Louisville *Daily Journal*, January 23, 25, 1866.

52. Merrill to Ely, April 1, 1866, LRACO, Tenn., box 7, BRFAL, RG 105; Graham to R.E. Johnson, February 1, 1867, LS, Covington, no. 93, *ibid.*; Raphael, "Health of Kentucky Black People," 152-54; Covington *Journal*, March 21, 1868.

53. R.E. Johnson to Ely, June 30, 1866, LS, Lexington, no. 122, BRFAL, RG 105; R.E. Johnson to Runkle, July 31, 1868, LRACO, box 18, *ibid.*; Kay to Ely, September 30, 1867, LRACO, box 12, *ibid.*; Bailey to Ely, May 1, 1867, Thomas Cheaney to Lt. Wells S. Bailey, June 4, 1867, Bailey to Ely, July 13, 1867, Catlin to Runkle, November 1, 1867, LRACO, box 7, *ibid.*; Cheaney to Ely, April 11, 1866, LRACO, box 1, *ibid.*; A.B. Brown to Runkle, September 30, 1868, LRACO, box 15, *ibid.*; Raphael, "Health of Kentucky Black People," 153-55.

54. *House Ex. Doc.* No. 70, 211; Louisville *Daily Journal*, February 21, March 16, 1866; Burnett to James H. Rice, April 17, 1866, Ely to H.C. Swartzwelder, June 2, 1866, LSACO, vol. 14, BRFAL, RG 105; Fowles to Ely, April 6, 1866, Frederick to Ely, April 30, 1866, LRACO, box 2, *ibid.*; Frederick to Ely, April 11, 1866, PCLS, Louisville, vol. 139, *ibid.*; Merrill to Burnett, June 30, 1866, LRACO, box 5, *ibid.*

55. A.M. York to Fisk, September 1, 1865, ULRACO, Tenn., box 15, BRFAL, RG 105; Donovan to Ely, May 4, 1866, LRACO, box 1, *ibid.*; John F. Smith to Donovan, June 19, 1866, LS, Paducah, no. 179, *ibid.*; Buckner to Hunter, March 18, 1868, RLR, Russellville, box 61, *ibid.*

56. *Third Annual Report, FASMEC*, 6; *Fourth Annual Report, ibid.*, 5; *Fifth Annual Report, ibid.*, 13; *American Freedmen* 1 (May 1866): 25-26; Louisville *Daily Democrat*, May 2, 1866.

57. Fisk to Howard, October 17, 1865, PC, LSACO, Tenn., vol. 15, BRFAL, RG 105; Henry M. Laing to Ely, March 3, 1866, LRACO, box 1, *ibid.*; Ely to Annie Biddle, September 29, 1866, Ely to Laing, December 5, 22, 1866, LSACO, vol. 15, *ibid.*; Narrative Report of Bureau Operations for January 1868 (hereafter cited NR), February 15, 1868, ACO, box 36, *ibid.*; R.E. Johnson to Runkle, December 31, 1867, LS, Lexington, no. 124, *ibid.*; *House Ex. Doc.* No. 329, 2. The disposition of the funds collected at Camp Nelson is not known.

58. *House Ex. Doc.* No. 70, 211; Fisk to John D. Black, January 24, 1866, PC,

LSACO, Tenn., vol. 9, BRFAL, RG 105; Ely to Davis, August 15, 1866, LSACO, vol. 14, *ibid.*; Runkle to Burbank, November 15, 1867, LSACO, vol. 18, *ibid.*; Howard to Runkle, April 7, 1869, LSACO, box 21, *ibid.*

59. NR, February 15, 1868, ACO, box 36, BRFAL, RG 105; Runkle to Catlin, February 10, 1868, LSACO, vol. 18, *ibid.*; Runkle to R.E. Johnson, February 14, 1868, LR, Lexington, box 48, *ibid.*; Raphael, "Health of Kentucky Black People," 149-50.

60. *House Ex. Doc.* No. 329, 2, 12, 14; Runkle to Burbank, April 10, May 12, 1868, Burbank to Howard, October 14, 1868, LSACO, vol. 19, BRFAL, RG 105; Runkle to Burbank, December 12, 1867, Runkle to Bvt. Brig. Gen. M.P. Small, February 10, 1868, LSACO, vol. 18, *ibid.*; Ely to Davis, November 5, 1866, vol. 15, *ibid.* Most whites who received rations were in the Refugee's and Freedmen's Hospital.

61. Catlin to Runkle, March 2, 1868, LRACO, box 16, BRFAL, RG 105; Bailey to Ely, January 31, 1867, LRACO, box 7, *ibid.*; Howard to Burbank, February 29, 1868, LRACO, box 17, *ibid.*; *House Ex. Doc.* No. 329, 6, 10.

62. Bell to Dr. John A. Octerlony, July 28, 1868, F.S. Town to Edwards, August 22, 1866, Circular No. 7, August 27, 1866, Town to Davis, January 1, 1867, LSMD, vol. 55, BRFAL, RG 105; Burbank to Howard, June 23, 1868, Burbank to the Judges of the County Courts, August 3, 1868, LSACO, vol. 19, *ibid.*; Octerlony to Ely, November 1, 1866, LRACO, box 5, *ibid.*; Runkle to Whittlesey, July 20, 1869, LSACO, vol. 21, *ibid.*; Raphael, "Health of Kentucky Black People," 144-46n, 150-51. Some patients remained at the hospital into 1869. Gaines M. Foster's "The Limitations of Federal Health Care for Freedmen, 1862-1868," *JSH* 48 (1982): 349-72, describes bureau health services for the entire South as rather like that in Kentucky. See also Marshall S. Legan, "Disease and the Freedmen in Mississippi During Reconstruction," *Journal of the History of Medicine and Allied Sciences* 28 (1973): 257-67; Howard N. Rabinowitz, "From Exclusion to Segregation: Health and Welfare Services for Southern Blacks, 1865-1890," *Social Services Review* 48 (1974): 327-54; and Paul Skeels Pierce, *The Freedmen's Bureau: A Chapter in the History of Reconstruction* (Iowa City, Iowa, 1904).

63. Louisville *Daily Democrat*, February 3, 1866; Merrill to Burnett, June 10, 1866, Octerlony to Ely, October 9, November 1, 1866, LRACO, box 5, BRFAL, RG 105; Bell to Octerlony, July 28, 1868, Town to Edwards, August 22, 1866, LSMD, vol. 55, *ibid.*; Runkle to Whittlesey, July 20, 1869, LSACO, vol. 21, *ibid.*; Ross Webb, "Runkle," 353.

64. Ely to Davis, January 20, 1867, LSACO, vol. 15, BRFAL, RG 105; Bell to Runkle, March 12, 1868, LRACO, box 15, *ibid.*; Ely to Burbank, March 13, April 20, June 1, 1867, LSACO, vol. 16, *ibid.*; Runkle to Whittlesey, July 20, 1869, LSACO, vol. 21, *ibid.*; Burbank to Howard, October 14, 1868, LSACO, vol. 19, *ibid.*; Raphael, "Health of Kentucky Black People," 151.

65. Ely to Davis, January 20, 1867, LSACO, vol. 15, BRFAL, RG 105; Town to Edwards, February 9, 1867, W.R. DeWitt to Dr. Fred Hassig, April 11, 1867, Bell to Runkle, May 18, 1868, DeWitt to Kay, June 17, 1867, Bell to Edwards, December 10, 1867, March 31, 1868, LSMD, vol. 55, *ibid.*; Ely to Burbank, March 13, June 1, 1867, LSACO, vol. 16, *ibid.*; Bell to Runkle, March 12, box 15, *ibid.*; Burbank to Howard, October 14, 1868, LSACO, vol. 19, *ibid.*; Raphael, "Health of Kentucky Black People," 153.

66. Town to Edwards, August 22, 1866, LSMD, vol. 55, BRFAL, RG 105; Ely to Burbank, March 13, 1867, Burnett to Kay, June 24, 1867, LSACO, vol. 16, *ibid.*; Ely to Davis, August 15, 1866, LSACO, vol. 14, *ibid.*; Frederick to Ely, April 11, 1866, PCLS, Louisville, vol. 139, *ibid.*; Runkle to Burbank, March 13, 1868, Burbank to Howard, October 14, 1868, LSACO, vol. 19, *ibid.* Statistics are derived from monthly reports of the Refugee's and Freedmen's Hospital. About 10 percent of the hospital's patients were white.

67. Town to Ely, September 21, 1866, LRACO, box 6, BRFAL, RG 105; Frederick to

Davis, February 15, 1867, LRACO, box 8, *ibid.*; Ely to R. Winterspoon, August 11, 1866, LSACO, vol. 14, *ibid.*; Special Order No. 30, March 13, 1868, LRMD, box 36, *ibid.*; Runkle to Ely, August 20, 1867, IRACO, vol. 37, *ibid.*

68. Runkle to Burbank, March 13, July 10, August 11, 1868, Burbank to Howard, October 14, 1868, Runkle to Burbank, December 15, 1868, LSACO, vol. 19, BRFAL, RG 105; Bell to Edwards, December 10, 1868, LSMD, vol. 55, *ibid.*; Runkle to Whittlesey, July 20, 1869, LSACO, vol. 21, *ibid.*; T.W. Chamberlin to Runkle, November 20, 1868, LRACO, box 16, *ibid.*

69. Donovan, "Kentucky Law Regarding the Negro," 57, 59-60; Runkle to Whittlesey, May 9, 1868, Runkle to Burbank, June 16, August 11, September 14, 19, 1868, LSACO, vol. 19, BRFAL, RG 105; Bell to Runkle, July 17, 1868, Runkle to Speed, July 21, 1868, Bell to Octerlony, July 28, 1868, LSMD, vol. 55, *ibid.*; Runkle to Whittlesey, January 20, 1869, LSACO, vol. 21, *ibid.*; J.S. Atwell to Bell, August 10, 1868, LRACO, box 15, *ibid.*; R.E. Johnson to Runkle, July 17, 1868, Disbursing Officer, LRACO, box 27, *ibid.*; Runkle to Burbank, September 19, 1868, LRACO, box 17, *ibid.*; *House Ex. Doc.* No. 329, 3, 24.

70. *House Ex. Doc.* No. 70, 202, 204-5, 207.

71. Louisville *Daily Democrat*, January 14, 1866; Donovan to John Boyd, April 16, 1866, LS, Paducah, no. 176, BRFAL, RG 105; Graham to Ely, May 27, 1866, LRACO, box 2, *ibid.*; John Peyton to Ely, August 26, 1866, James Nesbit to Davis, September 22, 1866, Peyton to Davis, September 24, 1866, LRACO, box 5, *ibid.*; Donovan to Ely, June 1, 1866, LRACO, box 1, *ibid.*; True to R.E. Johnson, November 27, 1867, LS, Maysville, no. 158, *ibid.*

72. Kentucky *Acts* (1865-66), 49-50; Catlin to Ely, September 5, 1867, LRACO, box 7, BRFAL, RG 105; Kay to Ely, January 31, 1867, LS, Paducah, no. 176, *ibid.*; Frederick to Ely, September 19, 1866, LRACO, box 2, *ibid.*; Margaret Baker to Col. ? Davis, December 19, 1866, LR, Covington, no. 91, *ibid.*

73. Elisha Green, *Life*, 37; Louisville *Commercial*, May 1, 1874; J.W. Hazelrigg to [Adj. Gen. of Kentucky], July 10, 1866, Records of the Kentucky Adjutant General, Department of Military Affairs, Military Records and Research Library, Frankfort, Ky.; Faney Wakefield to [Adj. Gen. of Kentucky], March 30, 1879, *ibid.*; E.K. Clemmer to Adj. Gen. of Kentucky, March 22, 1875, *ibid.*; Bruner, *A Slave's Adventures*, 47-48.

74. Kentucky *Acts* (1865-66), 37; Donovan, "Kentucky Law Regarding the Negro," 41-42; *General Orders*, Circular No. 3, June 26, 1866.

75. H.G. Thomas, "General Condition of the Freedmen," to Runkle, March 31, 1868, LS, Danville, no. 100, BRFAL, RG 105; R.E. Johnson to Ely, June 30, 1866, LS, Lexington, no. 122, *ibid.*; A.B. Brown, "General Conditions of Freemen," September 30, 1868, LS, Bowling Green, no. 69, *ibid.*; E.O. Brown to Runkle, February 27, 1868, LRACO, box 15, *ibid.*; J.H. Johnson to James H. Rice, April 10, 1866, LR, Lexington, box 49, *ibid.*; Donovan, "Kentucky Law Regarding the Negro," 40-41; *House Ex. Doc.* No. 329, 7; Berlin et al., *Black Military Experience*, 673-75. Freedmen's Bureau officials considered the number of abandoned children from racially mixed relationships alarming.

76. Nain to James H. Rice, July 20, 1867, LS, Nicholasville, no. 168, BRFAL, RG 105; J.E. Jacobs to J.B. Gowen, February 19, 1866, Jacobs to R.P. Haley, February 21, 1866, PC, LSACO, Tenn., vol. 10, *ibid.*; J.H. Johnson to James H. Rice, April 10, 1866, LR, Lexington, box 49, *ibid.*; Merrill to Burnett, May 4, 1866, LRACO, box 5, *ibid.*; Ely to A.L. Robinson, August 10, 1866, LSACO, vol. 14, *ibid.*; Berlin et al., *Black Military Experience*, 676-79.

77. Howard, *Black Liberation*, 125; Lammermeier, "Urban Black Family," 443, 451, 455.

## 9. Post-Civil War Religion, 1865-1891

1. J.J. Jepson, *History of the First Baptist Church of Sulphur Spring and Sulphur Spring Missionary Baptist Church* (Frankfort, Ky., 1938), 8; History Committee, *A History of First Baptist Church Somerset, Kentucky 1799 to 1974* (Wolf City, Texas, 1974), 16; D.P. Browning, *One Hundred Years of Church History* ([Lewisburg, Ky.], 1922), 19.

2. W.O. Carver, *History of the New Salem Baptist Church* (Louisville, 1901), 6; Minutes of the Pleasant Grove Baptist Church, Jefferson County, Kentucky, August 15, 1868 (FC); Masters, *Baptists*, 368.

3. Paris, *Black Churches*, 9; Elisha Green, *Life*, 26; Parrish, *Golden Jubilee*, 89-90, 187; Masters, *Baptists*, 174, 233, 238, 347; Spencer, *Baptists*, 2:660.

4. Parrish, *Golden Jubilee*, 90-93; *Minutes of the General Association of Colored Baptists in Kentucky . . . 1880* (Louisville, Ky., 1880), 9; H. Lyman Morehouse, ed., *Baptist Home Missions in North America . . .* (New York, 1883), 85-87; Spencer, *Baptists*, 2:661.

5. Elisha Green, *Life*, 26; Parrish, *Golden Jubilee*, 90-95, 105, 107-8; Masters, *Baptists*, 348; *Minutes, Gen. Assn., 1869* (Louisville, Ky., 1869), 12, 16; *ibid., 1882* (Louisville, Ky., 1883), 31-33; *ibid., 1887* (Louisville, Ky., 1888), 59; *ibid., 1893* (Louisville, Ky., 1894), 81.

6. Spencer, *Baptists*, 2:660-61; Masters, *Baptists*, 349; Parrish, *Golden Jubilee*, 94, 96, 103; J. William Snorgrass, "America's Ten Oldest Black Newspapers," *Negro History Bulletin* 36 (1983): 11-12; Armistead Scott Pride, "A Register and History of Negro Newspapers in the United States: 1827-1950" (Ph.D. diss., Northwestern University, 1950), 95; Gibson and Crogman, *Colored American*, 443. For a brief history of Roger Williams University, see Morehouse, *Baptist Home Missions*, 445-48.

7. Parrish, *Golden Jubilee*, 94, 97-98, 104; *Minutes, Gen. Assn., 1873* (Louisville, Ky., 1873) 27; *ibid., 1875* (Shelbyville, Ky., 1875) 13; *ibid., 1877* (Louisville, Ky., 1877), 26; Spencer, *Baptists*, 2:661-62; Minutes, Fifth Street Baptist Church, 2: October 13, 1874; Minutes, Green Street Baptist Church, 1: September 11, 1864.

8. *Minutes, Gen. Assn., 1878* (Louisville, Ky., 1878), 15; Morehouse, *Home Baptist Missions*, 85.

9. *Minutes, Gen. Assn., 1879* (Louisville, Ky., 1880), 16; *ibid., 1882* (Louisville, Ky., 1883), 12; Spencer, *Baptists*, 2:662.

10. Marrs, *Life*, 120-22, 126-27, 129; Parrish, *Golden Jubilee*, 162; *Minutes, Gen. Assn., 1887*, 19-20.

11. Parrish, *Golden Jubilee*, 182-83; *Minutes, Gen. Assn., 1881* (Louisville, Ky., 1882), 19; Paul W.L. Jones, *A History of the Kentucky Normal and Industrial Institute* (Lexington, Ky., 1912), 14-15n.

12. *Minutes, Gen. Assn., 1881*, 19-20; Nobel Lovely Prentis, *Southern Letters* (Topeka, Kan., 1881), 10; Simmons, *Men of Mark*, 765.

13. *Minutes, Gen. Assn., 1881*, 19; *ibid., 1892* (Louisville, Ky., 1893), 22; Parrish, *Golden Jubilee*, 162, 165, 172-73; Baptist Normal and Theological Institute *Catalog* (hereafter cited BNTI *Catalog* with date), 1881-1882, box 1, Simmons Bible College Records, RG 105 (UL); State University *Catalog*, 1884-1885, 1892-1893 (hereafter cited SU *Catalog* with date), *ibid.*, 8; S.E. Smith, *Anti-Separate Coach Movement*, 174; Louisville *Defender* (supplement), February 18, 1982; I. Garland Penn, *The Afro-American Press, And Its Editors* (Springfield, Mass., 1891), 412; Indianapolis *World*, October 22, 1892.

14. New York *Freeman*, April 24, 1886; *Minutes, Gen. Assn., 1885* (Louisville, Ky., 1886), 21; *ibid., 1889* (Louisville, Ky., 1890), 19, 35, 37; George C. Wright, *Life Behind A Veil: Blacks in Louisville, Kentucky, 1865-1930* (Baton Rouge, 1985), 165.

15. BNTI *Catalog*, 1881-1882, 15; SU *Catalog*, 1884-1885, 12; *ibid.*, 1892-1893, 21;

*American Baptist,* November 12, 1880; Indianapolis *World,* October 22, 1892; Parrish, *Golden Jubilee,* 173; *Minutes, Gen. Assn., 1883* (Louisville, Ky., 1884), 15; *ibid., 1893,* 37.

16. BNTI *Catalog, 1881-1882,* 8-9, 14; SU *Catalog, 1884-1885,* 14-15; *ibid., 1892-1893,* 35-36.

17. Parrish, *Golden Jubilee,* 106; BNTI *Catalog, 1881-1882,* 14-15; SU *Catalog, 1892-1893,* 9-12, 18-20.

18. Owen D. Pelt and Ralph Lee Smith, *The Story of the National Baptists* (New York, 1960), 88-91; Lawrence H. Williams, *Black Education in Kentucky, 1879-1930: The History of Simmons University* (Lewiston, Me., 1987), 165.

19. New York *Freeman,* March 13, 20, April 17, 1886; SU *Catalog, 1884-1885,* 12-14, 20; *ibid., 1892-1893,* 32-34; *Minutes, Gen. Assn., 1885,* 21.

20. *American Baptist,* November 12, 1880, January 1, 1887; New York *Freeman,* December 11, 1886; Louisville *Courier-Journal,* June 19, 1887.

21. George C. Wright, *Life Behind A Veil,* 128, 159; Prentis, *Southern Letters,* 11; Minutes, Fifth Street Baptist Church, 3: November 9, 1881, July 18, December 12, 1888; Louisville *Bulletin,* September 24, 1881; New York *Freeman,* November 18, 1885; *American Baptist,* November 12, 1880; Parrish, *Golden Jubilee,* 105, 108, 139, 143-44; Lawrence H. Williams, *Black Higher Education,* 54-55.

22. Marrs, *Life,* 121-23; *Minutes, Gen. Assn., 1881,* 16; *ibid., 1885,* 21; *ibid., 1889,* 35, 37; *ibid., 1890,* 22; Morehouse, *Baptist Home Missions,* 85; Masters, *Baptists,* 350; Parrish, *Golden Jubilee,* 106.

23. George C. Wright, *Life Behind A Veil,* 161; *Minutes, Gen. Assn., 1892,* 22; *ibid., 1893,* 37; S.E. Smith, *Anti-Separate Coach Movement,* 171-72; Minutes, Fifth Street Baptist Church, 4: October 15, 1890; Parrish, *Golden Jubilee,* 127-28; SU *Catalog, 1892-1893,* 8.

24. Minutes, Fifth Street Baptist Church, 2: April 19, May 10, 15, 29, 1871, January 3, 1873; *ibid.,* 3: October 13, November 10, 1886, February 21, 1887; Louisville *Commercial,* November 5, 1872. In addition to paying for an annuity, the church paid the back salary owed Adams.

25. Gibson, *Historical Sketch,* 18; Marrs, *Life,* 141-42; Parrish, *Golden Jubilee,* 195, 272-74.

26. Marrs, *Life,* 129-34; Parrish, *Golden Jubilee,* 187, 197-98, 203, 217-18, 254, 282-83; Perrin, *Bourbon, Scott, Harrison and Nicholas Counties,* 198, 298.

27. Louisville *Courier-Journal,* June 1, 1887; Underwood, *Colored Churches of Frankfort,* 4-5, 16-18.

28. Peter, *Fayette County,* 471; Parrish, *Golden Jubilee,* 244-47, 271; Scott, *State Street Baptist Church,* 20, 28, 30; Diamond Jubilee Commission, *Diamond Jubilee Of The General Association Of Colored Baptists In Kentucky* (Louisville, 1943), 194; *American Baptist,* November 12, 1880.

29. Parrish, *Golden Jubilee,* 198-200; Simmons, *Men of Mark,* 595-97. For a brief account of Allensworth's all-black community in California, see Department of Parks & Recreation, *Allensworth Feasibility Study* (Sacramento, Calif., 1971).

30. Minutes, Green Street Baptist Church, 1: November 2, 1865; *ibid.,* 2: July 1, 31, August 8, September 18, October 7, 10, 1873, January 20, 1876; *ibid.,* 3: December 4, 1882; Minutes, Fifth Street Baptist Church, 1: July [no day] 1866; *ibid.,* 3: September 11, 1878, February 12, 1879; *ibid.,* 4: March 13, 20, 1889; George C. Wright, *Life Behind A Veil,* 37; *American Baptist,* November 12, 1880; Elisha Green, *Life,* 27.

31. Minutes, Fifth Street Baptist Church, 2: January 13, May 11, June 8, 1870, February 15, May 15, 29, 1871, January 3, 1873, January 17, October 13, 1874, June 17, 1875; *ibid.,* 3: July 17, 1878, January 8, 1879, March 12, 1880, November 9, 1881, February 8, 1882, March 9, 1883; *ibid.,* 4: June 12, 1889, February 19, March 12, 1890; Minutes, Green Street Baptist Church, 2: March 12, 1869, October 11, 1872, March 6, 1873,

May 11, September 11, 1874, January 12, 1877; *ibid.*, 3: October 12, 1877, May 10, 1889, January 10, 1890; Louisville *Commercial*, September 29, 1870.

32. Fifth Street Choir Record, October 7, 1873, September 3, 1874; Minutes, Fifth Street Baptist Church, 4: December 12, 1888, January 9, 1889, February 19, March 12, July 9, October 15, 1890, February 11, 1891; Minutes, Green Street Baptist Church, 2: May 8, December 11, 1874; *ibid.*, 3: February 8, 1880; New York *Freeman*, November 28, 1885; Louisville *Bulletin*, September 24, 1881; Louisville *Commercial*, August 9, 1872.

33. George C. Wright, *Life Behind A Veil*, 37; Louisville *Commercial*, November 9, 1875; Minutes, Green Street Baptist Church, 2: August 3, 1870, February 7, 1874; New York *Freeman*, May 15, 1886.

34. *AME Christian Recorder*, May 27, 1865; Harry V. Richardson, *Dark Salvation: The Story of Methodism as It Developed Among Blacks in America* (Garden City, N.Y., 1976), 210; General Conference Handbook, *Historical and Illustrated, 25th Quadrennial Session of the A. M. E. Zion Church* . . . (Louisville, Ky., 1916), 17 (hereafter cited *AME Zion Church*); David M. Jordan, Sr., "The Lexington Conference and Negro Migration," 1-4; Harry D. Tinsley, *History of No Creek, Ohio County, Kentucky; with a Genealogy and Biographical Section* (Frankfort, Ky., 1953), 83-84.

35. *AME Christian Recorder*, March 25, 1865; Louisville *Courier-Journal*, June 28, 1874, September 6, 1888; New York *Freeman*, May 16, 1885; Weeden, *History*, 49; Gibson, *Historical Sketch*, 9-10.

36. *AME Zion Church*, 17, 106-7; Weeden, *History*, 43, 53, 56; Johnston, ed., *History of Louisville*, 2:224; Louisville *Courier-Journal*, June 26, 1887; New York *Freeman*, May 16, 1885.

37. Walters, *Life*, 28-30, 34-35, 37, 85-86; Simmons, *Men of Mark*, 221-22; Rule, *Light Bearers*, 170. Kentucky native Albery Allson Whitman, born a slave in Munfordville, also acquired fame as a poet, but after leaving the state in 1870. For an assessment of his career, see Blyden Jackson, "Albery Allson Whitman (1851-1901)," in *Fifty Southern Writers Before 1900*, ed. Robert Bain and Joseph M. Flora (Westport, Conn., 1987), 514-23.

38. Perrin, *Bourbon, Scott, Harrison and Nicholas Counties*, 198, 298; Anonymous, *Daviess County*, 384; William Henry Perrin, ed., *County of Christian, Kentucky: Historical and Biographical* (Chicago and Louisville, Ky., 1884), 240.

39. *AME Christian Recorder*, March 25, May 27, 1865, November 19, 1870; New York *Freeman*, May 16, 23, 1885, January 1, 1887; George C. Wright, *Life Behind A Veil*, 130; Louisville *Ohio Falls Express*, July 11, 1891; Louisville *Commercial*, August 16, 1870; Gibson, *Historical Sketch*, 53; Marjorie Norris, "An Early Instance of Nonviolence: The Louisville Demonstrations of 1870-71," *JSH* 32 (1966): 491-92.

40. King, "Free Negroes," 87-88; Louisville *Courier-Journal*, June 28, 1874; B.W. McDonnold, *History of the Cumberland Presbyterian Church* (Nashville, Tenn., 1899), 432-36, 439, 455; Thomas D. Campbell, *One Family Under God: A Story of Cumberland Presbyterians In Black And White* (Memphis, Tenn., 1982), 36-37, 45-47; Anonymous, *The Bowling Green and Warren County, Ky., Immigration Society* (Bowling Green, Ky., 1885), 12. McDonnold estimates that there were twenty thousand black Cumberland Presbyterians in 1860.

41. Protestant Episcopal Church, "The Colored Episcopal Mission, Louisville, Kentucky," April 6, 1861, broadside (FC); Johnston, *History of Louisville*, 2:185; Louisville *Daily Courier*, August 19, 1868; Gibson, *Historical Sketch*, 21; George C. Wright, *Life Behind A Veil*, 130-31.

42. Ella Lord Hopson, ed., *Memoirs Dr. Winthrop Hartly Hopson* (Cincinnati, 1887), 185-88.

43. John T. Brown, *Churches of Christ* . . . (Louisville, Ky., 1904), 173-74; Simmons, *Men of Mark*, 189, 191; New York *Freeman*, September 11, October 9, 1886; Louisville *Courier-Journal*, July 10, 1887.

44. Anna C. Minogue, *Pages from a Hundred Years of Dominican History* (Cincinnati, 1921), 149-51; John T. Gillard, *The Catholic Church and the American Negro* . . . (New York, 1968; orig. pub. 1929), 142; *The Record, Official Publication of the Diocese of Louisville*, February 27, 1936, February 23, 1970; Gibson, *Historical Sketch*, 22; George C. Wright, *Life Behind A Veil*, 131.

45. Calico, *Garrard County*, 317-18; Sears, *Practical Recognition*, 77-78; Newberry, *Sanitary Commission*, 527-28; John G. Fee to M.E. Strieby, May 18, 1865, AMA.

46. Fee to George Whipple, December 16, 1865, January 25, February 11, 1867, AMA; Fee to Strieby, May 18, 1865, *ibid.*; Gabriel Burdett to E.M. Cravath, November 20, 1870, *ibid.*; Sears, *Practical Recognition*, 23, 77.

47. Burdett to Strieby, July 18, 1877, AMA; Burdett to Cravath, November 20, 1870, July 1, 1871, February 19, 1872, December 5, 13, 1873, November 26, 1875, *ibid.*; Burdett to Whipple, December 29, 1875, *ibid.*; Fee to Cravath, May 7, 1872, January 20, 1873, *ibid.*

48. Burdett to Cravath, February 1, June 1, December [no day], 11, 1872, AMA; Burdett to Strieby, February 1, May 12, 15, 1877, *ibid.*; Burdett to E.P. Smith, May 21, 1867, *ibid.*; Burdett to Whipple, May 6, 1876, *ibid.*; Burdett to William Whiting, May 1, 1871, *ibid.*; Sears, *Practical Recognition*, 41.

49. Burdett to Strieby, July 18, 1877, AMA; *American Missionary* 37 (1883): 71; *ibid.*, 35 (1881): 276; George C. Wright, *Life Behind A Veil*, 130, 134; "Normal School," undated printed flier, box 4, RG 1.2, John G. Fee Papers (BC).

## 10. Post-Civil War Education, 1865-1891

1. Thomas James to George Whipple, January 13, 24, 1865, AMA; Abisha Scofield to M.E. Strieby, July 15, 1865, *ibid.*; B.B. Smith to Strieby, February 24, 1865, *ibid.*; E.P. Smith to Strieby, October 4, 1865, *ibid.*; C.J. True to R.E. Johnson, September 30, 1866, LS, Maysville, no. 157, BRFAL, RG 105; H.C. Howard to Dr. Rush, LS, Mt. Sterling, no. 162, *ibid.*; T.K. Noble to J.W. Alvord, July 8, 1867, Monthly School Reports, Kentucky (hereafter cited MSR with dates; all references are to Kentucky), roll 20, Microfilm 803 (35 rolls, frames unnumbered), *ibid.*; Louisville *Daily Union Press*, February 7, 1865; Louisville *Daily Journal*, January 20, 1866. Kentucky blacks were typical of southern freedmen in their desire for education following the Civil War. See James D. Anderson, *The Education of Blacks in the South, 1860-1935* (Chapel Hill, N.C., 1988), 5-12.

2. *American Missionary* 8 (1864): 263; John G. Fee to Whipple, January 2, February 25, 1865, AMA; Fee to Strieby, November 30, 1866, *ibid.*; Ann E.W. Williams to Strieby, May 22, 1865, *ibid.*; Belle Mitchell to AMA, January [no day] 1866, *ibid.*; J.W. Alvord, *Fourth Semi-Annual Report on Schools for Freedmen, July 1, 1867* (Washington, D.C., 1867), 73.

3. Alvord, *Fourth Report*, 73; Wells A. Bailey to Benjamin P. Runkle, December 13, 1867, LRACO, box 7, BRFAL, RG 105; J.G. Nain to J.H. Rice, December 26, 1866, February 8, 1867, LS, Lexington, box 47, *ibid.*; J.S. Catlin to J.S. Stansberry, October 23, 25, 29, 1868, LS, Louisville, no. 141, *ibid.*; J.C. Rodriquez to C.F. Johnson, July 8, 1867, LRACO, box 11, *ibid.*; Noble to Runkle, February 26, 1868, LRACO, box 19, *ibid.*; Kimball, "Freedom's Harvest," 275-76; B.B. Smith to Whipple, February 9, 1865, AMA; B.B. Smith to Strieby, February 24, 1865, *ibid.*; James, *Autobiography*, 27-28. The female teacher opposed was Belle Mitchell.

4. Victor B. Howard, "The Struggle for Equal Education in Kentucky, 1866-1884," *Journal of Negro Education* 46 (1977): 315-16; *Kentucky Documents* (1866), No. 3, 23 (hereafter cited *Ky. Doc.* with year and Doc. No.); *ibid. (1867)*, No. 31, 42; A.W. Lawwill to John Ely, September 21, 1866, LRACO, box 6, BRFAL, RG 105; Lawwill to Ely, January

31, 1867, LRACO, box 12, *ibid.*; James M. Fidler to Ely, September 30, 1867, LRACO, box 8, *ibid.*; True to Runkle, October 24, 1867, LRACO, box 11, *ibid.*; Fee to Whipple, June 9, 1865, AMA.

5. *Report of the Commissioners of the Bureau of Refugees, Freedmen and Abandoned Lands for the Year 1867* (Washington, D.C., 1867), 72.

6. Richard B. Drake, "The American Missionary Association" (Ph.D. diss., Emory University, 1966), 156; Ely to Annie Biddle, September 29, 1866, Ely to Davis, October 15, 1866, LSACO, vol. 15, BRFAL, RG 105; Ely to H.A. Dike, August 11, 1866, LSACO, vol. 14, *ibid.*; Noble to Alvord, January 13, 1869, LSACO, vol. 21, *ibid.*; Runkle to Alvord, September 19, 1870, MSR, roll 21, *ibid.*; Noble to Alvord, MSR, roll 20, *ibid.*; *Third Annual Report, FASMEC,* 6; *Fourth Annual Report, ibid.,* 5; *Fifth Annual Report, ibid.,* 13; *American Freedman* 1 (May 1866): 25-26; Alvord, *Fourth Report,* 70-71; J.W. Alvord, *Sixth Semi-Annual Report on Schools of Freedmen, July 1, 1868* (Washington, D.C., 1868), 52.

7. John Ogden to Clinton B. Fisk, December 31, 1865, LRACO, Tenn., box 8, BRFAL, RG 105.

8. *Kentucky Acts* (1865-66), 51; *ibid. (1867),* 2 vols. (Frankfort, Ky., 1867), 1:94-95; Donovan, "Kentucky Law Regarding the Negro," 44-46; *Ky. Doc.* (1867), No. 31, 277.

9. *Ky. Doc.* (1866), No. 3, 22-23; Noble to Alvord, February 11, 1867, LSACO, vol. 16, BRFAL, RG 105; Noble to Alvord, October 30, 1868, LSACO, vol. 19, *ibid.*; A.B. Brown to Runkle, March 31, 1868, LRACO, box 15, *ibid.*; A.B. Brown to R.E. Johnson, August 25, 1867, LR, Lexington, box 48, *ibid.*; *Ky. Doc.* (1869), No. 18, 71-72; *Kentucky Acts* (1871), 18; Kimball, "Freedom's Harvest," 273n. The superintendent of public instruction reported distribution of tax funds to thirteen black schools in 1866.

10. Noble to Alvord, January 13, 1869, LSACO, vol. 21, BRFAL, RG 105; Noble to G.D. Elliot, December 31, 1867, LSACO, vol. 18, *ibid.*; J.W. Alvord, *Eighth Semi-Annual Report on Schools For Freedmen, January 1, 1869* (Washington, D.C., 1869), 65; *idem, Tenth Semi-Annual Report on Schools For Freedmen, July 1, 1870* (Washington, D.C., 1870), 44.

11. Noble to S.C. Hale, February 27, 1868, LSACO, vol. 19, BRFAL, RG 105; Ogden to Fisk, December 31, 1865, John Harlan to Rev. D. Stevenson, May 23, 1866, LRACO, Tenn., box 8, *ibid.*; Alvord, *Fourth Report,* 74. The attitudes expressed by bureau and aid society officials working in Kentucky were not philosophically different from the motives of those laboring among blacks in the Lower South. See Jacqueline Jones, *Soldiers of Light and Love: Northern Teachers and Georgia Blacks, 1865-1873* (Chapel Hill, N.C., 1980), 49-50.

12. Ogden to Fisk, April 22, 1865, LRACO, Tenn., box 8, BRFAL, RG 105; Noble to Alvord, January 13, 1869, LSACO, vol. 21, *ibid.*; R.E. Johnson to Runkle, March 2, 1868, LRACO, box 18, *ibid.*; Noble to Sidney Burbank, November 28, 1868, LSACO, vol. 19, *ibid.*; *House Ex. Doc.* No. 329, 5; *ibid.,* No. 1, 1055; *General Orders,* Circular No. 8, September 26, 1866; Alvord, *Sixth Report,* 50.

13. Noble to Alvord, November 6, 1867, LSACO, vol. 18, BRFAL, RG 105; Runkle to Burbank, June 16, 1868, Runkle to John L. Graham, March 28, 1868, Burbank to Howard, October 14, 1868, LSACO, vol. 19, *ibid.*; Noble to Rev. Spencer Taylor, January 22, 1867, LSACO, vol. 15, *ibid.*; Noble to Alvord, June 1, 1867, MSR, roll 20, *ibid.*; Noble to Alvord, March 11, 1867, LSACO, vol. 16, *ibid.*; Ely to R.E. Johnson, August 21, 1866, LSACO, vol. 14, *ibid.*; Noble to Alvord, January 13, 1869, LSACO, vol. 21, *ibid*. The absence of a uniform system for reporting expenditures complicates reconciling monthly and yearly figures.

14. Noble to Mrs. L.L. Alexander, August 31, 1868, Noble to E.S. Bussett, September 1, 1868, Noble to Cravath, September 23, 1868, Burbank to Howard, October 14,

1868, LSACO, vol. 19, BRFAL, RG 105; Noble to Fee, November 18, 1867, LSACO, vol. 18, *ibid.*; Lawwill to Ely, September 21, 1866, LRACO, box 6, *ibid.*; Noble to Ely, May 6, 1867, Noble to Alvord, May 15, 1867, LSACO, vol. 16, *ibid.*; Lawwill to Ely, June 20, 1867, LRACO, box 12, *ibid.*; Howard to Runkle, August 11, 1869, LRACO, box 21, *ibid.*; Alvord, *Sixth Report*, 50; J.W. Alvord, *Seventh Semi-Annual Report on Schools For Freedmen, January 1, 1869* (Washington, D.C., 1869), 48-49; *idem, Eighth Report,* 66-67; *idem, Ninth Semi-Annual Report on Schools For Freedmen, January 1, 1870* (Washington, D.C., 1870), 54; *idem, Tenth Report,* 44.

15. Ogden to Fisk, December 31, 1865, LRACO, Tenn., box 8, BRFAL, RG 105; J.W. Alvord, *Report on Schools and Finances of Freedmen: for July 1866* (Washington, D.C., 1866), 17-18.

16. Alvord, *Fourth Report,* 70, 72; *idem, Fifth Semi-Annual Report on Schools For Freedmen, January 1, 1868* (Washington, D.C., 1868), 13; *idem, Sixth Report,* 7; 51-53; *idem, Seventh Report,* 7; *idem, Eighth Report,* 7; *idem, Ninth Report,* 7; *idem, Tenth Report,* 7; Noble to Cravath, September 23, 1868, Burbank to Howard, October 14, 1868, LSACO, vol. 19, BRFAL, RG 105; Noble to Alvord, January 13, 1869, Runkle to Whittlesey, March 23, 1869, LSACO, vol. 21, *ibid.*; Kimball, "Freedom's Harvest," 287-88.

17. Ely to Dike, August 11, 1866, LSACO, vol. 14, BRFAL, RG 105; Ogden to Fisk, December 31, 1865, LSACO, Tenn., box 8, *ibid.*; Noble to Alvord, February 11, 1867, LSACO, vol. 16, *ibid.*; Noble to Alvord, March 1, 1868, LSACO, vol. 19, *ibid.*; Kimball, "Freedom's Harvest," 282; Alvord, *Fourth Report,* 72; *idem, Sixth Report,* 50; Thomas Calvin Venable, "A History of Negro Education in Kentucky" (Ph.D. diss., George Peabody College For Teachers, 1953), 112. Criticisms regarding school quality were not leveled at the urban, long-standing church schools. For a comparison with teachers in other Freedmen's Bureau schools, see Robert C. Morris, *Reading, Riting, and Reconstruction: The Education of Freedmen in the South, 1861-1870* (Chicago, 1976), 85-130.

18. J.W. Alvord, *Third Semi-Annual Report on Schools For Freedmen, January 1, 1867* (Washington, D.C., 1867), 34; Kimball, "Freedom's Harvest," 281; Ely to Davis, August 15, 1866, LSACO, vol. 14, BRFAL, RG 105; Catlin to Stansberry, October 29, 1868, LS, Louisville, no. 141, *ibid.*; Noble to Alvord, May 15, 1867, LSACO, vol. 16, *ibid.*; Noble to E.P. Smith, June 18, 1868, Noble to Alvord, September 10, 1868, LSACO, vol. 19, *ibid.*; Noble to Alvord, September 1, 1867, MSR, roll 20, *ibid.* For a survey of fluctuations in attendance, see Noble's monthly correspondence with Alvord, MSR, rolls 20-21, BRFAL, RG 105.

19. *Report of the Commissioners of the BRFAL,* 72; Soloman Littlefield to W. James Kay, May 31, 1867, RLR, Smithland, no. 191, BRFAL, RG 105; Kay to Runkle, February 5, 1868, LS, Paducah, no. 177, *ibid.*; Burbank to Howard, October 14, 1868, LSACO, vol. 19, *ibid.*; Alvord, *Fourth Report,* 73, 76; *idem, Fifth Report,* 12-13; *idem, Sixth Report,* 6-7; *idem, Seventh Report,* 7; *idem, Eighth Report,* 6-7, 67; *idem, Ninth Report,* 6-7; *idem, Tenth Report,* 6-7.

20. Alvord, *Fourth Report,* 76; *idem, Fifth Report,* 12-13; *idem, Sixth Report,* 6-7; *idem, Seventh Report,* 6-7; *idem, Eighth Report,* 6-7; *idem, Ninth Report,* 6-7; *idem, Tenth Report,* 6-7; Noble to A.S. Barnes and Company, January 23, 1867, LSACO, vol. 15, BRFAL, RG 105; Cravath to Noble, March 10, 1868, LRACO, box 6, *ibid.*; James to Whipple, February 17, 1865, AMA. Black heroes in these texts included Phillis Wheatley, Troussaint L'Ouverture, and Frederick Douglass. See Robert C. Morris, ed., *Freedmen's Schools and Textbooks,* 2 vols. (New York, 1980), 2: introduction and contents. For an extensive discussion of instructional content at freedmen's schools, see *idem, Reading, Riting, and Reconstruction,* 174-212.

21. Kimball, "Freedom's Harvest," 280.

22. Noble to Alvord, March 1, November 16, 1868, LSACO, vol. 19, BRFAL, RG 105; Ely to Davis, August 15, 1866, LSACO, vol. 14, *ibid.*; Noble to Runkle, November

8, 1867, LSACO, vol. 18, *ibid.*; Noble to Alvord, September 10, 1868, MSR, roll 20, *ibid.*; Henry Lee Swint, *The Northern Teacher in the South, 1862-1870* (New York, 1967), 131; Howard, "Equal Education," 309; Alvord, *Sixth Report*, 52.

23. Minutes, Fifth Street Baptist Church, 1: May 19, 1865; *National Freedman* 1 (1865): 130, 189; Louisville *Daily Union Press*, April 15, 1865; Minutes, Green Street Baptist Church, 1: April 7, May 12, December 21, 1865.

24. Sara G. Stanley to Rev. Samuel Hunt, June 7, 1866, AMA; Louisville *Daily Union Press*, April 15, 1865; *National Freedman* 1 (1865): 130; *ibid.* 1 (1865): 189; *AME Christian Recorder*, June 3, 1865; Wilson, "Negro Education in Louisville," 24.

25. B.B. Smith to Whipple, February 9, 1865, James to Whipple, February 10, 1865, AMA; Louisville *Daily Union Press*, April 15, 1865; *Freedmen's Journal* 1 (1865): 72; Noble to Ely, May 6, 1867, LSACO, vol. 16, BRFAL, RG 105; Gibson, *Historical Sketch*, 20-21; Louisville *Daily Courier*, August 19, 1868. After leaving Louisville, Straker became professor of common law at Allen University in Columbia, S.C. See Louisville *Courier-Journal*, September 24, 1883.

26. Ogden to Fisk, December 31, 1865, LRACO, Tenn., box 8, BRFAL, RG 105; Noble to Alvord, January 1, May 1, 1868, MSR, roll 20, *ibid.*; Louisville *Daily Courier*, April 7, 1868; *American Missionary* 12 (1868): 147.

27. Noble to Alvord, May 1, 1868, LSACO, vol. 19, BRFAL, RG 105; Noble to Alvord, January 13, 1869, LSACO, vol. 21, *ibid.*; Simmons, *Men of Mark*, 597.

28. James to Whipple, January 13, 1865, AMA; E.P. Smith to Strieby, October 4, 1865, *ibid.*; Ely to Davis, October 15, 1866, LSACO, vol. 15, BRFAL, RG 105; Fouse, "Educational History," 40.

29. E.P. Smith to Strieby, October 4, 1865, AMA; James Monroe to E.P. Smith, November 18, 1865, *ibid.*; Mitchell to William E. Whiting, September [no day] 1865, *ibid.*; Mitchell to AMA, January [no day] 1866, *ibid.*; Mitchell, Teacher's Monthly Reports, February 8-March 8, 1866, *ibid.*; Mitchell to Strieby, March 14, 1866, *ibid.*; Fouse, "Educational History," 42-43.

30. Peter, *Fayette County*, 475; *American Missionary* 11 (1867): 129, 198-99; Ely to Davis, October 15, 1866, LSACO, vol. 15, BRFAL, RG 105.

31. *American Missionary* 11 (1967): 129, 198; January 1867, February and May 1871 Attendance Reports, Howard School, AMA; Peter, *Fayette County*, 475; King, "Free Negroes," 102; M.J. Hawey to Runkle, May 7, 1869, LRACO, box 22, BRFAL, RG 105.

32. Fee to Whipple, January 2, 1865, Fee to Strieby, March 7, 1865, AMA; Scofield to Strieby, August 18, October 31, 1865, Scofield to AMA, December 30, 1865, *ibid.*; *Sanitary Reporter* 2 (1864): 61; Richard Sears, "John G. Fee, Camp Nelson, and Kentucky Blacks, 1864-1865," *Register* 85 (1987): 33, 35-36.

33. Ann Williams to Strieby, May 22, 1865, AMA; Fee to Fisk, July 29, 1865, LRACO, Tenn., box 2, BRFAL, RG 105; *American Missionary* 9 (1865): 247.

34. Fee to Strieby, May 30, 1865, Fee to Whipple, June 9, 1865, AMA; W.W. Wheeler to Whipple, August 31, 1865, *ibid.*; Mitchell to Strieby, March 14, 1866, *ibid.*; W.D. Johnson, *Biographical Sketches*, 68. See also Sears, *Practical Recognition*, 31-35.

35. *House Ex. Doc.* No. 329, 14; Isaac M. Newton to Noble, December 16, 1868, LRACO, box 19, BRFAL, RG 105; Noble to Alvord, January 13, 1869, LSACO, vol. 21, *ibid.*

36. Newberry, *Sanitary Commission*, 526; H.G. Thomas to Runkle, LS, Danville, no. 100, BRFAL, RG 105; J.W. Alvord, *Letters from the South, Relating to the Conditions of Freedmen Addressed to Major General O.O. Howard* (Washington, D.C., 1870), 36; *Proceedings of the State Convention of Colored Men, Held at Lexington, Kentucky, in the A. M. E. Church, November 26th, 27th, and 28th, 1867* (Frankfort, Ky., 1867), 5; Noble to Alvord, July 10, 1868, LSACO, vol. 19, BRFAL, RG 105; H.C. Howard to Runkle, LS, Mt. Sterling, no. 163, *ibid.*; Graham to R.E. Johnson, April 25, 1868, LS, Covington, no. 93,

*ibid.*; True to Runkle, October 24, 1867, LS, Maysville, no. 158, *ibid.*

37. Ogden to Fisk, April 22, 1865, LRACO, Tenn., box 8, BRFAL, RG 105; Ely to Davis, October 15, 1866, LSACO, vol. 15, *ibid.*; True to Cravath, December 19, 1866, LS, Maysville, no. 157, *ibid.*; True to Ely, May 31, 1867, True to Runkle, October 24, 1867, True to R.E. Johnson, April 21, 1868, LS, Maysville, no. 158, *ibid.*; H.C. Howard to R.E. Johnson, June 27, 1867, LS, Mt. Sterling, no. 163, *ibid.*

38. Marrs, *Life*, 77-78, 80-83; Ely to George W. Harbeson, February 20, 1867, LR, Louisville, box 53, BRFAL, RG 105; Noble to Marshall W. Taylor, March 12, 1868, Burbank to Howard, October 14, 1868, LSACO, vol. 19, *ibid.*; Indianapolis *Freeman*, March 9, 1889. Joseph Cotter was one of Taylor's students. See Rule, *Light Bearers*, 170.

39. Owensboro *Monitor*, October 31, 1866; Lawwill to Ely, October 18, 1866, LRACO, box 5, BRFAL, RG 105; Burbank to Howard, October 14, 1868, LSACO, vol. 19, *ibid.*; agent to Ely, April 21, 1867, agent to Runkle, February 29, 1868, LS, Owensboro, no. 173, *ibid.*; Lawwill to Ely, September 30, 1867, LRACO, box 12, *ibid.*; Noble to Runkle, February 26, 1868, LRACO, box 19, *ibid.*; Herbert Aptheker, ed., *A Documentary History of The Negro People in the United States* (New York, 1951), 560-61.

40. Louis A. Reynolds to Noble, January 20, 1868, LS, Bowling Green, no. 69, BRFAL, RG 105; "Report of facilities for the establishment of schools in the Southern Sub-District of Ky.," [January 1867], C.F. Johnson to Noble, February 16, 1867, LS, Bowling Green, no. 68, *ibid.*

41. "Report of facilities for the establishment of schools in the Southern Sub-District of Ky.," [January 1867], C.F. Johnson to Noble, February 16, 1867, LS, Bowling Green, no. 68, BRFAL, RG 105; *Proceedings of the State Convention 1867*, 6; Noble to Alvord, October 1, 1867, MSR, roll 20, *ibid.*; A.B. Brown to Runkle, March 31, April 3, 1868, LRACO, box 15, *ibid.*; A.D. Jones to Rodriquez, July 8, 1867, LRACO, box 11, *ibid.*; Rodriquez to C.F. Johnson, April 9, 1867, LS, Bowling Green, no. 70, *ibid.*; Alvord, *Fourth Report*, 70.

42. Nelson C. Lawrence to C.F. Johnson, July 27, 1867, ULR, Russellville, box 42, BRFAL, RG 105; H.A. Hunter to A.B. Brown, March 16, 1868, M.E. Billings to A.B. Brown, April [no day], 16, 23, 1868, LS, Russellville, no. 187, *ibid.*; Noble to Moses T. Weir, July 11, 1868, LSACO, vol. 19, *ibid.*

43. Bailey to Ely, December 22, 1866, LRACO, box 1, BRFAL, RG 105; Thomas Cheaney to Bailey, June 4, 1867, LRACO, box 7, *ibid.*; A.B. Brown to Runkle, September 20, 1868, LS, Paducah, no. 178, *ibid.*; *Ky. Doc.* (1866), No. 3, 22.

44. Ogden to Fisk, December 31, 1865, LRACO, Tenn., box 8, BRFAL, RG 105; Kay to Noble, April 4, 1867, LS, Paducah, no. 176, *ibid.*; Noble to Runkle, March 9, 1868, Burbank to Howard, October 14, 1868, Noble to Alvord, October 14, 1868, LSACO, vol. 19, *ibid.*; Kay to Runkle, February 5, 1868, LS, Paducah, no. 177, *ibid.*; Noble to Alvord, April 16, 1867, LSACO, vol. 16, *ibid.*; James F. Bolton to Kay, December 12, 25, 1867, LS, Columbus, no. 87, *ibid.*; William McCluskey to Bolton, October 15, 1866, RLR, Columbus, no. 86, *ibid.*; Jennie Fyfe to "My Dear Nell," December 29, 1865, February 22, 1866, Fyfe Family Papers (Bentley Historical Library, University of Michigan, Ann Arbor, Michigan); *American Missionary* 11 (1867): 133.

45. *Proceedings of the State Convention 1867*, 3-5; flier "To the Colored People of Kentucky," July 14, 1869, Runkle to Whittlesey, July 20, 1869, MSR, roll 21, BRFAL, RG 105; Runkle to Whittlesey, July 20, 1869, Runkle to Alvord, August [16], 1869, LSACO, vol. 21, *ibid.*; *Kentucky State Colored Educational Convention, Held At Benson's Theater, Louisville, Ky. July 14, 1869* ([Louisville, Ky., 1869]), 1, 3, 17, 29-30, 33, 36-41; Kimball, "Freedom's Harvest," 286; Louisville *Courier-Journal*, July 17, 1869. Several well known white supporters of black education helped defray the convention's expenses.

46. Runkle to Alvord, September 19, 1870, MSR, roll 21, BRFAL, RG 105; Louisville *Commercial*, August 16, 17, 1870.

47. Ford and Ford, *Ohio Falls Cities*, 1:414; Weeden, *History*, 32; Louisville *Courier-Journal*, June 28, 1874.

48. Weeden, *History*, 32-33; Louisville *Commercial*, November 8, 1871; Horace Morris to Cravath, September 5, October 12, 20, November 8, 1871, June 11, August 14, 1872, AMA.

49. Louisville *Courier-Journal*, September 23, November 11, December 2, 1873, June 28, 1874; Louisville *Commercial*, September 24, 1874; Fifth Street Choir Record, September 3, 1874.

50. Fifth Street Choir Record, October 7, 1873; Louisville *Courier-Journal*, October 7, 9, December 2, 1873; Louisville *Commercial*, October 8, 1873.

51. Ford and Ford, *Ohio Falls Cities*, 1:414; Louisville *Courier-Journal*, December 2, 1873; Weeden, *History*, 34.

52. Alvord, *Fourth Report*, 75; Fouse, "Educational History," 42-44, 55-57; King, "Free Negroes," 107, 111-12; Peter, *Fayette County*, 476.

53. Anonymous, *Daviess County*, 362-63; Kentucky Acts (1873), 205, 222; Starling, *Henderson County*, 425-26; Frank L. McVey, *The Gates Open Slowly: A History of Education in Kentucky* (Lexington, Ky., 1949), 150, 263.

54. Marrs, *Life*, 91-92, 101-6, 108-9.

55. Mattie E. Anderson to Whipple, January 8, February 25, March 5, May 29, September 30, 1878, AMA; *Charles Emerson's Frankfort Directory, 1884-85* (Frankfort, Ky., 1884), 233.

56. Miscellaneous Black History Collection, typescript, boxes 4, 7, XVII-5, 7, RG8 (Loretto Archives, Nerinx, Kentucky); Nathaniel E. Green, *Silent Believers*, 45; Minogue, *Dominican History*, 149-51; Annals of St. Monica Convent, Bardstown, Kentucky (Nazareth Archival Center, Nazareth, Kentucky).

57. DeBoer, "Afro-Americans in the AMA," 501; Drake, "AMA," 298; Gabriel Burdett to Cravath, March 6, 1871, February 1, 19, September 16, December 11, 1872, December 13, 1873, January 20, 1874, AMA; Burdett to D.E. Emerson, March 7, 1873, ibid.

58. Sears, *Practical Recognition*, 45-49, 52, 54; Angus A. Burleigh, *John G. Fee, Founder of Berea College* (Berea, Ky., n.d.), 9-10; E.H. Fairchild, *Inauguration of Rev. E.H. Fairchild, President of Berea College, Kentucky. Wednesday, July 7th, 1869* (Cincinnati, 1870), 9.

59. Sears, *Practical Recognition*, 53-54; Wheeler to Whipple, November 22, 1866, AMA; "The induction of colored pupils into Berea College," in undated miscellaneous writings, box 3, Fee Papers, RG 1.2 (BC); Mortimer to Fee, May 25, 1869, box 2, ibid.; Noble to Howard, May 25, 1867, LSACO, vol. 16, BRFAL, RG 105; John A.R. Rogers, *Birth of Berea College: A Story of Providence* (Philadelphia, 1970; orig. pub. 1903), 111-12. The time required to fulfill graduation requirements was probably typical for blacks at other schools. See *American Missionary* 44 (1890): 126-27.

60. Minutes, Board of Trustees, Berea College, April 24, 1865, July 23, 1866, box 1, RG 2 (BC), hereafter cited Minutes, BTBC, RG 2; Minutes, Prudential Committee of the Board of Trustees, Berea College (hereafter cited Minutes, PC, BTBC) December 6, 1869, September 22, October 7, 1871, September 10, 1872, ibid.; Fairchild, *Inauguration*, 13; Alvord, *Letters from the South*, 38; Fee to Burleigh, April 25, 1867, Angus A. Burleigh file, RG 8 (BC); Noble to Howard, May 25, 1867, LSACO, vol. 16, BRFAL, RG 105.

61. Elisabeth Peck, *Berea's First Century, 1855-1955* (Lexington, Ky., 1955), 42, 44-46; E.H. Fairchild, *Berea College, Ky. An Interesting History*, (Cincinnati, 1875), 44; Minutes, BTBC, July 1, 1872, June 28, 1894, Fee Papers, box 2, RG 2; Minutes, BTBC, typescript "Report of Clerk of Faculty to Trustees," June 30, 1874, and "Resolutions of Alumni," June 20, 1889, box 1, ibid.; Nelson, "Experiment in Interracial Education at Berea College," 17-18; Klotter, "The Black South and White Appalachia," 846; Frank L. Williams's

response to questionnaire, 1924, Black File, RG 13 (BC); William H. Gibson to Fee, April 25, 1876, Frank L. Williams to Fee, September 3, 1893, box 2, Fee Papers, RG 1.2; Ernest G. Dodge to William G. Frost, April 11, 1925, William G. Frost Papers, box 13, RG 3.3 (BC).

62. Peck, *Berea*, 46-47; W.D. Johnson, *Biographical Sketches*, 37; Fee to Cravath, September 3, 1867, AMA; *American Missionary* 32 (1878): 275-76; ibid. 34 (1880): 242; ibid. 37 (1883): 231; ibid. 38 (1884): 234; clipping from *Congregationalist*, July 15, 1875, E.H. Fairchild Papers, box 1, RG 3.1 (BC). Hathaway resigned from Berea in 1893, embittered because he did not receive a professorship.

63. Thomas Burton, *Autobiography*, 43-44, 47-51, 57.

64. Peck, *Berea*, 43; Anonymous, *Historical Sketch of Berea College*, 1904 (Berea, Ky., 1904), 27; *American Missionary* 32 (1878): 275-76; ibid. 36 (1882): 240-41.

65. Louisville *Commercial*, January 25, 1873; Howard, "Equal Education," 319-20; Penn, *Afro-American Press*, 317.

66. *Ky. Doc.* (1869), No. 18, 70-71; ibid. (1871), No. 5, 21; ibid. (1872), No. 2, 45-46; Donovan, "Kentucky Law Regarding the Negro," 50, 136.

67. *Kentucky Acts* (1873-74), 63-66.

68. *Ky. Doc.* (1874), No. 1, 29-30; ibid. (1871), No. 5, 25; ibid. (1876), No. 1, 19; ibid. (1887-88), No. 7, 118, 147.

69. *Ibid.* (1875), No. 3, 105; ibid. (1887-88), No. 7, 147; U.S., *Report of the Commissioner of Education for the Year 1877* (Washington, D.C., 1879), 74; U.S., *Report of the Commissioner of Education for the Year 1881* (Washington, D.C., 1883), 81; U.S., *Report of the Commissioner of Education for the Year 1883-'84* (Washington, D.C., 1885), 97.

70. *Ky. Doc.* (1891-92), No. 34, 139, 146.

71. *Ibid.* (1887-88), No. 7, 147; *Report Commissioner of Education, 1883-'84*, 97; U.S., *Report of the Commissioner of Education for the Year 1886-87* (Washington, D.C., 1888), 875; U.S., *Report of the Commissioner of Education for the Year 1888-89*, 2 vols. (Washington, D.C., 1891), 2:1431; U.S., *Report of the Commissioner of Education for the Year 1889-90*, 2 vols. (Washington, 1893), 2:1074; *Ky. Doc.* (1891-92), No. 34, 133-34, 141. The average attendance of blacks was about one percent higher than that of whites for both 1885-86 and 1888-89. There are occasional slight statistical variations in both state and federal reports.

72. *Ky. Doc.* (1891-92), No. 34, 67, 71, 119, 123, 127, 140-42; Laine, "My Life," 2. Black school buildings and furnishings were valued at under 10 percent of those of white schools.

73. *American Missionary* 37 (1883): 45, 72; ibid. 39 (1885): 45; ibid. 40 (1886): 40; ibid. 41 (1887): 45; ibid. 42 (1888): 39; ibid. 43 (1889): 41-42; ibid. 44 (1890): 51-52; DeBoer, "Afro-Americans in the AMA," 501; *Kentucky Acts* (1873-74), 65; *Ky. Doc.* (1891-92), No. 34, 103, 107, 133, 135-38. While some urban areas already required certification of black teachers, the Commonwealth did not require the examination of black instructors until 1874; certification standards for black teachers remained lower than those for whites until 1894. See Louisville *Commercial*, November 16, 1873, and Venable, "Negro Education in Kentucky," 111. For comparison, 23 percent of white teachers held first-class certificates, 40 percent second-class, and 38 percent third-class. Seventeen percent of whites who took the teacher's exam failed; 24 percent of blacks. See *Ky. Doc.* (1891-92), No. 34, 51, 55.

74. Louisville *Courier-Journal*, September 2, 1879; Venable, "Negro Education in Kentucky," 113-14; *Ky. Doc.* (1891-92), No. 34, 135-36.

75. *Ky. Doc.* (1881), No. 20, 146; ibid. (1891-92), No. 34, 97, 132, 142; Laine, "My Life," 2; Venable, "Negro Education in Kentucky," 112.

76. Lexington *American Citizen*, November 13, 1875.

77. Paul Jones, *Normal and Industrial Institute*, 9-10; Howard, "Equal Education,"

321-22n; Harvey C. Russell, *The Kentucky Negro Educational Association, 1877-1946* (Norfolk, Va., 1946), 8. Henderson did not appear at the first meeting.

78. Louisville *Courier-Journal*, September 1, 1879; Russell, *KNEA*, 8; Howard, "Equal Education," 321-22.

79. Howard, *Black Liberation*, 171-74; J. Morgan Kousser, "Making Separate Equal: Integration of Black and White School Funds in Kentucky," *Journal of Interdisciplinary History* 10 (1980): 402-6.

80. Owensboro *Semi-Weekly Messenger*, July 21, 1882; Owensboro *Messenger and Examiner*, August 30, September 20, 1882, May 9, 1883; *Claybrook v. Owensboro*, 16 *Federal Reports*, 297 (1883); ibid., 23 *Federal Reports*, 634 (1884); *Dawson v. Lee*, 83 *Kentucky Reports*, 49 (1884). I am indebted to Dr. Lee A. Dew of Kentucky Wesleyan College for use of his unpublished paper, "*Claybrook v. Owensboro*: An Early Victory for Equal Education Opportunity in Kentucky."

81. Paul Jones, *Normal and Industrial Institute*, 9-16; *Ky. Doc.* (1891-92), No. 34, 232-34. See also C.L. Timberlake, "The Early Struggle for Education of Blacks in the Commonwealth of Kentucky," *Register* 71 (1973): 233-34.

82. Barksdale Hamlet, *History of Education in Kentucky* (Frankfort, Ky., 1914), 287-88; *Ky. Doc.* (1891-92), No. 34, 235-37; Paul Jones, *Normal and Industrial Institute*, 19.

83. Russell, *KNEA*, 11, Part 1, 1-3, 7-8, 14-16, 18-19, 21-22, 25-28, 30-32, 34-35, 37-39; *Ky. Doc.* (1889), No. 1, 127.

84. *Berea Evangelist* 1 (October 15, 1884): 2; ibid. 1 (June 1, 1885): 4; ibid. 2 (September 15, 1885): 1; W.D. Johnson, *Biographical Sketches*, 35-36; *Ky. Doc.* (1889), No. 1, 124, 126-27, 129; ibid. (1887-88), No. 7, 69, 73, 77; ibid. (1891-92), No. 34, 238.

85. Louisville *Commercial*, April 6, 1875; *Louisville Municipal Reports for the Fiscal Year Ending August 31, 1886* (Louisville, Ky., 1887), 216, 226, 228, 231, 234, 237, 240, 243, 246, 249, 260-61 (hereafter cited LMR with date); *LMR 1887* (Louisville, Ky., 1888), 290, 294; *LMR 1888* (Louisville, Ky., 1889), 425, 428; *LMR 1889* (Louisville, Ky., 1890), 346, 350, 352; *LMR 1890* (Louisville, Ky., 1891), 161; *LMR 1891* (Louisville, Ky., 1892), 224, 228; New York *Freeman*, October 17, 1885; Louisville *Courier-Journal*, September 6, 1888, October 8, 1889; George C. Wright, *Life Behind A Veil*, 66; Weeden, *History*, 34, 58; Louisville *Ohio Falls Express*, July 11, 1891.

86. New York *Freeman*, November 6, 1886; George C. Wright, *Life Behind A Veil*, 67-69; W.D. Johnson, *Biographical Sketches*, 25, 50; Louisville *Courier-Journal*, September 6, 1888; Louisville *Ohio Falls Express*, July 12, 1884.

87. Louisville *Courier-Journal*, October 9, 1874, October 17, 1882, September 9, 1886; *LMR 1886*, 261; Joseph Seamon Cotter, *Links of Friendship* (Louisville, Ky., 1898), iii-iv; Weeden, *History*, 10; New York *Freeman*, November 14, 1885, January 16, 30, February 13, March 13, 1886; *LMR 1888*, 428; *LMR 1889*, 350; *LMR 1890*, 352; *LMR 1891*, 228.

88. J.H. Jackson to E.H. Fairchild, December 5, 10, 1878, AMA; Jackson to Strieby, May 21, December 6, 1878, ibid.; King, "Free Negroes," 112; Fouse, "Educational History," 41-42; *Ky. Doc.* (1889), No. 1, 126.

89. *American Missionary* 37 (1883): 72-73; ibid. 38 (1884): 237-38; ibid. 42 (1888): 305-6; ibid. 44 (1890): 51, 278; ibid. 45 (1891): 175.

90. Perrin, *Bourbon, Scott, Harrison and Nicholas Counties*, 54, 119; *Ky. Doc.* (1889), No. 1, 124; Burdett to Cravath, May 5, 1876, AMA; Burdett to Whipple, May 6, 1876, ibid.; *American Missionary* 36 (1882): 44; M.M. Robe to Fee, May 16, 1889, Fee Papers, box 2, RG 1.2; undated printed flier entitled "Normal School," box 4, ibid.; Sears, *Practical Recognition*, 76; S.E. Smith, *Anti-Separate Coach Movement*, 157-58.

91. Anonymous, *Daviess County*, 367; William Foster Hayes, *Sixty Years of Owensboro, 1883-1943* (Owensboro, Ky., 1946), 247-49.

92. Anonymous, *Bowling Green and Warren County*, 10; *Ky. Doc.* (1887-88), No. 7, 77-78; ibid. (1889), No. 1, 130.

93. Perrin, *County of Christian*, 252; *Ky. Doc.* (1887-88), No. 7, 70; *ibid.* (1889), No. 1, 125-26; Starling, *Henderson County*, 425-26; *Bennett & Co.'s Henderson City Directory, for 1891-1892* (Henderson, Ky., 1891), 11.

## 11. Labor, Living Conditions, and Recreation, 1865-1891

1. Thomas, "Victims of Circumstance," 266; John L. Graham to R.E. Johnson, April 18, 1867, LS, Covington, no. 93, BRFAL, RG 105; R.E. Johnson to John Ely, June 30, 1866, LRACO, box 3, *ibid.*; J.H. Johnson to James H. Rice, April 10, 1866, LR, Lexington, box 49, *ibid.*; *National Anti-Slavery Standard*, September 16, 1865; Berlin et al., *Black Military Experience*, 277; Robert Anderson, *From Slavery To Affluence*, 48.

2. John G. Fee to George Whipple, July 18, 1865, AMA; Fee to Clinton B. Fisk, July 18, 1865, RLRACO, Tenn., box 2, BRFAL, RG 105; Legislative Records of Louisville, Board of Aldermen Minutes, July 18, 1867, Reel 15.

3. Howard, *Black Liberation*, 100, 104-5.

4. Elisha Green, *Life*, 24-25.

5. Marrs, *Life*, 77; Rule, *Light Bearers*, 167, 169.

6. Samuel McKee to Ely, July 20, 1866, LRACO, box 5, BRFAL, RG 105; Howard, *Black Liberation*, 97, 99; Donovan, "Kentucky Law Regarding the Negro," 66-68. An 1871 state law ended the provision which held that a contract had to be fulfilled to be valid.

7. Ely to John H. Donovan, June 25, 1866, Ely to J.C. Davis, August 15, 1866, LSACO, vol. 14, BRFAL, RG 105; *General Orders*, Circular No. 3, June 26, 1866, no. 7, September 19, 1866; *Report of the Commissioners of the BRFAL*, 72. Contracts were to be enforced in Freedmen's Bureau courts. For a comparison of the labor conditions of black Kentuckians with those of Deep South workers, see Daniel A. Novak, *The Wheel of Servitude: Black Forced Labor after Slavery* (Lexington, Ky., 1978), 9-43.

8. Labor Contracts, ACO, box 41, BRFAL, RG 105; Howard, *Black Liberation*, 98-99.

9. A.W. Lawwill to Ely, September 30, 1866, LRACO, box 5, BRFAL, RG 105; Lawwill to Ely, September 30, 1867, LRACO, box 12, *ibid.*; A.B. Brown to Benjamin P. Runkle, June 30, 1868, LS, Henderson, no. 109, *ibid.*; *House Ex. Doc.* No. 1, 1057; Howard, *Black Liberation*, 98-99.

10. Labor Contracts, ACO, box 41, BRFAL, RG 105; R.E. Johnson to Ely, June 30, 1866, LRACO, box 3, *ibid.*; Freedmen's Contracts, Louisville, no. 150, *ibid.*; *House Ex. Doc.* No. 1, 1057. Salaries varied widely by season and from region to region.

11. Labor Contracts, ACO, box 41, BRFAL, RG 105; Freedmen's Contracts, Louisville, no. 150, *ibid.*

12. J.S. Catlin to Ely, September 5, 1867, LRACO, box 7, BRFAL, RG 105; Y.A. Woodward to Ely, December 31, 1866, LRACO, box 12, *ibid.*; R.E. Johnson to Ely, June 30, 1866, LS, Lexington, vol. 122, *ibid.*; James M. Fidler to Ely, August 31, September 30, 1867, LRACO, box 8, *ibid.*; *Louisville Daily Journal*, May 22, 1867.

13. Catlin to Runkle, November 1, 1867, LRACO, box 7, BRFAL, RG 105; Fidler to Ely, August 31, 1867, LRACO, box 8, *ibid.*; Wells S. Bailey to Ely, May 1, 1867, LRACO, box 7, *ibid.*; Donovan to Ely, August 3, 1866, LRACO, box 1, *ibid.*; McKee to Ely, July 20, 1866, LRACO, box 5, *ibid.*

14. Howard, *Black Liberation*, 126; J.E. Jacobs to Fidler, February 24, 1866, PC, LSACO, Tenn., vol. 10, BRFAL, RG 105; Donovan, "Kentucky Law Regarding the Negro," 64; *Kentucky Acts* (1865-66), 49-50. Skills apprentices were to learn included the "trade or business of Farming," "House keeping and sewing," "Housekeeping and serving," "general work about the house and drug store," Indentures of Apprenticeship, LS, Columbus, no. 87, BRFAL, RG 105; "the duties of housewifery," and "the

duties of waiter and Os[t]ler," Indentures, Louisville, no. 149, *ibid.*

15. *Kentucky Acts* (1865-66), 49-50; W. James Kay to Ely, January 31, 1867, LS, Paducah, no. 176, BRFAL, RG 105.

16. Howard, *Black Liberation*, 126; Bailey to Ely, July 31, 1867, LRACO, box 7, BRFAL, RG 105.

17. *American Missionary* 10 (1866): 18; Sears, *Practical Recognition*, 24, 39. A few blacks thought that it was only fair for owners to share their land with their former slaves. See *American Missionary* 8 (1864): 94.

18. Fee to Whipple, June 9, 1865, AMA; Fee to Whipple, March 11, 18, 1868, LRACO, box 16, BRFAL, RG 105; Howard, *Black Liberation*, 94; Sears, *Practical Recognition*, 39, 47-49.

19. Lexington *Kentucky Statesman*, June 28, 1867; Kellogg, "Black Residential Areas in Lexington," 32-33; Smith and Raitz, "Negro Hamlets," 226-29.

20. Kellogg, "Black Residential Areas in Lexington," 29, 32-33, 35, 37, 42; Thomas, "Victims of Circumstance," 264; Elisha Green, *Life*, 25.

21. Thomas, "Victims of Circumstance," 256-57, 260, 263-66; Kellogg, "Black Residential Areas in Lexington," 38-40, 49-51.

22. George C. Wright, *Life Behind A Veil*, 32, 44-45, 103, 106, 110; Louisville *Daily Journal*, September 25, 1866; Weeden, *History*, 28, 58; Joseph S. Cotter, *25th Anniversary of the Founding of Colored Parkland or "Little Africa," Louisville, 1891-1916* (Louisville, 1934), 8; Lammermeier, "Urban Black Family," 446.

23. Louisville *Courier-Journal*, October 8, 1873; Carl R. Osthaus, *Freedmen, Philanthropy, and Fraud: A History of the Freedman's Savings Bank* (Urbana, Ill., 1976), 129; Weeden, *History*, 28, 58; Louisville *Commercial*, February 4, 1875, July 1, 1877. Brownstown was named after the first person to move into the area.

24. George C. Wright, *Life Behind A Veil*, 103, 106, 110; Louisville *Times*, November 13, 1885.

25. Weeden, *History*, 28, 58; Louisville *Commercial*, February 4, 1875; Louisville *Courier-Journal*, June 28, 1874. George C. Wright, in *Life Behind A Veil*, 112, concluded that the quality of housing for whites was similar to that of blacks.

26. Osthaus, *Freedman's Savings Bank*, 128-29.

27. Collins, *History*, 174, 198; *Bureau of Agriculture, Horticulture & Statistics Report*, in Ky. Doc. (1879), No. 1 (3 vols.), 2:484-85, 488-89, 492-93, 496-97, 516-17, 528-29, 532-33; New York *Freeman*, December 5, 1885. Poor wages led some Kentucky blacks to seek better-paying jobs as domestics in northern states. See David M. Katzman, *Seven Days A Week: Women and Domestic Service in Industrializing America* (New York, 1978), 76-77.

28. Rawick, *The American Slave*, 16:45; Anonymous, *Daviess County*, 186; George C. Wright, *Life Behind A Veil*, 33, 79-80; Thomas, "Victims of Circumstance," 260, 264, 266; New York *Freeman*, October 17, 1885, September 11, 1886; Raphael, "Health of Kentucky Black People," 147.

29. H.G. Thomas to Runkle, April 30, 1868, LS, Danville, no. 100, BRFAL, RG 105; George C. Wright, *Life Behind A Veil*, 33, 84-86; Alvord, *Letters from the South*, 41; Thomas, "Victims of Circumstance," 269; Indianapolis *Freeman*, October 3, 1891; Louisville *Commercial*, July 3, 1874. James Brown was reportedly worth ten thousand dollars.

30. T.K. Noble to Fidler, September 18, 1868, LSACO, vol. 19, BRFAL, RG 105; Indianapolis *Freeman*, October 3, 1891; G.F. Richings, *Evidence of Progress among Colored People* (Philadelphia, 1899), 321, 325; Walters, *Life*, 40; Louisville *Commercial*, July 3, 1874; Gibson, *Historical Sketch*, 28-29; Thomas, "Victims of Circumstance," 269; Weeden, *History*, 7.

31. Simmons, *Men of Mark*, 191.

32. Thomas, "Victims of Circumstance," 266-69; Louisville *Courier-Journal*, September 6, 1888; Louisville *Commercial*, July 3, 1874; Gibson, *Historical Sketch*, 29; Walters,

*Life*, 30, 40; George C. Wright, *Life Behind A Veil*, 86; New York *Freeman*, May 16, 1885; R.E. Johnson to Runkle, March 2, 1868, LRACO, box 18, BRFAL, RG 105; Howard, *Black Liberation*, 99-100; Cloyd Herbert Finch, Jr., "Organized Labor in Louisville, Kentucky, 1880-1914" (Ph.D. diss., University of Kentucky, 1965), 25, 75; Thomas Burton, *Autobiography*, 49.

33. Thomas, "Victims of Circumstance," 267-69; *AME Zion Church*, 121; New York *Freeman*, May 16, 1885; George C. Wright, *Life Behind A Veil*, 34; Louisville *Commercial*, July 3, 1874; Gibson, *Historical Sketch*, 28-29; Louisville *Bulletin*, September 24, 1881; Kellogg, "Black Residential Areas in Lexington," 49; Weeden, *History*, 28; Louisville *Courier-Journal*, September 6, 1888.

34. *American Baptist*, November 12, 1880; New York *Freeman*, May 16, 1885; Thomas, "Victims of Circumstance," 268; Louisville *Commercial*, February 4, 1875; King, "Free Negroes," 130.

35. Louisville *Commercial*, July 3, 1874; George C. Wright, *Life Behind A Veil*, 33, 82; Kellogg, "Black Residential Areas in Lexington," 49; New York *Freeman*, May 16, 1885, April 17, November 27, 1886; Thomas, "Victims of Circumstance," 267.

36. Weeden, *History*, 48; Gibson, *Historical Sketch*, 29; Louisville *Commercial*, July 3, 1874; New York *Freeman*, May 16, 1885; George C. Wright, *Life Behind A Veil*, 95-96; Walters, *Life*, 40-42; King, "Free Negroes," 136.

37. Finch, "Organized Labor," 75; George C. Wright, *Life Behind A Veil*, 81, 87; Louisville *Commercial*, July 3, 1874; Walters, *Life*, 30, 32; Louisville *Courier-Journal*, September 6, 1888.

38. Strother, "Negro Culture in Lexington," 29-30, 85, 87-88.

39. *Kentucky's Black Heritage*, 66; Chicago *Tribune*, July 10, 1885; *Guide To Kentucky Historical Highway Markers* (Frankfort, Ky., 1969).

40. Alice Allison Dunnigan, *A Black Woman's Experience: From Schoolhouse to White House* (Philadelphia, 1974), 473-74; Strother, "Negro Culture in Lexington," 85; *Kentucky's Black Heritage*, 66.

41. Runkle to Edwin Whittlesey, July 20, 1869, MSR, roll 21, BRFAL, RG 105; Osthaus, *Freedman's Savings Bank*, 23, 108-9, 133; Ross Webb, *Reconstruction*, 53; King, "Free Negroes," 135; Louisville *Commercial*, July 3, 1874.

42. Osthaus, *Freedman's Savings Bank*, 111-12; Runkle to Whittlesey, July 20, 1869, MSR, roll 21, BRFAL, RG 105; Gibson, *Historical Sketch*, 55; Louisville *Commercial*, July 3, 1874; Alvord, *Letters from the South*, 34.

43. Ross Webb, *Reconstruction*, 52-54; Louisville *Commercial*, April 2, 1870; John Fowles to Ely, April 6, 1866, LRACO, box 2, BRFAL, RG 105; Louisville *Courier-Journal*, June 28, 1874; Alvord, *Ninth Annual Report*, 67.

44. Louisville *Daily Union Press*, December 23, 1865; Alvord, *Letters from the South*, 34; Runkle to Whittlesey, July 20, 1869, MSR, roll 21, BRFAL, RG 105; Alvord, *Ninth Annual Report*, 67; idem, *Tenth Annual Report*, 45; Osthaus, *Freedman's Savings Bank*, 107-8; Louisville *Courier-Journal*, June 28, 1874.

45. Osthaus, *Freedman's Savings Bank*, 37-38, 120-21, 169; Ross Webb, *Reconstruction*, 53; J.G. Hamilton to E.M. Cravath, August 11, 1873, AMA.

46. Ross Webb, *Reconstruction*, 54; Louisville *Commercial*, December 17, 18, 1874; October 30, 1875; Weeden, *History*, 28; Minutes, Fifth Street Baptist Church, 4: February 19, 1890.

47. New York *Freeman*, March 13, 1886; King, "Free Negroes," 58, 136; S.E. Smith, *Anti-Separate Coach Movement*, 151, 164; Simmons, *Men of Mark*, 370; Weeden, *History*, 6, 10; George C. Wright, *Life Behind A Veil*, 92.

48. James S. Hathaway "History Repeated" Speech, 1884, Faculty File, RG 9 (BC); William W. Brown, *Narrative*, xv-xvi; George C. Wright, *Life Behind A Veil*, 77; New York *Freeman*, January 9, March 13, 20, 1886.

49. Louisville *Commercial*, December 13, 1873; Louisville *Courier-Journal*, July 4, 1874.

50. Legislative Records of Louisville, Board of Aldermen Minutes, January 11, 1883, Reel 18; New York *Freeman*, May 2, July 25, 1885, February 13, March 20, November 20, December 18, 1886; Indianapolis *Freeman*, February 21, 1891.

51. Gibson, *Historical Sketch*, 53-55; New York *Freeman*, March 20, May 15, June 19, 1886; Finch, "Organized Labor," 25; Philip S. Foner, *Organized Labor and the Black Worker, 1619-1973* (New York, 1974), 50. For a discussion of blacks and the Knights of Labor, see Melton A. McLauren, *The Knights of Labor in the South* (Westport, Conn., 1978), 131-48.

52. Finch, "Organized Labor," 25-26, 37, 49, 75; New York *Freeman*, May 15, June 5, August 21, 1886; Louisville *Ohio Falls Express*, July 11, 1891.

53. Louisville *Commercial*, December 30, 1873; *American Baptist*, November 12, 1880; New York *Freeman*, December 11, 1886.

54. Roy Garvin, "Benjamin, or 'Pap' Singleton and His Followers," *JNH* 33 (1948): 9.

55. Gabriel Burdett to M.E. Strieby, November 11, 1876, May [no day], 3, 12, 15, July 30, 1877, AMA; Nell Irvin Painter, *Exodusters: Black Migration to Kansas after Reconstruction* (New York, 1977), 149-52; Glen Schwendemann, "Nicodemus: Negro Haven on the Solomon," *Kansas Historical Quarterly* 34 (1968): 13-14; Garvin, "Pap Singleton," 16, 21-22; Louisville *Commercial*, July 1, 1877; Robert G. Athearn, *In Search of Canaan: Black Migration to Kansas, 1879-80* (Lawrence, Kan., 1978), 63, 76-78, 277-78.

56. Minutes, Fifth Street Baptist Church, 2: December 18, 1872; Louisville *Ohio Falls Express*, July 12, 1884; *American Baptist*, November 12, 1880; New York *Freeman*, July 10, 1886.

57. Louisville *Commercial*, July 4, 1873; Louisville *Ohio Falls Express*, July 12, 1884, July 11, 1891; New York *Freeman*, July 10, November 6, 1886; Louisville *Courier-Journal*, May 31, 1885.

58. New York *Freeman*, September 11, October 2, 1886; Louisville *Ohio Falls Express*, July 11, 1891; *American Baptist*, November 12, 1880.

59. Indianapolis *Freeman*, October 3, 1891; George C. Wright, *Life Behind A Veil*, 60; Strother, "Negro Culture in Lexington," 26.

60. Marrs, *Life*, 85-86; *Ky. Doc.* (1879), 2: No. 1, 419; Louisville *Commercial*, September 21, 1872, September 10, 11, 1874; Frankfort *Commonwealth*, August 11, 1871; King, "Free Negroes," 134-35; Richmond *Kentucky Register*, September 12, 1879; New York *Freeman*, October 2, 1886.

61. W.D. Johnson, *Biographical Sketches*, 79, 81-84; Strother, "Negro Culture in Lexington," 21-29, 80; Indianapolis *Freeman*, October 3, 1891; Fouse, "Educational History," 78-79; *Rules and Regulations of the Annual Fair of the Colored A. & M. Association, Inc.* (Lexington, Ky., 1897), 5-19.

62. Louisville *Commercial*, September 11, 1874. Each Louisville team had chosen names that were popular in northern cities. See New York *Freeman*, January 22, 1887, and Robert Peterson, *Only the Ball was White* (Englewood Cliffs, N.J., 1970), 34, 38.

63. New York *Freeman*, April 14, 17, July 3, 24, September 4, November 27, 1886, January 22, February 19, April 2, 1887; Peterson, *Only the Ball was White*, 26-27; Louisville *Courier-Journal*, September 6, 1888.

### 12. Civil Rights, Politics, and Society, 1865-1891

1. Donovan, "Kentucky Law Regarding the Negro," 25, 27-33, 36-37; Victor B. Howard, "The Breckinridge Family and the Negro Testimony Controversy in Ken-

tucky, 1866-1872," *FCHQ* 49 (1975): 38; Kentucky *Acts* (1865-66), 39, 42. Relief of Confederate veterans was a common post-Civil War theme in the southern states. See John Hope Franklin, "Public Welfare in the South During the Reconstruction Era, 1865-80," *Social Service Review* 44 (1970): 381-82.

2. J. Rogers Hollingsworth and Bell I. Wiley, eds., *American Democracy: A Documentary Record*, 2 vols. (New York, 1962), 2:22, 54. The 1875 Civil Rights Act was declared unconstitutional in 1883. See James M. McPherson, *Ordeal By Fire* (New York, 1982), 576-77. For a discussion of Kentucky post-Civil War violence involving blacks and whites, see Hambleton Tapp and James C. Klotter, *Kentucky: Decades of Discord, 1865-1900* (Frankfort, Ky., 1977), 377-409.

3. M.B. Belknap to Benjamin H. Bristow, February 25, 1871, Benjamin H. Bristow Papers (Library of Congress, Washington D.C.); Louisville *Commercial*, September 5, October 12, 1870, January 27, July 9, 1871; Fairchild, *Berea*, 94-96.

4. Richards, *Bath County*, 235-36; Louisville *Commercial*, September 4, 1887; George C. Wright, *Racial Violence in Kentucky*, 41, 307-16; New York *Freeman*, July 25, 1885. Two whites, also held in the Flemingsburg jail for rape, went unmolested by the mob. An article in the Louisville *Commercial*, July 26, 1871, cited, without reference to race, 106 murders during the first six months of 1871; Tapp and Klotter, in *Decades of Discord*, 408, state that more than eight homicides, involving both races, occurred weekly in 1890.

5. Louisville *Commercial*, March 28, 1870, April 9, 1875; George C. Wright, *Life Behind A Veil*, 71; Louisville *Courier-Journal*, June 28, 1874; Louisville *Bulletin*, September 24, 1881; New York *Freeman*, July 18, September 12, December 19, 1885, November 6, 1886.

6. Louisville *Commercial*, July 21, 1870; E.H. Fairchild, *Baccalaureate Sermon by E.H. Fairchild, of Berea College, Preached June 30, 1878* (Boston, 1878), 7; Louisville *Bulletin*, September 24, 1881; Anonymous, *Daviess County*, 428-29; New York *Freeman*, July 3, November 27, 1886.

7. Louisville *Commercial*, September 25, 1872; New York *Freeman*, May 23, October 10, 1885, April 3, October 2, 1886, January 15, 1887.

8. Peterson, *Only the Ball was White*, 22-23; George C. Wright, *Life Behind A Veil*, 60, 62; New York *Freeman*, March 23, October 17, 1885, September 25, 1886.

9. *Proceedings of the State Convention 1867*, 7; Louisville *Daily Journal*, February 8, 1866; New York *Freeman*, September 4, October 9, 16, 1886; Louisville *Bulletin*, September 24, 1881. Black protests led one company to announce that black women could ride in the first-class section, but objections by whites led to a policy reversal after only two months. See George C. Wright, *Life Behind A Veil*, 63.

10. Louisville *Bulletin*, September 24, 1881; Fairchild, *Sermon*, 7.

11. Elisha Green, *Life*, 51-52, 54-55, 57-58; New York *Freeman*, January 15, 1887; Kentucky *Acts* (1891-93), 63; Charles Henry Phillips, *From the Farm to the Bishopric: An Autobiography* (Nashville, Tenn., 1932), 122-24. In explaining his treatment of the crippled, sixty-five-year-old minister to the Maysville *Daily Bulletin*, Bristow said that he merely "tapped the darkey with" a "light satchel."

12. Norris, "Louisville Demonstrations of 1870-71," 491-95, 498-502; Louisville *Commercial*, April 2, May 14, November 4, 30, 1870, May 14, 16, 1871; New York *Freeman*, July 31, 1886; George C. Wright, *Life Behind A Veil*, 54.

13. Louisville *Daily Journal*, January 20, 1866; Cincinnati *Daily Gazette*, January 19, 1866; King, "Free Negroes," 33; Louisville *Daily Courier*, January 25, 1866.

14. Cincinnati *Daily Gazette*, March 27, 1866; Victor B. Howard, "Negro Politics and the Suffrage Question in Kentucky, 1866-1872," *Register* 72 (1974): 113-14, 120; August Meier, *Negro Thought in America, 1880-1915: Racial Ideologies in the Age of Booker T. Washington* (Ann Arbor, Mich., 1963), 6.

15. Lexington *Kentucky Statesman,* November 8, 22, December 3, 1867; Howard, "Black Testimony," 155-56; Howard, *Black Liberation,* 140; King, "Free Negroes," 39-40; *Proceedings of the State Convention 1867,* 4, 8-10.

16. Louisville *Commercial,* October 18, 1871; S.E. Smith, *Anti-Separate Coach Movement,* 145; Marrs, *Life,* 140; New York *Freeman,* October 31, December 5, 1885. The legislature refused a request from blacks to hold their 1870 convention in the House chamber. See King, "Free Negroes," 43-44.

17. Howard, *Black Liberation,* 138, 147-48, 150, 153-54, 206-note 74; Louisville *Daily Journal,* January 4, 1866, January 2, 1867; Louisville *Courier-Journal,* January 3, 4, 1869; Louisville *Commercial,* May 7, 1870, July 6, 1872; Marrs, *Life,* 86-87; Gibson, *Historical Sketch,* 62-63.

18. Minutes, Fifth Street Baptist Church, 2: February 7, 1874; *American Baptist,* November 12, 1880; Howard, "Negro Politics," 115, 120-22; Thomas Lewis Owen, "The Formative Years of Kentucky's Republican Party, 1864-1871" (Ph.D. diss., University of Kentucky, 1981), 50-51, 67, 115, 117; Louisville *Daily Courier,* August 11, 1866.

19. Fairchild, *Berea,* 86; Owen, "Republican Party," 67-68, 72-73, 77-78, 150; Ross Webb, *Bristow,* 54-58; Gillette, "Anatomy of a Failure," 273, 276; Howard, "Negro Politics," 112-17, 119, 122.

20. Howard, "Negro Politics," 124-25; Louisville *Commercial,* February 25, 1870; Paris *True Kentuckian,* March 2, 1870.

21. Alfred H. Kelly and Winfred A. Harbison, *The American Constitution: Its Origins and Development* (New York, 1970), 1092; Owen, "Republican Party," 68; Howard, *Black Liberation,* 156. Other blacks who stumped for Republican candidates in 1870 included Henry Hastings and Elijah P. Marrs. See King, "Free Negroes," 46.

22. Collins, *History,* 1:227; Howard, *Black Liberation,* 115, 158-59; Owen, "Republican Party," 69-70, 77, 117; New York *Freeman,* October 23, 1886, January 15, 1887.

23. Gabriel Burdett to M.E. Strieby, August 25, 1876, AMA; Howard, "Negro Politics," 126, 130; New York *Freeman,* March 13, December 4, 1886; S.E. Smith, *Anti-Separate Coach Movement,* 147-48; New York *Globe,* September 29, 1883; *American Baptist,* November 12, 1880.

24. Howard, "Negro Politics," 129; Donovan, "Kentucky Law Regarding the Negro," 128-29; Thomas D. Clark, *Kentucky,* 583-84; Owen, "Republican Party," 70-71, 156.

25. Connelley and Coulter, *Kentucky,* 2:919; Thomas D. Clark, *Kentucky,* 584; Louisville *Commercial,* August 2, 1870, January 6, 1874; Owen, "Republican Party," 71; Kirk Harold Porter, *A History of Suffrage in the United States* (Chicago, 1918), 201; S.E. Smith, *Anti-Separate Coach Movement,* 172. According to Porter, *Suffrage,* 202-3, state authorities winked at obstructionist tactics.

26. Gillette, "Anatomy of a Failure," 276; Owen, "Republican Party," 72; Burdett to Strieby, November 11, 1876, AMA; L.F. Johnson, *Franklin County,* 176; Louisville *Commercial,* August 3, 4, 1870, August 12, 1874.

27. Louisville *Commercial,* August 4, 1870; Collins, *History,* 1:216; Louisville *Post,* August 8, 1882.

28. Owen, "Republican Party," 68, 72-75, 114; Malcolm E. Jewell and Everett W. Cunningham, *Kentucky Politics* (Lexington, Ky., 1968), 5.

29. Owen, "Republican Party," 73-75; S.E. Smith, *Anti-Separate Coach Movement,* 141, 148; W.D. Johnson, *Biographical Sketches,* 43-44; Gibson, *Historical Sketch,* 75; Louisville *Commercial,* August 8, September 12, 1872; King, "Free Negroes," 46-47, 52.

30. Marrs, *Life,* 86, 116-18, 140, 143; King, "Free Negroes," 47; Louisville *Commercial,* July 29, 1870.

31. Burdett to George Whipple, May 6, August 2, 1876, AMA; Burdett to E.M. Cravath, November 20, 1870, June 1, 8, September 16, October 7, 1872, May 5, 1875,

*ibid.*; Burdett to Strieby, August 25, November 4, 11, 1876, July 30, 1877, *ibid.*; John G. Fee to Cravath, January 20, 1873, *ibid.*; King, "Free Negroes," 52.

32. Howard, "Negro Politics," 125; King, "Free Negroes," 56-58; Owen, "Republican Party," 76.

33. George C. Wright, *Life Behind A Veil*, 178-79, 181; Ross Webb, "Kentucky," 142; Louisville *Commercial*, July 31, August 2, 1870, November 1, 1872, March 27, 1873, June 8, 1875; Weeden, *History*, 7; New York *Globe*, September 29, 1883. The Republicans won their first victory in Louisville in 1894.

34. New York *Freeman*, August 8, 1885, June 5, 12, 26, July 24, August 14, October 23, November 13, 20, 1886, February 5, 1887; Louisville *Courier-Journal*, June 1, 3, 1887; King, "Free Negroes," 55-56.

35. S.E. Smith, *Anti-Separate Coach Movement*, 183; George C. Wright, *Life Behind A Veil*, 179.

36. Gilbert Thomas Stephenson, *Race Distinctions in American Law* (New York, 1910), 243.

37. Elijah P. Marrs to Secretary of War E.M. Stanton, February 1, 1868, T.D. Eliot Papers, box 19, BRFAL, RG 105; Berlin et al., *Black Military Experience*, 822; Louisville *Commercial*, October 18, 1871; Howard, "Black Testimony," 149; Owen, "Republican Party," 50; King, "Free Negroes," 49-50; Norris, "Louisville Demonstrations of 1870-71," 493-94.

38. Howard, *Black Liberation*, 133-34, 141, 143-44.

39. Johnston, *History of Louisville*, 2:27; *Kentucky Acts* (2 vols., 1881), 1:15; Meacham, *Christian County*, 209; New York *Freeman*, October 17, 31, November 7, 14, 1885, January 16, 1886. In November 1885, Horace Morris and Austin Hubbard were two of the first five blacks chosen to serve on a Louisville jury. Some black civic leaders complained bitterly when four of the six blacks chosen for jury duty in January 1886 asked to be excused.

40. Louisville *Commercial*, February 25, 1870; Louisville *Courier-Journal*, July 15, 1869; Gibson, *Historical Sketch*, 84; Isaac Johnson, *Slavery Days*, 40; Weeden, *History*, 59-60.

41. Donovan, "Kentucky Law Regarding the Negro," 59-60; Venable, "Negro Education in Kentucky," 95-96; Weeden, *History*, 43-44.

42. Donovan, "Kentucky Law Regarding the Negro," 57-58; *Kentucky Acts* (2 vols., 1876), 1:101, 112.

43. Robert G. Crawford, "A History of the Kentucky Penitentiary System" (Ph.D. diss., University of Kentucky, 1955), 147-49, 151; George W. Cable, *The Silent South: Together with the Freedman's Case in Equality and the Convict Lease System* (New York, 1885), 144-47; *American Missionary* 32 (1878): 136.

44. Louisville *Commercial*, December 30, 1873; Louisville *Bulletin*, September 24, 1881; Louisville *Ohio Falls Express*, July 11, 1891; *Union Benevolent Society*, 15-16; Perrin, *Bourbon, Scott, Harrison and Nicholas Counties*, 298; Donovan, "Kentucky Law Regarding the Negro," 59; *LMR 1869* (Louisville, Ky., 1870), "Report of Louisville Alms House," 7, 10. For example, Hopkinsville formed its first "benevolent society" in 1868; in 1881 that town's blacks organized a branch of the Union Benevolent Society, the fifty-sixth chapter. See William T. Buckner to H.A. Hunter, RLR, Russellville, box 61, BRFAL, RG 105, and newspaper clipping in *Union Benevolent Society*.

45. Louisville *Commercial*, November 30, 1872; Oliver H. Strattan, ed., *That Business of Mine . . .* (Louisville, Ky., 1879), 39-41.

46. Weeden, *History*, 20, 22-24; Gibson, *Historical Sketch*, 19-20, 72-73; Louisville *Bulletin*, September 24, 1881; Louisville *Ohio Falls Express*, July 12, 1884; W.D. Johnson, *Biographical Sketches*, 69.

47. Donovan, "Kentucky Law Regarding the Negro," 59-60; Louisville *Commercial*,

August 19, 1873, February 1, 1874, August 14, 20, 1875; Weeden, *History,* 36-37. The Industrial Home was sometimes called the House of Refuge.

48. Weeden, *History,* 37; *LMR 1886,* 260, 332, 345-46; *LMR 1887,* 245, 258; *LMR 1888,* 363; *LMR 1889,* 359, 373; *LMR 1890,* 537, 550-51; *LMR 1891,* 83-84, 89, 110-11; Louisville *Courier-Journal,* September 6, 1888, January 9, 1891.

49. Gibson, *Historical Sketch,* 71; Indianapolis *Freeman,* October 18, 1890, January 3, 1891; George C. Wright, *Life Behind A Veil,* 144.

50. Minutes, Green Street Baptist Church, 3: May 10, 1889; Minutes, Fifth Street Baptist Church, 4: March 12, 1890, February 11, 1891; Gibson, *Historical Sketch,* 20, 73; Weeden, *History,* 24, 26, 28; Indianapolis *Freeman,* December 12, 1891.

51. Minutes, Fifth Street Baptist Church, 3: May 9, 1883; McKee and Bond, *Anderson County,* 212; Weeden, *History,* 46-47.

52. New York *Freeman,* May 16, 1885; George C. Wright, *Life Behind A Veil,* 99-101.

53. Agnes Geraldine McGann, *Mother Columba Carroll: Sister of Charity of Nazareth 1810-1878* (Nazareth, Ky., 1973), 17-18n; William Montague Cobb, "Henry Fitzbutler," *Journal of the National Medical Association* 44 (1952): 403; Leslie L. Hanawalt, "Henry Fitzbutler: Detroit's First Black Medical Student," *Detroit in Perspective: A Journal of Regional History* 1 (1973): 131, 133, 135; *AME Christian Recorder,* March 6, 1873.

54. Alvin Fayette Lewis, *History of Higher Education in Kentucky* (Washington, D.C., 1899), 301-2; Louisville *Ohio Falls Express,* July 12, 1884; Weeden, *History,* 48; New York *Freeman,* May 16, 1885; Louisville *Bulletin,* September 24, 1881.

55. Oliver Lucas, ed., *General Ordinances of the City of Louisville* . . . (Louisville, Ky., 1889), 238-40; Cobb, "Fitzbutler," 403, 405-6; Indianapolis *Freeman,* April 11, 1891; Hanawalt, "Fitzbutler," 136; George C. Wright, *Life Behind A Veil,* 99; Louisville *Ohio Falls Express,* July 11, 1891. LNMS received official recognition from the State Board of Health in 1894. Lewis, *Education,* 302. Hanawalt, "Fitzbutler," 136, concluded that though LNMS's "Standards could not have been high," graduates automatically received a license to practice in Kentucky. According to Cobb, "Fitzbutler," 403, 407, existing records of the state medical examining board, 1903-11, indicate that eleven of twenty-nine graduates passed. LNMS closed in 1912.

56. S.E. Smith, *Anti-Separate Coach Movement,* 144, 167-68, 178; *The National Cyclopedia of The Colored Race* (Montgomery, Ala., 1919), 176; *Bulletin of the Kentucky Historical Society* 14 (August 1988): 2; Indianapolis *Freeman,* September 26, 1891; Lawrence Harris, *The Negro Population of Lexington in the Professions, Business, Education and Religion* (Lexington, Ky., 1907), no page; Richings, *Progress,* 325.

57. Hickman *Courier,* December 2, 1871; Ross Webb, *Reconstruction,* 61; Harris, *Negro Population,* no page; S.E. Smith, *Anti-Separate Coach Movement,* 163, 182-83; New York *Freeman,* May 16, 1885, June 5, 1886; Indianapolis *Freeman,* February 21, 1891; Weeden, *History,* 44.

58. New York *Freeman,* May 16, June 27, October 24, November 14, 1885; Weeden, *History,* 44; Louisville *Courier-Journal,* September 21, 1884; Louisville *Commercial,* February 4, 1875; *AME Zion Church,* 141.

59. Indianapolis *Freeman,* August 9, 1890; Louisville *Commercial,* May 3, 1881; Penn, *Afro-American Press,* 317; Gibson, *Historical Sketch,* 65; Louisville *Ohio Falls Express,* July 12, 1884, July 11, 1891; *Ky. Doc.* (1875), No. 3, 107-8; *American Baptist,* November 12, 1880. Fitzbutler claimed that when a patron asked for "yesterday's liar," at a newsstand, the vendor handed him a copy of "the Courier Journal."

60. Louisville *Bulletin,* September 24, 1881; Louisville *Ohio Falls Express,* July 12, 1884, July 11, 1891; Lexington *American Citizen,* November 13, 1875.

61. Pride, "Negro Newspapers," 95-96; Penn, *Afro-American Press,* 317; Cobb, "Fitzbutler," 404-5; Louisville *Ohio Falls Express,* July 11, 1891; Louisville *Commercial,* May 3, 1881; New York *Freeman,* April 25, June 27, 1885; Indianapolis *Freeman,* August 9, 1890,

February 21, 1891; Gibson, *Historical Sketch*, 65-66; Weeden, *History*, 44.

62. *American Baptist*, November 12, 1880; Indianapolis *Freeman*, February 23, 1889; Penn, *Afro-American Press*, 378; George C. Wright, *Life Behind A Veil*, 171-72; Louisville *Commercial*, July 3, 1874; Weeden, *History*, 6. For an account of W.H. Steward's postwar career, see George C. Wright, "William Henry Steward: Moderate Approach to Black Leadership," in *Black Leaders of the Nineteenth Century*, ed. Leon Litwack and August Meier (Urbana and Chicago, 1988), 275-89.

63. Lexington *American Citizen*, November 13, 1875; Thomas, "Victims of Circumstance," 268-69; Indianapolis *Freeman*, August 9, 1890; Marrs, *Life*, 139; S.E. Smith, *Anti-Separate Coach Movement*, 151, 184; W.D. Johnson, *Biographical Sketches*, 37, 40; Penn, *Afro-American Press*, 254; New York *Globe*, September 29, 1883.

64. Penn, *Afro-American Press*, 120, 254, 368-73, 378, 380, 384, 386, 400, 408, 410, 412, 415-16, 418; Meacham, *Christian County*, 103; Simmons, *Men of Mark*, 606; Louisville *Defender*, February 18, 1982; Indianapolis *Freeman*, February 23, 1889; King, "Free Negroes," 114.

65. Louisville *Commercial*, May 4, 1870, July 31, August 9, 1872; New York *Freeman*, May 23, 1885, February 20, November 6, 1886; Minutes, Fifth Street Baptist Church, 4: January 9, 1889; Parrish, *Golden Jubilee*, 199-200; Minutes, Green Street Baptist Church, 2: May 8, 1874; Burdett to D.E. Emerson, March 7, 1873, AMA.

66. Louisville *Commercial*, January 14, 1870, February 14, 1872; Minutes, Fifth Street Baptist Church, 4: April 16, May 14, 1890; New York *Freeman*, December 19, 1885, January 9, June 5, July 24, November 6, 1886, April 2, 1887; Indianapolis *Freeman*, March 2, 1889; Louisville *Ohio Falls Express*, July 12, 1884, July 11, 1891; George C. Wright, *Life Behind A Veil*, 135-37, 152; Marrs, *Life*, 90-91; Louisville *Bulletin*, September 24, 1881. For a more extensive look at club activities, see Gerda Lerner, "Early Community Work of Black Club Women," *JNH* 59 (1974): 158-67.

67. Starling, *Henderson County*, 502; Louisville *Bulletin*, September 24, 1881; Anonymous, *Daviess County*, 400-401; Ford and Ford, *Ohio Falls Cities*, 1:576. For additional information on Kentucky lodges, see Edward M. Palmer, "Negro Secret Societies," *Social Forces* 23 (1944): 207-12, and W.H. Grimshaw, *Official History of Freemasonry Among the Colored People of North America* (New York, 1969; orig. pub. 1903), 231-32.

68. Gibson, *Historical Sketch*, 42-43, 45-46; Louisville *Courier-Journal*, June 28, 1874; Lousville *Bulletin*, September 24, 1881; Weeden, *History*, 26, 52; Indianapolis *Freeman*, April 26, 1890; W.H. Gibson, *History of the United Brothers of Friendship and Sisters of the Mysterious Ten* (Louisville, Ky., 1897), 65-67; George C. Wright, *Life Behind A Veil*, 133.

69. Simmons, *Men of Mark*, 369; Weeden, *History*, 8, 44, 55; Louisville *Commercial*, August 19, 1870; Gibson, *Historical Sketch*, 74.

70. Gibson, *Historical Sketch*, 60-61; Weeden, *History*, 45-46, 49, 55; New York *Freeman*, February 20, July 10, September 11, 1886; *AME Zion Church*, 140; Louisville *Commercial*, June 23, 1872; Louisville *Courier-Journal*, October 7, 1873, June 19, 1887.

71. Eileen Southern, *The Music of Black Americans* (New York, 1971), 274, 341; Louisville *Ohio Falls Express*, July 12, 1884; New York *Freeman*, September 26, 1885, January 1, 1887; Gibson, *Historical Sketch*, 57-61; Louisville *Daily Courier*, April 7, 1868; Louisville *Courier-Journal*, September 25, 1883.

# BIBLIOGRAPHY

*Primary Sources*

**Manuscripts**
American Missionary Association Manuscripts. Microfilm. Amistad Research Center, Dillard University, New Orleans, Louisiana.
Annals of St. Monica Convent. Nazareth Archival Center, Nazareth, Kentucky.
Birney, James G. Emancipation Document. Microfilm. Kentucky Department for Libraries & Archives, Frankfort, Kentucky.
Black File. Berea College Archives, Berea, Kentucky.
Bristow, Benjamin H. Papers. Manuscript Division, Library of Congress, Washington, D.C.
Browder, George R. Diary. Kentucky Library, Western Kentucky University, Bowling Green, Kentucky.
Brown Family Papers, 1799-1846. Manuscript Division, Filson Club, Louisville, Kentucky.
Brown, Orlando. Papers. Manuscript Division, Filson Club, Louisville, Kentucky.
Bullitt Family Letters. Special Collections, University of Kentucky, Lexington, Kentucky.
Burleigh, Angus A. File. Berea College Archives, Berea, Kentucky.
Carlisle Family Papers. Bentley Historical Library, University of Michigan, Ann Arbor, Michigan.
Clay, Brutus Janius. Papers. Special Collections, University of Kentucky, Lexington, Kentucky.
Coleman, J. Winston, Jr. Papers on Slavery, 1780-1940. Special Collections, University of Kentucky, Lexington, Kentucky.
Davidson, James. Letter. Special Collections, University of Kentucky, Lexington, Kentucky.
Dicken-Troutman-Balke Family Papers. Special Collections, University of Kentucky, Lexington, Kentucky.
Draper MSS. Microfilm, Western Kentucky University, Bowling Green, Kentucky. Originals located at State Historical Society of Wisconsin,

Madison, Wisconsin.
Duncan Family Papers. Special Collections, University of Kentucky, Lexington, Kentucky.
Evans Family Papers. Special Collections, University of Kentucky, Lexington, Kentucky.
Faculty File. Berea College Archives, Berea, Kentucky.
Fairchild, E.H. Papers. Berea College Archives, Berea, Kentucky.
Fayette County Records. Microfilm. Special Collections, University of Kentucky, Lexington, Kentucky.
Fee, John G. Papers. Berea College Archives, Berea, Kentucky.
Fifth Street Choir Record. Fifth Street Baptist Church safe, Louisville, Kentucky. Microfilm copy located at University of Louisville Archives, Louisville, Kentucky.
Frost, William G. Papers. Berea College Archives, Berea, Kentucky.
Fyfe Family Papers. Bentley Historical Library, University of Michigan, Ann Arbor, Michigan.
Godbey, Duke Marion. Papers. Microfilm. Special Collections, University of Kentucky, Lexington, Kentucky.
Goulding, E.H. Letter. Special Collections, University of Kentucky, Lexington, Kentucky.
Halbersham, Joseph. Letter. Microfilm. Kentucky Historical Society, Frankfort, Kentucky.
Harris, M.A. Small Collection. Kentucky Library, Western Kentucky University, Bowling Green, Kentucky.
Kennedy, Jesse. Small Collection. Kentucky Library, Western Kentucky University, Bowling Green, Kentucky.
Legislative Records of Louisville, Kentucky, 1781-1929. Microfilm. University of Louisville Archives, Louisville, Kentucky.
Lewis-Starling Collection. Kentucky Library, Western Kentucky University, Bowling Green, Kentucky.
Lyle Family Papers. Special Collections, University of Kentucky, Lexington, Kentucky.
McElroy, William Thomas. Journal. Manuscript Division, Filson Club, Louisville, Kentucky.
Miller, Howard. Diary. Manuscript Division, Filson Club, Louisville, Kentucky.
Minutes, Board of Trustees, Berea College. Berea College Archives, Berea, Kentucky.
Minutes, Prudential Committee of the Board of Trustees, Berea College. Berea College Archives, Berea, Kentucky.
Minutes of the Fifth Street Baptist Church, Louisville, Kentucky. Fifth Street Baptist Church safe, Louisville, Kentucky. Microfilm copies currently located at University of Louisville Archives, Louisville, Kentucky.
Minutes of the First [Walnut Street] Baptist Church, Louisville, Kentucky. Walnut Street Baptist Church, Louisville, Kentucky.
Minutes of the Green Street Baptist Church, Louisville, Kentucky.

Microfilm. University of Louisville Archives, Louisville, Kentucky.
Minutes of the Pleasant Grove Baptist Church, Jefferson County, Kentucky. Manuscript Division, Filson Club, Louisville, Kentucky.
Minutes of the Trustees for the City of Bowling Green, Kentucky. Kentucky Library, Western Kentucky University, Bowling Green, Kentucky.
Miscellaneous Black History Collection. Loretto Archives, Nerinx, Kentucky.
The Negro in the Military Service of the United States 1639-1886. Microfilm. National Archives, Washington, D.C.
Perry, Fountain, and Rodrick Perry. Papers. Special Collections, University of Kentucky, Lexington, Kentucky.
Piper, James. Papers. Special Collections, University of Kentucky, Lexington, Kentucky.
Pratt, William. Diary. Special Collections, University of Kentucky, Lexington, Kentucky.
Records of the U.S. Adjutant General's Office. Record Group 94, National Archives, Washington, D.C.
Records of the Educational Division of the Bureau of Refugees, Freedmen, and Abandoned Lands, 1865-1871. Microfilm. Record Group 105, National Archives, Washington, D.C.
Records of the Bureau of Refugees, Freedmen, and Abandoned Lands. Record Group 105, National Archives, Washington, D.C.
Records of the Kentucky Adjutant General. Department of Military Affairs. Military Records and Research Library, Frankfort, Kentucky.
Records of the U.S. Provost Marshal General's Bureau, 1863-1866. Record Group 110, National Archives, Washington, D.C.
Records of the U.S. Army Continental Commands. Record Group 393, National Archives, Washington, D.C.
Shelby Family Papers. Special Collections, University of Kentucky, Lexington, Kentucky.
Trustees Minute Book, Lexington, Kentucky. Microfilm. Special Collections, University of Kentucky, Lexington, Kentucky.
Underwood, Warner L. Collection. Kentucky Library, Western Kentucky University, Bowling Green, Kentucky.
Weis, Daniel K. "Reminiscences of Eastern Kentucky." Microfilm. Special Collections, University of Kentucky, Lexington, Kentucky.
Wickliffe, Robert. Will. Microfilm. Kentucky Department for Libraries and Archives, Frankfort, Kentucky.
Yandell Family Papers, 1823-1887. Manuscript Division, Filson Club, Louisville, Kentucky.

**Printed Documents**
Alvord, J.W. *Semi-Annual Report on Schools For Freedmen*, 3rd-10th reports. Washington, D.C., 1867-70.
_____. *Letters from the South, Relating to the Conditions of Freedmen Addressed to Major General O.O. Howard*. Washington, D.C., 1870.

————. *Report on Schools and Finances of Freedmen: for July 1866.* Washington, D.C., 1866.
*Annual Report of the Freedmen's Aid Society of the Methodist Episcopal Church,* 3rd-5th reports. Cincinnati, 1869, 1871-72.
Aptheker, Herbert, ed. *A Documentary History of The Negro People in the United States.* New York, 1951.
Baptist Normal and Theological Catalog. 1881-82. Simmons Bible College Records. UL.
Basler, Roy P., ed. *The Collected Works of Abraham Lincoln.* 8 vols. New Brunswick, N.J., 1953.
*Bennett & Co.'s Henderson City Directory, for 1891-1892.* Henderson, Ky., 1891.
Berlin, Ira et al., eds. *Freedom: A Documentary History of Emancipation 1861-1867. Selected From The Holdings of The National Archives of The United States. Series 1. Volume 1: The Destruction of Slavery.* Cambridge, England, 1985; and *Series 2: The Black Military Experience.* Cambridge and New York, 1982.
*Bosworth v. Brand,* Kentucky Reports, 1 Dana 377, Fall Term 1833.
Catterall, Helen T. *Judicial Cases Concerning American Slavery and the Negro.* 5 vols. Washington, D.C., 1926-37.
*Charles Emerson's Frankfort Directory, 1884-85.* Frankfort, Ky., 1884.
*Claybrook v. Owensboro,* 16 Federal Reports 297 (1883).
*Claybrook v. Owensboro,* 23 Federal Reports, 634 (1884).
*Commonwealth v. Bird* (a slave), Barren Circuit Court (1846).
*Congressional Globe.*
*Constitution and By-Laws of the Colored People's Union Benevolent Society, No. 1, of Lexington, Ky., Organized May 1, 1843.* Lexington, Ky., 1877.
*Dawson v. Lee,* 83 Kentucky Reports 49 (1884).
Department of Parks & Recreation. *Allensworth Feasibility Study.* Sacramento, Calif., 1971.
Hollingsworth, J. Rogers, and Bell I. Wiley, eds. *American Democracy: A Documentary Record.* 2 vols. New York, 1962.
*Free Frank and Lucy v. Denham's Administrator,* 5 Littell 330 (1824).
General Conference Handbook. *Historical and illustrated, 25th Quadrennial Session of the A.M.E. Zion Church* . . . Louisville, Ky., 1916.
*General Orders, Circulars, Etc. Asst.-Commissioner, Bu. R., F., & A. L. Kentucky. 1866-68.* Louisville, Ky., 1869.
*Guide To Kentucky Historical Highway Markers.* Frankfort, Ky., 1969.
Kentucky Acts (1809-12, 1825, 1834, 1849-51, 1865-68, 1871, 1873-74, 1876, 1881, 1891-93).
Kentucky. *Bureau of Agriculture, Horticulture, & Statistics Report.* Kentucky Documents 1879.
Kentucky. *House Journal* (1833, 1863-64).
Kentucky. *Superintendent of Public Instruction Report* . . . Kentucky Documents 1867, 1869, 1871-72, 1874-76, 1881, 1887-89, 1891.
Kentucky. *The Revised Statutes of Kentucky* . . . 1851 and 1852. Frankfort, Ky.
*Kentucky State Colored Educational Convention, Held At Benson's Theater,*

Louisville, Ky. July 14, 1869. Louisville, Ky., 1869.
*Kyler and Wife* v. *Dunlap, Kentucky Reports*, 18 B. Monroe 561 (1857).
Legislative Records of Louisville, Kentucky. Microfilm. UL.
Littell, William, ed. *The Statute Law of Kentucky* . . . 5 vols. Frankfort, Ky., 1809-19.
Littell, William, and Jacob Swigert, eds. *A Digest of the Statute Laws of Kentucky* . . . Frankfort, Ky., 1822.
Louisville, Kentucky. *Louisville Municipal Reports for the Fiscal Year Ending August 31, 1869, 1886, 1887, 1888, 1889, 1890, 1891.* Louisville, Ky., 1870-92.
Louisville Library Collection. Mimeograph. 5 vols. Louisville Free Public Library, Louisville, Kentucky.
Minutes of the Bardstown Trustees. Reprinted in the Bardstown *Kentucky Standard*, September 17, 1936.
*Minutes of the Elkhorn Association of Baptists, Kentucky, 1785-1870.* Microfilm. n.p., n.d.
*Minutes of the General Association of Colored Baptists in Kentucky* . . . Louisville, Ky., 1869-94.
*Minutes of the Long Run Association of Baptists, 1803-1894.* Microfilm. 2 vols. Louisville, Ky., 1803-94.
Morehead, C.S., and Mason Brown, eds., *Digest of the Statute Laws of Kentucky* . . . 2 vols. Frankfort, Ky., 1834.
Morris, Robert C., ed. *Freedmen's Schools and Textbooks*. 2 vols. New York, 1980.
*Proceedings of the State Convention of Colored Men, Held at Lexington, Kentucky, in the A.M.E. Church, November 26th, 27th, and 28th, 1867.* Frankfort, Ky., 1867.
Protestant Episcopal Church. "The Colored Episcopal Mission, Louisville, Kentucky." April 6, 1861, broadside.
*Report of the Commissioners of the Bureau of Refugees, Freedmen and Abandoned Lands for the Year 1867.* Washington, D.C., 1867.
*Rules and Regulations of the Annual Fair of the Colored A. & M. Association, Inc.* Lexington, Ky., 1897.
State University *Catalog*. 1884-85, 1892-93.
U.S. *Census of the United States*, 1st-9th, 11th. Philadelphia, New York, Washington, D.C., 1791, 1801, 1821, 1841, 1853, 1864, 1865 (orig. pub. 1832), 1867 (orig. pub. 1811), 1875, 1895.
U.S. Department of Education. *Report of the Commissioner of Education* . . . Washington, D.C., 1868, 1879, 1883, 1885, 1888, 1891, 1893.
U.S. *House Ex. Doc.* No. 1, 40 Cong., 3 Sess. (Serial 1367); No. 70, 39 Cong., 1 Sess. (Serial 1256); No. 329, 40 Cong., 2 Sess. (Serial 1346).
U.S. *Official Army Register of the Volunteer Force of the United States Army for the Years 1861, '62, '63, '64, '65.* 8 vols. Washington, D.C., 1865-67.
U.S. *Senate Doc.* No. 49, 42 Cong., 2 Sess. (Serial 1467).
U.S. *Senate Ex. Doc.* No. 27, 39 Cong., 1 Sess. (Serial 1238); No. 28, 38 Cong., 2 Sess. (Serial 1209).
U.S. *Statistical View of the United States* . . . Washington, D.C., 1854.

U.S. *Statistics of the Population of the United States at the Tenth Census (June 1, 1880)* . . . Washington, D.C., 1883.
U.S. *Statistics of the United States in 1860* . . . Washington, D.C., 1866.
U.S. *The War of the Rebellion: A Compilation of the Official Records of the Union and Confederate Armies.* 128 vols. Washington, D.C., 1880-1901.
Young, Bennett H. *History and Texts of the Three Constitutions of Kentucky* . . . Louisville, Ky., 1890.


**Autobiographies, Memoirs, Travel Accounts**
Abdy, E.S. *Journal of a Residence and Tour in the United States* . . . 3 vols. London, 1835.
Anderson, Robert. *From Slavery To Affluence* . . . Hemingford, Neb., 1927.
Anonymous. *Historical Sketch of Berea College, 1904.* Berea, Ky., 1904.
Armstrong, Orlan K. *Old Massa's People: The Old Slaves Tell their Story.* Indianapolis, Ind., 1931.
Baxter, J.H., comp. *Statistics, Medical and Anthropological* . . . 2 vols. Washington, 1875.
Bernhard, Karl. *Travels through North America* . . . 2 vols. Philadelphia, 1828.
Bibb, Henry. *Narrative of the Life and Adventures of Henry Bibb* . . . New York, 1849.
Blassingame, John W., ed. *Slave Testimony: Two Centuries of Letters, Speeches, Interviews, and Autobiographies.* Baton Rouge, La., 1977.
Brown, Thomas. *Brown's Three Years in the Kentucky Prisons* . . . Indianapolis, Ind., 1857.
Brown, William W. *Narrative of William W. Brown A Fugitive Slave Written By Himself.* Edited by Larry Gara. Reading, Mass., 1969; orig. pub. 1848.
Bruner, Peter. *A Slave's Adventures Toward Freedom* . . . Oxford, Ohio, 1918.
Buckingham, J.S. *The Eastern and Western States of America.* 3 vols. London, 1842.
Burleigh, Angus A. *John G. Fee, Founder of Berea College.* Berea, Ky., n.d.
Burton, Thomas William. *What Experience Has Taught Me: An Autobiography* . . . Cincinnati, 1910.
Campbell, Madison. *Autobiography* . . . Richmond, Ky., 1895.
Campbell, Israel. *Bond and Free: or, Yearnings for Freedom* . . . Philadelphia, 1861.
Clarke, James Freeman. *Anti-Slavery Days.* New York, 1883.
_____. *James Freeman Clarke: Autobiography, Diary and Correspondence.* Boston, 1899.
Clarke, Lewis. *Narrative of the Sufferings* . . . Boston, 1845.
_____, and Milton Clarke. *Narratives of the Sufferings of Lewis and Milton Clarke* . . . Boston, 1846.
Clay, Cassius Marcellus. *The Life of Cassius Marcellus Clay* . . . Cincinnati, 1886.
Coffin, Levi. *Reminiscences* . . . London and Cincinnati, 1879.
Cotter, Joseph Seamon. *Links of Friendship.* Louisville, Ky., 1898.

_____. *25th Anniversary of the Founding of Colored Parkland or "Little Africa," Louisville, 1891-1916.* Louisville, 1934.
Cuming, F[ortesque]. *Sketches of a Tour to the Western Country* . . . Pittsburgh, 1810.
Darlington, William M., ed. *Christopher Gist's Journals* . . . Pittsburgh, 1893.
Diamond Jubilee Commission. *Diamond Jubilee Of The General Association of Colored Baptists In Kentucky.* Louisville, 1943.
Drew, Benjamin. *A North-Side View of Slavery* . . . New York, 1968; orig. pub. 1856.
Fairbank, Calvin. *Rev. Calvin Fairbank, During Slavery Times.* Chicago, 1890.
Fairchild, E.H. *Baccalaureate Sermon by E.H. Fairchild, of Berea College, Preached June 30, 1878.* Boston, 1878.
_____. *Berea College, Ky. An Interesting History.* Cincinnati, 1875.
_____. *Inauguration of Rev. E.H. Fairchild, President of Berea College, Kentucky. Wednesday, July 7th, 1869.* Cincinnati, 1870.
Fedric, Francis. *Slave Life in Virginia and Kentucky* . . . London, 1863.
Fee, John G. *Autobiography of John G. Fee, Berea, Kentucky.* Chicago, 1891.
Filson, John. *The Discovery, Settlement And Present State of Kentucke* . . . Wilmington, Del., 1784.
Flint, James. *Letters from America* . . . New York, 1970; orig. pub. 1822.
Frederick, Francis. *Autobiography of Rev. Francis Frederick, of Virginia.* Baltimore, 1869. See above Francis Fedric, alternate spelling.
Gibson, W.H. *Historical Sketch of the Progress of the Colored Race, in Louisville, Ky.* Louisville, Ky., 1897.
_____. *History of the United Brothers of Friendship and Sisters of the Mysterious Ten.* Louisville, Ky., 1897.
Green, Elisha W. *Life of the Rev. Elisha W. Green* . . . Maysville, Ky., 1888.
Green, Jacob D. *Narrative* . . . Huddersfield, England, 1864.
Harris, Lawrence. *The Negro Population of Lexington in the Professions, Business, Education and Religion.* Lexington, Ky., 1907.
Haviland, Laura S. *A Woman's Life Work* . . . Grand Rapids, Mich., 1881.
Hayden, William. *Narrative of William Hayden* . . . Cincinnati, 1846.
Henson, Josiah. *An Autobiography of Reverend Josiah Henson.* Edited by Robin Winks. Reading, Mass., 1961; orig. pub. 1849.
Hopson, Ella Lord, ed. *Memoirs Dr. Winthrop Hartly Hopson.* Cincinnati, 1887.
Jackson, Andrew. *Narratives and Writings* . . . Miami, Fla., 1969; orig. pub. 1847.
James, Thomas. *The Autobiography of Rev. Thomas James.* Rochester, N.Y., 1975; orig. pub. 1887.
Jocelyn, Stephen. *Mostly Alkali: A Biography.* Caldwell, Idaho, 1953.
Johnson, Isaac. *Slavery Days in Old Kentucky.* Ogdensburg, N.Y., 1901.
Johnson, W.D. *Biographical Sketches of Prominent Negro Men and Woman of Kentucky* . . . Lexington, Ky., 1897.
Laine, Henry Allen. "My Life." Museum, Eastern Kentucky University.
Lyell, Charles. *A Second Visit to the United States of North America.* 2 vols. New York, 1849.

Marrs, Elijah P. *Life and History of the Rev. Elijah P. Marrs, First Pastor of Beargrass Baptist Church, and Author.* Louisville, Ky., 1885.

Marryat, Fred. *A Diary in America* . . . 3 vols. London, 1839.

Mason, Richard Lee. *Narrative of Richard Lee Mason in the Pioneer West, 1819.* New York, 1915.

Massie, James William. *America: The Origin of Her Present Conflict* . . . Miami, Fla., 1969; orig. pub. 1864.

Melish, John. *Travels in the United States* . . . 2 vols. Philadelphia, 1812.

Morton, M.B. *Kentuckians are Different.* Louisville, Ky., 1938.

Neal, Mary Julia, ed. *The Journal of Eldress Nancy* . . . Nashville, Tenn., 1963.

Newberry, J.S. *The U.S. Sanitary Commission in the Valley of the Mississippi, During the War of the Rebellion, 1861-1866.* Cleveland, 1871.

Olmsted, Frederick Law. *A Journey in the Seaboard Slave States, With Remarks on their Economy.* New York, 1856.

Osofsky, Gilbert, ed. *Puttin' On Ole Massa: The Slave Narratives of Henry Bibb, William Wells Brown, and Solomon Northrup.* New York, 1969.

Owen, Robert Dale. *The Wrong of Slavery the Right of Emancipation* . . . New York, 1969; orig. pub. 1864.

Palmer, John M. *Personal Recollections of John M. Palmer* . . . Cincinnati, 1901.

Payne, Daniel A. *History of the African Methodist Episcopal Church.* New York, 1969; orig. pub. 1891.

Pease, Theodore Calvin, and James G. Randall, eds. *The Diary of Orville Hickman Browning.* 2 vols. Springfield, Ill., 1925.

Pickard, Kate E.R. *The Kidnapped and the Ransomed* . . . New York and Auburn, 1856.

Polk, J.J. *Autobiography* . . . Louisville, Ky., 1867.

Prentis, Nobel Lovely. *Southern Letters.* Topeka, Kan., 1881.

Pulszky, Francis, and Theresa Pulszky. *White, Red, Black* . . . 2 vols. New York, 1853.

Rawick, George P., ed. *The American Slave: A Composite Autobiography.* 19 vols. Westport, Conn., 1972; orig. pub. 1856.

Reed, Andrew, and James Matheson. *A Narrative of the Visit to the American Churches* . . . 2 vols. New York, 1835.

Rogers, John A.R. *Birth of Berea College: A Story of Providence.* Philadelphia, 1970; orig. pub. 1903.

Shaler, Nathaniel S. *The Autobiography of Nathaniel S. Shaler.* Boston, 1909.

Simmons, William J. *Men of Mark: Eminent, Progressive, and Rising.* Chicago, 1970; orig. pub. 1887.

Smith, Harry. *Fifty Years of Slavery in the United States of America.* Grand Rapids, Mich., 1891.

Smith, S.E., ed. *History of the Anti-Separate Coach Movement* . . . Evansville, Ind., [1894].

Speed, Thomas. *Records and Memorials of the Speed Family* . . . Louisville, Ky., 1892.

Stirling, James. *Letters from the Slave States.* London, 1857.

Trotter, Isabella. *First Impressions of the New World* . . . London, 1858.

Troutman, Richard L., ed. *The Heavens Are Weeping: The Diaries of George Richard Browder, 1852-1886.* Grand Rapids, Mich., 1987.

Toulmin, Harry. *The Western Country in 1793: Reports on Kentucky and Virginia.* San Marino, Calif., 1948; orig. pub. 1792.

Tower, Philo. *Slavery Unmasked . . .* Rochester, N.Y., 1856.

Walters, Alexander. *My Life and Work.* New York, 1917.

Webb, William. *The History of William Webb, Composed by Himself.* Detroit, 1873.

Weeden, H.C. *Weeden's History of the Colored People of Louisville.* Louisville, Ky., 1897.

Weld, Theodore Dwight. *American Slavery As It Is: Testimony of a Thousand Witnesses.* New York, 1969; orig. pub. 1839.

Wiley, Bell I., ed. *Slaves No More: Letters from Liberia, 1833-1869.* Lexington, Ky., 1980.

Yetman, Norman R., ed. *Voices from Slavery.* New York, 1970.

Young, Chester Raymond, ed. *Westward Into Kentucky: The Narrative of Daniel Trabue.* Lexington, Ky., 1981.

*Secondary Sources*

**Newspapers and Magazines**
*African Repository.*
*American Baptist.*
*American Freedman.*
*The American Missionary.*
Baltimore *Sun.*
Bardstown *Kentucky Standard.*
Berea *Evangelist.*
Chicago *Tribune.*
Cincinnati *Daily Gazette.*
Frankfort *Commonwealth.*
*Freedmen's Journal.*
Hopkinsville *Semi-Weekly South Kentuckian.*
Indianapolis *Freeman.*
Indianapolis *World.*
Lexington *American Citizen.*
Lexington *Intelligencer.*
Lexington *Kentucky Gazette.*
Lexington *Kentucky Reporter.*
Lexington *Kentucky Statesman.*
Lexington *Observer & Reporter.*
Lexington *Western Luminary.*
*The Liberator.*
Louisville *Bulletin.*
Louisville *Commercial.*
Louisville *Courier-Journal.*

Louisville *Daily Courier.*
Louisville *Daily Democrat.*
Louisville *Daily Journal.*
Louisville *Daily Union Press.*
Louisville *Defender.*
Louisville *Ohio Falls Express.*
Louisville *Sanitary Reporter.*
Louisville *Times.*
Maysville *Daily Bulletin.*
*National Anti-Slavery Standard.*
New York *Freeman.*
New York *Globe.*
New York *National Freedman.*
New York *Times.*
New York *Tribune.*
*Niles' Weekly Register.*
Owensboro *Messenger and Examiner.*
Owensboro *Monitor.*
Owensboro *Semi-Weekly Messenger.*
Paris *Western Citizen.*
Philadelphia *AME Christian Recorder.*
*The Record, Official Publication of the Diocese of Louisville.*
Richmond *Kentucky Register.*
Sandwich, Canada, *The Voice of the Fugitive.*

**Books**
Allen, James Lane. *The Blue-Grass Region of Kentucky.* New York, 1892.
Anderson, James D. *The Education of Blacks in the South, 1860-1935.* Chapel Hill, N.C., 1988.
Anonymous. *The Bowling Green and Warren County, Ky., Immigration Society.* Bowling Green, Ky., 1885.
_____. *History of Daviess County, Kentucky . . .* Chicago, 1883.
Aptheker, Herbert. *American Negro Slave Revolts.* New York, 1943.
Athearn, Robert G. *In Search of Canaan: Black Migration to Kansas, 1879-80.* Lawrence, Kan., 1978.
Axton, W.F. *Tobacco and Kentucky.* Lexington, Ky., 1975.
Bakeless, John. *Master of the Wilderness, Daniel Boone.* New York, 1939.
Ballagh, Curtis. *A History of Slavery in Virginia.* [Baltimore, 1902].
Bancroft, Frederic. *Slave-Trading in the Old South.* Baltimore, 1931.
Barrett, Leonard E. *Soul-Force: African Heritage in Afro-American Religion.* Garden City, N.Y., 1974.
Benedict, David. *A General History of the Baptist Denomination in America and Others Parts of the World.* New York, 1848.
Bentley, George R. *A History of the Freedmen's Bureau.* New York, 1970; orig. pub. 1955.
Berlin, Ira. *Slaves Without Masters: The Free Negro in the Antebellum South.*

New York, 1974.
Birdwhistell, Ira S. *Gathered at the River: A Narrative History of Long Run Association.* Louisville, Ky., 1978.
Bishop, Robert H. *An Outline History of the Church in the State of Kentucky . . .* Lexington, Ky., 1824.
Blassingame, John W. *The Slave Community: Plantation Life in the Antebellum South.* 2d ed. New York, 1979.
Bohannan, Paul, and Philip Curtin. *Africa and Africans.* Garden City, N.Y., 1971; orig. pub. 1964.
Boles, John B. *Black Southerners, 1619-1869.* Lexington, Ky., 1983.
_____. *Religion in Antebellum Kentucky.* Lexington, Ky., 1976.
Boyd, L. *Chronicles of Cynthiana and other Chronicles.* Cincinnati, 1894.
Brown, John T. *Church of Christ . . .* Louisville, Ky., 1904.
Browning, D.P. *One Hundred Years of Church History.* [Lewisburg, Ky.], 1922.
Burton, Orville Vernon. *In My Father's House are Many Mansions . . .* Chapel Hill, N.C., 1985.
Cable, George W. *The Silent South: Together with the Freedman's Case in Equality and the Convict Lease System.* New York, 1885.
Calico, Forrest. *History of Garrard County Kentucky and its Churches.* New York, 1947.
Campbell, Stanley W. *The Slave Catchers: Enforcement of the Fugitive Slave Law, 1850-1860.* Chapel Hill, N.C., 1968.
Campbell, Thomas D. *One Family Under God: A Story of Cumberland Presbyterians In Black And White.* Memphis, Tenn., 1982.
Carleton, George W. *The Suppressed Book About Slavery!* New York, 1864.
Carver, W.O. *History of the New Salem Baptist Church.* Louisville 1901.
Caswell, Henry. *America and the American Church.* London, 1839.
Channing, Steven A. *Kentucky: A Bicentennial History.* New York, 1977.
Clark, Thomas D. *A History of Kentucky.* New York, 1937.
Clark, Victor S. *History of Manufacturing in the United States.* 2 vols. New York, 1929.
Cofer, Ella. *History of Severn's Valley Baptist Church.* [Elizabethtown], Ky., 1931.
Coleman, J. Winston, Jr. *Slavery Times in Kentucky.* Chapel Hill, N.C., 1940.
_____. *The Springs of Kentucky . . .* Lexington, Ky., 1955.
_____. *Stage-Coach Days in the Bluegrass . . .* Louisville, Ky., 1935.
Collins, Lewis, and Richard H. Collins, *History of Kentucky . . .* 2 vols. Frankfort, Ky., 1966; orig. pub. 1874.
Conkwright, S.J. *History of the Churches of Boone's Creek Baptist Association of Kentucky.* Winchester, Ky., 1923.
Connelley, William Elsey, and E.M. Coulter, *History of Kentucky.* 5 vols. Chicago and New York, 1922.
Connelly, Emma M. *The Story of Kentucky.* Boston, 1890.
Coulter, E. Merton. *The Civil War and Readjustment In Kentucky.* Gloucester, Mass., 1966; orig. pub. 1926.
Coward, Joan Wells. *Kentucky in the New Republic: The Process of Constitution*

*Making*. Lexington, Ky., 1979.
Curry, Leonard P. *The Free Black in Urban America, 1800-1850: The Shadow of the Dream*. Chicago, 1981.
Dabney, Wendell P. *Cincinnati's Colored Citizens* . . . New York, 1970; orig. pub. 1926.
Darnell, Ermina Jett. *Forks of Elkhorn Church*. Louisville, Ky., 1946.
Davenport, Garvin. *Ante-Bellum: Kentucky A Social History, 1800-1860*. Oxford, Ohio, 1943.
Davis, David Brion. *The Problem of Slavery in Western Culture*. Ithaca, N.Y., 1966.
Dick, Robert C. *Black Protest: Issues and Tactics*. Westport, Conn., 1974.
Dorris, Jonathan Truman, and John Cabell Chenault. *Old Cane Springs* . . . Louisville, 1937.
Dunnigan, Alice Allison. *A Black Woman's Experience: From Schoolhouse to White House*. Philadelpha, 1974.
Eaton, Clement. *The Freedom-of-Thought Struggle in the Old South*. 2d ed., New York, 1964.
―――――. *Henry Clay and the Art of American Politics*. Boston, 1957.
Elliott, Charles. *Sinfulness of American Slavery* . . . 2 vols. Cincinnati, 1850.
Ellis, John H. *Medicine in Kentucky*. Lexington, Ky., 1977.
Ellis, William E., H.E. Everman, and Richard D. Sears. *Madison County: Two Hundred Years in Retrospect*. Richmond, Ky., 1985.
Egerton, John. *Generations: An American Family*. Lexington, Ky., 1983.
Epstein, Dena. *Sinful Tunes and Spirituals: Black Folk Music to the Civil War*. Urbana, Ill., 1977.
Escott, Paul D. *Slavery Remembered: A Record of Twentieth-Century Slave Narratives*. Chapel Hill, 1979.
Ezell, John Samuel. *The South Since 1865*. New York, 1963.
Fackler, Calvin Morgan. *A Chronicle of the Old First*. Louisville, Ky., 1946.
Federal Writers Project, Works Progress Administration. *Military History of Kentucky*. Frankfort, Ky., 1939.
Fields, Barbara Jeanne. *Slavery and Freedom on the Middle Ground: Maryland during the Nineteenth Century*. New Haven, 1985.
Fogel, Robert William, and Stanley L. Engerman. *Time on the Cross: The Economics of American Negro Slavery*. 2 vols. Boston, 1974.
Foner, Philip S. *Organized Labor and the Black Worker, 1619-1973*. New York, 1974.
Ford, Kate, and Henry A. Ford. *History of the Ohio Falls Cities and their Counties, with Illustrations and Biographical Sketches*. 2 vols. Cleveland, 1882.
Fox, Early Lee. *The American Colonization Society, 1817-1840*. Baltimore, 1919.
Frazier, E. Franklin. *The Negro Church in America*. New York, 1963.
Frederickson, George M. *The Black Image in the White Mind: The Debate on Afro-American Character and Destiny, 1817-1914*. New York, 1971.
Gara, Larry. *The Liberty Line: The Legend of the Underground Railroad*. Lexington, Ky., 1961.
Genovese, Eugene D. *Roll, Jordan, Roll: The World The Slaves Made*.

New York, 1972.
Gibson, J.W., and W.H. Crogman. *The Colored American: From Slavery to Honorable Citizenship.* Atlanta, Ga., 1906.
Gillard, John T. *The Catholic Church and the American Negro . . .* New York, 1968; orig. pub. 1929.
―――――. *Colored Catholics in the United States . . .* Baltimore, 1941.
Grimshaw, W.H. *Official History of Freemasonry Among the Colored People of North America.* New York, 1969; orig. pub. 1903.
Gutman, Herbert. *The Black Family in Slavery and Freedom, 1750-1925.* New York, 1976.
Hamilton, Thomas. *Men and Manners in America.* New York, 1968; orig. pub. 1833.
Hamlet, Barksdale. *History of Education in Kentucky.* Frankfort, Ky., 1914.
Harrison, Lowell H. *The Civil War in Kentucky.* Lexington, Ky., 1975.
―――――. *The Antislavery Movement in Kentucky.* Lexington, Ky., 1978.
―――――. *John Breckinridge: Jeffersonian Republican.* Louisville, Ky., 1969.
Hayes, William Foster. *Sixty Years of Owensboro, 1883-1943.* Owensboro, Ky., 1946.
Hedrick, Charles Embury. *Social and Economic Aspects of Slavery in the Transmontane Prior to 1850.* Nashville, Tenn., 1927.
Herskovits, Melville J. *The Myth of the Negro Past.* Boston, 1958; orig. pub. 1941.
History Committee. *A History of First Baptist Church Somerset, Kentucky, 1799 to 1974.* Wolf City, Texas, 1974.
Hodge, William J. *Historical Sketch of the Fifth Street Baptist Church.* Louisville, 1969.
Hopkins, James F. *A History of the Hemp Industry in Kentucky.* Lexington, Ky., 1951.
―――――  et al., eds. *The Papers of Henry Clay.* 11 vols. Lexington, Ky., 1959-92.
Howard, Victor B. *Black Liberation in Kentucky: Emancipation and Freedom, 1862-1884.* Lexington, Ky., 1983.
Howington, Arthur F. *What Sayeth The Law: The Treatment of Slaves and Free Blacks in the State and Local Courts of Tennessee.* New York and London, 1986.
Hundley, D.R. *Social Relations in Our Southern States.* New York, 1860.
Ireland, Robert M. *The County Courts in Antebellum Kentucky.* Lexington, Ky., 1972.
Jackson, Bruce, ed. *The Negro and His Folklore in Nineteenth-Century Periodicals.* Austin, Texas, 1967.
Jepson, J.J. *History of the First Baptist Church of Sulphur Spring and Sulphur Spring Missionary Baptist Church.* Frankfort, Ky., 1938.
Jewell, Malcolm E., and Everett W. Cunningham. *Kentucky Politics.* Lexington, Ky., 1968.
Jillson, Willard Rouse. *Kentucky Hemp . . .* Versailles, Ky., 1942.
Johnson, E. Polk. *A History of Kentucky and Kentuckians: The Leaders and Representative Men in Commerce, Industry and Modern Activities.* 3 vols. Chicago and New York, 1912.

Johnson, L.F. *History of Franklin County, Ky.* Frankfort, Ky., 1912.
Johnston, J. Stoddard, ed. *Memorial History of Louisville From Its First Settlement to the Year 1896.* 2 vols. Chicago, 1896.
Jones, Jacqueline. *Soldiers of Light and Love: Northern Teachers and Georgia Blacks, 1865-1873.* Chapel Hill, N.C., 1980.
Jones, Paul W.L. *A History of the Kentucky Normal and Industrial Institute.* Lexington, Ky., 1912.
Jordan, Lewis G. *Negro Baptist History U.S.A., 1750-1930.* Nashville, Tenn., 1930.
Jordan, Winthrop D. *White Over Black: American Attitudes Toward the Negro, 1550-1812.* Chapel Hill, N.C., 1968.
Joyner, Charles. *Down by the Riverside: A South Carolina Slave Community.* Urbana and Chicago, 1984.
Katzman, David M. *Seven Days A Week: Women and Domestic Service in Industrializing America.* New York, 1978.
Kelly, Alfred H., and Winfred A. Harbison. *The American Constitution: Its Origins and Development.* New York, 1970.
*Kentucky's Black Heritage . . .* Frankfort, Ky., 1971.
Kimbrough, B.T. *The History of the Walnut Street Baptist Church Louisville, Kentucky.* Louisville, 1949.
Klotter, James C. *The Breckinridges of Kentucky, 1760-1981.* Lexington, Ky., 1986.
Levine, Lawrence E. *Black Culture and Black Consciousness: Afro-American Folk Thought from Slavery to Freedom.* New York, 1977.
Lewis, Alvin Fayette. *History of Higher Education in Kentucky.* Washington, D.C., 1899.
Litwack, Leon F. *Been in the Storm So Long: The Aftermath of Slavery.* New York, 1979.
Lucas, Oliver, ed. *General Ordinances of the City of Louisville . . .* Louisville, Ky., 1889.
Masters, Frank M. *A History of Baptists in Kentucky.* Louisville, Ky., 1953.
Mbiti, John S. *Introduction to African Religion.* New York, 1975.
McDonnold, B.W. *History of the Cumberland Presbyterian Church.* Nashville, Tenn., 1899.
McDougle, Ivan E. *Slavery in Kentucky, 1792-1865.* Lancaster, Pa., 1918.
McDowell, Robert Emmett. *City of Conflict: Louisville in the Civil War, 1861-1865.* Louisville, Ky., 1962.
McFarlan, Arthur C. *Geology of Kentucky.* Lexington, 1943.
McGann, Agnes Geraldine. *Mother Columba Carroll: Sister of Charity of Nazareth, 1810-1878.* Nazareth, Ky., 1973.
McKee, Lewis W., and Lydia K. Bond. *A History of Anderson County.* Frankfort, Ky., 1936.
McLauren, Melton A. *The Knights of Labor in the South.* Westport, Conn., 1978.
McPherson, James M. *Ordeal By Fire.* New York, 1982.
McVey, Frank L. *The Gates Open Slowly: A History of Education in Kentucky.* Lexington, Ky., 1949.

Meacham, Charles Mayfield. *A History of Christian County Kentucky from Oxcart to Airplane.* Nashville, Tenn., 1930.

Meier, August. *Negro Thought in America, 1880-1915: Racial Ideologies in the Age of Booker T. Washington.* Ann Arbor, Mich., 1963.

Merrill, Boynton, Jr. *Jefferson's Nephews: A Frontier Tragedy.* 2d ed. Lexington, Ky., 1987.

Miles, John L., Jr., ed. *Calvary Baptist Church: A Century and Forty, 1829-1969.* Louisville, Ky., 1969.

Minogue, Anna C. *Loretto: Annals of the Century.* New York, 1912.

———. *Pages from a Hundred Years of Dominican History.* Cincinnati, 1921.

Mohr, Clarence L. *On the Threshold of Freedom: Masters and Slaves in Civil War Georgia.* Athens, Ga., 1986.

Mooney, Chase C. *Slavery in Tennessee.* Bloomington, Ind., 1957.

Morehouse, H. Lyman, ed. *Baptist Home Missions in North America . . .* New York, 1883.

Morris, Robert C. *Reading, Riting, and Reconstruction: The Education of Freedmen in the South, 1861-1870.* Chicago, 1976.

Morrison, Toni. *Beloved: A Novel.* New York, 1987.

Neal, Julia. *By Their Fruits: The Story of Shakerism in South Union, Kentucky.* Chapel Hill, N.C., 1947.

*94th Anniversary Program, Oct. 17-21, 1945.* Lexington, Ky., [1945].

Novak, Daniel A. *The Wheel of Servitude: Black Forced Labor after Slavery.* Lexington, Ky., 1978.

*The National Cyclopedia of The Colored Race.* Montgomery, Ala., 1919.

Olmsted, Frederick Law. *Cotton Kingdom . . .* Edited by Arthur M. Schlesinger. New York, 1953.

Osthaus, Carl R. *Freedmen, Philanthropy, and Fraud: A History of the Freedman's Savings Bank.* Urbana, Ill., 1976.

Owens, Leslie Howard. *This Species of Property: Slave Life and Culture in the Old South.* New York, 1976.

Painter, Nell Irvin. *Exodusters: Black Migration to Kansas after Reconstruction.* New York, 1977.

Paris, Peter J. *Social Teaching of the Black Churches.* Philadelphia, 1985.

Parker, Thomas H. *History of the 51st Regiment . . .* Philadelphia, 1869.

Parrish, C.H., ed. *Golden Jubilee of the General Association of Colored Baptists in Kentucky . . .* Louisville, Ky., 1915.

Patterson, Caleb Perry. *Negro in Tennessee.* Austin, Texas, 1922.

Pease, William H., and Jane H. Pease. *Black Utopia: Negro Communal Experiments in America.* Madison, Wisc., 1963.

Peck, Elisabeth. *Berea's First Century, 1855-1955.* Lexington, Ky., 1955.

Pelt, Owen D., and Ralph Lee Smith. *The Story of the National Baptists.* New York, 1960.

Penn, I. Garland. *The Afro-American Press, And Its Editors.* Springfield, Mass., 1891.

Perrin, William Henry, ed. *County of Christian, Kentucky: Historical and Biographical.* Chicago and Louisville, Ky., 1884.

———. *History of Bourbon, Scott, Harrison and Nicholas*

Counties, Kentucky . . . Chicago, 1882.
Peter, Robert. *History of Fayette County* . . . Edited by W. Henry Perrin. Chicago, 1882.
Peterson, Robert. *Only the Ball was White.* Englewood Cliffs, N.J., 1970.
Phillips, Charles Henry. *From the Farm to the Bishopric: An Autobiography.* Nashville, Tenn., 1932.
Phillips, Ulrich Bonnell. *Life and Labor in the Old South.* New York, 1929.
Pierce, Paul Skeels. *The Freedmen's Bureau: A Chapter in the History of Reconstruction.* Iowa City, Iowa, 1904.
Porter, Kirk Harold. *A History of Suffrage in the United States.* Chicago, 1918.
Posey, Walter Brownlow. *Frontier Mission: A History of Religion West of the Southern Appalachians to 1861.* Lexington, Ky., 1966.
Postell, William Dosite. *The Health of Slaves on Southern Plantations.* Gloucester, Mass., 1970; orig. pub. 1951.
Quarles, Benjamin. *The Negro in the Civil War.* New York, 1968; orig. pub. 1953.
Raboteau, Albert J. *Slave Religion: The "Invisible Institution" in the Antebellum South.* New York, 1978.
Ramage, James A. *Rebel Raider: The Life of General John Hunt Morgan.* Lexington, Ky., 1986.
Ranck, George W. *Boonesborough* . . . Louisville, Ky., 1901.
_____. *"The Traveling Church": An Account of the Baptist Exodus from Virginia* . . . Louisville, Ky., 1910.
Rice, Otis K. *Frontier Kentucky.* Lexington, Ky., 1975.
Richards, J.A. *A History of Bath County, Kentucky.* Yuma, Arizona, 1961.
Richardson, Harry V. *Dark Salvation: The Story of Methodism as It Developed Among Blacks in America.* Garden City, N.Y., 1976.
Richings, G.F. *Evidence of Progress among Colored People.* Philadelphia, 1899.
Ridenour, George L. *Early Times in Meade County Kentucky.* Louisville, Ky., 1929.
Riley, Walter H. *Forty Years in the Lap of Methodism: History of Lexington Conference of Methodist Episcopal Church.* Louisville, Ky., 1915.
Rone, Wendell H., Sr. *An Historical Atlas of Kentucky and Her Counties.* Owensboro, Ky., 1965.
Rule, Lucien V. *The Light Bearers.* Louisville, 1926.
Russell, Harvey C. *The Kentucky Negro Educational Association, 1877-1946.* Norfolk, Va., 1946.
Savitt, Todd L. *Medicine and Slavery: The Diseases and Health Care of Blacks in Antebellum Virginia.* Urbana, Ill., 1978.
Scott, Mingo, Jr. *History of the State Street Baptist Church, 1883-1973.* Bowling Green, Ky., [1973].
Sears, Richard D. *The Day of Small Things: Abolitionism in the Midst of Slavery, Berea, Kentucky, 1854-1864.* New York, 1986.
_____. *"A Practical Recognition of the Brotherhood of Man": John G. Fee and the Camp Nelson Experience.* Berea, Ky., 1986.
Sernett, Milton C. *Black Religion and American Evangelicalism* . . . Metuchen, N.J., 1975.

Siebert, Wilbur H. *The Underground Railroad from Slavery to Freedom.* New York, 1967; orig. pub. 1898.
Silverman, Jason H. *Unwelcome Guests: Canada West's Response to American Fugitive Slaves, 1800-1865.* Millwood, N.Y., 1985.
Singer, J.W., ed. *The Negro Members of the Stamping Ground Baptist Church.* Stamping Ground, Ky., 1967.
Smith, John David, and William Cooper, Jr., eds. *Window on the War: Frances Dallam Peter's Lexington Civil War Diary.* Lexington, Ky., 1976.
Sobel, Mechal. *"Trablin' On": The Slave Journey to an Afro-Baptist Faith.* Westport, Conn., 1979.
Southern, Eileen. *The Music of Black Americans.* New York, 1971.
Spalding, Martin J. *Sketches of Early Catholic Missions of Kentucky . . .* New York, 1972; orig. pub. 1844.
Spencer, J.H. *History of Kentucky Baptists.* 2 vols. Cincinnati, 1885.
Stampp, Kenneth M. *The Peculiar Institution: Slavery in the Ante-Bellum South.* New York, 1956.
Starling, E.L. *History of Henderson and Henderson County, Ky.* Henderson Ky., 1887.
Starobin, Robert S. *Industrial Slavery in the Old South.* New York, 1970.
Stephenson, Gilbert Thomas. *Race Distinctions in American Law.* New York, 1910.
Stowe, Harriet Beecher. *Uncle Tom's Cabin; or, Life Among the Lowly.* 2 vols. Boston 1852.
Strattan, Oliver H., ed. *That Business of Mine . . .* Louisville, Ky., 1879.
Sweet, William Warren. *Religion on the American Frontier: The Baptists, 1783-1830.* New York, 1931.
Swint, Henry Lee. *The Northern Teacher in the South, 1862-1870.* New York, 1967.
Tadman, Michael. *Speculators and Slaves: Masters, Traders, and Slaves in the Old South.* Madison, Wisc., 1989.
Tapp, Hambleton, and James C. Klotter. *Kentucky: Decades of Discord, 1865-1900.* Frankfort, Ky., 1977.
Taylor, John. *A History of Ten Baptist Churches . . .* Bloomfield, Ky., 1827.
Taylor, Orville W. *Negro Slavery in Arkansas.* Durham, N.C., 1958.
Tinsley, Harry D. *History of No Creek, Ohio County, Kentucky; with a Genealogy and Biographical Section.* Frankfort, Ky., 1953.
Townsend, W.H. *Lincoln and His Wife's Home Town.* Indianapolis, Ind., 1929.
Underwood, E.E. *A Brief History of the Colored Churches of Frankfort, Kentucky.* Frankfort, Ky., 1906.
Wade, Richard C. *The Urban Frontier: The Rise of Western Cities, 1790-1830.* Cambridge, Mass., 1959.
Walker, Juliet E.K. *Free Frank: A Black Pioneer on the Antebellum Frontier.* Lexington, Ky., 1983.
Webb, Ross A. *Benjamin Helm Bristow: Border State Politician.* Lexington, Ky., 1969.
_____. *Kentucky in the Reconstruction Era.* Lexington, Ky., 1979.
Webber, Thomas L. *Deep Like the Rivers: Education in the Slave Quarter*

*Community, 1831-1865.* New York, 1978.
Wells, J.W. *History of Cumberland County.* Louisville, Ky., 1947.
Wharton, Vernon Lane. *The Negro in Mississippi, 1865-1890.* New York, 1965; orig. pub. 1947.
Wheeler, Jacob D. *A Practical Treatise on the Law of Slavery.* New York, 1968; orig. pub. 1837.
White, Deborah Gray. *Ar'n't I A Woman?: Female Slaves in the Plantation South.* New York, 1985.
Wiggins, William H., Jr. *O Freedom!: Afro-American Emancipation Celebrations.* Knoxville, Tenn., 1988.
Williams, George W. *History of the Negro Race in America . . .* 2 vols. New York, 1882.
Williams, Lawrence H. *Black Education in Kentucky, 1879-1930: The History of Simmons University.* Lewiston, Me., 1987.
Williams, Sherley Anne. *Dessa Rose.* New York, 1986.
Williamson, Joel. *After Slavery . . .* Chapel Hill, N.C., 1965.
Wilmore, Gayraud S. *Black Religion and Black Radicalism.* New York, 1972.
Wilson, Calvin D. *Negroes Who Owned Slaves.* [New York], 1912.
Wilson, Joseph T. *The Black Phalanx: A History of the Negro Soldiers of the United States in the Wars of 1775-1812, 1861-'65.* Hartford, Conn., 1888.
Winks, Robin W. *The Blacks in Canada: A History.* New Haven, Conn., 1971.
Wood, Norman B. *The White Side of A Black Subject . . .* Cincinnati, 1894.
Woodson, Carter G., ed. *Free Negro Owners of Slaves in the United States in 1830 . . .* Washington, D.C., 1924.
Wright, Carroll D. *The History and Growth of the United States Census . . .* Washington, D.C., 1900.
Wright, George C. *Life Behind A Veil: Blacks in Louisville, Kentucky, 1865-1930.* Baton Rouge, 1985.
_____. *Racial Violence in Kentucky 1865-1940: Lynchings, Mob Rule, and "Legal Lynchings."* Baton Rouge and London, 1990.
Wright, Ray H., and Elsie S. Wright. *History of Cox's Creek Baptist Church.* Cox's Creek, Ky., 1935.
Young, Bennett H., and S.M. Duncan. *A History of Jessamine County, From Its Earliest Settlement to 1898.* Louisville, Ky., 1898.

**Articles**
Allen, Jeffrey Brooke. "Were Southern White Critics of Slavery Racist? Kentucky and the Upper South, 1794-1824." *JSH* 44 (1978): 169-90.
Bailey, David Thomas. "A Divided Prism: Two Sources of Black Testimony on Slavery." *JSH* 46 (1980): 381-404.
Barnhart, John D. "Frontiersmen and Planters in the Formation of Kentucky." *JSH* 7 (1941): 19-36.
Berlin, Ira. "The Structure of the Free Negro Caste in the Antebellum United States." In *The Southern Common People: Studies in Nineteenth-Century Social History,* edited by Edward Magdol and Jon L. Wakelyn. Westport, Conn., 1980.

Blassingame, John W. "The Recruitment of Colored Troops in Kentucky, Maryland and Missouri, 1863-1865." *Historian* 29 (1967): 533-45.
*Bulletin of the Kentucky Historical Society* 14 (August 1988).
Burton, Orville Vernon. "Hiring Out." In *Dictionary of Afro-American Slavery*, edited by Randall M. Miller and John David Smith. New York, 1988.
Cade, John B. "Out of the Mouths of Ex-Slaves." *JNH* 20 (1935): 294-337.
Calderhead, William. "How Extensive Was the Border State Slave Trade? A New Look." *Civil War History* 18 (1972): 42-55.
―――――. "The Role of the Professional Slave Trader in a Slave Economy: Austin Woolfolk, A Case Study." *Civil War History* 23 (1977): 195-211.
Clark, Thomas D. "The Slave Trade Between Kentucky and the Cotton Kingdom." *MVHR* 21 (1934): 331-42.
Cobb, William Montague. "Henry Fitzbutler." *Journal of the National Medical Association* 44 (1952): 403-7.
Coleman, J. Winston, Jr. "Delia Webster and Calvin Fairbank, Underground Railroad Agents." *FCHQ* 17 (1843): 129-41.
―――――. "Lexington's Slave Dealers and Their Southern Trade." *FCHQ* 12 (1938): 1-23.
Conrad, Alfred H., and John R. Meyer. "The Economics of Slavery in the Ante-Bellum South." *The Journal of Political Economics* 66 (1958): 95-130.
Dew, Charles B. "Black Ironworkers and the Slave Insurrection Panic of 1856." *JSH* 41 (1975): 321-39.
Dorris, J.T., ed. "Early History of Madison County." *Register* 30 (1932): 119-61.
Eaton, Clement. "Slave Hiring in the Upper South." *MVHR* 46 (1960): 663-78.
Flanigan, Daniel J. "Criminal Procedure in Slave Trials in the Antebellum South." *JSH* 40 (1974): 537-64.
Foster, Gaines M. "The Limitations of Federal Health Care for Freedmen, 1862-1868." *JSH* 48 (1982): 349-72.
Franklin, John Hope. "Public Welfare in the South During the Reconstruction Era, 1865-80." *Social Service Review* 44 (1970): 379-92.
Garvin, Roy. "Benjamin, or 'Pap' Singleton and His Followers." *JNH* 33 (1948): 7-23.
Gillette, William. "Anatomy of a Failure: Federal Enforcement of the Right to Vote in the Border States during Reconstruction." In *Radicalism, Racism and Party Realignment: The Border States during Reconstruction*, edited by Richard O. Curry. Baltimore, 1969.
Green, David C., comp. "1860 Madison County, Kentucky Mortality Records." *Heritage Highlights* 2 (Spring 1990): [6-7].
Hanawalt, Leslie L. "Henry Fitzbutler: Detroit's First Black Medical Student." *Detroit in Perspective: A Journal of Regional History* 1 (1973): 126-40.
Harrison, Lowell H. "The Folklore of Some Kentucky Slaves." *Kentucky Folklore Record* 17 (1971): 25-30.
―――――, ed. "John Breckinridge's Bluegrass Plantation, Agreement to Operate, 1806." *FCHQ* 31 (1957): 104-14.

———. "John Breckinridge of Kentucky: Planter, Speculator, and Businessman." *FCHQ* 34 (1960): 205-27.
Hite, Roger W. "Voice of the Fugitive: Henry Bibb and Ante-bellum Black Separatism." *Journal of Black Studies* 4 (1974): 269-84.
Howard, Victor B. "The Black Testimony Controversy in Kentucky 1866-1872." *JNH* 58 (1973): 140-65.
———. "The Breckinridge Family and the Negro Testimony Controversy in Kentucky, 1866-1872." *FCHQ* 49 (1975): 37-56.
———. "Negro Politics and the Suffrage Question in Kentucky, 1866-1872." *Register* 72 (1974): 111-33.
———. "The Struggle for Equal Education in Kentucky, 1866-1884." *Journal of Negro Education* 46 (1977): 305-28.
Hughes, Sarah S. "Slaves for Hire: The Allocation of Black Labor in Elizabeth City County, Virginia, 1782-1810." *William and Mary Quarterly* 3rd ser., 35 (1978): 260-86.
Jackson, Blyden. "Albery Allson Whitman (1851-1901)." In *Fifty Southern Writers Before 1900*, edited by Robert Bain and Joseph M. Flora. Westport, Conn., 1987.
Jordan, David Morris, Sr. "The Lexington Conference and Negro Migration." Mimeograph. Louisville Conference Collection, Kentucky Wesleyan College, Owensboro, Ky.
Kellogg, John. "The Evolution of Black Residential Areas in Lexington, Kentucky, 1865-1887." *JSH* 47 (1982): 21-52.
Kimball, Philip Clyde. "Freedom's Harvest: Freedmen's Schools in Kentucky After the Civil War." *FCHQ* 54 (1980): 272-88.
Kiple, Kenneth F., and Virginia H. Kiple. "Black Tongue and Black Men: Pellagra and Slavery in the Antebellum South." *JSH* 43 (1977): 411-28.
———. "Slave Child Mortality: Some Nutritional Answers to A Perennial Puzzle." *Journal of Social History* 10 (1977): 284-309.
Klotter, James C. "The Black South and White Appalachia." *Journal of American History* 66 (1980): 832-49.
———. "Slavery in Louisville, Ky." In *Dictionary of Afro-American Slavery*, edited by Randall M. Miller and John David Smith. New York, 1988.
Kousser, J. Morgan. "Making Separate Equal: Integration of Black and White School Funds in Kentucky." *Journal of Interdisciplinary History* 10 (1980): 399-428.
Lammermeier, Paul J. "The Urban Black Family of the Nineteenth Century: A Study of Black Family Structure in the Ohio Valley, 1850-1880." *Journal of Marriage and The Family* 35 (1973): 440-56.
Landon, Fred. "Henry Bibb, A Colonizer." *JNH* 5 (1920): 337-47.
Legan, Marshall S. "Disease and the Freedmen in Mississippi During Reconstruction." *Journal of the History of Medicine and Allied Sciences* 28 (1973): 257-67.
Lerner, Gerda. "Early Community Work of Black Club Women." *JNH* 59 (1974): 158-67.
Mathias, Frank Furlong. "Slave Days." In *History of Nicholas County*, edited by Joan Weissinger Conley. Carlisle, Ky., 1975.

Margo, Robert A., and Richard H. Steckel. "The Heights of American Slaves: New Evidence on Slave Nutrition and Health." *Social Science History* 6 (1982): 516-38.
Messmer, Charles. "Louisville on the Eve of the Civil War." *FCHQ* 50 (1976): 249-89.
Morris, Richard B. "Measure of Bondage in the Slave States." *MVHR* 41 (1954): 219-40.
Nash, A.E. Keir. "Slave Trials." In *Dictionary of Afro-American Slavery*, edited by Randall M. Miller and John David Smith. New York, 1988.
Nelson, Paul David. "Experiment in Interracial Education at Berea College, 1858-1908." *JNH* 59 (1974): 13-37.
Norris, Marjorie. "An Early Instance of Nonviolence: The Louisville Demonstrations of 1870-71." *JSH* 32 (1966): 487-504.
Palmer, Edward M. "Negro Secret Societies." *Social Forces* 23 (1944): 207-12.
Post, Edward M. "Kentucky Law Concerning Emancipation or Freedom of Slaves." *FCHQ* 59 (1985): 344-67.
Rabinowitz, Howard N. "From Exclusion to Segregation: Health and Welfare Services for Southern Blacks, 1865-1890." *Social Services Review* 48 (1974): 327-54.
Raphael, Alan. "Health and Social Welfare of Kentucky Black People, 1865-1870." *Societas: A Review of Social History* 2 (1972): 143-578.
Schwendemann, Glen. "Nicodemus: Negro Haven on the Solomon." *Kansas Historical Quarterly* 34 (1968): 10-31.
Sears, Richard. "John G. Fee, Camp Nelson, and Kentucky Blacks, 1864-1865." *Register* 85 (1987): 29-45.
Smith, John David. "Kentucky Civil War Recruits: A Medical Profile." *Medical History* 24 (1980): 185-96.
―――. "The Recruitment of Negro Soldiers in Kentucky, 1863-1865." *Register* 72 (1974): 364-90.
Smith, Peter C., and Karl B. Raitz. "Negro Hamlets and Agricultural Estates in Kentucky's Inner Bluegrass." *Geographical Review* 64 (1974): 217-34.
Snorgrass, J. William. "America's Ten Oldest Black Newspapers." *Negro History Bulletin* 46 (1978): 11-14.
Stewart, Charles. "My Life As A Slave." *Harper's New Monthly Magazine* 69 (1884): 730-38.
Sutch, Richard. "The Breeding of Slaves for Sale and the Westward Expansion of Slavery, 1850-1860." In *Race and Slavery in the Western Hemisphere: Quantitative Studies*, edited by Stanley L. Engerman and Eugene D. Genovese. Princeton, N.J., 1975.
―――. "The Care and Feeding of Slaves." In *Reckoning with Slavery: A Critical Study in the Quantitative History of American Negro Slavery*, edited by Paul A. David et al. New York, 1976.
Tadman, Michael. "Slave Trading in the Ante-Bellum South: An Estimate of the Extent of the Inter-regional Slave Trade." *Journal of American Studies* 13 (1979): 195-220.
Thomas, Herbert A., Jr. "Victims of Circumstance: Negroes in a Southern

Town, 1865-1880." *Register* 71 (1973): 252-71.
Timberlake, C.L. "The Early Struggle for Education of Blacks in the Commonwealth of Kentucky." *Register* 71 (1973): 225-52.
"To Stop A School." *Green County Review* 2 (1979): 59.
Toppin, Edgar A. "Humbly They Served: The Black Brigade in the Defense of Cincinnati." *JNH* 47 (1963): 75-97.
Turner, Wallace B. "Kentucky Slavery in the Last Ante Bellum Decade." *Register* 58 (1960): 291-307.
Venable, W.H. "Down South Before the War: Record of a Ramble to New Orleans in 1858." *Ohio Archaeological and Historical Quarterly* 2 (1889): 461-84.
Volpe, Vernon L. "Squirrel Hunting for the Union: The Defense of Cincinnati in 1862." *CWH* 33 (1987): 242-55.
Walker, Juliet E.K. "The Legal Status of Free Blacks in Early Kentucky, 1792-1825." *FCHQ* 57 (1983): 382-95.
Wax, Darold D. "Robert Ball Anderson, A Kentucky Slave, 1843-1864." *Register* 81 (1983): 255-73.
Webb, Ross A. "Kentucky: 'Pariah Among the Elect.' " In *Radicalism, and Party Realignment: The Border States during Reconstruction*, edited by Richard O. Curry. Baltimore, 1969.
_____. " 'The Past Is Never Dead, It's Not Even Past': Benjamin P. Runkle and the Freedmen's Bureau in Kentucky, 1866-1870." *Register* 84 (1986): 343-60.
Wilson, George D. "A Century of Negro Education in Louisville, Kentucky." Typescript report. Works Progress Administration. Louisville, Ky., n.d.
Wright, George C. "William Henry Steward: Moderate Approach to Black Leadership." In *Black Leaders of the Nineteenth Century*, edited by Leon Litwack and August Meier. Urbana and Chicago, 1988.
Yanuck, Julius. "The Garner Fugitive Slave Case." *MVHR* 40 (1953): 47-66.

**Unpublished Works**
Bennett, Charles Raymond. "All Things To All People: The American Colonization Society in Kentucky, 1829-1860." Ph.D. diss., University of Kentucky, 1980.
Byrd, Pratt. "The Kentucky Frontier in 1792: Slavery, Land Holding and the State Constitution." M.A. thesis, University of Wisconsin, 1947.
Carlesimo, Peter Carlesimo. "The Refugee Home Society: Its Origin, Operation and Results, 1851-1876." M.A. thesis, University of Windsor, Canada, 1973.
Conner, Eloise. "The Slave Market in Lexington, Kentucky, 1850-1860." M.A. thesis, University of Kentucky, 1931.
Cook, Michael Anthony. "The Health of Blacks During Reconstruction, 1862-1870." Ph.D. diss., University of Maryland, 1983.
Crawford, Robert G. "A History of the Kentucky Penitentiary System." Ph.D. diss., University of Kentucky, 1955.

De Boer, Clara Merritt. "The Role of Afro-Americans in the Origin and Work of the American Missionary Association: 1839-1877." Ph.D. diss., Rutgers University, 1973.

Donovan, Mary Sudman. "Kentucky Law Regarding The Negro, 1865-1877." M.A. thesis, University of Louisville, 1967.

Drake, Richard B. "The American Missionary Association." Ph.D. diss., Emory University, 1966.

Finch, Cloyd Herbert, Jr. "Organized Labor in Louisville, Kentucky, 1880-1914." Ph.D. diss., University of Kentucky, 1965.

Fouse, William Henry. "Educational History of the Negroes of Lexington, Kentucky," M.A. thesis, University of Cincinnati, 1937.

Hedrick, Charles E. "Negro Slavery in Kentucky Before 1850." M.A. thesis, University of Chicago, 1915.

King, Cyrus Baldwin. "Ante-bellum Free Negroes as Race Leaders in Kentucky and Virginia during Reconstruction." M.A. thesis, University of Kentucky, 1949.

O'Brien, Mary L. "Slavery in Louisville During the Antebellum Period: 1820-1860. A Study of the Effects of Urbanization on the Institution of Slavery as it Existed in Louisville, Kentucky." M.A. thesis, University of Louisville, 1979.

Owen, Thomas Lewis. "The Formative Years of Kentucky's Republican Party, 1864-1871." Ph.D. diss., University of Kentucky, 1981.

Pride, Armistead Scott. "A Register and History of Negro Newspapers in the United States: 1827-1950." Ph.D. diss., Northwestern University, 1950.

Stafford, Hanford Dozier. "Slavery in a Border City: Louisville, 1790-1860." Ph.D. diss., University of Kentucky, 1982.

Strother, William Bruce. "Negro Culture in Lexington, Kentucky." M.A. thesis, University of Kentucky, 1939.

Troutman, Richard L. "The Social and Economic Structure of Kentucky Agriculture, 1850-1860." Ph.D. diss., University of Kentucky, 1958.

Turner, Wallace B. "Kentucky In A Decade of Change, 1850-1860." Ph.D., diss., University of Kentucky, 1954.

Venable, Thomas Calvin. "A History of Negro Education in Kentucky." Ph.D. diss., George Peabody College For Teachers, 1953.

Wickenden, Homer E. "History of the Churches of Louisville with Special Reference to Slavery." M.A. thesis, University of Louisville, 1921.

# INDEX

Given names which appear without a surname refer to slaves or free persons who had no surname or for whom none could be found.

Aaron, 20
Aberdeen, Ohio, 77
Abram, 158
Adair County, Ky., 156, 165
Adam, xi
Adams, Cyrus, 320
Adams, E.P., 214
Adams, Henry, 123-26, 135, 142, 164, 211-12, 219, 237, 320
Adams, John, 320
Adams, Lottie, 246-47
Adams, Susie, 246
Adams, Willis, 279
Adcock, Henry, 172
Add, 54
Advisory Board, Lexington, Kentucky, 248
African (Colored) Baptist Church, Louisville. *See* Fifth Street Baptist Church
African Baptist Church, Henderson, 129
African Methodist Episcopal Church: Lexington, 244; Louisville, 247; mentioned, 223
African Methodist Episcopal Zion Church, Louisville, 128, 223-24
Africanisms, 131-33
Alabama, 23, 207, 219
Alexander, Edward, 278
Alexander, Elias, 271
Alexander, Henry, 112
Alfred, 168
Allen, 31, 105
Allen, Dudley, 281
Allen, G.T., 98
Allensville, Ky., 155, 244

Allensworth, Allen, 11, 20, 221, 239, 245
Allensworth, James L., 320-21
Allensworth, Levi, 20
Allensworth, Phyllis, 20
Allison, Peter, 318
American Baptist Home Missionary Society, 218-19, 221
*American Baptist*, 212, 320
American Missionary Association, 164, 221, 226-28, 230-31, 237, 238-41, 246, 250, 257, 265-66, 286-87, 315
American National Baptist Convention, 217
American Tract Society, 236
Amhurstburgh, Canada, 73
Anchorage, Ky., 300
Anderson, Agga, 24
Anderson, Bill, 24
Anderson, E.J., 214
Anderson, Elijah, 68
Anderson, Emma, 24
Anderson, Mattie E., 249
Anderson, Robert, 10, 13-14, 24, 34-35, 160
Anderson, Silva, 24
Anderson, Wash, 127
Anderson, William, 24, 60
Anderson County, Ky., 165
Anthony, 27
Appalachian Mountains, 1
Appomattox Court House, Virginia, 178, 214
Apprenticeships. *See* Slave children and Employment, post-Civil War
Arch, 155
Ariel Academy (Ariel Normal School),

Camp Nelson, 241, 250, 266
Aristides (horse), 282
Arkansas, 49
Arteburn brothers, 90
Asbury Chapel Methodist Church (formerly, Fourth Street Methodist), Louisville, 92, 128, 136, 142, 144, 183, 223, 225, 237, 300
Asbury Methodist Episcopal Church, Lexington, 123, 223, 239
"Ashland," 5
Athens, Ky., 35, 293
Atkins, Reuben, 191
Atwell, Joseph S., 205, 225, 238
Auburn, Ky., 191
Aunt Rachel, 69
Ayers, Malcolm, 183, 281

Baker, Margaret, 206
Ballard, Bland, 238
Ballard County, Ky., xxi, 306
Balls, Joseph, 194
Baltimore, Maryland, 128, 142
Bancroft, Frederic, 20
Banton, Betsy, 22
Baptist Normal and Theological Institute, Louisville, 213-14, 216, 287-88
Baptist Union Theological Seminary, Chicago, 219
Baptist Women's Educational Convention, 218
Barber's Union, 286
Bardstown, Ky., 24, 35, 116, 224, 249, 288
Barren County, Ky., xix, 5, 49
Barren River, 9, 173
Barrett, Captain, 300
Barrett, David, 44, 63
Barry, A., 213
Barry, H.W., 160
Bascom, Sam, 293
Bath County, Ky., xvii, 8, 60, 194, 293
Battle of New Orleans, 48
Batts, Alexander, 242
Bear Grass Baptist Church, Louisville, 32, 220
Bedford, Ky., 65, 81
Beech Fork River, 3, 152
Bell, Andrew, 323
Belle, Arian, 90
Belle, Melissa, 90
Ben-Brush (horse), 281
Benevolent societies. *See* individual societies

Benevolent Society of Winchester, 302
Berea College: and teacher preparation, 254, 258; black students admitted to, 251; racial atmosphere at, 253; supports black political rights, 302; mentioned, 143, 212-13, 235, 250, 252, 259-60, 262-63, 273, 295, 320-21
Berea Literary Institute, 235, 250-51
Berea, Ky., 143, 250, 274, 302
Berry, M.P., 214
Betsy, 27
Bibb, A.J., 246
Bibb, George, 119
Bibb, Henry, 7, 16-18, 20, 23, 51, 62, 65, 80-82, 86, 92, 97, 99, 131, 142, 244
Bibb, Lewis, 44
Bibb, Malinda, 18, 81, 86
Bibb, Mary Frances, 81-82
Big Sandy River, 198
Big Springs military engagement, Breckinridge County, Ky., 172-73
Bill, 50
Birney, James G., 54
Black Ann, 27
Black Brigade, Cincinnati, Ohio, 151
Black John, 9, 16
Black Mary, 40
Black Republican party. *See* Republican party
Black, I.E., 318
Blackfish, xi, xii
Blair, Richard, 271-72
Blassingame, John W., 19
Bloomington, Illinois, 76
Blue Lick Hills, 22
Blue Ridge Mountains, xi
Blue, Rolla, 112, 115
Bly, Wiley, 243
Board of Examiners, 245
Board of Visitors. *See* Committee on Colored Schools
Bob, 158
Bogie, Dan, 13
Bonaparte, Napoleon, 246
Boone County, Ky., 63, 66, 70, 74, 206
Boone, Daniel, xi, xii, 84
Boone, James, xi
Boone, Squire, xi
Boston Resolutes Baseball Club, Boston, Massachusetts, 290
Boston Vigilance Committee, 73
Bourbon Colored Mutual Savings and Loan Association, 280
Bourbon County, xvii, xviii, 46, 73, 85, 88, 98-99, 154, 156-57, 159, 179, 266,

288
Bourbon Iron Works Company, 8
Bowling Green Institute, 225
Bowling Green *Watchman*, 320
Bowling Green, Ky., xxi, 8, 19, 27, 29, 61, 74, 144, 154-55, 160, 167-68, 171-76, 181, 185, 195, 198-99, 221, 243, 248, 266, 299, 320-21, 324
Bowling-Green *Democrat*, 320
Boyd, Ann E., 206
Boyd, Henry, 12, 71
Boyd, Peter, 321
Boyd, William H., 206
Boyle County, Ky., 30, 145, 154, 156-57, 192, 241, 287-88, 304, 309
Boz, 192
Bracken County, Ky., 54, 73, 155
Bragg, Braxton, 144, 150
Bramlette, Thomas E., 152
Branford, Peter, 191
Braxton, Frederick, 122, 221
Breckinridge County, Ky., 242
Brents, George, 123
Bridwell, James, 208
Brisee, Armstage, 34
Bristow, Benjamin, 302
Bristow, E.L., 296
Bristow Station, Ky., 243
British West Indies, 132
Britton, Julia, 253, 323
Britton, Mary E., 321
Brooks, Thomas, 237
Brother January, 123
Browder, George, 135
Brower, Linda, 244
Brower, Rose, 244
Brown, Dinah, 206
Brown, Edward "Brown Dick," 281
Brown, G.W., 246
Brown, J.C., 116
Brown, James Seay, 278
Brown, John, 116, 139
Brown, Mary Jane, 206
Brown, Mary, 206
Brown, Robert 80
Brown, Thomas, 70
Brown, William Wells, 99
Brown County, Ohio, 69
Brownstown, Louisville, 275-76
Brucetown, Lexington, 274
Bruner, Peter, 9, 11, 20, 45, 57, 62, 66, 96, 155, 170, 207
Bryant, C.M., 324
Buckingham, James S., 32
Buckner, E.P., 165-66

Buckner, George W., 13, 155, 278
Buffalo, New York, 6, 77, 79
Bullitt, Sandy, 156, 167, 171
Bullitt County, Ky., 32, 219, 272
Burbank, Sidney, 185-87
Burbridge, Stephen G., 163, 174
Burdett, Gabriel, 194, 226-28, 241, 250, 253, 266, 286-87, 299, 308-9
Burdette, Clarissa, 190
Burdette, Elijah, 190
Bureau of Refugees, Freedmen, and Abandoned Lands. *See* Freedmen's Bureau
Burleigh, A.A., 245, 251, 253
Burney, W.A., 317
Burnside, John, 193
Burris, Charlotte, 56
Burton, Thomas, 13, 254
Butler, Thomas, 157, 167
Butler, W.F., 298-99

Cabell, Edmund, xiii
Cadiz, Ky., xxi, 60
Caldwell County, Ky., 8
California district, Louisville, 275
California Elementary School, Louisville, 264
California, 44, 221
Callie, 48
Calvary Baptist Church (formerly York Street), Louisville, 183, 220, 315, 353
Camp Nelson, Ky.: blacks acquire land at, 273-74; Elijah P. Marrs brings refugees to, 174; John G. Fee at, 162-63, 250-51; refugee treatment at, 160-63; mentioned, 154-57, 159, 166-70, 175, 179, 181, 184-85, 191, 193-94, 196-97, 200, 226-27, 229, 240-41, 266, 286, 299, 308
Camp Nelson Church of Christ, 227-28
Camp Nevin, Hart County, 148
Campbell, Alexander, 123
Campbell, Daniel, 21
Campbell, David, 21
Campbell, Green, 18
Campbell, Israel, 57
Campbell, Jackson, 20
Campbell, Lucy, 20
Campbell, Lydia, 21
Campbell, Madison, 11, 19-21, 37, 137, 139, 141, 220, 241, 254
Campbell, Samira, 18
Canada, 12, 31, 43-46, 55, 62-69, 78-83, 152, 206
Cane Springs, Ky., 219

Caribbean Sea, 132
Carlisle, Ky., 76, 105, 226
Carr, Yarmouth, 280
Carroll County, Ky., 60, 64
Carter, John, 87
Casey, William, 70-71
Cash, 139
Cassilly, 58
Cathedral of the Assumption, Louisville, 226
Catholic Churches, 119, 226
Catlettsburg, Ky., 198
Catlin, J.S., 238
Cave City, Ky., 155, 172, 243
Center Street Methodist Church, Louisville, 127-28, 142, 165, 183, 223, 237, 246, 300
Center Street School, Louisville, 237
Central School, Louisville, 247-48, 264
Centre College, 73
Chandler, Phebe, 266
Chandler Normal School, Lexington, 266
Channing, Steven A., 3
Charles, xi, 192
Charlotte, 68
Chicago, Illinois, 185, 211, 282, 288, 324
Children's Home and Polytechnic Academy at the Falls of the Ohio, 315
Chiles, James A., 318
Christian Bible College, New Castle, Ky., 226
Christian Church, Lexington, Kentucky, 123, 239
Christian County, Ky., xix, 5-6, 8, 49, 59, 93, 267
*Christian Index*, 320
Christian Mutual Association, 314
Christine, 15
Church of Our Merciful Savior, Episcopal, Louisville, 225
Churches
—during slavery: African missions in, 135, 352; African religion in, 132-33; controversies in, 136-38; demand independence for, 124; desire to separate from white churches, 119, 121; first state organization of, 140; ministers in, 119-24, 133-34; sermons and theology in, 133-35; social concerns of, 135-36, 140; unequal position in white controlled, 118-19; whites harass, 138-39. *See also* Conjuring and individual churches
—post-Civil War: and African missions, 222; and politics, 222, 360; blacks and whites, 210, 212; black Baptist convention of, 211; conservative theology of, 221-22; social concerns of, 200. *See also* individual churches
Churchill, Worden, 320
Cincinnati Branch of the Western Freedmen's Aid Association, 231
Cincinnati Choral Association, Cincinnati, Ohio, 324
Cincinnati, Ohio, 1-2, 12, 27, 44, 61, 64, 66-71, 74, 77-78, 81, 106, 150-52, 179, 200, 206, 221, 231, 247, 254, 264, 266, 280
Civil Rights: Acts, 190, 293, 312, 384; and court testimony, 299, 312; and jury sitting in Kentucky, 313, 386; and Kentucky's discriminatory legal code, 292-93; and voting, 299-300, 305-7; protests, 298-301; mentioned, 312-13. *See also* Colored educational conventions; Segregation; and Elections
Civil War: arrival of federal troops during, 146-49; blacks attend school during, 169; blacks enrolled as substitutes, 153, 157, 358; black soldiers contact relatives, 168; black troops and labor assignments in, 169-70; black volunteers in, 151, 153-56, 166, 170, 176; bounties, 153-54, 283; changes in slave behavior during, 147, 159-60; decline in crop and property values during, 160; federal military policy toward blacks in, 148-50, 153-54, 156-57, 160-63; harassment of black troops during, 156, 174-76; join military outside Kentucky during, 151-53, 358; medical examinations of recruits in, 165-66, 361; new opportunities during, 147; occupations of black inductees in, 165; recruiting, impressing black troops during, 149-59, 359; religion among black troops during, 167-68; slaveholders attempt to reclaim slaves during, 149, 156-57, 161; slaves and their families enter federal camps during, 147-49, 158-64; slaves freed during, 160, 164-65; treatment of soldiers' families by slaveholders, 157-59; white attitudes toward black troops, 153, 156, 174-76; wives and children of soldiers freed during, 159; mentioned, 8, 21, 42, 52, 54, 56, 61,

100, 111-12, 121, 123-24, 126, 128-29, 139-42, 144, 177, 179, 182, 184-85, 187, 193, 196, 208-10, 214, 219-21, 223-26, 229-30, 234, 240, 250, 268, 272, 280, 292-93, 301, 309, 313, 326, 327. *See also* United States Colored Troops
Claget, Laura, 301
Clark, Peter H., 254
Clark, Roxe, 244
Clark County, Ky., 8, 16, 96, 288
Clarke, Alexander, 22
Clarke, Archy, 22
Clarke, Cyrus, 22, 77
Clarke, Delia, 22-23, 27, 86
Clarke, Dennia, 22
Clarke, Lewis George, 10, 11, 15-17, 22-23, 27, 42, 44, 58, 62, 77-78, 105
Clarke, Milton, 7-8, 22, 31, 62, 64, 106-7
Clarksville, Tennessee, 27, 152, 157-158
Clary, 27
Clay County, Ky., 8
Clay, Cassius M., 6, 22, 48, 116
Clay, David, 80
Clay, Henry, 5-6, 36
Clay, Ward, 207
Claybrook, Edward, 262
Clear Creek Baptist Church, 135
Cleveland, Ohio, 77-78, 243
Clinton, W.Y., 127
Clinton, Ky., xxii
Clinton County, Ky., xvii, 307
Clinton Street High School, Frankfort, 266
Cloverport, Ky., 61, 224, 250
Coates, Charles, 323
Coffin, Levi, 65, 68-70
Colcester, Canada, 79
Coleman, 159
Coleman, Charles, 294
Coleman, Dick, 24
Coleman, J. Winston, Jr., 20, 33, 43
Coleman, Lucretia Newman, 321
Collins, John, Sr., 125
Colored Baptist Church (later First Baptist), Frankfort, 130, 211, 220
Colored Baptist Church, Louisville. *See* Fifth Street Baptist Church
Colored educational conventions, 244-46
Colored Ladies' Soldiers' Aid Society, Louisville, 164, 169, 184
Colored Men's State Convention, 303
Colored Methodist Episcopal Church, South, 223
Colored Musical Association, Louisville, 324
Colored People's Union Benevolent Society of Lexington, 136, 302, 314
Colored Soldiers' Aid Society of Fifth Street Baptist Church, 163, 169
Colored Soldiers' Aid Society, 169
Colored Teachers' State Association, 260, 262
Columbus, Ky., xxi, 148-49, 155, 175, 189, 194, 200, 207, 244
*Commercial*, 308, 310
Committee on Colored Schools, Louisville, 246
Confederate invasion of 1862, 150-51
Conjuring, 130-31
Connelley, William E., 42
Connelly, Emma, 42
Conrad, George, Jr., 7, 40, 131, 155
Conrad, Rufus, 317
Contraband, 148, 357
Cook, J.H., 237
Cook, Mary V., 168, 215, 219, 321
Corydon, Ky., 224
Cotter, Joseph S., 68, 141, 224, 265, 269
Cotter, Mrs. Joseph, 68
Coulter, E. Merton, 42
County court day, 94
Covington, Ky., 8, 61, 64, 74, 154, 165, 181, 195-96, 199, 202-3, 206, 241, 248, 281-82
Cowan, Eliza, 324
Cowan, John, xv
Coward, Bob, 25
Coward, Jane, 190
Crab Orchard, Ky., xiii
Crane, Mary, 15, 25
Cranshaw, Frank, 92, 93
Cravath, E.W., 238
Creditt, William A., 220, 263
Crittenden, John J., 73
Crittenden County, Ky., 8, 61
Crutcher, David, 324
Cumberland County, Ky., 8, 85, 243
Cumberland Gap, 2
Cumberland Presbyterians, 225
Cumberland River, 9, 155, 157
Cumberland, Maryland, 1
Cunningham, J., 157
Cunningham, J.R., 324
Currey, E.H., 223
Curry Chapel Zion Church, Louisville, 223
Curtis, Isaac, 141, 309
Curtis, Samuel, 318
Cynthia, 27, 114-15
Cynthiana, Ky., 103, 155, 157, 192, 220,

224, 241, 307
Cynthiana Baptist Church, 220
Cynthiana Methodist Church, 224

Daily, Dick, 64
Daniel, 59
Danville, Ky., xviii, 30, 54, 72, 110, 112, 183-84, 186, 192, 194, 220, 241, 250, 305, 307, 320
Danville Baptist Church, 220
Danville *Tribune*, 320
Daughters of Samona, 323
Daughters of Zion, Louisville, 169
Davenport, Eliza, 323
David, Miss _____, 142
Daviess County, Ky., xix, 2, 5, 17, 192, 195, 242
Davis, Moses A., 263, 185-87
Davis, W.R., 214
Davis, William, 123
DeBaptist, Richard, 211
DeBaptiste, Georgia Mable, 321
Declaration of Independence, 300, 308, 327
DeGruy, Eugene, 279
Delphia, 90
Democratic party (Democrats), 284, 302, 304-5, 311
Dennehy, D.D., 237
Dick, xv
Dickenson, Stephen, Jr., 9
Dickey, James H., 96
Dickson, William M., 151
Dinah, 98
Dinkins, Charles S., 215, 219-20
Dinwiddie, W.T., 318
Disciples of Christ, 225-26, 228
Ditson, William H., 223
Doc, 15
Dolly, 158
Dorum, Tom, 69
Douglass, Frederick, 134
Doyle, E.J. "Patrick," 73
Drake, _____, 310
Drakes Creek, Ky., 243
DuBoise, W.E.B., 251
Dudley, John, 286
Dumas Literary Club, 322
Dumas, Alexandre, 322
Duncan, Carey, 297
Dunn, George, 44
Dupee, George W., 25, 31, 123, 130, 138-41, 212-13, 220, 245, 298, 321
Dupee, Henry, 26
Dupee, Logan, 26

Dupuy, Charles, 5

Eastern School, Louisville, 247, 264
Eastern State Asylum, Lexington, 314
Ebenezer Baptist Church, Chicago, 221
Eckstein Norton Institute, 219
Ed, 159
Education
—antebellum: and harassment, 141-42; churches center of, 140, 142; success of, 144-45, 356
—immediate post-Civil War: black contribution to, 234; at Camp Nelson, 240, 266; Catholic Schools, 249-50; conventions, 244-46; desire for, 229; high school, 264-66; Kentucky laws on, 231-32, 255, 261; Kentucky's financial support of, 231-32; Lexington, 239-40; Louisville, 236-39; northern philanthropy, 230-32, 244, 250; obstacles to, 230; schools, teachers, and pupils 1865-74 in, 234-44; rural, 241-44; white hostility to, 230, 236
—public system of: Bowling Green, 266-67; funding of, 255-56, 260-61; Henderson, 267; Lexington, 248; 265-66; Louisville, 246-48, 264-65; night schools, 264-65; pressure on legislature for, 254-55; quality of, 257-58, 263-65, 378; rural, 266-67; segregated schools and, 261; student increase in, 255-57, 378. *See also* Berea College; Baptist Normal and Theological Institute; Freedmen's Bureau; and State Normal School
Edward, William, 12, 20
Elections: 1866, 302; 1872, 304, 310; and violence, 305-7, 385
Elijah, 48
Elite Club, The, 322
Elizabethtown, Ky., 32, 155, 172-73
Elkhorn Baptist Association, 122
Elkton, Ky., 243
Ellen, 158
Ely, John, 238
Ely Normal School, Louisville, 221, 238-39, 242, 246
Ely School, Owensboro, 242
Emancipation Day, 299-300
Emancipation Proclamation, 151, 187, 300
Emancipation, xiv, 5, 12, 21, 23, 26, 51-54, 82
Emily, 6

Emma, 168, 171
Employment, post-Civil War: agricultural, 270-72; and labor unions, 285-86; and landowning, 273-77, 381; apprenticeship in, 206, 272-73; as businessmen, 278-80, 282; as domestics, 277; as farmers, 276-77; as horsemen, 281-82; as laborers, 277-78; as service providers, 280-81; contracts in, 271-72, 380; in government service, 284; problems in, 268, 278, 284-86; self-help in, 268-69, 300; as sharecroppers, 270-71
England, 44
Ennis, C.H., 290
Episcopalians, 142, 225, 231, 237-38
Ermine, Grace, 321
Estill County, Ky., 190, 293
Estill's Station, xiii, xiv
Eubanks, John, 17
Evans, Eugene, 220-21, 311
Evansville, Indiana, 152, 207
Excelsior Cornet Band, Bowling Green, 324
Excelsior Jubilee Singers, 226

Fairbank, Calvin, 70-72
Fairchild, E.H., 258
Fairfield, John, 70
Falls City Band, 238
Falls City's Baseball Team, Louisville, 290
Fancy girls. See Slave trade
Fanny, 19
Fantasma Club, The, 322
Faulkner, T.M., 214
Fauquier County, Va., 1
Fayette County, Ky., xvii-xviii, xxii, 28, 31, 44, 47-48, 50, 58, 73, 85, 90, 113, 122, 141, 144-45, 154, 159, 194, 249, 258, 287, 293, 307, 309
Fayette County Colonization Society, 54
Fayette County Justice Association, 312
Fayette National Bank, 282
Fee, Howard, 241
Fee, John G., 54, 130, 162-63, 168, 185-86, 212, 226-27, 229, 240-41, 250-51, 253, 268, 273-74, 290, 300
Ferguson, Joseph M., 247
Fern Creek, Ky., 34
Ferrill, London, 19, 32, 110, 122, 134, 136-37, 144
Fields, Eliza, 159
Fields, Jackson, 208
Fields, Mary, 159

Fields, Sarah, 208
Fietus, Tally, 169
Fifteenth Amendment, 299-301, 303, 305, 307-8
Fifteenth Street AME Zion Church, Louisville, 223-24
Fifth Street Baptist Church (formerly, First Colored Baptist), Louisville, 32, 124-26, 135-38, 142, 163, 169, 183, 200, 211, 218-19, 221-22, 237, 246-47, 322-23, 355
Fifth Street Baptist School, Louisville, 237
Filson, John, xv
Finney, Jordan, 190
First African Baptist Church (later the black First Baptist Church), Lexington, 25, 121-22, 135-38, 144, 211-12, 214, 220-221, 239-40
First African Baptist Church, Maysville, 129-30, 220
First African Baptist Church, Paris, 130, 220
First Baptist Church (white), Bowling Green, 129
First Baptist Church, Frankfort, 220
First Baptist Church, Georgetown, 123
First Baptist Church (white), Louisville, 124-26
First Colored Baptist Church, Louisville. See Fifth Street Baptist Church
First Presbyterian Church (white), Danville, 130
Fisk Jubilee Singers, 295
Fisk, Clinton B., 185, 200
Fitzbutler, Henry, 310, 317, 319-20, 322
Fitzbutler, Sarah, 317
Fleming County, Ky., 8, 192, 206
Flemingsburg, Ky., 242, 294
Florence, Ky., 59
Forees, Henrietta, 168
Forks of the Elkhorn Baptist Church, Woodford County, 129
Fort Anderson, Paducah, 160
Fort Boonesborough, xi-xiv
Fort Donelson, Tennessee, 152
Fort Smith, Bowling Green, 173
Foster, Stephen, 35
Fourteenth Amendment, 262
Fourth Street Methodist Church, Louisville, 92, 128, 136, 142, 144. See also Asbury Chapel
Fourth Street School, Lexington, 248
Fowles, John, 200
Fox, Robert C., 280, 297

Fox, Samuel, 297
Frank, 23, 56, 106
Frank, John H., 219
Frankfort, Ky., xviii, 8, 32, 62, 67, 72, 110, 116, 130, 141, 144, 189, 211, 249, 266, 296, 303-5, 307, 311, 318
Frankfort Baptist Church, 211
Frankfort Female High School, 249
Franklin County, Georgia, 123
Franklin County, Ky., 192, 249, 266, 288, 306
Franklin, Ky., xxi, 155, 171, 210, 243, 262
Frazier, E. Franklin, 132
Frederick, Francis, 1, 10, 19, 38-39, 44-45, 63, 68
Frederick Douglass Lyceum, 322
Free Baptist Mission of Providence, Rhode Island, 231
Free blacks: and family life, 109; attempt to rescue children, 54; concentrate in urban areas, 108, 110; education of, 145; employment of, 110-13; freedom papers of, 12, 113; legal rights and harassment of, 108-9, 113-16, 312, 340; purchase families, 109, 112; statistics, 107-8. *See also* Palmer passes
Free Frank, 112, 115
Freedmen's Aid Association, Columbus, Ky., 200
Freedmen's Aid Society of the Methodist Episcopal Church, 200, 250
Freedmen's Bureau: and education, 232-34, 241-44, 246; provides assistance, 201-5; officials, 185-86, 190; mentioned, 187-88, 193, 195, 206, 208, 221, 229-30, 238-39, 249, 252-53, 267, 270-73, 278, 295, 313-14
Freedmen's Sanitary Commission, Paducah, 200
Freedmen's Savings Bank, 277, 283
Freedmen: and family problems, 182-83, 205-9; and post-Civil War celebrations, 183-85, 299-301; helped to acquire land, 273-75; call for economic assistance for, 268, 273; confused status of, at war's end, 178, 182; driven from homes, 194-95; post-Civil War economic problems of, 185, 268; visit slave homes, 182; post-Civil War housing, 181, 196-98
Freedom celebrations, 183, 299-301
Freeman's Chapel Methodist Church, Hopkinsville, 224
Free Zibe, 112

Frey, Nellie L., 323
Friends Association of Pennsylvania, 200, 231
Froman, Alfred, 320
Fry, Speed S., 161
Fugitives: attempt to free families, 70, 80-82; attempt to kill children, 74; in Canada, 79-81; seek help in black neighborhoods, 66-67, 69, 77; mentioned, 27, 42, 43, 44, 46, 58, 61, 65, 68, 73, 75-76, 78, 149. *See also* Running away
Fugitive Slave Law, 61-62, 70, 107, 116, 147
Fulton County, Ky., xxi
Fulton Elementary School, Louisville, 264

Gaddie, Daniel A., 212, 220, 245
Gaines, Henry, 191
Gaines, Horace P., 309
Galena, Illinois, 126
Gallatin, Tennessee, 152
Gallatin County, Ky., 25, 195, 199, 241
Galveston, Texas, 31
Garner, Margaret, 74
Garner, Robert, 74
Garnett, J.H., 219
Garrard County, Ky., xvii, 11, 13, 114, 139, 165, 194, 208, 226-27, 287, 307
Garrett, Frank, 290
Garrison, Matthew, 82, 92
General Association of Colored Baptists, 140, 211-13, 219-21
Genovase, Eugene D., 3
George and Dan's Restaurant, 279
George, 7, 47, 94, 106, 158
Georgetown, Ky., xviii, 7, 123, 138, 220, 224
Georgia, 2, 28, 42, 123
Gibson, William H., Jr., 144
Gibson, William H., Sr., 140, 142, 144, 226, 237, 245, 282, 284-85, 294, 301, 310-11, 323-24
Gilbert, Miss A.G., 215
Gillespie, Shelby, 315
Gist, Christopher, xi
Gist, Nathaniel, 23
Givens, George, 206
Givens, Mark, 206
Glasgow, Ky., 61, 172, 243
Glass, E.W., 321
Glenn, John, 157-58
Glenn, Robert, 17, 46, 182
Goodlowtown, Lexington, 274

Gooley, 26-27
Gordon, Henry, 98
Gordon Baseball Club, Chicago, Illinois, 290
Gordonsville, Ky., 243
Gould, G.T., 296
Grand Encore Concert Troupe, 226
Granger, Gordon, 149
Granger, William R., 215
Grant County, Ky., 27, 241
Grant, Ulysses S., 302, 308
Graves County, Ky., xxi
Graves, Ham, 141
Gray, Frank, 279
Grayson County, Ky., xix
Greeley, Horace, 304
Green County, Ky., xix, 8, 13, 32, 141, 156, 190
Green Street Baptist Church (formerly Second Colored Baptist, Louisville), 32, 126-27, 136-39, 142, 169, 183, 219-20, 222, 237
Green, Amanda, 183
Green, Caroline, 183
Green, Elisha, 21-22, 31, 51, 97, 106, 113-14, 129-30, 138, 183, 206-7, 220, 269, 274, 290, 296, 299
Green, Elvira C., 246
Green, Henry, 130
Green, Jacob D., 76-77
Green, John, 22
Green, Maria, 183
Green, Susan, 21
Greenbrier Plantation, 5
Greensburg, Ky., 141
Greenup, Ky., 98
Greenup County, Ky., 98
Greenupsburg, Ky., 155, 195
Griffin, Isaac, 9, 51
Griffin, Pierce, 89
Griffith, George A., 303-4, 318
Gross, Tabb, 44, 56
Guard, Timothy, 9
Guwn, Betty, 13

Hackney, George W., 243
Hale, S.C., 240
Hall, 57
Hall, T.E., 163
Halleck, Henry W., 149
Hall's Gap, Ky., 194
Hamilton, J.G., 283
Hamilton, John, 71, 239
Hamilton County, Ohio, 69
Hancock County, Ky., 46, 70, 156, 248

Hand Primary School, Lexington, 266
Hardin, Billy, 20
Hardin, Mahala, 20
Hardin County, Ky., 96
Hardinsburg, Ky., 98-99, 242, 250
Harlan, John M., 302, 307
Harlan, Robert, 44
Harper, James, 128, 142, 144
Harper, Nathaniel R., 223, 313, 318-20, 323-24
Harpers Ferry, Virginia [W. Va.], 139
Harriet, 58
Harris, _____, 192
Harris, Virgie, 267
Harrison County, Ky., 7, 40, 73
Harrod's Fort, xv
Harrodsburg, Ky., xviii, 44
Harrodsburg Springs Hotel, 106
Harry, 73
Hart County, Ky., 9, 148, 286
Harvard University, 251
Hassig, Fred, 204
Hatfield, John, 67
Hathaway, James, 253, 320
Haviland, Laura S., 70
Hawes, Richard, 55
Hawesville, Ky., xix
Hawkins, Horace, 81
Hayden, Lewis, 63, 71, 73
Hayden, William, 7, 14, 52, 55, 106-7, 141
Hazelton, William, 323
Heady, Mr. _____, 15
Health care: slaves, 39-42, 333, 338; freedmen, 196, 198-200, 317-18; mentioned, 8, 24, 51, 54, 76
Heath, Andrew, 219
Helen, 6
Henderson, Erskin, 282
Henderson, H.A.M., 255, 260
Henderson, Ky., xix, xxi, 29, 70, 96, 155, 158, 186, 195, 199, 225, 248, 267, 324
Henderson County, Ky., xix, 5, 11, 59-60, 157
Henry, 27, 45, 106, 158
Henry County, Ky., 158-59, 194, 226, 293
Henson, Amos, 1
Henson, Josiah, 1, 9, 17, 27, 31, 56-57, 63, 65, 78-79
Henson, Tom, 65
Herskovits, Melville, 131-32
Hickman, Ky., 244
Hillsborough, Ky., 76
Hind, Richard, xiv

Hines, C.W., 290
Hines, Duncan, 135
Hod Carriers Union, 285
Hodgenville, Ky., 183
Hoffman, J.W., 215
Hopkins, Ohio, 71
Hopkins County, Ky., 244
Hopkinsville, Ky., xxi, 50, 59-61, 155, 307
Hopkinsville *Baptist Monitor*, 320
Hopkinsville Benevolent Society, 200, 386
Hopkinsville *Indicator*, 321
Hopkinsville *Kentucky News*, 321
Hopson, W.H., 225-26
Houser, C.W., 264
Housing: for slaves, 12-14; immediate post-Civil War, 181, 196-98. *See also* Lexington and Louisville
Howard, Oliver O., 185, 239, 252
Howard Hall, Berea College, 252, 254
Howard School, Lexington, 239-40, 248, 265
Howard University, Washington, D.C., 264
Hubbard, Austin H., 56, 298
Hughes, Michael, 89
Hughes, Thomas, 6, 97
Hughes and Downing, 89
Humphrey, 168
Hunter, John E., 318
Hurd, Babe, 282
Hutchinson, Gertie, 214
Hynes, Mandy, 250

Ida, 158
Illinois, 152
Imes, B.A., 250
Independent (Corinthian) Baptist Church, Frankfort, 220
Independent Baptist Church, Lexington, 283
Independent Church of Christ, 226-28
Independent Order of Good Samaritans, 323
Independent Party of the Colored Race, 311
Independent Sons of Honor, 323
Indiana, 59, 70, 99, 152, 195, 224, 254
Indiana State Normal College, 264
Indianapolis, Indiana, 144, 225, 288
Irvine, John S., 137

Jackson, Andrew (slave), 19, 74-76
Jackson, Andrew, xxi
Jackson, John H., 245, 257, 260, 262-63, 265
Jackson, John J., 253
Jackson, Jordan C., 245, 253, 280-81, 283-84, 309, 320
Jackson, William, 55, 107
Jackson County, Ky., xvii, 108
Jackson Purchase, xxi, xxii, 108, 195, 244, 307
Jackson Street Methodist Church, Louisville, 142, 183, 223, 237, 246
Jacob, 28, 50
Jacob Street Tabernacle, Louisville, 223
James, Thomas, 164-65, 183-84, 290
Jane, 48
January's Tom, 19
Jefferson, Thomas, 47
Jefferson County, Ky., xvii-xviii, 32, 144-45, 245, 276, 285, 287, 298-300
Jeffersonville, Indiana, 73
Jennings, Cornelia A., 238
Jerry, 19
Jess, 27-28
Jessamine County, Ky., xvii, 113, 135, 154, 191, 193, 240, 307
Jesse, 49-50
Jim, 7, 48, 107
Jocelyn, Stephen, 176
Joe, 103
Joe Cotton (horse), 281
John, 67
Johnny, 7
Johnson, Ambrose, 25
Johnson, E. Polk, 42
Johnson, Eddie, 25
Johnson, Eli, 63
Johnson, Isaac, 3, 25, 44, 46, 93, 152, 182
Johnson, Laura, 243
Johnson, Mary A., 246
Johnson, Peter, 212
Johnson, Swift, 168
Johnson, W.D., 320
Joint Committee on Education, 260
Jones, A.D., 243
Jones, A.T., 3
Jones, Aby, 55
Jones, Joseph, 53
Jones, Q.B., 220, 245
Jones, William, 159
Joyce, Ida, 262-63
Judith, 27
Julett, 54
Juvenile delinquency, 315-16, 386-87

Kansas, 228, 286-87

Kelly, William, 90
Kennedy, Paul H., 155
Kenton County, Ky., 10, 69, 74
Kentucky Bar Association, 312
Kentucky Colonization Society, 53-54
Kentucky Constitutions of 1792 and 1799, 108
Kentucky Court of Appeals, 114-15, 305, 312
Kentucky Derby, 281
Kentucky Emancipation Convention, 72
*Kentucky Industrialist*, 286
Kentucky Institute for the Education of the Blind, 313
Kentucky River, xiii, 154
Kentucky State Board of Education, 245
*Kentucky v. Jesse Ellis*, 261
Kidnapping, 90, 92-93
Kilgore, W.E., 242
King, Henry, 288, 299
Kingman (horse), 281
Kinkeadtown, Lexington, 275
Kirby Smith, Edmund, 150
Kite, Elijah, 74
Knights of Labor, 285-86
Knox, Sergeant, 184
Ku Klux Klan, 188, 293
Kyler, Steve, 114

Ladies Sewing Circle, 315
Ladies' Hall School, Lexington, 248
Lafayette, Ky., 59
Lago, Willis, 31, 68
LaGrange, Ky., 242, 249
LaGrange School, 249
Laine, Henry Allen, 257-58
Lake Erie, 78-79
Land ownership, 273-75
Lander, Robert, 318
Lane, Robert M., 144
Langston, John M., 184
Larue County, Ky., 25, 182, 199
Latonia Derby, 282
Laurel County, Ky., 93
Law League, 302, 312
Lawrenceburg, Indiana, 71
Lawson, J.H., 318
Lawson, W.H., 310
Lawyers, 318-19
League of Colored Base Ball Clubs, 290
Lebanon, Ky., 154, 156, 165, 202, 249
Lee, Annie, 142
Lee, Letty, 26
Lee, Nancy, 26
Lee, Reuben, 220

Lee, Robert E., 175
Lee, Tony, 26
Lee County, Ky., 307
Lee's Row, Lexington, 275
Leitchfield, Ky., 250
Levi, 6
Lewis, Alpheus, 46
Lewis, Isaac, 282
Lewis, Isham, 47
Lewis, Lilburn, 47
Lewis, Margaret, 46
Lewis, Mary, 169
Lewis, Oliver, 282
Lewis, Peter, 111, 237, 315
Lewisburg, Ky., 210
Lewis County, Ky., xvii, 87
Lexington, Ky.: education in, 239-40, 248, 265-66; free blacks in, 108, 110, 112; post-Civil War housing, 274-75, 381; slave hiring in, 102, 105, 107; slavery in, xvii-xviii, 8-9, 11, 13, 26, 30, 32, 35, 44, 46-47, 58-59, 63, 71, 77, 88, 102, 110, 112, 121-22; mentioned, 2, 22-24, 27-28, 31, 34, 43, 48, 59, 61, 67, 73, 81, 86-87, 89, 96, 107, 116, 123, 134, 138, 141-42, 144, 154, 158-59, 166, 168, 170-71, 174, 181, 185, 194-96, 199, 201-3, 205, 212, 229, 233, 248, 250, 253, 260, 262, 265-66, 268, 278-82, 284, 289, 294, 296, 299-300, 302, 305-7, 312, 314-15, 318, 320-22, 325
Lexington *American Citizen*, 258-60, 320-21
Lexington Colored Agricultural and Mechanical Association, 288-89
Lexington and Frankfort Railroad Company, 30
Lexington *Herald*, 321
Lexington *Intelligencer*, 24
Lexington *Standard*, 320
Liberal Republican party, 304
Liberia, Africa, 26, 53-54
Licking River, 151
Lilly, Lilborn, 271
Lincoln, Abraham, 97, 146, 151-52
Lincoln, Mary Todd, 122
Lincoln County, Ky., 52, 161
Lincoln University, Pennsylvania, 235
Lindsay, J.W., 97
Livingston County, Ky., 31, 47, 105
Lodges, 183-84, 322-23
Logan, Joseph, 22
Logan, Judith, 22
Logan County, Ky., xix, 1, 27, 40, 74,

116, 158-59, 182, 189, 243
London, xii
London, Ky., 165
Lord Baltimore's Baseball Club, Baltimore, Maryland, 290
Loretto, Ky., 119
Louisa, Ky., 154, 160
Louisiana, 6, 82, 90, 97, 234
Louisville, Ky.: Alms House, 314; free blacks in, 108, 110-13, 115-16; post-Civil War housing in, 275-76; refugee camp in, 163-65; slave hiring in, 102-3, 107; slavery in, xvii-xviii, 10, 14, 25, 29, 32, 55, 60, 68, 73, 76-77, 82, 90, 92, 97, 102, 110-12, 135; mentioned, 6, 8-9, 11, 13, 20, 24, 27, 29, 31, 40, 44, 48, 51, 54, 58, 61, 64, 67, 81, 86, 93, 96, 98, 106, 124-28, 138-42, 144, 147, 150, 154-59, 167-70, 174-75, 179, 181, 183-85, 191, 194-96, 198-206, 208-10, 213, 218-26, 229-30, 236, 239, 245-51, 254, 260-61, 264-66, 268-69, 278, 279-84, 286-88, 290, 293, 295-96, 298-305, 308-9, 313, 315-17, 319-22, 325
Louisville Bar Association, 312
Louisville Bible School, 225-26
Louisville Board of Health, 317
Louisville *Bulletin*, 320
Louisville Cemetery Association, 317
Louisville *Champion*, 320
Louisville Choral Society, 324
Louisville *Commercial*, 308
Louisville *Courier-Journal*, 276, 320
Louisville *Examiner*, 13
Louisville *Indicator*, 321
Louisville *Informer*, 320
Louisville *Kentuckian*, 320
Louisville *Kentucky News*, 321
Louisville Law League, 302, 312
Louisville & Nashville Railroad, 8, 171, 288
Louisville National Medical School, 317-18, 387
Louisville *Ohio Falls Express*, 319
Louisville *Planet*, 320
Louisville Real Estate and Mutual Relief Association, 276, 319
Louisville Sanitary Commission, 283
Louisville School of Pharmacy, 318
Louisville *Times*, 276
Louisville *Weekly Journal*, 24
Love, Homer L., 173
Loving, Nelson, 221
Lowndes County, Mississippi, 28

Lucinda, 159
Lucy, 56, 112, 115, 158
Lunwood Club, 322
Lyell, Sir Charles, 135
Lyon County, Ky., 206
Lytle, Henry H., 32, 123, 223

Mack, Albert, 316
Macklin, Jim, 192
Madinglay, John, 93
Madison, Indiana, 64-65
Madison County, Ky., xiv, xvii, 3, 10, 15, 18, 27, 37, 46, 51, 57, 77, 80, 93, 129, 154, 165, 168, 241, 250, 257, 293, 307
Madison University, New York, 214
Madisonville, Ky., xix, xxi, 61, 199, 244
Mahan, John B., 69
Maiden Lane School, Louisville, 264
Main Street Baptist Church, Lexington, 122, 221, 239
Main Street Elementary School, Louisville, 264
Major Hughes Baseball Club, Louisville, 290
Mammoth Cave, Ky., 9
Marion County, Ky., xvii, 154, 156, 176, 189, 226
Marrs, Elijah P., 141, 146, 155-57, 167-75, 191, 213-15, 218, 220, 242, 245, 249, 269, 288, 308, 320
Marrs, Henry C., 170, 213-14, 245, 269, 288, 303
Marshall County, Ky., xxi, xxii
Martha, 46
Martin, Robert, 220
Martin County, Ky., 307
Mary Elizabeth, 27
Mary, 6, 23, 48, 67
Maryland, xiv, 1, 31, 56, 89
Mason, Harriet, 16
Mason, John, 267
Mason, Martha, 267
Mason County, Ky., xvii, 1, 8, 19, 65, 69, 81, 93, 112, 207
Masons, 323
Massachusetts, 73, 152, 251, 266
Massey, Reuben D., 166
Mato, 21
Maxwell, J.M., 247, 260, 264
Mayfield, Bert, 4, 11, 16
Mayfield, Ky., 61
Mayo, William, 266
Mayslick, Ky., 21, 77, 114, 242
Maysville, Ky., 1, 8, 21, 27, 31-32, 61, 62, 70, 96-97, 110, 113, 144, 155, 183,

195, 198, 220, 229, 242, 254, 296
McClintock, William, 12
McCracken County, Ky., 48
McDougal, Thomas, 182-83
McDougle, Ivan E., 42-43
McDowell, C.C., 320
McKee, Sam, 302
McKinley, J.J.C., 320
McLean, George, 135
McRoberts, Al, 192
Meade County, Ky., xix, 61, 165, 195
Meaux, Jordan, 130
Megowan, Thomas B., 89
Meharry Medical College, Nashville, Tennessee, 318
Memphis Eclipse Baseball Club, Memphis, Tennessee, 290
Mendelssohn Singing Association, 324
Mercer County, Ky., 154, 191
Merriwether, Jesse, 246
Methodist Episcopal Church, South. *See* Colored Methodist Episcopal Church, South
Meulder, Father Francis De, 249
Meyzeek, A.E., 264
Michigan, 142, 244
Military District of Kentucky, 163
Military engagements of Kentucky black troops, 171-76
Mill Springs, 149
Miller, Ada, 246
Miller, Henry, 237
Miller, Joseph, 161
Millersburg, Ky., 71, 226, 296
Milly, 63
Minnesota, 264
Minnis, Madison, 323
Mississippi, 1, 27, 42, 98
Mississippi River, 9, 96-97, 102, 104, 106, 111, 149, 263
Missouri, 2, 18, 82
Mitchell, E. Belle, 239, 241
Mitchell, Robert, 221
Monk, xiv
Monroe, C.C., 262-63
Monroe, James, 130, 140, 211, 220-21, 239
Monroe, Mary B., 262
Monroe County, Ky., 45
Montgomery County, Ky., 8
*Monthly Methodist*, 320
Moore, Richard, 58
Morehead, Henry, 63, 141
Morgan County, Ky., 145
Morgan, Charles, 323

Morgantown, Virginia [W. Va.], 31, 105
Morrill Act, 263
Morris, Charles, 318
Morris, Horace, 68, 246-47, 260, 282-84, 298, 303, 310, 320
Morris, John, 246
Mortimore, R.G., 144, 245
Morton, Martha, 243
Mose, 48
Moses, 50
Mozart Society, 140
Mt. Sterling, Ky., xiv, 36, 102, 105, 195, 198-99, 204, 226, 242, 278, 301
Mt. Vernon, Ky., 96, 294
Muhlenberg County, Ky., 54
Muldraugh Hill, 173
Munfordville, Ky., 160, 172, 181
Murphy, Isaac, 281-82
Murphy, Ruben, 270
Murrow, Florence, 246
Myers, Bill, 93

Narcissa, 56
Nashville, Tennessee, 152, 166, 171-72, 221, 226-27, 249
Nat Turner Club, 322
Natchez, Mississippi, 89-90, 97, 99
National Freedmen's Relief Association, 231
National Freedmen's Savings and Trust Bank, 282-84
National Negro Democratic Conference, 305
National Road, 1
Nature and distribution of slave ownership, 2
Neal, Nelson, 280
Ned, 141
Nelson County, Ky., 3, 5, 44, 93, 182, 195, 210, 226, 288
New Albany, Indiana, 32, 169, 317
New Castle, Ky., 147, 249
New Castle School, 249
New Eureka Grocery Company, 279
New Haven, Ky., 249
New Orleans, Louisiana, 7, 10, 23-24, 27, 31-32, 41, 71, 82, 86, 90, 92, 96-99, 218
New Salem Baptist Church (white), Nelson County, Kentucky, 210
New York, 9, 70, 164, 201
New York *Freeman*, 280, 290, 294
New York Gothams Baseball Club, 290
New York *Times*, 158
New York *Witness*, 218

Newport, Indiana, 69
Newport, Ky., 202
Newport, Rhode Island, 6
Newspapers, 212, 218, 259-60, 319-21, 387
Newton, Isaac M., 241
Nicholas, 158
Nicholas County, Ky., 12, 25, 85, 93, 105, 156, 205, 241, 288
Nicholasville, Ky., 32, 129, 162, 169, 174, 192, 206, 305
Nichols, William, 172
Nicodemus, Kansas, 287
Ninth Street Methodist Church, Louisville, 142, 237
Noble, T.K., 232, 236, 238, 251
Noble School, Hardinsburg, 242
Non-importation act of 1833, 15, 86, 88, 345
Normal Hill. *See* State Normal School
North Carolina, 49
Northern freedmen's aid societies, 200-201
Northwestern Freedmen's Aid Commission of Chicago, 200, 231, 244
Norton, Peter, 60
Nutter, Henry, 112

Oates, Will, 20
Oberlin, Ohio, 76, 152, 184
Oberlin College, 71, 112, 143, 219, 234-35, 237, 239, 243, 250, 283
Octerlony, John A., 203, 317
Odd Fellows, 323
Ohio, 8, 12, 54, 61, 63, 70-71, 74, 78, 81, 144, 152, 178-79, 195, 207, 234, 241, 243-44, 261
*Ohio Falls Express*, 319
Ohio River, xi, xiv, xvii, xxii, 1, 2, 9, 30, 42, 51, 54-56, 61-62, 64-65, 67-69, 73-78, 82, 96-98, 104, 106, 111, 113, 115, 146, 150, 152, 155, 159, 178-79, 194-95, 250
Ohio River Valley, 31
Old Captain (Peter), 121-23
Old Folks Home, Louisville, 224
Old Kemp, 50
Oldham County, Ky., xxii, 18, 308
Oldham County Republican Club, 308
Olivet Baptist Church, Louisville, 213
Olmsted, Frederick Law, 19
Orphans Home Society, 314-15
*Our Women and Children*, 321
Owensboro, Ky., xix, xxi, 24, 61, 154-55, 165-66, 195, 198-99, 204, 207, 224, 242, 248, 261-62, 266, 284
Owensboro AME Church, 266
Owensboro Freedmen School Committee, 242
Owingsville, Ky., 293

Paducah, Ky., xxii, 8, 61, 96, 139, 154, 160, 165-66, 175, 181, 185, 194-95, 199-200, 202, 204, 206, 212, 235, 244, 261, 321
Paducah *Baptist Herald*, 212, 321
Page, Yancy & Company, 279
Palmer passes, 178-79
Palmer, Cyrus O., 174
Palmer, John M., 164-65, 178, 181, 183-84, 187
Panic of 1873, 276
Paris, Ky., 22, 29, 30-31, 93, 96, 110, 130, 179, 192, 220, 226, 241, 274, 280, 296, 305, 307, 311
Paris Baptist Church, 130
Paris *Western Citizen*, 24
Parker, James, 306
Parrish, Charles H., Sr., 215, 219-20
Parrish, James H., 220
Patsy, 159
Patterson, George, 214, 220
Patterson, Solomon, 125
Payne, Daniel A., 142, 247
Pearce, Horace, 297
Peggy, 23
Penick, Thomas, 243
Pennsylvania, xiv, 84
Perry, 113
Perry, Abe, 281
Perry, William H., 264
Peter. *See* Old Captain
Petersburg, Virginia, 166, 214, 225
Petit, William B., 98
Peyton, W.T., 264
Philadelphia, Pennsylvania, 2, 214
Philadelphia Institute, 238
Philadelphia Pythians Baseball Club, 290
Philanthropic associations: northern, 200-201, 218-19, 231, 244, 250; freedmen, 199-201, 238
Physicians, 317-18
Pittsburgh, Pennsylvania, 70
Pittsburgh Keystones Baseball Club, 290
Pleasant Green Baptist Church, Lexington, 25, 122-23, 239
Plymouth Congregational Church, Louisville, 228
Polk, J.K., 212

Polly, 51
Polytechnic Preparatory School, 314
Pompey, xi-xii
Pope, J.D., 246
Pope, Fausie, 169
Poplar Street School, Owensboro, 266
Population: in antebellum Kentucky, xiv-xxii; movement in post-Civil War, 178-84; sold south, 99
Porter, B.F., 317
Porter, E.S., 215, 317
Porter, J.M., 311
Porter, Jeff, 304
Porter, Will, 280
Porter & Jackson, Undertakers, 280
Portland, Louisville, Ky., 316
Portland Elementary School, Louisville, 247, 264
Portsmouth, Ohio, 78, 90
Post-Civil War racial violence: and elections, 305-7, 385; and lynchings, 191-92, 364; and police brutality, 294; statistics on, 187-89, 294, 364; mentioned, 190, 193-95, 293. See also Ku Klux Klan
Post-Civil War social services: cemetery associations, 317; for orphans, 205, 314-15; mentioned, 313, 317
Post-Civil War society and culture, 321-25
Powell, Thomas, 90
Pralltown, Lexington, 274
Pratt, William, 25-26, 135, 159, 212
Presbyterians, 225
Prestley, 73
Preston, 49
Price, Nathaniel, 243
Priest, James, 135
Prisons, 314
Prohibition party, 304
Protestant Episcopal Aid Society, 231, 238
Pulaski County, Ky., 56, 106, 112, 115, 307
Pullum, William A., 89

Quid Nunc Club, 322
Quills, Harry, 137
Quinn Chapel African Methodist Episcopal Church, Louisville, 128, 136, 144, 183-84, 223-24, 237, 245, 297, 353

R.C. Fox & Brothers, 280
Ramsey, George, 80

Randall, William H., 302
Raywick, Ky., 250
Rebellions. See Slave conspiracies
Recreation: and baseball, 289-90, 295; at A & M fairs, 288-89; excursions, 287-88; mentioned, 33-39, 105, 287, 291
Red River Iron Company, 293
Refugee Home, 80, 240
Refugee Home Society, 80
Refugee's and Freedmen's Hospital, 201-5
Regulators, 194-95
Reid, T. Augustus, 226
Renting slaves. See Slave hiring
Republican party (Republicans): ambiguous relationship of blacks with, 302-4, 309-11; and black candidates, 309-10; mentioned, 284, 287-88, 301, 305-8, 312, 319
Reuben, 106
Revels, Hiram R., 128
Revels, Willis R., 128
Richardson, Mary Jones, 142
Richmond, Ky., xi, 144, 220, 241, 254, 293
Richmond Baptist Church, 220
Ridley, N.J., 318
Riley, Catherine, 182
Riley, J.R., 246
Robards, Lewis C., 89-90
Robins, O.H., 239
Robinson, A., 168
Robinson, Alfred, 5-6
Robinson, Ferdinand, 279
Robinson, Perry, 318
Robinson, Tom, 129
Rockcastle County, Ky., 106
Rockefeller, John D., 219
Roger Williams University, Nashville, 213, 221, 249
Rogers, J.A.R., 143
Ross, J. Allen, 304-5
Rowlett, James, 286
Roxborough, Miss _____, 237
Runkle, Benjamin P., 186-87, 232, 234, 238, 245
Running away: in large numbers, 73-74; obstacles to, 64-65; temporarily, 57; mentioned, 6, 27, 42, 48, 61-63, 66-72, 75-79, 82. See also Fugitives
Russellville, Ky., xxi, 60, 168, 171, 195, 198
Ruth, William, 80

Index / 427

Salem, Indiana, 73
Sally, 47, 69, 103
Saltville, Virginia, 175-76
Sam, xi, 23, 30
San Francisco, California, 224
Sandusky, Ohio, 79
Sanitary Commission. *See* United States Sanitary Commission
Satchell, Charles, 126-27
Schafer, George A., 144
Scioto River, xi
Scofield, Abisha, 193, 241
Scott County, Ky., xvii, 191, 287, 309
Scroggins, George, 304
Scroggins, Henry, 260, 284, 288, 309, 320
Seal, Dennis, 112
Seales, Enoch, 250
Second Colored Baptist Church, Louisville. *See* Green Street Baptist Church
Segregation: and harassment in transportation, 295-99, 384; mentioned, 261, 294, 314. *See also* Housing; Recreation.
Seguin, Texas, 219
Seleka, Madame, 324
Semple, Jeremiah, 54
Shacklett family, 195
Shadrack, 73
Shakertown, 74
Shanks, Orrin, 126
Shawnee Indians, xi, xii
Shelby County, Ky., 141, 146, 168, 271, 288, 299-300, 308
Shelby County A & M Fair, 288
Shelbyville, Ky., 32, 116, 191, 213
Sherman, William T., 148
Shirley, Edd, 43, 46
Siddles, Aaron, 9
Sidney, Allen, 69
Simmons, William J., 214-19, 221, 253, 262, 321
Simpson, James E., 264
Simpsonville, Ky., 156, 167, 242
Sims, John, 293
Sisters of Charity of Nazareth, 249
Sisters of Loretto, 249-50
Sisters of the Mysterious Ten, 323
Slater Fund, 219
Slaughter, Isaac, 130
Slaughter, Linton, 243
Slave catchers, 67, 69-70, 74, 76, 79
Slave children, xiv-xv, 2, 4, 9-14, 17, 19, 21-26, 33, 35, 44-45, 47, 50, 54, 56, 58, 64-65, 85, 90, 91
Slave clothing, 14, 16-17, 35, 52, 63, 65, 74, 77, 334
Slave conspiracies, 59-61, 98
Slave diet, 10, 14-16, 34, 333
Slave families: attempts to maintain contact after separation of, 26-28; disrupted by hiring-out practices, 21-24, 100; viability of, 20; separation of, 23-27; mentioned, 1, 2, 11-15, 17-19, 24-25, 33-34, 51, 54, 56-57, 63-65, 70-71, 78-81, 98
Slave hiring, 23-24, 101-7
Slave labor: as domestic and personal servants, 5-7; bargaining for, 7-8; harsh treatment of, 6-7; in manufacturing, 8; on farms, 2-5; skilled, 7-9; mentioned, xi, xiii, xv-xvi, xx, 1-4, 10-12, 22-23, 28, 38-39, 41-42
Slave marriage: and slave "breeding," 19-20, 335; tenuousness of, 17, 19; mentioned, 18, 21, 26, 28, 56, 334
Slave mobility: and passes, 30-32, 54, 337; and regulations, 29-30, 61-62, 336-37; mentioned, 5, 8, 22, 33, 50, 56, 74, 77, 82
Slavery: and migration to Kentucky, xiv-xv, 1-2; and racial prejudice, xiv; and 1798; slave code, xiv, 29, 49, 61, 105, 333; and slave owners in 1850, 2; before statehood, xv; *idee fixe* of, 51; in Boonesborough, xi-xiv; in Bowling Green, xxi, 29, 74, 144, 149; in Cadiz, xxi, 60; in Danville, xviii, 30, 54, 110; in the mountains, xvii, xix-xx, xxii; in Frankfort, xviii, 106, 110, 116; in Franklin, xxi; in Georgetown, xviii, 7; in Hardinsburg, 98-99; in Henderson, xix, xxi, 29, 59-60, 70; in Hopkinsville, xxi, 50, 59-60; in Indian fighting, xi-xiv; in Madisonville, xix, xxi; in Maysville, 110, 144; in Owensboro, xix, xxi, 24; in Paducah, xxii, 110; in Paris, 22, 24, 30-31, 110; in Richmond, xi, 27, 144; in Russellville, xxi, 60; in the Bluegrass, xvii-xix, 5, 7, 11, 14, 31, 35, 40, 61; in the Jackson Purchase, xx-xxii; in Versailles, xviii, 140; in western Kentucky, xix-xxi; on the frontier and race relations, xi-xv, 1; statistics 1790-1860, xv-xxii, 99, 107-8; transferred from coastal areas, xiv

Slaves anticipate freedom, 51, 146
Slaves purchase freedom, 9, 21-22, 26-27, 32, 44, 51, 54-57, 120
Slave trade: auctions, 10, 22, 24-26, 47, 63, 71, 76, 93-94; children sold south in, 21, 24-25, 64, 94, 335-36; coffle, 94, 96-98; elderly slaves sold in, 85-86; families commonly broken up in, 23-26, 82, 94; fancy girls, 85-86, 89; prices, 84-86; statistics, 99-100; universally accepted, 86; mentioned, xiv, 28, 41, 87-92, 95-98
Slave traders: jails of, 89, 92-93; slaves rebel against, 98-99; universal denunciation of, 88-89; mentioned, 3, 23-26, 54, 57, 63, 73, 90-91, 94-97, 100, 102, 345
Slave violence against owners, 57-59
Smith, 56
Smith, B.E., 318
Smith, Z.F., 255
Smith, Adam, 192
Smith, Benjamin B., 237-38
Smith, Billy, 60
Smith, Eliza, 315
Smith, Harriet, 208
Smith, Harrison, 208
Smith, Harry, 13, 44
Smith, J.D., 225-26
Smith, Josie, 249
Smith, Lucy W., 321
Smith, Madison, 112, 279
Smith, Mary V., 226, 324
Smith, William, 123, 297
Smithland, Ky., 8, 61, 155
Smithtown, Lexington, 275
Smoketown, Louisville, 275-76
Sneed, Charles F., 215, 219
Sneed, Lavinia B., 215
Sneethen, Richard, 126-27, 211, 219
Soldier's Aid Societies, 139, 169
Soldiers League of Lexington, 302
Sons and Daughters of the Morning, Louisville, 169
South America, 132
South Carolina, 27, 123, 214
Spalding, Father J. Lancaster, 226
Spanish-American War, 221
Spears, John, 280
Speed, James, 238, 303
Spencer, Moses, 280
Spirituals, 131-32, 134
Spradling, Washington, 68, 112-13, 128, 200
Springfield, Ky., 250

Springfield, Missouri, 225
Squire, 25
St. Augustine Church, Louisville, 226; school of, 250
St. Catherine's School, New Haven, 249
St. James Old Folks' Home, Louisville, 224, 316
St. Louis, Missouri, 126, 217
St. Mark's Episcopal Church, Louisville, 142, 225, 237-38
St. Monica's School, Bardstown, 249
St. Paul's African Methodist Episcopal Church, Lexington, 123
St. Stephen's Episcopal Church, Petersburg, Virginia, 205
Stamping Ground Baptist Church, 129
Stampp, Kenneth M., 20
Stansberry, J.B., 303-4, 311
Starlight Club, 322
State Convention of Colored Baptists, 211
State Normal College, Indiana, 264
State Normal School, Frankfort, 262-63
State Street Baptist Church, Bowling Green, 129, 221
State University, Louisville: course of study at, 216-17; faculty of, 214-15; fundraising at, 218; leadership of, 217-19; mentioned, 213-14, 220-29, 254, 287-88, 318
Steel, Armisted, 140
Steward, Mamie E., 323
Steward, William H., 142, 320, 323
Still, Alfred, 23
Still, Levin, 2, 23
Still, Peter, 2, 23-24
Stone, Edward, 93, 98
Stone, James, 151-52
Stowe, Harriet Beecher, 42
Stowers, Mary, 24, 207
Stowers, Willis, 24, 207
Straker, D.A., 238
Strother, Thomas, 184
Stumm, C.C., 220-21, 320
Susan, 158
Sykes, William, 242

Talbert, Lewis, 64-65
Talbott, William F., 90-91
Tamar, 73
Taylor, Bartlett, 142, 242, 299
Taylor, J.H., 280
Taylor, Marshall W., 242, 320, 323
Taylor, Preston, 226, 278
Taylor, W.W., 220, 315

Taylor Barracks, Louisville, 167
Taylor County, Ky., 60, 156
Taylortown, Lexington, 275
Temple, J.G., 203
Tennessee, xvii, xix, 8, 49, 59, 144, 153, 185
Tennessee River, xix, xxi, 9
Terre Haute, Indiana, 264
Texas, 227
Third Street AME Church, Owensboro, 224
Thirteenth Amendment, 178, 185, 206
Thomas, George H., 171
Thomas, J.F., 221
Thomas, Jonathan, 51
Thomas, Lorenzo, 154, 157, 160, 163
Thomas, Warren, 244
Thompson, John, 214
Thompson, P.J., 243
Thompson, Thornton, 279
Thompson, William, 290
Thomson, Edward, 223
Tilghman, Miss A.L., 324
Tobias, 21
Todd County, Ky., xix, 5, 243
Tolbot, Hanson, 223
Tolbot, Willis, 278
Toledo, Ohio, 295
Tom, 31, 192
Tompkinsville, Ky., 43
Topeka, Kansas, 287
Toronto, Canada, 77
Traveling Church, 121
Treatment of slaves: abusive, 45-49; and white violence, 60-61; believed better than in Deep South, 42-43; typical, 45-46; mentioned, 23-24, 32-33, 43, 50-51, 58, 63, 80
Treble Clef Club, 323
Trigg, Leroy, 243
Trigg County, Ky., xix, 206, 285
Triggs, Ned, 243
Trimble County, Ky., 9, 51, 65, 82, 142, 155
Trotter, Isabella, 32
*True American*, 116
Turner, Caroline, 47
Turner, James, 239, 245, 248, 288
Turpin, William, 306

*United States* v. *Buntin*, 261
*Uncle Tom's Cabin*, 42, 66
Underground Railroad: black abolitionists and the, 67-70; white abolitionists and the, 68-74; mentioned, 65-66, 77
Underwood, Edward E., 318
Underwood, J.T., 25
Union Baptist Church, Cincinnati, 221
Union Benevolent Society, 314
Union Cement & Lime Company, 279
Union Church, Nicholasville, 129
Union County, Ky., xix, 70, 75, 157
Union Relief Committee, 314
United Brothers of Friendship, 316, 323
United Relief Committee, 314
United States Constitution, 247
United States Colored Troops, 166-76, 183-84
United States District Court, 297
United States Sanitary Commission, 161-62, 167-69, 200, 283
University of Pennsylvania, 264
Utica, New York, 76

Van Zandt, John, 69-70
Vanceburg, Ky., 98
Varian, Richard, 284
Vermont, 71, 148
Versailles, Ky., xviii, 2, 220, 250
Versailles African Baptist Church, 140, 220
Virginia, xiv, xvii, 2, 17, 70, 84, 89, 122, 126, 136, 182, 238
*Voice of the Fugitive*, 80
Volney, Ky., 60

Walker, Moses Fleetwood, 295
Walker, Smart Edward, 10, 44, 63
Walker, William, 282
Walker, Willis, 129
Wallace, James B., 243
Wallace, Lew, 151
Waller, William I., 225
Walters, Alexander, 20, 224, 281
Walters, Harriet, 20
Walters, Henry, 20
Walton, Ky., 190
Ward, W.H., 309-10
Waring, P.M., 247
Warren County, Ky., xix, 49, 158, 189, 243
Warsaw, Ky., 195
Washington, Booker T., 217
Washington, D.C., 5, 148, 205, 324
Washington, Jane, 141
Washington Capital Citys Baseball Club, Washington, D.C., 290
Washington County, Ky., 226, 307
Washington Street Colored Baptist

Church, Paducah, 123, 212, 220
Waters, J.C., 225
Watson, Washington, 246
Watson, William, 280
Watterson, Henry, 320
Watts, Cato, 35
Wayne County, Ky., 17, 20
Webb, William, 1, 42
Webster County, Ky., 206
Webster, Delia A., 71
Weeden, Henry C., 249, 284, 320
Weir, Moses T., 243
Wells, Erasmus, 311
Wells, George, 126-27, 137-38
Wells, Ida B., 321
Wesley Chapel, Georgetown, 224
Western Freedmen's Aid Commission, 200, 231, 244
Western School, Louisville, 247, 264
Wheat, John L., 279
Wheelbanks, Silas, 76
Wheeler, Ellen, 251
Wheeler, W.W., 251
Wheeling, Va. [W. Va.], 1
White, Father John, 226
White, J.F., 45
White, John, 70
White, Samuel L., 111, 116, 140
White, William, 18
Whitney, Jackson, 80
Wichita, Kansas, 286
Wickliffe, Robert, 54
Widows' and Orphans' Home, 316
Wilberforce University, 144
Wilderness Trail, 2
Wilkinson, R.S., 215
William, 158-59
Williams, Frank L., 253
Williams, George, 62
Williams, Henry, 140
Williams, S.W., 324
Williams University, Nashville, 221
Wilson, Elias, 272
Wilson, Laura, 237
Wilson, Mary, 272
Winchester, Ky., 94, 207, 286, 302
Wisconsin, 76
Wolford, Frank L., 153
Wood, Ione E., 215, 219, 321
Woodford County, Ky., xvii-xviii, xxii, 68, 129, 191, 208, 249, 306
Woodson, Alice, 237
Woodson, Marshall, 246
Wright, George C., 189, 294
Wyandot Indians, xiii

Xenia, Ohio, 207, 241, 247

Yazoo County, Mississippi, 27
York Street Baptist Church, Louisville, 183, 220, 315
Young Men's Christian Association, 316
Young, Henry J., 300, 301, 313
Young, Robert, 243
Young, S.P. 212, 221
Young, Solomon, 60

Zanesville, Ohio, 76
Zibe, Free, 112
*Zion's Banner*, 320

www.ingramcontent.com/pod-product-compliance
Lightning Source LLC
Chambersburg PA
CBHW022055150426
43195CB00008B/149